CW00621086

Professional and Practice-based Learning

Volume 14

Series editors

Stephen Billett, Griffith University, Griffith, Australia
Christian Harteis, University of Paderborn, Paderborn, Germany
Hans Gruber, University of Regensburg, Regensburg, Germany

Professional and practice-based learning brings together international research on the individual development of professionals and the organisation of professional life and educational experiences. It complements the Springer journal *Vocations and Learning: Studies in vocational and professional education.*

Professional learning, and the practice-based processes that often support it, are the subject of increased interest and attention in the fields of educational, psychological, sociological, and business management research, and also by governments, employer organisations and unions. This professional learning goes beyond, what is often termed professional education, as it includes learning processes and experiences outside of educational institutions in both the initial and ongoing learning for the professional practice. Changes in these workplaces requirements usually manifest themselves in the everyday work tasks, professional development provisions in educational institution decrease in their salience, and learning and development during professional activities increase in their salience.

There are a range of scientific challenges and important focuses within the field of professional learning. These include:

- understanding and making explicit the complex and massive knowledge that is required for professional practice and identifying ways in which this knowledge can best be initially learnt and developed further throughout professional life.
- analytical explications of those processes that support learning at an individual and an organisational level.
- understanding how learning experiences and educational processes might best be aligned or integrated to support professional learning.

The series integrates research from different disciplines: education, sociology, psychology, amongst others. The series is comprehensive in scope as it not only focusses on professional learning of teachers and those in schools, colleges and universities, but all professional development within organisations.

More information about this series at http://www.springer.com/series/8383

Lina Markauskaite • Peter Goodyear

Epistemic Fluency and Professional Education

Innovation, Knowledgeable Action and Actionable Knowledge

 Springer

Lina Markauskaite
Centre for Research on Learning
 and Innovation (CRLI), Faculty
 of Education & Social Work
The University of Sydney
Sydney, NSW
Australia

Peter Goodyear
Centre for Research on Learning
 and Innovation (CRLI), Faculty
 of Education & Social Work
The University of Sydney
Sydney, NSW
Australia

ISSN 2210-5549   ISSN 2210-5557   (electronic)
Professional and Practice-based Learning
ISBN 978-94-007-4368-7   ISBN 978-94-007-4369-4   (eBook)
DOI 10.1007/978-94-007-4369-4

Library of Congress Control Number: 2016936367

Printed on acid-free paper

This Springer imprint is published by Springer Nature
The registered company is Springer Science+Business Media B.V. Dordrecht

Are we made of habits, compressed by time,
like layered rocks?
   (Ben Okri, 2014, The Age of Magic*)*

Series Editors' Foreword

An ability to respond to the changing requirements of occupations, work tasks and workplaces has being conceptualised in a range of ways. Sometimes, such capacities are referred to as expertise which has been the subject of decades of enquiry within cognitive science. Along the way, considerations have been given to whether those capacities are of a general kind, specific to a particular domain of activity (e.g. an occupation) or those required for effective performance situationally. Then, there is the call for adaptability and flexibility among workers that governments have long made and is expected of graduates from tertiary education, who should be job-ready. More recently, in some countries this requirement is captured as the capacity to be innovative. This focus on understanding the capacities which can adopt or adapt to changing requirements are central to workplace effectiveness, efficacy of occupational practices and individuals' career trajectories. Hence, these capacities are salient to conceptions of workplace performance, and how individuals might come to learn and develop the capacities, and are highly consistent with the concerns of this book series. Without accounts of these kinds of capacities, the project of professional and practice based learning is stymied.

This volume offers fresh conceptions and accounts about both the qualities and the characteristics of those capacities and how they might be learnt. Peter Goodyear and Lina Markauskaite coin the term epistemic fluency to describe these capacities drawing upon a range of socially-oriented theoretical propositions. Within this conception, they emphasise the importance of actionable knowledge which is used to enact the routine and non-routine professional activities, yet which is more than behaviours which can be observed and measured. Instead, it is a product of learnt processes that are not easily articulated or captured. In essence, it places a strong focus upon the kinds of knowledge which are needed for actions of the kind that are responsive to and secure legacies from engaging in changing professional activities. As such, these conceptions inform how professional education might be considered, organised and ordered. Such is the project of this book.

To make and advance its case, a range of contributions from diverse disciplines are utilised as both bases for the propositions advanced and to indicate why these concepts have been selected in response to unsatisfactory or incomplete accounts provided elsewhere. Advanced in this elaboration across the initial four chapters are two distinct contributions; firstly personal knowing, actions and being, and, secondly, the demarcations of what constitutes particular occupations. These contributions are seen as being reciprocal and interdependent, which includes the role of the personal in mediating these developments.

Given the extent and scope of its charter, it is not surprising perhaps that the authors offer elaborate and lengthy deliberations about the concepts which support it. These stretch over 20 chapters that initially set out some premises for seeking to understand these conceptions and accounts and the way they differ from what is proposed elsewhere and how they draw upon other ideas and propositions. The reader is provided with specific terminologies and their elaboration within these chapters. These include considerations of the mind and thinking of the kind that is characterised as being epistemic, which is followed by a consideration of artefacts and objects that could draw upon and shape epistemic actions. Then, a clear departure from cognitive accounts is the term 'inscription' which refers to the representation of knowledge that has been secured through the processes of experiencing, as well as of particular roles that socially-derived artefacts play within that securing. Here are rehearsed the roles and contributions of these artefacts, and how they are engaged resourcefully through learners' activity and engagement. Then, considerations for how these ideas fit within educational visions for work and the professions complete its argued case.

In all of this, new ground is trod, and existing ideas re-examined and rehabilitated within the authors' account. In this way, the many chapters of this volume contribute individually and collectively to an understanding about professional practice, its learning and how it fits within the broader education project. As such, it makes a valuable contribution to this book series.

Griffith University   Stephen Billett
Griffith, QLD, Australia
University of Paderborn   Christian Harteis
Paderborn, Germany
University of Regensburg   Hans Gruber
Regensburg, Bayern, Germany
February 2016

Acknowledgements

It has been a delight to work with two very talented postdocs during the course of researching for, and writing, this book. Dr Agnieszka Bachfischer worked with us on many of the data collection processes. Dr Dewa Wardak helped us with the final stages of preparing the manuscript, redrew many of the figures, checked references and in many other ways made the difference between a terminating and nonterminating procedure. Our thanks also go to Sonia Bartoluzzi, whose editing and organisational skills made a crucial difference to our work on the book at difficult times.

Some of the most rudimentary ideas about epistemic fluency in higher education got an airing in keynote addresses by Peter Goodyear at conferences in Leuven (1997), Maastricht (1998) and Lancaster (2006). A few sharp-eyed colleagues picked up the essence and, in so doing, provided encouragement to pursue things further. Special thanks here to Paul Kirschner, Chris Jones and Ray Land. Early outings in print can be found in Goodyear and Ellis (2007), Goodyear and Zenios (2007), Goodyear and Markauskaite (2008, 2009) and Markauskaite and Goodyear (2009, 2014b, 2014c). Earlier versions of some material in Chapters 2, 3, 4 and 20 appeared in Markauskaite and Goodyear (2014a).

This is a good opportunity to thank our co-authors, editors and others who provided kind, convincing and encouraging feedback – in appropriate measures. Our thanks to Rob Ellis, Maria Zenios, Stephen Billett, Angela Brew and Judyth Sachs. It is also a great pleasure to acknowledge Yael Kali – who worked with us on some of our early research on epistemic fluency in educational design teams – and to thank other academic visitors to Sydney who read parts of drafts of the book: Nina Bonderup Dohn, Crina Damşa and Monika Nerland.

Several of our PhD students have been carrying out research and leading us to new ideas and authors – directly or indirectly shaping some of our thinking and writing. Thank you to Pippa Yeoman, Natalie Spence, Shaista Bibi, Catherine Smyth, Anindito Aditomo, David Ashe and Gilbert Importante. Members of the broader CoCo team have been wonderfully supportive, sympathetic and encouraging – also forcing us to air and defend some critical ideas and explanations. Our particular thanks to Kate Thompson, Lucila Carvalho, Mary-Helen Ward, Melinda Lewis and Peter Reimann. We also acknowledge the support of colleagues from the Faculty of Education and Social Work: Louise Sutherland, Fran Waugh, Lindsey Napier, Robyn Ewing and Gabrielle Meagher. Without their collegial encouragement, support and patience this project would have been impossible.

We also gratefully acknowledge the academic staff involved in running the professional education courses that we studied. Their expertise that they so generously shared with us made this book. It is unfortunate that we cannot mention their names.

Funding for the original research came from the Australian Research Council (ARC) through grant DP0988307 to Peter Goodyear and Lina Markauskaite ('Professional learning for knowledgeable action and innovation: The development of epistemic fluency in higher education'). We are also very pleased to acknowledge subsequent financial support from the ARC through grant FL100100203 to Peter Goodyear ('Laureate Fellowship – Learning, technology and design: Architectures for productive networked learning') and from the University of Sydney through a Thomson Fellowship to Lina Markauskaite ('Epistemic fluency in professional learning and scientific inquiry: The origins of resourcefulness for knowledgeable action'), which allowed us to dedicate some extra time to writing the book.

Contents

About the Authors

Lina Markauskaite is an associate professor in the Centre for Research on Learning and Innovation (CRLI), the University of Sydney. Lina has been carrying out studies in the areas of technology-enhanced teaching and learning, professional knowledge and methodological innovation since the mid-1990s. She has published more than 80 refereed papers and an edited book. Her most recent work spans two related areas. Her primary area is concerned with understanding the nature of capabilities involved in complex inter-professional knowledge work and learning. Her formulated theoretical accounts of professional knowing bring into a single framework insights from psychology, neuroscience, anthropology, design, linguistics, organisational studies and science and technology studies (STS). The second research area is emerging interdisciplinary research methods. Her recent work includes the coedited book *Methodological Choice and Design: Scholarship, Policy and Practice in Social and Educational Research* (2011, Springer, coedited with Peter Freebody and Jude Irwin) and a special issue of the British Journal of Educational Technology *e-Research for Education: Applied, Methodological and Critical Perspectives* (2014, coedited with Peter Reimann).

Peter Goodyear is professor of education and Australian Laureate Fellow at the University of Sydney in Australia. He is the founding codirector of the Centre for Research on Computer Supported Learning and Cognition (CoCo) and now also leads the University's Sciences and Technologies of Learning research network, a multi-faculty network involving over 80 academic staff and PhD students. He has been carrying out research in the field of learning, technology and higher education since the early 1980s. Peter's research focusses on networked learning, the nature of professionals' 'working knowledge' and complexity in educational design. He has published nine books and over 100 journal articles and book chapters. His most recent books are *The Architecture of Productive Learning Networks* (Routledge, coedited with Lucila Carvalho), *Handbook of Design in Educational Technology* (2013, Routledge, coedited with Rose Luckin and colleagues), *Technology-Enhanced Learning: Design Patterns and Pattern Languages* (2010, Sense, coedited with Simeon Retalis) and *Students' Experiences of e-Learning in Higher Education: The Ecology of Sustainable Innovation* (2010, Routledge, co-authored with Rob Ellis).

Peter and Lina have been jointly working on projects investigating professional learning, design knowledge, knowledgeable action, innovation and epistemic fluency for the last 7 years. Findings from their joint work provide the empirical basis for this book.

Chapter 1
Introduction

What does it take to be a productive member of a multidisciplinary team working on a complex problem? What enables a person to integrate different types and fields of knowledge, indeed different ways of knowing, in order to make some well-founded decisions about actions to be taken in the world? What personal knowledge resources are entailed in analysing a problem and describing an innovative solution, such that the innovation can be shared in an organisation or professional community? How do people get better at these things; and how can teachers in higher education help students develop these valued capacities? The answers to these questions are central to a thorough understanding of what it means to become an effective knowledge worker and of how the preparation of students for a profession can be improved.

Working on real-world problems usually requires the combination of different kinds of specialised and context-dependent knowledge, as well as different ways of knowing. People who are flexible and adept with respect to different ways of knowing about the world can be said to possess *epistemic fluency*.

This book is intended to make a contribution to our shared understanding of epistemic fluency in some of the core activities of professional workers. It uses data from a 4-year project investigating the boundaries between (university-based) professional education and professional practice, with the aim of analysing the epistemic nature of such professional work and identifying some key sources of capability that people need if they are to engage successfully in it. These embrace a range of mental resources, including conceptual, perceptual and experiential resources, and, especially, the epistemic resources that help people to recognise and switch between different ways of knowing and forms of knowledge. Such resources also help people participate in the creation of new knowledge that can be represented and shared in their professional culture(s).

The book is part of a general move to build upon, and integrate, cognitivist, sociocultural and other accounts of learning, knowing and acting (Billett, 2014; Billett, Harteis, & Gruber, 2014; Billett & Henderson, 2011; Collins, 2007; Dall'Alba, 2009; Edwards, 2010; Farrell & Fenwick, 2007; Fenwick & Nerland,

© Springer Science+Business Media Dordrecht 2017
L. Markauskaite, P. Goodyear, *Epistemic Fluency and Professional Education*,
Professional and Practice-based Learning 14, DOI 10.1007/978-94-007-4369-4_1

2014; Kemmis & Smith, 2008; Sawyer, 2014; Schatzki, Knorr Cetina, & von Savigny, 2001; Sternberg & Horvath, 1999). It draws on research into professional learning carried out in continental Europe, Britain, North America and Australia. It connects this with two previously discrete streams of theorisation about learning and thinking which originate in (a) research on science education and 'resource-based' epistemology, originating in America, and (b) research on the materiality of knowledge work, originating in France.

The book's synthesis of recent research into the nature of professional learning, knowledge work and personal mental resources offers a new and powerful conceptualisation of epistemic fluency in professional practice. It links the social and material investigation of purposeful activity with the exploration of key features of mental resourcefulness in knowledge work. Results from our empirical studies are used to illustrate and develop this conceptual framework and to shed light on practical ways in which the development of epistemic fluency can be recognised and supported – in higher education and in the transition to work. We hope that the ideas will be of interest to an international audience of researchers, as well as to curriculum leaders and other practitioners in the areas of professional education and continuing professional development.

1.1   The Social Importance of Professional Education

Our concern for university education and training for the professions may, at first glance, seem esoteric, or even elitist. Why would one choose to focus on the education of a cadre of highly paid people, like lawyers and doctors, when there are glaring cases of social disadvantage in education crying out for better research? One aspect of our answer is that everyone who calls on the services of professional people wants to be able to depend upon their specialist knowledge and skills. Their abilities, in 'normal' times, are important to the rest of us. This is a reasonably straightforward reason for studying professional work and professional education. We want professionals to be effective and efficient.

A more subtle aspect of our answer is that people in professional roles are very influential in helping society adapt in changing times – and also in helping resist some changes (Grace, 2014). The ways in which professionals conceive of, and approach, their work and the ways they engage in the reconfiguration of work and services over time have pervasive effects. They alter people's expectations, for example, of what healthcare can offer to people in old age. They affect national expenditure. They have powerful shaping effects on our day-to-day lives, in domains as diverse as health and medicine, education, legal matters, the economy and taxes, transport and housing. In short, professional people play a significant role in mediating our responses to major changes, such as those associated with globalisation and innovations in technology.

As the world struggles to deal with climate change, war and migration, food scarcity, peak oil, drug-resistant bugs and other 'wicked' problems, many political, social and economic responses will be influenced by the ways in which professional people do their work – such as in implementing legislation or devising local strategies for ameliorating the effects of environmental change. So a better understanding of how professionals (learn to) do what they do, and what their expertise consists of, can illuminate the unfolding of a number of important societal issues. Dealing with these global changes will also require professionals from different specialisms to work effectively together. The disruptive, pervasive and complex nature of many of these changes also means that professionals will have to examine ever more closely the ethical aspects of their decisions.

Returning to the issue of elitism, we also note that, in many countries, access to the professions has played an important part in social (im)mobility and in the reproduction of economic advantage. Universities face an important equity issue here – not just in opening up entry to professional education programs but also in making changes to their programs to reduce the effects of social and economic background on completion and employment rates. This is good for society, not just for the individuals who find themselves able to access new opportunities. It is good for all of us if universities, and the professions, are able to draw on a bigger pool of talent – hiring people without regard to their origins. And there are social benefits to having a demographic profile in each profession that resembles the profile of the populations being served.

If universities are to become more successful at selecting from a broader range of people and better at supporting their learning once they are enrolled, then the staff managing the admissions; designing courses, curricula and assessments; and doing the teaching will be better able to discharge their responsibilities if they have a good, evidence-based understanding of what to assess and teach.

We do not want to imply that university staff who are engaged in professional education do not know what they are doing. On the contrary, we think that some of the best work on curriculum innovation and assessment can be found in professional education faculties. But the nature of professional work is changing quite rapidly, and there are signs that some of the established ways of distributing professional education between the university and the workplace are in crisis. Employers and their friends in government express deep concerns about the capacity of universities to prepare graduates who are ready for work. For example, in teacher education in a number of countries, there are moves to shift the balance of initial teacher education from universities to schools. Other professions that are relatively new to academia may also find their location becoming a matter of debate and uncertainty once more.

We also want to argue that society needs to be able to rely on *universities* to play their part in the provision of high-quality professional education. This is not something that can be left to employing organisations and/or the market. We do not want to romanticise universities or the education they provide: some are living through tough times and making compromises to survive. However, we take the view that society needs to be able to *place trust* in universities, to do some important things in a disinterested fashion, including professing what is worth knowing and attesting to the capabilities of people for whom they set examinations.

Against this background of uncertainty, change and contestation, we take a firm view that those who manage, and advocate for, university-based professional education programs need a much stronger knowledge base that they can use for making decisions and, especially, for defending the changes they make.

In sum, we are arguing that preparing people to become effective, adaptable, innovative and trustworthy professionals means taking *professional knowledge* much more seriously. *Really* understanding the nature and demands of professional work is a necessity for anyone who needs to assess and support the learning of would-be professionals. Opening up entry to the professions to a wider talent pool depends upon having valid and reliable forms of assessment and a sharp appreciation of how to design and manage a properly supportive learning environment. It also means that staff in universities – and in workplaces – need to understand what can be learnt where and not to harbour unrealistic expectations on that score.

1.2   Patterns in Professional Work: Introducing Epistemic Forms and Games

Research in such diverse fields as sociology, anthropology, cultural studies, psychology and information technology has increasingly acknowledged that human behaviour, at least in part, can be characterised by certain characteristic patterns and structures that appear repeatedly in the physical, social and mental realms and on a range of levels (e.g. Anderson, 1983; Bourdieu, 1977; Giddens, 1984; Schank & Abelson, 1977; Simon, 1979; Sweller, van Merrienboer, & Paas, 1998).

The literature on everyday thinking and workplace practices consistently argues that real-world problems do not come represented for us in one particular shape. As Belth (1977) puts it:

> The problems of the world do not come so well formulated, so consistently structured, that we can learn a tactic of unstructuring the form of that problem, looking into it rapidly, and coming out with the proper conclusions. The dreadful fact about thinking is that it takes time, *and it demands action.* <...> Indeed, the world's problems are what we form them to be, and thus are as unique as the individual minds that create them. (Belth, 1977, p. xxi, original emphasis)

These problems can be reformulated in many different ways, and their solutions typically require working with different kinds of knowledge and different ways of knowing. Explaining how people deal with complex questions in different domains, such as psychology or physics, Minsky (2006) argued:

> ... we find ourselves forced to split those domains into 'specialities' that use different kinds of representations to answer different kinds of questions. (Minsky, 2006, p. 303)

Each such representation is then related to a certain, somewhat different, 'way to think' – that is more likely to help in finding a solution. While Minsky's concern was a broad one – how the mind works – others have argued, in a similar vein, that such characteristic forms of knowledge and patterns of thinking are necessary generic tools for effective *inquiry*. Perkins (1997) puts it thus:

> When people engage in investigations – legal, scientific, moral, political, or other kinds – characteristic moves occur again and again. An anthropologist, a literary critic, or an astronomer may profile an observation in words or classify it into a category system. A judge, a sociologist, or a philosopher may explain something by analogy or explain it as the lawful outcome of a general rule applied to a particular case (covering rule explanation). A physicist, a historian, or a lawyer may justify a conclusion by appealing to one critical observation or an aggregate of observations with a statistical trend, as in DNA testing. Indeed, a practitioner of any of these professions might proceed at one time or another in almost any of these ways. (Perkins, 1997, pp. 50–51)

Collins and Ferguson (1993) and Perkins (1997) called the characteristic forms of outcome that people use to structure the outcomes of their inquiries 'epistemic forms' and the characteristic patterns of action 'epistemic games':

> In part, the term games is suggested by the conspicuous involvement of goals, moves, and rules; in part by the recognition that these patterns of inquiry are not static templates but action systems; in part by the fact that often epistemic games are played competitively, as in the adversarial system of justice or scientific debates; and in part in allusion to Wittgenstein's notion of language games. (Perkins, 1997, pp. 51–52)

Morrison and Collins (1996) argued that the capability to recognise and practice a culture's epistemic games, with their associated epistemic forms, is one of the essential skills for becoming a member of a community of practice. They called this capability 'epistemic fluency'.

In the empirical studies reported in this book, we saw many such tacit and explicit epistemic games and a variety of professional epistemic forms. For example, we observed pharmacists conducting medication reviews, school counsellors carrying out behavioural assessments and preservice teachers developing lesson plans. In nursing, the phrase 'thinking like a nurse' turned out to involve some component epistemic games. While the goal expressed by this phrase ('thinking like an X') has some explicable components and it has a model behind it, many important aspects of what is desired remain uncertain. Perkins and others give us some language and constructs which we can use to become clearer about what is involved in the epistemic games of professional practice. 'Native speakers' often find themselves unable to speak explicitly about the rules and grammar of their language, but they do notice *mistakes* and can correct them. Experienced nurses and nurse educators – indeed all experienced professionals and professional educators – can do the same. Part of what our research offers is the chance to find and articulate the games, their rules and characteristic moves. However, our book goes far beyond the initial ideas about 'epistemic games' and 'epistemic fluency', which were originally rooted in school education. It delves deeply into the very nature of the capabilities that enable professionals to engage skilfully and knowledgeably in complex, dynamic, and often *inter*-professional, work. It describes how to develop these capabilities in university and other educational settings. By doing this, we also significantly extend and refine the notion of 'epistemic fluency'.

1.3 Seeing Through the Changing Surface of Professional Work and Knowledge

Changes in the way that work gets done – whether these are due to advances in technology, new divisions of labour, disaggregation of the value chain, new ways of relating to clients, new laws or regulatory frameworks or other causes – mean that many of the elements that constitute professional practice, and the tools and resources that enable it, are on the move. They are not just developing into new versions of themselves (e.g. when Office 2007 becomes Office 2010). They are also shifting across categories. For example, what was once part of a professional person's tacit knowledge (at time1) gets articulated as a written procedure (at t2), which later becomes encoded in a computer-based performance support tool (t3), which then means that the task can be delegated to a less skilled worker (t4), whose job is outsourced to a cheaper provider overseas (t5). These kinds of shifts are occurring in shorter and shorter cycles. Working out the implications for initial and continuing professional education is far from straightforward. An awareness of the diminishing half-life of specific professional tools and procedures has coloured initial professional education for a long time. It has placed those staff who design curricula in situations where they have to find workable compromises between teaching more abstract knowledge that stands a chance of being longer lived and knowledge tied to current work practices that helps with a sense of 'workplace readiness' but which can leave the new professional underprepared when the workplace changes.

A firm belief underpinning the approach we are taking in this book is that people who are in charge of professional education programs need ways of conceptualising professional work that can cut through the superficial appearance of things and get to the fundamentals. For example, if, when taking a common-sense approach, one habitually and unreflectively sees X as a physical tool and Y as an idea, then one is less well equipped to see how an idea becomes a tool and to distinguish between what has changed and what has stayed the same when this happens:

> If we truly understand cognitive systems, then we must be able to develop designs that enhance the performance of operational systems; if we are to enhance the performance of operational systems, we need conceptual looking glasses that enable us to see past the unending variety of technology and particular domains. (Woods & Sarter, 1993, p. 156)

We will feel this book has been useful if it helps staff involved in designing and managing professional education programs to find sharper ways of analysing professional work in context. We aim to provide some robust ideas that can be used in such analytic work and some language that may help program teams create a shared understanding of their joint enterprise.

Having deeper ways of viewing these flighty things is important in the design of worthwhile assessment tasks and professional learning experiences more generally.

1.4 Research on Education, Learning and Expertise: From Shifts in Fashion to an Integrated Account

The educational research knowledge base on which staff engaged in professional education might hope to draw is not seen by many people as being accessible, reliable or cumulative (Biesta, 2007; DETYA, 2000; Furlong, 2012). Sceptics might say its evolution over the last 50 years has been characterised by twists and turns of fashion, that educational theories are more a matter of taste than the outcome of rational argument, coherent analysis and reliable evidence. Over this period, research into education, expertise, teaching and learning has borne witness to a succession of 'turns':

- A cognitive turn, away from behaviourism
- A practice turn, away from cognitivism
- A linguistic turn
- A material or socio-material turn
- A neuro- or 'brain science' turn

The opening up of each of these new lines of work can be understood as a reasonable response to the neglect of some key areas of human experience and/or scientific insights. (It can also sometimes relate to the 'drying up' of an existing line of work, as it struggles to make headway with certain problems.)

But because the phenomena being studied are very complex, and researchers doing empirical work understandably tend not to bite off too much, each turn has tended to marginalise, rather than build on, what was dominant before.

Of course, there are some deep issues of theoretical and conceptual incompatibility at work here too, but it is also fair to say – with Lehtinen (2012) and Sfard (1998) – that we really *do* need accounts that bring together research on the brain, the mind, tools, discourse, semiotics, culture, praxis, context, the material and so on. We actually need *all* of these, to understand the complexities of what professionals do, how they do it, how they came to be able to do it, how others might be helped along similar paths and so on.

Our book takes this integrative challenge very seriously, which means you, the reader, will need to follow us in what are sometimes quick passages from familiar to unfamiliar territory and back again.

1.5 Our Empirical Research

Most of the chapters in this book include illustrations that are drawn from empirical work that we conducted in four areas of preparation for the professions: nursing, pharmacy, educational psychology (school counselling) and teacher education. Our focus has been unashamedly on less prestigious professions – what Nathan Glazer might have referred to as 'minor professions' (see Chap. 2). They are strongly oriented towards the social – many would place them among the 'caring professions'. Our research looked most closely at experiences on the boundaries of the practicum (also known as placement, clinical placement, internship, etc.). Assessment tasks that are set for students in and around the practicum tell us a lot about the relations between academic and professional knowledge and ways of knowing. Hence, some of our empirical examples are drawn from this fruitful area and from interviews with the professional education staff who set and marked such assignments. We also worked with students who were making preparations for their placement tasks, looking at how they planned and spoke about their planning for practice.

In linking outcomes from our empirical work with the explanation of theoretical ideas, we have used what seemed to us to be the most appropriate examples in each case. For some parts of the book, however, we decided not to jump around between professions and to use single examples to make a number of connected points. For example, Chaps. 8 and 9 draw their data from nurse education, Chaps. 14 and 15 (on epistemic games) use material from pharmacy education and Chaps. 17 and 18 use an extended analysis of the planning activity of some preservice primary school teachers. We think that this may make it easier for the reader to focus on the unfolding ideas, without needing to keep track of multiple empirical sites.

1.6   Overview of the Book: Key Ideas

In this section, we provide a summary of each of the chapters in the book. In so doing, we also introduce a number of core concepts, around which the main arguments of the book are woven.

The book is divided into four parts. Part 1 (Chaps. 1 and 2) is scene-setting. Part 2 (Chaps. 3, 4, 5, 6 and 7) is where we provide an explanation of the theoretical ideas needed to understand actionable knowledge, knowledgeable action and epistemic fluency in professional work and learning. Part 3 (Chaps. 8, 9, 10, 11, 12, 13, 14, 15, 16, 17 and 18) is still theoretically oriented, but each of the chapters includes some significant use of material from our empirical studies – mainly to illustrate the key points that we are trying to make.

In these chapters, we explore professional knowing and learning from six perspectives, each of which helps construct an understanding of epistemic fluency, actionable knowledge and knowledgeable action. These are:

- Object-oriented perspective (Chaps. 8 and 9)
- Inscriptional perspective (Chaps. 10 and 11)
- Infrastructural perspective (Chaps. 12 and 13)
- Epistemic game perspective (Chaps. 14 and 15)
- Socio-material-embodied perspective (Chap. 16)
- Personal resourcefulness perspective (Chaps. 17 and 18)

Finally, Part 4 (Chaps. 19 and 20) draws the book to a close, with some thoughts about educational approaches that are conducive to the development of epistemic fluency, including an extended, integrative conception of epistemic fluency that we present in Chap. 20.

1.6.1 Part 1

Chapter 2, 'Professional Work in Contemporary Contexts', sets the scene for the rest of the book by discussing key changes in workplaces and in higher education that underline the need to rethink knowledge, knowing and epistemic fluency. We see the perspective and insights described in this book as being applicable to many modern workplaces, not just to areas of work that have historically been labelled as 'the professions'. The book is therefore relevant to education that prepares people for all those workplaces: for example, to debates about the generic graduate attributes that all university students should be helped to develop and demonstrate. In the broadest analysis, our book has something to say for everyone who is interested in the dynamics of contemporary knowledge work, where performance of the job regularly involves finding new ways of working, new ways of framing problems, new working relationships, etc.

That said, we are conscious of the fact that a major location for substantial curriculum reform is in the faculties that prepare people for the professions. So, some of the groundwork in Chap. 2 speaks directly to questions about the nature of professional activity, including as it is seen in commentaries on the history and sociology of the professions. A major driver for our work on this book, and indeed for the research project on which it draws, is that contemporary workplaces have changed and are changing, in ways that we do not yet see properly reflected in the mainstream literature of professional education. Alongside processes that have intensified scrutiny, and tightened accountability, of professions and employers to society and government – processes which *have* been subjects of a good deal of research and writing – we see a less frequently and deeply discussed set of processes that place other demands on professional workers and the organisations they work for. So in addition to the discourse of 'workplace readiness', so beloved of the bodies that advocate for employers' interests, we see a need for much more sophisticated attention to be paid to *workplace innovation* – how professionals learn to participate in processes which create new ways of working, new procedures, new working relationships and so on.

In its second part, the chapter switches focus from the demands of contemporary workplaces and organisations to the organisation of professional education programs within universities. It gives very brief sketches of some of the best-understood approaches to professional education – looking at such examples as case-based learning, problem-based learning, learning through inquiry, reflection on practice, induction into a community of practice, inter-professional education programs, etc.

1.6.2 Part 2

Chapter 3, 'Defining the Problem: Four Epistemic Projects in Professional Work and Education', summarises ideas about four core challenges that have to be faced in professional learning. In brief, we can describe these as:

- Linking theory with practice
- Fine-tuning professional skills and developing a professional identity
- Creating knowledge for the future (dealing with a changing world)
- Learning how to work with people from other professional specialisms, as well as with clients (as knowledgeable partners)

The central part of Chap. 3 contains four sections, each of which draws together some ideas from the literature of professions, workplaces, knowledge and learning. Chapter 3 also offers a way of framing the four *epistemic projects* that can be mapped to these challenges. We draw out a distinction that plays a deep role throughout the book – between *representational* and *performative* views on professional learning. Representational views focus on the relations between professional action and articulated knowledge: this is a place for us to touch on Schön's critique of classical assumptions about rational-scientific knowledge and professional reflection, for example. Performative views do not underestimate the importance of professional knowledge, but they see knowing as tightly bound to action in the world – an intrinsic part of the ongoing process of *being in* the world. Both representational and performative accounts need to deal with change and innovation. In Chap. 3, we talk about this in terms of learning to work on two kinds of boundaries: temporal and spatial. The 'temporal' refers to engagement in the development of new ideas and practices, needed to survive and succeed in a changing world. What is involved in such knowledge creation and how do professional learn to build new knowledge? The 'spatial' boundaries are those where the professional worker has to find (and create) ways of working with people from outside their specialism, including with clients, other members of the public and other professionals. This is a place to consider implications for inter-professional education, for example. The chapter concludes by drawing an additional distinction, which becomes crucial as we move further into the book. This is the distinction between the knowledge used in work and the knowledge used to improve the knowledge used in work: a distinction between *knowledge work* and *epistemic work*. We begin to sketch what skilled professionals know and use when they are tackling epistemic tasks – creating new knowledge and improving on existing knowledge.

Chapter 4, 'The Shapes Taken by Personal Professional Knowledge', takes us more deeply into the nature of knowledge and knowing, seen (in this chapter) mainly from the perspective of the individual worker as knower. We distinguish between public, organisational and personal knowledge; between codified and non-codified knowledge; between the forms of knowledge involved in understanding (knowing that) and in getting things done (know how). We also take a look at knowledge (as a possession) and knowing (as a process – as part of the action). We discuss tacit knowledge and explain some important distinctions between different kinds of tacit knowledge, as well as some relations between tacit and explicit forms of knowledge. The chapter ends on another of our key themes: the nature of *knowledgeable action* and of *actionable knowledge*. We use some illustrative material from our empirical research to draw a map of the involvement of different kinds of knowledge and ways of knowing in the lesson-planning action of a trainee teacher. A key goal of this chapter is to argue that actionable knowledge – knowledge which helps get things done in practical situations – needs to be understood as taking a complex form. It is used to establish functional connections between environment, self and action. It is partly tacit, but there is a special role here for explicit knowledge, which allows one to make, and reflect on, these connections knowledgeably.

Whereas Chap. 4 focusses mainly on ways of understanding an individual professional's knowledge, Chap. 5, 'Professional Knowledge and Knowing in Shared Epistemic Spaces: The Person-Plus Perspective', introduces some ideas that become particularly useful, indeed necessary, once one acknowledges that much professional work is a *collective* accomplishment. The trajectory of the argument, as we move from Chap. 4 to Chap. 5, touches on the kinds of knowledge that individuals need in order to work with others – especially when working on the boundaries of their areas of expertise. It then begins to look more deeply at how professional cultures create intellectual spaces in which such joint work can be accomplished effectively and efficiently. In the formation of such spaces, professional cultures draw together a variety of resources, including material resources and also language. We develop the notion of *objects* and the various roles they can play in helping organise and reproduce collective professional work. We also begin to capture how *assemblages* of objects turn out to be intimately involved in both routine knowledge work and epistemic practices that create better ways of coming to know. We draw on Karen Knorr Cetina's ideas (e.g. Knorr Cetina, 1999) about epistemic cultures – providing the machinery for the production of new knowledge – and outline the different kinds of epistemic spaces in which professionals need to (learn to) work. For example, inter-professional problem-solving depends upon an ability to construct, and function within, shared epistemic spaces. Chapter 5 helps capture what is entailed in such activity and what this might mean for the capabilities that novice professionals need to develop.

Chapter 6, 'Understanding the Mind', lays out our argument for the necessity of combining insights, into the nature of the human mind, that derive from a number of scientific and philosophical traditions. We look at what is said about the mind from phenomenological, neuropsychological, environmentalist, situated/sociocultural and mentalist perspectives. We argue that each of these perspectives explains a part of what needs to be known about the human mind if one is to be able to understand how professionals do what they do. We draw upon some relatively recent lines of research in the area known as 'grounded cognition' to illuminate some of the connections between the mind, brain, body, culture and environment. We also delve more deeply into relationships between experiential knowledge and knowledge that is learnt through formal instruction. Our interest in actionable knowledge means that ways have to be found of reclaiming experience as a source of useful knowledge, rather than as something that usually has to be corrected via formal instruction. This has implications for thinking about conceptual change and knowledge transfer. In particular, we argue that accounts of conceptual change and transfer that insist upon an 'all or nothing' approach are missing important aspects of human knowledgeability. Among other things, this has implications for the status of *threshold concepts* in higher education practice (Land, Meyer, & Smith, 2008).

This carries us neatly to Chap. 7, *Epistemic thinking*, which starts by exploring what happens when epistemic resources are added to a conceptual system, opening up a capacity for epistemic agency. We review several lines of research into students' personal epistemologies, but in so doing we are less interested in merely describing what a person may believe about the nature of knowledge and more interested in the possibilities for action that emerge from the *use* of epistemic resources – how they enable a person to work in novel ways with knowledge. Some of the literature we use here will be familiar to colleagues who are interested in school and university students' beliefs about knowledge and learning. We go some way beyond this to show how epistemic cognition and epistemic flexibility are crucially important in dealing with novel problems in professional practice. Part of the novelty of our account here is to explore the idea of *epistemic affordances*, and the skills needed to take up what they offer, and to extend ideas in the literature on cognitive flexibility to embrace epistemic flexibility. In both cases – epistemic affordances and epistemic flexibility – we extend the account from the purely mental to the embodied.

1.6.3   Part 3

Chapter 8, 'Objects, Things and Artefacts in Professional Learning and Doing', is the first chapter in the book in which we combine the development of ideas introduced in Part 2 with material from our empirical studies. This material illustrates the application of the ideas to an area of practical importance in professional education. In the case of Chap. 8, that focus is on assessment tasks – especially the kinds of assessment tasks that students who are training for a profession are asked to do in/around their practicum experiences. We start with the notion of 'object' (introduced in Chap. 4) and sketch some relations between objects, learning and work, drawing on activity theory and ideas about mediation in explaining objectual practice in contexts of learning and work. We sort out some confusion about object-oriented activities (in the literature) that can be traced back to two meanings of the word 'object' in the foundational writing of Leontiev: object as motive, goal or purpose and object as real, material stuff. We look at a range of objects that can be found when students are tackling assessment tasks and attend to their nature and purposes in both learning and work. We then provide an extended description of the development of a complex *epistemic artefact* in an assessment task undertaken by some nursing students. We illustrate some useful distinctions made by Wartofsky (1979), between primary, secondary and tertiary artefacts, and show how artefacts are used to preserve, transfer and change skills and ways in which professional practice is carried out in the physical world. We complement this account by drawing on Bereiter's notion of conceptual artefacts in knowledge work, finding some significant differences between his sense of scientific knowledge building and our sense of innovation in professional work and knowledge (Bereiter, 2002).

Chapter 9, 'Epistemic Tools and Artefacts in Epistemic Practices and Systems', can be seen as an extension of Chap. 8. It extends the account by following tools and artefacts into their broader contexts – into larger practices and systems. As with Chap. 8, we use material from our empirical studies to illustrate the main points – this time, analysing the epistemic qualities of some artefacts produced by student nurses as Nursing Guidelines. Chapter 9 is also a place in which we explore some of the distinctive qualities of the university as a site in which to learn professional knowledge – as a hybrid space where the three epistemic cultures of learning, research and professions come together, in what should be creative ways.

Chapters 10 and 11 explore the role of *inscriptions* in professional work and learning. The term 'inscription' is used to cover all instances of representations that are produced in *external media*. (While representations may be 'in the mind' or 'outside the mind', this usage makes it clear that inscriptions exist 'outside the mind' – e.g. tally marks on a stick, print on the pages of a book.)

Chapter 10, 'Inscribing Professional Knowledge and Knowing', takes some ideas about the characteristics, properties, uses, etc., of inscriptions that have been advanced in studies of scientific practices and translates these to help understand the role of inscriptions in professional work and in learning to be a professional. We draw on our empirical data to present an example of a task tackled by someone learning to be a school counsellor. In particular, we show that much of what happens in this task is closely bound up with inscriptions. That is, we present the *inscriptional practices* implicated in this task. We move on from this to discuss a variety of types of inscriptions and the roles they have in workplaces and in learning to practice in those workplaces. We distinguish between *projective* inscriptions (inscriptions *for* practice), *productive* inscriptions (inscriptions *in* practice) and *illuminative* inscriptions (inscriptions *of* practice), explaining the different roles these play in learning and work. Finally, the chapter develops the construct of '*enactive* inscriptions' to show how students can be helped to see inscriptional work as part of how they learn *and* how they help the systems in which they are embedded get better at doing what they do. For professional educators, a key message from this chapter is that the kinds of inscriptional tasks that students find themselves tackling are not always well aligned with our educational goals for them. Understanding how inscriptions vary is a prerequisite for improving this alignment.

Chapter 11, 'Inscriptions Shaping Mind, Meaning and Action', complements Chap. 10 by showing what inscriptions mean in professional learning and work and how they mean what they mean. Where the perspective in Chap. 10 was largely *functional*, Chap. 11 takes a *semiotic* perspective. We use examples from our research with nurse educators and teacher educators to explain knowledge production as semiotic work and to account for what slices of knowledge and ways of knowing get inscribed and for what purposes. As we argue in Chap. 11, the traditional semiotic account of the functioning of signs is incomplete, with respect to the role of signs in the creation of new ideas and in innovative work more generally. One of the roles for inscriptions is in enabling work that involves degrees of conceptual complexity that overwhelm the biological capacities of the unaided human mind. In the later parts of the chapter, we look at how inscriptions play a role in various kinds of conceptual integration, blending and enacting that are entailed in tackling complex professional tasks – especially those that involve the generation of new ideas.

In Chap. 12, 'Epistemic Tools, Instruments and Infrastructure in Professional Knowledge Work and Learning', we turn from artefacts to the instrumental ensemble or epistemic infrastructure in which artefacts are produced, from the semiotic features of inscriptions to epistemic features of tools and arrangements within which this inscriptional work is done. We use the work of ergonomist Pierre Rabardel on *instrumental genesis* (Rabardel & Beguin, 2005) to link epistemic tools and epistemic games – defining as an 'instrument' the combination of a tool and an action scheme for using it (a.k.a. a personal rendering of a socially produced game). The chapter looks at tools in professional work and especially at the reasons why invention of new tools is so difficult. We move on to illustrate the idea of epistemic infrastructures by drawing once more on the case of the school counsellor conducting a behavioural assessment, showing how the tools she uses fit together within, and depend upon, a professional infrastructure for supporting inquiry. As the chapter points out, the epistemic work undertaken in professional practice is not the same as epistemic work undertaken in scientific disciplines; nor is it identical with, or reducible to an enactment of, codified professional standards and guidelines. That is why we are interested in discovering what tools are used (and how) in the performative and representational practices of everyday professional work – and also in instances of innovation.

Chapter 13, 'Taxonomies of Epistemic Tools and Infrastructures', maps the landscape of epistemic tools and infrastructures, capturing the main kinds of each and identifying some of their interrelationships. We start by noting that tool use typically involves a tweaking of problems to make them 'doable' as well as a selection of the tools best fitted to working on that doable problem. We draw on De Landa (2011) to focus on the properties, capacities and functions of different kinds of tools and infrastructures in professional work and learning. For example, *codes* turn out to be important in infrastructures for professional work. Different kinds of codes – such as codes of practice and competence codes – have different intrinsic features and they play different roles in professional practices. They affect practice in different ways, and the relationships between codes and practices need to be understood (by novice professionals) in nuanced ways. What complicates this further is the realisation that codes are not, in any simple sense, technologies for representing realities. They are enacted in local practices. The chapter concludes with some thoughts about how students can be helped to learn to master epistemic tools, configured in – and constituting – epistemic infrastructures. In this regard, we find that the habit, in university education for the professions, of splitting disciplinary knowledge from skills and from social practices is deeply unhelpful. This perspective on professional work and learning obscures the very essence of professional knowledge and the epistemic complexity of professional action. Becoming more conscious of, and articulate about, a profession's epistemic tools and infrastructures is one important step on the way to creating professional learning experiences that stand a chance of doing better than 'sitting by Nelly' in the workplace.[1]

In Chap. 14, 'Professional Epistemic Games', we return to the notion of reconfiguring problems to make them 'doable'. We discuss the idea of epistemic games as patterns of inquiry – dynamic structures that guide thought and action in the pursuit of new understandings. In professional work, we see an epistemic game as a form of action that entangles rules of thought and rules of culture with affordances and constraints of the epistemic, social, symbolic and material spaces with(in) which it plays out. We explore the nature and variety of epistemic games in professional practice. Since one of our main contributions is to take the idea of epistemic games from its origins in science education into professional education, we offer a taxonomy of epistemic games to be found in professional work. This taxonomy depends upon the following constructs: what sort of knowledge the game produces (its epistemic focus), what the game aims to achieve (its epistemic agenda), the nature of the epistemic object around which the game unfolds and the sorts of knowledge and skills that expert players of the game use. We distinguish six main types of epistemic game, to be found in professional work. It turns out that epistemic games are rarely played one at a time. Rather, skilled professional thinking and action commonly involve multiple 'tools for thought' and therefore need a fluent interweaving of several epistemic games, as well as an interweaving of the epistemic, social and material.

This is the core subject matter of Chap. 15, 'Weaving Ways of Knowing'. In Chap. 15, we analyse what is involved in learning to weave together multiple epistemic games and material and social-bureaucratic infrastructures, in carrying out what – for experienced pharmacists – is a demanding yet commonplace task. We show how mundane yet skilful professional work depends upon an ability to recognise and use a range of epistemic tools, play a range of epistemic games, switch neatly between games and weave them together in a timely, focussed, efficient way.

We explore this more deeply in Chap. 16, 'Rethinking the Material, the Embodied and the Social for Professional Education', in which we develop the argument that professional knowledge work and knowledgeable action are constitutively entangled with embodied practices in the material and social worlds. To take this further, we look more closely at how matter matters in professional work and how thinking is shared with others – using the notion of the socially extended mind. This has

---

[1] 'Sitting by Nelly' refers to informal learning on the job, done by watching a more experienced worker perform the tasks to be done.

significant implications for what it is sensible to try to teach through replication of workplaces in university settings. In particular, it helps identify the limitations of techniques like role play and simulation and through that points to some more productive ways in which such techniques can be used. The chapter concludes with an explanation of a more nuanced notion of mediation, one that emerges most distinctly when one distinguishes between the self as subject and the self as knower.

Chapter 17, 'Conceptual Resourcefulness and Actionable Concepts: Concepts Revisited' turns to conceptual knowledge that is often seen as central in higher education. The chapter makes a crucial distinction between (a) concepts as they are thought to exist in the mind and (b) concepts as they appear in discourse. The two are not the same. Distinguishing between kinds of concepts – abstract, contextual and situated – allows us to focus more clearly on relations between abstract conceptual knowledge and situated action and to advance a case for the importance of *actionable concepts* in professional work. To be capable of making use of relevant concepts of appropriate kinds, in the flow of demanding professional work, is to exhibit conceptual resourcefulness. This chapter makes use of our analysis of the planning discourse of some preservice teachers to illustrate key points in the argument for understanding conceptual resourcefulness – and of how concepts function in such work.

Building on the distinction we made between conceptual and epistemic resources, we develop a parallel argument in Chap. 18, 'Epistemic Resourcefulness for Actionable Knowing'. In this chapter, we examine how epistemic resources feature in discourse and in accounts of the mind and explain how the two come together in accounts of epistemic thought and action. We examine epistemic action and introduce ideas about *framing*: how sense-making and other processes entail epistemic work that asks 'what is going on here?' The chapter shows how epistemic resourcefulness is constituted by an ability to *coordinate* diverse ways of knowing.

1.6.4 Part 4

Chapter 19, 'Teaching and Learning for Epistemic Fluency', takes us to the question of how the development of epistemic fluency can be supported in higher education. We offer an analysis of four broad educational approaches that we see as having high potential for use in professional education. We are 'importing' a number of these from areas outside of preparatory professional education at the university level. Indeed, some relevant and inspiring innovations come from school science education and from work with experienced professionals. We examine (a) knowledge integration and cognitive flexibility, (b) playing epistemic games, (c) designerly work on knowledge building and (d) approaches in which students learn to design inquiry itself. The chapter claims that well-designed tasks for professional learning are simultaneously professional and epistemic. They involve knowledge that is coherent and contingent, structured and experiential, explicit and tacit, systemic and systematic.

Chapter 20, 'Creating Epistemic Environments: Learning, Teaching and Design', has two main functions. It presents a fifth epistemic project and discusses some approaches to professional education that align with this conception. The focus here is on the capabilities needed to assemble and reconfigure one's epistemic environment. The chapter reflects on approaches to design for learning, making an important move from seeing design as work done outside the learning system to its inhabitants to seeing design as something to be done consciously and conscientiously by the inhabitants.

1.7   Reading the Book: Online Glossary and Abbreviations

We have written this book in a way that assumes the reader will work through it sequentially, skimming sections that are familiar or skipping empirical cases and illustrations if a quicker sense of core arguments is needed. We have tried to explain what can sometimes be complex ideas in situ – though we have also created an online glossary at the *Epistemic Fluency* website: http://www.epistemicfluency.com.

We hope this website will be active for a number of years, and we will be happy to receive feedback, debate ideas and expand and improve our glossary, as the need arises.

Some quotations from our empirical studies have been lightly edited for clarity, but in such a way as to preserve what we believe to be the intended meaning. In the quotes, abbreviated full sentences or clauses are indicated with '<...>' and abbreviated words or short phrases are indicated with '...'.

References

Anderson, J. (1983). *The architecture of cognition*. Cambridge, MA: Harvard University Press.

Belth, M. (1977). *The process of thinking*. New York, NY: David McKay.

Bereiter, C. (2002). *Education and mind in the knowledge age*. Mahwah, NJ: Lawrence Erlbaum Associates.

Biesta, G. (2007). Bridging the gap between educational research and educational practice: The need for critical distance. *Educational Research and Evaluation, 13*(3), 295–301.

Billett, S. (2014). *Mimetic learning at work: Learning in the circumstances of practice*. Heidelberg, Germany: Springer.

Billett, S., Harteis, C., & Gruber, H. (Eds.). (2014). *International handbook of research in professional and practice-based learning* (Vol. 2). Dordrecht, The Netherlands: Springer.

Billett, S., & Henderson, A. (Eds.). (2011). *Developing learning professionals*. Dordrecht, The Netherlands: Springer.

Bourdieu, P. (1977). *Outline of a theory of practice* (R. Nice, Trans.). Cambridge, MA: Cambridge University Press.

Collins, H. (2007). *Rethinking expertise*. Chicago, IL: Chicago University Press.

Collins, A., & Ferguson, W. (1993). Epistemic forms and epistemic games. *Educational Psychologist, 28*(1), 25–42.

Dall'Alba, G. (2009). *Learning to be professionals*. Dordrecht, The Netherlands: Springer.

De Landa, M. (2011). *Philosophy and simulation: The emergence of synthetic reason*. London, UK: Continuum.

DETYA (Ed.). (2000). *The impact of educational research*. Canberra, Australia: Higher Education Division, Dept of Education, Training & Youth Affairs.

Edwards, A. (2010). *Being an expert professional practitioner: The relational turn in expertise*. Dordrecht, The Netherlands: Springer.

Farrell, L., & Fenwick, T. (Eds.). (2007). *Educating for the global workforce: Knowledge, knowledge work, and knowledge workers*. London, UK: Routledge.

Fenwick, T., & Nerland, M. (Eds.). (2014). *Reconceptualising professional learning: Sociomaterial knowledges, practices and responsibilities*. London, UK: Routledge.

Furlong, J. (2012). *Education – an anatomy of the discipline: Rescuing the university project?* London, UK: Routledge.

Giddens, A. (1984). *The constitution of society: Outline of the theory of structuration*. Berkeley, CA: University of California Press.

Grace, G. (2014). Professions, sacred and profane: Reflections on the changing nature of professionalism. In M. Young & J. Muller (Eds.), *Knowledge, expertise and the professions*. London, UK: Routledge.

Kemmis, S., & Smith, T. (Eds.). (2008). *Enabling praxis: Challenges for education*. Rotterdam, The Netherlands: Sense.

Knorr Cetina, K. (1999). *Epistemic cultures: How the sciences make knowledge*. Cambridge, MA: Harvard University Press.

Land, R., Meyer, J., & Smith, J. (Eds.). (2008). *Threshold concepts within the disciplines*. Rotterdam, The Netherlands: Sense.

Lehtinen, E. (2012). Learning of complex competences: On the need to coordinate multiple theoretical perspectives. In A. Koskensalo, J. Smeds, A. Huguet, & R. de Cillia (Eds.), *Language: Competencies – contact – change* (pp. 13–28). Berlin, Germany: LIT Verlag.

Minsky, M. (2006). *The emotion machine: Commonsense thinking, artificial intelligence, and the future of the human mind*. New York, NY: Simon & Schuster.

Morrison, D., & Collins, A. (1996). Epistemic fluency and constructivist learning environments In B. Wilson (Ed.), *Constructivist learning environments: Case studies in instructional design* (pp. 107–119). Englewood Cliffs, NJ: Educational Technology Publications.

Perkins, D. N. (1997). Epistemic games. *International Journal of Educational Research, 27*(1), 49–61.

Rabardel, P., & Beguin, P. (2005). Instrument mediated activity: From subject development to anthropocentric design. *Theoretical Issues in Ergonomic Science, 6*(5), 429–461.

Sawyer, K. (Ed.). (2014). *The Cambridge handbook of the learning sciences* (2nd ed.). Cambridge, MA: Cambridge University Press.

Schank, R., & Abelson, R. (1977). *Scripts, plans, goals, and understanding: An inquiry into human knowledge structures*. New York, NY: Psychology Press.

Schatzki, T., Knorr Cetina, K., & von Savigny, E. (Eds.). (2001). *The practice turn in contemporary theory*. London, UK: Routledge.

Sfard, A. (1998). On two metaphors for learning and the dangers of just choosing one. *Educational Researcher, 27*(2), 4–12.

Simon, H. A. (1979). *Models of thought* (Vol. 1–2). New Haven, CT: Yale University Press.

Sternberg, R., & Horvath, J. (Eds.). (1999). *Tacit knowledge in professional practice: Researcher and practitioner perspectives*. Mahwah, NJ: Lawrence Erlbaum Associates.

Sweller, J., van Merrienboer, J., & Paas, F. (1998). Cognitive architecture and instructional design. *Educational Psychology Review, 10*(3), 251–296.

Wartofsky, M. (1979). *Models: Representation and the scientific understanding*. Dordrecht, The Netherlands: D. Reidel.

Woods, D. D., & Sarter, N. B. (1993). Evaluating the impact of new technology on human-machine cooperation. In J. Wise, V. D. Hopkin, & P. Stager (Eds.), *Verification and validation of complex systems: Human factors issues* (pp. 133–158). Berlin, Germany: Springer.

Chapter 2
Professional Work in Contemporary Contexts

Some of the things about which we are writing in this book will appear unfamiliar and strange to many people who are involved in the practicalities of professional education. This chapter is intended to create bridges between some of the main ideas in recent writing about professional work and the central concerns of this book. The chapter draws on literature about the professions, professional work and professional education and emphasises the growing importance, and changing nature, of knowledgeable action in professional work settings.[1] Section 2.1 introduces some key themes from the literature on professions and professional work, drawing on a number of classic accounts of professionalism. Section 2.2 sketches a few of the main challenges of contemporary professional workplaces and activities. These challenges include the need for more professional workers to be able to participate in innovation: developing new areas of professional knowledge and working practices, to cope with a dynamic external environment, for example. Challenges also emerge from the need to participate in inter-professional work and in work that more deliberately shares responsibilities with lay people (clients, customers, etc.). Section 2.2 uses these ideas about the intensifying demands placed on professional workers and helps tighten the focus further onto the qualities of knowledge work in the professions. Section 2.3 provides a brief overview of principal themes in writing about preparation for the professions, and Sect. 2.4 surveys a number of contemporary approaches to professional education, connecting some of their salient features to our key themes of knowledgeable action and actionable knowledge.

---

[1] It is important to note that many jobs that are not normally classified as 'professional' involve substantial amounts of knowledge work, including the creation of new knowledge. The core ideas in this book are relevant to knowledge work in general; we do not see them as restricted to phenomena that are unique to professional workplaces (Gorman & Sandefur, 2011). We speak of 'professional education' in quite a pragmatic way – what western universities currently deem to be professional education provides a space within which our empirical work is situated and also provides us with a sense of audience for this book.

© Springer Science+Business Media Dordrecht 2017
L. Markauskaite, P. Goodyear, *Epistemic Fluency and Professional Education*,
Professional and Practice-based Learning 14, DOI 10.1007/978-94-007-4369-4_2

wide range of commentators on the nature of contemporary professional work, and on programs of preparation for the professions, are in agreement about core distinguishing features and issues, though their language and theoretical perspectives may vary. What may once have been relatively stable areas of occupational practice are no longer so. Information, knowledge, networks, mobility and other dynamic processes that characterise contemporary society are accompanied by the 'decline of routine action' (Archer, 2007). What were once seen as integral parts of a job are being outsourced to skilled workers in cheaper countries or are completely or partially automated with the use of IT-based systems. Entirely new jobs and even professions emerge and older ones dwindle. The role of professional shifts from fount of authority to sense-maker, from 'legislator' to 'interpreter' (Archer, 2007; Bauman, 1987; Dall'Alba, 2009; Ekbia & Nardi, 2014; Guile, 2014; Nerland, 2012). As we will argue, the ability to thrive in such a rapidly changing world needs much more than a disposition for lifelong learning. It needs a deep understanding of how knowledge works, the capacity to participate in the creation of actionable knowledge and a sense of how to reconfigure the world in order to see what matters more clearly and enable oneself, and others, to act more knowledgeably.

2.1 Professions and Professional Work

It is not easy to pin down the meanings of the terms 'profession', 'professional' and 'professional knowledge'. The core term – profession – has denoted different occupations at different times and in different places. Its interpretation is coloured by its association with medicine and law – fields often seen, in the literature and in higher education, as the archetypal professions. In recent years, in Western countries, other occupations have been added to the list: engineer, architect and scientist, for example. Others have pushed to join the club. Some succeed. Some are consoled with titles like 'para-profession' or 'minor profession'. Moreover, the very idea of profession has to be seen as historically, spatially and linguistically located (Sciulli, 2005). If one traces the history of occupational fields in China, India or other non-Western countries, some very different ideas of profession and professional hierarchy emerge (Unschold, 2010).

Very broadly speaking, the literature on professions and professional work falls into two main areas – sociological studies of *the growth and position* of professions in society and studies which focus more closely on *the specific demands* of professional work and workplaces. These latter studies draw on a range of disciplines, including anthropology, psychology, ergonomics and behavioural science. They often have a practical goal of improving the design of work and workplaces or of enhancing professional education, whereas the former corpus of sociologically inspired research on the professions exhibits a preference for showing how professions function in competitions for status, wealth and power (Evetts, 2014).[2]

Developing this distinction a little further, we might also point to substantial differences in conceptions of professional work that are associated with (a) functionalist and (b) critical research traditions.

Functionalist accounts explain the existence of professions as a solution to the problem of the social control of expertise:

> ... the professions 'strike a bargain with society' in which they exchange competence and integrity against the trust of client and community, relative freedom from lay supervision and interference, protection against unqualified competition as well as substantial remuneration and higher social status. (Rueschemeyer, 1983, p. 41)

As Eraut (1994) points out, the social dilemma emerges because experts are needed by people who are not knowledgeable enough to make *a priori* judgements about the soundness of claims to relevant expertise. Professions have emerged to solve this problem, with powers of self-regulation that have varied between states and over time. On this view, a professional is:

> ... someone trusted and respected, an individual given class status, autonomy, social elevation, in return for safeguarding our well-being and applying their professional judgement on the basis of a benign moral or cultural code. (Dent & Whitehead, 2002, p. 1)

Critical accounts of the professions take a different view. Rather than seeing professions as a rational solution to a shared social problem, they tend to focus on the ways professions operate to protect the interests of their members: they provide an apparatus for seeing off competition and reproducing advantage (Abbott, 1988). Hearn (1982), for example, points to the dominance of middle-class males in the higher status professions and to the 'masculinisation' of the lower status professions, within which women may be more numerous, but find themselves managed by men.

It is worth spending some time trying to get a clearer view of this terrain, even though it is changing and contested. In the end, whether or not an occupation merits the title 'profession' is less relevant to our book and its argument than the forms of knowledge and ways of knowing implicated in the daily practices of the workers involved. It turns out that many occupations reveal occasional examples of the kinds of knowledge work in which we have a special interest. But some occupations are suffused with such work.

To reduce the sense of slipperiness, we can draw upon some classic, and more recent, analyses of the scope and nature of 'professions' and 'professionals'.

Early work in the area interpreted a profession to be a vocation based on prolonged and specialised intellectual training, allowing a particular service to be rendered (Carr-Saunders & Wilson, 1933). Scholars of the professions often refer to

---

[2] Indeed, it can be argued that sociological research on the professions has been blind to a number of very significant developments. The growth of inter-professional work is one good example (Guile, 2014).

the work of the American sociologist Talcott Parsons to advance a simple definition: a profession involves the provision of a service, based upon a body of expert,
scientific knowledge (e.g. Parsons, 1968). Other early authors added a range of
characteristics that are typically, but not universally, associated with professional
status – including having one or more organisations that support and safeguard
professional work and status, having an explicit, shared code of conduct, and having
a shared apparatus for testing and certifying competence to practice (Millerson,
1964).

The possession of expert knowledge is used to explain and justify higher levels
of remuneration. In some of the less traditionally class-conscious societies, expertise turns out to be strongly associated with occupational prestige. For example,
working with data from Israel, Adler and Kraus (1985) conclude:

> ... we find that the knowledge and skills requisite for an occupation is the best single
> predictor of the prestige assigned to it. Value to society ... has no predictive value of
> prestige over and above the other dimensions considered. (Adler & Kraus, 1985, p. 36)

The history and sociology of professions alerts us to the ways in which professions
defend their territories, using the possession of specialist professional knowledge as
both a test of entry and a defence against unqualified individuals offering services at
cheaper rates. So while professional knowledge enables professional action, it is
also embroiled in the marketplace of services, being used to resist a downward
spiral of remuneration levels. Such powerful forces cannot leave professional
knowledge, and its definition, untouched:

> The designation 'profession' is not a permanent monopoly of a few occupations. The term
> refers to a comparative status level attained after deliberate action by an occupation.
> (Millerson, 1964, p. 9)

Wilensky (1964) examined the historical development of occupations and identified a number of key stages or milestones in their evolution, notably (a) when they
first became full-time occupations, (b) when they acquired training schools or
university schools/programs, (c) when they formed professional associations,
(d) when they became protected by law and (e) when they adopted a formal code
of ethics.

The notion that not all professions are the same recurs throughout the literature.
For example, Moore and Rosenblum (1970) proposed a 'scale of professionalism'
to which professions approximate in varying degrees. There were six elements to
this scale: full-time occupation, commitment to a calling, formal organisation,
esoteric but useful knowledge or skills acquired through education/training, an
orientation to service and autonomy/self-regulation.

Hickson and Thomas (1969) conducted a major empirical study of 43 professional associations in the UK and constructed a 'professionalisation index' which
turned out to correlate well with the age of each association ($r = 0.41$, $p < 0.01$),
lending some support to Wilensky's historical model. Hickson and Thomas also
remarked that certain attributes were very common across their set of professional
associations. These included such features as a requirement on gaining work
experience between formal training and the granting of full professional status,

Table 2.1 The 1960s hierarchy of professions, compiled from Hickson and Thomas, based on their 13 criteria for distinguishing professional bodies (1969, pp. 44–45)

Met criteria (out of 13)	Professions
13/13	Obstetricians and gynaecologists, physicians and surgeons
11/13	GPs, civil engineers, solicitors and architects
10/13	Electrical engineers
9/13	Town planners and barristers
8/13	Mechanical engineers, chartered accountants and company secretaries
7/13	Aeronautical and marine engineers
6/13	Pharmacists
5/13	Chiropodists and medical social workers
2/13	Radiographers and advertising executives
Not on the list	Teachers, nurses, military and church

the power of the professional association to act over non-professional conduct and other misdemeanours, defined lengths of professional preparation and agreed levels for professional fees and prohibitions on members undercutting one another. A subset of features distinguished the more prestigious and older professions, notably in medicine and the law. Table 2.1 presents the hierarchy of professions based on the Hickson and Thomas professionalism scale.

Hickson and Thomas's analysis may say more about the mode and degree of organisation of professional bodies than it says directly about the professions themselves – hence, for example, the placing of solicitors above barristers in Table 2.1 and the absence of clerics and the military.

Such portrayals of status hierarchies represent a teasing out of a dichotomy which has been around in the literature on the professions for many years. Glazer (1974), for example, makes a sharp distinction between the major and minor professions:

> The major professions are medicine and the law: the minor professions are all the rest. <...> One of the major differences between the major and minor professions is that practitioners of the minor professions do not possess knowledge at the same level of technical complexity and of the same importance to an individual's life as that possessed by the classic major professions. (Glazer, 1974, pp. 347–348)

The writings of a number of other influential authors also capture this notion of 'major' and 'minor' professions, and some even cast doubt on whether the 'minor' professions are really professions at all, labelling them as 'semi-professions' or 'quasi-professions' (Denzin & Mettlin, 1968; Etzioni, 1969; Glazer, 1974).

The centrality of high-level, specialist knowledge in defining professional positioning is not universally endorsed. For some authors, and not just those adopting a 'critical' position, the ways in which members of one professional group manage their own work and the work of others are at least as crucial. Informed particularly by the organisation of professional work in the USA, Leicht and Fennell (1997) conclude:

> ... the prestige of a profession is often dictated by the ability of professionals to determine the organizational form under which service will be delivered. If medicine represents one

extreme where (traditionally) there are strong institutionalized norms dictating appropriate organizational forms for professional practice, engineering may be at the other extreme. (Leicht & Fennell, 1997, p. 225)

Turner's (1995) classification of the health professions is another case in point. Turner places medicine at the pinnacle – as the 'dominant' profession – and then identifies two other health profession groupings: the 'limited' and the 'subordinated'. The 'limited' health professions are those, like dentists, opticians and pharmacists, whose practice is *legally restricted* to specific kinds of practice and/or areas of the body. The 'subordinated' health professions, such as nurses and physiotherapists, are those in which work is normally *delegated* by members of the dominant profession. While the details of practice and autonomy may vary from state to state, and over time, the underpinning structural arrangements are important to note. Among other things, they have strong implications for the arrangement of inter-professional working and the distribution of knowledge within care teams. More recently, Saks (2015) has added a fourth category – the 'marginalised' professions such as complementary medicine. These bear a relation to healthcare, but their role and status are placed in doubt, especially by members of the dominant groups. It is necessary to remember that the status of these marginalised groups also varies from time to time and place to place. As Saks and others point out, the relations between members of dominant, limited, subordinated and marginalised professional groupings become very significant for clients at times when they need to be able to benefit from the close cooperation of professionals distributed across several of these groups.

A further consideration in distinguishing between kinds of professions, or between ways of enacting professional work, involves the extent to which such work is tackled in a narrowly prescribed way, or – in contrast – as an expansive, inventive enterprise. Carr (2014) uses the notions of restricted and extended professionalism to capture this – being careful not to assert that such a stance is either determined by a profession or entirely susceptible to the outlook and energy of each professional person. Carr speaks of the restricted professional as one who works to a set agenda, within set hours, taking little or no responsibility for the advancement of shared professional practice. In contrast, the extended professional is a:

... pro-active agent who is prepared to take time – outside any and all minimally prescribed working hours – to engage in discussion, enquiry and research regarding the progressive development of professional principles and procedures ... to assist with the education and training of junior colleagues, to take individual responsibility and initiative ... in circumstances of professional uncertainty and dilemma. (Carr, 2014, p. 19)

As we will see later in this book, extended professionalism – especially engaging in the development of innovative practice and expanding the knowledge base of the profession – requires particular kinds of skills for working with knowledge.

Provision of a professional service is normally associated with both a degree of disinterested altruism and remuneration to the professional – either directly or through an employing organisation such as a professional service firm (PSF) or a public sector institution: a hospital or school district, for example (Evetts, 2014; Faulconbridge & Hall, 2009).

This issue of disinterested working – of the *client's* best interests coming first – has long been seen as sitting in tension with remuneration, and this tension is part of the explanation for the ways in which professional associations have formed to safeguard professional standards, quash malpractice and regulate competition (Minnameier, 2014). That said, the moral basis of professional work is at its core:

> ... the very idea of professional service is a fundamentally *moral* one; that issues and questions about the promotion of this or that aspect of human good or flourishing are central to the conduct of any and all occupations meriting professional status; and that any theoretical or technical knowledge which professional agents may indeed require for the effective prosecution of the various moral ends or goals of professional service are at least normatively secondary to or subservient of such ends. (Carr, 2014, p. 21, original emphasis)

Gerald Grace (2014) reminds us that the origins of professional work are to be found in religious callings – vocations – and that professional practice has to be understood as a site in which complex, competing forces are worked out. To allow professional action to be reduced to the mere expression of expert technical knowledge is to lose sight of its distinctive social purpose. Professional action needs to be imbued with a sense of moral purpose; knowledgeable action is not merely technical – it seeks to promote the best interests of others, against the forces of rampant markets or overbearing states:

> Established professions ... are presented with ideological and political challenges to their professional ethics, values and commitments to common good service. What we are witnessing in contemporary society is an attempted market culture colonisation of all forms of social service in order to sharpen the overall efficiency and competitive edge of the total social formation and not simply the sphere of business. (Grace, 2014, p. 23)

In Grace's view – and ours – professions need to find ways of working that provide leadership in changing and uncertain times, both through advocacy and in the day-to-day accomplishment of professional tasks. Professional work entails the use and creation of 'moral know-how'.

From the ideas presented in this section, we need to emphasise the following:

- Professions can be understood as a social response to the problem of unevenly distributed expertise, particularly expertise that relates to core areas of human well-being.
- As organisational forms, professions also 'take on a life of their own' – they have to find ways of resolving tensions between professional, client and broader social interests; in working on and with such tensions, professional knowledge plays a shaping role, but is also reshaped over time.
- Many professionals find themselves working in complex organisational settings, on tasks that depend upon colleagues from other professions. They operate in circumstances where their own professional knowledge is insufficient for success and their own professional practices have to adapt to the practices of others.
- Professional knowledge and action are rooted in a moral framework. Professional action is always action on behalf of others; professional expertise includes an ability to integrate and advance moral and technical reasoning.

In the next section, we shift the focus to some characteristics of contemporary professional work and workplaces that place new or sharper demands on professionals and on programs of professional education. Donald Schön's (1983) remarks, made 30 years ago, about the crisis of professionalism, help frame this transition. Schön was commenting on the uncertainties that arise when serious questions are asked about the foundations of professional competence – once one rejects the notion that professional practice is simply the enactment of specialist technical knowledge:

> Professionals have been disturbed to find that they cannot account for processes they have come to see as central to professional competence. It is difficult for them to imagine how to describe and teach what might be meant by making sense of uncertainty, performing artistically, setting problems, and choosing among competing professional paradigms, when these processes seem mysterious in the light of the prevailing model of professional knowledge. We are bound to an *epistemology of practice* which leaves us at a loss to explain, or even to describe, the competences to which we now give overriding importance. (Schön, 1983, pp. 19–20, emphasis added)

2.2   Demands of Contemporary Professional Work

In Sect. 2.2, we summarise three main sets of concerns that emerge from consideration of the demands of contemporary professional work and which connect to the core themes of this book. These concerns are as follows:

- The entrenched public and policy discourse criticising the adequacy of (university-based) preparation for the professions; graduates are not seen as being 'workplace ready'; there are frequent comments that they lack important general-purpose capabilities, such as being able to work in a team, communicate effectively, etc.
- The rise of performance monitoring, accountability, surveillance, regulation, litigation and other pressures, set amidst an intensification of professional work.
- New and emerging 'epistemified' demands – the necessity to engage in new and more complex kinds of knowledge work, with new and more intelligent tools and with changing distributions of expertise and labour.

As we will go on to point out, there is also a growing mismatch between the public, employer and governmental discourse about what is needed in the workplace and what close-up research is revealing about how work is actually done. Professional education curricula that respond too timidly to espoused needs may turn out to serve nobody's interests.

2.2.1   *Workplace Readiness*

There is a long history of employers' organisations – and governments, on their behalf – criticising universities for their failure to create work-ready graduates

(Hinchliffe & Jolly, 2011; Knight & York, 2004; Tholen, 2014). Some of the arguments resolve around claims that universities privilege narrow disciplinary knowledge over broader capabilities that employers say are necessary for success in the modern workplace. In practical terms, this has resulted in a number of initiatives – national and local – to develop so-called transferable skills or generic graduate attributes (Barrie, 2007; Bennett, Dunne, & Carre, 2000; Kalfa & Taksa, 2015). Coupled with this economic and social concern is an anxiety that universities are much better at teaching abstract conceptual knowledge ('theory') than they are at preparing students to work on real-world problems ('practice').

In the context of professional education, these disputes about the 'theory–practice' gap and about the degree to which graduates are 'workplace ready' have prompted a number of studies that have attempted to assess how well programs of professional preparation succeed in readying the graduate for the demands of their first workplace. Methods vary, but there is a body of empirical research that uses recent graduates' self-reports of how well their courses prepared them for the workplace (see, e.g. Keeve, Gerhards, Arnold, Zimmer and Zollner (2012) in dentistry, Schlett et al. (2010) in medicine, Hart and Macnee (2007) for nurse practitioners and Yu et al. (2013) for accountancy).

Outcomes from such studies are very varied, and much can depend on emphases in curriculum design, pedagogy and assessment. Even then, relations between broad educational approach and outcomes can be surprising. For example, Keeve et al. (2012) and Schlett et al. (2010) took a similar approach to eliciting the views of graduates from German universities of (a) the capabilities they had found of most value in their work and (b) the capabilities they felt had been relatively well developed or rather poorly developed in their professional preparation programs. Keeve et al. studied case-based learning (CBL) in dentistry and Schlett et al. problem-based learning (PBL) in medicine. Both studies reported that students felt their CBL/PBL programs left them underprepared to deal with business issues and that – perhaps surprisingly – they did not feel they had graduated with strong enough research skills. That said, in overall terms, graduates in both studies felt well prepared for most areas of practice. This contrasts with outcomes from similar studies in other professional fields – studies where graduates are asked to rate areas of capability that are (a) important in their work and (b) well or badly developed in their professional preparation. Hart and Macnee (2007), for example, report that only 10 % of the nurse practitioners in their sample felt very well prepared for practice and half felt 'minimally' or only 'somewhat' prepared. They were especially concerned about the lack of rigour in their preparations for clinical work and (like in the Keeve and Schlett studies) felt poorly prepared for the business and organisational aspects of their job:

> Physicians receive a much more rigorous educational experience and come out ready to practice. We do not and are embarrassed by our lack of clinical preparedness. (Hart & Macnee, 2007, p. 38)

A number of studies have been able to survey both employer and student/graduate views of the fit between professional education and workplace needs. For instance,

Yu et al. (2013) report a quasi-longitudinal study which captured views of students and their employers just after an internship and also views from alumni of the same program 1 year out from graduation. Comparing the interns' views with their employers' views revealed that, in most areas of capability, employers rated the interns' skills at a lower level than the interns' rated their own level of preparation – this was particularly the case for communication skills: a common complaint among employers, though something which is rarely subjected to close scrutiny or precise definition. One year after graduation, the alumni in this study have more moderate views than their corresponding interns – with more study and work experience, the alumni self-assessments come closer to the assessments of employers.

Studies *within* specific professions and of specific kinds of professional preparation program are necessary if one aims to improve alignment between workplace needs, assessment and curriculum design, pedagogy and so on. To get a more general sense of the relations between employers' views on workplace needs and what professional education programs are achieving depends on being able to summarise across what can be quite diverse studies. The feasibility of obtaining that general sense also depends upon complex issues about the nature of the capabilities that can be developed in university and workplace settings. For example, summarising a number of studies of employers' views, Hinchliffe and Jolly (2011) conclude that:

> ... employers prize most highly those skills that can only be feasibly developed in the workplace. (Hinchliffe & Jolly, 2011, p. 565)

Part of our motivation in producing this book has been to help clarify some issues about the fundamental nature of workplace capabilities, so that everyone can be clearer about what is wanted and what is really needed. In short:

- What kinds of knowledge can be learnt on campus, and what needs to be learnt during internships?
- How should we conceive of the development of workplace capabilities – especially when recent research suggests that this is not simply a matter of adding practical skills to a theoretical foundation. Rather, it seems clear, substantial *transformations* of knowledge occur when learning to use knowledge in real workplaces, on real problems.

Our research has a lot to say about the challenges of 'weaving' together different kinds of knowledge, including formal conceptual and experiential knowledge.

2.2.2 Managerialism, Performativity and Organised Professionalism

The classic accounts of professional work and professional ways of using knowledge were written in very different economic times. In the last 30 years or so, professional work in many countries has intensified substantially – with longer hours worked and/or higher levels of productivity expected (Green & McIntosh, 2001; Kelliher & Anderson, 2010).[3] Alongside this, there has been a major shift in the employment patterns for professionals, with many more people being employed to do professional work within large employing organisations (Evetts, 2014). Modes of control have shifted from professional self-regulation towards a greater interference by the state and also to greater control by managers, exercised through performance measures of various kinds (de Bruijn, 2002, 2010; Fitzgerald, 2008). In part, state intervention has been prompted by headline-grabbing failures in professional self-regulation, but it can be argued that there has also been a secular decline in trust (Allsop, 2006; Grace, 2014). Alongside this, we see growing concern about the possibilities of litigation in response to perceived failures to adhere to professional standards and a growing apparatus of measures to protect employing organisations from such risks.

Noordegraaf (2011) cautions against taking the simple opposition between professionalism and managerialism at face value. In short, he argues that a multiplicity of factors is strengthening the connections between organisations and professional work and that research on, and education for, professional work needs to consider the special qualities of 'organised professionalism' – professional practices that embody organisational logics. For one thing, there is a new generation of 'managerial professionals' who do not offer front-line services but who organise the rendering of those services. In addition, the complexity of the problems professionals find themselves facing requires organisational infrastructures – for example, to enable efficient multi-professional work and to manage risk:

> ... it is difficult to have one-to-one relations between professionals and clients. Clients might be empowered, or professionals must cooperate in order to provide effective services. This legitimises the rise of new *organizational* arrangements: joined-up services, multi-disciplinary and multi-agency teams, multi-professional and multi-agency partnerships, inter-professional collaboration, multi-professional practices, integrated services and the like. (Noordegraaf, 2011, p. 1360, original emphasis)

Noordegraaf predicts that organised professionalism will shift the balance of demands on the capabilities required of new entrants to each profession – with an increased emphasis on communication, cooperation and learning skills, an openness to learning the vocabularies, techniques and routines of other professional groups, to experiment with new service models and reflect on successes and failures:

---

[3] Intensification of work is not a simple phenomenon. In some countries – notably in Europe – new legal restrictions have been placed on the length of the working week, with major consequences for working practices in areas such as healthcare. Ongoing reductions in the real resources available for professional work in the public sector, and increasing competition in the private sector, nevertheless apply pressure to raise productivity and throughput, with accompanying stresses on the workforce. In contrast, increasing participation by women in areas of professional work previously dominated by men is often being accompanied by pressures to attain greater flexibility and control over work–life balance (Heiligers & Hingstman, 2000; Kelliher & Anderson, 2010).

... professional fields need to initiate cooperative projects and products, which include procedures, guidelines and formats for restructuring everyday work forms in the light of *coordinated action.* (op. cit., p. 1363, emphasis added)

In sum, the changing nature of organisational life for many professionals means that the programs that support their formation need to pay closer attention to inter-professional working and to the identification and development of skills (etc.) that professionals use to invent new working relationships and working methods.

2.2.3 The Mounting Demands of Epistemic Work

The rapidly widening use of information technology in contemporary work has made much more visible the fact that knowledge is produced in a multitude of places and that it flows rapidly across organisational, disciplinary and national boundaries (Gibbons et al., 1994; Nerland & Jensen, 2014). As Nerland and Jensen (2014) explain, rendering knowledge into abstract and symbolic forms makes it easier for it to travel – to be decontextualised and recontextualised, to circulate rapidly and to be applied in unforeseen circumstances. Knowledge is no longer bound to place:

... the knowledge worlds in which professional learning is embedded are becoming more extensive and complex ... students are presented with knowledge and ways of thinking that are linked with dynamic and geographically dispersed ecologies of knowledge. These wider worlds contribute to defining relevant knowledge and competencies ... we cannot take for granted that practitioners' engagement with knowledge is bounded to given sites. (Nerland & Jensen, 2014, p. 612)

Professional capability has long been associated with a mix of specialist, abstract codified knowledge (gained largely in the university) and tacit, experiential knowl-edge of processes, rules, cases and practices (gained largely in workplaces). The ability to use specialist codified knowledge in the dynamic, complex circumstances of practice is not the only requirement in contemporary work sites. As Jens-Christian Smeby (2012) puts it:

Theoretical knowledge, therefore, is not just a basis for professional problem-solving; professionals also have to provide scientifically based arguments to defend their diagnoses and decisions to a greater extent than previously. Thus the manner in which professional knowledge is developed in higher education is at the very heart of professionalism. (Smeby, 2012, p. 49)

Social expectations about professional accountability are thereby placing extra knowledge burdens on those training for the professions.

On top of this, the dynamics of professional work situations are such that professionals have not only to work with knowledge and use knowledge to justify their action; they also need to be adept at practices of creating and testing new, applicable knowledge. In this sense, *professional cultures* are taking on more of the qualities and practices of *epistemic cultures* – they have to become more knowledgeable about knowledge (Nerland, 2012; Nerland & Jensen, 2014). This includes developing strategies for creating new knowledge, of relevance to professional problems, and also strategies for redesigning ways of working – for example, to get the best out of working with other professional specialists, in new combinations, on new projects.

David Guile (2014) draws on a case study by Rogers Hall and colleagues (2002) to provide an illustration of how mixed groups of professionals have to invent ways of working with one another, almost on a project-by-project or case-by-case basis. Hall's example is from architecture – in particular, the remodelling of two historic libraries. The work was actually accomplished by architects, structural engineers, historic building preservationists and librarians. In thinking about implications for inter-professional education (IPE), Guile draws out the following points:

- Teams which form on such a case-by-case basis are best described using Engeström's notion of 'knotworking' – that is, their work entails a process of tying, untying and retying what appear to be separate threads of activity (Engeström, 2008, p. 194).
- The teams are also involved in what Victor and Boynton (1998) call 'co-configuration' – a process in which producers and users and products are engaged in ongoing relationships, through which the application of users' intelligence improves the working of products and their fit with users' needs. (We discuss this in more detail in Chap. 3.)
- Teams negotiate their own working processes, bring tensions to the surface (to broaden the inputs to the solutions chosen), reframe the problem as presented and problematise what each professional/disciplinary perspective sees as insoluble.
- In so doing, they need to create the conditions in which each professional can understand the others – their ideas, needs, perspectives and so on.

Guile draws from this the implication that inter-professional working is always a *situated* accomplishment: it depends upon social and material resources that come together in the doing of the work. This raises troubling questions about how students may be prepared for such work (Guile, 2014, p. 130; and see Chap. 19).

On a related tack, Roger Dunston (2014) talks of the 'co-production' of healthcare, a phrase which connotes:

> ... practices that are purposefully, 'strongly' and expansively focused on incorporating the service user(s) as competent and knowledgeable partners across all areas of health service design, development, delivery and evaluation. (Dunston, 2014, p. 141)

which also implies:

> ... new relational configurations in which the roles, rules and relationships that governed the way in which 'practitioners' and 'service users' interacted [are] profoundly reshaped. (op. cit., p. 142)

On this view, professionals also need to learn to create new methods for working with other partners – not just professionals from other specialties but also clients and their families.

In addition to this, professional knowledge work has become increasingly entangled with knowledge embedded in smart machines. We hear more and more about smart medical alarms, smart technologies for the disabled and the elderly, intelligent expert systems, smart hospitals, smart cities, etc. This saturation of social life and work with smart devices and systems also invites a rethinking of the shape of professional work and knowledge. Richard Susskind's (2010) *The End of Lawyers? Rethinking the Nature of Legal Services* provides a good illustration. He asks whether legal work cannot be done differently – more quickly, more cheaply and to a higher quality – and what sort of knowledge lawyers are likely to need when their work becomes even more suffused with the use of legal databases and intelligent legal systems and indeed becomes more global. While such arguments are sometimes pressed too hard – romanticising technology and ignoring the resilience of organisational forms and practices – the reality is undeniable. The availability of new technologies makes a difference to expectations about how work can be done, how work is distributed and what kinds of professional knowledge are needed.

2.3   Preparation for the Professions in Higher Education

Preparation for the professions has been part of university missions for a very long time. Professional education has been of great material importance to universities and has played a significant role in shaping questions about the purpose of the university. Many universities these days are heavily reliant on fees and related income associated with professional preparation – not just in business, but in a wide range of specialisms. The focus and evolution of universities cannot be understood as merely a concern for the reproduction of an *academic* workforce. This economic importance of professions to the university applies to both professional formation programs and certification. In return, university certification of a person's readiness to enter a profession is of great importance to the person and the profession. It is part of how the profession's status and competitive advantage are protected.

In short, the relations between the knowledge taught in universities and professionals' activity in the workplace are of great material importance for both the professionals and the universities. As just one instance, Michael Eraut (1994) comments on how universities' predilection for testing through formal examinations boosted the importance of codified knowledge:

> ... most examinations guaranteed only that knowledge they were able to test; and this seldom extended to practical competence. Hence one of the main consequences of their introduction was the transformation of large areas of the professional knowledge base into codified forms which suited the textbooks needed to prepare students for what were from the outset very traditional exams. (Eraut, 1994, p. 7)

Such matters give extra edge to debates about (a) relationships between explicit understanding, tacit knowledge and knowing in professional action; (b) different kinds of tacit knowledge; (c) the meaning of explicit, articulated, formal knowledge; and (d) the location of various forms of disciplinary knowledge in this debate. Hence, we focus on these issues carefully in Chaps. 3, 4 and 5.

As the book unfolds, we will try to show that some common approaches to understanding and fostering 'workplace capabilities' in higher education miss the importance of 'actionable knowledge' – knowledge capable of informing action in organisational and other workplace settings. 'Knowledge work' in higher education and 'actionable knowledge' in organisational settings are based on rather divergent notions of the various kinds of knowledge involved and of the relationships between them. The notion of epistemic fluency provides a conceptual basis for framing and exploring what are often hidden relationships between the contingent nature of professional work and ways of knowing adopted in professional communities and used in organising professional knowledge work.

2.4 Approaches within Professional Education

There is a rich, varied and rapidly growing literature on professional education, workplace learning, work-integrated learning, practice-based education and so on. We do not aim to reflect that literature here.[4] Rather, our aim is to offer some simple structuring of the main approaches in the field, as a way of connecting to core concerns explored later in this book.

Michael Eraut (1994, pp. 6–7) summarises the main modes of preparation for the professions as follows, indicating that most people's experiences involve a combination of several of these, in variable order: (a) a period of pupillage or internship; (b) enrolment in a professional college (outside the university system); (c) a qualifying exam – normally set by a professional association; a period of university study, normally resulting in an academic qualification; and (d) collection of evidence of practical competence – e.g. through a portfolio. In the past 20 years, many university schools and faculties that have a serious engagement in professional education have focussed efforts on achieving a better integration of workplace experience and academic study, in ways that are both stimulated and constrained by the actions of professional bodies. Indeed, a key consideration for academic staff managing programs that prepare students for a profession is how the combination of academic and workplace experiences can improve upon what students might learn merely through immersion as an apprentice in the professional workplace: what exactly is the added value of academic study, over and above the knowledge obtainable in the workplace? As Billett (2014) has pointed out, looking over the span of human history, direct instruction is a novel method for helping people learn how to work, and it is not at all clear that the kinds of learning that are best

---

[4] For general summaries, see Billett, Harteis and Gruber (2014).

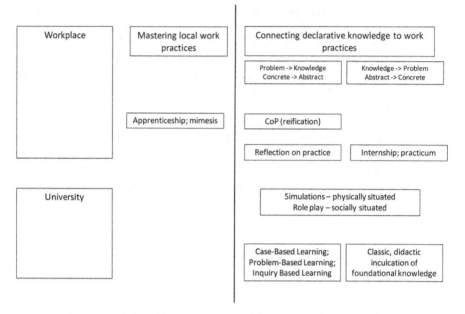

Fig. 2.1 Schema for approaches to professional formation

supported by formal educational processes are particularly important when it comes to getting things done.

A growing consciousness of the precarious relationships that may exist between academic study and workplace performance provides fertile ground for experimentation with new ways of linking the lecture hall and workplace. It is not merely that more and more workplace experience is seen as necessary; rather the search is for educational processes that help each student professional make connections between workplace and academia. The rest of this section provides a necessarily brief overview of some of the main approaches that are used to do this. Figure 2.1 provides one way of giving shape to the field.

The vertical dimension in Fig. 2.1 is broadly spatial, referring to the organisational setting for work-related learning. We can divide this roughly into university-based learning and workplace learning, while acknowledging that communication technologies make it impossible to insist on a sharp boundary between the two.

The horizontal dimension in Fig. 2.1 is knowledge oriented. On the left, we locate learning for work that is undertaken in circumstances where little or no explicit attention is paid to declarative or propositional knowledge.[5] In everyday language, we might say this involves a focus on practice, with little attention to theory. It values local 'know-how' over generalisable 'know that' and tacit

---

[5] Chapter 4 explains different kinds of knowledge.

knowledge over articulated knowledge and contribution to the productive work of the organisation over personal learning. Much of what is learnt is learnt through imitation (mimesis) and is a by-product of engagement in productive work (Billett, 2014). Of course, workplace learning can be done differently, and it may indeed involve structured opportunities to connect local practice to more general principles (Fuller & Unwin, 2014). However, such forms of apprenticeship start to move us to the right-hand side of the figure, where serious attention is paid to connecting 'theory and practice'. On this side of the figure, we distinguish educational arrangements on the basis of the direction of the relationship between problems of work and declarative knowledge. So on the far right of the figure, we see approaches that focus on the application of previously learnt declarative knowledge ('theory') – the movement being from abstract to concrete. Nearer the middle, we have approaches that use problems as the starting point, with the movement being from concrete to abstract, from 'practice' to 'theory'.

Thus, for example, we can locate the use of approaches based on 'communities of practice' (CoPs) in a space that is close to the workplace and where a characteristic activity involves capturing and sharing knowledge that is embedded in practice through processes of 'reification' – making things which represent and/or embody that knowledge (Wenger, 1998). The use of simulations and role-play activities is located near the interface between 'workplace' and 'university' in Fig. 2.1. In a literal sense, such learning activities are typically located in the university. But for educational purposes, they bring some affordances of the workplace to the university. For instance, the use of simulators instead of real equipment allows learning activity to proceed as if it was physically situated in the workplace – at least, to an acceptable degree of workplace fidelity. Role plays can serve a parallel function with respect to an experience that depends upon qualities of the social situation – on social resources for professional problem-solving that would not normally be found in academia. In the bottom right-hand corner of the figure, we have much-maligned classic 'academic' approaches to professional preparation, of the kind where a high value is placed on inculcation of foundational theoretical knowledge, the application of which is somebody else's problem.

Inter-professional education (IPE) is a vitally important area but hard to locate within this scheme. This is partly because the need for skills and knowledge to work across professional boundaries is now well recognised in workplaces, but the definition and learning of such skills are still in flux. We return to this shortly.

In the next three subsections, we give very brief summaries of three closely related and quite widely practised approaches to professional education that sit together in the 'university-based, problem-driven' area: case-based, problem-based and inquiry-based learning.

2.4.1   Case-Based Learning

Case-based learning (CBL) is one of the older pedagogical inventions in professional education. Its roots are in nineteenth-century legal education at Harvard, where it was introduced to overcome difficulties with the two then dominant modes of training lawyers – apprenticeship in a legal firm and lecture courses in a law school (Williams, 1992). The first of these was held to be very uneven in its outcomes and the second lacking in practicality. Under the case method, students' training involved consideration of authentic cases from the legal records, with discussion led by a law professor who also had deep, extensive practical professional experience. Students were challenged to make sense of legal language, procedures and constructs with little or no direct instruction or theoretical framing. Reports of their early learning experiences attest to long periods of confusion before an ability to understand and analyse the merits of cases developed. The case method spread to other Harvard faculties and – with variations – to other universities. Christensen and Hansen (1987) describe the Harvard case method in business education as follows:

> A case is a partial, historical, clinical study of a situation which has confronted a practicing administrator or managerial group. Presented in narrative form to encourage student involvement, it provides data – substantive and process – essential to an analysis of a specific situation, for the framing of alternative action programs, and for their implementation recognizing the complexity and ambiguity of the practical world. (Christensen & Hansen, 1987, p. 27)

While case-based learning was deemed, in law, to be necessitated by the structure of the law itself, in other professions, it is the vividness, concreteness and contextual specificity of the case that count (Merseth, 1996). This is held to assist in constructing a more nuanced understanding of professional principles: wrestling with authentic cases necessarily involves integrating diverse sources of knowledge, making subtle judgements and difficult decisions. More recently, case-based forms of learning have been the subject of a further line of innovation (Kolodner, 2006). Cases are not only considered as a pedagogical method – to learn more contextualised kinds of knowledge; they are seen as a distinct *way of reasoning* underpinned by a particular way of organising knowledge and particular cognitive processes that support expert resolution of complex issues. (We discuss this further in Chap. 19.) Experience in the use of case-based education methods has also proven to be an important foundation for innovations in problem-based learning.

2.4.2 Problem-Based Learning

Problem-based learning (PBL) has made substantial inroads into programs of professional preparation, especially in medicine, other health professions, engineering and law (Barrows & Tamblyn, 1980; Boud & Feletti, 1997; Schmidt, Rotgans, & Yew, 2011). PBL takes a number of forms, but its core characteristics include using problems to trigger learning; students working in small self-directed problem-focussed groups, with access to tutor guidance; and a shift of time demands away from lectures and towards self-study. PBL is motivated by an ambition to help students develop knowledge of a domain in a particular way – one which is aimed at helping students to connect knowledge that they learn to problems in the field of application (Schmidt et al., 2011). While some critics have argued that poorly guided PBL can be ineffective (Kirschner, Sweller, & Clark, 2006), there is substantial empirical evidence to indicate that, well implemented, it provides effective support for the development of *actionable knowledge* as well as practice in developing strategies for ongoing learning and inquiry (Albanese & Mitchell, 1993; Dochy, Segers, Van den Bossche, & Gijbels, 2003).

2.4.3   Inquiry-Based Learning

Inquiry-based learning (IBL) places a strong emphasis on the need to generate new knowledge, and/or to hone skills for independent learning and research (Aditomo, Goodyear, Bliuc, & Ellis, 2013; Doane & Varcoe, 2008; Spronken-Smith et al., 2011). It is rarely used for whole professional programs, but has a significant role in a range of professional courses. Depending on the ways in which IBL is implemented, it can be seen as a version of collaborative knowledge building (Bereiter, 2002; Moen, Mørch, & Paavola, 2012), which we explore in more detail in Chaps. 3 and 19. As we saw earlier in this chapter (Sect. 2.2.1), graduates of some case-based and problem-based learning programs expressed the view that while their education had equipped them with lifelong learning skills, it had not set them up well for *research* – for creating knowledge new to their practice. IBL has the potential to help here and, as we show in Chap. 19, is core to the development of professional education that equips new professionals to innovate.

In the next three sections, we move upwards on Fig. 2.1 to summarise some key ideas in the professional education literature related to learning in the workplace. Section 2.4.4 discusses the use of internships or various kinds. Internship on its own can be a valuable way of learning to apply theoretical knowledge on problems of practice. Section 2.4.5 describes reflective ways of learning. While reflective learning is not limited to the workplace, if experiential learning is also meant to build more general personal understanding, then it is commonly coupled with requirements to engage in structured forms of reflection. Section 2.4.6 outlines the educational use of ideas associated with communities of practice.

2.4.4   Internships

On a longer-term historical perspective, one might argue that learning in the workplace is the norm and that attempting to train people for work in schools and universities is a modern aberration (Billett, 2014; van Woerkom & Poell, 2010). University-based formation of professionals has been justified on a number of grounds, including the rapid growth in technical knowledge and the need to develop capabilities that question and can transform existing working practices (Eraut, 1994; Glazer, 1974; Guile, 2014). That said, university-based courses are invariably complemented with more or less structured workplace experiences. These go under a variety of names, including practicum, clinical placement, internship and externship. The rationale for work experience in general is rarely questioned, but in any single example, there is likely to be a mix of motivations. These include an ability to test theoretical ideas in circumstances of practice, gaining experience in recognising and framing messy, complex, practical problems, learning to work with others, learning from experienced colleagues, working with real clients, learning to navigate the geography of real worksites, learning local rules and procedures, mastering the technical equipment of the workplace and so on.

Internships – whatever label is used for them – usually require some forms of pedagogical structuring and support. For example, there may be a designated workplace mentor whose role is to help the novice intern through a process of induction into the workplace and who may also be involved in assessing the intern's workplace capabilities. In addition, the intern may be required to complete tasks that are not part of the normal work – such as keeping a reflective journal or portfolio. We analyse a number of structured tasks of this kind throughout the book, particularly in Chaps. 13 and 14.

2.4.5 Reflective Practice

The notion of reflection in and on one's professional learning and action has a long pedigree, going back through the work of Donald Schön (1983, 1987) to John Dewey (1910) and others. We discuss notions of reflection more thoroughly in Chap. 3. For now, it is important to note that the immediate, surface appeal of reflection as an activity in professional education, and its incorporation into the production of educational artefacts such as portfolios, has been accompanied by a conceptual dilution of the term. For some, it now means little more than 'thinking about what happened'. Part of the problem can be seen in significant differences between Dewey's and Schön's notions of reflective practice. Also, the two very different meanings of Schön's terms 'reflection in action' and 'reflection on action' have added to the confusion. The second of these has achieved wider currency in professional education programs, but in its travels, it has lost or stretched its connections with Schön's distinctive notions of professional action. Schön's conception of the reflective practicum gave a significant role to the teacher (or coach/ mentor) – discussion between student and coach being an important site and resource for reflection (Schön, 1987, Chap. 7). This has also disappeared from many instances of the use of reflection in professional education programs. In short, educational practice has tended to treat 'reflection' loosely and unproblematically. Furthermore, changes in the nature of professional work since the times in which Schön was writing have raised serious questions about the power of individual reflection to equip a new graduate for contemporary workplaces, especially for inter-professional work (Eraut, 1994, pp. 147–148; Boud, 2010; Frost, 2010; Guile, 2014). This realisation has given rise to new forms of collective reflective practices that increasingly are embedded in organisational change and learning processes (Checkland & Poulter, 2006; Senge, 2006). That said, they have not yet made a significant impact in professional preparation programs generally. (We discuss them more extensively in Chap. 19.)

2.4.6 Communities of Practice

The term 'community of practice' derives from the work of Jean Lave and Etienne Wenger on situated learning (Lave & Wenger, 1991; Wenger, 1998). It began as a way of referring to naturally occurring social practices and helped explain how skills are learnt, and identity is developed, in traditional community settings. Like reflective practice, this apparently simple and accessible idea has been taken up enthusiastically in professional education – and in education more broadly – while at the same time losing some of its core characteristics (Barton & Tusting, 2005; Fuller, Hodkinson, Hodkinson, & Unwin, 2005; Henderson, 2015; Quinn, 2010). An important question is whether a community of practice (CoP) is necessarily a naturally occurring, self-managing group of people, united in shared practices, or whether CoPs can be set up by educators, for educational purposes. For Wenger in particular, the ways CoPs create objects that embody valued practical knowledge – a process of *reification* – are an important resource for the development of capability, for individual workers, for the community as a whole and for other communities (Wenger, Trayner, & de Laat, 2011). Another significant issue is whether understandings of who learns from whom in a relatively stable, traditional CoP necessarily apply in contemporary workplaces, where newly arrived junior workers are often used as a source of updating by 'old timers' (see, e.g. Fuller et al., 2005). In addition to these more traditional communities of practice, new forms of (open and global) communities of innovation, professional networking and learning have been emerging. In such networked communities, the boundaries are not set so tightly around particular professions or workplaces. They include much more heterogeneous relationships and simultaneous processes of innovation and learning (Carvalho & Goodyear, 2014: Wenger et al., 2011). Students' participation in such communities tends to be unacknowledged in formal education settings (Nerland, 2012).

2.4.7 Inter-Professional Education

The need for more and better inter-professional education (IPE), to improve collaboration across professional specialisms, has been recognised for some years, particularly in the health sector (WHO, 2010). As we argued earlier in this chapter, the ability to work across boundaries – with other specialists and with clients who are taking on more responsibility for the co-production of outcomes – is becoming a more salient feature of work in many professions. Guile (2014) sees this as creating a paradox within professional education, where the need to develop the abilities for such boundary-crossing work is marginalised by discussions that insist on the importance of 'foundational' disciplinary knowledge. Tensions between disciplinary knowledge, professional specialist knowledge and the knowledge needed to collaborate effectively with others – each of which needs space in a packed curriculum – make it harder to resolve an appropriate focus for IPE:

> IPE aims to encourage different professionals to meet and interact in learning to improve collaborative practice and the health care of patients/clients, and therefore has more potential for enhancing collaborative practice than a programme of multiprofessional education (where professionals share their learning experiences but do not interact with one another, such as a joint lecture) or uniprofessional education (where professionals learn in isolation from one another). (Reeves et al., 2008, p. 3)

While approaches to IPE vary considerably, there is consistency around the point that getting students to engage in collaborative work across their professional specialisms needs to be approached in a carefully planned and structured way; it is not enough to simply place students from different professions in the same classroom or practicum context (IOM, 2013). As we will explain in Chap. 3, inter-professional working requires and develops what Anne Edwards (2010) calls 'relational expertise'. Serendipitous encounters between novices from different professions are a very inefficient and unreliable way of helping grow the knowledge needed to function effectively within an inter-professional team, especially if the novice professionals are also very focussed on exercising their own specialist skills and learning the routines of an unfamiliar workplace.

Research on high-functioning teams in healthcare settings underlines the importance of everyone in the team having a shared sense of purpose – understanding the collective goal and how to attain it – as well as having good levels of understanding of each other's roles and unique professional capabilities and high levels of mutual trust (Mitchell et al., 2012). In short, IPE has aims that depend upon an ability to interweave high-level conceptual knowledge, specialised skills, professional identity, personal knowledge and trust. How experienced professionals weave such apparently disparate resources in the execution of their work is an important theme in much of this book.

2.5 Concluding Points

In this chapter we have tried to sketch some territory which will be familiar to readers who are engaged in professional education, whether as teachers of professionals or as researchers of the field. Our main concern is to create some connections from this familiar territory to the core concerns of knowledgeable action, actionable knowledge and the nature and development of epistemic fluency which permeate the rest of the book. The following points may help strengthen these connections:

- Professional work has always involved an ability to blend codified knowledge with experiential knowledge. This is becoming more challenging as (a) codified knowledge expands and changes and (b) workplaces and work practices become more complex and dynamic.
- Professional education approaches that optimise for teaching codified knowledge cannot be relied upon to provide good foundations for either knowledgeable action or the development of new knowledge and innovative work practices. This latter kind of knowledge is deeply entrenched in the relationships between one's personal capability and the capabilities of others, abstract forms of knowledge and situated practice.
- Professional preparation needs to change, and this change needs to be informed by sharper understandings of knowledge, knowledgeable action and actionable knowledge. As we argue throughout this book, professional preparation needs to shape, and be shaped by, an understanding of how professionals weave together diverse forms of knowledge and diverse ways of knowing – that is to say, by an understanding of epistemic fluency.

References

Abbott, A. D. (1988). *The system of professions: An essay on the division of expert labor*. Chicago, IL: University of Chicago Press.

Aditomo, A., Goodyear, P., Bliuc, A. M., & Ellis, R. A. (2013). Inquiry-based learning in higher education: Principal forms, educational objectives, and disciplinary variations. *Studies in Higher Education, 38*(9), 1239–1258. doi:10.1080/03075079.2011.616584.

Adler, I., & Kraus, V. (1985). Components of occupational prestige evaluations. *Work and Occupations, 12*, 23–39.

Albanese, M., & Mitchell, S. (1993). Problem-based learning: A review of the literature on its outcomes and implementation issues. *Academic Medicine, 68*(1), 52–81.

Allsop, J. (2006). Regaining trust in medicine: Professional and state strategies. *Current Sociology, 54*(4), 621–636. doi:10.1177/0011392106065093.

Archer, M. (2007). *Making our way through the world: Human reflexivity and social mobility*. Cambridge, NY: Cambridge University Press.

Barrie, S. (2007). A conceptual framework for the teaching and learning of generic graduate attributes. *Studies in Higher Education, 32*(4), 439–458.

Barrows, H. S., & Tamblyn, R. M. (1980). *Problem-based learning: An approach to medical education*. New York, NY: Springer.

Barton, D., & Tusting, K. (Eds.). (2005). *Beyond communities of practice: Language, power and social context*. Cambridge, UK: Cambridge University Press.

Bauman, Z. (1987). *Legislators and interpreters*. London, UK: Polity Press.

Bennett, N., Dunne, E., & Carre, C. (2000). *Skills development in higher education and employment*. Buckingham, UK: SRHE/Open University Press.

Bereiter, C. (2002). *Education and mind in the knowledge age*. Mahwah, NJ: Lawrence Erlbaum Associates.

Billett, S. (2014). *Mimetic learning at work: Learning in the circumstances of practice*. Heidelberg, Germany: Springer.

Billett, S., Harteis, C., & Gruber, H. (Eds.). (2014). *International handbook of research in professional and practice-based learning (2 Vols)*. Dordrecht, The Netherlands: Springer.

Boud, D. (2010). Relocating reflection in the context of practice. In H. Bradbury, N. Frost, S. Kilminster, & M. Zukas (Eds.), *Beyond reflective practice: New approaches to professional lifelong learning* (pp. 25–36). London, UK: Routledge.

Boud, D., & Feletti, G. (Eds.). (1997). *The challenge of problem based learning* (2nd ed.). London, UK: Kogan Page.

Carr, D. (2014). Professionalism, profession and professional conduct: Towards a basic logical and ethical geography. In S. Billett, C. Harteis, & H. Gruber (Eds.), *International handbook of research in professional and practice-based learning* (pp. 5–28). Dordrecht, The Netherlands: Springer.

Carr-Saunders, A., & Wilson, P. (1933). *The professions*. Oxford, UK: Clarendon.

Carvalho, L., & Goodyear, P. (Eds.). (2014). *The architecture of productive learning networks*. New York, NY: Routledge.

Checkland, P., & Poulter, J. (2006). *Learning for action: A short definitive account of soft systems methodology and its use for practitioners, teachers, and students*. Hoboken, NJ: John Wiley & Sons.

Christensen, C., & Hansen, A. (1987). *Teaching and the case method*. Boston, MA: Harvard Business School Press.

Dall'Alba, G. (2009). *Learning to be professionals*. Dordrecht, The Netherlands: Springer.

de Bruijn, J. A. (2002). *Managing performance in the public sector*. London, UK: Routledge.

de Bruijn, J. A. (2010). *Managing professionals*. London, UK: Routledge.

Dent, M., & Whitehead, S. (2002). *Managing professional identities: Knowledge, performativity and the 'new' professional*. London, UK: Routledge.

Denzin, N. K., & Mettlin, C. J. (1968). Incomplete professionalization: The case of pharmacy. *Social Forces, 46*(3), 375–381.

Dewey, J. (1910). *How we think*. Boston, MA: D. C. Heath.

Doane, G. H., & Varcoe, C. (2008). Knowledge translation in everyday nursing: From evidence-based to inquiry-based practice. *Advances in Nursing Science, 31*(4), 283–295. doi:10.1097/01. ANS.0000341409.17424.7f.

Dochy, F., Segers, M., Van den Bossche, P., & Gijbels, D. (2003). Effects of problem-based learning: A meta-analysis. *Learning and Instruction, 13*(5), 533–568.

Dunston, R. (2014). Arrangements of co-production in healthcare: Partnership modes of inter-professional practice. In T. Fenwick & M. Nerland (Eds.), *Reconceptualising professional learning: Sociomaterial knowledges, practices and responsibilities* (pp. 140–154). London, UK: Routledge.

Edwards, A. (2010). *Relational agency: Learning to be a resourceful practitioner*. Dordrecht, The Netherlands: Springer.

Ekbia, H., & Nardi, B. (2014). Heteromation and its (dis)contents: The invisible division of labor between humans and machines. *First Monday, 19*(6). http://firstmonday.org/article/view/5331/4090

Engeström, Y. (2008). *From teams to knots: Activity-theoretical studies of collaboration and learning at work*. Cambridge, NY: Cambridge University Press.

Eraut, M. (1994). *Developing professional knowledge and competence*. London, UK: Falmer Press.

Etzioni, A. (Ed.). (1969). *The semi-professions and their organization*. New York, NY: Free Press.

Evetts, J. (2014). The concept of professionalism: Professional work, professional practice and learning. In S. Billett, C. Harteis, & H. Gruber (Eds.), *International handbook of research in professional and practice-based learning* (pp. 29–56). Dordrecht, The Netherlands: Springer.

Faulconbridge, J. R., & Hall, S. (2009). Educating professionals and professional education in a geographical context. *Geography Compass, 3*(1), 171–189. doi:10.1111/j.1749-8198.2008. 00176.x.

Fitzgerald, T. (2008). The continuing politics of mistrust: Performance management and the erosion of professional work. *Journal of Educational Administration and History, 40*(2), 113–128. doi:10.1080/00220620802210871.

Frost, N. (2010). Professionalism and social change: The implications of social change for the 'reflective practitioner'. In H. Bradbury, N. Frost, S. Kilminster, & M. Zukas (Eds.), *Beyond reflective practice: New approaches to professional lifelong learning* (pp. 15–24). London, UK: Routledge.

Fuller, A., Hodkinson, H., Hodkinson, P., & Unwin, L. (2005). Learning as peripheral participation in communities of practice: A reassessment of key concepts in workplace learning. *British Educational Research Journal, 31*(1), 49–68. doi:10.1080/0141192052000310029.

Fuller, A., & Unwin, L. (2014). Nurturing occupational expertise in the contemporary workplace: An 'apprenticeship turn' in professional learning. In T. Fenwick & M. Nerland (Eds.), *Reconceptualising professional learning: Sociomaterial knowledges, practices and responsibilities* (pp. 85–98). London, UK: Routledge.

Gibbons, M., Limoges, C., Nowotny, H., Schwartzman, S., Scott, P., & Trow, M. (1994). *The new production of knowledge: The dynamics of science and research in contemporary societies.* London, UK: Sage.

Glazer, N. (1974). Schools of the minor professions. *Minerva, 12*(3), 346–364.

Gorman, E. H., & Sandefur, R. L. (2011). "Golden age", quiescence, and revival: How the sociology of professions became the study of knowledge-based work. *Work and Occupations, 38*(3), 275–302. doi:10.1177/0730888411417565.

Grace, G. (2014). Professions, sacred and profane: Reflections on the changing nature of professionalism. In M. Young & J. Muller (Eds.), *Knowledge, expertise and the professions.* London, UK: Routledge.

Green, F., & McIntosh, S. (2001). The intensification of work in Europe. *Labour Economics, 8*(2), 291–308. http://dx.doi.org/10.1016/S0927-5371(01)00027-6.

Guile, D. (2014). Interprofessional working and learning: A conceptualization of their relationship and its implications for education. In T. Fenwick & M. Nerland (Eds.), *Reconceptualising professional learning: Sociomaterial knowledges, practices and responsibilities* (pp. 125–139). London, UK: Routledge.

Hall, R., Stevens, R., & Torralba, T. (2002). Disrupting representational infrastructure in conversations across disciplines. *Mind, Culture, and Activity, 9*(3), 179–210.

Hart, A. M., & Macnee, C. L. (2007). How well are nurse practitioners prepared for practice: Results of a 2004 questionnaire study. *Journal of the American Academy of Nurse Practitioners, 19*(1), 35–42.

Hearn, J. (1982). Notes on patriarchy, professionalization and the semi-professions. *Sociology, 16,* 184–202.

Heiligers, P. J. M., & Hingstman, L. (2000). Career preferences and the work–family balance in medicine: Gender differences among medical specialists. *Social Science & Medicine, 50*(9), 1235–1246. http://dx.doi.org/10.1016/S0277-9536(99)00363-9.

Henderson, M. (2015). The (mis)use of community of practice: Delusion, confusion and instrumentalism in educational technology research. In S. Bulfin, N. F. Johnson, & C. Bigum (Eds.), *Critical perspectives on education and technology* (pp. 127–140). New York, NY: Palgrave Macmillan.

Hickson, D., & Thomas, M. (1969). Professionalization in Britain: A preliminary measurement. *Sociology, 3,* 37–53.

Hinchliffe, G. W., & Jolly, A. (2011). Graduate identity and employability. *British Educational Research Journal, 37*(4), 563–584. doi:10.1080/01411926.2010.482200.

IOM (Institute of Medicine). (2013). *Interprofessional education for collaboration: Learning how to improve health from interprofessional models across the continuum of education to practice.* Washington, DC: The National Academies Press.

Kalfa, S., & Taksa, L. (2015). Cultural capital in business higher education: Reconsidering the graduate attributes movement and the focus on employability. *Studies in Higher Education, 40* (4), 580–595. doi:10.1080/03075079.2013.842210.

Keeve, P. L., Gerhards, U., Arnold, W. A., Zimmer, S., & Zollner, A. (2012). Job requirements compared to dental school education: Impact of a case-based learning curriculum. *GMS Zeitschrift für Medizinische Ausbildung, 29*(4), 1–14.

Kelliher, C., & Anderson, D. (2010). Doing more with less? Flexible working practices and the intensification of work. *Human Relations, 63*(1), 83–106. doi:10.1177/0018726709349199.

Kirschner, P. A., Sweller, J., & Clark, R. E. (2006). Why minimal guidance during instruction does not work: An analysis of the failure of constructivist, discovery, problem-based, experiential, and inquiry-based teaching. *Educational Psychologist, 41*(2), 75–86. doi:10.1207/s15326985ep4102_1.

Knight, P., & York, M. (2004). *Learning, curriculum and employability in higher education.* London, UK: RoutledgeFalmer.

Kolodner, J. L. (2006). Case-based reasoning. In K. Sawyer (Ed.), *The Cambridge handbook of the learning sciences* (pp. 225–242). Cambridge, NY: Cambridge University Press.

Lave, J., & Wenger, E. (1991). *Situated learning: Legitimate peripheral participation.* Cambridge, UK: Cambridge University Press.

Leicht, K. T., & Fennell, M. L. (1997). The changing organizational context of professional work. *Annual Review of Sociology, 23*(1), 215–231. doi:10.1146/annurev.soc.23.1.215.

Merseth, K. (1996). Cases and case methods in teacher education. In J. Sikula (Ed.), *Handbook of research on teacher education* (2nd ed., pp. 722–744). New York, NY: Macmillan.

Millerson, G. (1964). *The qualifying associations: A study in professionalization.* London, UK: Routledge.

Minnameier, G. (2014). Moral aspects of professions and professional practice. In S. Billett, C. Harteis, & H. Gruber (Eds.), *International handbook of research in professional and practice-based learning* (pp. 57–77). Dordrecht, The Netherlands: Springer.

Mitchell, P., Wynia, M., Golden, R., McNellis, B., Okun, S., Webb, C. E., … von Kohorn, I. (2012). Core principles & values of effective team-based health care: Discussion paper. Washington, DC: Institute of Medicine. Retrieved April 17, 2016 from http://iom.edu/Global/Perspectives/2012/TeamBasedCare.aspx.

Moen, A., Mørch, A., & Paavola, S. (Eds.). (2012). *Collaborative knowledge creation: Practices, tools, concepts.* Rotterdam, The Netherlands: Sense.

Moore, W., & Rosenblum, G. (1970). *The professions: Roles and rules.* New York, NY: Russell Sage.

Nerland, M. (2012). Professions as knowledge cultures. In K. Jensen, L. C. Lahn, & M. Nerland (Eds.), *Professional learning in the knowledge society* (pp. 27–48). Rotterdam, The Netherlands: Sense.

Nerland, M., & Jensen, K. (2014). Learning through epistemic practices in professional work: Examples from nursing and engineering. In T. Fenwick & M. Nerland (Eds.), *Reconceptualising professional learning: Sociomaterial knowledges, practices and responsibilities* (pp. 25–37). London, UK: Routledge.

Noordegraaf, M. (2011). Risky business: How professionals and professional fields (must) deal with organizational issues. *Organization Studies, 32*(10), 1349–1371. doi:10.1177/0170840611416748.

Parsons, T. (1968). Professions. In D. Shils (Ed.), *International encyclopedia of the social sciences* (Vol. 12, pp. 536–547). New York, NY: Macmillan.

Quinn, J. (2010). *Learning communities and imagined social capital: Learning to belong.* London, UK: Continuum.

Reeves, S., Zwarenstein, M., Goldman, J., Barr, H., Freeth, D., Hammick, M., & Koppel, I. (2008). Interprofessional education: Effects on professional practice and health care outcomes. *Cochrane Database of systematic reviews, 1.* http://onlinelibrary.wiley.com/doi/10.1002/14651858.CD002213.pub2/pdf/

Rueschemeyer, D. (1983). Professional autonomy and the social control of expertise. In R. Dingwall & P. Lewis (Eds.), *The sociology of the professions: Lawyers, doctors and others* (pp. 38–58). London, UK: Macmillan.

Saks, M. (2015). Inequalities, marginality and the professions. *Current Sociology, 63*(6), 850–868. doi:10.1177/0011392115587332.

Schlett, C., Doll, H., Dahmen, J., Polacsek, O., Federkeil, G., Fischer, M., et al. (2010). Job requirements compared to medical school education: Differences between graduates from problem-based learning and conventional curricula. *BMC Medical Education, 10*(1), 1–8.

Schmidt, H. G., Rotgans, J. I., & Yew, E. H. J. (2011). The process of problem-based learning: What works and why. *Medical Education, 45*(8), 792–806. doi:10.1111/j.1365-2923.2011.04035.x.

Schön, D. A. (1983). *The reflective practitioner: How professionals think in action.* New York, NY: Basic Books.

Schön, D. A. (1987). *Educating the reflective practitioner.* London, UK: Jossey-Bass.

Sciulli, D. (2005). Continental sociology of professions today: Conceptual contributions. *Current Sociology, 53*(6), 915–942. doi:10.1177/0011392105057155.

Senge, P. M. (2006). *The fifth discipline: the art and practice of the learning organization* (Rev. and updated ed.). Milsons Point, Australia: Random House Business Books.

Smeby, J. C. (2012). The significance of professional education. In K. Jensen, L. C. Lahn, & M. Nerland (Eds.), *Professional learning in the knowledge society* (pp. 48–67). Rotterdam, The Netherlands: Sense.

Spronken-Smith, R., Walker, R., Dickinson, K., Closs, G., Lord, J., & Harland, T. (2011). Redesigning a curriculum for inquiry: An ecology case study. *Instructional Science, 39*(5), 721–735. doi:10.1007/s11251-010-9150-5.

Susskind, R. E. (2010). *The end of lawyers? Rethinking the nature of legal services.* Oxford, MA: Oxford University Press.

Tholen, G. (2014). Graduate employability and educational context: A comparison between Great Britain and the Netherlands. *British Educational Research Journal, 40*(1), 1–17. doi:10.1002/berj.3023.

Turner, B. (1995). *Medical power and social knowledge.* London, UK: Sage.

Unschold, P. (2010). *Medicine in China: A history of ideas.* Oakland, CA: University of California Press.

van Woerkom, M., & Poell, R. (Eds.). (2010). *Understanding learning in the workplace: Concepts, measurement and application.* London, UK: Routledge.

Victor, B., & Boynton, A. C. (1998). *Invented here: Maximizing your organization's internal growth and profitability.* Boston, MA: Harvard Business School Press.

Wenger, E. (1998). *Communities of practice: Learning, meaning, and identity.* Cambridge, NY: Cambridge University Press.

Wenger, E., Trayner, B., & de Laat, M. (2011). *Promoting and assessing value creation in communities and networks: A conceptual framework* (Vol. 18). Heerlen, The Netherlands: Open Universiteit.

WHO (World Health Organization). (2010). Framework for action on interprofessional education and collaborative practice. Retrieved April 17, 2016 from http://www.who.int/hrh/resources/framework_action/en/ index.html.

Wilensky, H. (1964). The professionalization of everyone. *American Journal of Sociology, 70*(2), 142–146.

Williams, S. M. (1992). Putting case-based instruction into context: Examples from legal and medical education. *The Journal of the Learning Sciences, 2*(4), 367–427. doi:10.2307/1466615.

Yu, S., Churyk, N. T., & Chang, A. (2013). Are students ready for their future accounting careers? Insights from observed perception gaps among employers, interns, and alumni. *Global Perspectives on Accounting Education, 10*, 1–15.

Chapter 3
Defining the Problem: Four Epistemic Projects in Professional Work and Education

> So they don't just become a registered nurse – they're always looking at improving their education, looking at evidence based practice, doing in-service when they're working. Always looking at making it more effective. <...> [F]rom the very first semester, the idea behind the practice development was to instil that that this is what you do for ever as a registered nurse. This is the practice we want you to be thinking about. (Nursing Practice Coordinator)

3.1 Crafting Expert Practitioners

When we asked university teachers to describe what students learn in professional practice courses, we were struck by a *commonality* in their teaching agendas and by the *diversity* of their answers about how they do this. Many teachers started to describe their courses by explaining recent 'paradigm shifts' in their respective professional areas. The examples that they gave included a shift from dispensing medications to improving the quality of the use of medicines and improving overall community health (in pharmacy education), the introduction of a new conceptual framework that entirely restructures the arts teaching curriculum (in teacher education) and a shift to continuous improvement of patient-centred care (in nursing education):

> There is a significant push, not only [here], but internationally, to reduce the amount of remuneration pharmacists receive for dispensing a medicine, and instead, remunerate them for improving quality use of medicines or health outcomes. So it's a major paradigm shift within the profession. (Pharmacy Lecturer)

How do university teachers prepare students for a changing world? Some of the aims and tasks associated with the professional practice courses featured in our research looked fairly mundane (e.g. to dispense a medication, to design an assessment task, to administer a literacy test), but some of them were much more future oriented and challenging (e.g. to design an ideal pharmacy layout, to create

© Springer Science+Business Media Dordrecht 2017
L. Markauskaite, P. Goodyear, *Epistemic Fluency and Professional Education*,
Professional and Practice-based Learning 14, DOI 10.1007/978-94-007-4369-4_3

an evidence-informed nursing guide for manual handling, health assessment or infection control).

Broadly speaking, all of the examples uncovered in our empirical research differed in their details, but all were aimed at achieving something along one or more of the following four lines. That is, they were underpinned by one or more of the following rationales:

1. Giving form to the combination of professional 'mind' and 'action', that is, mapping and mixing 'theories' and 'evidence' learnt at university with certain kinds of practical knowledge. Examples included such tasks as reflecting on professional experiences or developing a plan or strategy.
2. Climbing into a professional 'skin': getting the body, mind and materials to act together (e.g. getting the pitch of one's voice right when teaching), doing what professionals do and feeling how they feel (e.g. thinking and feeling like a nurse).
3. Challenging students' minds with future-oriented ideas and with changing conceptions of their professions (e.g. creating an ideal pharmacy layout, developing a disease state management service).
4. Going 'outside the box' of professional skill and knowledge and engaging with practices at the intersections between different professional fields, with their different ways of knowing (e.g. for trainee pharmacists, talking with a doctor; for preservice teachers, knowing who the school social worker is and what they do).

All of the examples we observed involved grappling with some 'wild' – untamed and complex – challenges characteristic of their professions: the diversity of students', patients' and other clients' needs, multiple policy requirements, discrepancies between evidence and demands, contingency of professional decisions, etc. When 'wrapped' into simple specifications for student assignments, the tasks we observed clearly reflected some key practical and epistemic challenges in professional learning. On the one hand, there is the need to 'pack' the diversity of professional issues into a manageably small number of shapes and responses that students can learn. On the other hand, there is the challenge of adding to any form of professional knowledge the possibilities for infinite variation that will be encountered in real-world professional practice:

> People don't realise school counsellors cover from basically from three and half year olds to 18 year olds. So all of primary and secondary and special education – kids with disability. So it's really wide. So to fit all that expertise and range is very hard. <...> I don't expect them [students] to leave the university fully formed. I expect them to leave fully qualified to do it. But I'm not expected – I've covered everything – it's just impossible because it's such a wide ranging job. So I don't feel that it all hangs on that [Tasks that students do in the course]. (School Counselling Lecturer and Program Director)

In a variety of ways, the professional educators with whom we spoke tried to help students render the real world so that it looked more compactly 'conceptual' and render the conceptual world to make it feel more diverse, realistic and concretely 'material'. The teaching aims of these courses were underpinned by a notion of the 'mindful professional' – someone able to fuse theoretical knowledge with a

Table 3.1   Four epistemic projects of professional learning

	Rationale underlying tasks set for students	Challenges for professional learning	Epistemic projects
1	Giving form to mind and action	Linking theory with practice	Reflective rational
2	Donning a professional skin	Forming fine-tuned professional skills and identity	Reflective embodied
3	Challenging minds with future developments	Creating knowledge for the future	Knowledge building
4	Going outside one's professional box	Working with other professionals and clients	Relational expertise

common-sense grasp of the situation, formal rules with creativity, standards with improvisation and reason with intuition.

How can students learn to think and act as professionals? Indeed, how can they come to *be* professionals? Most of the things that students find hard to learn in their professions tend to be concentrated around four challenges, each of which is linked to the four lines sketched above: linking theories with practice, developing professional skills and identity, designing professional artefacts for the future and working with other professionals and clients. In light of such challenges, how do universities 'craft' future professionals? How do students craft themselves as professionals? How do they participate in the collective crafting of future professions?

Table 3.1 summarises the four kinds of professional learning tasks and associated challenges that we identified in our observations and interviews with professional educators. (These tasks are primarily distinguished by their respective rationales.) The table also connects these to what we are calling the four main 'epistemic projects' in professional education. Each of these epistemic projects can be thought of as a kind of learning journey: a reimagining of professional knowledge and practice, through which one learns/inhabits this knowledge and practice. The relationship between these four epistemic projects is captured in Fig. 3.1, which can be understood as follows.

We start by drawing on the work of Pickering (1995) and Mulcahy (2011b), to contrast two views of professional learning: the *representational* and the *performative*. Each involves distinct kinds of 'epistemic tricks'[1] that students are supposed to master.

We can think of them thus:

- Representational: linking doing with knowing
- Performative: linking doing with being

The *representational* view emphasises the building of bridges between one's professional actions and articulated forms of knowledge. In contrast, the

---

[1] We use the phrase 'epistemic tricks' because it suggests mastering skills that are usually somewhat hidden in the fluent work of experienced professionals: tricks which can appear 'magical' or 'mystical' for a lay observer until explicated.

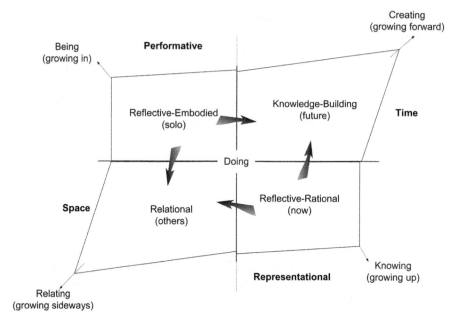

Fig. 3.1 Relations between the four epistemic projects

performative view foregrounds linking one's engagement with activities in the world to the development of the existential qualities of being a professional – qualities such as values and dispositions. While the representational view also acknowledges the critical role of professional qualities, it sees professional ways of being as emergent from knowledgeable action, rather than a direct focus for learning. Similarly, the performative view does not neglect the importance of professional knowing; rather, it sees knowing as emergent from professional coping with the world and becoming a professional, rather than being a direct focus for learning.

Next, we suggest that students have to go beyond *self*-representation and *self*-performance. They are also challenged to engage in professional work on the boundaries of their professions. One set of boundaries is *temporal* – extending doing and knowing from the past and present into the future. The other set of boundaries is *organisational* or *spatial* – extending doing and being from 'assembling the professional self' (Mulcahy, 2011b) to working across the boundaries of professional fields, crafting new professional assemblages and dwelling in what might be called 'trans-epistemic' spaces.

We argue that working in such dynamic spaces involves mastering all four sets of epistemic 'tricks' together. This capacity is one way of understanding what we mean by *epistemic fluency*. At the end of the book, we will extend this view by proposing a fifth project that connects the other four.

In the next part of this chapter, we describe in some detail these four reimaginings of professional learning, drawing connections where appropriate to existing writing about professional work and professional education. It may help to know in advance that our account moves towards a key idea about innovation in professional work that is fundamental to the book: the knowledge involved in a capability is not sufficient to improve that capability. We explain the significance of this in Sect. 3.7.

3.2   The Reflective-Rational Project: From Rational Knowledge to Reflective Practice to Rational Reflection

> In real-world practice, problems do not present themselves to practitioners as givens. They must be constructed from the materials of problematic situations that are puzzling, troubling, and uncertain. In order to convert a problematic situation to a problem, a practitioner must do a certain kind of work. He must make sense of an uncertain situation that initially makes no sense. (Schön, 2002, p. 47)

In broad terms, this first epistemic project can be traced back to the intersection of two lines of thought about (a) the link between theory and practice and (b) reflective thinking (cf. Dewey, 1910, 1938; Eraut, 1994; Schön, 1983, 1985). The pioneers of the pragmatic turn in education critiqued the positivist model of professional knowledge as an epistemic canon and made a distinction between reflective thinking and technical-rational thinking (Dewey, 1938; Schön, 1983). From the technical rationality perspective, practical knowledge is a form of applied science, and professionals should learn general problem-solving principles provided for them by the basic sciences and then develop skills in applying these principles in rigorous, proceduralised ways to the professional problems they encounter. The reflective project opposed this view, pointing to the uncertainty, uniqueness, value conflicts and other epistemic complexities of practical phenomena encountered in professional work. Real-world situations are irreducible to direct application of scientific principles; and, as Schön (1983) argued, practical knowledge involves a capacity to name the elements and frame encountered situations as problems. On this view, the epistemology of practice involves doing and thinking 'on one's feet'. Schön argued it is not only rigour but also relevance that should be the basis for professional knowledge. He suggested that such knowledge is best learnt by combining 'the teaching of applied science with coaching in the artistry of reflection in action' (Schön, 1987, p. xii). From this reflection-in-action perspective:

> ... professionals must be equipped with epistemological tools that can help them raise useful hypotheses, experiment with different candidate solutions and evaluate results. (de Souza, 2005, p. 32).

Schön (1987) also argued that professionals reflect not only 'in action' but also 'on action', suggesting that there is another layer of professional knowledge, knowing and learning – such as general principles – which is different from the knowledge involved in the rapid decisions of concrete problem-solving and which requires a different kind of reflection. In relation to both reflection in action and reflection on action, Schön opposed the technical-rational view of a 'systematic knowledge base of a profession', seen as one that is:

> ... specialized, firmly bounded, scientific, and standardized. (Schön, 1983, p. 23).

Practical problems do not present themselves as neat cases or instances of scientific generalisations. Even when practitioners take time for reflection, they still think about problems in the language of practice and relevance, not in the language of scientific inquiry and rigour.

Schön's views on reflective practice are now widely recognised in higher education. However, they are not seen as universally applicable, and the reflective turn takes a number of modified forms.

For example, Schön (1987) was primarily interested in designers' work and 'designery' ways of knowing in action that, paraphrasing Latour (1990), are done by 'shuffling' papers: being 'thin' and 'slow' on the physical plane of action, but 'thick' on the epistemic plane of mental work:

> ... interacting with the model, getting surprising results, trying to make sense of the results, and then inventing new strategies of action on the basis of the new interpretation. (Schön & Bennett, 1996, p. 181)

Such thinking and action are not characteristic of all professions, particularly those that frequently require fast responses, such as in teaching, nursing and other health professions. Eraut (1994) and some others (e.g. Usher, Bryant, & Johnston, 1997) have questioned if, and how, reflection in action may happen in more dynamic professional work, arguing that Schön essentially overlooked some psychological realities of reflective thinking and underestimated pressure of time as a critical factor. Eraut (1994) noted that many practical decisions have to be made quickly and the scope for reflective thought is extremely limited in such situations. In these conditions, as Eraut argued:

> ... reflection is best seen as a metacognitive process in which the practitioner is alerted to a problem, rapidly reads the situation, decides what to do and proceeds in a state of continuing alertness. (Eraut, 1994, p. 145).[2]

Eraut also did not agree with Schön's clear-cut distinction between the theoretical or propositional knowledge invoked by 'technical rationality', in Schön's sense, and knowledge used in practical situations. As Eraut claimed:

> ... the use of such theoretical knowledge may not always be in the application mode stressed by the technical rationality model, but in the interpretative mode where it is more

---

[2] Eraut (1994) makes an explicit distinction between two meanings of reflection: 'metacognition' and 'deliberation'. Metacognition denotes alertness to, and control of, the ideas received from perception and sensations, but it does not involve deliberative consideration. Only 'deliberation' refers to serious consideration and deeper reflective thought 'the process of bringing personal knowledge under critical control' (p. 156).

> difficult to detect. Moreover, just because busy professionals do not use a particular idea, does not imply that they should not: that remains to be argued. (op. cit., pp. 103–104)

For Eraut, there *is* no clear-cut distinction between theory and practice. He agrees that the knowledge and knowing that underpin professional action should be of central importance in professional learning. He also agrees that the use of theoretical (propositional) knowledge in practical decisions requires considerable time and significant intellectual effort. But, in contrast to Schön, he argues that propositional knowledge needs to undergo significant transformation before it enters practice. So the process of interpreting and personalising theoretical propositions needs considerable support during professional education.

In higher education, these quite diverse views of knowledge and learning usually come in one 'pedagogical package' of *rational reflection*. This aims to use professional propositions and disciplinary concepts as lenses to reflect on professional phenomena and performance (Eraut, 1994, 2009; Roth, 2010; Schön, 1987; Wenger, 1998). In this way, the propositional kinds of theoretical and applied knowledge are linked with skill and performed practice.

Despite this commitment to action and practical knowledge, this view assumes that there is a canonical knowledge base of propositional or practical knowledge that all practitioners in a community should acquire. Examples would be the knowledge bases for teaching identified by Shulman (1986, 1987), and Shulman and Shulman (2004) or the professional competencies that need to be demonstrated and articulated for gaining professional accreditation in many professions.

This representational project underpins a range of well-known models of professional learning which are often regarded as very different, even incompatible, with each other (cf., Ericsson, 2006; Lave & Wenger, 1991; Schön, 1987). For example, as Mulcahy (2011b) notes, even the community of practice model (Lave & Wenger, 1991; Wenger, 1998), which articulates the idea of mutual constitution of meaning through a process of legitimate peripheral participation and negotiation, nevertheless carries a similar representational assumption and also assumes an ontological autonomy of the practitioner's understanding from in situ performance:

> . . . participation in a community of practice implies that the professional who is making her becoming needs to *achieve a 'fit'* with an established and somewhat enclosed structure. (Mulcahy, 2011b, p. 225, emphasis added)

Whether informed by action and a community-driven view of knowledge, foundational theories or sociopolitical concerns for accountability, the pedagogical account that underpins this representational view focusses on developing a certain relatively well-defined set of knowledge and skills that needs to be enacted, practised and fine-tuned to a variety of situations. Despite the focus on knowledge in practice, as Guile (2010) notes these pedagogies of reflection maintain a clear ontological separation between the mind and the world, and between theory and practice.

3.3   The Reflective-Embodied Project: Skill
and the Ontological Turn in Practice

> . . . we do not primarily access things conceptually or intellectually, but, instead, through being constantly immersed in activities, projects and practices with things and others. We organise entities and creatures within these projects: breed livestock and prepare food for our families, for example. We also alter or construct things, such as fell trees and build houses, or re-orient streams and rivers. To be this way requires that we are open to the possibilities of things—the qualities of timber or fresh produce, for example, and what those qualities enable. Things, in turn, need to be receptive to our manipulations. (Dall'Alba & Barnacle, 2007, p. 681)

A more radical turn, not only away from technical rationality but also from the 'intellect' as cognitive capacity, can be observed in other recent writings on the topic. This turn is towards the ontological project of professional practice and learning as 'being' (Barnett, 2004; Dall'Alba, 2009; Dall'Alba & Barnacle, 2007) and 'becoming' (Scanlon, 2011) – from *representation* to *performativity*. These writings have different roots: ranging broadly from existentialist ideas about 'receptive spontaneity' (e.g. Dall'Alba, 2009) to accounts that are more grounded in the physical world and socio-material practices of 'assembling a professional self' (Mulcahy, 2011a). This turn is primarily based on the assumption that the knowledge and skills that will be needed in future workplaces cannot be known, in advance, in detail or with any great certainty; thus, attention to 'knowing the world' and 'skills for doing' appears to be an unproductive focus for educating future professionals in higher education. Rather, 'being in the world' – pulling disparate elements of practice together into one 'assemblage of self' – needs to be at the centre of university teaching. As Barnett (2004) puts it:

> After all, if the future is unknown, what kind of learning is appropriate *for* it. <. . .> [T]he way forward lies in construing and enacting a pedagogy for human being. In other words, learning for an unknown future has to be a learning understood neither in terms of knowledge or skills but of human qualities and dispositions. (Barnett, 2004, p. 247)

Dall'Alba and Barnacle (2007) similarly question whether there is a universal form of professional knowledge, disconnected from experience, and they turn to a more contextually constructed and more pluralistic view of knowledge. They argue that (a) the current emphasis in higher education on knowledge and skills that are decontextualised from the practices to which they relate is flawed and (b) there is no one absolute universal knowledge; rather, there are knowledges that are situated, localised and 'socially constructed in relation to specific knowledge interests' (Dall'Alba & Barnacle, 2007, p. 680). This view challenges the primary focus of higher education on intellect, knowledge and transfer and suggests an alternative account of knowing that dislodges mind and reason from any kind of privileged – detached from the body and the world – position:

> Where a conventional account of knowing has treated it as restricted to an ideal realm of thoughts, ideas and concepts, we want to situate knowing within the materiality, and spatial and temporal specificity, of being-in-the-world. In other words, knowing is not reducible to thought or the discursive. Instead, knowing is always situated within a personal, social,

historical and cultural setting, and thus transforms from the merely intellectual to something inhabited and enacted: a way of thinking, making and acting. Indeed, a way of being.
(Dall'Alba & Barnacle, 2007, p. 682)

This line of thinking holds that professional education has become too concerned
with epistemology, at the expense of ontology – a concern for the nature of being
and the existential aspects of the profession. However, Dall'Alba's and Barnacle's
'ontological turn' is not so much the turn from epistemology to ontology, but to
more ontological forms of knowing:

... from epistemology in itself to epistemology in the service of ontology. <...> In other
words, learning is not confined to the heads of individuals, but involves integrating ways of
knowing, acting and being within a broad range of practices. (Dall'Alba & Barnacle, 2007,
p. 683)

Some others have extended this ontological twist to lifelong learning – from 'being'
to 'becoming' – emphasising the evolving and accumulative nature of knowledge
and knowing (Scanlon, 2011). However, this performative project does not deny, in
any strong sense, the existence of a knowledge base, foundational skills and core
competences. As Scanlon (2011) claims:

The acquisition of this recipe knowledge is a critical step in becoming a professional within
the context of practice. (Scanlon, 2011, p. 15)

Dall'Alba (2009) similarly explains:

Aspiring professionals need to develop necessary knowledge, routines and procedures for
entering into appropriate caring relations with those whom they provide a service; ontology
and epistemology are both implicated. For example, accountants need to develop knowledge and skills in accounting in order to provide ethical accounting services that respect the
needs of their clients. (Dall'Alba, 2009, p. 141)

What is more at stake is the question of *what else* is needed when recipe principles
and core knowledge fail to provide a sufficient basis for acting effectively as an
expert professional practitioner. The main pedagogical suggestion that underpins
this onto-epistemic project is that curriculum should be organised around core
professional practices, meaning-making, reflexivity and identity:

Allowing students to encounter and reflexively dwell in this dynamism and complexity.
(Dall'Alba & Barnacle, 2007, p. 688)

There are several takes on this view of professional knowledge and learning. More
existential accounts emphasise critical–reflective capabilities – so as to question
professional assumptions and practices (e.g. Dall'Alba, 2009). In contrast, more
socio-materialistic accounts emphasise the construction of the professional self
across 'different discourses, material practices and positions' (Mulcahy, 2011b,
p. 226). Nevertheless, the core pedagogical proposition is underpinned by a shared
notion of performance: getting body, mind and hands (and heart) to act together in a
coherent dynamic ensemble with the environment and the ongoing action. Mind
and knowledge are not ontologically separated, by rational reflection, from the

world, embodied experiences and action. Knowing is being in the body and in the world: acting and reflecting. Accordingly, as Mulcahy (2011b) suggests, a curriculum for professional learning should be organised around the core professional practices, where skills, knowledge, identity and other professional qualities are developed 'in the process of learning to practice' (p. 240).

3.4 Representational and Performative Accounts and the Need to Cross Boundaries

The representational and performative views of professional knowledge and learning have significant similarities. Both projects acknowledge that professional expertise involves a certain set of 'core' skills and knowledge, and neither project questions the fundamental role of doing and experience in learning. Yet, the performative account of learning offers a pathway towards professional expertise that unfolds in a different direction from the representational account. The representational account starts from doing as a tacit form of practical knowing and proceeds *outwards* towards more articulated, explicit understandings which are independent from the situated action and environment. In contrast, the performative account starts from doing (and even articulated forms of recipe knowledge as a precondition for professional understanding) and proceeds *inwards* towards the existential, fusing understanding with the situated action and environment.

Both representational and performative accounts capture the nature of expertise and learning that might happen in (well defined) epistemically bounded knowledge spaces. In such spaces, professional knowledge is something that is already out of there in the form of explicit knowledge – expressed in symbolic representations or community discourses – or in the world, in its socio-material practices and arrangements. Thus, this knowledge either waits to be 'acquired' and 'transferred' or 'lived' and 'assembled' into a personal understanding and professional self. However, what kinds of knowledge and learning underpin expertise in a more *dynamic* and *epistemically diverse* professional world?

Being open to novelty and change requires engagement with innovation and multi-professional work. So we now offer two extensions of the representational and performative views of professional knowledge and learning: *temporal*, moving from what is known to creating new knowledge, and *organisational or spatial*, moving across epistemic spaces. These are the third and fourth epistemic projects represented in Table 3.1 and Fig. 3.1.

3.5   The Knowledge-Building Project: From Practice as Knowledge Transfer to Knowing as Epistemic Practice

> ... new knowledge is created also by professionals in practice, though this is often of a different kind from that created by researchers. Moreover, in some professions nearly all new practice is both invented and developed in the field, with the role of academics being confined to that of dissemination, evaluation and post-hoc construction of theoretical rationales. In others, knowledge is developed by practitioners 'solving' individual cases and problems, contributing to their personal store of experience and possibly that of their colleagues but not being codified, published or widely disseminated. (Eraut, 1985, p. 129)

It is now widely acknowledged that a range of professional innovations and organisational knowledge emerges from professional practices and problem-focussed design activity, rather than developmental work driven by basic research (Gibbons et al., 1994). Knowledge creation, innovation and transformation capacities have been seen as important qualities of successful practitioners and organisations (Argyris & Schön, 1996; Bresnen & Burrell, 2012; Engeström, 2008; Nonaka, 2004; Victor & Boynton, 1998). Some professions, such as architecture, engineering or computer programming, claim that such knowledge-building work is a part of everyday practice (Ewenstein & Whyte, 2009). Other professions aim to create similar practical knowledge, by trying to render current practices into codified forms (Goodyear & Steeples, 1998; Falconer & Littlejohn, 2009; Szymanski & Whalen, 2011). Knowledge that emerges from practice-based innovation is different in form and nature from the normative accounts of scientific knowledge; and the process through which such practical knowledge is created is distinct from the orderly normative models of scientific inquiry that (at least in theory) guide the production of formal scientific knowledge.[3]

It is often assumed that practical innovation and knowledge creation largely rest either on chance ('dumb luck' or serendipitous discovery) or on substantial amounts of experience. Either way, this makes innovative capability a quite esoteric, hard-to-learn skill. On this view, it would be difficult, if not impossible, to develop such capacities among university students who have little or no practical experience. For example, Nonaka and colleagues suggest that practical innovation depends on the conversion of tacit knowledge to explicit knowledge (Nonaka & Takeuchi, 1995; Nonaka & Toyama, 2007). Such knowledge gets created through continuous social interaction and is articulated, codified and made available for use in other settings. This knowledge creation process nevertheless tends to be quite mysterious, difficult to pin down and with tenuous links to pre-existing knowledge.

---

[3] We should emphasise that this argument primarily applies to *the normative* accounts of knowledge creation practices in research institutions. When we look at a range of ethnographies conducted in scientific laboratories (e.g. Goodwin, 1994; Knorr-Cetina, 1999; Latour & Woolgar, 1979; Lynch, 1988; Nersessian, 2006), it becomes more doubtful if the internal workings of scientific practices are very different from situated, contingent, messy and negotiated problem-solving in professional workplaces (e.g. Engeström & Middleton, 1996; Mol, 2002).

In contrast, Bereiter (2002a, 2002b), drawing on Whitehead's (1925/1948) ideas, argues that one of the distinguishing qualities of innovation over the last two centuries has been its *sustained* character (see also Mokyr, 2009). This kind of innovation is based on a 'disciplined progress' – 'a process of disciplined attack upon one difficulty after another' (Whitehead, 1925/1948, p. 92, cited in Bereiter, 2002a, p. 321). Bereiter illustrates this by describing the evolution of the television receiver since the mid-twentieth century – a process based on a series of small improvements:

> ... the basic design was established early; there were no further dramatic innovations in design, but instead a vast number of minor innovations. The end result ... was a device that continued to be structurally very similar to its prototype but with enormously improved performance and reliability. (Bereiter, 2002a, p. 321)

In more dynamic domains of professional work, such as the provision of new business solutions and other services, knowledge creation is a more mundane activity, not very different from individual, group and organisational learning (Argyris & Schön, 1996; Bereiter, 2002a, 2002b; Engeström & Sannino, 2012; Miettinen & Virkkunen, 2005). Moreover, on this view, knowledge creation can guide learning, and how to create knowledge can be learnt in formal education (Bereiter, 2002a, 2002b; Muukkonen & Lakkala, 2009; Muukkonen, Lakkala, & Paavola, 2011; Paavola & Hakkarainen, 2005; Paavola, Lipponen, & Hakkarainen, 2004).

The 'trialogical knowledge creation' (Paavola & Hakkarainen, 2005) or 'knowledge-building' (Bereiter, 2002b) approaches offer an initial framework for understanding the epistemic principles that underpin this view. As Paavola et al. (2004) explain:

> Learning could be understood as a collaborative effort directed toward developing some mediated artefacts, broadly defined as including knowledge, ideas, practices, and material and conceptual artefacts. The interaction among different forms of knowledge or between knowledge and other activities is emphasised as a requirement for this kind of innovativeness in learning and knowledge creation. (Paavola et al., 2004, pp. 569–570)

From this perspective, knowledge not only is the property of an individual mind but is embedded in mediating or conceptual artefacts – such as plans, theories, ideas and models – that are public and have an independent 'social life'. As Bereiter (2002a) argued, through joint work on conceptual artefacts, students can make their personal understanding explicit and accessible for further collaborative improvement. Students enhance their 'personal knowledgeability' by improving such 'public manifestations' of things they have in their minds. (Chapter 8 goes into much more detail about conceptual artefacts.)

The knowledge-building project is sometimes described in a romanticised way: extolling the virtues of the knowledge age, knowledge society and knowledge intensive economy. To hard-nosed sceptics, there is a credibility gap separating the innovation rhetoric of the knowledge economy and the mundane activities of everyday work. Talk of knowledge building may then seem a long way from the realities of practice and from the need to help students understand the propositions and principles germane to the profession or foster the skills of professional behaviour. Nevertheless, skilful and mindful tweaking of ideas and building new material and conceptual tools for professional work are recognisable elements of everyday practice, though they are often overlooked in professional education (Bresnen & Burrell, 2012). Eraut (1985) argues that knowledge creation and knowledge use cannot easily be separated in practitioner problem-solving:

> The interpretative use of an idea in a new context is itself a minor act of knowledge creation. (Eraut, 1985, p. 129)

From this perspective, working on shared conceptual artefacts provides a meeting point between routine practice and innovation.

3.6 The Relational Project: From Individualistic to Relational Expertise

> All learning involves boundaries. Whether we speak of learning as the change from novice to expert in a particular domain or as the development from legitimate peripheral participation to being a full member of a particular community (Lave & Wenger, 1991), the boundary of the domain or community is constitutive of what counts as expertise or as central participation. When we consider learning in terms of identity development, a key question is the distinction between what is part of me versus what is not (yet) part of me. (Akkerman & Bakker, 2011, p. 132)

The discontinuities and tensions discussed above, particularly in relation to the first two epistemic projects, have emerged *within* the epistemological boundaries inherent in each professional domain. One can think of sociocultural discontinuities between university and workplace settings, or between different kinds of knowledge that constitute the internal workings and knowledge base of the profession, or between theory and practice, knowing, doing and being – these boundaries are *within* the epistemic space of the profession, thus internal to a broader notion of becoming an expert practitioner *within* one's professional domain.[4] Crossing these 'internal boundaries' – between school and work, learning and doing, etc. – has

---

[4] Akkerman and Bakker (2011) define boundaries 'as sociocultural differences that give rise to discontinuities in interaction and action' (p. 139). They identify two kinds of boundaries *within* and *across* domains and use *physical* sites with distinct sociocultural practices as the main criterion for locating the external boundary (i.e. boundaries *within* a school or *within* a work setting, but *between* school and work). In this book, we use an *epistemic* space of a profession, rather than a physical space or site of action, for demarcating the internal (within) and the external (across) boundaries of professional learning and expertise. That is, the internal workings shared within a profession for generating professional knowledge, learning, doing and being are the main criteria for deciding what is 'within' and what is 'between' and what is 'beyond' the boundaries of the profession. Thus, on our definition, the boundaries between the sociocultural sites that are located in the same professional space – such as between university and workplace, between different workplaces or between different levels of expertise (i.e. a novice and an expert) – are *internal* to the profession, whereas the boundaries between two professions (e.g. a nurse and a doctor) or between people who do not operate within the same epistemic space (e.g. a nurse and a patient, a teacher and a child) are *external* boundaries, across epistemic spaces. These external boundaries are the main focus of our discussions of the relational project.

dominated the literature on professional learning in higher and vocational education for decades (Billett, 2010; Eraut, 1994; Sternberg & Horvath, 1999; Tuomi-Grohn & Engeström, 2003). However, as Akkerman and Bakker (2011) note:

> ... various types of professional work (science, technology design, and teaching) are heterogeneous in that they involve multiple actors representing different professional cultures. <...> Hence, working and learning are not only about becoming an expert in a particular bounded domain but also about crossing boundaries. (Akkerman & Bakker, 2011, p. 134)

The expanding scale of such boundary work has been demonstrated in numerous studies of interdisciplinary, inter-professional, lay and professional and other kinds of joint work (e.g. Derry, Schunn, & Gernsbacher, 2005; Engestrom, 2004, 2008), Engeström & Middleton, 1996; Hutchins, 1995; Star & Griesemer, 1989). In some domains, such as architecture, design, media, healthcare, social work and other areas of public service, this kind of boundary expertise is not reserved to a specific group of people (such as a sales or customer relations team), but is a core part of professional competence. New accounts of professional expertise that includes the capacities needed to work on such epistemic boundaries have been emerging in a variety of professional and scientific domains (e.g. Collins & Evans, 2007; Edwards, 2010; Guile, 2010, 2011). Thus, the notion of professional learning has to be expanded to include the capacity to work on the epistemic boundaries of professional expertise, in trans-epistemic spaces.

Edwards (2005, 2010) has offered the idea of 'relational agency' or 'relational expertise' and defined it as:

> ... an additional form of expertise which makes it possible to work with others to expand understandings of the work problem as an object of joint activity, and the ability to attune one's responses to the enhanced interpretation to those being made by other professionals. (Edwards, 2010, p. 13)

She explains that this kind of expertise primarily arises from two dynamically interrelated sources: (a) recognising other professionals as resources and understanding what is salient for them and what they bring when they interpret the joint object of activity and (b) aligning one's own responses and actions to the emergent interpretations and actions of others. She argues that relational expertise involves both purposeful inter-professional activity and 'weaving' clients' private knowledge into professional decisions. While such decision-making does not necessarily involve established procedures or pre-existing ideas, such relational expertise can be learnt by working alongside others. That said, Edwards is very clear that core professional expertise is essential and she warns against 'the dilution of personal specialist expertise' (Edwards, 2010, p. 15).

This extension of professional competences and practices into trans-epistemic spaces is distinct from, and goes beyond, the *self*-assembling practices implied in the performative and representational accounts of learning. Boundary practices not only spill out beyond preconfigured epistemic space but also involve 'weaving in' other ways of knowing that assume particular languages, particular ways of seeing and particular forms of reasoning, doing and being. From the instructional point of view, this relational practice goes beyond the self-assembling implied in the performative accounts of learning, to include assembling dynamically a *shared* material and epistemic space in ways that enable mutual understanding (Engeström, 2004; Goodwin, 2005). This view shifts the focus from reflective forms of learning to shared activities, discourse and objects that constitute the boundary infrastructure for the joint activity and meaning-making.

There are several views on what kinds of skills and understandings could provide a basis for such relational expertise (e.g. Bromme, Kienhues & Porsch, 2010; Collins & Evans, 2007; Guile, 2010, 2011). Some claim that such shared intelligibility rests on shared knowledge that precedes joint work – such as an 'interactional expertise' that involves enough practical understanding and ability to participate in the *discussion* of certain practices without having the knowledge or skills to *contribute* to those practices (Collins & Evans, 2007). Others claim that relational expertise requires an ability to bring knowledge that resides outside the practice of others into shared action and discourse during joint activity. For example, Guile (2011) suggests that such inter-professional work and learning becomes possible by giving and asking for reasons, and making judgements, in ways that are intelligible to people outside the professional field. In all cases, language, the understanding of the rules that people who come from a particular domain use to make sense and generate meanings and typical shapes in which knowledge gets expressed, play an integral role in developing the competences needed to work in trans-epistemic spaces.

The importance of such 'boundary' capabilities is widely recognised in higher education. For example, increasing attention is paid in professional courses to such things as nurses' and pharmacists' abilities to communicate with doctors, to teaching health professionals to communicate with patients and to creating opportunities for preservice teachers to engage in classroom management interactions before entering a real classroom. However, creating environments for authentic work with other experts or clients presents a significant challenge when one tries to engage students in *genuine* epistemic practices and to develop this competence in university settings. Linguistic practices, social interactions and the material affordances of heterogeneous practice settings (e.g. a classroom with children, interactions with a patient at home) cannot be easily simulated in conventional university learning environments. As Goodwin (2005) suggests, social and material authenticity matters as joint epistemic spaces are created not only by talk but also by juxtaposing tools and practices and jointly inhabiting a material environment.

3.7   Combining the Four Epistemic Projects: Knowledge for Doing and Knowledge for Innovation and Learning

... we try and get them out of – not only physically but mentally – out of the pharmacy. But more and more so, disease management is about prevention. And pharmacists can help in that way. So it's really, as healthcare is changing, in a way, so is the role the pharmacist can change with that. <...> It's part of also relationship building with their clients, their customers. Customer loyalty and all that kind of stuff, develops out of providing something extra. (Pharmacy Practice Coordinator)

The four epistemic projects outlined above point to different notions of the knowledge that is needed for professional practice and different ways of learning it. But what kinds of knowledge and ways of knowing might underpin the very capacity to learn and change? We need to share some ideas from Victor and Boynton's (1998) book *Invented Here* to advance our argument. Victor and Boynton offer an insightful heuristic that depicts knowledge and processes on which organisations draw for maximising their internal capability and growth. They see organisational capability advancing along a path that goes through five stages – craft, mass production, process enhancement, mass customisation and co-configuration – and note that there is a tight link between the nature of capabilities, values and knowledge in each stage (Fig. 3.2).

Craft primarily draws on the tacit knowledge of individual workers. This stage of organisational capability values the uniqueness, novelty and invention that emerge from personal experiences and mastery of techniques and tools. In contrast, *mass production* is based on articulated knowledge. It is good at producing standard, low-price commodities, and this success is achieved by standardised processes, divisions of labour, specialised work and effective management and control systems. *Process enhancement* draws on practical knowledge that emerges from doing similar tasks repeatedly and tight links between doing and thinking. This stage of organisational capability values the quality of work and its outcomes and

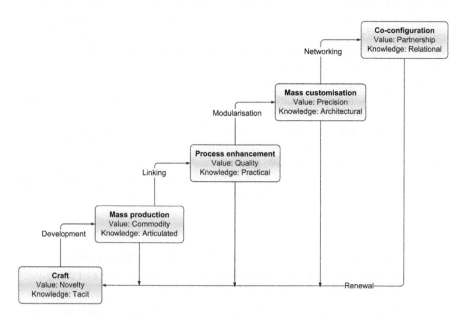

Fig. 3.2 Capabilities and transformations in organisational growth (Adapted from Victor & Boynton, 1998, p. 121, p. 233)

focusses on shared commitment to improving work processes – to continuing quality enhancement. *Mass customisation* draws on the architectural knowledge which tightly couples deep understanding of the products and processes. It values precision and focusses on producing things that are well suited to the diverse needs of different customers, through affordable, 'made-to-order' products and services. Such outcomes are achieved through analysing and breaking up products and work processes, such as by creating a network of easy-to-assemble elements. *Co-configuration* draws on relational knowledge to tailor products and services to better match customers' dynamically changing needs, allowing professionals together with customers to co-configure and reconfigure things. This capability focusses on creating 'customer-intelligent' products and services that are actively responsive and continuously adapt in synch with evolving customer requirements. Such an outcome is achieved by creating products that can be upgraded, enhanced or altered in other ways without replacing them and by establishing enduring partnerships with the customers that permit just-in-time responsiveness to their changing needs.

According to Victor and Boynton (1998), organisational growth is achieved by going through four (sequential) transformations: development, linking, modularisation and networking (or integration). Each stage draws on the previous capability, and specific tools, for achieving each transformation. During the *development* transformation, tacit craft knowledge is articulated and solidified into the development of processes and tools for mass production. It draws on various tools and techniques for articulation, such as product and process engineering. During the *linking* transformation, the practical knowledge acquired during the mass production process is used for improving this process. This transformation involves collaboration across teams, identification of inefficiencies, documentation, team building and other techniques and tools for process improvement. During the *modularisation* transformation, work capabilities are reconfigured into a network of modular units. This draws on architectural principles for identifying such modules, building their networks and creating ways to assemble finished products. During the *networking* transformation, knowledge about products and knowledge about customers are combined in a series of dynamic interactions. As Victor and Boynton put it:

> With co-configuration, there are no final products; no service is ultimately delivered. Instead, the boundaries between learning and work, customer and product, customer and company disappear. What replaces those boundaries are tightly coupled linkages, which feature constantly shared information, ideas, and experiences around the product or service experience. (Victor & Boynton, 1998, p. 207)

Each stage of capability is not only a reflection of organisational maturity but a more complex configuration of what customers value and what kinds of capabilities are most appropriate for delivering the best outcomes. For example, as Victor and Boynton show, in some service provision domains, customers may have privacy concerns and may not be willing to engage and provide sufficient information for configuring products and services dynamically to their changing needs. In some production industries, such as car manufacturing, the co-configuration of complex mechanical products may be too risky and expensive. In short, one capability may be more appropriate than another when it comes to achieving the best value for the organisation and its customers.

However, none of the capabilities are static as, without the change, organisations cannot sustain their capacity to meet their clients' expectations in changing market conditions. Thus, one of the essential processes that underpins *all* capabilities is *renewal*. During such changes, organisations use their limited capabilities to serve certain clients by direct invention. They go back to the craft work that creates tacit knowledge. As Victor and Boynton say:

> ... the ultimate origin of all value: the unique insights and inspiration of the craftsperson – the human font of creativity. (op. cit., p. 182)

> ... tacit knowledge is real, but hard to describe. <...> Craft workers intuitively figure out how to respond to shifting customer demands and diverse market needs using a set of tools at their disposal, sense the urgency to react to a novel market, and have the freedom and motivation to do so. (op. cit., p. 22)

The dynamic depicted in this view draws on knowledge entailed in all four of the epistemic projects we sketched earlier in this chapter, including links between tacit, articulated and practical knowledge in the two reflective projects and architectural and relational knowledge in the knowledge-building and relational projects. It underlines the fact that a new capability draws on experience, skill and existing knowledge.

However, Victor and Boynton's account also makes it clear that knowledge *for work* (e.g. tacit and articulated knowledge) is not the same as knowledge *for improvement of work* (e.g. development and linking, respectively). The *capability for enhancing capability* does not emerge solely from accumulated experience or bold creativity. Rather, it involves the use of certain kinds of *tools*; it happens in certain *environments* and requires certain kinds of *knowledge*.

The knowledge, tools and environments needed *for* this change and learning are different from the knowledge, tools and environments entailed in the production of goods and services. They are *epistemic* knowledge, tools and environments: entailed in the production of *knowledge*. In making such transformations that underpin organisational growth, knowledge for *doing* work is weaved with knowledge for *constructing* this knowledge – i.e. epistemic knowledge.

Victor and Boynton primarily emphasise the nature of knowledge that underpins each organisational capability, but we also need to recognise that each capability is also underpinned by *a particular way of knowing*. These ways of knowing are particularly central in the organisations that *produce knowledge* as a part of their daily work. They include *epistemic intuitions* that underpin knowledge craft, *formal epistemic concepts and structures* that enable mass knowledge production, *epistemic practices* that underpin the skilful enhancement of existing ways of knowing, *epistemic infrastructures* that may be customised and adapted flexibly for knowledge work in particular situations, *epistemic sensitivity* that supports knowledge creation in partnership with others and *epistemic fluency* that allows professionals to understand, switch between and coordinate different ways of knowing with awareness, sensitivity to the situation and skill.

In organisations that rely on dynamic change, these epistemic capacities become central skills for knowledgeable action and innovation in everyday work. They enable a shift from disruptive cyclical transformations and renewal to a more sustainable and continuous process of ecological innovation, change and professional learning.

As Cook and Brown (1999) claim, when apprentices engage in work practices – be it baking, flute making or designing copying machines – they develop not only knowledge but also *ways of knowing*. However, drawing on Geoffrey Vickers, they observe:

> It's funny what's happened to this word *knowing*. <...> The actual *act* of apprehending, of making sense, of putting together, from what you have, the significance of where you are – this [now] oddly lacks any really reliable, commonly used verb in our language ... [one] meaning the *activity* of knowing. <...> [Yet], every culture has not only its own set *body* of knowledge, but its own *ways* of [knowing]. (Vickers, 1976, cited in Cook & Brown, 1999, p. 381, original emphasis)

Indeed, the epistemic abilities needed to engage fluently with different *ways of knowing* are not salient in the literature and practices of professional learning.

This kind of fluency provides the basis for extending co-configurational forms of work. It also allows *personal* and *organisational* growth and renewal to be a more organic part of everyday practice, rather than a set of unique transformations that break with the past (Fig. 3.3).

Each of the accounts summarised in this chapter adds a new dimension to the epistemic puzzle of professions: what kinds of knowledge underpin professional action? What kinds of knowledge, skills and other qualities provide a sufficient

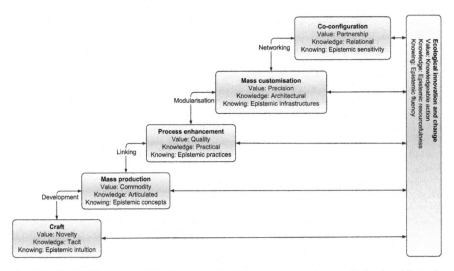

Fig. 3.3 Capabilities for sustainable, ecological innovation and change (Following Victor & Boynton, 1998)

basis for the development of skilful performance and professional expertise? The word 'development' is essential here. It would be foolish to think that preservice education in universities can create fully formed expert professionals. But it is reasonable to expect universities to prepare graduates who are competent to *start* doing the job and *capable of becoming* expert professionals. To lay the foundations for this professional development, university courses need to pay sharper attention to the constitutive elements of knowledge and the means by which professionals create new knowledge.

References

Akkerman, S. F., & Bakker, A. (2011). Boundary crossing and boundary objects. *Review of Educational Research, 81*(2), 132–169.

Argyris, C., & Schön, D. A. (1996). *Organizational learning II: Theory, method and practice.* Reading, MA: Addison-Wesley.

Barnett, R. (2004). Learning for an unknown future. *Higher Education Research & Development, 23*(3), 247–260.

Bereiter, C. (2002a). Design research for sustained innovation. *Cognitive Studies: Bulletin of the Japanese Cognitive Science Society, 9*(3), 321–327.

Bereiter, C. (2002b). *Education and mind in the knowledge age.* Mahwah, NJ: Lawrence Erlbaum Associates.

Billett, S. E. (2010). *Learning through practice: Models, traditions, orientations and approaches.* Dordrecht, The Netherlands: Springer.

Bresnen, M., & Burrell, G. (2012). Journals à la mode? Twenty years of living alongside Mode 2 and the new production of knowledge. *Organization, 20*(1), 25–37.

Bromme, R., Kienhues, D., & Porsch, T. (2010). Who knows what and who can we believe? Epistemological beliefs are beliefs about knowledge (mostly) to be attained from others. In L. D. Bendixen & F. C. Haerle (Eds.), *Personal epistemology in the classroom: Theory, research, and implications for practice* (pp. 163–193). Cambridge, UK: Cambridge University Press.

Collins, H., & Evans, R. (2007). *Rethinking expertise.* Chicago, IL: The University of Chicago Press.

Cook, S. D. N., & Brown, J. S. (1999). Bridging epistemologies: The generative dance between organizational knowledge and organizational knowing. *Organization Science, 10*(4), 381–400.

Dall'Alba, G. (2009). *Learning to be professionals.* Dordrecht, The Netherlands: Springer.

Dall'Alba, G., & Barnacle, R. (2007). An ontological turn for higher education. *Studies in Higher Education, 32*(6), 679–691. doi:10.1080/03075070701685130.

de Souza, C. S. (2005). *The semiotic engineering of human-computer interaction.* Cambridge, MA: MIT Press.

Derry, S. J., Schunn, C. D., & Gernsbacher, M. A. E. (2005). *Interdisciplinary collaboration: An emerging cognitive science.* Mahwah, NJ: Lawrence Erlbaum Associates.

Dewey, J. (1910). *How we think.* Boston, MA: D. C. Heath.

Dewey, J. (1938). *Logic: The theory of inquiry.* New York, NY: Henry Holt.

Edwards, A. (2005). Being an expert professional practitioner: The relational turn in expertise. *International Journal of Educational Research, 43*(3), 168–182.

Edwards, A. (2010). *Relational agency: Learning to be a resourceful practitioner.* Dordrecht, The Netherlands: Springer.

Engeström, Y. (2004). New forms of learning in co-configuration work. *Journal of Workplace Learning, 16*(1/2), 11–21.

Engeström, Y. (2008). *From teams to knots: Activity-theoretical studies of collaboration and learning at work*. Cambridge, NY: Cambridge University Press.

Engeström, Y., & Middleton, D. E. (Eds.) (1996). *Cognition and communication at work*. Cambridge, NY: Cambridge University Press.

Engeström, Y., & Sannino, A. (2012). Concept formation in the wild. *Mind, Culture, and Activity, 19*(3), 201–206. doi:10.1080/10749039.2012.690813.

Eraut, M. (1985). Knowledge creation and knowledge use in professional contexts. *Studies in Higher Education, 10*(2), 117–133.

Eraut, M. (1994). *Developing professional knowledge and competence*. London, UK: Falmer Press.

Eraut, M. (2009). Understanding complex performance through learning trajectories and mediating artefacts. In N. Jackson (Ed.), *Learning to be professional through a higher education e-book* (Ch. A7, pp. 1–17). Guildford, UK: Surrey Centre for Excellence in Professional Training and Education (SCEPTrE). Retrieved from https://www.learningtobeprofessional. pbworks.com

Ericsson, K. A. (2006). The influence of experience and deliberate practice on the development of superior expert performance. In K. A. Ericsson, N. Charness, P. J. Feltovich, & R. R. Hoffman (Eds.), *The Cambridge handbook of expertise and expert performance* (pp. 683–703). New York, NY: Cambridge University Press.

Ewenstein, B., & Whyte, J. (2009). Knowledge practices in design: The role of visual representations as 'epistemic objects'. *Organization Studies, 30*(1), 7–30.

Falconer, I., & Littlejohn, A. (2009). Representing models of practice. In L. Lockyer, S. Bennet, S. Agostinho, & B. Harper (Eds.), *Handbook of research on learning design and learning objects* (pp. 20–40). Hershey, PA: Idea Group.

Gibbons, M., Limoges, C., Nowotny, H., Schwartzman, S., Scott, P., & Trow, M. (1994). *The new production of knowledge: The dynamics of science and research in contemporary societies*. London, UK: Sage.

Goodwin, C. (1994). Professional vision. *American Anthropologist, 96*(3), 606–633.

Goodwin, C. (2005). Seeing in depth. In S. J. Derry, C. D. Schunn, & M. A. Gernsbacher (Eds.), *Interdisciplinary collaboration: An emerging cognitive science* (pp. 85–121). Mahwah, NJ: Lawrence Erlbaum Associates.

Goodyear, P., & Steeples, C. (1998). Creating shareable representations of practice. *Association for Learning Technology Journal, 6*(3), 16–23.

Guile, D. (2010). *The learning challenge of the knowledge economy*. Rotterdam, The Netherlands: Sense.

Guile, D. (2011). Interprofessional learning: Reasons, judgement, and action. *Mind, Culture, and Activity, 18*(4), 342–364.

Hutchins, E. (1995). *Cognition in the wild*. Cambridge, MA: MIT Press.

Knorr-Cetina, K. (1999). *Epistemic cultures: How the sciences make knowledge*. Cambridge, MA: Harvard University Press.

Latour, B. (1990). Drawing things together. In M. Lynch & S. Woolgar (Eds.), *Representation in scientific practice* (pp. 19–68). Cambridge, MA: MIT Press.

Latour, B., & Woolgar, S. (1979). *Laboratory life: The social construction of scientific facts*. Beverly Hills, CA: Sage.

Lave, J., & Wenger, E. (1991). *Situated learning: Legitimate peripheral participation*. Cambridge, UK: Cambridge University Press.

Lynch, M. (1988). The externalized retina: Selection and mathematization in the visual documentation of objects in the life sciences. *Human Studies, 11*(2), 201–234.

Miettinen, R., & Virkkunen, J. (2005). Epistemic objects, artefacts and organizational change. *Organization, 12*(3), 437–456.

Mokyr, J. (2009). *The enlightened economy: An economic history of Britain 1700–1850*. New Haven, CT: Yale University Press.

Mol, A. (2002). *The body multiple: Ontology in medical practice.* Durham, NC: Duke University Press.

Mulcahy, D. (2011a). Assembling the 'accomplished' teacher: The performativity and politics of professional teaching standards. *Educational Philosophy and Theory, 43*, 94–113.

Mulcahy, D. (2011b). Teacher professional becoming: A practice-based, actor network theory perspective. In L. Scanlon (Ed.), *"Becoming" a professional: An interdisciplinary analysis of professional learning* (pp. 219–244). Dordrecht, The Netherlands: Springer.

Muukkonen, H., & Lakkala, M. (2009). Exploring metaskills of knowledge-creating inquiry in higher education. *International Journal of Computer-Supported Collaborative Learning, 4*(2), 187–211. doi:10.1007/s11412-009-9063-y.

Muukkonen, H., Lakkala, M., & Paavola, S. (2011). Promoting knowledge creation and object oriented inquiry in university courses. In S. Ludvigsen, A. Lund, I. Rasmussen, & R. Säljö (Eds.), *Learning across sites: New tools, infrastructures and practices* (pp. 172–189). Oxon, OX: Routledge.

Nersessian, N. J. (2006). The cognitive-cultural systems of the research laboratory. *Organization Studies, 27*(1), 125–145.

Nonaka, I. (2004). The knowledge creating company. In H. Takeuchi & I. Nonaka (Eds.), *Hitotsubashi on knowledge creation* (pp. 29–46). Singapore, Singapore: John Wiley & Sons.

Nonaka, I., & Takeuchi, H. (1995). *The knowledge-creating company: How Japanese companies create the dynamics of innovation.* New York, NY: Oxford University Press.

Nonaka, I., & Toyama, R. (2007). Why do firms differ? The theory of the knowledge creating firm. In K. Ichijo & I. Nonaka (Eds.), *Knowledge creation and management: New challenges for managers* (pp. 13–31). Oxford, UK: Oxford University Press.

Paavola, S., & Hakkarainen, K. (2005). The knowledge creation metaphor – an emergent epistemological approach to learning. *Science & Education, 14*(6), 535–557.

Paavola, S., Lipponen, L., & Hakkarainen, K. (2004). Models of innovative knowledge communities and three metaphors of learning. *Review of Educational Research, 74*(4), 557–576.

Pickering, A. (1995). *The mangle of practice: Time, agency, and science.* Chicago, IL: University of Chicago Press.

Roth, W.-M. (2010). Learning in praxis, learning for praxis. In S. Billett (Ed.), *Learning through practice: Models, traditions, orientations and approaches* (pp. 21–36). Dordrecht, The Netherlands: Springer.

Scanlon, L. E. (2011). *"Becoming" a professional: An interdisciplinary analysis of professional learning.* Dordrecht, The Netherlands: Springer.

Schön, D. A. (1983). *The reflective practitioner: How professionals think in action.* New York, NY: Basic Books.

Schön, D. A. (1985). *The design studio: An exploration of its traditions and potentials.* London, UK: RIBA Publications for RIBA Building Industry Trust.

Schön, D. A. (1987). *Educating the reflective practitioner.* London, UK: Jossey-Bass.

Schön, D. A. (2002). From technical rationality to reflection-in-action. In R. Harrison, F. Reeve, A. Hanson, & J. Clarke (Eds.), *Supporting lifelong learning: Perspectives on learning* (Vol. 1, pp. 40–61). London, UK: RoutledgeFalmer.

Schön, D. A., & Bennett, J. (1996). Reflective conversation with materials. In T. Winograd, J. Bennett, L. D. Young, & B. Hartfield (Eds.), *Bringing design to software* (pp. 171–184). New York, NY: ACM Press.

Shulman, L. S. (1986). Those who understand: Knowledge growth in teaching. *Educational Researcher, 15*(2), 4–14.

Shulman, L. S. (1987). Knowledge and teaching: Foundations of the new reform. *Harvard Educational Review, 57*(1), 1–22.

Shulman, L. S., & Shulman, J. H. (2004). How and what teachers learn: A shifting perspective. *Journal of Curriculum Studies, 36*(2), 257–271.

Star, S. L., & Griesemer, J. R. (1989). Institutional ecology, 'translations' and boundary objects: Amateurs and professionals in Berkeley's museum of vertebrate zoology. *Social Studies of Science, 19*(4), 387–420.

Sternberg, R. J., & Horvath, J. A. (1999). *Tacit knowledge in professional practice: Researcher and practitioner perspectives*. Mahwah, NJ: Lawrence Erlbaum Associates.

Szymanski, M. H., & Whalen, J. E. (2011). *Making work visible: Ethnographically grounded case studies of work practice*. Cambridge, UK: Cambridge University Press.

Tuomi-Grohn, T., & Engeström, Y. E. (2003). *Between school and work: New perspectives on transfer and boundary-crossing*. Amsterdam, The Netherlands: Pergamon Press.

Usher, R., Bryant, I., & Johnston, R. (1997). *Adult education and the postmodern challenge*. London, UK: Routledge.

Vickers, G. (1976). *Technology and culture, invited paper given at the Division for Study and Research in Education*. Cambridge, MA: Massachusetts Institute of Technology.

Victor, B., & Boynton, A. C. (1998). *Invented here: Maximizing your organization's internal growth and profitability*. Boston, MA: Harvard Business School Press.

Wenger, E. (1998). *Communities of practice: Learning, meaning, and identity*. Cambridge, UK: Cambridge University Press.

Whitehead, A. N. (1925/1948). *Science and the modern world* (Mentor ed.). New York, NY: New American Library.

Chapter 4
The Shapes Taken by Personal Professional Knowledge

Before we can speak further about epistemic fluency, we need to say more about what we mean by *knowledge* and *knowing*. It is impossible to describe professional knowledge in a simple uniform way. The fundamental message coming from research is quite consistent. Human beings, including professional workers and experts, draw upon a *variety* of knowledge types; they learn this knowledge and draw upon it in their professional practice in a *variety* of ways (Argyris, 1993; Bereiter, 2002; Collins & Evans, 2007; Collins, 2010; Davenport, 2005; Eraut, 1985, 1994, 2010; Ericsson, 2009; Farrell, 2006; Gromman, 1990; Harper, 1987; Hoffmann & Roth, 2005; Schön, 1995).

When it comes to describing what constitutes *personal professional knowledge*, it becomes clear that, from a cognitive standpoint, this knowledge is not so dissimilar from the *general knowledge* that one develops through, and draws upon in, everyday life. In fact, almost all the types of knowledge that are used to characterise expertise have their counterparts in accounts of general knowledgeability. For example, Bereiter's (2002) dissection of the main aspects of knowledgeability – stable, episodic, implicit, impressionistic and regulative knowledge and skill – has much in common with Eraut's (1994, 2009, 2010) depiction of professional personal knowledge and capability: codified knowledge, accumulated memories, personal understandings, self-knowledge, metaprocesses and know-how (see Table 4.1). These aspects of knowledgeability are closely associated with distinct kinds of memory, and, as Donald (2010) notes, they are likely to stand as functionally identifiable cognitive subsystems which have different learning and retrieval characteristics and could function with some degree of independence. For example, episodic memories usually result from a single encounter, while skills are learnt gradually through repetition.

However, there is more controversy about how these different aspects of knowledgeability are implemented by the human brain and how they relate to each other. There are even deeper differences about what counts as knowledge and about how what one knows connects to language, perception and action, both individual and collective. How does *culture*, with its particular symbolic and material structures

© Springer Science+Business Media Dordrecht 2017
L. Markauskaite, P. Goodyear, *Epistemic Fluency and Professional Education*,
Professional and Practice-based Learning 14, DOI 10.1007/978-94-007-4369-4_4

Table 4.1 Some common aspects of general knowledgeability and personal professional knowledge, drawing on Bereiter and Eraut

Aspects of knowledgeability (Bereiter, 2002)	Personal professional knowledge (Eraut, 1994, 2009, 2010)[a]
Stable knowledge – knowledge that can be made explicit in various forms, such as sentences, diagrams, formulas, stories or enactments. This knowledge is a counterpart of abstract knowledge objects in one's mind	*Codified knowledge* or *propositional knowledge* – discipline-based theories and concepts, generalisations of practical principles
Episodic knowledge – remembered episodes which typically can be retrieved and considered and applied in new, similar situations. In essence, reasoning based on cases uses this kind of knowledge	*Accumulated memories* of episodic events and specific propositions about particular cases, decisions and actions
Implicit understanding – knowledge that people have and use but cannot easily state. It characterises intelligent relationships to things or situations in the world. It is knowledge based on experience, and as Bereiter argues, 'it probably owes little or nothing to formal education' (p. 139)	*Personal understandings* of people and situations, *practical wisdom, tacit knowledge* and other aspects of personal expertise. Includes *personal knowledge and the interpretation of experience* – knowledge that people learn without there being an intended educational purpose and without propositional knowledge being drawn to their attention
Impressionistic knowledge includes feelings and impressions which influence choices and actions. Bereiter argues that this knowledge often works in situations when a reason or evidence gives little guidance	*Self-knowledge, attitudes, values and emotions* – sense of the meaningfulness of the purpose, sense of choice, extent to which one feels supported, encouraged or discouraged
Regulative knowledge includes personal metacognition – which pertains to one's own activity – and regulative ideas that pertain to collective activity (group metacognition, in some accounts)	*Metaprocesses* – process knowledge for directing one's own behaviour and controlling one's engagement in other processes. Includes agency and reflection
Skill is a type of knowledge that includes the cognitive part or 'know-how' and sub-cognitive part, that is, change in performance which takes place with practice, becoming easier, faster, smoother and more automatic through repetition	*Know-how or process knowledge* – knowing how to conduct the various processes that contribute to professional action, skills and practices

[a] Note that Eraut (1994, 2009, 2010) identifies different types of personal professional knowledge across his writings. Here, we have attempted to integrate his earlier map of professional knowledge (Eraut, 1994) with his more recent categorisations (Eraut, 2009, 2010). The earlier map included only three knowledge types: (a) propositional knowledge, (b) processes and (c) impressions, personal knowledge, and the interpretation of experience. More recent categorisations by Eraut identify more knowledge types, but do not explain them in detail. The term 'metaprocess' is based on Eraut (1994). The rest come from Eraut (2009)

and representations, and how do *workplace settings*, with their tools and physical environments, shape and get shaped by (professional) ways of knowing? These questions are far from trivial. Getting the right answers is very important for educators who are helping university graduates and practitioners to develop professional knowledgeability that links the (largely representational) knowledge usually learnt in classroom environments with the (largely performative) knowledge relevant to workplaces.

To provide a general sense of what kinds of capacities professional knowledge may involve, this chapter summarises some useful distinctions made in the literature about different kinds of knowledge and what those differences may entail.[1] We focus on knowledge and ways of learning that are related to the epistemic challenges discussed in Chap. 3 and address the following question:

> What kinds of problems underpin the relationships between theory and practice, general capabilities and situated performance, and are the right questions being asked by those trying to resolve such tensions?

We start this chapter by introducing our notion of knowledge and how it is entangled with action and professional practice. While our main focus in this chapter is personal knowledge, successful performance in modern workplace settings cannot be understood by isolating the personal capacities of individuals from broader institutional contexts. So in Sect. 4.2, we introduce some other notions of knowledge in professional work and discuss the relationships between personal, public and organisational knowledges. After setting this background, we turn to the question above. In Sect. 4.3, we discuss some dichotomies between learning for doing and learning for understanding that are common in the representational accounts of knowledge which we presented in Chap. 3. After that (Sect. 4.4), we elaborate on this dichotomy by making a shift to the performative accounts of knowledge and discuss the relationships between knowledge as possessed and knowing as skilful performance. As much of the discussion about the challenges in professional learning and performance revolve around the links between explicit and tacit knowledge, in Sect. 4.5 we turn to these two kinds of knowledge. We point out that traditional views of tacit knowledge obscure some important qualities of tacitness and make learning and teaching of some kinds of actionable knowledge unnecessarily covert and disconnected from explicit knowledge. In Sect. 4.6, we bring these key theoretical insights together and provide an example of how different kinds of knowledge and ways of knowing lean on each other in situated knowledgeable performance. We argue that *knowledgeable action* and *actionable knowledge* blur the boundaries between understanding and doing. However, various kinds of knowledge and knowing *can* be distinguished, and a better understanding of their nature and relations can improve designs for professional education.

---

[1] In this chapter, we only address differences that are important for our argument. There is a substantial literature that addresses the topic in more comprehensive and nuanced ways (e.g. Bereiter, 2002; Collins, 2010; Eraut, 1994; Ericsson, Charness, Feltovich, & Hoffman, 2006). However, it is important to note that in much of the literature, conceptions of knowledge are still dominated by a few sharp dichotomies and are not always comprehensive. For example, as Bereiter (2002) observes, much of the literature makes a clear-cut distinction between procedural and declarative knowledge, but underestimates the importance of episodic knowledge.

4.1   What Knowledge Is

Questions of knowledge and knowing have been central concerns in many domains of study, and in this chapter we will draw particularly on philosophy and cognitive science. Philosophers mainly focus on fundamental theoretical questions about knowledge, such as its limits, sources and nature, and related notions of truth, belief and justification. Cognitive scientists mainly focus on empirical questions about human thinking, such as cognitive processes and structures, beliefs, motivation, learning and performance. More recently, questions of knowledge have become a major concern in the field of *psychological epistemology*, which integrates philosophical and cognitive interests in human knowledge, knowing, learning and performance (Chinn, Buckland, & Samarapungavan, 2011; Muis, Bendixen, & Haerle, 2006; Royce, 1974):

> Knowledge, then, is defined as those cognitions of an organism's cognitive structure (psychological perspective) that are epistemologically justifiable (philosophical perspective). (Muis et al., 2006, p. 11)

However, the question of what counts as justification is far from straightforward when one refers to knowledge that underpins professional performance. Much of this knowledge is expressed in terms of skill, action and relations with the external environment, rather than in validated and justified explicit statements. For example, Hoy and Murphy (2001) note that 'knowledge' often refers to factual, externally verified 'content' which is organised in certain logical ways and justified, whereas 'belief' usually refers to propositions and ideas that individuals feel to be true, irrespective of external validation or justification.

However, as Southerland, Sinatra, and Matthews (2001) state:

> Distinctions between knowledge and belief, complex and confusing at the theoretical level, seem to become hopelessly blurred at the empirical level. (Southerland et al., 2001, p. 348)

This particularly applies to professional knowledge, where logically and experientially[2] organised ways of knowing revealed through skill and action are intertwined with value judgements, dispositions, conceptions and other psychological constructs which are neither necessarily logical nor particularly rational and which rarely gain the status of 'knowledge' in the rigid philosophical treatments or rational operationalisations of expert knowledge.

Following other research on professional practice and expertise, we use the term 'knowledge' in the broadest sense, to include justified propositions, hunches, beliefs, know-how, skills, habits, tacit knowledge and other constructs of human thought and behaviour expressed in language, action and other kinds of perfor-

---

[2] By 'experientially organised ways of knowing', we refer to such things as habits, routines and other persistent, though not necessary logical or fully conscious, kinds of action. They are common and important in learning and professional performance (Hoffmann & Roth, 2005, 133–134).

mance (Eraut, 1994; Hoffmann & Roth, 2005; Hoy & Murphy, 2001; Murphy & Mason, 2006; Southerland et al., 2001). These constructs include entities that have different epistemological status – such as externally verified facts, beliefs, values and moral judgements – which involve different relationships between phenomena and what is thought to be true, as well as how things might be known.

The meaning of one's propositions or behaviours is not defined solely by individual words or by a particular state of mind but also by the activity in which one is engaged and the totality of the judgements available. Intelligibility – making sense of something as being such and such – is inherited against a background of prior understandings and experiences, in relation to which one comes to make sense of the situation and to know new things:

> ... what we believe is not a single proposition, it is a whole system of propositions. (Light dawns gradually over the whole.). (Wittgenstein, 1969, p. 21 §141)[3]

> And only within this system has a particular bit the value we give it. (op. cit., p. 52, §410)

In order to make sense of actions and statements, we must share a background with (in) which we interpret them and attach meanings. Practices, by being socially and historically constructed, constitute 'fields of action intelligibility' (Nicolini, 2013, p. 172) which provide shape to the situation and inform practitioners about what makes sense and how they should proceed next. Practice, thus, provides a background with(in) which one distinguishes between what is reasonable and what is not, or, in a strong sense, what is true and what is false.

So, practical knowledge is not so much defined by an objective certainty of propositions, as by shared ways of seeing, a shared sense of relevance and similar ways of responding – a shared 'form of life' (Wittgenstein, 1953/2009, 94e, §241). Professional knowledge, from this perspective, is a tool for interaction with the world: a tool that is used, mastered and produced in situated knowing (Cook & Brown, 1999; Nicolini, 2013):

> ... knowledge is conceived largely as a form of mastery that is expressed in the capacity to carry out a social and material activity. Knowledge is thus always a way of knowing shared with others, a set of practical methods acquired through learning, inscribed in objects, embodied, and only partially articulated in discourse. Becoming part of an existing practice thus involves learning how to act, how to speak (and what to say), but also how to feel, what to expect, and what things mean. (Nicolini, 2013, p. 5)

Learning such knowledge is not only a matter of acquiring shared meanings but rather of developing capacities for establishing functional relationships between meanings, environment and activity. Brown, Collins and Duguid (1989) put this neatly, in explaining how people learn, and learn to use, conceptual knowledge, in a tool-like way:

> People who use tools actively rather than just acquire them, by contrast, build an increasingly rich implicit understanding of the world in which they use the tools and of the tools

---

[3] Wittgenstein's published work is referenced by page number in the cited edition, followed by section number (§).

themselves. The understanding, both of the world and of the tool, continually changes as a result of their interaction. Learning and acting are interestingly indistinct, learning being a continuous, life-long process resulting from acting in situations.

Learning how to use a tool involves far more than can be accounted for in any set of explicit rules. The occasions and conditions for use arise directly out of the context of activities of each community that uses the tool, framed by the way members of that community see the world. The community and its viewpoint, quite as much as the tool itself, determine how a tool is used. (Brown et al., 1989, p. 33)[4]

Such knowledge is not simply a matter of mind and skill, or of environment and activity. Rather, it arises from relationships created between mind, skill, environment and activity (Yinger & Hendricks-Lee, 1993).

A corollary of this position is that we do not bother much about specific distinctions between expertise, competence, capability and other such terms that are used to describe different levels of proficiency in specific professional domains (see, e.g. Eraut, 2007, 2010). Rather, following Collins and Evans (2007), we adopt a more flexible, socially shaped and situated view of expertise, acknowledging that expertise includes various kinds of specialised knowledge and performance: from 'ubiquitous expertise' that exists broadly within a culture and can often be taken for granted through 'interactional expertise' that allows one to participate in a specialised discourse and to 'contributory expertise' that allows one to actually *do* professional work. (We develop this in more detail later in the chapter.) Expertise, from this perspective, is skilful performance informed by particular kinds of knowledge and ways of knowing, recognised within a culture.

4.2 Public, Personal and Organisational Knowledge

Expertise needs to be understood in terms of a relationship between professional work and professional knowledge. In this section, we distinguish between public and personal knowledge and then introduce the idea of organisational knowledge. Public knowledge is knowledge that is made broadly available within a culture, including within a profession. Personal knowledge is what an individual knows and is able to do. Organisational knowledge (including group knowledge) is knowledge that is available to everyone within a specific organisation or group. Organisational knowledge emerges at the intersection between, and as an entanglement of, the public and the personal. Understanding these three kinds of knowledge – and their interactions – offers an important insight into professional performance.

---

[4] We develop this idea of a tool further, drawing on the theory of instrumental genesis, in Chap. 12.

4.2.1 Public Knowledge

Public knowledge is what Bereiter (2002) calls *knowledge outside the mind*. It includes both codified and non-codified knowledge.

Codified public knowledge includes all the knowledge that is captured in some inscribed form.[5] Thus, it can be shared and used beyond the communities, sites and people involved in its origination. It includes knowledge that is associated with publications in books and journals, with special value being given to knowledge that has been peer reviewed and which has gained the level of *acceptance* needed for incorporation into a discipline or profession's knowledge base (Eraut, 2010). It also includes knowledge embedded in other material inscriptions that are available to members of a professional community, including resources used within programs of education, qualification standards, professional databases and informal resource collections. Broadly, this knowledge has the qualities that Bereiter (2002) associates with 'conceptual artefacts' (see Chap. 8).

Non-codified public knowledge is knowledge that is usually described as embedded in cultural practices. It is what professionals learn through participation. People usually describe this knowledge as cultural knowledge and take it for granted. Some of this knowledge has a sociocultural character and is embedded in the discourses and practices of professional communities. Some of it is situated and emerges from engagement in local activities – relationships among the people, tools, artefacts, historical, cultural, material and social environment in which practice takes place. In both cases, this knowledge is not available beyond the communities and practices concerned and can be learnt only by socialisation and engagement.

Much public knowledge has both codified and non-codified qualities. For example, Cook and Brown (1999) describe knowledge that is used to produce flutes in some world-class flute manufacturing companies. They note that there is a body of shared knowledge, such as concepts about the parts of the instrument, how they function and are connected together, rules describing how a job should be done and which tool should be used for which function. There are many dimensions and tolerances in how different parts should work and fit together. However, many of those dimensions are not used by experienced flute makers and are not taught directly to apprentices. Rather, the quality of the instrument is judged by hand or eye, by passing the flute back and forth from one flute maker, who works on one part of the instrument, to another flute maker, reworking the flute until both agree that the flute has the 'right feel'. The flutes produced by such companies have a distinct quality and character, and knowledgeable flautists around the world can recognise the feel of the flutes produced by world-class brands. Such flute making is impossible without the individual skills needed to produce instruments with the 'right feel'.

---

[5] Because it is inscribed, it is shareable and mobile. However, the inscription, by itself, is not the knowledge.

4.2.2   Personal Knowledge

Personal knowledge refers to personal attributes, capacities and other qualities that underpin what Bereiter (2002) calls *well-rounded knowledgeability*. As Eraut (2010) suggests, such knowledge can be described as 'the individual-centred counterpart to cultural knowledge' (p. 38). There are various types of personal knowledge, such as procedural knowledge, propositional knowledge, practical knowledge, skills and know-how.

In specific professional contexts, personal knowledge can be described more narrowly – 'what individual persons bring to the situation that enables them to think, interact and perform' (Eraut, 2010, p. 37) or what Yinger and Hendricks-Lee (1993), drawing on Harper (1987), call 'working knowledge': the kind of knowledge that is 'particularly useful to get things accomplished in practical situations' (Yinger & Hendricks-Lee, 1993, p. 100). Other terms have been used for similar kinds of knowledge and knowing, such as 'knowing in action' (Schön, 1995), 'actionable knowledge' (Argyris, 1999), 'action-oriented understanding', 'personal practical knowledge' (Clandinin, 1985) and 'metis' (Baumard, 1999).

Some personal knowledge can be *explicit*, that is, available to consciousness, or able to be put into words when the need arises. However, some personal knowledge is *tacit* or implicit, that is, one might know or be able to do something without an explicit awareness, and one may not be able to describe how one does something. (Explicit and tacit could be broadly seen as personal – embodied and embrained – counterparts of codified and non-codified public knowledge: the former is available to consciousness, reflection or discourse; the latter is enacted in doing.)

Public and personal and explicit and tacit are interrelated (Billett, 2008; Cook & Brown, 1999). Cook and Brown's (1999) example of flute makers using and creating new individual and company knowledge in making flutes, and passing them back and forth between master flute makers and apprentices, is a good illustration of this. A part of flute makers' knowledge is in those interactions themselves – it is a kind of 'organisational knowledge'.

4.2.3   Organisational or Group Knowledge

There are some other kinds of knowledge that occupy a large space between public and personal knowledge: such as community knowledge, organisational knowledge and group knowledge. Given this book's concern with professional work and the fact that much professional activity occurs within organisational settings, we refer to this category of knowledge as 'organisational knowledge'. Organisational knowledge can be seen as a dynamic assemblage of cultural knowledge that is made available to everyone within an organisation or group and a dynamic collection of personal knowledges that jointly define what an organisation collectively brings to the situation and is capable of doing. It will normally include both explicit and tacit elements. The explicit knowledge may take the form of shared symbolic artefacts, such as rules, codes, organisational routines and codified propositions embedded in organisational artefacts. As Argyris and Schön (1996) put it:

> When organizations are large and complex, their members cannot rely entirely on face-to-face contact to help them compare and adjust their private images of organizational theory-in-use. Even in face-to-face contact, private images of organization often diverge. Individuals need external references to guide their private adjustments. (Argyris & Schön, 1996, p. 16)

Such knowledge may be inscribed in records, such as files, message boards, manuals, databases, information systems and other kinds of organisational recordings. It can also exist in non-codified forms in established ways of acting or routines. As Nelson and Winter (1982) state:

> ... the routinization of activity in an organization constitutes the most important form of storage of the organization's specific operational knowledge. Basically we claim that organizations *remember by doing*. (Nelson & Winter, 1982, p. 99, original emphasis)

This enacted organisational knowledge has two distinct aspects: collective capacity and individual capacity. On the one hand, this knowledge can be seen as a distinct emerging property of an organisation or a group (e.g. Kay, 1993). That is, organisational knowledge is more than the sum of the individual knowledges and related capacities of those who work in the group. Such knowledge is profoundly collective and cannot be reduced to discrete individuals. From this collectivist view:

> ... organizational knowledge is the set of collective understandings embedded in a firm, which enable it to put its resources to particular uses. (Tsoukas & Vladimirou, 2001, p. 981)

On the other hand, Tsoukas and Vladimirou (2001) observe that the open-endedness of the world 'gives knowledge its not-as-yet-formed character' (p. 989). Drawing on Polanyi's claim that '*All* knowing is personal knowing' (Polanyi & Prosch, 1975, p. 44, original emphasis), they argue that it is individuals who put shared knowledge into action and there is always some improvisation in how people make sense of organisational propositions and how they enact this organisational knowledge in specific contexts and situations (see also Cook & Brown, 1999; Orlikowski, 2002, 2007; Weick, 1995, 2001; Weick, Sutcliffe, & Obstfeld, 2005):

> Such knowledge may be formally captured and, through its casting into propositional statements, may be turned into organizational knowledge. While this is feasible and desirable, the case still remains that, at any point in time, abstract generalizations are in themselves incomplete to capture the totality of organizational knowledge. In action, an improvisational element always follows it like shadow follows an object. (Tsoukas & Vladimirou, 2001, p. 988)

From this point of view, an organisation's working knowledge can be seen as a capability arising from its members' joint capacities to make sense of situations and carry out their work. While this capability is a characteristic of an organisation, it is impossible without individual understandings and actions that constitute and materialise it. This knowledge is not a static property of individual or collective minds.

Rather it emerges dynamically from the shared propositions and collective performance of individuals across contexts and situations over time.

4.2.4 Sociopolitical Knowledge

One special kind of knowledge that mixes the organisational and the public is *sociopolitical knowledge* – such as qualification standards and ethical codes. This kind of knowledge is not 'conceptual knowledge', in the sense that it does not add understanding to the professional knowledge base, yet it plays an important role in defining and shaping the 'expertise space' (Lampland & Star, 2009; Mulcahy, 2011). Eraut (2009) points to this kind of knowledge when he makes a distinction between competence and capability. He explains that *competence*, from the socio-cultural perspective, is based on the notion of 'meeting other people's expectations' (p. 6) and 'being able to perform the tasks and roles required to the expected standard' (loc. cit.). This expectation is socially defined, it varies across contexts and over time and the expected standard for competence may be a moving target related to a person's years of experience, organisational roles and responsibilities. In contrast, *capability* is 'everything that a person or group or organisation can think or do' (loc. cit.). Eraut (2009) argues that competence can be seen as necessary for capability, but the reverse is not true. People and organisations usually have additional capabilities that go beyond the definition of their competences.[6]

Nevertheless, socio-materialistic accounts remind us that sociopolitical knowledge, such as standards, can play quite distinctive roles in knowing in practice. For one thing, as Timmermans and Epstein (2010) observe, different standards and agreements – such as the ISO 9000 quality standards that provide the basis for integrating firms and products on an international level – can form a fundamental infrastructure for coordinating shared work and modern life in general. But also, some standards may be very remote from knowledge enacted in professional performance. For example, in summarising his insights into how textbooks for teacher education programs have been revised after the introduction of new professional and occupational standards in the UK, Tummons (2011) remarks:

> What is noteworthy, if you read and then compare different textbook editions from this period of time, is that the content of different editions remains relatively unchanged: certainly, the imposition over the last decade or so of two – quite different – sets of professional standards does not seem have impacted on the content of the books, apart from the fact that as such books are updated, the relevant standards are 'plugged in', in a manner akin to the ways in which I have to install new plug-ins for my web browser before I can access some forms of online content. (Tummons, 2011, p. 28)

---

[6] In this book, we often use these words 'competence', 'capability' and even 'expertise' interchangeably in a broader 'capability' sense. In cases where we want to specifically associate the term 'competence' with the sociopolitical notion of meeting *formal* standards and requirements, we say so explicitly.

4.3 Doing and Understanding

> If successful task performance were impossible without correct understanding, human culture could not have gotten started. <...> In fact, all the technologies that brought the human race out of subsistence – metal working, leather preparation, the manufacture of cloth and glass, navigation, waterwheels and windmills, sailing boats, bread baking, brick making – had to be invented and developed in the absence of deep understanding, because such understanding has only become available since the scientific revolution, three centuries or so ago. (Ohlsson, 1995, p. 49)

Ohlsson (1995) makes a useful comparison between practical and declarative knowledge.[7] *Practical knowledge* broadly covers conventional notions of practice and practical reasoning – what Ohlsson describes as the knowledge needed for accomplishing something in a convenient way. Such knowledge includes sensori-motor skills (e.g. riding a bike or driving a car), cognitive skills (e.g. calculating or playing chess) and a disposition to act in a particular way when one tries to achieve a certain goal in given circumstances (e.g. to move a car wheel when one wants to make a turn). The main outcome of learning such knowledge is *competence*[8] or 'know-how' – which leads to effective goal attainment. Ohlsson argues that such learning starts from general methods (e.g. analogical reasoning) and increasingly becomes a more automatic, less conscious, simple, domain-specific skill. Such competence is generally acquired through extensive practice, and the medium for it is action.

He describes *declarative knowledge* as 'knowing that', which includes both concrete facts and abstract (higher-order) knowledge, such as concepts, ideas, theories, schemas and principles.[9] He argues that such 'higher-order' learning proceeds in the opposite direction to that taken in skill acquisition. It starts from a prior, poorly articulated understanding and increasingly becomes more conscious, explicit, elaborate and abstract. The main outcome of mastering such knowledge is *understanding* or 'know-that'. Such knowledge is acquired mainly through reflection, and the medium for it is discourse.

Ohlsson's distinction is a useful starting point, but it distracts attention from the fact that elements of 'knowing how' and 'knowing that' are usually entangled in any specific (nontrivial) example of understanding or capability. It also obscures some differences between various kinds of expertise and between different types of explicit and tacit knowledge (see, e.g. Collins & Evans, 2007, and Sects. 4.5 and 4.6). However, it does shine a light on some important discontinuities between practice

---

[7] This dichotomy, or close variants upon it, can be found in a diverse array of literature. For example, it has echoes in Anthony Giddens' distinction between practical and discursive consciousness (see, e.g. Giddens, 1984) and in Gilbert Ryle's (1945) distinction between 'knowing how' and 'knowing that'.

[8] Here, the term 'competence' is used by Ohlsson to refer to a higher level of ability in a rational, technical sense, not in the sociopolitical sense discussed in the previous section.

[9] 'Declarative knowledge' is also often called 'theoretical knowledge', 'propositional knowledge', 'formal knowledge' and 'conceptual knowledge'. In some contexts, these terms refer to different things, but they are often used as synonyms (e.g. Eraut, 1994, 2010).

and theory or, as Ohlsson puts it, between 'learning to do' and 'learning to under-stand'. In short, knowledge involved in the ability 'to do' is not the same as 'higher-order' understanding of fundamental principles that may be relevant to such action, but which are not (in reality) either necessary or sufficient for the action concerned. Successful performance does not imply understanding, nor does understanding guarantee successful action – it is possible 'to perform *any* task without understand-ing, by learning and doing the right actions' (Ohlsson, 1995, p. 50, emphasis added).

Miettinen and Virkkunen (2005) make a similar statement:

> Whereas the traditional epistemology defined knowledge in terms of symbolically represented, declarative knowledge (theories, models, concepts, facts), behavioural theo-ries of organization define competencies in terms of established ways of action using the concept of routine. (Miettinen & Virkkunen, 2005, p. 439)

They point to further parallels between action and routine, symbolic knowledge and innovation, and argue that concepts, models and other symbolic forms of knowl-edge are instrumental in inducing learning and change in human practices. Eraut (2010), on the basis of an empirical study of early career professionals' learning in workplace settings in the UK, draws similar conclusions and adds that fusing practice and theory, action and understanding requires effort:

> ... learning to practice and learning to use knowledge acquired in education settings do not happen automatically. <...> Learning to use formal knowledge in practical situations is a *major learning challenge* in its own right – it is not a natural consequence of learning knowledge on its own, and trying to employ that knowledge in practice without critical questioning of its appropriateness and effectiveness will not meet the challenge. Such learning also requires both *time* and *support*. (Eraut, 2010, p. 51, original emphasis)

What is the role of theoretical knowledge in practice? Ohlsson (1995) argues that declarative knowledge is fundamental for understanding, and there is increasing empirical evidence to suggest that this understanding supports and sometimes provides foundations for practice. For example, experts and novices, *when they solve complex or unfamiliar problems*, draw on large amounts of domain-specific propositional knowledge (Collins, 2011; Woods, 2007).[10]

The challenge in education, as Ohlsson observes, is that surprisingly little is known about how declarative knowledge is learnt and used.[11] Ohlsson makes two

---

[10] Bereiter (2002), drawing on Scribner's (1984) and Saxe's (1991) studies of school mathematics, also observes that novices in fact do use formal knowledge to do new tasks in workplace settings. While novices do these tasks more slowly than experienced peers, who execute them without engaging in formal manipulations, it is this knowledge that allows novices to start a job right away, without a long period of apprenticeship. Further, formal knowledge has an advantage of being more transferable across contexts. While 'know-how' developed in specific situations may be more effective, it is less transferable across contexts.

[11] The emerging line of research on threshold concepts works broadly in this direction (Land, Meyer, & Smith, 2008; Meyer & Land, 2006). Some other studies try to pin down the kinds of knowledge people use (and how) when they encounter complex professional problems (e.g. Collins, 2011; Hoffmann & Roth, 2005). We discuss this further in Chap. 6. However, Ohlsson's observation about the lack of understanding of declarative knowledge and higher-order learning still stands.

additional important points about why the propositional knowledge taught in educational institutions may not meet the needs of action. First, he makes a distinction between simple descriptive knowledge (facts) and higher-order principles, concepts, ideas, schemas, theories and so on. He argues that more attention is paid to teaching the former, whereas it is the latter that really capture fundamental features of the domain. Second, he argues that understanding of general principles is learnt through, and used in, practices that are different from those involved in learning and exercising skills:

> ... *human beings employ their understanding, not in action, but in the generation of symbols* <...> Abstract concepts, ideas and principles find their primary expression in cultural products, not in goal attainment. In particular, there is a deep connection between abstract knowledge and discourse. The study of higher-order learning might therefore begin by asking what people do when they produce discourse. What are the canonical tasks that people carry out when they talk and write? (Ohlsson, 1995, p. 51, original emphasis)

Ohlsson suggests a set of general epistemic activities (such as describing, arguing and defining) for engaging in discourse that leads to higher-order learning. We discuss such activities in more depth in Chaps. 12, 13, 14 and 15.

However, one should note that what Ohlsson (1995) calls 'understanding' primarily refers to 'scientific understanding' of underpinning fundamental principles. This is different from 'practical understanding' of underpinning principles to support action, such as useful heuristics, analogies or cases that are not necessarily grounded in scientific laws. But, as de Souza (2005) notes, even the latter kind of knowledge is different from the knowledge that underpins practitioners' 'know-how'. Practical decision-making and understanding draw on two different ways of knowing and acting and two different forms of discourse:

> Supporting decisions is not the same as supporting understanding and cognition, although the latter undeniably contributes to the former. One of the clearest distinctions between the two is perhaps that knowledge and action to support understanding is usually formatted in *positive* terms – explanations about how to achieve goals, how to carry out tasks and perform operations; information about the meaning of terms, the function and behavior of objects; and so on. Knowledge and action to support decisions is usually formatted in *comparative* and sometimes even *negative*, terms – analyses of costs and benefits involved in making choices, troubleshooting hypotheses, instructions for how to diagnose failure, and so on. (de Souza, 2005, p. 63, original emphasis)

4.4 Knowledge and Knowing

Ohlsson's (1995) distinction is clear-cut – knowledge for understanding is not the same as knowledge for doing. Explicit knowledge is different from tacit. Learning and knowing for understanding are not the same as learning or knowing for doing:

> understanding is a state of mind, not a process. There is *no intrinsic connection* between that state and any particular action. (Ohlsson, 1995, p. 50, emphasis added)[12]

---

[12] Ohlsson draws here on the representational view of knowledge and learning and puts it in sharp contrast to the performative view that we discussed in Chap. 3.

Tim Ingold (2011) offers a complementary perspective on two rather different epistemological views of knowledge in practice. Drawing on Rubin (1988), he makes a (metaphorical) distinction between the view of knowledge as 'complex structure' and as 'complex process'. From the *complex structure* viewpoint, knowledge is a certain configuration of mental representations that are acquired by an individual through some mechanism similar to 'copying' or 'replication', prior to the time at which they step into the world of practice. The application of such knowledge is relatively straightforward – one simply needs to match the structures in the mind and structures in the world through a mechanism that establishes the homogeneity between the two. From the *complex process* viewpoint, priority is given to the very act of knowing rather than structures or properties of the mind – 'people know *by way* of their practice' (p. 159, original emphasis):

> ... far from being copied, ready-made, into the mind in advance of its encounter with the world, knowledge is perpetually 'under construction' within the field of relations established through the immersion of the actor-perceiver in a certain environmental context. Knowledge, in this view, is not transmitted as a complex structure but it is the emergent product of a complex process. It is not so much *replicated* as *reproduced*. (Ingold, 2011, p. 159, original emphasis)

Ingold notes that the distinction between the two viewpoints goes back to two different meanings of the word 'process'. In the complex structure view, the verb 'process' is used in *a transitive* sense – knowing starts with perceived bodily sensations of the structures in the world and ends with the representations in the head. In the complex process view, the word 'process' is used in an *intransitive* sense. It does not have a clearly articulated beginning and end, but continually unfolds within practice:

> It is equivalent to the very movement – the *processing*. (loc. cit., original emphasis)

However, once one looks at understanding and doing in professional work in organisational settings, the relationship between the two becomes more complicated.

Cook and Brown (1999) make a useful distinction between the 'epistemology of possession' and 'epistemology of practice'. They explain that, historically, different forms of 'what is known' have been treated as something people or organisations *possess*, be it tacit or explicit, individual or group knowledge. While such knowledge is important, it does not account for what one *can do*. For example, when a mechanic fixes a car, his knowledge involves not only what he has and applies but also things he is doing:

> ... the epistemic work done, [which] needs to include both the knowledge he possesses and the actions he carries out. (Cook & Brown, 1999, p. 53)

Cook and Brown extend the view of *knowledge as possessed* with the view of *knowing as a part of action*:

> ... understanding of the epistemological dimension of individual and group action requires us to speak about both knowledge *used in* action and knowing as *part of* action. (loc. cit., original emphasis)

The former focusses on *knowledge* as understanding *employed* for making sense of the world and action; the latter focusses on *knowing* as understanding *created* in this very moment of sense-making and action. It requires one to master a distinct kind of knowledge which is *ways of knowing*. They further note that knowledge and knowing form a dynamic couple with each other:

> Knowing does not sit statically on top of knowledge. Quite the contrary, since knowing is an aspect of our interaction with the world, its relationship with knowledge is dynamic. Each of the forms of knowledge is brought into play by knowing when knowledge is used as a tool in interaction with the world. Knowledge, meanwhile, gives shape and discipline to knowing. (op. cit., pp. 70–71)

Therefore, some aspects of actionable professional knowledge, including ways of knowing, can be learnt in advance, prior to practice. However, learning for knowledgeable action necessarily involves practising, as some epistemic work is inevitably done and learnt in action and by action:

> When a part [of a flute] is handed back to a previous worker, for example, it can come with a comment such as 'this is a clunky one'. The flutemakers then hand the piece back and forth discussing its 'clunkiness'. <...> [I]t is typical for an apprentice to work on flutes starting on his or her first day in the shop: he or she engages in the practice of flutemaking, and begins to acquire not only knowledge but also ways of knowing. An apprentice may be told explicitly that 'these keys need to work more solidly'. But it is only through practice, through actual working jointly with other flutemakers on the piece, that he or she will 'get a feel' for what 'solidly' actually means in that shop ('solidly' could mean quite a different thing at one of the other workshops). When a master flutemaker says something such as 'this is what we call clunky' an apprentice can only know what that means by learning what it feels like – and a master flutemaker can only agree that an apprentice's work ultimately feels right by feeling the piece. (op. cit., pp. 75–76)

We can illustrate the point with related observations from a different area: from studies of preoperative anaesthesia teams and apprenticeship in operating theatres (Hindmarsh & Pilnick, 2007; Koschmann, LeBaron, Goodwin, & Feltovich, 2011). A surgeon or anaesthetist cannot participate in an operation without substantial, explicit, high-order understanding: of the medical condition involved and of operating protocols. However, learning to participate in such work also involves developing nuanced perception and complex manual skills, such as how to make the right incision. Furthermore, performance and real-time coordination of a team's work in the operating theatre is inseparable from what Hindmarsh and Pilnick (2007) call 'intercorporeal knowing':

> ... participants become expert in knowing the bodily conduct of others in the anaesthetic room as one resource to coordinate their contributions to the team's work. (Hindmarsh & Pilnick, 2007, p. 1398)

In summary, knowledgeable action and actionable knowledge blur the boundaries between declarative and procedural knowledge, between understanding and doing and between knowledge as possessed and knowing in practice.

4.5   Tacit Knowledge and Explicit Learning

Tacit, largely unarticulated kinds of knowledge and ways of knowing have often been considered as essential to fluent action (Atkinson & Claxton, 2000; Collins, 2010; Ingold, 2011; Sternberg & Horvath, 1999) and also as the main source for professional innovation (Nonaka & Takeuchi, 1995; Victor & Boynton, 1998). Such knowledge is usually considered to be deeply personal, developed through practice and, in essence, impossible to teach in explicit ways. However, there is more than one kind of tacit knowledge. Recognising these different kinds means that one can be more certain about relations between tacit knowledge and explicit learning.[13] We follow Harry Collins (2010) in distinguishing three kinds of tacit knowledge, which he calls 'weak' (or relational), 'medium' (or somatic) and 'strong' (or collective).

Weak tacit knowledge is knowledge that is (in principle) explicable, but generally is tacit because of its relational character – that is, because of relations between people in society. For example, some knowledge is concealed (professionals may want to keep it secret), unrecognised (one may fail to appreciate someone else's need to know), ostensive (it is easier to communicate by showing rather than explaining) or logically demanding (taking a long time to explain and learn). In short, weak tacit knowledge is tacit only because of social contingencies, not because it *cannot* be made explicit and thereby rendered in a form that can be communicated, taught and learnt. It is often merely a matter of applying effort or willingness to make relational tacit knowledge explicit and shareable.

Medium tacit knowledge is perhaps the most familiar kind of tacit knowledge – it is somatic. It too *can* be made explicit, but it is 'inscribed' in the human body and brain. Thus, there is a 'somatic limit', and this knowledge cannot be learnt easily because of the way the human body and brain work (e.g. a person can read a description of how to ride a bicycle, but the knowledge in use while balancing the bike is somatic; a teacher can be shown how to use a new interactive whiteboard, but it will take time for her to fine-tune her hand movements to the device and to integrate its use, with minimal conscious attention, into the flow of classroom action). Complex somatic learning usually involves significant practice, yet various learning strategies that make somatic knowledge more explicit, such as physical and emotional awareness and cognitive reflection, usually enhance this process (Green, 2002).

Strong tacit knowledge is so called because it is a collective tacit knowledge and is not reducible to the personal or explicit. It depends on a sensitivity to social context and moment-to-moment interaction. The 'right' way to do certain things can only be learnt through experience and through socialisation with others in a similar context (e.g. learning how close one may stand to a stranger in a queue,

---

[13] Consequently, there are also significant implications for task analysis, curriculum design, assessment and recruitment/selection processes. Some kinds of tacit knowledge are easier to specify and assess than others.

learning how to drive in dense traffic). An example from our own research on preparation for school teaching could be resolving whether a particular pedagogical method would be acceptable, given what is mandated in the national curriculum, the likely willingness of the students to cooperate, the views of other teachers, etc.

Action involving tacit knowledge may involve all three kinds of tacitness. For example, consider the tacit knowledge involved in a teacher's ability to manage a classroom effectively. Some of it may be weak tacit (e.g. an experienced teacher may be able to explain his/her key classroom management principles), some may be medium (e.g. even knowing these principles, a young teacher may need time to practice his voice pitch, tone, volume and other embodied skills) and some may be strong (e.g. the classroom management strategies may need significant adjustment if the teacher moves from a boys to a girls school). While some parts of this might be learnt separately (e.g. a teacher may learn motor skills to control his voice level before going into the classroom), they still have to be coordinated together into a more complex skill (e.g. using motor skills in a socially sensitive way).[14]

Drawing on the example of riding a bicycle, Harry Collins (2011) further notes:

> No amount of explanation will enable the novice to get on a bike and ride it at the first time of trying. The skill of bicycle-*balancing* (as opposed to *riding* in traffic) is individually embodied rather than collectively embodied. Physical skills of this kind require *changes in the material form of body and brain*. The same is true of what we might call 'embrained' abilities such as mathematically expressed theorizing – this requires 'mental muscles' to be trained and exercised as the tacit abilities are acquired. (Collins, 2011, p. 282, emphasis added, author's footnote omitted)

Collins points out that 'bicycle balancing' is not the same as 'bicycle riding', as the latter involves social conventions of traffic and is therefore a much more complicated skill. Nevertheless, he notes that even basic learning usually involves language:

> Imagine finding a bike for the first time on a desert island! How would one come to understand that this spindly thing could be balanced and ridden? (op. cit., p. 295)

He notes the importance of being aware of different 'muscles' and of training those 'muscles' that are not strong enough. However, these 'muscles' should be trained in a social ensemble, by linking physical skill and language in practical understanding. He puts the relationship between discourse and physical practice and individual and social performance in this way: seeing language as essential in the individual

---

[14] Collins (2010, pp. 123–124) compares his view of tacit knowledge with the well-known Dreyfus and Dreyfus (1980) five-stage model of skill acquisition – which describes how learners progress from novice to advanced beginner, to competent practitioner, to proficient worker and up to an expert. Collins observes that Dreyfus and Dreyfus do not discuss the step change between bodily skills and social skills. Further, Collins suggests that skill learning should not be seen as a stage-by-stage process but as a process that involves phases in which previously acquired skills are fused with new capabilities. A narrow emphasis on perception, decision-making and semi-automated, routinised behaviour in the Dreyfus model has been also criticised by Eraut (1994, pp. 124–128). Eraut argues that progress beyond competence depends on situational apprehension ('reading the situation') and also on a deeper, holistic understanding which is informed by theoretical learning.

acquisition of practical understanding and physical practice as central for learning practical language:

> ... language is, and must be, more central than physical practice in individual acquisition of practical understanding. <...> Physical practice remains central to human culture but its influence is at the collective level at which languages are formed, rather than the individual level at which practical abilities are acquired. (op. cit., p. 271)

Collins' view of tacit knowledge contrasts with many traditional views that see the tacit as (primarily) embodied and unarticulated skill: as a complete opposite of the explicit. Collins (2010) rejects this boldly: 'The tacit depends on the explicit!' (p. 7). He goes on to say:

> ... many of the classic treatments of tacit knowledge – those that have to do with bodily skills or the way the human brain works in harmony with the body – put the emphasis in the wrong place. What the individual human body and human brain do is not much different from what cats, dogs, and, for that matter, trees and clouds have always done. While humans encounter bodily abilities as strange and difficult because we continually fail in our attempts to explicate them, there is nothing mysterious about the knowledge itself. It is knowledge that, *in principle*, can be understood and explicated by the methods of scientific analysis. In practice it may be hard to describe the entire picture but it is hard to develop a complete scientific understanding of many things. (Collins, 2010, pp. 7–8, original emphasis)

Collins acknowledges the importance of the body in the acquisition of knowledge, but he argues that this has to do with the *nature of human beings* not the *nature of knowledge* itself. He shifts the source of complexity of certain kinds of knowledge from the individual to the collective level:

> ... the nature of the body does, to a good extent, provide the conceptual structure of our lives, but that conceptual structure is located at the collective level, not the individual. (op. cit., p. 8)

This gives some useful insights into some of the challenges of the *performative* project (linking doing with being) (Chap. 3). While performance may well help build expertise for doing tasks and interacting with others, it may not build an explicit understanding or deliberative problem-solving knowledge. It is difficult to apply concepts for reflecting on actions, if they were not applied in learning those actions in the first place. However, a narrowly focussed *representational* project (linking doing with knowing) is unlikely to succeed in helping students to learn the hardest parts of actionable knowledge, unless representations are seen as emerging, dynamic tools. Rather than positioning representations as final states, they are better seen as dynamically constituted, within collective and inherently situated performance – a process of *(re)presenting*.

In the last main section of this chapter, we want to bring these insights together by illustrating how different kinds of knowledge and ways of knowing – which are often seen as ontologically distinct and incompatible – are related to, and lean on, each other in skilful professional performance.

4.6 Actionable Knowledge

Ohlsson (1995) primarily focussed on how people learn two types of knowledge: declarative and procedural. It is also important to think about how professionals create knowledge for action, such as analyses of complex situations, problem–solutions and other kinds of *explicit* knowledge that support practical decisions and help attune their actions in performance – that is, creating declarative knowledge to support practice.[15]

As Yinger and Hendricks-Lee (1993) argue, bringing intelligence to bear on activity requires 'working knowledge' – which we prefer to call *actionable knowledge, knowledge that helps getting things accomplished in practical situations.* Such knowledge does not exist independently of a person, but neither is it solely a matter of an individual and their mind. Rather, it involves a relationship between an individual, place and action. From a personal perspective, such knowledge primarily involves an ability to establish functional relationships between various aspects of the environment, self and action. Explicit knowledge, from this perspective, provides a repertoire of tools for making these connections knowledgeably.

For analytical purposes, it may be helpful to understand some further epistemic discontinuities between knowledge that *underpins* conceptual understanding, knowledge *for action* and knowledge entangled *in action.*

As we mentioned before, Eraut (2010) notes that *time* is a critical factor in professional practice: some decisions have to be made quickly, with limited deliberation before the action. In other words, some actions rely on perceptual sensorimotor knowledge and strategies at hand (e.g. reflex and intuitive skill), rather than more time-consuming deliberative, analytic or reflective thinking or the cognitive skills of problem-solving and decision-making (see de Souza, 2005). Thus, when one lacks time, habit takes over and substitutes the reflexive skill and the body for the reflective mind.[16]

Further, as Harry Collins (2010) notes, explicit knowledge involves different levels of explicitness and, accordingly, requires different levels of interpretation. For example, some knowledge may be already embedded in the physical environment and situation, such that it does not require significant explanation and interpretation (e.g. a teacher generally knows how to use a blackboard or how to introduce a new concept to students). Alternatively, some explication could be embedded in the design of affordances (e.g. an interactive whiteboard may have

---

[15] Ohlsson (1995) puts cognitive and sensorimotor skills into one 'skill acquisition' category and describes them afterwards as one thing (procedural knowledge). This makes it harder to distinguish between how the mind learns and how the body learns and how the mind supports the body. Learning to understand and performing different tasks that may already draw upon this understanding are different things. Linking to Collins and Evans's (2007) different kinds of expertise, on which we elaborate in Chap. 5, the former is a part of 'interactional expertise' and the latter of 'contributory expertise'. Practical decoupling (for analysis of performance, teaching and learning) can be facilitated by the theoretical decoupling which we aim to provide here.

[16] From a different perspective, Kahneman (2011) distinguishes between thinking fast and slow; the former is intuitive and error-prone; the latter involves effortful interpretive work.

additional help features for assisting a teacher to understand how it works; a new textbook could provide a sequence of activities). However, some kinds of explicit knowledge may require communication and interpretation (e.g. a teacher may not know how to use an interactive whiteboard effectively even if she knows how it works or may not know how to implement a Jigsaw technique effectively even though she knows what it consists of). Even procedural knowledge, which is the main focus of Collins' argument, may involve not only simple mechanical descriptions that mimic human actions but rather what he calls 'scientific explanations' of mechanical causes and effects. For example, an interactive whiteboard or a Jigsaw teaching technique can be applied in teaching in various ways. Understanding the instructional and psychological principles underlying the effectiveness of a tool or technique may allow one to adapt them flexibly to different situations. For example, knowing that a Jigsaw technique is effective because it promotes students' engagement in self-explanation and active cognitive processing of information may help a teacher to modify various aspects of this instructional technique, while preserving its core educational qualities. Such underpinning 'scientific knowledge' enables more flexibility in application – the possibility of responding to opportunities, constraints and other cues encountered in various situations. However, more flexible kinds of knowledge also require more time to do interpretational work. It is worth noting that this knowledge of 'scientific explanations' behind the causes of practical effects is still not the same as *understanding* the theoretical principles that underpin these effects, which would more closely approach declarative knowledge in Ohlsson's (1995) terms (i.e. a teacher may still not know why self-explanation causes deeper learning).

Like Ohlsson (1995), de Souza (2005) and Perkins (1997) take the view that problem-solving and decision-making do not guarantee understanding and may not necessarily be a consequence of it. While knowledge work for building declarative knowledge (what Ohlsson calls 'epistemic tasks') can be seen mainly as a discursive activity, including use of the language and inscriptions of a professional domain, knowledge work for supporting action usually involves *an entanglement* of intelligent problem-solving, engagement with the material and social environment and perceptual sensorimotor skill (e.g. thinking how to teach, creating an environment for teaching, adapting instructions to existing logistical constraints and teaching). While many aspects of this knowledge require fine-tuned perception and skills that as a rule develop slowly and require practice, this does not mean that these skills are firmly tacit and cannot be supported by explicit knowledge.

The distinctions between (a) learning *to understand*, (b) learning *to do interpretational work* and create knowledge that underpins action, (c) learning *in doing* in a concrete social and material setting and (d) learning to know *while doing* become clear if we map the epistemic activities that are central to some of the main kinds of human knowledge and ways of knowing side by side (Table 4.2).

Table 4.2 Linking learning for understanding and working knowledge for problem-solving, making and action

Kind of knowledge and way of knowing	Aspect of knowledgeability						
	Declarative			Procedural and meta-procedural		Relational	
	Propositional ('know-That')	Structural ('know-How')ᵃ	Explanatory ('know-Why')	Procedural ('know-how')	Regulative ('know-for')	Experiential ('know -what')	Contextual ('know-when')
Conceptual knowledge – knowing as building conceptual understanding	What are the main elements of the conceptual construct?	How do these conceptual elements relate to each other?	Why does this conceptual construct work in this way?	How to construct appropriate conceptual understanding for the task	How could the knowledge-building process be monitored?	What do I know from my experience and feel about the conceptual phenomena that I encounter?	In and for which context am I constructing this knowledge; and in which context does this conceptual solution make sense?
Problem-solving knowledge – knowing as constructing understanding for action	What are the main elements of the problem and its solution?	How should the elements of the problem and its solution connect to each other?	Why should the problem be solved in this way?	How to solve the problem	How could problem-solving be monitored?	What do I feel and know from my experience about inappropriate and appropriate solutions of similar problems?	In and for which context am I solving this problem; and in which context does this problem solution make sense?
Social knowledge – knowing as orchestration of social arrangements	What are the elements of the social relationships and interactions that are related to the activity?	How do various social elements of social arrangements relate to each other?	Why do these social arrangements function in this way?	How to orchestrate social interactions	How could the appropriateness of social interactions be monitored?	How do I feel, experience and perceive social relationships?	In and for which context am I acting; and in which context does this social organisation and my interactions make sense?

(continued)

Table 4.2 (continued)

Kind of knowledge and way of knowing	Aspect of knowledgeability						
	Declarative			Procedural and meta-procedural		Relational	
	Propositional ('know-That')	Structural ('know-How')[a]	Explanatory ('know-Why')	Procedural ('know-how')	Regulative ('know-for')	Experiential ('know-what')	Contextual ('know-when')
Material knowledge – knowing as co-configuration of material environment	What are the elements of the material environment that are related to the activity?	How do various elements of material environment join with each other?	Why do these material arrangements work in this way?	How to configure the material environment	How could the appropriateness of material arrangements be monitored?	How do I feel, experience and perceive material environment?	In and for which context am I acting; and in which context do these material arrangements make sense?
Somatic knowledge – knowing as attunement to the situation and coordination of perception, bodily skill, and action	Which aspects of sensorimotor performance are important for this task?	How do these somatic aspects relate to each other and overall performance?	Why do these somatic aspects relate in this way?	How to attune ones sensorimotor performance to the task and situation	How could sensorimotor performance and unfolding situation be monitored?	How do I feel, experience and perceive myself, my performance and the situation?	What are the qualities of the situation in which my actions, reactions and interactions make sense?

[a] Together, these 'Knowing That', 'Knowing How' and 'Knowing Why' represent understanding of the principles underlying a phenomenon. 'How' with capital 'H' is different from 'how' with small 'h'. The former represents an understanding of intrinsic/internal generative mechanisms that constitute phenomena; the latter represents extrinsic/external generative processes that produce phenomena

4.6.1 An Example: Knowledge in Teaching

Let us illustrate this by mapping out 'the architecture' of a teacher's knowledge, and ways of knowing, involved in preparing for a lesson and teaching it. Let us imagine the teacher is planning to introduce a new scientific concept to primary school students – *material properties* – and wants to engage students in deep, authentic learning. Her choice is to do this by designing small inquiry tasks in which groups of students explore different materials and then consolidate each group's findings (and students' learning) using a Jigsaw technique. On what kinds of knowledge would she draw in making this decision?[17]

To get started, let us use our earlier classification of the main aspects of personal professional knowledgeability (Table 4.1) and map the main aspects of the teacher's professional knowledge involved in this work. We start with the teacher's stable or codified knowledge, which is a direct counterpart to Ohlsson's (1995) *declarative knowledge*. Such knowledge, in scientific and technical domains, is usually seen as having several main parts (e.g. Perkins, 1986; Schwab, 1978):

- *Propositional* (What are the main elements of a phenomenon?)
- *Structural* (How are these elements related?)
- *Explanatory* (Why do things function in this particular way?)

Together, these three knowledges – 'knowing That', 'knowing How' and 'knowing Why' – represent understanding of the principles underlying a phenomenon. It is what Bereiter (2002) called 'stable' aspect of knowledgeability: 'That', 'How' and 'Why' are inherent in the phenomenon rather than the knower. (To emphasise this, we use capital letters: 'knowing How', 'knowing That', etc.).

To put this knowledge into practice, the teacher needs *procedural knowledge* of suitable strategies, principles and other tacit and explicit 'know-hows' for performing relevant tasks (How should I do this and that?) and *regulative knowledge* for monitoring and adjusting her performance (How do I monitor what I do? What criteria do I use to evaluate outcome and performance?). This 'know-how' and 'know-for' represent understanding of the generative processes that produce the phenomenon (Garud, 1997). They are primarily dynamic aspects of a person's knowledgeability, as these – 'how' and 'for' – are deeply inherent in the knower and her performance rather than in the phenomenon. (For this purpose, we use lower case letters: 'knowing how').

Even a novice teacher would bring to the situation at least some implicit and impressionistic knowledge derived from her experiences of similar situations and events – what do I know from my experience and what do I feel about it? Such *experiential knowledge* may lag behind her explicit thinking or rational justification, yet it turns out to be extremely influential in teachers' and other professionals'

---

[17] This example uses some pedagogical terms of art that may be unfamiliar to some readers (cognitive load, self-explanation, etc.). The example works, even if one doesn't know much about what these terms mean.

practical thinking (Olson & Bruner, 1996; Sternberg & Horvath, 1999). This knowledge, which Garud (1997) called 'know-what' knowledge, largely comes from learning by using and represents an appreciation of the kind of phenomena worth pursuing.

The teacher also needs to bring to the task her *contextual knowledge* of perceived affordances and constraints and her understandings of when her decisions and actions make sense (What do I know about the context? In what context do my intended actions make sense?). Such experiential and contextual knowledges often come from the memories of specific cases and other situated propositions and events. They often reside in the nexus between:

(a) The knowledge inhering in the phenomenon ('knowing That', 'knowing How' and 'knowing Why')
(b) A generative capacity for knowing ('knowing how' and 'knowing for')
(c) Sensitivity to the context for embodied situated performance ('knowing what' and 'knowing when').

Such 'knowing what' and 'knowing when' form a necessary part of the teacher's actionable knowledge. They allow her to make critical judgements about the relevance, feasibility and appropriateness of her declarative and procedural knowledge and to decide how to act.

Let us now look into the teacher's actions involved in designing and teaching such a lesson. What ways of knowing will be involved in the teacher's construction of actionable knowledge and making knowledgeable actions?

The first is knowledge for constructing a *conceptual understanding* that allows the teacher to assemble a (theoretically justified) foundation for a good lesson plan (see row 1 in Table 4.2). Borrowing from the classical design literature, such a conceptual assemblage could be called a 'design concept' (Cross, 2011). It draws on a sound understanding of the 'content knowledge' to be taught (e.g. material properties), pedagogical techniques to be applied (e.g. authentic inquiry, Jigsaw) and a web of other pedagogical and psychological concepts relevant to what and how this lesson will be taught (e.g. deep learning, active information processing, self-explanation, cognitive load). These declarative constructs would not be usable unless the teacher had *procedural knowledge* for assembling them into a new conceptual understanding[18] of how to teach about material properties using inquiry and Jigsaw. For example, such procedural knowledge could involve a range of strategies for choosing pedagogical techniques that would engage students in deep, authentic learning, while simultaneously avoiding cognitive overload. This knowledge work would also involve a *regulative aspect* as the teacher would need to make judgements about the appropriateness of her conceptual solution. The knowledge that underpins such decisions may build on explicit criteria for deciding if the cognitive load that students would experience during the inquiry and Jigsaw is

---

[18] This kind of teacher knowledge is usually called 'pedagogical content knowledge' (Shulman, 1986).

appropriate and the solution is, in general, good enough. However, the teacher is also likely to draw on her earlier experiences and *implicit feelings* of whether her blend of Jigsaw with various inquiry tasks would not overload students and, in general, feels right. The teacher's arguments for justifying her solution are unlikely to be formulated in absolute terms and unlikely to be put under rigorous experimental scrutiny. Rather, as with many things designed for specific and everyday use, this knowledge will be formulated and justified in relational terms – of whether the proposed solution is good enough in *the context* of her intended practical activity.

The constructed 'design concept' is just one aspect of the teacher's knowledgeable action, and alone would not necessarily result in a successfully designed lesson or classroom performance. To design the lesson, the teacher would also need to engage in practical *problem-solving* and put all the related conceptual constructs together into a more actionable form, such as a lesson plan. Such a plan could be implicit, but more likely will be expressed, at least in part, in a certain symbolic form and inscribed in a lesson planning document. While some elements of the knowledge involved in constructing conceptual understanding and in problem-solving inevitably overlap, this problem-solving activity also requires mastering some distinctive kinds of knowledge and ways of knowing (see row 2 in Table 4.2). For example, procedural knowledge for constructing conceptual understanding may involve various conceptual blending strategies that allow the teacher to see connections and integrate several conceptual constructs, such as active student engagement, cognitive load and Jigsaw. (That is, her students could engage in a deep, authentic exploration of just some aspects of the topic and learn other aspects from peers, which would reduce cognitive load and enhance deep learning through self-explanation.) Procedural knowledge for constructing the lesson plan, in contrast, would involve various strategies for designing, distributing and sequencing specific tasks for teaching specific content, using inquiry and Jigsaw to help achieve specific lesson aims in a specific context (e.g. use Jigsaw and authentic exploration for learning about material properties, but explain to students how to conduct a scientific experiment before they start authentic inquiry in groups). Problem-solving – which in this case is the lesson design – is a different way of knowing from constructing conceptual understanding for designing it. It draws on a distinct set of declarative knowledge about the elements, structure and function of a lesson plan and distinct procedural knowledge for designing all the elements of the lesson and distinctive relational knowledge which helps attune lesson planning to the context of the task.

To *teach* this lesson in a classroom setting, the teacher would further need knowledge that allows her to *think through the social and material* arrangements of the classroom and, drawing on her knowledge, skills and ways of engaging with the environment, to align her planned lesson with the social arrangements and material affordances of the specific setting, such as worksheets, blackboard position, room space, time, student bodies, habitual and explicitly orchestrated ways of interacting and doing things (rows 3 and 4 in Table 4.2). The actual teaching activity will further depend upon the teachers' *somatic knowledge* to carry out actions skilfully: such as motor skills, clarity of voice, sensory perception, spatial attention and reaction to students' behaviour (row 4 in Table 4.2). Social, material and somatic knowing draw on embodied, materially and socially situated, kinds of knowledge and ways of knowing. They are different from the conceptual and problem-solving knowledges which are usually expressed in formal vocabularies and grammars of disciplinary communities. Nevertheless, they are critical parts of a teacher's actionable knowledge. Johnson (1989) expressed this vividly:

> ... we need to view a person's understanding as their mode of being in, or having, a world. And this, of course, is not merely a matter of beliefs held and decisions made; instead, it is people's way of experiencing their world, and it involves sensory experiences, bodily interactions, moods, feelings, and spatio-temporal orientations. To sum up, teachers' personal practical knowledge would include the entire way in which they have a structured world that they can make some sense of, and in which they can function with varying degrees of success. (Johnson, 1989, pp. 362–363)

However, socio-materially situated and somatic knowledges are not entirely mysterious capabilities that can be learnt only by trial and error or rote copying and repetition. Even somatic capabilities, which are often considered as tacit and difficult to disentangle, can involve linguistic guidance and intelligent, mimetic *epistemic* actions that are attentive to the body and environment (see Table 4.2). Furthermore, different kinds of performative knowing are not independent and can be knowledgeably aligned with, and draw upon, each other in the teacher's action. For example, if the teacher knows that her voice is not strong enough to command the students' attention in a noisy classroom, especially when the students are working in groups, she could prepare handouts that describe the activity in more detail, so that at least part of this complex somatic work (and knowing) can be done by handouts (i.e. the combination of social and material knowing). But to be able to come to this decision, she must master a problem-solving strategy as well as construct conceptual knowledge that allows her to see the possibility of substituting some bodily skills (shouting) with the material and social affordances of a handout.

4.6.2 Drawing Some Implications for Professional Education

In summary, conceptual understanding, problem-solving, the skills needed to construct the material environment and orchestrate social arrangements and the somatic knowledge needed to act fluently are all aspects of knowledgeability, but, ontologically, they are distinct kinds of knowledge and ways of knowing. Epistemic activities for generating conceptual understanding cannot *substitute for* epistemic activities that underpin problem-solving, or one's actions in configuring the social and material arrangements or body intelligence and somatic skills. Most importantly, they cannot substitute for an ability to *integrate and coordinate* different kinds of knowledge and ways of knowing in one knowledgeable course of action.

This analysis gives some insight into why typical representational projects are incomplete: they simply engage professionals in epistemic activities for building conceptual understanding and problem-solving, but do not necessarily engage in the epistemic activities for perceiving, co-constructing and acting in the social and material world.

Unless these different kinds of knowledge are related to action in more explicit ways, then knowledge to understand, knowledge to do, knowledge to make and understanding in action quickly become disconnected from each other and from the practical world. There is not much natural overlap between different kinds of knowledge, except experiences ('know-what') and contexts ('know-when') that unite rather than split mind, action, social and material world and body into a single act of knowing and acting.

However, higher education courses often tear this context apart too. For example, in teacher education, conceptual knowledge of pedagogy and educational psychology will be covered (if at all) in *foundational courses* and assessed by getting student to write essays and do other 'conceptual' tasks. Problem-solving skills, such as lesson planning and the design of instructional materials, will be taught in *professional practice courses*, by giving students the task of constructing lesson plans and developing teaching and learning resources. Such plans and resources will usually be generic, thus not tweaked to specific social arrangements, physical spaces and other aspects of the environment in which one would learn social and material kinds of knowledge and knowing. Somatic knowledge would usually be learnt during *internships* and quite commonly through blunt performance and repetition, with minimal attention to explicit aspects of knowledgeability that underpin a teacher's bodily intelligence in the classroom. Reuniting these contexts, which are the main enablers for the development of tacit knowledge, would provide a viable starting point for integrating these different kinds of knowledge and ways of knowing.

That said, we should not forget that while different kinds of knowledge and ways of knowing are interconnected, they can be learnt and rehearsed individually. Merlin Donald (1990) reminds us that, as human beings, we have an extraordinary ability to 'parse' our own actions into their components and to practice, refine and then recombine and re-enact them in new events. This distinctive capability to parse and rehearse individual skills outside the practice is less clearly acknowledged than it should be in the performative projects of professional learning.

Various kinds of knowledge are discernible and useful for practitioners, and there is a benefit to learning different explicit ways of knowing that support various kinds of actionable understanding, including understanding how to make practical decisions, how to co-configure material setting, how to organise social interactions and how to adjust one's bodily skill and action to the environment – in short how to play different kinds of epistemic games. We will develop this theme later in Chaps. 12, 13, 14, 15 and 16.

Our discussion, in this chapter, has primarily looked at professional knowledge and knowing from the perspective of the individual student-practitioner – what David Perkins calls a 'person-solo' perspective (Perkins, 1993). In the next chapter, we extend this discussion by turning our attention to the shapes of professional knowledge in *collective* situated performance – involving other people, language, symbolic media and material environments – a 'person-plus' perspective.

References

Argyris, C. (1993). *Knowledge for action: A guide to overcoming barriers to organizational change*. San Francisco, CA: Jossey-Bass.
Argyris, C. (1999). Tacit knowledge in management. In R. J. Sternberg & J. A. Horvath (Eds.), *Tacit knowledge in professional practice: Researcher and practitioner perspectives* (pp. 123–140). Mahwah, NJ: Lawrence Erlbaum Associates.
Argyris, C., & Schön, D. A. (1996). *Organizational learning II: Theory, method and practice*. Reading, MA: Addison-Wesley.
Atkinson, T., & Claxton, G. (Eds.). (2000). *The intuitive practitioner: On the value of not always knowing what one is doing*. Buckingham, UK: Open University Press.
Baumard, P. (1999). *Tacit knowledge in organizations*. London, UK: Sage.
Bereiter, C. (2002). *Education and mind in the knowledge age*. Mahwah, NJ: Lawrence Erlbaum Associates.
Billett, S. (2008). Learning throughout working life: A relational interdependence between personal and social agency. *British Journal of Educational Studies, 56*(1), 39–58. doi:10.1111/j.1467-8527.2007.00394.x.
Brown, J. S., Collins, A., & Duguid, P. (1989). Situated cognition and the culture of learning. *Educational Researcher, 18*(1), 32–42.
Chinn, C. A., Buckland, L. A., & Samarapungavan, A. L. A. (2011). Expanding the dimensions of epistemic cognition: Arguments from philosophy and psychology. *Educational Psychologist, 46*(3), 141–167.
Clandinin, D. J. (1985). Personal practical knowledge: A study of teachers' classroom images. *Curriculum Inquiry, 15*(4), 361–385.
Collins, H. M. (2010). *Tacit and explicit knowledge*. Chicago, IL: The University of Chicago Press.
Collins, A. (2011). A study of expert theory formation: The role of different model types and domain frameworks. In M. S. Khine, & I. M. Saleh (Eds.), *Models and modeling* (pp. 23–40). Dordrecht, The Netherlands: Springer.
Collins, H. M. (2011). Language and practice. *Social Studies of Science, 41*(2), 271–300.
Collins, H. M., & Evans, R. (2007). *Rethinking expertise*. Chicago, IL: The University of Chicago Press.
Cook, S. D. N., & Brown, J. S. (1999). Bridging epistemologies: The generative dance between organizational knowledge and organizational knowing. *Organization Science, 10*(4), 381–400.
Cross, N. (2011). *Design thinking: Understanding how designers think and work*. Oxford, UK: Berg.
Davenport, T. H. (2005). *Thinking for a living: How to get better performance and results from knowledge workers*. Boston, MA: Harvard Business School Press.
de Souza, C. S. (2005). *The semiotic engineering of human-computer interaction*. Cambridge, MA: MIT Press.
Donald, M. (1990). *Origins of the modern mind: Three stages in the evolution of culture and cognition*. Cambridge, MA: Harvard University Press.
Donald, M. (2010). The exographic revolution: Neuropsychological sequelae. In L. Malafouris & C. Renfrew (Eds.), *The cognitive life of things: Recasting the boundaries of the mind* (pp. 71–79). Cambridge, UK: McDonald Institute Monographs.

Dreyfus, S. E., & Dreyfus, H. L. (1980). *A five-stage model of the mental activities involved in directed skill acquisition*. Berkeley, CA: University of California, Bekeley.

Eraut, M. (1985). Knowledge creation and knowledge use in professional contexts. *Studies in Higher Education, 10*(2), 117–133.

Eraut, M. (1994). *Developing professional knowledge and competence*. London, UK: Falmer Press.

Eraut, M. (2007). Learning from other people in the workplace. *Oxford Review of Education, 33* (4), 403–422.

Eraut, M. (2009). Understanding complex performance through learning trajectories and mediating artefacts. In N. Jackson (Ed.), *Learning to be professional through a higher education e-book* (Ch. A7, pp. 1–17). Guildford, UK: Surrey Centre for Excellence in Professional Training and Education (SCEPTrE). Retrieved from https://www.learningtobeprofessional. pbworks.com

Eraut, M. (2010). Knowledge, working practices and learning. In S. Billett (Ed.), *Learning through practice: Models, traditions, orientations and approaches* (pp. 37–58). Dordrecht, The Netherlands: Springer.

Ericsson, K. A. (Ed.). (2009). *Development of professional expertise: Toward measurement of expert performance and design of optimal learning environments*. Cambridge, UK: Cambridge University Press.

Ericsson, K. A., Charness, N., Feltovich, P., & Hoffman, R. R. (Eds.). (2006). *Cambridge handbook of expertise and expert performance*. Cambridge, UK: UK Cambridge University Press.

Farrell, L. (2006). *Making knowledge common: Literacy & knowledge at work*. New York, NY: Peter Lang.

Garud, R. (1997). On the distinction between know-how, know-why and know-what in technological systems. In J. Walsh & A. Huff (Eds.), *Advances in strategic management* (pp. 81–101). Greenwich, CT: JAI Press.

Giddens, A. (1984). *The constitution of society: Outline of the theory of structuration*. Berkeley, CA: University of California Press.

Green, J. (2002). Somatic knowledge: The body as content and methodology in dance education. *Journal of Dance Education. Special Issue: Somatics in Dance Education, 2*(4), 114–118.

Gromman, P. L. (1990). *The making of a teacher: Teacher knowledge and teacher education*. New York, NY: Teachers College Press.

Harper, D. (1987). *Working knowledge: Skill and community in a small shop*. Berkeley, CA: University of California Press.

Hindmarsh, J., & Pilnick, A. (2007). Knowing bodies at work: Embodiment and ephemeral teamwork in anaesthesia. *Organization Studies, 28*(9), 1395–1416. doi:10.1177/ 0170840607068258.

Hoffmann, M. H. G., & Roth, W.-M. (2005). What you should know to survive in knowledge societies: On a semiotic understanding of 'knowledge'. *Semiotica, 157*(1/4), 105–142.

Hoy, A. W., & Murphy, P. K. (2001). Teaching educational psychology to the implicit mind. In B. Torff & R. J. Sternberg (Eds.), *Understanding and teaching the intuitive mind: Student and teacher learning* (pp. 145–186). Mahwah, NJ: Lawrence Erlbaum Associates.

Ingold, T. (2011). *Being alive: Essays on movement, knowledge and description*. Oxon, OX: Routledge.

Johnson, M. (1989). Embodied knowledge. *Curriculum Inquiry, 19*(4), 361–377. doi:10.2307/ 1179358.

Kahneman, D. (2011). *Thinking, fast and slow*. New York, NY: Farrar, Straus and Giroux.

Kay, J. (1993). *Foundations of corporate success*. New York, NY: Oxford University Press.

Koschmann, T., LeBaron, C., Goodwin, C., & Feltovich, P. (2011). Can you see the cystic artery yet? A simple matter of trust. *Journal of Pragmatics, 43*(2), 521–541.

Lampland, M., & Star, S. L. (Eds.). (2009). *Standards and their stories: How quantifying, classifying, and formalizing practices shape everyday life*. London, UK: Cornell University Press.

Land, R., Meyer, J., & Smith, J. B. (Eds.). (2008). *Threshold concepts within the disciplines.* Rotterdam, The Netherlands: Sense.

Meyer, J. H. F., & Land, R. (Eds.). (2006). *Overcoming barriers to student understanding: Threshold concepts and troublesome knowledge.* London, UK: Routledge.

Miettinen, R., & Virkkunen, J. (2005). Epistemic objects, artefacts and organizational change. *Organization, 12*(3), 437–456.

Muis, K., Bendixen, L., & Haerle, F. (2006). Domain-generality and domain-specificity in personal epistemology research: Philosophical and empirical reflections in the development of a theoretical framework. *Educational Psychology Review, 18*(1), 3–54.

Mulcahy, D. (2011). Assembling the 'accomplished' teacher: The performativity and politics of professional teaching standards. *Educational Philosophy and Theory, 43*, 94–113.

Murphy, P. K., & Mason, L. (2006). Changing knowledge and changing beliefs. In P. A. Alexander & P. Winne (Eds.), *Handbook of educational psychology* (pp. 305–324). Mahwah, NJ: Lawrence Erlbaum Associates.

Nelson, R., & Winter, S. (1982). *An evolutionary theory of economic change.* Cambridge, MA: Belknap.

Nicolini, D. (2013). *Practice theory, work and organization: An introduction.* Oxford, UK: Oxford University Press.

Nonaka, I., & Takeuchi, H. (1995). *The knowledge-creating company: How Japanese companies create the dynamics of innovation.* New York, NY: Oxford University Press.

Ohlsson, S. (1995). Learning to do and learning to understand: A lesson and a challenge for cognitive modelling. In P. Reimann & H. Spada (Eds.), *Learning in humans and machines: Towards an interdisciplinary learning science* (pp. 37–62). London, UK: Pergamon Press.

Olson, D. R., & Bruner, J. S. (1996). Folk psychology and folk pedagogy. In D. R. Olson & N. Torrance (Eds.), *The handbook of education and human development new models of learning teaching and schooling* (pp. 9–27). Oxford, UK: Blackwell.

Orlikowski, W. J. (2002). Knowing in practice: Enacting a collective capability in distributed organizing. *Organization Science, 13*(3), 249–273.

Orlikowski, W. J. (2007). Sociomaterial practices: Exploring technology at work. *Organization Studies, 28*(9), 1435–1448.

Perkins, D. N. (1986). *Knowledge as design.* Hillsdale, NJ: Lawrence Erlbaum Associates.

Perkins, D. N. (1993). Person-plus: A distributed view of thinking and learning. In G. Salomon (Ed.), *Distributed cognitions: Psychological and educational considerations* (pp. 88–110). Cambridge, NY: Cambridge University Press.

Perkins, D. N. (1997). Epistemic games. *International Journal of Educational Research, 27*(1), 49–61.

Polanyi, M., & Prosch, H. (1975). *Meaning.* Chicago, IL: University of Chicago Press.

Royce, J. R. (1974). Cognition and knowledge: Psychological epistemology. In E. C. Carterette & M. F. Friedman (Eds.), *Handbook of perception. Historical and philosophical roots to perception* (Vol. 1, pp. 149–176). New York, NY: Academic Press.

Rubin, D. C. (1988). Go for the skill. In U. Neisser & E. Winograd (Eds.), *Remembering reconsidered: Ecological and traditional approaches to the study of memory* (pp. 374–382). Cambridge, UK: Cambridge University Press.

Ryle, G. (1945). Knowing how and knowing that. *Proceedings of the Aristotelian Society, 46,* 1–16. doi:10.2307/4544405.

Saxe, G. B. (1991). *Culture and cognitive development: Studies in mathematical understanding.* Hillsdale, NJ: Lawrence Erlbaum Associates.

Schön, D. A. (1995). *The reflective practitioner: How professionals think in action (New ed.).* Aldershot Hants, UK: Ashgate.

Schwab, J. J. (1978). *Science, curriculum, and liberal education: Selected essays.* Chicago, IL: University of Chicago Press.

Scribner, S. (1984). Studying working intelligence. In B. Rogoff & J. Lave (Eds.), *Everyday cognition: Its development in social context* (pp. 9–40). Cambridge, MA: Harvard University Press.

Shulman, L. S. (1986). Those who understand: Knowledge growth in teaching. *Educational Researcher, 15*(2), 4–14.

Southerland, S., Sinatra, G., & Matthews, M. (2001). Belief, knowledge, and science education. *Educational Psychology Review, 13*(4), 325–351.

Sternberg, R. J., & Horvath, J. A. (1999). *Tacit knowledge in professional practice: Researcher and practitioner perspectives*. Mahwah, NJ: Lawrence Erlbaum Associates.

Timmermans, S., & Epstein, S. (2010). A world of standards but not a standard world: Toward a sociology of standards and standardization. *Annual Review of Sociology, 36*(1), 69–89.

Tsoukas, H., & Vladimirou, E. (2001). What is organizational knowledge? *Journal of Management Studies, 38*(7), 973–993.

Tummons, J. (2011). Deconstructing professionalism: An actor-network critique of professional standards for teachers in the UK lifelong learning sector. *International Journal of Actor-Network Theory and Technological Innovation, 3*(4), 22–31.

Victor, B., & Boynton, A. C. (1998). *Invented here: Maximizing your organization's internal growth and profitability*. Boston, MA: Harvard Business School Press.

Weick, K. E. (1995). *Sensemaking in organizations*. Thousand Oaks, CA: Sage.

Weick, K. E. (2001). *Making sense of the organization*. Oxford, UK: Blackwell.

Weick, K. E., Sutcliffe, K. M., & Obstfeld, D. (2005). Organizing and the process of sensemaking. *Organization Science, 16*(4), 409–421.

Wittgenstein, L. (1953/2009). Philosophical investigations P. M. S. Hacker & J. Schulte (Eds.). (4th ed.), (G. E. M. Anscombe, Trans.). Chichester, UK: Wiley-Blackwell.

Wittgenstein, L. (1969). *On certainty* (D. Paul, & G. E. M. Anscombe, Trans.). Oxford, UK: Blackwell.

Woods, N. N. (2007). Science is fundamental: The role of biomedical knowledge in clinical reasoning. *Medical Education, 41*(12), 1173–1177.

Yinger, R., & Hendricks-Lee, M. (1993). Working knowledge in teaching. In C. Day, J. Calderhead, & P. Denicolo (Eds.), *Research on teacher thinking: Understanding professional development* (pp. 100–123). London, UK: Falmer Press.

Chapter 5
Professional Knowledge and Knowing in Shared Epistemic Spaces: The Person-Plus Perspective

Accounts of personal professional knowledge can appear to assume that professional knowledge for independent work and for collective work are not so different, at least that they do not differ at the level of the human cognitive structures and mechanisms that implement thinking and professional knowing. However, there are some serious practical and scientific challenges to this view.

From the practical perspective, one has to acknowledge that much professional work is intrinsically collective. Sharing knowledge and coordinating action make it possible to distribute labour across people with specialised professional skills. It is well recognised that engaging in various kinds of social interaction, group work and communication is an important professional attribute and prerequisite for employability. These 'soft skills' are often seen as generic attributes, whereas it may be more accurate to see them as *specialised* kinds of expertise, related to particular professional fields, which manifest themselves differently, and should be taught differently, in different disciplines (Jones, 2009).

From the scientific perspective, there is now sufficient evidence to suggest that the impact of collective life has had a far more profound effect on human cognition than just promoting the development of language and other means of communication (Donald, 1990, 2001; Tomasello, 2010, 2014). For example, Merlin Donald (1990) claims that the human mind, down at the level of its internal organisation, has been affected not only by its genetic inheritance and not only by the cognitive demands of tool making or spatial mapping – although these have been very important – but primarily by the demands of collective life and the evolution of human culture. Specifically, human cultural evolution has equipped the human species with three unique systems of memory representation:

- *Mimetic skill*, which draws on humans' ability to use their bodies as memory devices and as a means for sharing knowledge
- *Language*, which evolved with the development of speech and makes it possible to use verbal symbols for representation

© Springer Science+Business Media Dordrecht 2017
L. Markauskaite, P. Goodyear, *Epistemic Fluency and Professional Education*,
Professional and Practice-based Learning 14, DOI 10.1007/978-94-007-4369-4_5

- *External symbols* and *memory devices*, which draw on human abilities to read and write and which introduce radically new properties into the collective storage and retrieval of human knowledge, such as possibilities for formal theoretical thought

These systems are based on an inventive capacity, the products of which – gestures, social rituals, speech, images, symbols, etc. – continue to be invented, put to the test and regenerated in social arenas.

All three of these evolutionary adaptations of the human mind to cooperative social interaction coexist, and thinking and learning draw on a mix of all three. What comes through most strikingly from this perspective is that the implications of collective life and work for the overall organisation of the human cognitive system and knowledge are likely to be much more profound than merely adding 'soft skills' on top of an existing system of professional knowledge. As Merlin Donald (2001) argues, modern scientific and professional work, to a large extent, is a collective endeavour in which individual minds are hugely interconnected nodes in much larger, distributed cognitive systems, supported by external memory devices:

> Workers in such systems are, in their collective and professional identities, nodes in a distributed network. They may be active, intelligent people in their own right, absolutely convinced by their individuality, but they are nodes when they play their professional and corporate roles. <...> The creative spark of cognition still depends on the individual conscious mind, but even this statement has to be qualified because creativity cannot be exploited, or even defined, without a cultural context. (Donald, 2001, p. 299)

To provide a general sense of capacities for joint, skilful work, this chapter extends the discussion of professional knowledge and learning from individual to collective practices by addressing the following questions:

What kinds of knowledge do people need to work jointly? In particular, *what kinds of knowledge and skills enable professionals to work on the boundaries of their expertise: across different domains, on the frontiers of existing practice, inventing new ways of working?*

We aim to discuss those unique facets of knowledge which allow people to work, learn and innovate *collectively* with others, particularly with those people who have different areas of expertise and work across diverse settings. As a starting point, we take a distributed perspective which extends what counts as actionable knowledge beyond the isolated mind and body to other people and the environment. Several issues need to be reconsidered in making this turn to collective inter-professional work:

- What counts as expertise?
- What is the role of language and embodied practice in collective professional knowing and learning?
- How do professional cultures create shared intellectual spaces for joint knowledge work?

- How do professionals assemble their own social and material environments[1] for joint practices with(in) these spaces?

We examine how these aspects individually – and in combination – reconfigure the notion of professional knowledge and what the implications of these reconfigurations are for professional learning. In Sect. 5.1, drawing on Harry Collins' work, we discuss different kinds of expertise (Collins, 2011, 2013; Collins & Evans, 2007). In particular, we expand on what he called 'interactional expertise', which underpins capacities to work with others, and we point to the role of linguistic socialisation and embodied experiences in joint work. In Sects. 5.2, 5.3 and 5.4, we focus on mediating systems that set the conditions for joint professional knowledge work. We do this by expanding our focus from the environments and systems for fluid individual interactions and sense-making (i.e. mimetic, linguistic and symbolic representations – Sect. 5.2), to more enduring systems within activity settings (i.e. different kinds of objects – Sect. 5.3) and then on to shared systems of professional communities (i.e. knowledge cultures – Sect. 5.4). By drawing on Karen Knorr-Cetina's (1999, 2001, 2007) work, we bring these three systems back to the level of individual knowledge and embodied action within material settings, and we introduce the notion of epistemic culture. The two related notions of epistemic culture-as-practice and epistemic practice-as-culture nicely capture the essence of how actionable knowledge is co-constructed within different arenas of practice and culture. We argue that knowledge and skill for co-creating epistemic practice are at the centre of the inventive capability needed to work collectively on the boundaries of professional and other cultures. In the last three sections of the chapter (Sects. 5.5, 5.6 and 5.7), we look into the nature of *knowledge spaces* on these boundaries and at how professionals co-configure epistemic assemblages for their practices in those spaces. In the final Sect. (5.7) we explain the notion of *epistemic space* – which links objects back to the discourse and to other aspects of the assemblage and which thereby provides a useful focus for thinking about task and curriculum design in higher education.

With respect to professional education, the main claim that we make in this chapter is that learning to (co)create epistemic practice (and culture) is – or at least should be – an integral part of both learning and professional culture. Such learning involves the capacity to master representational devices – linguistic systems, objects and other cultural systems – and to assemble from them one's own epistemic environments for joint knowledgeable work.

---

[1] When we use 'environment' in this chapter, we mean something real and specific to a person or team working on a particular activity. The sense is of a 'task environment' – bounded in time and space by the requirements of the activity. We are interested in the ways in which professionals (learn to) assemble environments which are suited to their activity, especially to epistemic aspects of that activity. Such environments are usually a mix of elements and features that are deliberately co-configured and assembled, and elements that just happen to be there at the time.

5.1   Relational Expertise and Inter-professional Work

Harry Collins proposes a classification of expertise that he applies to practices in science and technology domains (Collins, 2011; Collins & Evans, 2007). It provides a good basis for reconsidering prevailing notions of expertise and approaches to developing professional competence for collective work in higher education.

Expertise is often treated as a unique capability that develops linearly through a gradual developmental progression from novice to expert (Dreyfus & Dreyfus, 1980) or through a spiral of decreasingly peripheral participation in a community of practice (Lave & Wenger, 1991). In contrast, as we mentioned in Chap. 4, Collins and Evans (2007) distinguish between three kinds of expertise: 'ubiquitous', 'interactional' and 'contributory'.

On one end of the continuum, *ubiquitous expertise* includes things that most people come to learn as they become members of a society. This includes such capacities as learning to speak one's mother tongue and basic knowledge of how to use written resources. On the other end of the continuum, *contributory expertise* includes the range of capacities needed to contribute fully to all aspects of a specialist domain of activity. It most closely resembles conventional notions of expertise and includes a tacit dimension of 'know how' that can only be acquired through engaging in the practices of the domain.

Interactional expertise occupies a middle space between ubiquitous and contributory expertise. It differs from contributory expertise in that interactional expertise involves some practical understanding, and an ability to participate in the *language* of practice, without having the expertise needed to engage successfully in the practice itself.[2] Collins and Evans claim that this kind of expertise can be acquired through 'linguistic socialisation' with experts. An example would be a science journalist who develops expertise in the language of scientists, even though he/she has never engaged in doing science.[3] Collins (2011, 2013) argues that interactional expertise plays a crucial role,

---

[2] The notion of 'interactional expertise' is closely associated with Anne Edwards (2005, 2010) 'relational expertise'. However, Collins and Evans (2007) state that their realist approach to expertise is different from relational accounts of expertise, arguing that expertise is real and substantial and not a matter of experts' relations with others. Being an expert as a native speaker of French persists as expertise in French in any country. It does not matter that French may not be counted as useful expertise outside francophone countries. We should also note that the term 'relational expertise' as used by Edwards (2005, 2010), though it differs somewhat from Collins' 'interactional expertise', does not carry the extreme relativistic connotations that one finds in the writing of Barnett (2004), for example, that expertise depends solely on the context of activity.

[3] As Collins (2013) notes, interactional expertise is also important in debates about the involvement of society in judgements that require technical understanding. It also gives productive insights into the difference between authentic construction of first-hand knowledge and one's 'epistemological sophistication' in judging second-hand knowledge (see Bromme, Kienhues, & Stahl, 2008). This is an increasingly important area of concern, given interest in evidence-informed professional work and learning, and we return to it in Chap. 7.

[It is] the main component in the acquisition of most practical abilities. (Collins, 2011, p. 274)

Without such expertise,

... we would be unable to cooperate and build common understandings and there would be no possibility of a sophisticated division of labour anywhere in society. (Collins, 2013, p. 255)

Collins acknowledges that this expertise is not easy to obtain and it comes only from participation in the language practices of specialist communities. Nevertheless, he argues that interactional expertise enables one to make practical judgements about the domain, solely as the result of linguistic socialisation.

Collins is very clear that interactional expertise involves only a limited kind of practical understanding which, on its own, is not sufficient to carry out expert action.[4]

Practical understanding developed though linguistic discourse alone does not, of course, carry with it the ability to *execute* embodied practices. (Collins, 2011, p. 282, original emphasis)

However, many studies show that 'boundary crossing' between communities primarily involves a *dialogue* between different parties (Akkerman & Bakker, 2011; Edwards, 2010; Engeström, 2008). Such dialogue does not necessarily imply homogeneity or symmetry of understandings and expertise. Rather, communication, learning and shared work among those with multiple perspectives are carried out by drawing on interactional expertise. Collins (2013) asks if current models of learning pay sufficient attention to the distinct role of language in professional learning and argues: 'The study of different educational practices and styles of apprenticeship must bear on the relative role of language and physical practice' (p. 269); the existence of interactional expertise 'forces one to *justify* the specific role of physical practice rather than simply assuming at the outset that learning a practice is all about practicing' (loc. cit., emphasis added).

Harry Collins (2013) emphasises the role of linguistic socialisation in developing interactional expertise. Nevertheless, other studies suggest that interactional expertise that is based solely on linguistic competences is *not sufficient* for professional collaboration and joint teamwork (Derry, Schunn, & Gernsbacher, 2005; Engeström & Middleton, 1996; Streeck, Goodwin, & LeBaron, 2011). For example, Goodwin (1994, 1996, 2005, 2013) has studied flight operations, courts of law, scientific expeditions in ships and other multi-professional places. His research shows that joint work activities in such heterogeneous workspaces (a) are mutually

---

[4] Collins (2011) is careful to acknowledge that there are different levels of interactional expertise as well. For example, a social researcher may be competent to interview a plumber, but may not necessarily be able to engage in a professional discussion with a plumber. As she acquires more experience and discursive competence in the domain, she becomes increasingly more capable of engaging in professional conversations. Nevertheless, even after gaining high levels of interactional expertise by participating in the discourse community, she will still not be able to carry out the plumber's work.

and dynamically constituted through the organisation of actions and interactions that (b) are tuned to the material structures of the workspace and by (c) appropriation of physical instruments and symbolic representations from each other's domains. In assembling such shared environments, language plays a constitutive, but not the only, role. These boundary spaces, at the intersections of different professions and ways of knowing, are not necessarily constructed every time from scratch ad hoc. Rather, many inter-professional practices are relatively enduring – such as between a nurse and doctor or a teacher and a school counsellor. This is also the case in a range of other professions that customarily work together to solve heterogeneous problems (Star, 1989). Indeed the ability to engage in such joint work is an integral part of professional competence in each of the professions involved.

Once we move from seeing knowledge solely as a property of the isolated mind, extending it to embrace the level of collective accomplishment and culture, the question of personal knowledge actually resurfaces again, but now from a different angle. What kind of *individual* capacities enable one to engage in *shared* knowledge practices – whether using existing, or developing new, collective knowledge? We now turn to this question.

5.2   (Re)presenting Knowledge and Shared Epistemic Labour

Vygotsky connected internal mental activity with the external world through 'psychological tools' and symbolic activity, including the use of language, and other representational systems and signs, such as

> ... different forms of numeration and counting, mnemotechnic techniques, algebraic symbolism, works of art, writing, schemes, diagrams, maps, blueprints, all sorts of conventional signs, etc. (Vygotsky, 1930, no page)

Echeverría and Scheuer (2009) note:

> External representations are not only avenues to knowledge; they are *forms* of knowing. (Echeverría & Scheuer, 2009 p. 2, our emphasis)

From this perspective, personal knowledge and knowing are not only a matter of a person's understanding of the external world – they also include the capacity to use representational tools and to participate in the representational practices of the field (Greeno & Hall, 1997; Hall, 1996; Hall, Stevens, & Torralba, 2002). Such tools do not consist of unrelated concepts or signs, but of different interconnected and at least partly shared ways of organising and presenting meanings.

Stuart Hall (1997) observes that people draw upon two kinds of interrelated representational systems when they construct and express their thoughts. The first is an internal system of concepts or 'mental representations'. This allows one to understand the world by constructing a set of correspondences between the external world and the mind. The second is the linguistic system of (external) representations. This provides people with 'shared language' and a possibility to exchange otherwise private meanings and mental representations with one another.[5] A linguistic system includes gestures, spoken words, written symbols, visual images and other ways of expressing meanings. It has several functions. First, humans use shared language for *representation, interpretation and sharing*: 'using signs we make distinctions, specify objects and relations, structure our observations, and organize societal and cognitive activity' (Hoffmann & Roth, 2007, p. 101). Second, we use these representational systems for *constructing new meanings*. As Gordin and Pea (1995) drawing on Toulmin (1953) argue: 'the representations provide a model complete with symbols that can be formally manipulated so that points of connection can be forged from the model to the phenomena' (Gordin & Pea, 1995, p. 257). The strength of symbolic constructions lies in productive analogies that create possibilities for new kinds of explorations which it would not be possible to conduct directly with or on the phenomena.

Goodwin (1994) specifically argues that it is the symbolic systems and material inscriptions that make knowledge work possible in professional practice.

> They [professionals] engage in active cognitive work, but the parameters of that work have been established by the system that is organizing their perception. (Goodwin, 1994, p. 609)

He identifies three major functions of such systems: they allow one to *structure the world* and to organise knowledge; they *shape perception* and future action; they *allow the creation* of external cognitive artefacts that encode knowledge in a form that is shaped through, and shapes, ongoing historical practices in the professional world. Mastering such systems is not a simple neurological process (though neurons are important), and knowledge that links symbols used in human discourse to the world is not a 'natural' phenomenon, but is established through social agreement and participation in collective representational practices (Deacon, 1997; Goodwin, 1994; Roth & McGinn, 1998).

> To many experts, the adequation ["making equal", from *adaequare* (Lat.)] of two different inscriptions is self-evident, intuitive, and straightforward. But these experts forget that the self-evident, intuitive, and straightforward way in which a series of data pairs are re-presented as sequences, as a table, or as a graph took years of training within specific social, historical, and cultural contexts. (Roth & McGinn, 1998, p. 41)

Engaging in discourse and representational practices in what we call 'shared epistemic spaces' constitutes a kind of knowledge and way of knowing that bridges

---

[5] Roth and McGinn (1998) make a distinction between the term 'inscriptions' – to refer to representations that exist in a material form – and 'representations' that are more general and may also refer to the mental content. In this book we use the word 'representations' in a broader sense. In particular, we often use the word representations to refer to expressions of human thought in spoken language, mimesis and other forms of discourse that are not inscribed in enduring material objects (i.e. are not inscriptions) but also cannot be reduced to 'mental representations' (i.e.' they are external, public). When we need to make it clear that we are referring to internal cognitive representations, we explicitly add a modifier: '*mental* representations'.

between the personal knowledge and public knowledge that we discussed in Chap. 4.

> Cognition and, by implication, all learning following this view is a social process at its root and involves the public production and interpretation of a wide diversity of representations that are in the world in a variety of material forms. (Henning, 2004, p. 162)

While these representational systems are shared, they are neither universal nor are they used in exactly the same way across different professional or other groups. As Säljö (1995) notes,

> Since modern society is characterized by a multitude of social and institutional practices in activity systems such as production, science, bureaucracies, schools, health care and many others, events and objects are construed in many different ways to serve different purposes. (Säljö, 1995, p. 88)

Different representational systems and different ways of representing make it possible to see different aspects of the world. When these systems are used in combination in joint (multi-professional) activities, they create opportunities to approach a problem from different perspectives and thereby enhance problem-solving (Echeverría & Scheuer, 2009; Greeno & Hall, 1997).

Learning for multi-professional and multidisciplinary professional work of this kind requires engagement in shared representational practices across epistemic spaces – becoming a fluent user of multiple representational systems.

However, it would be a mistake to see language and other representational capacities as a unique, wholly modern form of human 'higher-order' cognition, disconnected from other cognitive processes. As Deacon (2012) argues:

> The number of brain systems involved in language is surprisingly extensive, and the way that diverse brain systems can be recruited to support language under pathological or atypical task conditions indicates considerable plasticity. These attributes don't easily fit with claims about language-unique brain processes unrelated to other forms of cognition. (Deacon, 2012, p. 404)

What could be seen as a uniquely human and complex professional skill – to work with and create knowledge in shared epistemic spaces – should be seen as consti-tuted through, rather than isolated from, other much more general evolutionary changes. They are part and parcel of broader adaptations arising as the human body (including the brain) co-evolves with a heterogeneous, cultural, social and material environment.

5.3 Continuity of Practice and Innovation: Knowing with and Through Objects

What gives persistency to practice and joint activity in collaborative inter-profes-sional work? For a long time, professional knowledge that bridges understanding and practice and gives continuity to social orders in professional work has been associated with notions of recurrence, routine and habit (e.g. Bourdieu, 1990; Polanyi, 1966/2009). Drawing on the organisational literature, Miettinen and Virkkunen (2005) identify three perspectives on habits and routines as a basis for competent performance and knowledge.

The first perspective sees habits as standardised ways of focussing attention and acting (which could be called a 'blind habit'). According to this view 'Decision-making is more about following rules than about calculating outcomes' (Miettinen & Virkkunen, 2005, p. 439).

The second perspective focusses on the human ability to engage in predictable regular behavioural patterns and use tacit knowledge. It acknowledges a more open quality to human performance, which nevertheless involves intuitive and often unarticulated decisions and habitual performance. 'It [practice] also involves the making of numerous 'choices', often automatically' (loc. cit.).

The third perspective combines cognitive aspects with social orders and structures of routine behaviour. In this account,

> Routines are maintained both by pre-reflective consent by individuals and by the control systems and legitimation set up by organizations and institutions. <...> an innovation consists, to a substantial extent, of a recombination of previously existing routines. (op. cit., p. 440)

They conclude that an understanding of action that is based on the concept of knowledge as habit and routine cannot explain the relationship between continuity and change: how new practices are transformed and formed. As a way of overcoming unreflective habit, they draw on Dewey's (1938) ideas of reflective thought and inquiry 'that make a habit intelligent' (Miettinen & Virkkunen, 2005, p. 442).

> Dewey's basic thesis was that, although habits are necessary and constitute invaluable carriers of traditions and skills, reflective thought is needed when habitualized action confronts permanent difficulties as a result of changing circumstances. (op. cit., p. 451)

Discourse plays an important role in organising distributed work and, particularly, reflective thought and insight. However, as Nicolini, Mengis and Swan (2012, p. 613) argue, 'symbols alone do not resolve this puzzle' of continuity and change. Organisational studies (e.g. Engeström & Blackler, 2005; Ewenstein & Whyte, 2009; Miettinen & Virkkunen, 2005; Nicolini et al., 2012) and science and technology studies (Knorr-Cetina, 1999; Rheinberger, 1997; Star, 2010) commonly look for the foundations of enduring professional practices, discovery and innovation in *objects*.[6]

Objects can be defined as entities people *act towards* and/or *act with* (Star, 2010). Professional and expert communities in knowledge-generating settings are usually oriented towards exploring, assembling and developing knowledge or epistemic objects – 'complex problem-knowledge constellations around which

---

[6] This literature talks about both 'objects', 'things' and 'artefacts'. To keep a complex argument as simple as we can, we use the term 'objects' in this chapter. Chapter 8 offers an extensive discussion of objects, things and artefacts, their relations and differences.

practitioners gather and communities form' (Nerland & Jensen, 2014, p. 27, drawing on Knorr-Cetina, 2001, 2007).

However, as Nicolini et al. (2012) argue, objects have diverse roles in collective professional work: they provide infrastructure for activity, they help participants to work across various boundaries, and they give a direction to activity and motivate collaborative work. Accordingly, Nicolini and colleagues identify four kinds of objects that help organise shared work: *material infrastructures* that support collaboration, *boundary objects* that act as 'translation devices' and make cross-disciplinary collaboration possible, *epistemic objects* that organise joint desires and goals and *activity objects* that direct joint work by generating contradictions and triggering innovations.[7]

Spaces of joint professional practice are populated with different kinds of objects. Some of them are permanent, taken for granted and mundane infrastructures and translational devices that provide material and conceptual foundations and durability for joint work. Others are dynamic, full of tensions and incomplete carriers of collective activity and joint meaning-making that enable practical innovation and shared epistemic work. As Nerland and Jensen (2010) point out, objects also link everyday professional work with wider knowledge practices, and working with complex professional objects can serve as a vehicle for learning and professional innovation. Overall, one's understanding of, and ability to work with, the objects that are used for sharing and developing knowledge in workplace settings becomes a part of professional expertise.

However, shared knowledge practices do not just depend on team members' understandings of, and ability to work with, individual objects. More important is

---

[7] Different objects have different affordances and functions in cross-disciplinary work and innovation. *Material infrastructures* are mundane, rather settled, objects that support and shape cross-disciplinary collaboration, but often remain in the background of this shared work. They are taken for granted, are not seen as problematic and usually only become visible if something breaks down and needs to be repaired. *Boundary objects* act as devices for transition and transformation of knowledge between different disciplinary worlds (Nicolini et al. (2012) call them 'thought worlds'). They are objects that are created to make cross-disciplinary collaboration possible. These objects foreground differences and potential mismatches between the understandings and interests of different disciplines and/or collaborators, which need to be overcome in order to work jointly. Like material infrastructures, boundary objects are not the main purpose of the joint activity and innovation, rather they are enablers of it. *Epistemic objects* are objects that 'fuel collaboration and generate mutuality and solidarity' (p. 624) in solving a problem associated with the epistemic object. They are incomplete and emergent. They are the main focus of the joint activity and innovation. Distinctions and differences between disciplines are often invisible or at least temporarily suspended in joint work on such objects. The focus is on the shared pursuit. *Activity objects* motivate and direct collaboration by generating conflicts and contradictions. Differences between disciplines could be one of the sources for such contradictions. But overall the main focus of activity and innovation is to resolve contradictions which become apparent through activity objects. While both epistemic objects and activity objects are incomplete, dynamic and emergent, epistemic objects motivate collaboration by generating mutuality and agreement. In contrast, activity objects motivate collaboration and innovation by being the source of conflicts and tensions that need to be resolved.

their ability to participate in knowledge communities that assemble from these objects distinct arrangements, create distinct mechanisms and set up other parameters for what counts as knowledge and how to engage with knowledge work. While much of the attention in research and education has been on the objects themselves, as Nicolini et al. (2012) note, the key insight into shared knowledge work and learning comes not so much from understanding what sorts of objects are used in shared professional practice, but when and why these objects gain this particular status. In short, objects and practices with which, and through which, knowledge is generated cannot be understood in the absence of the cultures with(in) which these objects and practices are enmeshed.

5.4 Linking Epistemic Practice with Knowledge Culture

The different ways in which professional communities handle knowledge is a topic attracting increasing interest in studies of professional practices and professional learning (Fenwick & Nerland, 2014; Jensen, Lahn, & Nerland, 2012; Guile, 2010; Knorr-Cetina, 2007). The notion of *knowledge culture* – 'the whole set of structures and mechanisms that serve knowledge and unfold with its articulation' (Knorr-Cetina, 1999, pp. 7–8) – has become the main organising concept that provides a common referential foundation for joint professional work.

As Jensen et al. (2012) put it,

> As knowledge-based occupational groups, professional communities are constituted by their distinct ways of organising and managing knowledge. Their ways of producing, distributing, validating and approaching knowledge serve to give them integrative power. Moreover, these processes form profession-specific knowledge cultures which constitute a basis for work and learning. <...> They [knowledge cultures] serve to shape knowledge practices and strategies in certain ways, by providing a referential context within which practitioners relate to knowledge and engage in professional conduct. In this way they are also constitutive of the knower. Practitioners are shaped, and learn to see the world, through the qualities and lenses of their knowledge culture, and its technical and social arrangements form the basis for introducing newcomers to the professional domain. (Jensen et al., 2012, p. 25)

Nerland (2012) identifies a set of 'constitutive dimensions' of professional knowledge culture that structure both work practices and approaches to learning. They include ways in which knowledge is *produced*, which vary across professional fields in terms of their reliance on scientific achievements and personal reflexivity; ways in which knowledge is *accumulated*, which differ in terms of whether knowledge development is characterised by linearity and collectivity rather than richness and diversity of individual experiences; ways in which knowledge is *distributed*, which vary in the extent to which knowledge is bound to particular local settings or rests on written language, technologies and other infrastructures; and ways in which knowledge is *applied*, in particular, how professions handle the relationship between general knowledge and its local applications in particular settings. For example, knowledge for teaching and for computer engineering varies significantly across all these dimensions. Knowledge for classroom teaching turns out to be far more personal and experiential than is the case with knowledge for programming. Moreover, it is distributed through direct interaction and is differentiated across applications in various contexts. These dimensions operate together. They provide the means for students to learn to see their professional work. They shape the ways in which students engage with knowledge-related activities, including how they participate in the wider development of professional knowledge and how they learn throughout their professional life.

Learning to see the world 'through the lenses of a knowledge culture' and learning to engage in knowledge practices characteristic of their chosen discipline or profession are increasingly seen as an integral aspect of students' professional education and of the development of their professional identity (Trede, Macklin, & Bridges, 2011; Shaffer, 2004). For example, preservice teachers, as a part of their initial enrolment into the profession, often learn how to conduct action research projects and to engage in systematic reflection; software programmers learn how to comply with new technological and procedural standards; and pharmacists learn how to use pharmaceutical databases and keep up to date with new drugs and trends in the industry. Nevertheless, when students are learning to engage with professional knowledge practices, this is often associated with either traditional notions of *culture* or traditional notions of *practice*.

In contrast, Knorr-Cetina (2001), reflecting on changes in the knowledge society and work, notes that there are critical differences between traditional conceptions of 'practice' and 'epistemic practice' and between 'knowledge culture' and 'epistemic culture'. She argues that current conceptions of practice emphasise its routine habitual nature: 'recurrent processes governed by specifiable schemata of preferences and prescriptions' (p. 175). Acknowledging that such rule-governed and customary behaviours have a prominent place in organising social life, Knorr-Cetina notes that one of the characteristics of contemporary professional work is the frequency of encountering non-routine problems that demand non-routine solutions. One of the core features of many professions and organisations is that they have a substantial, growing knowledge base and their ways of working do not sit comfortably with the traditional, stable, notion of practice.

Knorr-Cetina draws our attention to 'epistemic practice' and characterises it as 'knowledge-centred' work that

> ... shifts back and forth between the performance of 'packaged' routine procedures and differentiated practice. (Knorr-Cetina, 2001, p. 187)

The central feature of such practices is 'a relational dynamics' that *extends the practice itself into the future in new, inventive and even disruptive ways.*

Further, Knorr-Cetina (2007) notes that attention has been on the knowledge culture – seen as a defining feature of how knowledge is constructed. What is more, such a notion locates culture at a broad level in society and focusses on universal features and structures that characterise knowledge production at a broad global scale, including such things as scientific 'paradigms' and other similar 'thought styles' of large social groups. This view of culture leaves the micro practices of workplace settings that produce knowledge 'black boxed'.

Knorr-Cetina contrasts 'knowledge culture' with an 'epistemic culture', characterised by the construction of *machineries* for knowledge construction. She defines 'epistemic culture' as

> ... those amalgams of arrangements and mechanisms – bonded through affinity, necessity, and historical coincidence which, in a given field, make up *how we know what we know*. (Knorr-Cetina 1999, p. 1, original emphasis)

In short, knowledge culture is a general feature of knowledge production itself, whereas epistemic culture is a feature of *the construction of machineries for knowledge production*. Epistemic culture brings the notion of culture to the level of micro practices in particular places and focusses on how different arrangements within local settings – including institutional structures and procedures, material objects, human bodies, signs and histories – work together to constitute a certain knowledge domain.

That is, in contrast to the traditional view of culture, this view foregrounds epistemic culture-as-practice. It does not reduce culture to the 'ideal', 'spiritual' and 'non-material', but focusses on the relationships between material and non-material arrangements and their enactments in concrete knowledge production activities. And in contrast to the traditional view of practice, this view does not reduce epistemic practices down to solely material regularities of knowledge construction. Rather, it sees epistemic practice as constitutive to, and constituted through, culture – including values, norms, identity, beliefs and other meanings. There are close, mutually shaping, connections between general culture, knowledge culture and various levels of epistemic culture.

It is impossible to understand practice without abandoning a priori assumptions about whether culture shapes human behaviours, objects and their agency or whether everyday meaning-making actions and objects shape culture.

> ... one may need to allow not only for multiple agencies but also for agency to rotate between constructs, depending on what is at stake and whose perspective is brought to bear. (Knorr-Cetina, 2007, p. 365)

Knorr-Cetina (1999, 2001, 2007) mainly describes cultures and practices within research communities and other large epistemic organisations (such as stock markets), where work demands constant adjustment to the continual inputs of new information and knowledge and, what she calls, 'the reordered conditions and dynamics of the chains of action of collective life' (Knorr-Cetina, 1999, p. 10). However, similar notions of epistemic culture and epistemic practice can also be applied to describe epistemic work in dynamic, highly differentiated workplace settings, such as schools, hospitals and social services. Epistemic practices, in such settings, require not only continuous adjustment to external reconfigurations (e.g. new policies, standards and other regulations) but also ongoing fine-tuning to the relentless flux of encountered situations (e.g. new clients with new problems).

A professional epistemic culture, once understood as process rather than fixed structure, can be seen as orienting itself by constantly moving between (a) 'packages' that characterise competent practice and (b) flexible reconfiguration – involving fine-tuned expert vision and the skills needed to adjust to changing problems, environments and working relationships.

In short, the notion of epistemic culture-as-practice nicely captures the different cultural layers with(in) which actionable knowledge is co-constructed. Yet, learning to embrace epistemic frameworks that organise the understandings, skills and values within and across professional cultures and learning to participate in epistemic practices on the boundaries of professional cultures are well outside most students' experiences of enrolment into professional knowledge-related work. One of the reasons for this is that learning to (co)create epistemic practice (and culture) is not usually seen as an integral part of both learning and culture, and the knowledge and skills needed for this are rather poorly understood.

In our view, it is necessary to understand professional learning as epistemic practice and culture, by extending the notion of professional epistemic culture at least one level down: to *skill* and the *mind* – to those infrastructures, machineries, arrangements and micro practices of professional learning settings in which culture, knowledge and practice come together into one *embodied* social, material and *cognitive* ensemble. To capture the dynamism and flexibility of this heterogeneous system – which goes all the way down from culture to human biology and cognition – one needs to extend the notion of epistemic practice in several directions.

Firstly, just as body and physical space are prerequisites for action and practice, so mind and epistemic space are prerequisites for epistemic action and practice. We can think of epistemic space as a domain of copresence of epistemic practice, as something that provides its necessary conditions and is dynamic, open to a multiplicity of trajectories, open for ongoing co-production. Such a space carries a history and opens up possibilities for certain kinds of epistemic (re)arrangements and certain kinds of epistemic practices and discourages others. We cannot reduce epistemic practice to cultural, or social, or cognitive processes. We should look for foundations for fluent epistemic work in the professional capabilities needed to co-configure epistemic environments for joint knowledge work within these spaces (we elaborate on this point in Sects. 5.5 and 5.6.).

Second, just as (collective) practice and expertise come into being through bodily movement and material (re)arrangements coordinated through fine-tuned skill and discourse, so epistemic practice and expertise in epistemic work come into being through cognitive (re)arrangements and flexible coordination of body and language with a skilful mind. Mind is not an abstract 'black-boxed' container, but, like body and language, has certain properties that define what it is, how it functions and what it can do. It is not only the symbolic and material affordances and arrangements of workplace settings that shape perception and foreground epistemically skilful performance and learning but also the resourcefulness of the mind and the dynamic reconfiguration of, and coordination with, 'affordances' of the practitioner's mind, body and brain (we elaborate on this argument in Chaps. 6 and 7).

5.5 Knowledge Space and Epistemic Assemblage

To describe our notion of an epistemic assemblage, we compare it with the idea of knowledge space. As Knorr-Cetina (2007) says, cultures concerned with knowledge are not one homogenous entity, but rather constitute, and are constituted by, different levels of cultures, including general knowledge culture, macro-epistemic culture and epistemic culture. Some of these cultures do not necessarily produce new knowledge in any deep sense, yet they play fundamental epistemic roles in the overall machinery that produces knowledge. For example, some organisations in different science domains or areas of the economy define the 'architecture' of the fields: they regulate the rules of conduct and mutual monitoring, define the epistemic rights and procedures of the respective units, define common technology and service standards, negotiate compatibilities between different administrations and political cultures and so on.

In short, they produce what we called, in Chap. 4, sociopolitical knowledge. While Knorr-Cetina notes that these units often work on the level of information and surface events, not on the level of 'underlying laws', nevertheless they are an important part of cultures that produce knowledge.

Turnbull (2000) pursues a similar line of argument, but elaborates it in relation to the spaces of heterogeneous multi-professional work. He argues,

> Knowledge is in effect 'motley'. The process of knowledge assemblage is a dialectical one in which forms of social space are coproduced. The interactive, contingent assemblage of space and knowledge, sustained and created by social labour, results in what I call 'knowledge space'. (Turnbull, 2000, p. 4)

Following Deleuze and Guattari (1987), he adopts the term 'assemblage' to describe

> ... the amalgam of places, bodies, voices, skills, practices, technical devices, theories, social strategies and collective work that together constitute technoscientific knowledge/practices. (Turnbull, 2000, pp. 43–44)

Knorr-Cetina (2007), Turnbull (2000) and others (e.g. Bowker & Star, 1999; Bowker, 2008; Howlett & Morgan, 2010; Lampland & Star, 2009) describe architectures for knowledge cultures and assemblages of knowledge spaces that allow the movement of knowledge from one local site, or from the moment of its production, to other places and other times. This involves the creation of global shared knowledge that can be used to build additional knowledge away from the sites of its origination. Turnbull (2000) argues,

> The standardisation and homogenisation required for knowledge to be accumulated and rendered truthlike is achieved through social methods of organising the production, transmission and utilisation of knowledge. (Turnbull, 2000, p. 20)

The assemblages of various social, technical and literary devices and strategies that allow the creation of equivalences, connecting, moving and engaging collectively with what would otherwise be isolated local knowledge, are essential for creating knowledge that can easily travel – leaving human bodies, material arrangements and situated minds behind. Turnbull emphasises the critical role of shared formal knowledge in professional practices:

> We cannot abandon the strength of generalisations and theories, particularly their capacity for making connections and for providing the possibility of criticism. (op. cit., p. 45)

However, Turnbull argues that rather than learning how knowledge gets from local to global, we also must learn how knowledge gets from local to local. In other words, how one knowledge that has origins in one setting is adapted to create other knowledges in other local settings. (In fact, not much is known about how global knowledge becomes local either.) This applies particularly to actionable knowledge. Turnbull notes that local knowledge is different from global knowledge:

> Local knowledge is not systematic in the nomological or law-like fashion of science, it does not lend itself to the standardisation and exact planning, but neither it is atheoretical and unsystematic. Being grounded in the specificities of local conditions and practice, it is the combination of diversity, complexity, vagueness and imprecision which gives it its essentially flexible, dynamic and strategic character. (op. cit., p. 32)

These epistemic assumptions are at the core of actionable knowledge and knowledgeable action, within today's professional practice settings. However, little is known about how this kind of knowledge is organised, created, passed, reshaped and used in local practices, and, consequently, little is known about how it is learnt and how to teach it. In order to teach, we first need to know how skilful workers assemble local epistemic environments for their embodied material epistemic practices in these broader knowledge spaces.

5.6 Creating Assemblages for Local Knowledge Work

Turnbull's (2000) insights into the historical evolution of technoscientific knowledge provide a good starting point. Summarising historic sources, on how Gothic cathedral were built, developments in Micronesian navigation and other manifestations of skilful work, Turnbull illustrates how much of the human knowledge that resulted in great practical achievements relied neither on universal laws of nature nor on carefully designed a priori plans. Rather, they were situated social and technical achievements. The medieval Gothic cathedrals, for example, were built without a general theory, without plans and without architects. A fully articulated structural theory, plans and architects as a profession, emerged and became commonplace only later. Three main elements – templates, talk and tradition – made these practical achievements possible. The main technological component for transmitting knowledge was a *template* and other simple representational technologies that permitted transmission of knowledge between masons and other craftsmen. This transmission was accompanied by tradition and talk, which permitted aggregation of different viewpoints and integration of norms and values. Constant exposure to new problems and new sites, and dynamic interaction between workers, enabled rapid changes in design, experimentation and the distribution of new solutions across sites, as well as the validation of innovations.

Turnbull (2000) acknowledges that scientific developments have indeed changed technical and social strategies, as well as the knowledge and skills used in work practices, in many domains. In the building industry, proportional analysis was changed to structural analysis. With increasing division of labour, and the appearance of architects as a profession requiring specialist education, design became separated from construction; the representation of knowledge became distinct from the performative side of making and knowing the world and expertise separated from skill. Nevertheless, Turnbull argues that social practices and devices which render theoretical and practical knowledge into concrete representational artefacts, as well as other conceptual means for coordinating various bits and forms of knowledge into an adequate joint frame of reference, remain 'profoundly constitutive of our thinking and our culture' (pp. 92–93). Such devices are an integral part of all epistemic practices, including scientific and professional work and education. They are a means for linking knowledge with practical work and also a means for moving knowledge back and forth between global and local, as well as between local sites.

Turnbull reminds us of four important qualities of practices and learning that recreate global and local knowledge in action. First, we must not overlook the performative side of knowledge, 'it is through the social work of creating the assemblages that science and society co-produce each other' (p. 101). Secondly, what counts as knowledge is not a purely conceptual problem but also political and moral. Thirdly, it is a mistake to overlook personal values and what an individual brings to the situation,

> ... at the individual level we do not behave like the ends/means optimization calculators that economic rationalism would have us believe we are. We are at least as interested in meaning, significance and personal values as we are in economic concerns. (Turnbull, 2000, p. 215)

Fourthly, while much knowledge comes from direct experience, people draw on a wide variety of knowledge sources:

> A considerable proportion of our knowledge derives from books, television, newspapers, journals, teachers, experts, and our community traditions. In other words our knowledge is a blend of the testimony of others, and our own experience of public and local knowledge. (loc. cit.)

Turnbull's analysis points to several significant aspects of knowledge practices that are somewhat overlooked in professional education and in more general thinking about professional knowledge:

- Knowledge and innovations that emerge from mundane practices do not necessarily take the form of abstracted universal 'lawlike' principles – they differ, in this regard, from some scientific knowledge products.

- People in various cultures have been inventing their own ways of assembling local knowledge, creating infrastructures (such as maps, standards and templates) that can hold heterogeneous pieces and practices together.
- It is conceptual and technical devices, as well as social strategies and practices that emerge around the use of those devices, that provide a shape for organising epistemic work in professions.
- While global and local knowledge, and theory and practice, have often been put in a dialectical opposition to one other, they are not such profoundly incompatible modes of knowing. In fact, as Turnbull claims, 'theory and practice are not distinct; theorising is also a local practice' (op. cit., p. 45).

We would argue that *theorising practice* is no less important than *practising theory* in professional work. This generative dialogue between practising and theorising is at the heart of learning for knowledgeable action and of innovation in actionable knowledge.

Each knowledge domain, including the modern sciences and the professions, is a field of interrelated cognitive, material and social practices, rather than a set of statements, skills and dispositions. So one's understanding of, and ability to engage with, those knowledge practices becomes a core part of the epistemic fluency needed for professional work and innovation. These practices include work in specific epistemic spaces, as well as in shared epistemic spaces created through negotiation, joint work and co-assembling.

This view does not privilege one form of knowledge and knowing over another: material over symbolic, mind over body. Rather, it accepts that people use diverse ways of knowing. In interdisciplinary and inter-professional knowledge work, much of how people understand and make connections comes from an ability to see the situation and think in the ways *insiders* think, from the insiders' point of view, rather than being locked in to an objective, external or critical *outsider's* way of knowing.

5.7   Knowledge and Knowing in Shared Epistemic Spaces

Our notion of epistemic space moves professional knowledge assemblages down a level from a global shared space to local sites of knowledge use, reuse, production and learning. At this lower level, the assemblages and machineries through which standardised and homogenised knowledge, and social methods and technical devices that render them universal, are adapted to the local situations, contingencies and needs, or, alternatively, local environments are adjusted to the larger architectures and infrastructures of knowledge.

As we are interested in professional learning, our focus is on local arrangements for learning (i.e. tasks and other material and social assemblages for them) rather than on arrangements that render what is learnt as some kind of universal 'professional knowledge' (e.g. professional standards and certification procedures). The former is not isolated from the latter, but the latter constitutes only one element of the epistemic space in which learning of professional knowledge occurs.

In short, our focus is on the assemblages and arrangements within which knowledge that has a universal status becomes part of a situated practice and situated practice becomes collective knowledge.

In the classical organisational literature, the power of objects and epistemic cultures is often associated with their stability and persistence – in contrast to the ephemerality of discursive practices and moment-to-moment engagement and interpretational work. In our view, this opposition obscures an important fact: that objects and discourse, culture and action are enmeshed with each other. Objects and culture are best understood with(in) shared discourse and activity. In fact, objects and culture are part of what makes shared meaning-making possible. However, knowledgeable work in shared epistemic spaces – particularly those that are dynamically co-assembled on the boundaries of different professional fields – weaves the permanency of objects with the dynamism of action and discourse. So, learning to work in such joint epistemic spaces involves mastering representational systems and other semiotic resources and inquiry tools and creating shared epistemic assemblages for joint meaning-making and knowledge work.

Extending parallels from the different kinds of objects to the representational systems and action, we can distinguish between three different kinds of epistemic spaces with(in) which professionals need to learn to work and within which they co-configure their epistemic environments: technical spaces, trans-epistemic spaces and open epistemic spaces.

Technical spaces are stable representational spaces that provide symbolic systems, concepts and frameworks for organising one's understanding, shaping professional vision, inquiry and action. Knowledge and learning from this perspective involves the ability to engage in the representational and inquiry practices of the domain (e.g. knowledge of the classification of diseases in medicine, common pedagogical frameworks and lesson plans in teaching, patient assessment procedures in nursing).

Trans-epistemic spaces are shared epistemic spaces in which multiple representational and inquiry practices coexist. Knowledge and learning in such epistemic spaces involve engaging with multiple practices simultaneously and establishing links between different ways of knowing and different perspectives. Such spaces also offer foundations for blended practices that provide the basis for translation of meanings. They emerge on the more stable boundaries between professional communities that are engaged in shared practices on an ongoing or permanent basis (e.g. discussions between a solicitor and a barrister or between a structural engineer and an architect, referral documents that carry communications between a general practitioner and a consultant).

Open epistemic spaces are spaces that organise inquiry. They make it possible to master practices and representational systems that help to structure perception and (re)frame problems. In turn, this makes it easier to conceive of related epistemic activities that may bring a solution closer and/or permit further inquiry and/or action. Knowledge, and learning to work in such epistemic spaces, involves an ability to engage in deliberative inquiry, problem-solving and action. As Rogers Hall (1996) points out, such representational activity often restructures not only the mental description of the situation but the situation itself. For example, it may involve creation of new tools, protocols or other resources and procedures that remain a part of the practice and setting (e.g. creating a disease management plan, for a patient with several chronic illnesses, to enable coordination of treatments between multiple health professionals; creating an online knowledge exchange repository to share knowledge between technical consultants and business consultants in an information technology company).

Learning for professional mobility, diversity and innovation requires a person to be flexible at working within and across these kinds of epistemic spaces. For example, Akkerman and Bakker (2011) identify four learning mechanisms that can engage when graduates and professionals move across different boundaries: *identification* (questioning of the core identity of intersecting sites, othering and legitimating coexistence), *coordination* (making communicative connections, translating and enhancing boundary permeability), *reflection* (perspective taking and perspective making) and *transformation* (reorganising a shared problem space).

We can then say that the technical space provides the foundation for identification, the trans-epistemic space provides the shared infrastructure for communication and reflection, and the open epistemic space provides the ground for transformation. The three spaces simultaneously link learning, practical inquiry and knowledge co-creation.

Seeing professionals as engaged in representational practices, inquiry and action in such heterogeneous epistemic spaces resolves the traditional tensions between learning, using knowledge and creating knowledge and between knowing as routine and habit and knowing as transformation and innovation.

The central shift that makes this view possible is seeing skilful professional work not in terms of doing vs. understanding or routine vs. innovation or work vs. learning but *as one epistemic practice* with(in) which professionals co-construct and co-inhabit a shared epistemic space, by creating epistemic assemblages for joint meaning-making, learning and work.

References

Akkerman, S. F., & Bakker, A. (2011). Boundary crossing and boundary objects. *Review of Educational Research, 81*(2), 132–169.

Barnett, R. (2004). Learning for an unknown future. *Higher Education Research & Development, 23*(3), 247–260.

Bourdieu, P. (1990). *The logic of practice*. Cambridge, UK: Polity Press.

Bowker, G. C. (2008). *Memory practices in the sciences*. Cambridge, MA: MIT Press.

Bowker, G. C., & Star, S. L. (1999). *Sorting things out: Classification and its consequences*. Cambridge, MA: MIT Press.

Bromme, R., Kienhues, D., & Stahl, E. (2008). Knowledge and epistemological beliefs: An intimate but complicate relationship. In M. S. Khine (Ed.), *Knowing, knowledge and beliefs:*

Epistemological studies across diverse cultures (pp. 423–441). Dordrecht, The Netherlands: Springer.

Collins, H. (2011). Language and practice. *Social Studies of Science, 41*(2), 271–300.

Collins, H. (2013). Three dimensions of expertise. *Phenomenology and the Cognitive Sciences, 12* (2), 253–273.

Collins, H., & Evans, R. (2007). *Rethinking expertise.* Chicago, IL: The University of Chicago Press.

Deacon, T. W. (1997). *The symbolic species: The co-evolution of language and the brain.* New York, NY: W. W. Norton.

Deacon, T. W. (2012). The symbol concept. In M. Tallerman & K. Gibson (Eds.), *The Oxford handbook of language evolution* (pp. 393–405). Oxford, UK: Oxford University Press.

Deleuze, G., & Guattari, F. (1987). *A thousand plateaus: Capitalism and schizophrenia.* Minneapolis, MI: University of Minnesota Press.

Derry, S. J., Schunn, C. D., & Gernsbacher, M. A. (Eds.). (2005). *Interdisciplinary collaboration: An emerging cognitive science.* Mahwah, NJ: Lawrence Erlbaum Associates.

Dewey, J. (1938). *Logic: The theory of inquiry.* New York, NY: Henry Holt.

Donald, M. (1990). *Origins of the modern mind: Three stages in the evolution of culture and cognition.* Cambridge, MA: Harvard University Press.

Donald, M. (2001). *A mind so rare: The evolution of human consciousness.* New York, NY: W.W. Norton.

Dreyfus, S. E., & Dreyfus, H. L. (1980). *A five-stage model of the mental activities involved in directed skill acquisition.* Berkeley, CA: University of California, Berkeley.

Echeverría, M. P. P., & Scheuer, N. (2009). External representations as learning tools. In C. Andersen, N. Scheuer, M. P. P. Echeverría, & E. V. Teuba (Eds.), *Representational systems and practices as learning tools* (pp. 1–17). Rotterdam, The Netherlands: Sense.

Edwards, A. (2005). Relational agency: Learning to be a resourceful practitioner. *International Journal of Educational Research, 43*(3), 168–182.

Edwards, A. (2010). *Being an expert professional practitioner: The relational turn in expertise.* Dordrecht, The Netherlands: Springer.

Engeström, Y. (2008). *From teams to knots: Activity-theoretical studies of collaboration and learning at work.* Cambridge, NY: Cambridge University Press.

Engeström, Y., & Blackler, F. (2005). On the life of the object. *Organization, 12*(3), 307–330.

Engeström, Y., & Middleton, D. (Eds.). (1996). *Cognition and communication at work.* Cambridge, NY: Cambridge University Press.

Ewenstein, B., & Whyte, J. (2009). Knowledge practices in design: The role of visual representations as 'epistemic objects'. *Organization Studies, 30*(1), 7–30.

Fenwick, T., & Nerland, M. (Eds.). (2014). *Reconceptualising professional learning: Sociomaterial knowledges, practices and responsibilities.* London, UK: Routledge.

Goodwin, C. (1994). Professional vision. *American Anthropologist, 96*(3), 606–633.

Goodwin, C. (1996). Seeing as a situated activity: Formulating planes. In Y. Engeström & D. Middleton (Eds.), *Cognition and communication at work* (pp. 61–95). Cambridge, NY: Cambridge University Press.

Goodwin, C. (2005). Seeing in depth. In S. J. Derry, C. D. Schunn, & M. A. Gernsbacher (Eds.), *Interdisciplinary collaboration: An emerging cognitive science* (pp. 85–121). Mahwah, NJ: Lawrence Erlbaum Associates.

Goodwin, C. (2013). The co-operative, transformative organization of human action and knowledge. *Journal of Pragmatics, 46*(1), 8–23.

Gordin, D. N., & Pea, R. D. (1995). Prospects for scientific visualization as an educational technology. *Journal of the Learning Sciences, 4*(3), 249–279.

Greeno, J. G., & Hall, R. P. (1997). Practicing representation: Learning with and about representational forms. *Phi Delta Kappan, 78*, 361–367.

Guile, D. (2010). *The learning challenge of the knowledge economy.* Rotterdam, The Netherlands: Sense.

Hall, R. (1996). Representation as shared activity: Situated cognition and Dewey's cartography of experience. *Journal of the Learning Sciences, 5*(3), 209–238.

Hall, S. (Ed.). (1997). *Representation: Cultural representations and signifying practices*. London, UK: Sage, in association with The Open University.

Hall, R., Stevens, R., & Torralba, T. (2002). Disrupting representational infrastructure in conversations across disciplines. *Mind, Culture, and Activity, 9*(3), 179–210.

Henning, P. H. (2004). Everyday cognition and situated action. In D. H. Jonassen (Ed.), *Handbook of research for educational communications and technology* (2nd ed., pp. 143–168). Mahwah, NJ: Lawrence Erlbaum Associates.

Hoffmann, M. H. G., & Roth, W.-M. (2007). The complementarity of a representational and an epistemological function of signs in scientific activity. *Semiotica, 164*(1/4), 101–122.

Howlett, P., & Morgan, M. S. (Eds.). (2010). *How well do facts travel?: The dissemination of reliable knowledge*. Cambridge, UK: Cambridge University Press.

Jensen, K., Lahn, L. C., & Nerland, M. (Eds.). (2012). *Professional learning in the knowledge society*. Rotterdam, The Netherlands: Sense.

Jones, A. (2009). Redisciplining generic attributes: The disciplinary context in focus. *Studies in Higher Education, 34*(1), 85–100.

Knorr Cetina, K. (1999). *Epistemic cultures: How the sciences make knowledge*. Cambridge, MA: Harvard University Press.

Knorr Cetina, K. (2001). Objectual practice. In T. R. Schatzki, K. Knorr-Cetina, & E. V. Savigny (Eds.), *The practice turn in contemporary theory* (pp. 175–188). London, UK: Routledge.

Knorr Cetina, K. (2007). Culture in global knowledge societies: Knowledge cultures and epistemic cultures. *Interdisciplinary Science Reviews, 32*, 361–375.

Lampland, M., & Star, S. L. (Eds.). (2009). *Standards and their stories: How quantifying, classifying, and formalizing practices shape everyday life*. London, UK: Cornell University Press.

Lave, J., & Wenger, E. (1991). *Situated learning: Legitimate peripheral participation*. Cambridge, UK: Cambridge University Press.

Miettinen, R., & Virkkunen, J. (2005). Epistemic objects, artefacts and organizational change. *Organization, 12*(3), 437–456.

Nerland, M. (2012). Professions as knowledge cultures. In K. Jensen, L. C. Lahn, & M. Nerland (Eds.), *Professional learning in the knowledge society* (pp. 27–48). Rotterdam, The Netherlands: Sense.

Nerland, M., & Jensen, K. (2010). Objectual practice and learning in professional work. In S. Billett, C. Harteis, & H. Gruber (Eds.), *Learning through practice* (Vol. 1, pp. 82–103). Dordrecht, The Netherlands: Springer.

Nerland, M., & Jensen, K. (2014). Learning through epistemic practices in professional work: Examples from nursing and engineering. In T. Fenwick & M. Nerland (Eds.), *Reconceptualising professional learning: Sociomaterial knowledges, practices and responsibilities* (pp. 25–37). London, UK: Routledge.

Nicolini, D., Mengis, J., & Swan, J. (2012). Understanding the role of objects in cross-disciplinary collaboration. *Organization Science, 23*(3), 612–629.

Polanyi, M. (1966/2009). *The tacit dimension*. Chicago, IL: University of Chicago Press.

Rheinberger, H. (1997). *Toward a history of epistemic things: Synthesizing proteins in the test tube*. Stanford, CA: Stanford University Press.

Roth, W.-M., & McGinn, M. K. (1998). Inscriptions: Toward a theory of representing as social practice. *Review of Educational Research, 68*(1), 35–59.

Säljö, R. (1995). Mental and physical artifacts in cognitive practices. In P. Reimann & H. Spada (Eds.), *Learning in humans and machines: Towards an interdisciplinary learning science* (pp. 83–95). London, UK: Pergamon Press.

Shaffer, D. W. (2004). Pedagogical praxis: The professions as models for postindustrial education. *Teachers College Record, 106*(7), 1401–1421.

Star, S. L. (1989). The structure of ill-structured solutions: Boundary objects and heterogenous distributed problem solving. In L. Gasser & M. N. Huhns (Eds.), *Distributed artificial intelligence* (Vol. 2, pp. 37–54). Pitman, CA: Morgan Kaufmann.

Star, S. L. (2010). This is not a boundary object: Reflections on the origin of a concept. *Science, Technology & Human Values, 35*(5), 601–617.

Streeck, J., Goodwin, C., & LeBaron, C. (Eds.). (2011). *Embodied interaction: Language and body in the material world.* New York, NY: Cambridge University Press.

Tomasello, M. (2010). *Origins of human communication.* Cambridge, MA: MIT Press.

Tomasello, M. (2014). *A natural history of human thinking.* Cambridge, MA: Harvard University Press.

Toulmin, S. (1953). *The philosophy of science: An introduction.* London, UK: Hutchinson's University Library.

Trede, F., Macklin, R., & Bridges, D. (2011). Professional identity development: A review of the higher education literature. *Studies in Higher Education, 37*(3), 365–384.

Turnbull, D. (2000). *Masons, tricksters and cartographers: Comparative studies in the sociology of scientific and indigenous knowledge.* Abingdon, OX: Routledge.

Vygotsky, L. S. (1930). The instrumental method in psychology. *Text of a talk given in 1930 at the Krupskaya Academy of Communist Education.* Retrieved from http://www.marxists.org/archive/vygotsky/works/1930/instrumental.htm.

Chapter 6
Understanding the Mind

Many of the educational challenges that university students face fall into three groups: (a) normal learning (gaining new knowledge and learning how to solve certain kinds of problems in work situations), (b) conceptual change (changing some part of existing knowledge, in order to shift from everyday beliefs to expert-like understanding) and (c) transfer (how to apply and extend existing knowledge to deal with new contexts and new situations). Learning to become an expert practitioner, and to innovate, necessarily involves all three aspects: normal learning, conceptual change and transfer. What sort of cognitive system can provide a reasonably plausible explanation of how these processes occur?

Any account of professional knowledge work, learning and innovation has to involve a discussion of the human mind. The questions of how the mind functions, on what sorts of mental entities it operates, and how change and transfer occur, have been examined from a variety of theoretical perspectives in education and in studies of learning and expertise (Chi & Roscoe, 2002; Ohlsson, 2011; Sinatra & Pintrich, 2003; Vosniadou (2008/2013). In this chapter, we revisit these questions from the perspective of actionable knowledge by exploring three main themes.

First, in Sects. 6.1 and 6.2, we provide a synthesis of what are often seen as competing views on the nature of the human mind. We start by using Stellan Ohlsson's (2011) summary of the five main approaches to understanding the human mind. Ohlsson's goal is to show how four of these approaches fail to provide an account of the mind, because they 'escape' through various routes outside the cognitive mechanisms that are inside the mind. He aims to 'stop the leaks' and thereby show that a fifth – mentalistic – approach offers the best way to achieve a scientific understanding of mind. Our account inverts the logic of Ohlsson's 'stopping off' move: we argue that a comprehensive account of the mind entails following the ways it 'leaks'. That is, if we are to understand the mind in a way which is sufficiently comprehensive to support the design of professional education programs, then we should adopt a perspective that *integrates* these views rather than reinforcing firm boundaries and sharp oppositions.

© Springer Science+Business Media Dordrecht 2017   127
L. Markauskaite, P. Goodyear, *Epistemic Fluency and Professional Education*,
Professional and Practice-based Learning 14, DOI 10.1007/978-94-007-4369-4_6

Second, in Sects. 6.3, 6.4, 6.5 and 6.6, we discuss some questions of conceptual knowledge and conceptual change, particularly as it pertains to knowledgeable action and professional learning. In Sect. 6.3, we review some debates surrounding the question of conceptual change, with a focus on relations between experiential knowledge and formal concepts. Our aim is to get at the questions of what changes in conceptual change and how this change happens, particularly when students learn conceptual knowledge that closely relates to their embodied experiences and professional actions. We then, in Sect. 6.4, extend this discussion to make connections with an area that has been very active in higher education research in the last decade – 'threshold concepts' and 'troublesome knowledge'. We show that this view, by attributing students' learning difficulties to their flawed mental models, creates an unproductive opposition between students' learning of formal articulated knowledge and their situated meaning-making. Section 6.5 revisits the relations between experience and conceptual knowledge by introducing the notion of 'situated concepts'. Drawing on contemporary cognitive literature, it proposes a rather different view of the human conceptual system and argues that much of conceptual knowledge is firmly grounded in situated human experiences of the world and support intelligent situated actions. Section 6.6 makes the next step and explores relationships between conceptual understanding and actionable knowledge.

Third, in Sects. 6.7 and 6.8, we address the question of transfer and learning for innovation.

6.1 Understanding the Human Mind and Learning: Experience, Brain, Environment and Culture

How does the human mind construct understanding? Ohlsson (2011) identifies five broad approaches in psychology that have tried, in different ways, to explain how the human mind works: phenomenological, neuropsychological, environmentalist, situated sociocultural and mentalist.[1]

The *phenomenological* tradition describes the mind as subjective experience – what one conceives, thinks and feels. The primary focus of such accounts of mind is human consciousness, thus how the mind operates and changes can be understood from the subjective experiences expressed in actions and discourse. While the phenomenologists acknowledge the limits of human consciousness – there is much more in human thinking, behaviour and feelings than a person can express – the key way to understand the mind is to depict those subjective phenomenological entities that present themselves in behaviour and discourse. Learning, from this perspective, involves increasing consciousness about the relationship between

---

[1] The descriptions of these five broad approaches, on this and the next few pages, are our summaries of Ohlsson's (2011) review and interpretation of each tradition. To each, we have added some extensions from other literature and some discussion of the implications of each approach for understanding learning.

oneself and the world, and change involves changes in human experience rather than in the mind:

> What it is that changes in conceptual change is the world perceived and the learner's capability of perceiving it. But these two things are actually two sides of the same thing: the experience of the world and the experienced world. (Marton & Pang, 2008, p. 542)

The *neuropsychological* account tries to understand the human mind by understanding the human brain. The focus is on those brain entities and processes that underpin human cognition, action, affect and other psychological processes. Neuropsychological accounts aim to explain human development and how the human mind operates by looking at the structures and regularities that can be observed at the physiological level, such as in the functioning of brain cells, the activation of neurons and the formation of synaptic connections. On this view, memory, learning and other cognitive processes are embedded in large networks of interconnected neurons that dynamically change their interconnections (Bransford, Brown, & Cocking, 1999; de Jong et al., 2009; Geake, 2009; Knowland & Thomas, 2014; OECD, 2007; Sousa, 2011). Over time, active connections are strengthened, while the inactive ones become weaker, increasingly tailoring the brain to fit the environment and producing a range of phenomena that underpin learning, change, expertise and skill development. From this perspective, learning and change are coupled with changes in the human brain's architecture, detectable by measuring brain activities at the neuropsychological level. On this view, knowing how the brain works allows one to set up appropriate conditions for learning:

> Guidance can be optimised by understanding the process of learning, the neurophysiological conditions that allow it and the changes that learning causes in the brain. (Knowland & Thomas, 2014, p. 101)

The *environmentalist* (or physically situated) accounts, in contrast, locate the agency and driving force for much of human behaviour *outside* the human skull – in the body and in the material environment. There are a number of different versions of the environmentalist view. For example, there are behaviourist accounts that see human behaviour and learning as a set of simple processes, coupling inputs from the environment (stimuli) with observable behaviours (responses) (Skinner, 1938). More complex accounts include the ecological approach to visual perception (Gibson, 1979) and embodied cognition and the extended mind (Anderson, 2003; Clark, 1999, 2012; Pecher & Zwaan, 2010). These see human action, perception and the body as fundamentally entangled with the material environment. The main assumption is that much of the information that accounts for human behaviour is located in the material environment. Then cognition that informs intelligent behaviour is underpinned by a human perceptual system that is responsible for aligning actions to the predictions derived from environmental regularities. Learning and change from this perspective are embodied in the very flexibility of human perception: an ability to sense the affordances of the environment and align actions and the body with the dynamically changing situation (Gibson & Pick, 2000; Smith, 2005). As Noë (2004) succinctly puts it,

... perceiving is a way of acting. Perception is not something that happens to us, or in us. It is something we do. (Noë, 2004, p. 1)

Situated sociocultural (or socially situated) accounts look for patterns and processes that can describe human behaviour in the *social* environment and culture. This perspective ranges from accounts that say that much of what we think of as the human mind is based on internalised patterns of human social behaviour to more extreme formulations associated with situated cognition that generally assume no specific internal mechanisms are necessary to describe human behaviour (Cole, Engeström, & Vasquez, 1997). On this view, learning happens on an inter-psychological plane – by observing the behaviour of other people and by participating in communities of practice (Cole, 1996; Lave & Wenger, 1991; Rogoff & Lave, 1984; Scribner, 1997). In Jean Lave's (2012) words,

... 'knowledge' or 'knowledge-ability' must be understood as part of, and as taking meaning from and for, persons engaged as apprentices to their own changing practice across the multiple contexts of their lives. (Lave, 2012, p. 167)

Finally, the *mentalist* view aims to provide an explicit account of what kind of system the mind is: what entities make it up, what kinds of processes it carries out and what kinds of transformations it undergo. Ohlsson explains this account by detailing a symbolic architecture of the mind. Cognitive functions, such as action, seeing, learning, memory, thought and decision-making, are implemented by a range of cognitive processes (Atkinson & Shiffrin, 1968; Newell & Simon, 1972). Mind, therefore, has a central 'control executive' that represents intentions or goals and coordinates all the other simultaneously occurring mental processes. The main entities on which the intellect operates are *mental representations*. Most mental activity is constituted by three discrete steps: perception, thinking and action. Cognitive processes, including learning, belong to the 'think' part of the mind. Much of the 'think' part operates on representations encoded in long-term memory, from where they are retrieved, on demand, into short-term memory in order to perform an action. Learning and change occur through two broad categories of change processes that can be labelled 'monotonic change' and 'non-monotonic' change (Chi & Ohlsson, 2005). Monotonic change proceeds in modest increments, without disruptive effects on current knowledge structures. Non-monotonic change involves significant re-representation, reconfiguration or replacement in the structure of the learner's knowledge (Chi & Roscoe, 2002; Ohlsson, 2009).

As Ohlsson (2011) notes, these five different approaches tell a story about different aspects of human behaviour and cognitive change. The phenomenological approaches describe, but do not explain, the human mind. They equate mind with consciousness and subjective experience. Ohlsson argues that, 'The process that produces those experiences – retrieval from long term memory – is not itself conscious' (p. 25) and thus cannot explain mental events. In trying to reduce mind to brain, neuroscience offers accounts that are overwhelmingly complex and fundamentally uninteresting (p. 26). The environmentalist approaches locate the forces shaping behaviour outside the person, in the environment. However, Ohlsson notes that behaviour does not emerge from the environment, but from an interaction between the situation and personal goals. The structure of the mind does not necessarily mirror the structure of the environment, and behaviour cannot be explained without assuming that there is 'significant internal processing' (p. 27). The situated sociocultural approaches try to explain human practices without reference to the mind, but as Ohlsson asks: 'How does the mind work, such that a person can create and participate in social and cultural systems?' (p. 28). He argues that questions about how communities and groups behave do not say much about how new practices are adopted by novices or how the mind works when a person creates and engages in new practices.

Ohlsson concludes that 'Mind cannot be reduced to conscious experience, the brain, the material environment or sociocultural factors' (loc. cit.) and argues that none of these four approaches answer the fundamental question of how the mind works: only the mentalist approach will do this. He acknowledges that all the approaches ask valid questions but that they replace the task of describing how the mind works with something else: subjective experience, the brain, the material environment or social factors. He sees these patterns and regularities as operating at different levels of the system and suggests that if one is serious about providing an account of how the mind works, one needs to close off these (purported) explanatory 'escape routes' to consciousness, brain, environment and culture.

We broadly agree with Ohlsson's analysis of the mentalist model. The attempts to model processes that take place solely in the mind have proven useful in many domains of learning and human performance, such as reasoning and problem-solving (Newell & Simon, 1972), creativity and practical intelligence (Sternberg, 1985) and working memory and instructional design (Sweller, van Merrienboer, & Paas, 1998). In general, the mentalist approach suggests that humans have relatively stable schemas, models or frameworks that represent structures, causal and logical relationships and processes in the social and material world (Schraw, 2006). Such schemas support human understanding of various phenomena in the world – classic examples from research on learning being: how the human blood circulation system works (Chi, De Leeuw, Chiu, & Lavancher, 1994; Chi & Roscoe, 2002), the shape of the earth and how the day–night cycle functions (Vosniadou & Brewer, 1994) and anticipating how events will unfold and how one should act in social situations, such as in a restaurant (Schank & Abelson, 1977). Mentalistically oriented accounts of human cognition can be quite successful at explaining the mental part of much everyday situated activity (Vera & Simon, 1993). Moreover, teaching and learning using abstractions can be a useful way of gaining important knowledge that supports understanding and skill (Anderson, Reder, & Simon, 1996).

However, *our attempt to understand the resourceful and fluent mind goes in the opposite direction to Ohlsson* – aiming to *open up* the routes between the mind and the places to which, Ohlsson complains, accounts of the mind usually escape. As Barsalou, Breazeal and Smith (2007) note, in real-world, real-time cognition, it is impossible to understand cognitive processes in isolation from other processes, such as perception, action and emotion.

Indeed, understanding how a process coordinates with other processes may be as important, if not more important, than understanding the internal structure of the process itself. <...>

[T]he coordinated relationships between perception, action and cognition must be identified to characterise cognition adequately. (Barsalou et al., 2007, pp. 80–81)

In our view, the human mind

- Is constructed, in significant part, via introspection (thus, can be informed by the phenomenological perspectives)
- Operates in a human organism that underpins and extends beyond the mind (thus, the brain perspectives)
- Is embodied and, therefore, responds to the material environment (thus, the environmentalist perspectives)
- Evolves in communities and other social groups (thus, the situated sociocultural perspectives)
- Is able to operate with various kinds of mental representations and intentions (thus, the mentalistic perspectives)

It is simply *necessary* to consider all of these together if we are serious about understanding the knowledge that produces the knowledgeable action of the human body and mind in the real world. A productive flexible mind is in fact conscious, embedded, embodied and runs on the brain and in culture(s). These different facets of human cognition are not just different layers of a complex system. They are interacting elements from which cognition emerges. Daniel Siegel (2012) puts it like this:

A core aspect of the human mind is an embodied and relational process that regulates the flow of energy and information ... the mind is a process that emerges from the distributed nervous system extending throughout the entire body, and also from the communication patterns that occur within relationships ... human connections shape neural connections. (Siegel, 2012, p. 3)

One of the main functions of an intelligent mind is to be flexible enough to adapt and respond to changes in the other elements of the system, so that the overall performance of the system results in coordinated, fluent behaviour. To understand it, we need to understand all those elements and most importantly, what enables their interaction and fluent, mutual coordinated performance. In short, the human mind and practices change the body and the world, but the human body and the world change human practices and the mind.

Indeed, even those computer scientists and robotics engineers who are trying to create 'intelligent machines' are discovering the limitations of traditional mentalistic ways of tackling the question of human intelligence. It is no longer feasible to use models based on the idea of the mind as a 'symbolic machine' or a 'brain in a box', independent of bodily constraints, and depending upon explicit representations of the world (Brooks, 1991; Dreyfus, 1992, 2014). Real-world intelligence is intimately connected with real sensing and real action. As Brooks (1991) puts it:

When we examine very simple level intelligence we find that explicit representations and models of the world simply get in the way. It turns out to be better to use the world as its own model. (Brooks, 1991, p. 139)

... intelligence cannot be separated from the subjective experience of a body. (Brooks & Stein, 1994, p. 7)

We are not alone in feeling the need for a more integrative approach. A number of scholars interested in human development, learning and scientific and professional work have also found ways of going beyond traditional social vs. cognitive, mind vs. body and other such binary oppositions, producing their own adjustments and blends of different perspectives (see, e.g. Billett, 1996; Hutchins, 1995). Some of these approaches go under umbrella labels such as 'cognitive ecology' (Hutchins, 2010), 'grounded cognition' (Barsalou, 2008, 2010), 'environmental perspectives' (Nersessian, 2005) or 'enaction' (Stewart, Gapenne, & Paolo, 2010). Indeed, many other scholars who would consider their approaches, first and foremost, as anthropology, archaeology, sociology, linguistics, culture or philosophy are also providing fundamental insights into human behaviour, practice and mind (see, e.g. Boivin, 2008; Clark, 2011; Dreyfus, 2014; Ingold, 2011; Knorr-Cetina, 1999; Malafouris, 2013; Schatzki, Knorr-Cetina, & von Savigny, 2001; Sterelny, 2003, 2012; Szymanski & Whalen, 2011; Turnbull, 2000).

Much of our understanding of professional work and learning depends upon theoretical accounts in which the mind has a nontrivial role. The account of what mind is, how it contributes to intelligent performance, how it learns and can be taught and how it becomes capable of innovation all feature strongly. Our take, however, is a long way from the traditional mentalist view. It is not what many traditional cognitive psychologists would even regard as a 'cognitive account'. First, perception, action, affect and other aspects of human behaviour that traditional symbolic accounts of intelligence regard as a noncognitive part of human behaviour have a *constitutive* role in our thinking (Barsalou et al., 2007). Second, knowledgeable action is embedded and embodied in material and social settings and practices. This material and social world is not just a landscape in which cognition and action take place, but is the provider of resources from which higher-level cognition is constructed and the terrain *through and in which this construction* takes place (Hutchins, 2010). People learn using conceptual and material tools, and within environments, that have been historically constructed. They construct their understanding creating new social arrangements and material artefacts in the same environment. The content of the mind, the shape of mental resources, in broad terms, is the result of active engagement and sense-making within a rich and complex culturally configured material and social world (Malafouris, 2013; McGann, De Jaegher, & Di Paolo, 2013; Sterelny, 2012; Stewart et al., 2010).

However, what kinds of cognitive mechanisms could support such ways of thinking and learning? We turn to this question next.

6.2 From Cognition as Structure to Cognition as Coordination and Enaction

Theories of cognition and learning commonly focus on the achievement of stable expert performance, but intelligent professional action requires flexibility across situations. Smith (2005) notes that one established way of explaining stability in behaviour across situations, or over time, is to look for stability in the mind and a single central unit that can coordinate all actions. A typical putative source for such stability is the notion of a *concept* or other such stable mental representations – such as theories, mental models, beliefs and frameworks – that can guide, but exist independently of, perception and action. In contrast, Smith argues that much of the apparent stability in human behaviour emerges from the variability and coupling of individual elements distributed across the mind, the body and the world. Smith provides a vivid illustration, using the movements of a cat. A cat's locomotion is an apparently stable pattern of alternating limb movements. But when the animal moves through uneven terrain, its movements cannot be explained by the existence of a stable central pattern generator that is capable of producing similar alternating movement of the four limbs. The variability in the movements is extraordinary and essential – each move requires very different muscle firings, to keep the general pattern of the limb alternation stable when the cat moves across real terrain – grass, rocks, undergrowth – backwards, forwards, quickly, stealthily, etc. Smith claims that this emergent and apparently stable behaviour can be accounted for by a *dynamic systems approach*. From this perspective, there is no one central control mechanism that has a causal priority – be it a stable concept, theory or plan. The apparently coherent pattern emerges from the interaction and self-organisation of many elements in the system. The overall behaviour of such a self-organised system can be characterised by a relative stability or instability, but this behaviour emerges from the coordinated relationships among the components, not from the stable workings of one central control unit.

In experiments, Smith demonstrated that such stable constructs as 'a concept of an object' are generally not necessary to explain stabilities in children's cognition. The intelligence is not locked into the cognitive system, but emerges in real time by coupling perception and action. The (human) cognitive system is neither stationary in its external behaviour nor in its internal processes. It has its own dynamics, and changes in this system are driven by its history and its activity in the world; it is a part of much larger systems and is flexible and capable of responding differently to different situations.

This view shifts the focus of what is central in knowledgeable performance from stable constructs that can control knowledgeable actions (e.g. concepts, theories) to constructs that are rich in relationships and interactions with other external and internal elements of the system and which are thereby flexible enough to produce coordinated and coherent performance of the overall system.

The intelligence that makes alternating [cat's] leg movements is not strictly in the brain, not in the body, nor the world but in the interaction of a particularly structured body in a particularly structured world. (Smith, 2005, p. 286)

While Smith's example was primarily about the importance of outside systems in actions that seemingly don't place much demand on higher intelligence, she argues that 'Much of human intelligence resides in the interface between the body and the world' (loc. cit.). That is, people typically 'off-load' much of their intelligence to their environments:

This off-loading in the interface between body and world appears a pervasive aspect of human cognition and may be critical to the development of higher-level cognitive functions or in the binding of mental contents that are separated in time. (loc. cit.)

Such everyday functions as remembering and counting are usually performed, at least in part, in the world rather than solely in the head. In short, what might seem to be a person's stable concept[2] is better seen as the outcome of fluid interaction among a variety of systems, of which the conscious mind is merely one.

Recent accounts of cognition, building on evidence from developmental research, robotics, neuropsychology and other domains, increasingly show that higher-level cognition (creativity, anticipation, intuition, decision-making, etc.) – often seen as vital in professional work and innovation – is not just a result of independent processes created by a modular mind. Rather, they emerge from interactions among many other basic systems in the brain, such as perception, goal management, action, motivation, emotions and learning (Barsalou et al., 2007; Damasio, 2012). In the past, many of these processes have been seen as either subsidiary or noncognitive. They have been treated as separable from the key higher-order cognitive operations that have been given such a dominant place in the mentalist approaches on which key instructional theories have been built. Yet they turn out to be inseparable from the very act of thinking.

So what *is* the role of concepts, theories and other organised mental constructs that have been such a focus in education's use of ideas on human cognition? The grounded cognition view suggests that mental representations (i.e. what one knows) have a central role in human thinking (Barsalou, 1999, 2009; Pecher & Zwaan, 2010). However, this cognitive system is unlikely to mirror the abstract, self-contained mental constructs, such as concepts or theories, that operate in a closed symbolic system. Cognition is embedded in the physical world, and this world is the main source of resources from which the conceptual system is constructed and organised. People, when they think about goal-directed performance, are 'conceptually there': 'The conceptualiser is in the representation' (Barsalou, 2009, p. 245) – making inferences about the perceptual information, actions, introspective states,

---

[2] Or other such construct of higher-order cognition that putatively provides coherent guidance for their action.

perspectives and other aspects of the situation. When such situated information is not available, 'cognition suffers'.

Accounts of dynamic and grounded cognition do not say much about the nature and features of the cultural and material environments in which such coordinated performance becomes possible. However, there is a general acknowledgement that human cognition leans upon, and reflects, its social developmental processes. This includes the organisation of interactions, coordination and also interactions with material contexts that have themselves been shaped by social interactions (Smith & Gasser, 2005).

Some accounts of ecological cognition are helpful in this regard. As Hutchins (2010) asserts,

> For humans, the 'world' (in the now familiar 'brain-body-world' formulation) consists of culturally constructed social and material settings. <...> Human brain and human culture have coevolved. <...> Activity in the nervous system is linked to high level cognitive processes by way of embodied interaction with culturally organised material and social worlds. (Hutchins, 2010, pp. 711–712)

Social interactions are intimately involved in the learning of cognitively nontrivial social skills, such as working together.

> Humans probably learn important things more often through social interaction than they do from isolated individual interactions with inanimate stimuli. Furthermore, these socially acquired skills are intrinsic to coordinated activity in division-of-labour settings, and also in competitive activity in conflict situations. (Barsalou et al., 2007, p. 82)

Recent research in enactive psychology can help enrich and sharpen our understanding here (see, e.g. McGann et al., 2013). A distinguishing feature of the enactive approach is that the mind is not seen as located in, or a property of, an individual person. Rather, it emerges dynamically in the relationship between the individual and their physical and social surroundings (Varela, Thompson, & Rosch, 1991). This *engagement* – dynamic interaction between agent and environment – is central to the enactive view:

> ... enactive psychology is more interested in the dynamics of coupling between an agent and its environment than the stipulation of the characteristics of either. The idea of coupling is quite simply the mutual influence between the agent and the environment from which emerges the meaningful behavior into which we are seeking insight. (McGann et al., 2013, p. 204)

This notion of coupling makes *skill* vital in enactive accounts: skill is what enables an agent to act successfully and reliably in an environment – but it is through a flexible kind of coupling:

> ... in any given situation we are not merely reproducing previous patterns of behavior but *weaving* habitual actions into the details of the present situation ... as we become more skilled our perceptions and actions shift. Our goals and intentions begin to operate in different ways ... the coupling is of a different sort. The kind of meaning inherent in the activity is transformed ... it is in the relations between the embodied, motivated and skillful autonomous agent and its complex [physical and social] environment that the meaning of the engagement inheres, and to lose sight of that relational description is to lose sight of psychology. (op. cit., pp. 205–206, emphasis added)

One of the key implications of the account we are using here is that perception and action become as important as, and inseparable from, higher-order cognitive processes in the mind. So the critical element of learning complex knowledge and cognitive skill is not the construction of decontextualised symbolic structures in the mind, but the *very coordination* of what is the mind and what is outside of it, including perception, action, embodied skill and other forms of engagement with the environment and with other people. If we believe in the power of what is usually called 'deep knowledge' underpinned by conceptual understanding in knowledgeable action, then the central question for professional education is as follows. How do we help students build the 'grammar' connecting those theoretical constructs onto their multimodal experiences of sensing and acting – the experiences on which human cognition naturally builds and operates. In short, the focus of higher-order learning shifts from abstracted knowledge (and conception, as it is classically understood) to knowledge that allows the coordination of conceptual thought with situated experiences (i.e. perceiving, acting).

Students' experiences of engaging with the world, including their natural everyday experiences, are therefore foundational resources for constructing conceptual understanding. In the next section, we provide an outline of some ideas that extend the account of mind in ways that are helpful for understanding professional work, knowledge and learning: looking more closely at relations between formal concepts and experiential knowledge.

6.3 Learning and Conceptual Change: Formal Concepts and Experiential Knowledge

Students' minds are not empty containers. Transmissionist views of how to teach, which reduce learning to a mere accumulation of new information and knowledge structures (also known as 'accretion'), have been extensively, and not unreasonably, criticised in the constructivist literature (e.g. Bereiter, 2002; Papert, 1980). Such criticisms have been widely aired in adult and higher education, including professional education (e.g. Barrows & Tamblyn, 1980; Boud & Feletti, 1997; Brookfield, 1986; Jarvis, 2012; Savin-Baden, 2000). We have no intention of rekindling the debate over whether direct instruction is better than other forms of teaching (Kirschner, Sweller, & Clark, 2006) – there is always 'a time for telling' (Schwartz & Bransford, 1998) and the important pedagogical questions have always been about how to structure and scaffold students' learning, rather than about how little one can get away with (Jonassen, 2011; Kapur, 2008; Kuhn, 2007). As we explained in Chap. 3, otherwise diverse accounts of professional knowledge agree on the fact that students need to know the key ideas, conceptual structures, procedures and strategies that constitute an important part of the knowledge base of their profession (Clark, 2008; Perkins & Salomon, 1989).

However, this is far from being the full story. The declarative knowledge that can be taught through direct instruction is not enough to guarantee successful performance (Ohlsson, 1995). Various exceptional intellectual traits, such as inspiration and creativity (Sternberg, 2004), and various other personal traits, such as mindfulness and responsiveness (Dall'Alba, 2009; Dall'Alba & Barnacle, 2007) or dispositions (Barnett, 2004), also play an important role in expert performance. However, an explanation of professional resourcefulness as solely an inborn capacity, or an inner state, provides very little guidance about the sorts of mental constructs and mechanisms that may underpin these capacities and how they may develop. From an educational point of view, this is not particularly useful. Middle-ground views of learning as a gradual enhancement, restructuring and refinement of knowledge, skills and innate traits tend to offer a reasonable account of what kinds of changes may explain students' progress from everyday common sense, to novice professionals, to experts (diSessa & Sherin, 1998; Hallden, Scheja, & Haglund, 2008; Meyer & Land, 2006; Wagner, 2010). Nevertheless, even in this camp, there are some very different views of how learning occurs and what kinds of instructional approaches might be productive. The core of this debate has evolved around the nature of students' 'uneducated' experiential, intuitive knowledge and what educators should do about that (diSessa, 2006). We elaborate on this debate as a part of our discussion of conceptual change and transfer later in the chapter, but for now we provide a brief overview of its main implications for learning. We outline two broad views on this matter, which can be labelled 'negative rationalism' and 'positive empiricism'. Boiled down to the common core, these views see students' prior experiential knowledge as either (a) unhelpful and best replaced or (b) useful in the right circumstances and suitable for building upon.

6.3.1 Negative Rationalism: Students' Experiential Knowledge Seen as a Problem to Be Overcome

Some scholars have noted that much of the constructivist research on expertise and learning has been adhering to a line of theorisation that can be characterised as a 'negative rationalism' (e.g. Hallden et al., 2008; Perry, 1965; Rommetveit, 1978). This perspective acknowledges that prior knowledge has an influential role in students' learning. However, students bring to schools and universities a range of 'naïve ideas' about scientific or professional phenomena. Some of these ideas are incomplete, but basically correct, thus their enhancement requires normal 'monotonic' learning or small repairs. In contrast, other naïve ideas contradict the normative conceptions of phenomena that expert communities hold and sometimes require radical 'non-monotonic' change (Chi & Ohlsson, 2005; Chi & Roscoe, 2002). For example, Chi and Roscoe (2002) show that correcting students' misconception that the human circulatory system is a 'single loop' rather than a 'double loop' involves just a simple repair of their mental models, which may be corrected by incrementally learning additional details and revising earlier beliefs. But other misconceptions, such as thinking about electricity as a substance, that is 'stored', 'flows' and 'leaks', rather than as a process, require an ontological 'non-monotonic' shift. Crucially, some naïve misconceptions can be both incorrect and robust, as they are tightly bound into rich explanatory frameworks, cultural theories or myths that are reinforced by naïve perceptual experiences and/or by social discourse. For this reason, non-monotonic change often depends on confronting students with alterative views and changing belief systems or theories fundamentally. As an example, Keselman, Kaufman and Patel (2004) found that students' understandings of HIV were often flawed, but not because the students reasoned using superficial biomedical knowledge. Rather, they drew on false, causally complex, cultural and experiential theories about the disease. Kaufman, Keselman and Patel (2008) then argued that only 'sufficiently robust and coherent' (p. 316) biomedical knowledge provides a sufficient basis for correcting lay people's 'flaws in the logic of the myths' (loc. cit.).

Perry (1965) noted that much of the literature on expertise takes a radically negative view of common-sense knowledge, seemingly regarding all early experiences as crude, primitive and opposed to higher-level expert understanding. As he sarcastically concluded,

> The first intelligent step to the handling of our experience is to supersede commonsense.
> (Perry, 1965, p. 126)

This negative view of common-sense knowledge and everyday experience features in many accounts of expert learning. As Ohlsson (2011) argues, deep expert learning requires one to 'abandon, override, reject, retract or suppress' knowledge that has been gained through direct, personal experiences (p. 21). Broadly stated, this 'negative rationalism' tradition tends to attribute many common learning difficulties to a combination of (a) the intrinsic difficulty of some ideas and (b) students' developmental challenges (Meyer & Land, 2005; Perkins, 2007; Vosniadou & Ioannides, 1998). It emphasises shortcomings in, and fallibility of, students' prior understandings: such as flawed conceptual models and other deficiencies in thinking.

6.3.2 Positive Empiricism: Students' Experiential Knowledge as a Productive Resource

Other scholars have proposed an alternative account of learning. They argue that the negative rationalism tradition has at least three major shortcomings: (a) it offers a misleading account of what intuitive knowledge is, (b) it significantly oversimplifies the nature of conceptual change, and (c) it underestimates the value of students' common-sense understandings and their abilities to reason in sensible ways (diSessa, 1993; Kirsh, 2009; Säljö, 1991; Wagner, 2006). From this perspective, students' common-sense conceptual knowledge and skills – which they develop through experience and use in solving day-to-day problems that they encounter – do not necessarily resemble the theories or other coherent constructs that are implicated in normative accounts of experts' understanding and reasoning or that are captured in textbooks. Rather, such experiential knowledge is less systematic and more tightly coupled with tools and other external affordances available for reasoning within specific contexts and situations. Yet this knowledge is not necessarily misleading and, overall, can be perfectly sufficient for dealing with problems encountered in day-to-day work and life. For example, Hoyles, Noss and Pozzi (2001) show that even expert nurses, during drug administration, use a range of strategies to calculate required dosages. Nurses' ways of performing these calculations are tied to specific drugs, quantities, volumes, packaging and other material affordances of the environment. They do not draw on a single canonical, taught method, but their strategies are sufficiently correct to get the job done efficiently and without mistakes (see also Scribner, 1985, 1997; Rogoff & Lave, 1984; Lave, 1988).

This positive empiricist account emphasises the potentiality, productivity and variability of intuitive conceptual resources and skills. From this perspective, students' experiential concepts and experts' normative concepts can be seen as different constructs, which do not compete for the same space in students' or experts' minds (diSessa & Wagner, 2005; Gupta, Hammer, & Redish, 2010). Rather than abandoning prior experience and trying to fit all knowledge into one normative discourse, the challenge is to find ways of paying attention to the relationships between tasks, contextual details and other aspects of the situation and drawing on intuitive resources when it is productive. As Säljö (1991) argues, any attempt to equate students' cognitive performances to domain-specific knowledge and preformed competences obscures how students' competencies actually develop. A more productive view is to focus 'on understanding the resources – mental as well as practical – that people draw on when solving problems' (p. 117).

These two perspectives provide a point of departure for rethinking the conceptual understanding that underpins actionable knowledge and how it develops. However, what kinds of cognitive structures and mechanisms underpin development of conceptual understanding? We now need to look more closely at how these two perspectives address the question of conceptual change.

6.3.3 Conceptual Change: Coherent Structures and Knowledge-in-Pieces

This central debate in the conceptual change literature is outlined by diSessa (2006). He draws parallels with a dispute about the nature of scientific knowledge and human understanding between Thomas Kuhn and Stephen Toulmin. With respect to conceptual change, the difference can be summarised as a concern for (a) the systematic replacement of students' misconceptions or (b) strengthening the appropriate activation of fine-grained mental resources (diSessa, 2006; diSessa & Sherin, 1998; Özdemir & Clark, 2007).

The coherent structures and misconceptions perspective broadly follows Kuhn's view. It starts from the assumption that students' initial intuitive understandings and/or incomplete understandings are critical barriers that block further learning. Thus, students' conceptual development mirrors stages of the history of scientific theories – in which deep and sudden restructuring of knowledge occurs at several different developmental stages and/or when students' incorrect yet coherent ideas are replaced by a correct theoretical understanding. Such changes can be seen as rational, and the conditions for progress are broadly similar to the conditions that have to be met for scientific revolutions. These include (a) the student's dissatisfaction with their existing conception and (b) availability of a new, intelligible, plausible and fruitful conception.

The fine-grained mental resources, or 'knowledge-in-pieces', perspective broadly mirrors Toulmin's ideas. On this view, the student's intuitive ideas are not expected to have much global coherence. Rather, as diSessa (1988, 1993) argues, these intuitive ideas are composed of hundreds if not thousands of small fine-grained elements that he calls 'phenomenological primitives' or 'p-prims'. These pieces of knowledge are formed through everyday encounters and experiences of various phenomena in the world – including social and physical phenomena (diSessa, 2000; Philip, 2011). They are generally very contextualised and loosely organised, rather than coherent paradigms or theories. P-prims nevertheless play productive roles in constructing a normative conceptual understanding and play generative roles even in expert reasoning (Gupta et al., 2010). Indeed, they provide the very ground for constructing such understanding. Rather than rejecting these intuitive resources, they should be recognised and rewired in a more systematic kind of 'conceptual machinery'.

The fundamental distinction between the two views concerns what kinds of entities are involved, how they are organised and how they change in conceptual change. diSessa (2006) argues that most theories of conceptual change see the human conceptual system as constituted of at least two nested levels: lower-level 'entities', such as individual concepts, and higher-level 'systems', such as theories, frameworks and ontologies. The coherence perspective generally assumes that the relations at a higher-level constrain entities at a lower level. On this view, it is hard, if not impossible, to achieve conceptual change gradually – without a fundamental shift at the higher level. For example, Chi (2005; see also Chi & Roscoe, 2002) argues that understanding of 'emerging processes' – such as 'diffusion', 'electricity', 'temperature' and 'evolution' – causes learning difficulties because the emerging processes are *ontologically* different from the 'direct processes', such as 'blood circulation', that are generally implied in everyday conceptions. Thus, correcting such misconceptions involves a conceptual shift between the direct and the emergent processes at a higher ontological level, before correct understanding of individual concepts, or formulation of correct propositions using those concepts (i.e. beliefs), becomes possible.

In contrast, the 'knowledge-in-pieces' perspective sees the relationships between different levels as generally weak and diverse (diSessa & Sherin, 1998). The main challenges that students face grasping complex conceptual ideas emerge from the need to coordinate many diverse situation-specific knowledge elements into an organised system. The difficulties involved in such conceptual change are not particularly distinct from those that learners face when they learn conceptually new knowledge, as it involves coordinating an overarching conceptual understanding with situation-specific understandings of the phenomenon. In this case, lower-level experiential entities provide the actual basis for a well-integrated conceptual understanding. Rather than correcting or 'repairing' beliefs or theories at a system level, one should focus on helping students to get and coordinate the multiple elements first. In short, early intuitive ideas do not need to be dismantled and replaced by abstract normative concepts nor need they be replaced by new, better, experiential ideas for learning to occur. Successful learning dynamically emerges from all accumulated experiences, thus progress primarily involves contextualising and establishing more systematic relationships between (a) learnt normative concepts and ways of reasoning and (b) students' existing ideas and ways of reasoning.

The ideas expressed in the positive account provide an opportunity to look more deeply into students' experiential knowledge and the mechanisms that underpin conceptual development and transfer. There is no need to see conceptual learning as an 'all or nothing' or 'all or something' (cf. diSessa, 2006; Marton & Pang, 2008) change in abstract, decontextualised cognitive structures. It does not need to be seen as learning that happens in and through just one or a few phases of sudden change, in which contextual details and experience are suppressed. Rather, it can be seen as *a gradual systematisation and coupling* of experiential understandings with normative constructs. Resources that constitute actionable knowledge emerge from the instrumental relationship between experience and formal ways of knowing. In order to make such connections, both have to be in place. Experience is not sufficient for conceptual understanding nor is conceptual understanding sufficient for successful action. An *emerging* relationship between the 'expert concepts' and students' 'everyday concepts' (which they naturally develop through experience and employ in action) offers a productive way of understanding how students develop functional and actionable knowledge.[3] In a nutshell, professional learning, at its core, needs to connect *knowledge* and *action* – it needs to connect 'expert concepts' and experiential 'everyday concepts' rather than break these links and impose new conceptual structures that operate independently from, and above, situated experiences of the world.

---

[3] Our use of the term 'functional knowledge' is inspired by Greeno's (2012) term 'functional concept'. We discuss this in more detail in Chap. 17.

6.3.4 Summary: What Changes in Conceptual Change?

In professional education, we need to be able to talk about conceptual knowledge, skill, action and change almost simultaneously so we need a reasonably good account of the kinds of entities on which 'change' operates. It is possible to align ideas in the conceptual change literature with the five perspectives on how the mind operates that we introduced in Sect. 6.1.

The *neurobiological* perspective associates learning with changes in the brain. Thus the main concern is related to direct biological mechanisms underpinning cognition. The main questions about change and transfer relate to the issue of brain plasticity, which is usually seen as a function of age, previous experiences, short-term memory and other partly biological and partly developmental factors. Age is often seen as related to lower levels of brain plasticity, yet it is generally acknowledged that the brain continues to be plastic and that highly complex skills can be developed throughout the lifespan (Knowland & Thomas, 2014). There is also increasing evidence that brain processes associated with higher-order cognitions are connected with brain processes associated with biological regulation of the body: indeed that the former emerge from the latter (Damasio, 2012). Overall, mind and body, rationality and emotion and other cognitive and noncognitive processes are increasingly seen as not only inseparable from each other but also from the environment and social others (Goleman, 2006; Siegel, 2012).

In contrast, the classic *mentalist* approaches tend to start from the assumption that the human mind is constituted of symbolic mental structures that are generally self-contained and relatively coherent. Thus, conceptual change typically involves the (complete) restructuring or replacement of one symbolic entity by another. The implication is that a person can see the world in one way or another, but not in two contradictory ways.

The *phenomenological* approaches primarily see conceptual change as evolving consciousness, thus the process may be more gradual – moving feature-by-feature or step-by-step towards an expanded awareness or greater sophistication. There may occasionally be more radical change, yet the relationship between externally observable behaviours and experiences and the mind is generally maintained through reflection, rather than abandoned.

The *sociocultural, situated and environmentalist* approaches tend to shift the locus of explanation away from the mind and towards interaction and context. They look for the sources of patterns in human behaviour, and for the causes of change, in the culture or in the environment rather than in the mind.

Those who are in the 'mind and consciousness' focussed camps inevitably have to provide an account of how one mental structure replaces an earlier incorrect (yet possibly coherent) structure constructed in a person's mind. That is, how a 'folk theory' is replaced by an expert-like theory. Those who are in the environmentalist or sociocultural camps generally do not need (or aim) to provide detailed explanations of what changes in conceptual change at an individual cognitive level:

changes come from, and can be observed and explained at, an external behavioural level – discourse or skill.

Within and across these broad camps, there is still some appreciable diversity in theoretical positions. Whether we look at the human mind, consciousness, discourse or action, we can find a range of approaches distributed along a continuum. At one pole, each aspect is seen as generally well structured and stable – resembling theories, models, beliefs and habits. At the other pole, things are seen as more fragmented and fluid – with a quality of being coordinated and assembled on the spot, on demand, from different elements. Even those theorists who see the mind as a representational device do not necessarily agree with the classical, rule-based, symbolic memory architecture – instead proposing other alternative more flexible and dynamic models of human conceptual thought, such as situated simulations, feedforward nets and other more connectionist mechanisms (for a review, see Barsalou, 2003).

The meaning of conceptual change then follows from an understanding of what has to be changed: (a) coherent structures and rules or (b) assemblies of diverse individual elements. So the debate about coherent structures vs. dynamic coupling and coordination, in relation to conceptual change (and transfer), thus cuts across accounts of brain, mind, consciousness, discourse, environment and body. Table 6.1 provides a succinct summary.

Table 6.1 Coherent structures vs. dynamic coupling views across the theoretical accounts of mind

	Knowledge is in the:	Coherent structures	Dynamic coupling
Neuropsychological	Brain	Nonconscious and conscious brain processes are discontinuous (for a review, see Damasio, 1994)	Nonconscious and conscious processes are highly interrelated (Damasio, 2012)
Mentalist	Mind	Symbolic memory architecture (Anderson, 1983)	Connectionist nets (Bereiter, 1991)
Phenomenological	Consciousness, experience	Beliefs, theories, mental models (Chi & Roscoe, 2002)	Knowledge in pieces and other mental resources (diSessa, 2008)
Situated sociocultural	Culture and discourse	Cultural models, codes, habits, routines (Holland & Quinn, 1987)	Interaction, shared meaning-making, sense-making (Engeström, 2008)
Environmentalist	Skilful perception, coordination of environment, body, action	Classical skill acquisition theories (Colley & Beech, 1989), behaviourism (Skinner, 1938)	Extended, embodied, embedded, enacted cognition (Clark, 2011)

6.4   Troublesome Knowledge and Threshold Concepts

While many psychologists, over the last three decades, have been looking for generic answers to educational challenges by studying students' higher-order cognitions, university educators themselves have looked more closely at the core of the disciplines, trying to find solutions to students' learning troubles that depend upon discipline-specific concepts (e.g. Land, Meyer, & Smith, 2008).

The idea of 'threshold concepts' is underpinned by an insight that there are certain kinds of 'hard to get', epistemologically tricky, knowledge that are essential to the disciplines and professions. As Land, Meyer, and Baillie (2010) put it:

> ... the approach builds on the notion that there are certain concepts, or certain learning experiences, which resemble passing through a portal, from which a new perspective opens up, allowing things formerly not perceived to come into view. This permits a new and previously inaccessible way of thinking about something. It represents a transformed way of understanding, or interpreting, or viewing something, without which the learner cannot progress, and results in a reformulation of the learners' frame of meaning. The thresholds approach also emphasises the importance of disciplinary contexts. As a consequence of comprehending a threshold concept there may thus be a transformed internal view of subject matter, subject landscape, or even world view. (Land et al., 2010, p. ix)

Imagery relating to gateways, portals, thresholds and *liminality* (from the Latin for 'threshold') is widely used in this area of literature, within which threshold concepts are said to be:

Transformative: once understood, a threshold concept changes the way in which people see the subject. That is, such understanding results in a shift in their perspective, and perhaps even their values.

Irreversible: once understood, a threshold concept is not likely to be forgotten; it will be difficult to 'unlearn'.

Integrative: threshold concepts are likely to bring together different aspects of the subject that previously did not appear to be related.

Bounded: these concepts delineate a particular conceptual space and serve a specific purpose; they do not necessarily have a meaning beyond the specific discipline.

Troublesome: they can be troublesome for a number of reasons, which we explain below.

Threshold concepts are distinct from what university teachers describe as 'core concepts' – the traditionally acknowledged conceptual 'building blocks' that allow progress in understanding of the subject. These building blocks are essential, but they do not *necessarily* lead to a *conceptually different* view of the subject, and not all of them are troublesome. Threshold concepts, in contrast, are associated with certain deep learning difficulties and their learning involves 'transformation'.

The process of transformation generally includes three modes: preliminal, liminal and postliminal (Meyer, Land & Baillie, 2010). In the *preliminal* mode, students encounter the troublesome knowledge inherent in the threshold concept which instigates the transformation. This is followed by the *liminal* mode, in which students integrate new, and discard previous, understandings and undergo an ontological and epistemic shift. In this state, as Meyer et al. (2010) put it, 'an integration of new knowledge occurs which requires a reconfiguring of the learner's prior conceptual schema and a *letting go* or *discarding of any* earlier conceptual stance' (p. xi, emphasis added). The effects of this transformation are consequential. Thus, in the final *postliminal* mode, once learners cross the conceptual boundary, the transformation becomes irreversible and evident in changes in their thinking and discourse. Throughout this transformation process, students encounter a fourth *subliminal* mode, in which they start to recognise and understand the 'tacit underlying game' that underpins troublesome knowledge. As Land and Meyer (2010) say,

> There is variation in the extent of students' awareness and understanding of an underlying game or episteme – a 'way of knowing' – which may be a crucial determinant of progression (epistemological and ontological) within a conceptual domain. Such *tacit understanding or epistemic fluency* might develop in the absence of any formalised knowledge of the concept itself; it might for the learner represent a non-specialist way of thinking. (Land & Meyer, 2010, p. 64, emphasis added)

While this underlying way of knowing and epistemic fluency is considered to be critical, the subliminal mode is seen as a *tacit* mode, where changes just gradually happen:

> In what we might term the 'subliminal' mode, there is often an 'underlying game' in which ways of thinking and practising that are often left tacit come to be recognised, grappled with and gradually understood. (Meyer et al., 2010, p. xi)

The whole transformational process may involve some recursiveness and oscillation around the previous understanding, but generally such 'grappling' is considered to be a temporary 'perspective transformation' state. The transformation involves social repositioning of the learner; thus adopting the specialised expert discourse is seen as no less important than developing the conception. Meyer and Land (2005) emphasise

> ... the interrelatedness of the learner's identity with thinking and language. Threshold concepts lead not only to transformed thought but to a transfiguration of identity and adoption of an extended discourse. (Meyer & Land, 2005, p. 375)

The threshold concept perspective generally underscores the revolutionary nature of such transformations and the replacement of previous concepts and understandings with completely different views. 'The prevailing perception has to be let go of and eventually discarded so that a process of integration might begin' (Meyer et al., 2010, p. xiii), 'there can be no ultimate full return to the pre-liminal state' (Meyer & Land, 2005, p. 376). Rational reflection with an emphasis on affective processes is seen as the main pedagogical strategy through which this transformation is achieved.

Research on threshold concepts has generated interesting insights into the nature of knowledge in different specialities. The work moves beyond the seemingly narrow notion of a 'concept' to address broader questions of knowing, knowledge practices, ways of seeing, emotions and experiences. It turns out that university teachers *within* each discipline show some consensus around the threshold concepts in their own discipline. However, what those threshold concepts are, why they are threshold and troublesome and what kind of curriculum change is needed to teach them more successfully vary *across* disciplines. For example, Carmichael (2012) comments that in engineering this has been mainly about identifying specific troublesome or integrative concepts that are taught in fragmented ways and redesigning around them a more effective curriculum. In social anthropology, this has been related to the development of the notion of 'reflexivity', the categories of culture and gender, the ability to reflect, not so much about practices, but more about spaces in which problematic issues could be made visible and thought through. In theology, the focus has been on challenges associated with 'reading biblical texts as literature' and seeing things differently. In English literature, it has been related the notion of 'ethical reading'.

6.4.1   Issues with Threshold Concepts from a Grounded Perspective

In our view, there are two important challenges in understanding research on threshold concepts.

First, as Perkins (2006) argues, what is troublesome partly depends on other factors – for example, students' approaches to learning have a powerful influence, as some students will simply try to resolve 'troublesome' problems by relying on memory and routine procedures, rather than trying to achieve a deep 'insider' feel for the ideas. Furthermore, students may have challenges achieving deep understanding because of certain inherent features of the knowledge. Perkins identifies five types of *troublesome knowledge* that inhibit this deeper learning:

Ritual knowledge – has a routine and meaningless feel and character. It forms a part of social or individual rituals. Dates and names and other simple facts can also have this character.

Inert knowledge – knowledge that students know, but do not use actively, does not connect to the world around them and does not transfer to real problems and other contexts.

Conceptually difficult knowledge – including counter-intuitive scientific knowledge, such as Newton's laws. Students learn this kind of knowledge in a rote, ritualised way and apply it to quantitative questions in school; but they use their intuitive beliefs to tackle qualitative problems and problems encountered outside the classroom.

Foreign or alien knowledge – knowledge that conflicts with one's own understanding, like seeing historical events from a present-day perspective, understanding the different value systems of other cultures and ethnic groups from within one's own value system and recognising that many situations 'allow multiple serious, sincere, well-elaborated perspectives that deserve understanding' (Perkins, 2006, p. 39).

Tacit knowledge – knowledge about which people are only peripherally aware or are entirely unconscious (as when using language, or conducting inquiry, in a domain without being conscious of what they are doing). While tacit knowledge can be highly efficient, Perkins notes

> ... learners' tacit presumptions can miss the target by miles, and teachers' more seasoned tacit presumptions can operate like conceptual summaries that learners never manage to detect or track. (op cit., 40)

However, there is a sharp discontinuity between the nature of troublesome knowledge and the classical mode-based model of transformation adopted in the 'troublesome concept' pedagogies and research that we outlined above.

What is common across the five kinds of troublesome knowledge listed above is that they are all linked to what could be called 'grounded knowledge' – the kind of understandings that link what we know and how we act in the real world (see Sects. 6.2 above and 6.5 below). In contrast, the language describing (the learning of) threshold concepts and troublesome knowledge evokes ideas such as 'irreversibility', 'impossibility of progression' and the necessity of radical 'all or nothing' transformation in the students' minds. This assumption about students' *radically flawed* mental models or beliefs locks students' understanding up in their rational minds and invites teachers to draw upon the pedagogies of negative rationalism which discard students' intuitive knowledge: knowledge which is grounded in their experiences (see Sect. 6.3, above).

Disconnecting the embedded and embodied nature of troublesome knowledge and seeing a threshold concept as a deep-rooted 'flaw' in a student's intuitive mental model – one which needs to be eradicated and replaced – creates an unproductive opposition between knowing as intuitive situated action and articulated formal conceptual knowledge.

The key implication is that this view, by attributing students' learning difficulties to their minds (and mental models), significantly underestimates the extent to which troublesome knowledge and threshold concepts are *experiential* – that is, concepts grounded in situated experiences and students' mental resources.

The second issue we observe arises from the fact that concepts serve different purposes in human sense-making, problem-solving and inquiry (diSessa & Sherin, 1998; Keil & Silberstein, 1998). Indeed, Perkins (2006) lists several such functions:

Categorisers – most fundamentally, humans use concepts as conceptual categories for making sense of the world around them. 'They [concepts] carve up the world we already see and often posit the unseen or even the unseeable' (p. 41).

Frameworks and epistemic games – clusters of concepts set the stage for a more elaborate function. These clusters of concepts form activity systems or conceptual games. For example, the 'Freudean self' provides a broad scaffold for interpretation, diagnosis and treatment; styles of art (impressionism, surrealism, etc.) provide means for marking trends and tracing influences.

Many of the troubles relating to concepts do not arise from their *categorical* function (as described above), but from the larger *conceptual games* around them – 'the activity systems that animate concepts' (Perkins, 2006, p. 41). As Perkins says, it is easy to 'get' the concept of 'bias' in historical sources, but harder to use it in actually analysing historical sources or in making other decisions about historical evidence. Many troubles come from their tacit nature – teachers play the epistemic games of their disciplines fluently and automatically, so trouble arises from the fact that the games and their rules receive little explicit attention. However, threshold concept pedagogies that focus mainly on reflective discourse pay little attention to the material embodied nature of epistemic practices and epistemic games in many professions. We must not forget that experts become skilful at epistemic work not just by reflecting but by actually using the epistemic tools of the domain and playing the epistemic games of the profession (we develop these ideas further in Chap. 9 and after). We now return to the nature of the human cognitive system that underpins conceptual understanding.

6.5 Grounding Conceptual Knowledge in Experience: Situated Concepts

While conceptual knowledge accounts for only a part of what people know, it plays a fundamental role in *organising* human cognition. Just as human existence in a material world involves static, dynamic and emerging things (a chair, hammer, air, wind, rain, law, thought), similarly, human cognition is impossible without concepts for naming those things. That said, how the human conceptual system works and how it relates to experiences in the material and physical world are still not well understood.

A useful way of thinking about some of the fundamental differences between views of human knowledge and of how knowledge relates to the world can be found in Lawrence Barsalou's (2009) contrast between the *semantic* and *situated* views of conceptual systems; these dominate contemporary cognitive research.

The *semantic* view sees human memory as composed of two independent parts: (a) episodic memory, which contains records of experiential episodes with temporal and spatial relationships and other experiential details, and (b) semantic memory, which contains conceptual knowledge from which episodic details[4] have been filtered out. On this view, semantic memory is held to be relatively autonomous from episodic memory and operates independently from perception, action, emotions and other senses. Semantic knowledge is held to be represented in an internal symbolic (amodal) form that is different from (stripped of) the modalities of the

---

[4] Such as the circumstances in which the concepts were first encountered (e.g. the name and appearance of the physics teacher who first taught you Newton's laws).

external world, such as vision, action or affect. Semantic memory representations are relatively stable and generally shared among people.

Barsalou, drawing on recent neuroscientific evidence, rejects this semantic view and argues that human conceptual knowledge is *inherently situated*. He argues that human conceptual knowledge remains tightly linked ('packaged') with information from the background situations in which it was encountered. He specifically identifies four types of situated information that is stored together with conceptual categories: (a) selected properties of the conceptual category relevant to the current situation, (b) information about the background settings, (c) possible actions that could be taken and (d) perceptions of internal states that one might have experienced during previous encounters with the conceptual phenomena, such as affects, motivations, cognitive states and cognitive operations. Barsalou (2009) argues that the conceptual system is not abstract and detached, rather it

> ... constructs situated conceptualizations dynamically, tailoring them to the current needs of situated action ... [constructing experiences of] being there with category members. (Barsalou, 2009, p. 251)

These 'packages' prepare humans for situated action and can be used to guide a goal-directed activity that unfolds in a new situation. The concept is not separated from the conceptualiser. The actions and introspective states, which are *re-enacted* during the process of simulating a category, create for the conceptualiser the experience of being in the situation. In short, conceptual thinking does not involve processing of abstract, amodal symbols; rather, it is a creative, dynamic re-enactment of cognitive states that are distributed across modality-specific systems (e.g. audition, movement, emotion).

Barsalou argues that the conceptual system supports a range of 'online' and 'offline' cognitive activities. In online processing – that is, when people are engaged in a purpose-oriented physical activity – the conceptual system (a) supports perceptual processing via figure-ground segregation, anticipation and filling in gaps; (b) predicts the entities and events likely to be present; (c) produces mapping into categories of those entities and events; and (d) produces inferences, based on categorisations, about what they are likely to do next, how to interact with them and other actions.

In offline processing – that is, when people think about entities that are not present – the conceptual system supports memory, as it helps reconstruct things that are remembered; it supports language by supporting interpretation and generation of inferences; it supports thought as it represents entities, events and states that constitute the content of reasoning, decision-making and other similar cognitive tasks. Situated concepts play important roles in optimising cognitive processing and prediction as simulated representations are selective, episodic and simplify many tasks. Barsalou also notes that similar conceptualisation processes underpin concepts that have quite diverse origins, including concepts developed through experience and concepts established by means of reasoning. Overall, this conceptual system is highly flexible. Previously remembered concepts may be merged together during re-enactment in a variety of ways. Further, deliberative efforts to combine components and simulations of several conceptual instances can produce novel conceptual categories – that is, new knowledge.

Such a conceptual system is not a traditional representational device, rather it is a performative device for creating situated conceptualisations.

Conceptual knowledge is not a global description of a category that functions as a detached database about its instances. Instead, conceptual knowledge is the ability to construct situated conceptualizations of the category that serve agents in particular situations. (Barsalou, Kyle Simmons, Barbey, & Wilson, 2003, p. 89)

In research over the last three decades (or more), an unhelpful Cartesian divide has persisted, between understanding and doing, mind and body, representation and interaction, cognitive and sociocultural, symbolic and situated and material and conceptual. Recent research on grounded cognition is providing more and better evidence about the productive roles of experiences that are outside the 'symbolic mind' – including attitudes, social perception and emotion – in generating conceptual understanding and supporting ways of knowing that are beyond the situated, including conceptual knowledge, mindfulness and everyday creativity (Barsalou, 1999, 2008, 2009; Barsalou & Prinz, 1997).

What Barsalou has been saying persuasively, over the last 20 years, now seems obvious: human understanding, backgrounds, related actions and internal states are closely related aspects of the same conceptual system. In short, perception, understanding, doing and being are not separated by walls in the human mind or brain, but are separated by the situations in which people experience these different ways of knowing. Thinking and other conceptual mechanisms of the mind are inherently grounded in the situated experiences of the environment, the body and the act of perceiving and acting.

This view of human cognition as 'grounded' in situated experiences provokes the question of whether these Cartesian divides have not been merely 'threshold concepts' for educators and educational researchers, who have sought to replace students' situated experiences with abstract concepts and have missed the continuity between conceptual knowledge and practical experience. Conceptual knowledge for knowledgeable action can and should be grounded in local contexts and in 'hands-on' experiences. (Nurses do not just look after the abstract category of 'hypertension'; rather, they centre their work on, and think about, the patient with hypertension – a specific instance, if you like, of the situated concept.)

6.6   Conceptual Understanding and Actionable Knowledge

In order to help students develop actionable knowledge for professional work, we need to have a feasible account of a mechanism for how actionable knowledge operates and develops. What kinds of mental entities underpin the professional understanding that enables action? How are these entities entangled in action? How do they change? In short, what kinds of mental resources could provide students with a sufficient start for (a) fluent decisions and actions in more familiar, ordinary situations and (b) further changes and reconfigurations of knowledge and skills to cope with new situations and to innovate – that is, to help them be 'workplace ready' *and* prepared for lifelong learning and innovation in a changing work environment?

Few pedagogical models of professional education and expertise have been sufficiently careful in distinguishing between the human conceptual system, through which the mind brings forth meaning, and the normative conceptual system employed in expert discourse. Further, symbolic (information processing) accounts of the human conceptual system have informed, in a deep sense, much of the pedagogical thinking that has emerged in 'all or nothing' and 'something or nothing' accounts of conceptual change (e.g. Meyer & Land, 2005). Pedagogies for confronting troublesome knowledge and dislodging habituated skills – while they may have shifted some distance away from a purely rationalistic logic – have nevertheless maintained their deeply negative 'deficiency' view towards the intuitions students bring to higher education. However, such pedagogical ideas have not proved strong enough to account for the fluency and flexibility that is observed, needed and valued in the successful performance of expert (and novice) professionals in dynamically changing workplace settings. It is not a surprise that a common response to this conundrum has been to run away from conceptual knowledge and skills and look for answers solely in terms of students' dispositions and other 'human qualities' (Barnett, 2004).

In contrast, our account – broadly drawing on Greeno's (2012) notions of 'formal knowledge' and 'functional knowledge' – makes an explicit distinction between *normative* knowledge (and concepts that have formal definitions and formal uses in expert discourse) and *enacted* knowledge (and experiential concepts employed in human sense-making and skill). It builds on the fundamental assumption that actionable knowledge is grounded, dynamic knowledge. From this perspective, professional understanding and learning are a form of knowledge and knowing that draws upon, and constitutively entangles, (a) some core features of the common-sense understandings that underpin everyday sense-making and action and (b) the normative forms of knowledge embedded in the formal expert discourse of a professional community. Following this line of argument, we suggest that actionable knowledge is underpinned by a conceptual system of what we call *actionable concepts* – including *actionable conceptual and epistemic mental resources*. These actionable concepts project, blend and entangle the normative conceptual system of the professional field with the common-sense experiential concepts and ways of thinking developed through experiences and engagement with the world (they are absolutely not reducible to replacing the latter with the former).

'Action' and 'knowledge' play equally fundamental roles in the human conceptual system – so professional understanding and learning should constitutively entangle these two aspects of intelligent behaviour.

On the one hand, actionable knowledge is materially and socially *thick* knowledge – grounded in experiences, perception, introspection, affect and action. Such knowledge comes from (less articulated) empirical engagement with authentic situations. Thus, the human conceptual system that underpins sense-making and skill is, at least in part, intuitive, opportunistic and heuristic, closely coupled with the affordances of the situation, previous experiences, perception and action (Barsalou, 1999, 2009). It is therefore *not* predominantly abstract and rational.

On the other hand, professional understanding draws on substantial amounts of quite decontextualised knowledge, learnt via discourse, but extracted from the natural contexts in which it has been created and will be enacted in the future. To be clear, we are not underestimating the value of formal conceptual knowledge. On the contrary, we believe there is sufficient evidence, from such knowledge-intensive professions as medicine, engineering and the law, to be in no doubt that formal conceptual knowledge and formal reasoning strategies provide an important resource for expert decision-making in many complex, non-routine situations (e.g. Patel, Arocha, & Zhang, 2005). Indeed, the conceptual resources and ways in which experts draw upon this knowledge in solving problems in non-routine situations offer a good basis for thinking about what kinds of 'actionable conceptual system' (including strategies) may prove to be productive for students who are entering the professional field. (For novices, many situations are new and complex. Thus productive expert ways of thinking in unfamiliar circumstances have a reasonably good chance of overlapping with ways of thinking that might be helpful to novices initially and throughout their career.)

In short, a well-formed conceptual system for actionable knowledge should (a) draw upon and integrate different kinds of mental resources, from formal concepts of the domain to situated conceptualisations, construed in the here and now, through direct engagement with an encountered challenge and (b) be flexible, and well enough tuned, to attend to a variety of contexts and deal with situational variations. That is, conceptual thought for knowledgeable action cannot operate in a closed, decontextualised, conceptual space which does not have a solid connection to details of the situation. (We elaborate on this in Chaps. 17 and 18.)

6.7 Transfer

The two broad views on the nature of conceptual understanding and conceptual change permeating our analyses above can also be seen in the literature on transfer (diSessa & Wagner, 2005; Lobato, 2012; Wagner, 2006, 2010).

Those views which see conceptual learning and change as a sudden shift from one (incorrect) to another (correct) abstract and coherent conceptual system explain students' difficulties with transfer as a failure to assimilate a new situation into an existing abstract conceptual system. According to this view, the abstract conceptual structure should already be in place. Transfer can start once conceptual change is finished.

The knowledge-in-pieces perspective, in contrast, locates the issue of transfer rather differently (Wagner, 2006, 2010). From this perspective, the ability to use a concept in one context does not necessarily imply an ability to use the concept across all contexts. Learning a concept requires a coordination of a range of elements associated with a specific context,

To understand transfer and its problems more clearly, it is useful to look more deeply at the nature of the conceptual structures that underpin transfer. We outline three views on these structures: 'models', 'modules' and 'modalities'. As a part of the latter view, we introduce an actor-oriented view of transfer, which is particularly helpful in considering transfer in professional education and work (Lobato, 2012; Nemirovsky, 2011).

6.7.1   The Model Perspective

The model perspective is associated with mainstream cognitive research. From this perspective, transfer can be defined in terms of someone having a formal abstract concept and being able to apply it to diverse contexts by identifying abstract connections between new tasks and what is already familiar.[5] These connections can be made using one or more of a variety of mechanisms, ranging from a simple direct mapping between the abstract principles and the situation to a cognitively much more costly application of interpretative rules for translating previously learnt declarative knowledge into a set of procedures relevant for a task in a given situation (see, e.g. Nokes, 2009). A representative formulation of this model view can be found in Fuchs et al. (2003). They describe transfer as a two-stage process of abstraction and metacognition:

> To *abstract* a principle is to identify a generic quality or pattern across instances of the principle. In formulating an abstraction, a individual *deletes details across exemplars*, which are irrelevant to the abstract category (e.g., ignoring the fact that an airplane is metal, and that a bird has feathers, to formulate the abstraction of "flying things"). These abstractions are represented in symbolic form and avoid contextual specificity, so they can be applied to other instances or across situations. Because abstractions, or schemas, subsume related cases, they promote transfer. With *metacognition*, an individual *withholds* an initial response and, instead, deliberately examines the task at hand and generates alternative solutions by considering ways in which the novel task shares connections with familiar tasks. (Fuchs et al., 2003, p. 294, emphases added)

Lobato (2012) summarises the common features of this perspective on transfer:

> First, the formation of sufficiently abstract representations is a necessary condition for transfer (so that properties and relations can be recognized in both initial and transfer situations), where abstraction is conceived as a process of decontextualization ... Second, explanations for the occurrence of transfer are based on the psychological invariance of symbolic mental representations ... Finally, transfer occurs if the representations that people construct of initial learning and transfer situations are identical, overlap, or can be related via mapping. (Lobato, 2012, p. 233)

---

[5] Threshold concepts (Sect. 6.4) can also be thought of in this way.

As this perspective builds on the classic symbol-processing architecture, human perception and human conception are seen as two independent mechanisms of the human mind: one 'perceives' and the other does the 'thinking'. The transfer is the job of the former rather than the latter mechanism.

6.7.2 The Module Perspective

The second way is to see transfer as 'modular'. Rather than having one structure that accounts for a certain concept, this perspective posits a set of context-sensitive mental resources that allow one to see situations as similar and transfer knowledge from one context to another. Redish (2004) in physics and Wagner (2006, 2010) in mathematics illustrate this kind of transfer.

The main principle that underpins this view is that transfer does not happen via constructing and having 'expert-like' abstractions. Instead it involves constructing middle-ground phenomenological abstractions called 'coordination classes' which operate in specific contexts and then projecting them to a common 'expert-like' structure. These coordination classes are sets of 'systematically connected ways for seeing things in the world' (diSessa & Sherin, 1998, p. 117). They are grounded in experiences and contexts, but by being projected to generic structures, work as appropriate substitutes for formal ways of thinking in particular contexts. From this perspective,

> Transfer is understood not as the all-or-nothing transportation of an abstract knowledge structure across situations, but as the incremental growth, systematization, and organization of knowledge resources that only gradually extend the span of situations in which a concept is perceived as applicable. (Wagner, 2006, p. 10)

This view of transfer shifts the focus of conceptual learning from the formation of abstract representations to developing capacities to 'read out' contextual details and firmly link conceptual understanding with a growing diversity of situated experiences of the phenomenon in the world. As Wagner (2006) explains,

> ... transfer is the natural outgrowth of increased understanding, and understanding a principle is inseparable from developing appropriate readout strategies and coordination knowledge, as well as particular concept projections, that permit it to be useful in a variety of situations. The more complex and varied a particular knowledge frame grows, the more likely it is to be cued across many situations, and the more readily and flexibly it can be used to interpret any situation in which it is applied. (op. cit., pp. 64–65)

Attention to particularities of the context is the key to transfer in this 'module-like' organisation. It is not about formulating abstractions by deleting contextual details, but *specifically paying attention to them*, recognising similarities and differences between two contexts and projecting to a similar overarching concept. This perspective draws on the 'knowledge-in pieces' view of conceptual change and learning (diSessa 1988, 1993; and see Sect. 6.3.3). The initial context-specific abstractions may even be learnt without much formal teaching, but rather are gradually projected and integrated into a more coherent and coordinated conceptual machinery of complex conceptual thinking.

If we take this perspective on transfer seriously, the traditional view of transfer that is based on 'formal concepts' as assimilatory structures used by experts to 'see the world' is at odds with how transfer really happens.

> In this sense, the structure one perceives in a situation is actively constructed through an interaction of available contextual affordances and prior learning experiences, thereby denying a temporal sequence of *first* representing or structuring a situation and *then* applying prior knowledge. (Wagner, 2010, p. 448, original emphasis)

As Wagner (2010) argues – and others illustrate (Gupta et al., 2010) – even experts continue to use different non-formal, experientially constructed, conceptual projections for making sense of scientific phenomena. While abstract principles allow a scientific community to construct general theories and a shared understanding of various phenomena, these principles do not necessarily correspond to the cognitive mechanisms underpinning human reasoning and sense-making about these phenomenon.

> If different contexts cue different knowledge elements, and if different structural interpretations are more "natural" to different situations, there is no reason to expect that those varying forms of knowledge will be less useful or abandoned in the future. (Wagner, 2010, p. 475)

6.7.3 The Modality Perspective

The third way is to think about transfer of concepts in action from the situated conceptualisation perspective – a concept as modality coordination (Barsalou, 1999, 2009). In this case, the concept is not seen as situated in a one-dimensional context, as it is in the modular view. Rather, many cultural and action frames structure perception simultaneously, and a number of senses are involved: the concept and the context become multimodal.

> They [agents] perform sets of coordinated tasks that produce coherent behaviour. For example, organisms do not produce categorisation alone. Instead, they perform categorisation together with perception, inference, action, reward, and affect. (Barsalou et al., 2007, p. 83)

As Barsalou (1999, 2009) argues, such a system is grounded in perception and action. Multiple modalities of the phenomenon experienced in the world – via vision, touch, smell, audition, emotion and so on – are an integral part of knowledge representations and processes through which knowing becomes possible. For example, a pianist's ability to simulate action underlies their ability to recognise records of their own performances and synchronise with them (Keller, Knoblich, & Repp, 2007). Further, much of this cognition is closely coupled with specific background information in which the phenomenon was experienced. Barsalou (2009) illustrates this with the observation that when people encounter the word 'piano' in a sentence about moving pianos, they primarily activate information related to its modality of being 'heavy', whereas when they encounter the same word in a sentence about playing the piano, they think about a 'pleasant sound'. When asked to think about a scene that is not present, people usually infer background details. Further, this simulation extends to possible situated actions, emotions and other experiences.

Moreover, the concept is situated in the frame of a problem that is structured around the perception–action interface (following Barsalou). Thus, it is in the same conceptual neighbourhood as other concepts relevant to interpreting the situation. From this perspective, *transfer is not an application of a ready-made conceptual package but the process that emerges from blending different coordinated ways of structuring a situation* (a.k.a. frames) *and fusing different multimodal conceptual structures into one actionable concept* that guides perception of the situation and action.

This modality perspective closely resembles the view of Actor-Oriented Transfer (AOT), which is gaining some recognition in educational research (Lobato, 2012). This view of transfer similarly emphasises the highly interpretative nature of human conceptual thinking, particularly when people work with problems in complex, semantically rich domains. In such domains, problems are often open to multiple, usually idiosyncratic, ways of structuring various aspects of the situation and naturally lean to diverse interpretations and solutions. Perception and structuring of the encountered situation are seen as highly interactive and sensitive to the context process that heavily leans on personal goals, perceived affordances and diverse prior experiences:

> *Structuring* is contrasted with the view of extracting a *structure* from a situation, where . . . a closer correspondence between the external world and mental structures is often assumed. Relatedly, AOT is rooted in the notion of reflective abstraction, . . . which is a constructive rather than inductive formulation of abstraction. It focuses on the abstraction of regularities in records of experience in relationship to one's goals and expectations, rather than on regularities inherent in a situation or the encoding of common properties across instances. (Lobato, 2012, p. 243, original emphasis)

In contrast to the traditional model view that focusses on the transfer of well-defined strategies, or other knowledge, from one situation to another, the AOT perspective takes a holistic view and focusses on how students' prior experiences, independently from their origins, shape students' activity – constructing situated conceptualisations rather than transferring predetermined strategies. Transfer is about coordinating individual cognitive processes and social interaction in material, culturally shaped environments via 'noticing'. As Lobato emphasises:

> . . . transfer is a distributed phenomenon across individual cognition, social interactions, material resources, and normed practices. <. . .> By noticing, we do not mean simply "paying attention" but rather the selecting and processing of particular properties, features, or conceptual objects, when multiple sources of information compete for one's attention. (op. cit., pp. 241–242)

In professional work, this learning to notice, as Goodwin (1994) remarks, is not a simple psychological process but a complex, socially situated activity.

Table 6.2 Main features of the three perspectives on transfer

	Model view	Module view	Modality view
Mental constructs for transfer	Mental schemas, beliefs	Coordination classes and projections	Mechanisms for constructing multimodal situated conceptualisations
Main aspects that contribute to transfer	Mind	Mind and context	Mind, social interactions, language, cultural artefacts, normed practices
Nature of problems	Generic tasks with a rule-oriented, procedural focus	Common context-specific problems	Semantically rich problem domains
Point of view	An observer's view	Link between observer's and actor's views	An actor's view
What transfers	Well-defined strategies, solution methods, action schemas	Bottom-up constructed conceptualisations and solution methods	Construction of conceptualisations
Main difficulty of transfer	*Mapping* that relates features of representations constructed during initial learning and new transfer situations	*Projection* of various experiential concepts to the same abstract conceptual principle or category	*Noticing* – selecting, interpreting and working with particular features when multiple sources of information compete for attention

Table 6.2 summarises the main features of the model, module and modality views on transfer.

6.8   Dynamic Expertise, Transfer and Innovation

6.8.1   Dynamic Expertise as Coordination

The link between perception and conception tends to be very intimate and complex in professional knowledgeable action. Rules and logic do not replace fine-tuned perception in complex, situated, problem-solving. Understanding emerges from the coordination of the two.

This is nicely illustrated by Gupta et al. (2010) who show that expert physicists do not reason using one correct ontology that underpins deep properties of physical, non-material phenomena (such as light). Rather, they switch between ontologically correct ways of reasoning about the emergent processes and the matter-based reasoning that underpins 'surface' or 'naïve' intuitions. They argue,

> Our sense organs and our brain's tools for interpreting the data from these sense organs are an evolutionary 'satisfice'. (Gupta et al., 2010, p. 305)

Science tries to understand the world at a deeper analytical level. Scientific theories supplement our limited direct experiences and ontological categories. But the way they do this is by mixing and blending the observable and non-observable, context dependent and abstract, rather than by replacing one ontological category with another.

At the core of this way of reasoning, is what Gupta et al. call a 'dynamic perspective'

> [The] dynamic perspective emphasises the development of skills to evaluate the productiveness of multiple descriptions. <...> Developing expertise means that students become aware of the productiveness and limitations of the descriptions they use and the resources that they have at hand. (op. cit., p. 316)

Such mixing, switching and blending become evident in experts' and students' thinking. For example, teachers do not work with abstract theories or strategies that are based on a distinct ontology that underpins the concept 'constructivism'. They work in real classroom with real children – an ontology that underpins material and social arrangements. Similarly, a pharmacist does not dispense abstract chemical properties to a patient; she dispenses 'pills' and 'boxes' as medications. In essence, the conceptual is blended with the material, and concepts have a meaning in professional practice if they can travel across 'surface' material and 'deep' conceptual/ontological categories of professional knowledge (we illustrate this in Chaps. 17 and 18).

This contrasts with much of the threshold concepts' literature, which focusses on getting expert discourse 'straight' as the main objective of learning and which aims to suppress discourse and intuitions that do not fit this expert shape.

6.8.2 Dynamic Transfer and Innovation

Schwartz, Varma and Martin (2008) make an important observation noting that knowledge 'as repetition' and knowledge 'as use of prior learning' are not the same.

> Asking how people become more efficient via repetition is different from asking how people build on prior knowledge. (Schwartz et al., 2008, p. 482)

They go on to point out that education aims to equip students with knowledge that is 'ready for application' and also to prepare students to act as innovators in the future. They relate this to a discussion of transfer. They draw an explicit distinction between 'transfer for innovation' and change and 'transfer for repetition' – 'dynamic transfer' and 'similarity transfer' (see Table 6.3). *Similarity transfer* primarily concerns situations when knowledge learnt in one situation is deployed in another; *dynamic transfer* concerns situations when prior learning is used to create new knowledge. Dynamic transfer involves coordination of different sources of behaviour – mental, social and physical – and different types of knowledge, including different states of understanding and abilities.

Table 6.3 Comparison of similarity transfer and dynamic transfer

	Similarity transfer	Dynamic transfer
Purpose	Transfer for repetition	Transfer for change and innovation
Mechanism	'This is like that' – transfer by analogy, mapping	'This goes with that' – coordinating and making relationships among mental, social and physical systems
Concept	Well-formed before transfer	Formed during transfer
Formation	Concepts are formed in one situation, but applied in another, in new ways	Coordinate separate components to create a new concept first
Conceptual learning	'All or nothing'	An iterative process of building new relationships and new insights

After Schwartz et al. (2008)

How do people learn to be innovative? Schwartz et al. propose that innovative behaviour and thinking involve both similarity transfer and dynamic transfer. In their view, innovation is primarily about the mindset and about learning to see important environmental structures and create external representational resources that enable dynamic transfer.

> [The] ability to transfer and innovate grows from experiences where people gain insight into important environmental structures and their possibilities for interaction. (Schwartz et al., 2008, p. 502)

Keil and Silberstein (1998) make similar point, and link this kind of mindset and skill to the productive cognition of 'expert learners'.

> Expertise itself might require many years to develop if it is defined as requiring both ample experience and the ability to handle novel situations; but expert-like behavior can be exhibited by both novices and children. In such cases the learner is constantly trying to construct new and better knowledge structures for handling a problem, rather than merely trying to shoehorn the problem into older conceptions. <...> The expert learners, on the other hand, are able to create a new category to fit the novel style and try to incorporate it on its own terms. They are willing to expand the limits of their previous knowledge and adapt the knowledge to fit the data. (Keil & Silberstein, 1998, p. 636)

This kind of expertise draws on special kinds of mental constructs – epistemic rather than conceptual resources. We turn to these in the next chapter.

References

Anderson, J. R. (1983). *The architecture of cognition.* Cambridge, MA: Harvard University Press.

Anderson, M. L. (2003). Embodied cognition: A field guide. *Artificial Intelligence, 149*(1), 91–130. doi:10.1016/s0004-3702(03)00054-7.

Anderson, J. R., Reder, L. M., & Simon, H. A. (1996). Situated learning and education. *Educational Researcher, 25*(4), 5–11. doi:10.3102/0013189x025004005.

Atkinson, R. C., & Shiffrin, R. M. (1968). Human memory: A proposed system and its control processes. In K. W. Spence & J. T. Spence (Eds.), *The psychology of learning and motivation* (Vol. 2, pp. 89–195). New York, NY: Academic Press.

Barnett, R. (2004). Learning for an unknown future. *Higher Education Research & Development, 23*(3), 247–260.

Barrows, H. S., & Tamblyn, R. M. (1980). *Problem-based learning: An approach to medical education.* New York, NY: Springer.

Barsalou, L. W. (1999). Perceptual symbol systems. *Behavioral and Brain Sciences, 22,* 577–609.

Barsalou, L. W. (2003). Situated simulation in the human conceptual system. *Language and Cognitive Processes, 18*(5–6), 513–562. doi:10.1080/01690960344000026.

Barsalou, L. W. (2008). Grounded cognition. *Annual Review of Psychology, 59,* 617–645. doi:10.1146/annurev.psych.59.103006.093639.

Barsalou, L. W. (2009). Situating concepts. In P. Robbins & M. Aydede (Eds.), *The Cambridge handbook of situated cognition* (pp. 236–263). Cambridge, MA: Cambridge University Press.

Barsalou, L. W. (2010). Grounded cognition: Past, present, and future. *Topics in Cognitive Science, 2*(4), 716–724. doi:10.1111/j.1756-8765.2010.01115.x.

Barsalou, L. W., Breazeal, C., & Smith, L. (2007). Cognition as coordinated non-cognition. *Cognitive Processing, 8*(2), 79–91. doi:10.1007/s10339-007-0163-1.

Barsalou, L. W., Kyle Simmons, W., Barbey, A. K., & Wilson, C. D. (2003). Grounding conceptual knowledge in modality-specific systems. *Trends in Cognitive Sciences, 7*(2), 84–91. doi:10.1016/s1364-6613(02)00029-3.

Barsalou, L. W., & Prinz, J. J. (1997). Mundane creativity in perceptual symbol systems. In T. B. Ward, S. M. Smith, & J. Vaid (Eds.), *Creative thought: An investigation of conceptual structures and processes* (pp. 267–307). Washington, DC: American Psychological Association.

Bereiter, C. (1991). Implications of connectionism for thinking about rules. *Educational Researcher, 20*(3), 10–16.

Bereiter, C. (2002). *Education and mind in the knowledge age.* Mahwah, NJ: Lawrence Erlbaum Associates.

Billett, S. (1996). Situated learning: Bridging sociocultural and cognitive theorising. *Learning and Instruction, 6*(3), 263–280.

Boivin, N. (2008). *Material cultures, material minds: The impact of things on human thought, society and evolution.* Cambridge, UK: Cambridge University Press.

Boud, D., & Feletti, G. (Eds.). (1997). *The challenge of problem based learning* (2nd ed.). London, UK: Kogan Page.

Bransford, J. D., Brown, A. L., & Cocking, R. R. (Eds.). (1999). *How people learn: Brain, mind, experience, and school.* Washington, DC: National Academy Press.

Brookfield, S. (1986). *Understanding and facilitating adult learning.* Milton Keynes, UK: Open University Press.

Brooks, R. A. (1991). Intelligence without representation. *Artificial Intelligence, 47,* 139–159.

Brooks, R. A., & Stein, L. A. (1994). Building brains for bodies. *Autonomous Robots, 1,* 7–25.

Carmichael, P. (2012). Tribes, territories and threshold concepts: Educational materialisms at work in higher education. *Educational Philosophy and Theory, 44*(sup1), 31–42. doi:10.1111/j.1469-5812.2010.00743.x.

Chi, M. T. H. (2005). Commonsense conceptions of emergent processes: Why some misconceptions are robust. *Journal of the Learning Sciences, 14*(2), 161–199.

Chi, M. T. H., De Leeuw, N., Chiu, M.-H., & Lavancher, C. (1994). Eliciting self-explanations improves understanding. *Cognitive Science, 18*(3), 439–477. doi: http://dx.doi.org/10.1016/0364-0213(94)90016-7

Chi, M. T. H., & Ohlsson, S. (2005). Complex declarative learning. In K. J. Holyoak & R. G. Morrison (Eds.), *The Cambridge handbook of thinking and reasoning* (pp. 371–400). Cambridge, MA: Cambridge University Press.

Chi, M. T. H., & Roscoe, R. (2002). The processes and challenges of conceptual change. In M. Limon & L. Mason (Eds.), *Reconsidering conceptual change: Issues in theory and practice* (pp. 3–27). Dordrecht, The Netherlands: Kluwer.

Clark, A. (1999). Embodied, situated and distributed cognition. In W. Bechtel & G. Graham (Eds.), *A companion to cognitive science* (pp. 506–517). Oxford, UK: Basil Blackwell.

Clark, R. C. (2008). *Building expertise: Cognitive methods for training and performance improvement* (3rd ed.). San Francisco, CA: John Wiley & Sons.

Clark, A. (2011). *Supersizing the mind: Embodiment, action and cognitive extension.* Oxford, UK: Oxford University Press.

Clark, A. (2012). Embodied, embedded, and extended cognition. In K. Frankish & W. M. Ramsey (Eds.), *The Cambridge handbook of cognitive science* (pp. 275–291). New York, NY: Cambridge University Press.

Cole, M. (1996). *Cultural psychology.* Cambridge, MA: Harvard University Press.

Cole, M., Engeström, Y., & Vasquez, O. A. (Eds.). (1997). *Mind, culture, and activity: Seminal papers from the laboratory of comparative human cognition.* Cambridge, UK: Cambridge University Press.

Colley, A., & Beech, J. (Eds.). (1989). *Acquisition and performance of cognitive skills.* Chichester, UK: John Wiley & Sons.

Dall'Alba, G. (2009). *Learning to be professionals.* Dordrecht, The Netherlands: Springer.

Dall'Alba, G., & Barnacle, R. (2007). An ontological turn for higher education. *Studies in Higher Education, 32*(6), 679–691. doi:10.1080/03075070701685130.

Damasio, A. R. (1994). *Descartes' error: Emotion, reason, and the human brain.* New York, NY: G.P. Putnam.

Damasio, A. R. (2012). *Self comes to mind: Constructing the conscious brain.* New York, NY: Vintage Books.

de Jong, T., van Gog, T., Jenks, K., Manlove, S., van Hell, J., Jolles, J., . . . Boschloo, A. (2009). *Explorations in learning and the brain: On the potential of cognitive neuroscience for educational science.* New York, NY: Springer

diSessa, A. A. (1988). Knowledge in pieces. In G. Forman & P. Pufall (Eds.), *Constructivism in the computer age* (pp. 49–70). Hillsdale, NJ: Lawrence Erlbaum Associates.

diSessa, A. A. (1993). Toward an epistemology of physics. *Cognition and Instruction, 10*(2/3), 105–225.

diSessa, A. A. (2000). Does the mind know the difference between the physical and social worlds? In L. Nucci, G. B. Saxe, & E. Turiel (Eds.), *Culture, thought, and development* (pp. 141–166). Mahwah, NJ: Lawrence Erlbaum Associates.

diSessa, A. A. (2006). A history of conceptual change research: Threads and fault lines. In K. Sawyer (Ed.), *The Cambridge handbook of the learning sciences* (pp. 265–293). Cambridge, UK: Cambridge University Press.

diSessa, A. A. (2008). A bird's-eye view of the "pieces" vs. "coherence" controversy (from the "pieces" side of the fence). In S. Vosniadou (Ed.), *International handbook of research on conceptual change* (pp. 35–60). New York, NY: Routledge.

diSessa, A. A., & Sherin, B. L. (1998). What changes in conceptual change? *International Journal of Science Education, 20*(10), 1155–1191.

diSessa, A. A., & Wagner, J. F. (2005). What coordination has to say about transfer. In J. P. Mestre (Ed.), *Transfer of learning from a modern multidisciplinary perspective* (pp. 121–154). Greenwich, CT: Information Age.

Dreyfus, H. L. (1992). *What computers still can't do: A critique of artificial reason.* Cambridge, MA: MIT Press.

Dreyfus, H. L. (2014). *Skilful coping: Essays on the phenomenology of everyday perception and action.* New York, NY: Oxford University Press.

Engeström, Y. (2008). *From teams to knots: Activity-theoretical studies of collaboration and learning at work.* Cambridge, NY: Cambridge University Press.

Fuchs, L. S., Fuchs, D., Prentice, K., Burch, M., Hamlett, C. L., Owen, R., . . . Jancek, D. (2003). Explicitly teaching for transfer: Effects on third-grade students' mathematical problem solving. *Journal of Educational Psychology, 95*(2), 293–305.

Geake, J. (2009). *The brain at school: Educational neuroscience in the classroom.* Buckingham, UK: Open University Press.

Gibson, J. J. (1979). *The ecological approach to visual perception.* Boston, MA: Houghton Mifflin.

Gibson, E. J., & Pick, A. D. (2000). *An ecological approach to perceptual learning and development.* Oxford, UK: Oxford University Press.

Goleman, D. (2006). *Emotional intelligence.* New York, NY: Bantam Books.

Goodson-Espy, T. (2005). *Why reflective abstraction remains relevant in mathematics education research.* Paper presented at the annual meeting of the North American Chapter of the International Group for the Psychology of Mathematics Education.

Goodwin, C. (1994). Professional vision. *American Anthropologist, 96*(3), 606–633.

Greeno, J. G. (2012). Concepts in activities and discourses. *Mind, Culture, and Activity, 19*(3), 310–313. doi:10.1080/10749039.2012.691934.

Gupta, A., Hammer, D., & Redish, E. F. (2010). The case for dynamic models of learners' ontologies in physics. *Journal of the Learning Sciences, 19*(3), 285–321.

Hallden, O., Scheja, M., & Haglund, L. (2008). The contextuality of knowledge: An intentional approach to meaning making and conceptual change. In S. Vosniadou (Ed.), *International handbook of research on conceptual change* (pp. 509–532). New York, NY: Routledge.

Holland, D., & Quinn, N. (Eds.). (1987). *Cultural models in language and thought.* Cambridge, UK: Cambridge University Press.

Hoyles, C., Noss, R., & Pozzi, S. (2001). Proportional reasoning in nursing practice. *Journal for Research in Mathematics Education, 32*(1), 4–27.

Hutchins, E. (1995). *Cognition in the wild.* Cambridge, MA: MIT Press.

Hutchins, E. (2010). Cognitive ecology. *Topics in Cognitive Science, 2*(4), 705–715. doi:10.1111/j.1756-8765.2010.01089.x.

Ingold, T. (2011). *Being alive: Essays on movement, knowledge and description.* Abingdon, UK: Routledge.

Jarvis, P. (2012). *Adult learning in the social context* (Vol. 78). New York, NY: Routledge.

Jonassen, D. H. (2011). *Learning to solve problems: A handbook for designing problem-solving learning environments.* New York, NY: Routledge.

Kapur, M. (2008). Productive failure. *Cognition and Instruction, 26*(3), 379–424. doi:10.1080/07370000802212669.

Kaufman, D. R., Keselman, A., & Patel, V. L. (2008). Changing conceptions in medicine and health. In S. Vosniadou (Ed.), *International handbook of research on conceptual change* (pp. 295–327). New York, NY: Routledge.

Keil, F. C., & Silberstein, C. S. (1998). Schooling and the acquisition of theoretical knowledge. In D. R. Olson & N. Torrance (Eds.), *The handbook of education and human development* (pp. 621–645). Malden, MA: Blackwell.

Keller, P. E., Knoblich, G., & Repp, B. H. (2007). Pianists duet better when they play with themselves: On the possible role of action simulation in synchronization. *Consciousness and Cognition, 16*(1), 102–111. doi:10.1016/j.concog.2005.12.004.

Keselman, A., Kaufman, D. R., & Patel, V. L. (2004). "You can exercise your way out of HIV" and other stories: The role of biological knowledge in adolescents' evaluation of myths. *Science Education, 88*(4), 548–573. doi:10.1002/sce.10135.

Kirschner, P. A., Sweller, J., & Clark, R. E. (2006). Why minimal guidance during instruction does not work: An analysis of the failure of constructivist, discovery, problem-based, experiential, and inquiry-based teaching. *Educational Psychologist, 41*(2), 75–86. doi:10.1207/s15326985ep4102_1.

Kirsh, D. (2009). Problem solving and situated cognition. In P. Robbins & M. Aydede (Eds.), *The Cambridge handbook of situated cognition* (pp. 264–306). Cambridge, MA: Cambridge University Press.

Knorr-Cetina, K. (1999). *Epistemic cultures: How the sciences make knowledge.* Cambridge, MA: Harvard University Press.

Knowland, V. P., & Thomas, M. C. (2014). Educating the adult brain: How the neuroscience of learning can inform educational policy. *International Review of Education, 60*(1), 99–122.

Kuhn, D. (2007). Is direct instruction an answer to the right question? *Educational Psychologist, 42*(2), 109–113.

Land, R., & Meyer, J. H. F. (2010). Threshold concepts and troublesome knowledge (5): Dynamics of assessment. In J. H. F. Meyer, R. Land, & C. Baillie (Eds.), *Threshold concepts and transformational learning* (pp. 61–80). Rotterdam, The Netherlands: Sense.

Land, R., Meyer, J. H. F., & Baillie, C. (2010). Editors' preface: Threshold concepts and transformational learning. In J. H. F. Meyer, R. Land, & C. Baillie (Eds.), *Threshold concepts and transformational learning* (pp. IX–XLII). Rotterdam, The Netherlands: Sense.

Land, R., Meyer, J., & Smith, J. B. (Eds.). (2008). *Threshold concepts within the disciplines.* Rotterdam, The Netherlands: Sense.

Lave, J. (1988). *Cognition in practice.* Cambridge, MA: Cambridge University Press.

Lave, J. (2012). Changing practice. *Mind, Culture, and Activity, 19*(2), 156–171. doi:10.1080/10749039.2012.666317.

Lave, J., & Wenger, E. (1991). *Situated learning: Legitimate peripheral participation.* Cambridge, MA: Cambridge University Press.

Lobato, J. (2012). The actor-oriented transfer perspective and its contributions to educational research and practice. *Educational Psychologist, 47*(3), 232–247. doi:10.1080/00461520.2012.693353.

Malafouris, L. (2013). *How things shape the mind: A theory of material engagement.* Cambridge, MA: MIT Press.

Marton, F., & Pang, M. F. (2008). The idea of phenomenography and the pedagogy of conceptual change. In S. Vosniadou (Ed.), *International handbook of research on conceptual change* (pp. 533–559). New York, NY: Routledge.

McGann, M., De Jaegher, H., & Di Paolo, E. (2013). Enaction and psychology. *Review of General Psychology, 17*(2), 203–209.

Meyer, J. H. F., & Land, R. (2005). Threshold concepts and troublesome knowledge (2): Epistemological considerations and a conceptual framework for teaching and learning. *Higher Education, 49*(3), 373–388.

Meyer, J. H. F., & Land, R. (Eds.). (2006). *Overcoming barriers to student understanding: Threshold concepts and troublesome knowledge.* London, UK: Routledge.

Meyer, J. H. F., Land, R., & Baillie, C. (Eds.). (2010). *Threshold concepts and transformational learning.* Rotterdam, The Netherlands: Sense.

Nemirovsky, R. (2011). Episodic feelings and transfer of learning. *Journal of the Learning Sciences, 20*(2), 308–337.

Nersessian, N. J. (2005). Interpreting scientific and engineering practices: Integrating the cognitive, social, and cultural dimensions. In M. E. Gorman, R. D. Tweney, D. C. Gooding, & A. P. Kincannon (Eds.), *Scientific and technological thinking* (pp. 17–56). Mahwah, NJ: Lawrence Erlbaum Associates.

Newell, A., & Simon, H. A. (1972). *Human problem solving.* Englewood Cliffs, NJ: Prentice-Hall.

Noë, A. (2004). *Action in perception.* Cambridge, MA: MIT Press.

Nokes, T. J. (2009). Mechanisms of knowledge transfer. *Thinking & Reasoning, 15*(1), 1–36.

OECD. (2007). *Understanding the brain: The birth of a learning science.* Paris, France: Centre for Educational Research and Innovation.

Ohlsson, S. (1995). Learning to do and learning to understand: A lesson and a challenge for cognitive modelling. In P. Reimann & H. Spada (Eds.), *Learning in humans and machines: Towards an interdisciplinary learning science* (pp. 37–62). London, UK: Pergamon Press.

Ohlsson, S. (2009). Resubsumption: A possible mechanism for conceptual change and belief revision. *Educational Psychologist, 44*(1), 20–40. doi:10.1080/00461520802616267.

Ohlsson, S. (2011). *Deep learning: How the mind overrides experience.* Cambridge, MA: Cambridge University Press.

Özdemir, G., & Clark, D. B. (2007). An overview of conceptual change theories. *Eurasia Journal of Mathematics, Science & Technology Education, 3*(4), 351–361.

Papert, S. (1980). *Mindstorms: Children, computers, and powerful ideas.* New York, NY: Basic Books.

Patel, V. L., Arocha, J. F., & Zhang, J. (2005). Thinking and reasoning in medicine. In K. J. Holyoak & R. G. Morrison (Eds.), *The Cambridge handbook of thinking and reasoning* (pp. 727–750). Cambridge, MA: Cambridge University Press.

Pecher, D., & Zwaan, R. A. (Eds.). (2010). *Grounding cognition: The role of perception and action in memory, language, and thinking.* New York, NY: Cambridge University Press.

Perkins, D. (2006). Constructivism and troublesome knowledge. In J. H. F. Meyer & R. Land (Eds.), *Overcoming barriers to student understanding: Threshold concepts and troublesome knowledge* (pp. 33–47). London, UK: Routledge.

Perkins, D. (2007). Theories of difficulty. *BJEP Monograph Series II, Number 4 – Student Learning and University Teaching, 1*(1), 31–48.

Perkins, D. N., & Salomon, G. (1989). Are cognitive skills context-bound? *Educational Researcher, 18*(1), 16–25. doi:10.3102/0013189x018001016.

Perry, L. R. (1965). Commonsense thought, knowledge and judgement and their importance for education. *British Journal of Educational Studies, 13*(2), 125–138.

Philip, T. M. (2011). An "ideology in pieces" approach to studying change in teachers' sensemaking about race, racism, and racial justice. *Cognition and Instruction, 29*(3), 297–329. doi:10.1080/07370008.2011.583369.

Redish, E. F. (2004). *A theoretical framework for physics education research: Modeling student thinking.* Proceedings of the International School of Physics, "Enrico Fermi" Course CLVI, Amsterdam.

Rogoff, B., & Lave, J. (Eds.). (1984). *Everyday cognition.* Cambridge, MA: Harvard University Press.

Rommetveit, R. (1978). On negative rationalism in scholarly studies of verbal communication and dynamic residuals in the construction of human subjectivity. In M. M. P. Brenner & M. Brenner (Eds.), *The social contexts of method* (pp. 16–32). London, UK: Croom Helm.

Säljö, R. (1991). Piagetian controversies, cognitive competence, and assumptions about human communication. *Educational Psychology Review, 3*(2), 117–126. doi:10.1007/bf01417923.

Savin-Baden, M. (2000). *Problem-based learning in higher education.* Buckingham, UK: SRHE/Open University Press.

Schank, R. C., & Abelson, R. P. (1977). *Scripts, plans, goals, and understanding: An inquiry into human knowledge structures.* Hillsdale, NJ: Lawrence Erlbaum Associates.

Schatzki, T. R., Knorr-Cetina, K., & von Savigny, E. (2001). *The practice turn in contemporary theory.* London, UK: Routledge.

Schraw, G. (2006). Knowledge structures and processes. In P. A. Alexander & P. Winne (Eds.), *Handbook of educational psychology* (pp. 245–263). Mahwah, NJ: Lawrence Erlbaum Associates.

Schwartz, D. L., & Bransford, J. D. (1998). A time for telling. *Cognition and Instruction, 16*(4), 475–522. doi:10.2307/3233709.

Schwartz, D. L., Varma, S., & Martin, L. (2008). Dynamic transfer and innovation. In S. Vosniadou (Ed.), *International handbook of research on conceptual change* (pp. 479–508). New York, NY: Routledge.

Scribner, S. (1985). Knowledge at work. *Anthropology and Education Quarterly, 16*, 199–206.

Scribner, S. (1997). *Mind and social practice: Selected writings of Sylvia Scribner.* Cambridge, NY: Cambridge University Press.

Siegel, D. J. (2012). *The developing mind: How relationships and the brain interact to shape who we are* (2nd ed.). New York, NY: The Guilford Press.

Sinatra, G. M., & Pintrich, P. R. (Eds.). (2003). *Intentional conceptual change.* Mahwah, NJ: Lawrence Erlbaum Associates.

Skinner, B. F. (1938). *The behavior of organisms: An experimental analysis.* New York, NY: D. Appelton-Century.

Smith, L. B. (2005). Cognition as a dynamic system: Principles from embodiment. *Developmental Review, 25*(3–4), 278–298. doi:10.1016/j.dr.2005.11.001.

Smith, L. B., & Gasser, M. (2005). The development of embodied cognition: Six lessons from babies. *Artificial Life, 11*(1–2), 13–29. doi:10.1162/1064546053278973.

Sousa, D. A. (2011). *How the brain learns* (4th ed.). Thousand Oaks, CA: Corwin.

Sterelny, K. (2003). *Thought in a hostile world: The evolution of human cognition.* Oxford, UK: Blackwell.

Sterelny, K. (2012). *The evolved apprentice: How evolution made humans unique.* Cambridge, MA: MIT Press.

Sternberg, R. J. (1985). *Beyond IQ: A triadic theory of human intelligence.* Cambridge, UK: Cambridge University Press.

Sternberg, R. J. (2004). *Wisdom, intelligence, and creativity synthesized.* Cambridge, NY: Cambridge University Press.

Stewart, J., Gapenne, O., & Paolo, E. A. D. (Eds.). (2010). *Enaction: Toward a new paradigm for cognitive science.* Cambridge, MA: MIT Press.

Sweller, J., van Merrienboer, J. G., & Paas, F. W. C. (1998). Cognitive architecture and instructional design. *Educational Psychology Review, 10*(3), 251–296.

Szymanski, M. H., & Whalen, J. (Eds.). (2011). *Making work visible: Ethnographically grounded case studies of work practice.* Cambridge, MA: Cambridge University Press.

Turnbull, D. (2000). *Masons, tricksters and cartographers: Comparative studies in the sociology of scientific and indigenous knowledge.* Abingdon, OX: Routledge.

Varela, F., Thompson, E., & Rosch, E. (1991). *The embodied mind: Cognitive science and human experience* (6th ed.). Cambridge, MA: MIT Press.

Vera, A. H., & Simon, H. A. (1993). Situated action: A symbolic interpretation. *Cognitive Science, 17*(1), 7–48.

Vosniadou, S. (Ed.). (2008/2013). *International handbook of research on conceptual change* (1st and 2nd eds.). New York, NY: Routledge.

Vosniadou, S., & Brewer, W. F. (1994). Mental models of the day/night cycle. *Cognitive Science, 18*(1), 123–183. doi:10.1207/s15516709cog1801_4.

Vosniadou, S., & Ioannides, C. (1998). From conceptual development to science education: A psychological point of view. *International Journal of Science Education, 20*(10), 1213–1230. doi:10.1080/0950069980201004.

Wagner, J. F. (2006). Transfer in pieces. *Cognition and Instruction, 24*(1), 1–71.

Wagner, J. F. (2010). A transfer-in-pieces consideration of the perception of structure in the transfer of learning. *Journal of the Learning Sciences, 19*(4), 443–479.

Chapter 7
Epistemic Thinking

7.1 Knowledge and Knowing as an Open System

Contemporary views of learning and cognition that take dynamic ecological perspectives often describe human cognitive processes in systems-theoretic language: 'goal', 'agent', 'feedback', 'control', 'emergence', 'dynamic stability' and so on. However, such accounts can be constructed in two radically different ways: as an account of an *observed system* or as an account of an *observing* system (Banathy & Jenlink, 2004; von Foerster, 2003). von Foerster (2003) describes these two views in terms of answers to two simple questions:

> 'Am I *apart from* the universe?' Meaning whenever I *look*, I'm looking as if through a peephole upon an unfolding universe; or, 'Am I *part of* the universe?' Meaning whenever I *act*, I'm changing myself and the universe as well. (von Foerster, 2003, p. 293, original emphasis)

Indeed the answer to this question is critical for understanding actionable knowledge and knowing in the world. von Foerster continues:

> Whenever I reflect on these two alternatives, I'm surprised by the depth of the abyss that separates the two fundamentally different worlds that can be created by such a choice. That is to see myself as a citizen of an independent universe, whose regulations, rules and customs I may eventually discover; or to see myself as a participant in a conspiracy, whose customs, rules, and regulations we are now inventing. (op. cit., p. 294)

Without overstretching the links, we could draw a broad parallel between two fundamentally different views of human cognition and these two orders of cybernetics that evolved in modern systems sciences: the first order and the second order, respectively. From the first-order perspective, an account of cognitive processes is constructed from an external observer's point of view, as if the cognitive system's activity was independent from the meanings enacted within it and the system itself was unaware of its own functioning. In this case, the system is operationally 'closed' from its own cognitive performance, thus unable to purposefully modify it. From the second-order perspective, an account of cognitive processes is

© Springer Science+Business Media Dordrecht 2017

L. Markauskaite, P. Goodyear, *Epistemic Fluency and Professional Education*,
Professional and Practice-based Learning 14, DOI 10.1007/978-94-007-4369-4_7

constructed from the point of view of an observer who is a part of the system. In this case, the very process of meaning-making becomes a part of this cognitive system, and the observer (who is also observed) is aware of his or her viewpoint and the overall system performance. This awareness makes it possible to open the system and modify its action.

Current views of learning and cognition often take the 'first-order' cybernetic perspective. They see the relationships between human mind, body and action as a closed system. A view about how meanings are constructed – epistemology – is either seen as an implicit control structure or an emerging phenomenon, but generally it is not seen as something that an agent purposefully enacts or can independently modify. Adding *epistemic resources* to the very core of the action-able conceptual system opens this system up. In this case, cognition is the 'second-order' phenomenon; it depends on the actor's perspective, not just on a body–world–concepts coupling. If we see cognition in this way, then space is opened up to teach about disciplinary perspectives, productive stances, different ways to frame and approach tasks, about the importance of thinking how to link concepts to material and social contexts and embodied experiences. In short, it makes it possible to take human epistemic agency seriously.[1] Epistemology is not only a construct that can be used to describe human performance. It is also a construct that could be *purposefully enacted within* human performance.

Many of the concepts that refer to phenomena in the world are made explicit in teaching and learning, but *epistemic concepts* are often left implicit. (It seems they are often treated in an optimistic spirit of 'let's hope they will get it right'). One of the core limitations of education is that it pays very little explicit attention to helping students develop more articulated epistemic resources. Indeed, our every-day language is generally quite impoverished when it comes to naming the episte-mic constructs that people use in sense-making. For example, ask a student or even an experienced practitioner 'How do you know this or that', and they will quickly run out of words with which to answer the question. A relatively rich epistemic vocabulary has been developed by researchers, often for detecting 'flaws' in students' thinking. Some awareness about students' epistemic resources may be embedded in instructional approaches used by teachers. But epistemic concepts are rarely taught to students – which makes it harder for them to notice when there is a 'fault' and less able to correct things for themselves. Moreover, when students go into the professional field, there is no teacher standing by to help activate these productive epistemic resources.

In this chapter, we introduce questions of epistemic thinking and personal epistemic resourcefulness. In Sect. 7.2, we briefly review the main ideas and terminology, and in Sect. 7.3 introduce the main research approaches, in this field of work. In Sects. 7.4, 7.5, 7.6, 7.7, 7.8 and 7.9, we describe some recent extensions that bring established research on personal epistemology closer to how people think

---

[1] Epistemic agency can be understood as the capacity that enables one to engage deliberately in knowledge-producing activities (Damsa, Kirschner, Andriessen, Erkens, & Sins, 2010).

and act within specific cultural and material settings. These extensions provide the basis for the view on epistemic resourcefulness that we develop towards the end of the book.

7.2 Personal Epistemology, Epistemic Thinking and Epistemic Resources

Over the last four decades, educational psychology has extensively studied individuals' beliefs about the nature of knowledge, knowing and learning – under the general heading of 'personal epistemology' (Bendixen & Feucht, 2010; Brownlee, Schraw, & Berthelsen, 2011; Elen, Stahl, Bromme, & Clarebout, 2011; Hofer, 2001; Hofer & Pintrich, 2002; Khine, 2008; Kitchener, 1983; Perry, 1970; Royce, 1974). Studies have quite consistently reported that personal epistemology affects how people approach problem-solving and learning tasks and may be one of the main contributors to the capacities needed to solve more complex and diverse problems that require flexibility, sophisticated judgement or innovative solutions (Elen et al., 2011). However, the field offers quite a diverse range of answers to central questions such as what personal epistemology is, how it develops and how it actually functions in particular situations. Most importantly, one of the biggest challenges in this research domain is how to provide a richer insight into how personal epistemic understandings are intertwined with knowing in situated activities.

It is important to clarify core terminology.[2] In educational psychology, the terms 'epistemic beliefs' and 'epistemological beliefs' have often been used interchangeably to refer to people's commonsense ideas about knowledge and knowing. However, Kitchener (2002) notes that the terms 'epistemic' and 'epistemological' are not strict synonyms. 'Epistemic', which comes from the Greek word '*epistēmē*', means 'knowledge' and has a sense of a certain knowledge or understanding, even scientific knowledge.[3] The term 'epistemic beliefs', thus, implies beliefs about knowledge. 'Epistemology' refers to 'the theory of knowledge and understanding'[4] and, as with any 'theory', it implies a *system* of beliefs, in this case, 'epistemic beliefs'. Thus, 'epistemological beliefs' could be characterised as meta-level beliefs about epistemic matters – i.e. *beliefs* about epistemic *beliefs*. Kitchener (2002) observes, that, in the personal epistemology literature, when researchers refer to people's beliefs about knowledge (not their beliefs about theories of knowledge),

---

[2] If you don't care about terminological precision, you can safely skip to the start of Sect. 7.3. But don't then blame us for seeming to mix up the epistemic and the epistemological.

[3] '*episteme, n.*'. Oxford English Dictionary. Retrieved May 07, 2015 from http://www.oed.com/view/Entry/63540?redirectedFrom=Episteme

[4] '*epistemology, n.*'. Oxford English Dictionary. Retrieved May 07, 2015 from http://www.oed.com/view/Entry/63546?redirectedFrom=Epistemology

the term 'epistemological' is being used inappropriately.[5] However, this terminology has not been strictly adhered to in the domain of personal epistemology research and the term 'epistemological' continues to be used even when this word refers to people's ideas about knowledge and knowing (Elby & Hammer, 2010; Schommer-Aikins, 2011).

Some researchers tend not to use the term 'beliefs' and instead use the words 'epistemic' or 'epistemological' in different combinations with other words such as 'epistemological reflection' (Baxter Magolda, 2004), 'epistemological theories' (Hofer & Pintrich, 1997), 'epistemic cognition' (Chinn, Buckland, & Samarapungavan, 2011; King & Kitchener, 2002), 'epistemological understanding' and 'epistemological thinking' (Kuhn & Weinstock, 2002) or 'epistemological resources' (Hammer & Elby, 2002). Sometimes these terms are used as synonyms to the classical term 'epistemic beliefs', but often they imply a particular focus or particular conceptual take on what personal epistemology is.

In recent literature, terms such as 'epistemic cognition' (Chinn et al., 2011), 'epistemic thinking' (Barzilai & Zohar, 2014) and 'epistemological resources' (Elby & Hammer, 2010; Hammer & Elby, 2002) have become increasingly common. We explain these key terms in the sections that follow.

There is also significant disagreement about the *scope* of personal epistemology. Some scholars describe 'epistemic beliefs' as including students' beliefs and other cognitions about the nature of knowledge, knowing *and learning* (Elby & Hammer, 2010; Schommer, 1990). Others scholars categorically assert that beliefs about learning are outside the scope of personal epistemology and should be excluded from this construct (Hofer & Pintrich, 1997).

In the discussion of cognitive aspects of epistemic fluency, we generally try to maintain the distinction between 'epistemic' and 'epistemological', but when the two are inextricably intertwined, we use 'epistemic' as an umbrella term to refer to people's ideas and cognitions that are broadly related to matters of knowledge, knowing and learning, which sometimes include their meta-level ideas. However, when we review or draw upon existing literature, we usually use the original terminology adopted by the authors. We include in the scope of epistemology people's ideas related to learning, as, like others, we find that people's ideas and cognitions related to knowledge, knowing and learning are inextricably entangled (Elby, 2009; Elby & Hammer, 2010). This is particularly the case when people work on complex innovative tasks, which inevitably require drawing on cognitions for working with known ideas and figuring out new things: there is no a priori reason to locate learning outside other epistemic cognitions on which people naturally draw.

---

[5] From this perspective, when the term 'epistemological beliefs' is used to refer to people's beliefs about knowledge and learning-related questions, as is the case in one of the classical strands of personal epistemology research (Schommer, 1990), it is being used inaccurately. Instead, the more accurate term would be 'epistemic beliefs'.

7.3 Personal Epistemology: Classical Accounts

Broadly speaking, the established approaches to researching personal epistemology focus on (a) the (unidirectional) development of personal epistemologies or (b) the multidimensionality of personal epistemic beliefs. There are also some approaches which include elements of both. For reviews, see Hofer (2002, 2004b, 2008).

7.3.1 Epistemological Development

The developmental perspective primarily assumes that personal epistemology develops over time, in stages starting from simple/naïve and moving to increasingly more sophisticated epistemological judgements (e.g. Perry, 1970). The various developmental models suggest slightly different stages, but as Hofer (2008) concludes, four stages are quite well established: naïve realism, dualism, multiplicism and evaluatism.[6] During the *naïve realism* or *egocentric subjectivity* stage, which is usually observed in young children, a person's own perception is the only view that is accessible to them and the only one that is true for that person. Thus, 'what is true is what I believe is true'. During the next *dualism* or *absolutism* stage, people become increasingly aware that other views are also possible. At this stage, individuals start believing that there is an objective right answer, while all other answers must therefore be wrong. During the *multiplicism* stage, people come to understand that much knowledge is subjective and that different views might be possible; but they do not differentiate between different claims, believing that all of them have an equal validity. In the last *evaluatism* stage, individuals develop the means to judge the validity of different propositions, thereby starting to see differences between various claims, as well reconciling their own experiences with these external claims.

According to this account, epistemological development may be general or more domain-specific, and people are observed to operate at different levels of epistemological sophistication with respect to (say) physics, history, teaching and medicine or domains of personal taste, aesthetics and value judgements (Kuhn, Cheney, & Weinstock, 2000; Muis, Bendixen, & Haerle, 2006). People undergo a similar stagelike sequence of development in each domain. Once people reach a higher stage of development, then they generally do not go back, and they apply similar beliefs across all situations in the domain concerned. So on this view, if a trainee doctor holds a belief that scientific evidence *always* provides a better ground for decisions than one's own experience (i.e. the absolutist stage), then she would not

---

[6] It is appropriate to use the term 'epistemological development' rather than 'epistemic development' since the developmental stages refer to development in people's meta-beliefs about knowledge and knowing.

try to reconcile scientific evidence with personal experience until some later time, when she had attained a higher stage of epistemological development.

While some developmentally oriented researchers have focussed on the *structure* of beliefs about reality, knowledge and knowing, others have examined how people reason and make epistemic judgements, pointing out that the *process* of thinking may be as important as the nature of the beliefs and social context may play an important role. For example, one of Baxter Magolda's (2004) well-known models portrays the development of epistemic reflection as a journey through four stages: (a) 'following formulas', in which people focus on receiving and mastering knowledge; (b) 'crossroads', in which people recognise the need for internal self-definition and independent decision-making, but struggle to do this; (c) 'becoming the author of one's life', in which people increasingly take responsibility for their beliefs and identity; and (d) 'internal foundation', during which they become increasingly comfortable with their beliefs, identities and how they relate to other people. While studies may differ (e.g. in the number of stages identified or the study focus), this perspective generally assumes a similar *one-dimensional* and *unidirectional* pattern of epistemological development.

7.3.2   Epistemic Beliefs and Theories: Multiple Dimensions

The epistemic beliefs perspective assumes a different structure to beliefs, proposing that personal epistemology is a *multidimensional* construct. For example, Schommer's (1990) seminal work on beliefs about knowledge and learning suggested five dimensions: (a) *structure of knowledge*, ranging from a belief that knowledge is fragmented to a belief that it is organised into an interrelated system; (b) *stability of knowledge*, ranging from the belief that knowledge is unchanging to the belief that knowledge is evolving; (c) *ability to learn*, ranging from the belief that this ability is fixed to the belief that it can be improved; (d) *speed of learning*, ranging from the belief that learning happens immediately, or not-at-all, to the belief that learning can be gradual; and (e) *omniscient authority*, ranging from the belief that knowledge is passed on to the belief that one can create knowledge for oneself.

A core idea is that these dimensions may not necessarily develop at the same time. For example, a professional person may think that knowledge in their field is fragmented and evolving and may also believe that they can learn new knowledge in their field very quickly.

This perspective has been taken up and developed further in many other studies. Most studies emphasise two common components: the nature of knowledge and the nature of knowing (Hofer & Pintrich, 1997). Each of these components is seen as having two dimensions. *The nature of knowledge* is characterised in terms of certainty (knowledge is fixed vs. knowledge is fluid) and simplicity (discrete elements vs. highly interrelated concepts). *The nature of knowing* is characterised in terms of the source (received from outside vs. constructed by knower) and the means of justification (authority vs. reasoned justification). As with the developmental perspective, the epistemic beliefs perspective assumes that beliefs may be different in different domains, but overall there are relationships between the general and domain-specific beliefs that, once they develop, remain stable and are deployed quite consistently across situations and contexts within the domain (cf. Muis et al., 2006; Schommer & Walker, 1995). That is, they are *multidimensional*, but still *unidirectional*.

The so-called epistemological theories perspective integrates elements of the developmental and epistemic beliefs views sketched above. It suggests that individual beliefs may be multidimensional but also that these dimensions are likely to be interconnected and, as the developmental perspective suggests, will develop in stages (Hofer & Pintrich, 1997).

7.3.3   Commonalities and Extensions

A key claim of the developmental and epistemic beliefs perspectives is that personal epistemology is a coherent construct – that individuals deploy their beliefs about knowledge and knowing consistently across situations, within each domain. They also agree that such beliefs are hard to change and that generally they develop slowly.

Some recent developments in personal epistemology research have taken several directions that increase the relevance of research on personal epistemology to understanding personal capacities for professional learning, knowledge work and innovation. First, most new studies that build on the traditional perspectives increasingly recognise that personal epistemology is unlikely to be a universal construct. Beliefs may be different in different disciplinary domains (e.g. history vs. mathematics) and in different applied fields (e.g. education vs. engineering) (Hofer, 2006a, 2006b; Muis et al., 2006). They may also vary from culture to culture (Khine, 2008) or be related to the context in other ways (Hofer, 2004a). There is also increasing recognition that epistemic beliefs and cognitions are not separable from people's ontological beliefs about the nature of reality in general and in their specific domain of activity (Greene, Azevedo, & Torney-Purta, 2008; Schraw & Olafson, 2008).

Second, while most of the studies have been conducted in educational settings and focussed on traditional academic disciplines, some have begun to address the question of personal epistemology in professional knowledge construction and learning (e.g. Brownlee et al., 2011; Tillema & Orland-Barak, 2006). These explore how personal epistemology is intertwined with other constructs related to intellectual and personal development that extends throughout the career, such as identity and the development of relationships with others (Baxter Magolda, 2004).

7.4   Personal Epistemology Research: Critique and New Directions

Personal epistemology studies have provided useful evidence suggesting that personal epistemology can be an important predictor of, and contributor to, students' learning processes and learning outcomes. Nevertheless, they have also been sharply criticised, both within and outside the domain, for various theoretical and methodological limitations, and limited practical utility. Firstly, while studies have demonstrated relationships between the personal epistemology constructs and various measurements of learning and thinking processes and outcomes, the proportion of variance explained by the epistemological beliefs has been generally low (Chinn et al., 2011).

Second, many studies, particularly those in the epistemic beliefs strand, have been drawing on psychometric self-report questionnaires. There is growing concern that these instruments have significant measurement issues due to inadequate operationalisation of epistemic constructs (DeBacker, Crowson, Beesley, Thoma, & Hestevold, 2008; Limon, 2006) and/or because important aspects of personal epistemology are simply not covered (Chinn et al., 2011; Schraw & Olafson, 2008).

Third, studies have increasingly been finding that there are significant inconsistencies between *assessed* personal epistemologies and beliefs that individuals *enact* in practice (Olafson & Schraw, 2006). In particular, there is growing recognition that the established conceptualisations of personal epistemology are generally too insensitive to contexts (Chinn et al., 2011; Hammer & Elby, 2002) and are incompatible with situated conceptualisations of cognition (Sandoval, 2012). They cannot reveal ways in which cognition in action is intertwined with tools, artefacts and other material and social aspects inherent in human activity, and they are insensitive to the historically constructed environments that support the thinking of the students (and others) being researched. As Sandoval (2012) puts it,

> Personal epistemology researchers have largely ignored the culturally situated nature of knowledge and knowing, and thus the situated character of epistemic cognition and epistemological development. This is particularly apparent in how issues of "domain-specificity" are treated, which is almost entirely without reference to the practices of knowledge construction and evaluation of specific domains, such as history, math, or science. (Sandoval, 2012, p. 348)

7.5   The Division of Cognitive Labour: Epistemological Implications

Additional critiques of personal epistemology research have come from observations of the changing nature of knowledge and knowing in society and workplaces. Bromme, Kienhues and Porsch (2010) argue for a reconceptualisation of at least two aspects of what is often considered as sophisticated personal epistemology: authentic source of knowledge and autonomous justification and judgement.

In the literature on personal epistemology, knowledge constructed by others has been viewed negatively (as inauthentically constructed knowledge). 'Verbal knowledge' acquired from others has not been seen as indicating genuine understanding, whereas much higher epistemological credit has been given to direct experience and authentically constructed knowledge. Similarly, 'epistemically sophisticated' people have been conceived as those who are able to overcome existing divisions of cognitive labour – making their own judgements about knowledge claims, however specialised they may be.

In contrast, Bromme, Kienhues and Porsch argue that, in modern society, knowledge has become more specialised and professional work is increasingly characterised by a 'division of cognitive labour'. Reliance on the knowledge of experts in various specialised domains becomes a part of everyday life and of multidisciplinary professional work. Bromme et al. question the traditional assumption that a person's own knowledge is necessarily better than knowledge obtained from others. They remind us that first-hand evaluation (of knowledge claims) requires significant domain-specific knowledge and expertise and conclude that expecting autonomous judgement of knowledge in all domains is simply a 'utopian burden'.

They note that a more nuanced and context-sensitive understanding of epistemological sophistication is needed. As the first step, drawing on Sandoval (2005) and Hogan (2000), they observe that there is a difference between 'distal' (or 'formal') epistemology and 'proximal' (or 'practical') epistemology. They argue that students may hold and need different kinds of beliefs about how scientists produce and justify knowledge in various domains and about their own ways of acquiring and justifying knowledge when they deal with matters in those domains. First-hand evaluation ('What is true') and second-hand evaluation ('Whom to believe') draw on different kinds of expertise. The former requires domain knowledge and critical thinking; the latter requires knowledge of relevant and credible sources.

Overall, sophisticated second-hand epistemological judgements rely on knowledge about the division of cognitive labour: (a) who is responsible for which domain and (b) how to make decisions about different knowledge claims and sources. Bromme et al. assert that the domain or topic provides a critical context for epistemic meanings and decisions: explanation and justification in mathematics and social sciences are not the same, for example. A friend's explanation may be regarded as suitable for certain social topics, whereas mathematical calculations would be considered to be important for some math topics.

In short, while personal epistemology is traditionally considered to be in the domain of the individual mind, 'second-hand' epistemological sophistication tends to rely on understanding how knowledge is structured and organised in a society and in the local context: including understanding conceptual structures and distributions of expertise.[7] This relational and situated nature of epistemic beliefs poses an important challenge for traditional conceptualisations of personal epistemology.

---

[7] This kind of epistemological understanding relates closely to what Harry Collins and Robert Evans (2007) call 'interactional expertise' and which they distinguish from the 'contributory expertise' of professionals who do specialised work within a domain (see Chap. 4).

Attempts to address these issues have been coming from several directions. In the following sections, we summarise four recent lines of research that have been addressing conceptual and methodological questions particularly relevant for understanding professional knowledge and action. Firstly, we present some expansions of the scope of epistemic cognition that have been emerging from the convergence of this research domain with developments in contemporary philosophy (Sect. 7.6). Secondly, we introduce the 'epistemic resource' view that helps understand epistemic knowledge and thinking in action – the *diversity* of epistemic ideas on which people draw in sense-making within situated activities (Sect. 7.7). Thirdly, we argue that this epistemic thinking is firmly intertwined with the external environment; and, to explain this distributed view, we introduce the notion of 'epistemic affordances' (Sect. 7.8). We then describe some ideas about cognitive flexibility that aim to bring personal epistemology into closer relations with conceptual knowledge and the division of cognitive labour. We end the chapter by bringing together some ideas about mental resourcefulness for innovation and knowledgeable action (Sect. 7.9).

7.6   The Changing Scope of Epistemic Cognition

For a long time, personal epistemology researchers have been aiming to keep their view of epistemology consistent with the philosophical view of this term. As Hofer (2001) wrote,

> Although we are psychologizing about epistemology and are not philosophers, those of us working in this area have appropriated a term with a long history of meaning. If we want to talk about epistemological beliefs, development, theories, or resources, then it seems reasonable to delineate the construct by identifying those dimensions that fit within *the conventional* definition of epistemology, a philosophical field concerned with the nature of knowledge and knowing. (Hofer, 2001, p. 361, emphasis added)

However, mainstream research on personal epistemology drew on a *classical* view of epistemology which builds on the notion of knowledge as 'justified true belief' – a notion going back to Plato's ideas in antiquity (Silverman, 2014). But, contemporary philosophers, who have been increasingly interested in how people think in practice, rather than in abstract philosophical notions of knowledge, have moved beyond this idealised notion of knowledge (Steup & Sosa, 2005). They have been asking a much larger set of questions, such as 'How are we to understand the concept of justification?' 'What makes justified beliefs justified?' and 'Is justification internal or external to one's own mind?' (Steup, 2014).

In the *Stanford Encyclopedia of Philosophy*, Steup (2014) defines the scope of contemporary epistemology as follows:

> … epistemology is about issues having to do with the creation and dissemination of knowledge in particular areas of inquiry. (Steup, 2014, no page)

Further, a number of new philosophical lines have brought research in philosophy into closer contact with studies of the human mind in cognitive sciences. These include situated cognition and sociocultural perspectives. For example, *epistemological naturalism* investigates how individuals and communities generate knowledge. *Contextualism* examines how the meaning of the word 'know' varies from situation to situation. *Externalism* aims to understand how the content of a thought is shaped by the environment. *Virtue epistemology* asks questions about what it is reasonable to believe and focusses on understanding epistemic norms, values and evaluation. Work on the *embodied mind* brings questions about the role of the body into philosophical arguments about the nature of the human mind and cognition.

These contemporary philosophical developments are shifting away from seeing knowledge as an idealised construct, recasting it as a phenomenon of human cognition which contributes to human well-being and to practical concerns. As Kvanvig (2005) claims,

> Epistemology is the study of certain aspects of our cognitive endeavours. In particular, it aims to investigate *successful* cognition. (Kvanvig, 2005, p. 286, original emphasis)

Justified truth is not the primary epistemic aim; there are many other epistemic goals and values which people pursue, including

> knowledge, understanding, wisdom, rationality, justification, sense-making and empirically adequate theories in addition to getting to the truth and avoiding error. (op. cit., p. 287)

These recent developments in philosophy have only recently been noticed in educational psychology (Greene et al., 2008; Kitchener, 2011). A notable extension of established notions of personal epistemology, drawing on these trends, has been offered by Chinn et al. (2011) in their reconceptualisation of epistemic cognition. They define 'epistemic cognition' as 'an umbrella term encompassing all kinds of explicit or tacit cognitions related to epistemic or epistemological matters' (p. 141). Drawing on epistemological naturalism[8] and other branches of contemporary philosophical scholarship, they propose that epistemic cognition consists not of individual dimensions, but of a network of various kinds of cognition: (a) epistemic aims and epistemic values; (b) *structure* of knowledge[9]; (c) *sources and justification* of knowledge, together with related epistemic stances; (d) epistemic virtues and vices; and (e) reliable and unreliable processes for achieving epistemic aims.

This scoping of epistemology goes far beyond traditional concerns about the nature of knowledge and knowing (which are part of 'b' and 'c' in the paragraph above), as it has been understood in classic studies of personal epistemology. It brings the view of epistemic cognition much closer to the realities of epistemic practices in professional work. For our purposes, one of the most useful extensions is that epistemic aims include not only 'acquiring true belief' but also avoiding false beliefs, seeking understanding and constructing explanations. Moreover, the

---

[8] A useful summary of this broad philosophical view is presented in Kitchener's (2011) work.

[9] Chinn et al. (2011) use the phrase 'knowledge and other epistemic achievements' in order to include such things as 'understanding' and 'true beliefs'.

inclusion of epistemic values rules out the need to have an a priori set of (or to privilege) one particular epistemic aim or form of knowledge. It allows us to look more closely at what kinds of epistemic aims and other achievements are valued and which ways of knowing guide people's cognition in practice (e.g. in classical studies of personal epistemology, priority has typically been given to theoretically grounded, independently constructed knowledge rather than intuition or knowledge gained from others).

The proposed reconceptualisation also acknowledges that epistemic cognitions often vary across situations and emphasises the important role of fine-grained context-specific epistemic cognitions. For example, cognitions related to the structure of knowledge and other epistemic achievements go beyond a one-dimensional abstract classification of epistemological beliefs (along a continuum from simple to complex structures). This can be seen to include other aspects and specific structural forms of knowledge: such as the structure of models in mechanics, the structure of molecular mechanisms in molecular biology and the structure of causality. Similarly, epistemic virtues and vices, such as intellectual carefulness and open-mindedness, are not necessarily viewed as stable motivational dispositions, independent from the situation, but as contextual constructs that may vary from situation to situation. For example, intellectual carefulness, which includes a willingness to take care in gathering more evidence before taking a decision, could be seen as an epistemic virtue in some situations, but may become an epistemic vice in a situation requiring immediate action, such as in a medical emergency.

The application of this reconceptualisation of epistemic cognitions – in empirical investigations and practice – requires new 'intellectual tools' that permit movement beyond the large and stable epistemic units, such as epistemological beliefs, which have been investigated in classical personal epistemology studies. We turn to these finer-grained constructs in Sect. 7.7.

Chinn et al.'s (2011) extension provides a useful starting point for looking at epistemic aspects of professional knowledge and work in specific situated contexts. However, to provide a sufficient basis for epistemic cognition which brings forth meanings in embodied action, this view needs to be complemented in at least three additional ways.

Firstly, epistemic aims need to be expanded to go beyond the established intellectual aims – 'knowledge', 'understanding', 'having a minimally justified belief' and 'construction of explanation'. They need to include the epistemic purposes that practitioners often have in their work, in action, such as making sense of an encountered situation, making the best decision in particular circumstances, making the next step in a complex situation even if the final goal is not yet apparent, engaging in intellectual activities with others when there is no explicit epistemic agenda (e.g. sharing knowledge) and rehearsing a skill or other virtue (i.e. learning).

Second, Chinn et al. (2011) primarily provide an account of epistemic cognition that builds on the *representational* view of knowledge and knowing firmly targeted towards a particular articulated representational end. They claim,

Cognitions are epistemic *only* if they are directed at epistemic aims and accomplishments. (Chinn et al., 2011, p. 158, emphasis added)

Epistemic aims are *the end* to which all other epistemic beliefs and activities are directed. (op. cit., p. 147, emphasis added)

And explain,

Many beliefs *can be ruled out as nonepistemic* because they are not directed at epistemic aims. For example, a student's belief that "I like class work best when it really makes me think" ... is not epistemic because *no* epistemic aim is invoked; *mere* thinking is not an epistemic aim such as *knowledge or understanding*. (loc. cit., emphasis added)

Such a priori restrictions rule out of consideration embodied epistemic actions: the *processes of cognising* – 'finding', 'knowing', 'thinking', 'creating a psychologically healthy environment for one's cognition', 'liking to work together' and 'fine-tuning one's environment in ways that enhance one's cognition as well as the cognition of others' – which may be perfectly appropriate epistemic purposes in some, if not all, situations. This is particularly the case if one acknowledges the *performative* nature of knowing and sees cognition not only as the destination (e.g. knowledge) but also the journey (e.g. knowing). For example, thinking is a completely legitimate epistemic aim, particularly in a learning setting, if one sees one's *thinking* and maintaining a psychologically healthy environment which one *likes*, as the ongoing purposes within which cognition becomes possible. They are not only beliefs *about* processes and conditions under which processes of achieving epistemic aims are reliable (which would be the case if we apply this framework) but also conditions and processes that ought to be created and enacted within cognitive activity. Once we abandon a strong or exclusive representational definition of epistemic aims, then we can see these aims (and other cognitions) as emerging from within situated activities within specific epistemic cultures and practice settings, rather than being set a priori by others.

Thirdly, while Chinn et al.'s view provides a nuanced consideration of the context, it is rather weak at accounting for the embodied and enacted nature of human cognition, as if the embodied skills of perceiving, thinking and acting within this context were largely peripheral to epistemic cognitions implemented within the mind. Indeed, more recent ideas on the embodied mind that have emerged at the intersection of phenomenological philosophy, biology and neuroscience urge us to extend this notion of epistemic cognitions to the body and action in a very fundamental and deep sense (Clark, 1999, 2011; Dreyfus, 2014; Thompson, 2010; Varela, Thompson, & Rosch, 1991). Andy Clark (2012) gives the gist:

Human minds, it can hardly be doubted, are at the very least in deep and critically important contact with human bodies and with the wider world. Human sensing, learning, thought and feeling are all structured and informed by our body-based interactions with the world around us. <...> As active sensors of our world, possessed with bodies with specific shapes and characters, it is relatively unsurprising if what we think, do, and perceive all turn out to be deeply intertwined. Nor is it all that surprising if much of higher cognition turns out to be in some sense built on a substrate of embodied pseudo-motor capacities. <...> it [higher cognition] does a kind of ongoing intermingling of cognitive activity with the pseudo-motor matrix from which it putatively emerges. (Clark, 2012, pp. 275–276)

This pseudo-motor matrix provides the very basis through and within which epistemic cognition emerges and simultaneously brings forth the world and knowing.

Ingold (2011) makes an even a stronger point and asserts the primacy of the experiential world, questioning whether human relations with the environment are *necessarily* mediated by culture or internal symbolic representations. He specifically claims that nonhuman animals connect to the environment perfectly well, even though they do not share with humans the capacity to use symbolic representations. He draws on Whitehead, reminding us that humans, from birth, are involved in action without being able to articulate much of what they do. From this he comes to agree with the biosemiotics[10] argument that:

- Meaning is 'not in the correspondence between an external world and its interior representation, but in the immediate coupling of perception and action' (p. 77).
- Meaning is discovered in the very process of using tools and other affordances, as the quality of things is discovered from being drawn into activities.
- Meaning is an ongoing formation.

Acknowledging Ingold's point, we would add that humans are involved from birth in social interactions and in the worlds of internal and external representation. Rather than giving primacy to one over the other, it is more productive to think about them as being constitutively entangled. Acting is thinking through the world *and* by representing.

Dewey and Bentley (1949/1975) distinguish three fundamentally different forms of action that inform different views of the mind. These turn out to be helpful in understanding the separation between epistemic cognitions and embodied skill and action in the material world.

- *Self-action* – 'where things are viewed as acting under their own powers' (Dewey & Bentley, 1949/1975, pp. 132–133)
- *Inter-action* – 'where thing is balanced against thing in causal interconnection' (loc. cit.)
- *Trans-action* – 'where systems of description and naming are employed to deal with aspects and phases of action, without final attribution to "elements" or other presumptively detachable or independent "entities", "essences" or "realities" and without isolation of presumptively detachable "relations" from such detachable "elements"' (loc. cit.)

Self-actional views regard human knowledge and knowing as fundamental properties of the mind. Inter-actional views locate knowledge in the causal influences between mind and world. But these accounts nevertheless preserve a fundamental duality between world and mind. However, if we think about human learning and thinking as trans-action, then we cannot separate world and mind

---

[10] Biosemiotics is an interdisciplinary research field that investigates various forms of communication and signification in and between living systems.

anymore. This ongoing trans-action removes the boundary between acting and thinking, perceiving and conceiving, representing in the world and representing in the mind, performative mind and representational mind.

7.7   The Epistemic Resources View

David Hammer and Andrew Elby have proposed a rather different structure from the classical approaches for understanding the ontological basis of personal episte- mology (Elby & Hammer, 2010; Hammer & Elby, 2002). They argue that people are unlikely to have (or use) a coherent set of beliefs about knowledge and knowing and that they are unlikely to develop epistemic beliefs in a coherent, stagelike way. In contrast, they suggest that people hold lots of fine-grained 'epistemological resources' which are related to specific contexts.[11] These epistemological resources are largely experiential and intuitive and are activated, often subconsciously, when people solve tasks or learn. They are neither correct nor incorrect (in any absolute terms). Rather, depending on the circumstances, they may sometimes be activated appropriately and sometimes not. They are like building blocks, from which both lay people and experts construct the epistemological competence that they deploy in specific situations. Hammer and Elby suggest that people may have many such resources, but they also suggest that such resources can be seen as falling into four groups.

The first group is for *understanding the nature and sources of knowledge* – e.g. for recognising knowledge as passed on by others, created by oneself, created from existing knowledge, created by direct perception or ubiquitous inherent knowledge that is just 'common sense'.

The second group is for *understanding epistemological activities* through which people form or acquire knowledge. For example, most people have mental resources for understanding the accumulation of knowledge (e.g. gathering and retrieving), formation of knowledge (e.g. forming rules, forming stories, guessing, crafting), checking knowledge and applying knowledge in various knowledge tasks (e.g. comparing, sorting, naming).

The third group includes resources for *understanding epistemological forms* that are used in different epistemic activities. For example, most adults know that knowledge can take the form of a story, fact, picture, list, category, rule or rule system. These forms guide epistemic activity when someone is involved in pro- ducing knowledge of that particular form.

The fourth and last group consists of resources for *understanding epistemolog- ical stances*, such as believing, disbelieving, doubting, understanding, being puz- zled or accepting.

---

[11] This line of research on epistemological resources is a direct descendant of work on p-prims and knowledge-in-pieces (diSessa, 1988, 1993), which we discussed in Chap. 6.

In contrast to the classical views of personal epistemology, Hammer and Elby propose that many epistemological resources for understanding sources, activities, forms and epistemological stances are available from an early age or can be learnt relatively easily later on. A key idea is that *epistemological development generally consists of changes in the activation of resources* rather than significant changes in the stock of resources (or of the resources themselves). For example, the belief that nursing knowledge should be 'passed on' may mean that one activates and overuses epistemological resources related to accumulation, but counterproductively may underuse resources related to perception, formation and checking. In contrast, the belief that all nursing knowledge is acquired through *doing* nursing may be related to the over use of resources related to knowledge being inherent or directly perceived. However, the individual resources of 'accumulation' and 'perception' are not intrinsically incorrect – people do learn significant amounts of their knowledge in these two basic ways across the lifespan.

On this view, epistemological development consists of learning to recognise situations and activating those combinations of resources that are productive in that particular situation. It is not a matter of changing a simpler resource into a more sophisticated one. (For example, if you don't know how to carry out a specific procedure, is it better to learn this knowledge from colleagues, refer to manuals or make it up for yourself?)

The main educational implication is that learning and teaching should focus on designing tasks that prompt students to activate those epistemological resources that are productive in particular situations, rather than focussing on valuing and fostering particular types of beliefs (e.g. only the sophisticated ones).

Elby and Hammer (2010) suggest that epistemological resources form patterns – 'epistemological frames' – that are activated within similar contexts and across contexts. They note that framing and stability are achieved through three different mechanisms: *context* (i.e. setting, task or instructional materials cue a specific frame), *deliberative* (i.e. an individual is aware of a productive frame and deliberately maintains a productive stance during problem-solving) and *structural* (i.e. a contextual or deliberative pattern becomes internalised over time and reused without awareness). The first type of mechanism (context-cued), if used alone, might be said to belong with the primitive epistemological beliefs/theories addressed in the personal epistemology frameworks that we outlined earlier. However, the last two (deliberative and structural), if deployed consistently, would be indicative of more sophisticated beliefs. That said, if we focus exclusively on deliberative, conscious ways of thinking, we will overlook the productivity of other resources that come from direct experience and which can be appropriate in many situations. (As an example, think of a nurse carefully following the practices for giving an injection that she learnt by observing – relying on her own perception – without feeling a need to check for scientific evidence to validate the procedure.)

The 'epistemological resources' view provides a handy way of looking at epistemic resourcefulness in professional work and learning in concrete activities. That is, professional knowledgeable action usually draws on many kinds of knowledge and ways of knowing simultaneously and includes aims, values, virtues and other aspects of epistemic cognition in the broadest sense (Chinn et al., 2011). Drawing on the epistemological resources perspective, one can get an insight into ways of knowing that professionals enact in their practices by looking more closely at how they deploy different epistemological resources. Such resources may be very diverse (intuitive as well as formally learnt, primarily mental as well as strongly embodied), and they may be deployed in embodied professional action in combination with each other (and with affordances of the environment) in very different and flexible ways. For example, some epistemological resources can be intuitive, such as using direct perception and imitation for learning and performing a new skill. Some other resources can be more deliberative, such as creating a list of the main steps in a procedure to make sure that nothing is overlooked and everything is done in the right order. The intelligent activation and combination of these resources inherently relate to the dynamics between the complexity of the changing situation, one's experience, embrained capability to remember, skill to imitate and other aspects of one's biological capacity for perceiving, knowing and acting. We will return to this view and illustrate the nature of professional epistemic resourcefullness in Chap. 18. However, professional epistemic resourcefullness cannot be understood in isolation from the affordances of the environments within which professionals engage in learning and knowing.

7.8 Epistemic Affordances

The idea of 'affordance' originates in Gibson's (1979) ecological psychology, where it emerged as a way of talking about what an environment offers (to an organism, such as a person). For Gibson, affordances are directly perceived: no processes of mental mediation need to be invoked. Differently from this, Jim Greeno's (1994) account of affordances stresses the connection between features of the environment and abilities (of the organism), saying that these are fundamentally intertwined and relational.

> An affordance relates attributes of something in the environment to an interactive activity by an agent who has some ability, and an ability relates attributes of an agent to an interactive activity with something in the environment that has some affordance. The relativity of affordances and abilities is fundamental. Neither an affordance nor an ability is specifiable in the absence of specifying the other. (Greeno, 1994, p. 338)

While acknowledging the importance of direct perception, Greeno has noted that direct perception alone is insufficient to perceive all the kinds of affordances of the environment and to interact with the environment skilfully. Such interaction inevitably involves certain kinds of mental constructs – Greeno called them 'mental symbols' – and is likely to depend on more complex perceptual processes that involve interactions between the external world and internal mental constructs. For example, Greeno argues that the ability to recognise that a mailbox affords sending letters cannot be explained by direct perception of the thing. The process of perceiving this affordance includes recognising some cues that permit recognition of the object as a mailbox.

> The information required for that classification has to be visually available, of course, but the process of classification includes, I should think, a mental state that has the epistemic status of a symbol that designates the property of being a mailbox. (op. cit., p. 341)

The involvement of internal mental symbols and processes in perception of the environment departs from the core notion of direct perception of affordances that Gibson created to refer to non-mediated ways of cognising. Many others have adopted broadly similar Post-Gibsonian notions of 'affordance' and agree that ways in which material things are perceived – and come to be used in practical interactions – involve both direct and indirect aspects of perception, the latter being mediated by culture, experience and action (e.g. Cook & Brown, 1999; Knappett, 2004; Zhang & Patel, 2006).

7.8.1   A Distributed View of Affordances

Zhang and Patel (2006) offer a further extension and fuse the notion of 'affordance' with the framework of 'distributed cognition' – cutting across multiple internal and external representations, across multiple modalities of things and action spaces. They note that Gibson (1979) developed the notion of affordance to capture fundamental aspects of visual cognition. He was not tackling the whole cognitive system, distributed across multiple structures of the external environment and multiple internal features of the organism. Zhang and Patel observe that affordances should not be seen as one homogenous mode of visual perception, but as distributed systems that extend across multiple external and internal representations – the knowledge and structure – in the environment and in the organism. Broadly, the external representations are diverse kinds of attributes of the objects in the environment, such as chemical processes, physical configurations, spatiotemporal layouts and symbolic structures. They correspond to certain internal features (or abilities) of the organism – such as biological mechanisms inside the body, the physique of the organism, the perceptual system and cognitive structures and processes of the mind, respectively – creating distinct categories of affordances.

These categories include *biological affordances* that are based on the biological functions of the organism (e.g. an appropriate medication affords healing); *physical affordances* that are provided and constrained by physical structures (e.g. the layout of a lecture room affords one-to-many communication); *perceptual affordances* which are mainly provided by spatial mappings (e.g. an image of a flame on a container affords the meaning of a flammable substance); *cognitive affordances* that are provided for, and constrained by, cultural conventions (e.g. a red cross on a car affords the understanding that this is an ambulance; a chemical symbol system affords understanding of the chemical structure of substances); and *mixed affordances* that include various combinations of the above (e.g. a mailbox is a mix of the physical affordance that affords dropping letters into it and the cognitive affordance that conveys culturally agreed functions of the mailbox).

Zhang and Patel (2006) have introduced five categories of affordance. We argue that this list is far from complete and the notion of affordance can be extended to other ways of sensing and cognising through which humans interact with the environment and construct their understandings of it. For example, touch, hearing, smell, taste and affect come into play. (A bleeding wound *affords* – for many lay people – the experience of fear.) Furthermore, external and internal spaces do not necessarily map neatly onto each other. (Seeing a 'bleeding wound' is based on direct perceptual processes, but internal processes that afford the experience of 'fear' cut across many modalities, including the *cognitive*, perceiving 'a sign' of pain; *biological*, a release of certain hormones; and *cultural*, a trained paramedic would not necessarily experience fear.)

7.8.2 Pragmatic Affordances and Epistemic Affordances

Carl Knappett (2004) notes another inherent duality in human perception. When a person interacts with the environment, perception cuts across *reactive responses* involved in the execution of action that draws on affordances and constraints that support it and *active exploration* involved in the evaluation of affordances and constraints available in the environment for action. Knappett remarks that Gibson's (1979) theory of direct perception focusses on the *reactive* side of engagement with affordances and execution, rather than more active evaluation. However, when people solve pragmatic problems they act in ways that *explore* affordances of the situation (Kirsh, 2009; Kirsh & Maglio, 1994). Knappett uses the example of a person trying to assemble a jigsaw puzzle. The person's actions involve *execution* – trying to fit pieces into the right positions – but also a range of other actions that do not fit into a sequence of direct perception and execution, such as putting on one side all the pieces with straight edges or grouping pieces with similar colours together. These actions support perception and cognition. In mainstream cognitive science, the direct execution processes would be considered as external and physical, while the evaluation processes would be regarded as internal and mental. But in fact both processes involve external actions and manipulation of physical objects and both are direct and indirect, unmediated and mediated. Drawing on Kirsh and Maglio's (1994) work, Knappett (2004) makes the distinction between *pragmatic actions* and *epistemic actions*. While pragmatic actions change the world directly, epistemic actions change the environment *in order to enhance cognition*. On what kinds of affordances do these epistemic actions draw?

Using Zhang and Patel's (2006) distributed view of affordances, we can say that material environments also have 'epistemic affordances' – on which people draw to support their 'intelligent' perception. As with other affordances, epistemic affordances have:

- An *external* component – such as reconfigurations in the space that reduce the complexity of the situation by using certain salient features (such as shapes and colours of jigsaw pieces)
- An *internal* component – such as the abilities of the perceiver to see those salient features in the environment and link them with the pragmatic follow-up action (such as to try to assemble a region from pieces with similar colour)

Just as affordances can be seen as relations between the abilities of the organism and features of the environment, so epistemic affordances can be seen as relations between the epistemic abilities of humans – to engage in certain kinds of knowledge activities – and epistemic features of the environment that afford those kinds of epistemic actions. These epistemic affordances are multimodal.

7.9 Cognitive and Epistemic Flexibility

In this section we address the relationship between conceptual and epistemic aspects of knowledge and knowing in making flexible professional judgements that are informed by conceptual knowledge and in other kinds of knowledgeable professional actions. Some years ago, Rand Spiro and colleagues suggested that professionals who face complex ill-structured problems need to develop a special cognitive ability related to the conceptual understanding of their domain (Spiro & Jehng, 1990; Spiro et al., 1988/2013). They called this 'cognitive flexibility', meaning

> ... the ability to spontaneously restructure one's knowledge, in many ways, in adaptive response to radically changing situational demands (both within and across knowledge application situations). (Spiro & Jehng, 1990, p. 165)[12]

For example, when doctors look for possible treatments of such diseases as hypertension, whose etiology is largely unknown, better outcomes can be crafted by combining clinical and basic science approaches (Coulson, Feltovich, & Spiro, 1997). Spiro further describes 'cognitive flexibility' as,

> ... a function of both the way knowledge is *represented* (e.g., along *multiple* rather than single conceptual dimensions) and the processes that operate on those mental representations (e.g., processes of schema *assembly* rather than intact schema retrieval). (Spiro & Jehng, 1990, pp. 165–166, original emphasis)

The notion of cognitive flexibility has been extended over time, such that it is not restricted to static aspects of knowledge (related to specific domain representations and assembly in the mind), but now embraces the whole cognitive system that is used when working in dynamic interaction with a continuously changing environment and/or making complex judgements to arbitrate between competing claims (see, e.g. Elen et al., 2011). Overall, many instructional approaches in this domain

---

[12] We take a longer look at cognitive flexibility in relation to professional education in Chap. 19.

focus on two main cognitive processes: *knowledge representation*, as suggested by Spiro, and *attentional processes*, acknowledging that an ability to notice salient features of the environment is an integral part of one's ability to respond to changing situations and to restructure knowledge appropriately. As others have also argued, conceptual knowledge is not enough: beliefs, and particularly those that belong to personal epistemology, are important. There are two main approaches to understanding how conceptual knowledge relates to personal episte- mology: these echo the classical epistemic beliefs and the epistemological resources' views (described above). We explain them briefly here.

Coming from the epistemic beliefs perspective, Schommer-Aikins (2011) characterises cognitive flexibility as:

> . . . individuals considering and/or embracing alternative choices or responses in a balanced and mindful way. Here 'balanced' implies change that occurs after consideration of a wide array of choices or responses as opposed to a quick impulsive change. And 'mindful' implies the monitoring of the exploration process and the subsequent choices made. Hence, cognitive flexibility involves adaptability including the following: (a) seeing the potential need or benefit to change, (b) making changes after considering alternative choices, (c) monitoring the efficacy of change, and (d) presuming that the changes may not be permanent. (Schommer-Aikins, 2011, p. 62)

Schommer-Aikins primarily considers cognitive flexibility as a set of general 'higher-order' cognitive traits, rather than as knowledge related to a specific domain or context, and she concludes,

> In sum, cognitively flexible individuals are vigilant in monitoring for changes in situational demands and/or may seek change without provocation. <. . .> Broadly speaking, cognitive flexibility can be seen as a habit of the mind. Instead of automaticity being described as routine, mindless responses to set situations, individuals with cognitive flexibility automat- ically think deeply and adaptively. (loc. cit.)

She proposes that this cognitive flexibility is related to epistemological beliefs. Those people who hold more mature epistemological beliefs (about complexity, stability and connectedness of knowledge and gradual learning) will be more willing to spontaneously use strategies that support higher-order thinking. Epis- temological beliefs that enable cognitive flexibility are shaped by many factors, such as parenting, culture and social networks, but, overall, they include a set of general 'higher-order' cognitive traits that are generally independent from the knowledge related to a specific domain or situation in which a person encounters a problem. Thus, cognitively flexible individuals are those who already have mature epistemological beliefs and deploy them automatically across domains and situations.

In contrast, and coming from the epistemic resources perspective, Bromme, Kienhues and Stahl (2008; see also Stahl, 2011) see sophisticated epistemological judgements as involving topic-specific knowledge, therefore drawing on certain kinds of personal knowledge related to the discipline and topic. They identify three sources of cognitive flexibility: (a) epistemological beliefs; (b) topic-related knowledge, including knowledge of the discipline and knowledge of the research methods used in the production of this disciplinary knowledge; and (c) the ontological assumptions about the topic, a set of assumptions about reality, based on a certain perspective that constitutes a coherent body of knowledge – such as biology, medicine or lay people's belief systems about particular domains ('folk biology' or 'folk medicine'). Bromme and colleagues, extending Hammer and Elby's (2002) propositions, argue that when people make epistemological judgements, they activate different topic-related cognitive elements in combination with epistemological beliefs. They propose that epistemological sophistication involves

> ... 'flexibility' of epistemological judgements toward both different disciplines and different contexts. (Bromme et al., 2008, p. 425)

They also make it clear that the generative nature of epistemological beliefs is not located outside the conceptual field, but in fact intertwines both.

> Epistemological beliefs, ontological knowledge, and topic-related knowledge are the sources that can be activated within different contexts. They can complement or compensate each other to attain an epistemological judgement. (op. cit., p. 435)

In short, epistemological beliefs – which have the form of epistemological resources – are a part of what we could call the *conceptual–epistemic assemblage* for making judgements in specific contexts.

These three views offer very different interpretations of what kind of mental resourcefulness enables flexible decisions and what kind of generative mechanism lies behind this flexibility. Spiro and colleagues (Spiro & Jehng, 1990) locate this mechanism directly in the organisation of the conceptual knowledge and its retrieval. From this perspective, knowledge that enables flexibility of human decisions is not one uniform entity, but rather is distributed across multiple schema elements that can be reassembled to fit the needs of diverse problem-solving situations. This flexibility is generally acquired in advance as a part of conceptual learning by developing conceptual structures that integrate different representations of knowledge and allow mental crisscrossing of a complex knowledge domain (Fig. 7.1a).

Schommer-Aikins (2011) removes the main mechanisms that enable cognitive flexibility from the conceptual system and locates them in the sophistication of epistemological beliefs – in some sense, sitting 'above' conceptual knowledge and capable of regulating its functioning and change (Fig. 7.1b).

Bromme et al. (2008) speak of a joint generative mechanism that is constituted by conceptual (ontological and topic related) knowledge and epistemological beliefs: taking the form of dynamically interacting fine-grained context-sensitive resources rather than a large control system (Fig. 7.1c). While they acknowledge that these mental resources are sensitive to the context, nevertheless, they associate this flexibility primarily with a person's cognitive capacity and mental structures that operate inside the human mind.

Our view extends the third of these accounts, to connect with actionable knowledge. We extend the notion of cognitive flexibility in order to deepen the idea of epistemic fluency, proposing that epistemically fluent decisions that are

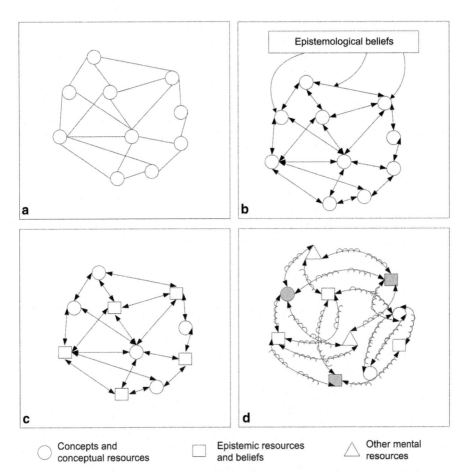

Fig. 7.1 Four ways of seeing flexibility: (**a**) cognitive flexibility as knowledge representation and schema assembly, (**b**) cognitive flexibility as sophisticated epistemological beliefs, (**c**) cognitive flexibility as co-activation of conceptual knowledge and context-sensitive epistemological resources and (**d**) cognitive flexibility as blending of diverse context-sensitive mental resources Notations: *Lines* represent relationships constructed a priori between knowledge elements; *arrows* represent the way that relationships between the conceptual elements are created and changed dynamically; *transparent elements* represent abstract mental entities; *shaded* elements represent the fact that mental entities are grounded in the external environment and in other embodied experiences; 'weaving' *arrows* indicate that the relationships between the elements involve their blending

sensitive to the situation are likely to draw on a much larger distributed collection of fine-grained mental resources – cognitive (including conceptual and epistemic) and noncognitive (including perception and feeling) – activated dynamically in a particular situation (Fig. 7.1d). Such mental resources are developed through numerous diverse experiences, such as engagement with the physical world, use of language and other symbols, social interaction and feeling. They are activated in interaction with material (what we have), symbolic (what we can figure out), social (what others know), affective (how we feel) and other features of the environment. They are blended, amalgamated and reconciled rather than just judged and selected. In short, human perception weaves mind, body and environment into fluent action (and understanding).[13] In defining 'fluency' we need to put context (or environment) first, and, in addition to the mind, we also need to include the body, matter, symbolic, social and other affordances of the environment in which action dynamically unfolds. We discuss this further in Chaps. 8, 9, 10 and 11.

We do not dismiss disciplinary knowledge. Indeed we argue that it is essential. But we want to say that professional knowledge and disciplinary knowledge are structured in different ways and that professional knowledge is more diverse in this regard. Nevertheless, different domains of inquiry – including professional fields – have their own ways of structuring knowledge and knowing to guide their inquiries. (These are publically shared and acknowledged in each field.) For example, teachers structure their understanding around such things as lessons and tasks, counsellors structure their understanding around various kinds of assessments and interventions, architects around drawings and plans and lawyers around cases. Professional ways of structuring the world, action, knowledge and knowing are not incompatible, but they are different from both the disciplinary ways and the ubiquitous (lay or 'naïve') ways of structuring knowledge and knowing associated with similar phenomena. For example, a parent may have a different understanding of what a good lesson looks like, and may use different criteria for evaluating it, than a teacher does. These two ways of thinking are not incompatible, but they are different. If one takes the structure of professional knowledgeable action and ways of knowing as a *primary* frame for structuring actionable knowledgeable and thinking about professional education, then one is better able to connect (a) the ways that professionals structure their inquiries to (b) other ways of knowing and understanding, including the various disciplines, other professional fields and ubiquitous ways of thinking among lay people. This sets the scene for the diverse epistemic forms and epistemic games to which we turn in Chaps. 12, 13, 14 and 15.

In sum, professional ways of seeing the world, with their conceptual resourcefulness, and ways of knowing the world, with their epistemic resourcefulness, are

---

[13] Actionable knowledge and knowledgeable action rarely start from knowledge, but from purpose, environment, perception and action. Thus, we need to swap knowledge and context, so that they are the other way around, and ground human knowledge in the world. We suggest that human understanding *starts* from perception of the situation (i.e. the purpose or object that guides action and the context) and *proceeds towards* sense-making and the knowledge needed for action. That is, professionals engage with knowing for understanding where it is needed for action and being, not merely for knowing 'in a vacuum'. It is the structure of *perception* that drives human *actions*, and it is the structure of *action* that drives knowing and understanding in professional work. Knowing starts from the situation and environment.

not disconnected from the flesh and structure of the material and symbolic world and the human body in which this knowledge is embedded, embodied, created and enacted. We explore this more thoroughly in Chaps. 16, 17 and 18.

References

Banathy, B. H., & Jenlink, P. M. (2004). Systems inquiry and its application in education. In D. H. Jonassen (Ed.), *Handbook of research for educational communications and technology* (2nd ed., pp. 37–57). Mahwah, NJ/London, UK: Lawrence Erlbaum Associates.

Barzilai, S., & Zohar, A. (2014). Reconsidering personal epistemology as metacognition: A multifaceted approach to the analysis of epistemic thinking. *Educational Psychologist, 49*(1), 13–35. doi:10.1080/00461520.2013.863265.

Baxter Magolda, M. B. (2004). Evolution of a constructivist conceptualization of epistemological reflection. *Educational Psychologist, 39*(1), 31–42.

Bendixen, L. D., & Feucht, F. C. (Eds.). (2010). *Personal epistemology in the classroom: Theory, research, and implications for practice.* Cambridge, UK: Cambridge University Press.

Bromme, R., Kienhues, D., & Porsch, T. (2010). Who knows what and who can we believe? Epistemological beliefs are beliefs about knowledge (mostly) to be attained from others. In L. D. Bendixen & F. C. Haerle (Eds.), *Personal epistemology in the classroom: Theory, research, and implications for practice* (pp. 163–193). Cambridge, UK: Cambridge University Press.

Bromme, R., Kienhues, D., & Stahl, E. (2008). Knowledge and epistemological beliefs: An intimate but complicate relationship. In M. S. Khine (Ed.), *Knowing, knowledge and beliefs: Epistemological studies across diverse cultures* (pp. 423–441). Dordrecht, The Netherlands: Springer.

Brownlee, J., Schraw, G., & Berthelsen, D. (Eds.). (2011). *Personal epistemology and teacher education.* New York, NY: Routledge.

Chinn, C. A., Buckland, L. A., & Samarapungavan, A. L. A. (2011). Expanding the dimensions of epistemic cognition: Arguments from philosophy and psychology. *Educational Psychologist, 46*(3), 141–167.

Clark, A. (1999). Embodied, situated and distributed cognition. In W. Bechtel & G. Graham (Eds.), *A companion to cognitive science* (pp. 506–517). Oxford, UK: Basil Blackwell.

Clark, A. (2011). *Supersizing the mind: Embodiment, action and cognitive extension.* Oxford, UK: Oxford University Press.

Clark, A. (2012). Embodied, embedded, and extended cognition. In K. Frankish & W. M. Ramsey (Eds.), *The Cambridge handbook of cognitive science* (pp. 275–291). New York, NY: Cambridge University Press.

Collins, H., & Evans, R. (2007). *Rethinking expertise.* Chicago, IL: The University of Chicago Press.

Cook, S. D. N., & Brown, J. S. (1999). Bridging epistemologies: The generative dance between organizational knowledge and organizational knowing. *Organization Science, 10*(4), 381–400.

Coulson, R., Feltovich, P., & Spiro, R. (1997). Cognitive flexibility in medicine: An application to the recognition and understanding of hypertension. *Advances in Health Sciences Education, 2* (2), 141–161. doi:10.1023/A:1009780229455.

Damsa, C. I., Kirschner, P. A., Andriessen, J. E. B., Erkens, G., & Sins, P. H. M. (2010). Shared epistemic agency: An empirical study of an emergent construct. *Journal of the Learning Sciences, 19*(2), 143–186.

DeBacker, T. K., Crowson, H. M., Beesley, A. D., Thoma, S. J., & Hestevold, N. L. (2008). The challenge of measuring epistemic beliefs: An analysis of three self-report instruments. *The Journal of Experimental Education, 76*(3), 281–312.

Dewey, J., & Bentley, F. (1949/1975). *Knowing and the known.* Westport, CT: Greenwood Press.

diSessa, A. A. (1988). Knowledge in pieces. In G. Forman & P. Pufall (Eds.), *Constructivism in the computer age* (pp. 49–70). Hillsdale, NJ: Lawrence Erlbaum Associates.

diSessa, A. A. (1993). Toward an epistemology of physics. *Cognition and Instruction, 10*(2/3), 105–225.

Dreyfus, H. L. (2014). *Skilful coping: Essays on the phenomenology of everyday perception and action.* New York, NY: Oxford University Press.

Elby, A. (2009). Defining personal epistemology: A response to Hofer & Pintrich (1997) and Sandoval (2005). *Journal of the Learning Sciences, 18*(1), 138–149.

Elby, A., & Hammer, D. (2010). Epistemological resources and framing: A cognitive framework for helping teachers interpret and respond to their students' epistemologies. In L. D. Bendixen & F. C. Feucht (Eds.), *Personal epistemology in the classroom: Theory, research, and implications for practice* (pp. 209–234). Cambridge, UK: Cambridge University Press.

Elen, J., Stahl, E., Bromme, R., & Clarebout, G. (Eds.). (2011). *Links between beliefs and cognitive flexibility: Lessons learned.* Dordrecht, The Netherlands: Springer.

Gibson, J. J. (1979). *The ecological approach to visual perception.* Boston, MA: Houghton Mifflin.

Greene, J. A., Azevedo, R., & Torney-Purta, J. (2008). Modeling epistemic and ontological cognition: Philosophical perspectives and methodological directions. *Educational Psychologist, 43*(3), 142–160.

Greeno, J. G. (1994). Gibson's affordances. *Psychological Review, 101*(2), 336–342.

Hammer, D., & Elby, A. (2002). On the form of a personal epistemology. In B. K. Hofer & P. R. Pintrich (Eds.), *Personal epistemology: The psychology of beliefs about knowledge and knowing* (pp. 169–190). Mahwah, NJ: Lawrence Erlbaum Associates.

Hofer, B. K. (2001). Personal epistemology research: Implications for learning and teaching. *Educational Psychology Review, 13*(4), 353–383.

Hofer, B. K. (2002). Personal epistemology as educational and psychological construct. In B. K. Hofer & P. R. Pintrich (Eds.), *Personal epistemology: The psychology of beliefs about knowledge and knowing* (pp. 3–14). Mahwah, NJ: Lawrence Erlbaum Associates.

Hofer, B. K. (2004a). Exploring the dimensions of personal epistemology in differing classroom contexts: Student interpretations during the first year of college. *Contemporary Educational Psychology, 29*(2), 129–163.

Hofer, B. K. (2004b). Introduction: Paradigmatic approaches to personal epistemology. *Educational Psychologist, 39*(1), 1–3.

Hofer, B. K. (2006a). Beliefs about knowledge and knowing: Integrating domain specificity and domain generality: A response to Muis, Bendixen, and Haerle (2006). *Educational Psychology Review, 18*(1), 67–76.

Hofer, B. K. (2006b). Domain specificity of personal epistemology: Resolved questions, persistent issues, new models. *International Journal of Educational Research, 45*(1–2), 85–95.

Hofer, B. K. (2008). Personal epistemology and culture. In M. S. Khine (Ed.), *Knowing, knowledge and beliefs: Epistemological studies across diverse cultures* (pp. 3–22). Dordrecht, The Netherlands: Springer.

Hofer, B., & Pintrich, P. (1997). The development of epistemological theories: Beliefs about knowing and their relation to learning. *Review of Educational Research, 67*(1), 88–140.

Hofer, B. K., & Pintrich, P. R. (Eds.). (2002). *Personal epistemology: The psychology of beliefs about knowledge and knowing.* Mahwah, NJ: Lawrence Erlbaum Associates.

Hogan, K. (2000). Exploring a process view of students' knowledge about the nature of science. *Science Education, 84*(1), 51–70.

Ingold, T. (2011). *Being alive: Essays on movement, knowledge and description.* Oxon, OX: Routledge.

Khine, M. S. (Ed.). (2008). *Knowing, knowledge and beliefs: Epistemological studies across diverse cultures.* Dordrecht, The Netherlands: Springer.

King, P. M., & Kitchener, K. S. (2002). The reflective judgment model: Twenty years of research on epistemic cognition. In B. K. Hofer & P. R. Pintrich (Eds.), *Personal epistemology: The psychology of beliefs about knowledge and knowing* (pp. 37–61). Mahway, NJ: Lawrence Erlbaum Associates.

Kirsh, D. (2009). Problem solving and situated cognition. In P. Robbins & M. Aydede (Eds.), *The Cambridge handbook of situated cognition* (pp. 264–306). Cambridge, UK: Cambridge University Press.

Kirsh, D., & Maglio, P. (1994). On distinguishing epistemic from pragmatic action. *Cognitive Science, 18*(4), 513–549. doi:10.1016/0364-0213(94)90007-8.

Kitchener, K. S. (1983). Cognition, metacognition, and epistemic cognition. A three-level model of cognitive processing. *Human Development, 26*(4), 222–232.

Kitchener, K. S. (2011). Personal epistemology and philosophical epistemology: The view of a philosopher. In J. Elen, E. Stahl, R. Bromme, & G. Clarebout (Eds.), *Links between beliefs and cognitive flexibility: Lessons learned* (pp. 79–101). Dordrecht, The Netherlands: Springer.

Kitchener, R. F. (2002). Folk epistemology: An introduction. *New Ideas in Psychology, 20*(2–3), 89–105.

Knappett, C. (2004). The affordances of things: A post-Gibsonian perspective on the relationality of mind and matter. In E. DeMarrais, C. Gosden, & C. Renfrew (Eds.), *Rethinking materiality: The engagement of mind with the material world* (pp. 43–51). Cambridge, UK: McDonald Institute Monographs.

Kuhn, D., Cheney, R., & Weinstock, M. (2000). The development of epistemological understanding. *Cognitive Development, 15*(3), 309–328.

Kuhn, D., & Weinstock, M. (2002). What is epistemological thinking and why does it matter? In B. K. Hofer & P. R. Pintrich (Eds.), *Personal epistemology: The psychology of beliefs about knowledge and knowing* (pp. 121–144). Mahway, NJ: Lawrence Erlbaum Associates.

Kvanvig, J. (2005). Is truth the primary epistemic goal. In M. Steup & E. Sosa (Eds.), *Contemporary debates in epistemology*. Malden, MA: Blackwell.

Limon, M. (2006). The domain generality-specificity of epistemological beliefs: A theoretical problem, a methodological problem or both? *International Journal of Educational Research, 45*(1–2), 7–27.

Muis, K., Bendixen, L., & Haerle, F. (2006). Domain-generality and domain-specificity in personal epistemology research: Philosophical and empirical reflections in the development of a theoretical framework. *Educational Psychology Review, 18*(1), 3–54.

Olafson, L., & Schraw, G. (2006). Teachers' beliefs and practices within and across domains. *International Journal of Educational Research, 45*(1–2), 71–84.

Perry, W. G. (1970). *Forms of intellectual and ethical development in the college years: A scheme.* New York, NY: Holt, Rinehart and Winston.

Royce, J. R. (1974). Cognition and knowledge: Psychological epistemology. In E. C. Carterette & M. F. Friedman (Eds.), *Handbook of perception. Historical and philosophical roots to perception* (Vol. 1, pp. 149–176). New York, NY: Academic Press.

Sandoval, W. A. (2005). Understanding students' practical epistemologies and their influence on learning through inquiry. *Science Education, 89*(4), 634–656.

Sandoval, W. A. (2012). Situating epistemological development. In J. V. Aalst, K. Thompson, M. J. Jacobson, & P. Reimann (Eds.), *Future of learning: Proceedings of the 10th international conference of the learning sciences* (Vol. 1, pp. 347–354). Sydney, Australia: International Society of the Learning Sciences.

Schommer, M. (1990). Effects of beliefs about the nature of knowledge on comprehension. *Journal of Educational Psychology, 82*(3), 498–504.

Schommer, M., & Walker, K. (1995). Are epistemological beliefs similar across domains? *Journal of Educational Psychology, 87*(3), 424–432.

Schommer-Aikins, M. (2011). Spontaneous cognitive flexibility and an encompassing system of epistemological beliefs. In J. Elen, E. Stahl, R. Bromme, & G. Clarebout (Eds.), *Links between beliefs and cognitive flexibility: Lessons learned*. Dordrecht, The Netherlands: Springer.

Schraw, G. J., & Olafson, L. J. (2008). Assessing teachers' epistemological and ontological worldviews. In M. S. Khine (Ed.), *Knowing, knowledge and beliefs: Epistemological studies across diverse cultures* (pp. 25–44). Amsterdam, The Netherlands: Springer.

Silverman, A. (2014). Plato's middle period metaphysics and epistemology. In E. N. Zalta (Ed.), *The Stanford encyclopedia of philosophy* (Fall 2014 ed.). Retrieved August 15, 2015 from http://plato.stanford.edu/entries/plato-metaphysics.

Spiro, R. J., & Jehng, J. (1990). Cognitive flexibility and hypertext: Theory and technology for the non-linear and multidimensional traversal of complex subject matter. In D. Nix & R. Spiro (Eds.), *Cognition, education, and multimedia* (pp. 163–205). Hillsdale, NJ: Lawrence Erlbaum Associates.

Spiro, R. J., Coulson, R. L., Feltovich, P. J., & Anderson, D. K. (1988/2013). Cognitive flexibility theory: Advanced knowledge acquisition in ill-structured domains. In D. E. Alvermann, N. J. Unrau, & R. B. Ruddell (Eds.), Theoretical models and processes of reading (6th ed., pp. 544–557). Newark, DE: International Reading Association.

Stahl, E. (2011). The generative nature of epistemological judgments: Focussing on interactions instead of elements to understand the relations between epistemological beliefs and cognitive flexibility. In J. Elen, E. Stahl, R. Bromme, & G. Clarebout (Eds.), *Links between beliefs and cognitive flexibility: Lessons learned* (pp. 37–60). Dordrecht, The Netherlands: Springer.

Steup, M. (2014). Epistemology. In E. N. Zalta (Ed.), *The Stanford encyclopedia of philosophy* (Spring 2014 ed.). Retrieved July 15, 2015 from http://plato.stanford.edu/archives/spr2014/entries/epistemology.

Steup, M., & Sosa, E. (Eds.). (2005). *Contemporary debates in epistemology*. Malden, MA: Blackwell.

Thompson, E. (2010). *Mind in life: Biology, phenomenology, and the sciences of mind*. Cambridge, MA: Harvard University Press.

Tillema, H., & Orland-Barak, L. (2006). Constructing knowledge in professional conversations: The role of beliefs on knowledge and knowing. *Learning and Instruction, 16*(6), 592–608.

Varela, F. J., Thompson, E., & Rosch, E. (1991). *The embodied mind: Cognitive science and human experience*. Cambridge, MA: MIT Press.

von Foerster, H. (2003). Ethics and second-order cybernetics. In *Understanding understanding: Essays on cybernetics and cognition* (pp. 287–304). New York, NY: Springer.

Zhang, J., & Patel, V. L. (2006). Distributed cognition, representation, and affordance. *Pragmatics Cognition, 14*(2), 333–341.

Chapter 8
Objects, Things and Artefacts in Professional Learning and Doing

... the hardest bit is to engage the students into *feeling* like nurses, feeling like they're *doing* nursing. <...> [T]rying to get them to *think* as a nurse, and that was the whole purpose behind doing this assignment too – to look at the fact that it's not just clinical skills that you need evidence behind what you're doing. (Nursing Practice Coordinator)

8.1 Assessment Tasks in Professional Education

As we pointed out in Chap. 2, if one takes an inventory of the time that students spend in university education, preparing for and completing assessments come high on the list. Assessment tasks are taken seriously by students.

Understanding the nature of assessment tasks can tell us a lot about what teachers are aiming to achieve, what students will experience, what they will come to know, what they will be able to do and what kinds of relationships they will form with knowledge practices in their professions. Of course, neither the goals set by teachers in assessment tasks nor the contexts in which the tasks are given can determine, in any strong sense, the specific ways in which students will approach these tasks, the epistemic practices in which they will engage or their learning outcomes. Students' approaches to the tasks they are set vary considerably, and what they actually do (their actual activity) determines what they learn (Biggs & Tang, 2007; Ginestié, 2008a; Goodyear, 2005; Hallden, Scheja, & Haglund, 2008; Prosser & Trigwell, 1999). That said, task and activity are not unrelated. They are dynamically interacting elements that play significant roles in the same complex system of learning. Assessment tasks can be regarded as 'critical agents' (or 'leverage points') in the overall ecology of learning: a small change in the specification of a task can bring about a big change in students' activities, experiences and outcomes.

Assessment tasks offer us a handy empirical focus. They provide an important gathering point where knowledge meets performance and observable outcome. To

© Springer Science+Business Media Dordrecht 2017
L. Markauskaite, P. Goodyear, *Epistemic Fluency and Professional Education*,
Professional and Practice-based Learning 14, DOI 10.1007/978-94-007-4369-4_8

make this more explicit, we can draw parallels while acknowledging some differences, between an expert practitioner's work, creating professional products, and a student's work, producing assessment artefacts. When we focus on students' work on specific tasks, learning activities and outcomes become 'well defined, goal oriented and concrete' and manifested in concrete actions and artefacts.

Our empirical focus in this chapter is assessment tasks that students complete in university courses as a part of preparing for professional practice. As we are interested in epistemic practices in professional learning, we have deliberately selected courses that are taught before or concurrently with students' short-term practical experiences, internships or work placements. (These courses often have titles like 'Craft knowledge', 'Professional practice' or 'Development of professional experience'.) This choice of empirical focus – on the boundary of professional learning and work – provides insights into:

- *Bridging epistemologies* that (aim to) link knowledge and ways of knowing in university with ways of thinking and doing in professional settings
- *Fundamental challenges* that future professionals, and their teachers, experience in making the shift from students' epistemic practices (ways of thinking and doing in university courses) to professional epistemic practices (ways of thinking, acting and being in workplaces)

Our conceptual perspective draws on the idea of *mediation*: object-focussed and artefact-focussed practice and knowing. We see artefacts as having multimodal dynamic affordances for knowing: knowledge and things yet to be known (see Chap. 7).

The ideas that inform our approach evolved on the boundaries between several theoretical traditions and have their empirical roots in developmental psychology, sociocultural studies, anthropology, science and technology studies (STS) and organisational research. The key concepts have been explored in a number of areas, but are perhaps most coherently developed through several generations of work in cultural–historical activity theory (CHAT).[1] More recently, they have surfaced in adjacent areas of research, such as:

- Studies on innovation, knowledge building and organisational change (Bereiter, 2002; Checkland & Poulter, 2006; Checkland & Scholes, 1999; Nonaka & Takeuchi, 1995; Nonaka & Toyama, 2007; Paavola & Hakkarainen, 2005; Paavola, Lipponen, & Hakkarainen, 2004)
- A range of anthropological studies of practices and cognition in scientific laboratories and other research settings (Knorr Cetina, 1999; Nersessian, 2006; Rheinberger, 1997), in low-tech and hi-tech workplaces (Goodwin, 1994, 1997, 2005; Hutchins, 1995; Ingold, 2000, 2010; Jensen, Lahn, & Nerland, 2012; Keller & Keller, 1996; Lave, 1988; Lave & Wenger, 1991; Scribner, 1997; Suchman, 2005, 2007) and in schools and other learning places (Sørensen,

---

[1] See, for example, Vygotsky (1978), Leontiev (1978, 1981) and Engeström (2001, 2008). For accessible reviews, see Engeström, Miettinen and Punamäki (1999) and Kaptelinin (2005).

2009; see also Fenwick & Edwards, 2010; Fenwick, Edwards, & Sawchuk, 2011)

Similar attention to objects of activity and recognition of the central role of artefacts in workplace, scientific and educational settings have generated some useful concepts for analysing phenomena on the boundaries between higher education and workplaces, in the relations between learning, knowing and doing.

In the next part of the chapter (Sects. 8.2 and 8.3), we introduce the notion of mediation and construct working definitions of 'object' – as material entity and as motive. We distinguish between 'neat' objects and 'shaggy' things and look at ways in which motives, material objects and things interrelate. We also introduce *epistemic* objects and artefacts. Next, in Sects. 8.4 and 8.5, we expand on the framework sketched above and makes some sharper comparisons between different kinds of artefacts. Using examples from our studies of professional, practice-related courses, we reveal some of the kinds of objects that guide university students' inquiries and the kinds of artefacts they produce. Then, we look more deeply at key features of these artefacts, how they are used for learning, what their relationships with professional knowledge and knowing practices are and what kinds of epistemic experiences these artefacts afford. Section 8.6 uses Wartofsky's (1979) work on how artefacts embody human skills and practices, or have these inscribed within them. Artefacts can thereby be used to preserve, transmit and imagine skills and working practices. We illustrate this in Sect. 8.7 with an analysis of the assessment tasks that students are asked to tackle, showing how different kinds of artefacts support different kinds of engagement with work and knowledge. Finally, we review Bereiter's (2002) treatment of conceptual artefacts, examining what happens when they travel between scientific and professional forms of knowledge work (Sect. 8.8).

Through this exploration, we develop three arguments. First, learning in higher education and doing in the workplace are inherently directed towards different kinds of (knowledge) objects, the former towards more abstract forms of knowledge that can travel across contexts and situations, the latter towards concrete products that are, or could be easily transformed into, specific outcomes in a specific context. Second, there is a trend for some professions to produce new kinds of epistemic artefacts for non-professional users (e.g. clients) and for specialists from other professions. These do not easily find a place in existing categorisations of epistemic artefacts, yet they play a fundamental role in shared knowledgeable actions, distributed across settings and people. Third, students learn professional knowledge not only by encountering the world through abstract qualities of artefacts but also by experiencing their social and material 'textures' – engaging with and making epistemic artefacts. Students encounter the world in this dual sense – 'objects as things' and 'things as objects'.

8.2   Knowing Through Objects: Objectual Practices in Learning and Work

We will now construct working definitions of the key theoretical term 'object' and derive some insights into the ambiguous nature of objects that are constructed on the boundaries between the university and the workplace. To begin our argument, we draw on the cultural notion of *mediation*.

Vygotsky (1978), offering the notion of mediation, argued that the higher psychological processes – going beyond the biological levels that we share with other animals – are made possible by the incorporation of artificial stimuli – tools, signs and other mediating objects. As Säljö (1995) says:

> We do not encounter the world as it exists in any neutral and objective sense outside the realm of human experience. We learn to interact with it by means of the signs and tools provided by our culture and in terms of which phenomena make sense. (Säljö, 1995, p. 84)

Säljö argues that, from this perspective, human cognitive development and learning can be regarded as a process of 'cognitive socialisation' – of 'appropriating' those tools and signs that originate in human cultures:

> In other words, the world is pre-interpreted for us by previous generations, and we draw on the experiences that others have made before us. (loc. cit.)

Tools, discourse and other signs serve as mediational objects in human sense-making. They allow inhabitants of the culture to find structure in the world and give distinct meaning to the phenomena encountered, which otherwise would be impossibly intricate and open to an infinite number of interpretations.

This notion of mediation has been embraced and extended in *object-focussed* interpretations of human practice, inquiry and knowledge building (e.g. Engeström, 2001, 2008; Engeström & Blackler, 2005; Knorr Cetina, 1999, 2001; Paavola et al., 2004; Paavola & Hakkarainen, 2005). Objects are seen as central in such work.

As Kaptelinin (2005) argues, every human activity is directed towards an object or goal that gives direction and structure to the activity:

> . . . the activity does not have a direction and does not really start until the object of activity is defined. (Kaptelinin, 2005, p. 16)

However, the notion of 'object' has different interpretations in different philosophical and research traditions that have evolved during the last two centuries.[2] As Engeström and Blackler (2005) point out, early attention to objects emerged because of their centrality in social life. The early Marxian tradition associated the notion of object with 'commodity' – that is, as something defined by social and labour relationships.

Later, this conception was overlaid or replaced by structuralist, semiotic, poststructuralist and other interpretative traditions that have emerged in social and cultural studies. These downplayed the materiality of objects and placed objects in the realm of human thought, social meaning-making and culture (Boivin,

---

[2] For reviews of the different interpretations of objects, see Akkerman and Bakker (2011), Engeström and Blackler (2005), Ewenstein and Whyte (2009), Miettinen (2005), Miettinen and Virkkunen (2005), Nicolini, Mengis, and Swan (2012) and Star (2010).

2008). The material world and objects were primarily seen as 'envelopes of meaning' – as symbols open for, and subjected to, discursive interpretation (Engeström & Blackler, 2005; Pels, Hetherington, & Vandenberghe, 2002).

Other scholars have questioned the conventional divide between human subjects and nonhuman objects (e.g. Barad, 2003; Latour & Woolgar, 1979). On this view, objects, like humans, take on the role of agents who, in 'ontological symmetry' with humans, can form relationships and participate in heterogeneous networks of humans and nonhumans.

These lines of thought have been combined in some 'practice theories' (e.g. Schatzki, Knorr Cetina, & von Savigny, 2001). Such theories tend to displace the human mind from its dominant place in social reality, including in knowledge work and inquiry, and put it in a dynamic relationship with other aspects of human practice and the world, including the material and symbolic, individual and collective and psychological and cultural. The 'backbone' of such practices is not the human mind and not the material, but the *entanglement* – between the subject and the object, the human and the material – that emerges in practice. Objects serve as centring and integrating devices for directing practice – they provide the 'glue' for professional work and discourse (Engeström, 2004; Knorr Cetina, 1997). Objects, when they are forming the backbone of practice, are both defined by existing meanings, material settings and practices and dynamically unfold, acquiring new meanings and material forms.

Knowledge, forms of practice and cognition, norms and other shared meanings in collective settings and communities cannot exist only in the form of intersubjective agreements. If they are to influence the course of collective action, they have to be 'objectified' (Miettinen & Virkkunen, 2005), 'reified'[3] (Wenger, 1998), 'inscribed' (Hall, Stevens, & Torralba, 2002; Roth & McGinn, 1998), 'represented' (Hall, 1997) or in some other way captured and instantiated in concrete material form. Such objects include artefacts embedded in the organisational environment, e.g. maps, memories and programs (Argyris & Schön, 1996), and other kinds of cultural artefacts – norms of action and cognition that are given concrete material expression (Miettinen & Virkkunen, 2005).

Enduring material quality is an essential characteristic of such objects and of how we depend upon them:

> ... consciousness does not exist as situated inside the head of the individual, but is rooted in the constant interaction between individuals and the world of objectified cultural artefacts. (Miettinen & Virkkunen, 2005, p. 443)[4]

A number of studies illustrate the central role of material objects in human cognition and epistemic activity, including professional practices and learning

---

[3] Wenger (1998) defines 'reification' as follows: 'the process of giving form to our experience by producing objects that congeal this experience. <...> [This creates] a point of focus around which the negotiation of meaning becomes organized. <...> [W]riting down a law, creating a procedure, or producing a tool is a similar process. A certain understanding is given form' (p. 59).

[4] There is more to be experienced in the world than 'objectified cultural artefacts', of course.

that fuse physical and intellectual activity (e.g. Ginestié, 2008b; Goodwin, 1994, 1997, 2005; Ludvigsen, Lund, Rasmussen, & Säljö, 2011; Sørensen, 2009). As Säljö (1995) argues:

> In a very fundamental sense, we think with and through artifacts. In human practices there is an intricate interplay between tools and physical activities. The experienced carpenter attempting to establish how much wood will be needed when repairing the wall of a wooden house *will make a drawing of the building and make his calculations by means of this paper and pencil version* of the house. There will be no need to measure the wall more than once, since the drawing – if done with adequate precision – mediates the wall in a functional manner. Most further reasoning can be done without measuring the real object. (Säljö, 1995, p. 90, emphasis added)

Miettinen and Virkkunen (2005), following Bruno Latour (1991), stress the importance of understanding these material objects:

> ... we should look for the foundations of social order and continuity not in the 'abstract' forms of sociality (norms, values, roles, shared meanings), but rather in enduring material objects, such as buildings, machines, traffic systems, laws, library collections, systems of classification, psychological tests and art works. (Miettinen & Virkkunen, 2005, p. 442)

This enduring nature of objects also points to some other important qualities, associated with how they are produced in organisations and in professional practices (Argyris & Schön, 1996; Engeström & Blackler, 2005; Knorr Cetina, 2001; Wenger, 1998). On the one hand, objects are not constructed on the spot, but have histories in professional and organisational cultures, tools and other material forms of organising and acting. In this sense, they are carriers of knowledge, habits and routines and provide for continuation of practice. On the other hand, objects are not just given or found, but are produced and reproduced by people as they make sense of the world, encounter challenges, name things and capture experiences, thoughts, wishes or goals.

In this sense, as Knorr Cetina (2001) argues, objects are both *meaning producing* and *practice generating*, as they provide for continuation, but also extension, of practice – what she called *objectual practice*. Objectual practice is a collective, culturally defined practice, as objects have a power to fuse meaning-making (discourse) and action together – directing attention and aligning actions. An important part of becoming a professional is learning to encounter the world with and through professional objects. As Goodwin (1994) says:

> Central to the social and cognitive organization of a profession is its ability to shape events in the domain of its scrutiny into the *phenomenal objects around which the discourse of the profession is organized*: to find archaeologically relevant events such as post holes in the color stains visible in a patch of dirt and map them or to locate legally consequential instances of aggression or cooperation in the visible movements of a man's body. (Goodwin, 1994, p. 626, emphasis added)

This section has introduced the first sense in which 'object' can be seen as a useful term in understanding objectual practices that are grounded in the material world. We want to distinguish two main senses – object as material entity and object as motive. These two senses are sometimes mixed up in the literature. We need to distinguish them clearly in order then to show how they are intimately related in objectual practices in professional learning. Some writers have introduced a third distinction – between material object and 'thing'.

In the next section, we shift attention to the second sense of 'object' – as *motive*. We will then distinguish between material objects and *things*, before looking at how the distinctions and relations between motives, objects and things can help analyse what is going on when students create *artefacts* in and for assessment tasks.

8.3   Motives, Objects and Things

Before we get too deeply involved in the nature, properties and roles of various kinds of material objects in professional learning, we need to point out some 'immaterial' qualities of objects and some disassociations (as well as connections) with their material counterparts. This difference between the material and immaterial, and different shades of materiality, is important for understanding the nature and qualities of the material objects produced in two different settings – educational and professional.

Kaptelinin (2005) reviews the two main traditions within activity theory – personal development (Leontiev, 1978, 1981) and organisational learning (Engeström, 2001, 2008).[5] Kaptelinin reminds us that Leontiev (1978), discussing individual development, defined the object of an activity in broad terms as a 'true motive' aroused by a certain need that gives to the activity a determined direction. This true motive may be material and present in perception, but it also could be ideal and present 'only in the imagination or thought'. The motive does not define specific goals or actions carried out by individuals for its realisation, but it does set a general direction and purpose. Leontiev illustrates this as follows. The motive of an individual may be to get food, but the actions carried out to achieve this may be directed towards various goals, such as preparing equipment for fishing, going fishing by herself or himself or giving the equipment to others and then obtaining a part of the catch.

As Kaptelinin explains, Leontiev developed his notion of 'object of activity' in the context of developmental psychology and was mainly interested in individual mental development in culturally mediated contexts. Therefore, he was concerned with motives and activities carried out by individuals rather than collectives (even if those activities were situated in a collective context). Specific actions may be carried out individually or collectively, but, on Leontiev's view, the 'true motive' – the object of this activity – is predominately individual. In relation to mental development, concrete actions, specific outcomes and relationships with others and the context are less significant than mental growth.

In contrast, Engeström (2001), elaborating some fundamental concepts of cultural–historical activity theory for organisational learning, defined the object

---

[5] See also Engeström (2001) for a review of the three generations of cultural–historical activity theory and Engeström, Miettinen and Punamäki (1999) for other extensions.

of activity in terms of a 'problem space' to which activity is directed. He called the object of activity a 'raw material' that is transformed, as a result of this activity, into a solution or outcome. In the context of organisational learning and change, specific actions are carried out by groups of individuals, and the object of activity is associated with the production of a specific outcome. Such an object has to have an objective physical existence and has to be realised in a certain material form.

8.3.1 Predmet and Objekt

Kaptelinin (2005) explains an important difference between two interpretations of the concept of 'object of activity' for which Leontiev (1978), in his original writings, used two different Russian words: *predmet* and *objekt*. These two words closely mirror the difference between two notions of the object described above. *Predmet* mainly refers to a broader target or content of a thought or action and denotes objective orientation of activity (i.e. a motive), while *objekt* has a narrower meaning and refers to material objective reality – entities that exist independently from one's mind.

This distinction between the two kinds of objects – or two kinds of qualities that may attach to objects – turns out to play an important role in analysing and understanding assessment practices in professional education. Professional preparation courses are guided by broad aims – a general, future-oriented, developmental motive – rather than by the need to seek specific solutions to specific work-based problems. Preparation for future professional work involves motives such as 'thinking like a nurse' or 'developing an ethical disposition'. Such broad objects are not easy to render into a specific or material form, without changing the object itself into something narrow and concrete – such as solving a specific problem of practice.

In short, learning for future practice is oriented towards *predmet* rather than *objekt(s)*. In contrast, learning activity is a specific activity. It has to be carried out via concrete tasks. Such activity may have an abstract motive – for example, to learn to understand and to do things in specific ways, such as to base decisions about the correctness of clinical procedures on available evidence. However, it has to have an object (*objekt*), i.e. has to be realised via specific tasks, so as to produce a specific artefact that gives a tangible form to some general capacities or understandings. An example of this could be a task to produce an induction guide for parents new to a school, drawing on evidence about home–school relations. Thus, concrete actions performed by students in concrete contexts and concrete realisations of objects in specific artefacts are oriented towards an *objekt*.

Kaptelinin (2005) argued that an object of activity is not necessarily determined by a single motive – humans may have multiple motives – thus, 'the object of activity is cooperatively determined by all effective motives' (p. 17), and 'objects of activities are dynamically constructed on the basis of various types of constraints' (loc. cit.). Moreover:

> The object of activity can be considered the "*ultimate reason*" behind various behaviors of individuals, groups, or organizations. In other words, the object of activity can be defined as

> *"the sense-maker,"* which gives *meaning* to and determines values of various entities and phenomena. (Kaptelinin, 2005, p. 5, emphasis added)

In short, objects are imbued with meanings, are well understood and are transparent. They encapsulate human motives and activities by giving meaning to daily actions. Further, objects have to be set before any effective or worthwhile action can really get underway.

As Kaptelinin and Nardi (2006) argue, objects are relatively 'long lived' and offer a certain degree of stability, allowing people to get on with the job, rather than challenge meanings. They oppose the view of seeing human professional activities as a series of (semi-)conscious decisions shaped by situational constraints rather than meanings. They criticise studies conducted in research laboratories that describe the research activities and fundamental research drivers as a series of solutions of 'doable' problems. Kaptelinin and Nardi (2006) assert that addressing some problems – such as those faced in collaborative scientific work in large laboratories – requires tremendous dedication, passion and desire: the description of *what* people are doing does not say much about *why* they are doing it:

> The use of terms such as "tinkering" (to describe working on doable problems) misses the mark when work is viewed in the wider context of motivated object-oriented activity. (Kaptelinin & Nardi, 2006, p. 285)

In short, the *what* of work does not help us understand the *why* of work – which creates the horizon for actions.

8.3.2   Objects and Things

In contrast, others question whether objects – named, explicit, fixed and transparent, as they are viewed in many socio-material perspectives – are so exclusively central in guiding skilful, knowledgeable actions. For example, Tim Ingold (2010) and Carl Knappett (2010) make a distinction between objects and *things*:

> Things are ambiguous and undefined; when you say 'pass me that green thing over there,' the thing is unintelligible in some way. Objects, on the other hand, are named, understood and transparent. (Knappett, 2010, p. 82)

Ingold (2010), rather like Kaptelinin and Nardi (2006), notes that *objects* offer a degree of stability and certainty; thus, if the environment was populated with objects, it would be easier to understand the world. However, Ingold (2010) asserts that the inhabited world is not so much composed of objects as of *things* – forms arise in flows of materials, rather than being set a priori, and 'stand against us'. He illustrates this by describing a tree in the open air and insists:

> ... the character of this particular tree lies just as much in the way it responds to the currents of wind, in the swaying of its branches and the rustling of its leaves, then we might wonder whether the tree can be anything other than a tree-in-the-air. <...> [T]he tree is not an object at all, but a certain gathering together of the threads of life. That is what I mean by a thing. (Ingold, 2010, p. 4)

As inhabitants of the world, we experience and construct our knowledge and skill not so much through confronting predefined static forms set by objects, but through joining the fluxes of materials that gather and hold together in one place as things. Ingold (2011) illustrates this by describing a carpenter sawing a plank of wood:

> Thus the carpenter himself, [is] obliged to follow the material and respond to its singularities. <...> No two strokes of the saw are quite alike, and each – far from following its predecessors like a beads on a string – grows out of the one before and prepares for the next. Thus the carpenter who has a feel for what he is doing is one who can harmonise the current variations with which he has to deal. (Ingold, 2011, pp. 216–217)

The plank is not so much an object as it is a thing. An experienced carpenter's knowledge and skill are not expressed as the imposition of preconceived forms onto material substances (whether static or dynamically constructed). Rather, they are expressed in the improvisatory and rhythmic quality of movement, which joins the currents of materials, through which forms are generated:

> ... thinking is a process that carries on, as do movement, speech and the materials of which things are made. (Ingold, 2012, p. 439)

Ingold mainly argues about the things, knowledge and skills embodied in manual work. Knappett (2010) makes similar claims, but argues for the 'cognitive life' of things, in the context of human epistemic work. He observes:

> ... in work that has focussed on the *cognitive* life of material culture, the emphasis appears to have fallen more on 'objects' – entities that have a clear functional role in a given task or set of tasks. <...> There is not much feeling for thingness in these cases, of stuff just being there, not fully perceived or understood. It is as if every entity around us in our material world can be precisely named and functionally ascribed. (Knappett, 2010, p. 82, original emphasis)

In contrast to those who place 'things' in opposition to 'objects' in human skilful and knowledgeable activity (cf. Ingold, 2010, 2011, 2012; Kaptelinin & Nardi, 2006), Knappett (2011) argues that *both* perspectives are necessary for a thorough understanding of invention and innovation. The 'thing perspective' provides a 'zoomed in' view. It is a way in which a practitioner (or a student) perceives the world and orients himself in the situated-embodied action of production. The 'object perspective' provides a 'zoomed out' view. It is a way in which an analyst (or a student) orients him/herself when he/she looks at a finished product and traces back to the sources and causes that produced the outcome. A creative 'configurational thinking' involves enmeshing these two perspectives – seeing objects and joining the currents of materials through things.

8.3.3   Motive, Material Object and Thing

Predmet, *objekt* and *thing*[6] are distinguishable but closely related. When we think about professional work and learning, there is a substantial difference between

---

[6] The closest Russian word for 'thing' would be 'vesch' (вещь).

broader capability – which aligns with *predmet* – and the ability to perform a specified sequence of operations on entities in the world. There is also a substantial difference between being able to manipulate well-behaved objects in the world (such as filling a syringe) and being able to give the right injection to a severely injured patient in the complex, turbulent world of the emergency room.

To develop broader capabilities – such as 'to think like a nurse' – is difficult and may be an impossible learning task within higher education. It cannot be achieved through learning the steps of the nursing tasks (or 'deconstructing nursing' as an analyst does). Nor can it be achieved through performing tasks as they appear in professional practice (i.e. 'doing nursing' as practitioners do).

There is a disassociation between *predmet*, *objekt* and *thing* in the learning context, which changes the entire learning activity. Instead of directly creating real professional artefacts, in order to learn, students often create artefacts that are not an intrinsic part of the profession, or they create modified artefacts, like 'nursing guidelines'. Yet, it seems such modified versions of artefacts reduce the gap between *predmet*, *objekt* and *thing*. How – we will elaborate later when we discuss qualities of epistemic artefacts, in Chap. 9.

Predmet, *objekt* and *thing* are not isomorphic in the academic context. Overall, successful completion of an assessment task does not necessarily imply expertise – or even the competence, in Eraut's (2009) terms, to carry out similar tasks in other contexts. The opposite can be true as well. An inability to complete an academic task that requires objectifying some skills in a material artefact that in a real professional context would not be embodied in such an artefact (e.g. in a portfolio) does not imply an inability to perform the action that requires this skill in a variety of contexts. Consider the example of nursing guidelines. An experienced nurse may not be able to create guidelines and may not be able even to articulate the actions that she performs, yet she may be competent to do the actual task in a variety of situations. A student, in contrast, may know the steps and may be competent to find and integrate the best evidence about 'why' this nursing procedure is done in a particular way and, accordingly, to produce the guidelines, but yet may not have the skills to actually perform the task: to feel like a nurse – *to work with the thing*.

This issue becomes more complicated when, using Kaptelinin and Nardi's (2006) vocabulary, the *constructed* or intended object is conflated with, or disassociated from, the *instantiated* object (i.e. an artefact in which this knowledge or skill is 'objectified') and the latter, rather than the former, becomes the focus of students' activity when they work on a given assessment task. That is, students may focus on the design of the final artefact (such as a presentation to peers or layout of the guidelines) and give insufficient attention to the knowledge or skill that they learn and represent. Or, vice versa, the students may focus on sense-making, meanings and skills, but undervalue the production of the artefact which instantiates their learning.

8.3.4   Knowledge Work, Epistemic Objects and Epistemic Artefacts

In the context of deliberative action and productive inquiry, an object is also not an immutable entity, but it is simultaneously both objective and projective: (a) the departure point for inquiry, something already given to perception and mind, and (b) an ultimate target or purpose (Adler, 2005; Miettinen, 2005, 2006; Miettinen & Virkkunen, 2005).

Adler (2005) illustrates the point:

> The object of the blacksmith's activity is simultaneously a piece of iron, an inert mass, and the mental image of the shape it should take, a goal. Indeed, it is the tension between the two that motivates the blacksmith's activity and thus serves as a starting point for understanding the form of organization assumed by that activity. (Adler, 2005, p. 403)

In the context of knowledge work, the notion of object becomes even more dynamic and stands in a more complex relationship with its material counterpart. Knowledge objects typically are characterised as incomplete, they stand for something that is not yet known, they often have multiple representations and they change. As Knorr Cetina (2001) says:

> ... objects of knowledge can never be fully attained, that they are, if you wish, never quite themselves. What we encounter in the research process are representations or stand-ins for a more basic lack of object. (Knorr Cetina, 2001, p. 181)

Objects of knowledge – which Knorr Cetina calls *epistemic objects* – are fundamentally different from the commodities or other fixed material or conceptual entities one finds in the literature on social and material culture. Openness, lack of completeness, flexibility and capacity to be woven into the dynamics of movement, perception, sense-making and action are key features of the objects through which knowledge is attained:

> The *lack in completeness of being* is crucial: objects of knowledge in many fields have material instantiations, but they must simultaneously be conceived of as unfolding structures of absences: as things that continually 'explode' and 'mutate' into something else, and that are as much defined by what they are not (but will, at some point have become) than by what they are. (op. cit., p. 182, original emphasis)

Complex problems can be represented from multiple perspectives and have multiple solutions. This generates a multiplicity of objects and their constitutive parts. As Suchman (2005) argues:

> A focus on the affiliative powers of objects orients as well to their multiplicity (see Law, 2002; Mol, 2002), both in the more obvious sense that complex objects can be understood as the alignment of their parts, and in the sense that objects are constituted always through specific sites and associated practices. The singularity of an object, correspondingly, is an outcome of discursive practices that render it coherent and stable, rather than a property that inheres in it *sui generis*. (Suchman, 2005, pp. 380–381)

In short, an *epistemic object* is all at the same time material and immaterial, fixed and dynamic, a naturally occurring entity and a creature of human thought. It is a form that stands against the perceiver and a gathering of materials in movement – a particular configuration that emerges through assembling together matter, form and flow – the object and the thing simultaneously (cf. Ingold, 2012).

Broadly, following Tweney's (2002) line of argument, we attribute to *epistemic artefacts* two related, yet distinct, functions. First, 'epistemic artefacts' – as is the case with 'epistemic objects' and 'epistemic things' – are products that build upon shared means for constructing knowledge that are consensually agreed upon by a certain community and often lead to finished products. In contrast to 'epistemic objects' and 'epistemic things' – which, as Tweney emphasises, do lead to new shared knowledge – 'epistemic artefacts' also serve as personal emerging 'thingy objects' that, through perception and action, matter and skill, bridge the gap between one's mind and (unknown) phenomena in the physical world.

We have casually introduced the word 'artefact', and we now need to explain a particular sense in which we want to use this term. 'Artefact' derives from a combination of classical Latin *arte* ('skill in doing something') and *factum* ('a thing done or performed'). It nicely captures the bond between human knowledge, skill and matter and emergent material and immaterial forms. In many standard uses, an 'artefact' is often seen as a finished product – rigid and encapsulated in a transparent and fixed form:

> If we reflect vpon the workes and artes of men, as, a good life, a commonwealth, an army, a house, a garden, all artefactes; what are they, but compositions *of well ordered partes*? (1644 K. Digby Two Treat. ii. viii. 411. Oxford English Dictionary Online, emphasis added)

However, if we bring the artefact back into the process of making, the fixedness disappears: a form becomes a movement; knowledge becomes knowing; the object becomes a thing (Fig. 8.1).

Figure 8.1 recapitulates the main distinctions and relationships we have discussed so far in this chapter. It shows the two senses of object ('objekt' and 'predmet') and introduces the notion of 'thing'. We place 'artefacts' in this picture as (a) a bringing together of the goal and its material locus, (b) understood from the perspective of active engagement, making and movement in the world. (One might say 'thingy objects'.)

8.4 Finding Objects for Professional Education and Reifying Them in Material Artefacts

How do university teachers find phenomenal objects around which the learning of 'professional vision' can be organised? In our empirical study, we investigated how university teachers 'objectify' course goals into specific assessment tasks. We found several common ways in which teachers did this.

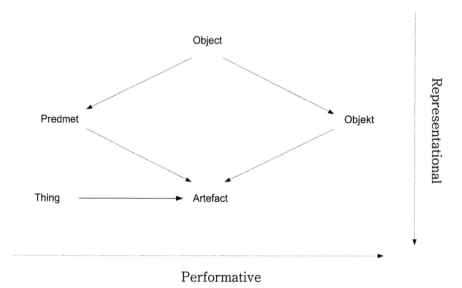

Fig. 8.1 Objects, artefacts and things

Overall, the objects chosen for assessment tasks varied in two ways:

(a) From *skill*, carrying out professional action; to *vision*, seeing the world in a particular way; to *making*, working with material things related to the profession (doing, seeing, making)
(b) From *everyday* to *unusual* practices

Table 8.1 helps schematise what we found.

Some tasks focussed on learning *specific key skills or knowledge* that require targeted development and repeated practice, such as fluent communication with clients and professionals from other fields, or performing complex assessment tasks that require attuned perception and skill. Some of the tasks did not call upon common skills and knowledge, but specifically involved *the hardest elements of professional practice*, such as designing a lesson plan for the most hard to teach topic in the curriculum and practising the teaching of this lesson in a simulated (peer-reviewed) setting.

Other tasks primarily focussed on students' use of *common frameworks of professional practice* that shape their vision and action in solving complex as well as more routine professional problems. In such tasks, the focus is less on an automatic fluent response to the situation and skill needed to perform an action, and more on the conscious ability to 'see' the situation and act through the overt professional ways of seeing and acting. Some tasks specifically focussed on those *elements of professional practice that are hidden* from lay perception – by teaching students to look at professional practices, spaces and artefacts, created by students or others, in specific professional ways.

Table 8.1 Finding objects for assessment tasks

Object of assessment task	Examples
Fine-tuning skill and knowledge	
Key specific skills and knowledge Tasks that involve important specific skills or knowledge that require targeted development	Communication role play with clients and professionals from other fields, medication dosage assessment, administering complex behavioural assessment tests
Hardest elements of professional practice Tasks that involve the hardest elements of professional practice	A lesson plan for the most difficult to teach topic plus practice in teaching this lesson in a simulated (peer-reviewed) setting
Shaping professional vision	
Core inquiry frameworks Tasks that involve the use of common frameworks of professional practice. This includes (a) typical tasks and (b) more complex tasks. In both cases, students are required to use and articulate each step or aspect of a generic inquiry 'script', even if it is not relevant in a specific situation	Doing a medication review following a generic framework – gather information, assess, recommend or deliver – which is also used in different situations in everyday pharmacy practice Doing a real child psychological assessment, but covering all elements of an 'ideal' assessment model and articulating all aspects of the typical report
Hidden elements of professional vision Tasks that involve understanding of professional artefacts or practices by using specific professional ways to look at them. These artefacts and practices could be created by other professionals or by students	Deconstructing a lesson plan from a social justice perspective, evaluating another student's lesson using given rubrics/criteria, reflecting on one's own practice in a structured way, unpacking the roles of an aboriginal officer, examining a pharmacy's layout, doing an inventory of medications available in the pharmacy for a specific disease
Making professional artefacts	
Production of everyday artefacts Tasks that require creation of specific everyday artefacts of, or for, professional practice, in an informed, systematic way (e.g. justify, try out, self-evaluate)	Designing an eResource for language teaching and learning, designing a disease state management service for a community pharmacy
Production of generic artefacts Tasks that require creation of generic artefacts for professional use, not necessarily for one's own practice	Creating guidelines for nursing informed by best evidence, developing a package for arts teaching, creating a kit for a school excursion

Some other tasks focussed on *production of common professional artefacts* that are used and produced in professional work for different purposes. Such tasks, while focussed on the artefact, usually maintained a strong focus on an informed, systematic mode of production, by asking students to justify their design decisions or test artefacts in practice and through self-evaluation. A set of tasks required students to *create artefacts for general professional use*. Such artefacts are not necessarily used in the student's own practice, but rather focus on reusable knowledge and materials that could be employed across a variety of other situations and sites.

In short, the *objects* chosen for assessment tasks varied from common core skills and knowledge to the hardest elements of professional practice; from learning to apply professional frameworks for guiding action to learning to use such frameworks for looking at, and being able to see, otherwise invisible features of practice; and from making specific everyday artefacts that are an integral part of professional practice to making generic artefacts for professional use beyond the immediate situation.

However, the link between an object and a task in which students engaged and the kind of artefact they produced were not straightforward. While most objects were clearly located in the domain of professional practice, artefacts that students constructed were far more diverse. Students were constructing three broad categories of artefacts: *accountability*, *pedagogical* and *professional* (Table 8.2).

Accountability artefacts include various formal tests and experience records, providing evidence that students have certain specific and measurable knowledge and skills, or have certain fieldwork or workplace experiences.

Pedagogical artefacts are artefacts that are produced specifically for learning purposes. These artefacts are not usually a part of the professional expert epistemic culture or workplace. Rather, they include various 'bridging' artefacts that students produce to learn and demonstrate that they have learnt certain knowledge and developed certain kinds of professional understanding or perception. Examples would include written reports, essays, reflections and presentations.

Professional artefacts include artefacts produced as a part of solving specific professional problems and planning, designing and producing things for professional practice. Some of these artefacts turn out to be common, everyday professional products, while others are rare or unusual to some degree. That said, all of them are genuine artefacts of professional practice.

Further details about, and examples from, each of these three categories can be found in Table 8.3.

Table 8.2 Categories of artefacts

Type of artefact	Hybrid learning for profession	Workplace-focused learning
Accountability	Formal tests	Experience records
Pedagogical	Educational artefacts	Deconstructive artefacts
Professional	Rare/hybrid professional artefacts	Common professional artefacts

Table 8.3 Examples of 'translational' artefacts created in professional university courses

Type of artefact and description	Examples
Accountability artefacts	
Formal tests Artefacts produced as a part of assessing well-defined knowledge and skills that, once learnt, could be checked and 'ticked off'. Often, they involve knowledge which is considered important but is epistemically simple. Tasks and assessments related to it are often compulsory 'add-ons' to professional courses	Professional law module and quiz in nursing, occupational health and safety tests and other tests that are a part of formal professional or institutional requirements
Experience records Artefacts created as a record of experience. They are based on the logic that time spent in professional field and encounters of common professional situations are a demonstration of professional competence	Practice logbooks, work placement portfolios
Pedagogical artefacts	
Educational artefacts All assignments that students do to demonstrate that they learnt specific (relatively complex) skill or content, and the artefact that they produce is an educational artefact that is not a part of the professional expert epistemic culture or workplace – i.e. exist in education only	Essays, concept maps, presentations on a specific topic
Deconstructive artefacts Assignments in which students construct artefacts that analyse settings, objects, practices or experiences from professional domain in order to get insight into specific aspect of professional field	Analyses and reflections on professional settings and practices, such as school report, community pharmacy report; analyses of professional artefacts, such as analysis of a medication information statement and deconstruction of a lesson plan from a social justice perspective; reflections on events, professional and learning experiences, such as a learning journal, a critical reflection 'wiki-maze'
Professional artefacts	
Common professional artefacts Artefacts that are common in professional practice. This includes (a) artefacts produced as a part of solving specific problems, planning, designing and producing things for professional action and (b) 'transient' or 'mimetic' artefacts and representations produced in action that encapsulates skill (not necessarily permanent changes in the matter)	Assessments, field case studies and recommendations, such as a child's behavioural assessment and recommendations by a school counsellor, a family assessment by a social worker, a medication dosage assessment by a pharmacist, patient's surgical assessment and pre- and post-operative teaching plan; plans and other designs, such as a lesson plan or an excursion plan; artefacts for professional work, such as eResource for language teaching, an assessment task for assessing a specific topic Simulated professional practices, such as dispensing prescription role play, oral communication role play, clinical performance appraisal in on-campus clinical simulated settings

(continued)

Table 8.3 (continued)

Type of artefact and description	Examples
Rare and hybrid professional artefacts Artefacts that are not commonly produced in everyday professional practice, but exist and used in profession, and mixed artefacts that fuse features of different types of the artefacts described above	Nursing guidelines, a medication review, an action learning project in teacher internship, an artist case study for teaching arts, a design of a health promotion program for a community pharmacy

8.5 A Case: Assembling Objects and Things in an Epistemic Artefact

As we explained above, Kaptelinin (2005) pointed out that many human activities are driven by multiple needs and have multiple motives. The object, in such poly-motivated activity, 'is cooperatively *determined* by all effective motives' (p. 17, emphasis added). He expressed the relationship between multiple needs and motives, and a single activity, by arguing that such activity starts once the poly-motivated object is defined (Fig. 8.2). He noted that an individual attempts to meet multiple needs 'in a given social context (SC), under certain conditions and having certain means (CM)' (op. cit., p. 149). How are such objects constructed in tasks performed by students in learning for knowledgeable action?

Consider an assessment task given in an Introduction to Nursing Practice course. In order to assist nursing students to develop practice thinking and master nursing craftsmanship, the course coordinator requested students to create nursing guidelines for a range of clinical practices, such as manual handling, health assessment, body care and infection control. The guidelines have to include pictures illustrating various steps in the clinical procedures. These are taken during students' group work in the labs, using high-fidelity mannequins and other equipment. The guidelines also have to be supported with evidence about why each procedure is done in the way that it is done. The course coordinator reflected on the rationales for giving this task to the students:

> ... this Nursing School didn't want to have a set of guidelines as such to give the students out of the books. They said we want the students to be *freer thinking*. And I watched the students struggle and I thought 'well, maybe often *they do need guidelines*.' I don't teach to guidelines. I teach to principles. But when you want them to go back and practice, they need guidelines. <...> So that's what I thought that a way of getting around that is if they developed their own guidelines.

The course coordinator emphasised the necessity of reconciling the two needs and related them to the following motives: (a) to help future nurses become 'freer thinkers', able to make independent critical choices, and (b) to help them to develop 'craft skills' – how to carry out particular clinical procedures in practice. The teacher noted two other needs and motives: (c) to engage the students in 'feeling like a nurse' by connecting to a 'real patient' and action and (d) to engage in

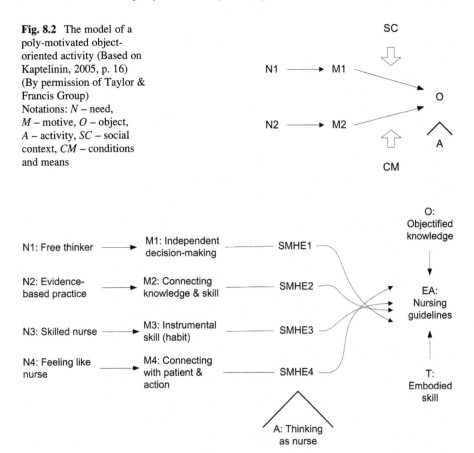

Fig. 8.2 The model of a poly-motivated object-oriented activity (Based on Kaptelinin, 2005, p. 16) (By permission of Taylor & Francis Group) Notations: *N* – need, *M* – motive, *O* – object, *A* – activity, *SC* – social context, *CM* – conditions and means

Fig. 8.3 A poly-motivated activity in constructing the nursing guidelines
Notations: *N* – need, *M* – motive, *O* – object, *A* – activity, *EA* – epistemic artefact, *T* – thing, *SMHE* – social, material and human entanglements, *SMHE1* – comparing sources, *SMHE2* – searching data bases, *SMHE3* – articulating 'turning points' of knowledgeable action in images, *SMHE4* – performing clinical procedures

evidence-based practice by connecting what nurses do to the knowledge behind the skill (Fig. 8.3):

> I think with a nursing practice course – my experience over the years has been we are not in the hospitals a lot, they go in and out, and the hardest bit is to *engage the students into feeling like nurses*, feeling like they're doing nursing. And to actually make their clinical practice in the simulation laboratories meaningful, rather than just doing things, you know, we just go in and we take a temperature or whatever. To actually to make it more meaningful and to get them to take responsibility for their learning and so I *think by getting them to think about it* and say 'ok what is it we're doing here?' and making them think about connecting – what have they learnt and how. <...> [T]rying to get them to think as a nurse and that was the whole purpose behind doing this assignment too – to look at the fact that it's not just clinical skills that *you need evidence behind what you're doing.*

All four motives were expressed in the task through the students' skills in carrying out specific grounded actions: (a) to critically evaluate different sources, (b) to find sources of evidence and connect this knowledge to 'craft skill', (c) to articulate the common patterns and key features of these clinical procedures and (d) to perform real clinical procedures:

> I suppose within any field too, but especially within nursing, *we have particular clinical skills* and you have text books and often you get to each text book and it's different. It's got different information, so the whole crux of this was to – because they had to make guidelines for a particular clinical skill, and *I asked them to use three different sources* and *talk about the discrepancies in those sources.* <...> And what was the better source. You know, talk about why you would do things in a particular way.

Further, each of these actions was firmly grounded in a social and material environment: (a) ways of evaluating different sources by making comparisons and relating evidence to context, (b) available databases, (c) images of the skills articulating 'what matters' in a clinical procedure and (d) laboratory settings and equipment.

The coordinator was not asked to explain those links, but in her responses firmly articulated how the students' skills and knowledge are expressed through their engagement with digital and physical tools and environments:

> So it's actually making them say ... or '*I can go to the sources that I've used. I know how to access databases. I know how to access information.*' Than 'I have to do it that way just because I was told to do it that way.'

> ... we wanted them [students] in the pictures that *they actually did it.* Not just grab it from a text book or somewhere else. *They connect with it.* And that's the thing – they would have *had to do it a number of times.* So then they *get to know how to actually do this procedure* and they've thought about 'ok, this is the right way to do it', 'this is the best way to do it'. 'I've read up on it. I know what I'm doing. And this is how I do it with best practice'.

The environment was not just a context or set of practical constraints that shaped possible pragmatic actions; rather, it was the very essence in which knowledge, skill and activity were expressed (e.g. if one removes the 'best evidence' databases from the environment, the entire activity, and perhaps even the very conception of nursing practice, will change).

The nursing guidelines constructed by the students are not the *object* of – in Kaptelinin's sense of the 'ultimate reason' for – the students' behaviours. Rather, they are the epistemic artefact that holds together diverse things and objects, through which actionable knowledge is constructed and expressed. In this sense, the activity is not so much *directed* towards a specific thing or object – 'the ultimate reason' – as it *is* this 'ultimate reason' of learning. This activity emerges through the entanglement of embodied human skill and knowledge with the social and material environment in which the actions take place.

In some views of practice and object-oriented activity, social contexts and material means are seen as the *background*, which may shape the object of activity, but are not *part of* the motives, needs, object or activity. In learning for knowledgeable action, however, the social and material context should not be seen as an

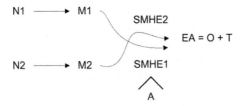

Fig. 8.4 The model of a poly-motivated artefact-oriented activity
Notations: N – need, M – motive, O – object, A – activity, EA – epistemic artefact, T – thing, $SMHE$ – social, material and human entanglement

inanimate background, but rather as the very matter through which motives are expressed and coordinated, and through which the objects come to life:

> I suppose the modus operandi behind it [the task] was to get them to *engage and connect* with what they're doing.

> . . . as they go on, I often ask them once they've done clinical, is if there was a patient, a real patient there, how would your patient respond to your practice, that sort of thing. So always taking it back to trying to get them to *connect* with what they're doing and not just coming in and being a student all the time.

The ultimate reason behind learning for knowledgeable action is connecting, rather than separating the object (why of work) and the thing (what of work). Such learning is achieved through carrying out *object-oriented (knowledgeable) actions* that presuppose the 'why', as well as through making *knowledgeable action-oriented* artefacts that connect 'what' and 'why' into 'know-how'. Such epistemic artefact-oriented learning can be seen as an activity that emerges from the simultaneous entanglement of social, material and human (embodied mind and skill) (Fig. 8.4).

8.6   Perception, Skill and Artefact

This part of the chapter addresses the following questions: Can actionable knowledge be learnt via creating artefacts? More precisely – what kinds of actionable knowledge can be learnt via creating specific kinds of (material and symbolic) artefacts? What kinds of artefacts do students create for learning professional knowledge?

We need to make several connections between the physical world and the symbolic world. These connections should clarify how (the learning of) actionable knowledge is related to, and situated within/between, these two worlds. In this section, we introduce Marx Wartofsky's (1979, 1987) account of the roles of *primary*, *secondary* and *tertiary artefacts*. We establish the relationship between professional skills and actions that are inherently embodied in the material world of practice and in associated symbolic artefacts. Note that our argument is about what might be called the 'material/embodied' professions (nursing, teaching, pharmacy, etc.) whose 'objects' are materially defined and situated in the physical world (patients, students, medications and pharmacy clients, etc.). Thus, action in the material world is an innate part of professional practice. We illustrate this with empirical examples in Sect. 8.7. In Sect. 8.8, we turn to Carl Bereiter's (2002) discussion of *conceptual artefacts*. We examine connections between conceptual knowledge, which is often seen as inherently immaterial, and 'thing-like' symbolic artefacts. Through this we also want to make an easily overlooked distinction between artefacts representing actions and artefacts representing the world.[7]

The links between professional skill, thought and the 'thing-like' representations of skills and thoughts are not obvious. Vygotsky's (1978) insights about the relationship and difference between 'natural memory' and 'culturally elaborated organisation of behaviour' provide a starting point for making the necessary links and distinctions. He wrote:

> A comparative investigation of human memory reveals that, even at the earliest stages of social development, there are two, principally different, types of memory. One, dominating in the behaviour of non-literate peoples, is characterized by the nominated impression of materials, by retention of actual experiences as the basis of mnemonic (memory), traces. We call this *natural memory*. <...> This kind of memory is very close to perception, because it arises out of the direct influence of external stimuli upon human beings. (Vygotsky, 1978, pp. 38–39, original emphasis)

Vygotsky noted that natural memory is not the only memory that people possess. He pointed out that people create and use artificial things to extend their natural cognitive capacities: thus, they have a culturally elaborated memory which has a different psychological structure than memory which is directly linked to experience:

> The use of notched sticks and knots, the beginnings of writing and simple memory aids all demonstrate that even at early stages of historical development humans went beyond the limits of the psychological functions given to them by nature and proceeded to a new culturally-elaborated organization of behaviour. <...> Even such comparatively simple operations as tying a knot or marking a stick as a reminder change the psychological structure of the memory process. They extend the operation beyond the biological dimensions of the human nervous system and permit it to incorporate artificial self-generated, stimuli, which we call *signs*. (op. cit., p. 39, original emphasis)

Vygotsky made these general points, about the role of signs and artefacts that humans use to extend their perception of the world, from the perspective of developmental psychology. Wartofsky (1979) has elaborated a complementary argument from a rather different perspective, which one might call 'historical epistemology'.

Wartofsky focussed on the link between perception, artefact and human skill. He distinguished two stages of perception development: ahistorical and human. *Ahistorical perception* is a universal characteristic. It is a sensorimotor apparatus that

---

[7] In a similar way, Vygotsky (1978) made a distinction between 'action and meaning' and 'object and meaning' (pp. 100–101).

allows any organism to experience the physical world. *Human perception* develops after the biological evolution of the sensory system is completed:[8]

> [It is] historically variable, and not an unchanging and universal feature of the species as such. It is universal only in its preconditions, i.e. in terms of the biologically evolved sensory system and the (undeveloped or native) sense modalities. (Wartofsky, 1979, p. 194)

Wartofsky did not separate action from perception and argued that action transforms perception while perception changes action:

> I take perception itself to be a mode of outward action; to be derived, in its genesis, from other direct forms of outward or motor-action or *praxis*; and to be, in perceptual practice itself, continuous with, or a part of such outward action or praxis. In this sense, it is perceptual activity *in* the world, and *of* a world as it is transformed by such activity. (loc. cit., 194, original emphasis)

He further argued that what is distinctive to human beings is that they create and reproduce conditions for existence by creating artefacts and tools. He noted that historical human perception is critical in the production and use of tools and artefacts. Wartofsky (1979, 1987) also made a distinction between *three kinds of artefacts* and linked them to *three kinds of human (historical) perception.*

Primary artefacts are specific things produced directly, using skills and tools, for the purpose of human existence. They include material things and tools themselves (such as buildings and hammers) as well as other more transient artefacts and tools that are instrumental for human existence and reproduction, including language, modes of social organisation and divisions of labour.

Secondary artefacts are created for preserving and transmitting skills that are used in the production and use of primary artefacts. These artefacts are objectified externalisations of skills and forms of action and are represented by symbolic means. They are not in the mind; they are external reflective embodiments that preserve and transmit modes of action in secondary ways. These representations are not restricted to specific modes (and modalities) and can take a range of permanent forms – such as prototypes and models – and more transient forms, such as gestures, rituals, language and music:

> The symbolic communication of such skills in the production, reproduction and use of artifacts – i.e. the teaching or transmission of such skills is the context in which *mimicry or the imitation of an action becomes a characteristic human mode of activity*. It is, in effect, this ability to *represent an action* by symbolic means which generates a distinctive class of artifacts, which we may call *representations*. <...> Such representations, then, are *reflexive* embodiments of forms of action or praxis, in the sense that they are symbolic externalizations or objectifications of such modes of action – 'reflections' of them, according to

---

[8] While Wartofsky (1979) closely integrated ahistorical and human perception, he still considered the development of those two kinds of perception as two distinct stages. Many ecological perspectives deny the possibility of such separation: 'we have no grounds for distinguishing between those capacities for action due to "biology" and those due to "culture"' (Ingold, 2000, p. 387).

some convention, and therefore understood as images of such forms actions – or, if you like, pictures or models of them. (Wartofsky, 1979, pp. 201–202, original emphasis)

He also noted that the symbolic nature of these artefacts makes them intrinsically linked to the canons of representation:

Canons of representation, therefore, have a large element of convention, corresponding to the change or evolution of different forms of action or *praxis*, and thus cannot be reduced to some simple notion of 'natural' semblance or resemblance. (op. cit., p. 202, original emphasis)

Tertiary artefacts are imaginary artefacts detached from specific use:

... the *formal* structures of the representation are taken in their own right as primary, and are abstracted from their use in productive praxis. (op. cit., p. 208, original emphasis)

He described this kind of perception as the 'rehearsal' for the real thing 'offline' that allows us to go beyond present actualities. It is 'imaginative praxis' and 'imaginative reenactment' (op. cit., p. 207). These artefacts operate because of their representational capacity and constitute the domain in which creation is possible, freed from the existing world of praxis. Tertiary artefacts constitute a domain in which imagination and free construction of alternative rules and operations are possible. They serve as tools for imagining rules and operations beyond those that exist in praxis.

As Miettinen and Virkkunen (2005) explain:

[Tertiary artefacts] constitute a domain in which a free construction, in the imagination, of alternative rules and operations is possible ... serving thus as tools for imagining and proposing alternatives. (Miettinen & Virkkunen, 2005, p. 445)

However, Wartofsky (1979) noted this free imagination is not completely disconnected from formal structures, forms and rules and ontologies of praxis that historically evolved through this praxis:

Such imaginary worlds I do not take as 'dreams' or 'in the head', but as embodied representations, or better, embodied alternative *canons* of representation: embodied *in* actual artifacts which express or picture this alternative perceptual mode. (Wartofsky, 1979, p. 209, original emphasis)

Wartofsky considered all three kinds of artefacts to be primarily related to skills and forms of action used in the production of goods for human existence. These artefacts preserve what we can call 'actionable' or 'working' knowledge. They represent movement or action rather than knowledge that preserves understanding of the world:

The mimetic character of such representations consists not simply in their imitation of natural objects or animals, but in their imitation and *representation of modes of action or praxis*. (op. cit., p. 202, emphasis added)

In summary, Wartofsky's historical epistemology provides a frame of reference for understanding the nature of artefacts that are used to preserve, transfer (teach and learn) and change skills and ways in which practice – including professional work – is carried out in the physical world. This includes skills that can be learnt via apprenticeship and direct professional practice, i.e. drawing on the *direct* perception of things, producing primary artefacts. It also includes skills and understandings that can be taught and learnt via creating 'objectified' representations of this practice, i.e. drawing on the *analytical* perception of objects and creating secondary artefacts. However, skills and modes of action are not immutable habits, and their representations do not necessarily emerge solely from practice in the physical world. Rather, artefacts that embody praxis can be a product of creative and deliberative improvement and change, i.e. tertiary artefacts. They emerge from this third kind of perception – an *epistemic* perception of the praxis.

8.7 Understanding Tasks and Artefacts

We will illustrate Wartofsky's ideas using our empirical data. Our results showed that, in terms of the *object* at which the students' activity is directed, assessment tasks include three distinct kinds of objects: (a) a concrete professional practice *problem to be solved*; (b) a concrete professional situation, artefact or other *professional practice to be understood*; or (c) a new (imagined) practice and/or *artefact to be created*. These are related to three distinct forms of tasks – problem, understanding and projective – and broadly mirror the three kinds of perception, primary, secondary and tertiary, in Wartofsky's terms. However, the artefacts produced by students rarely fit neatly into just one category.

In the professional problem tasks, students were using tools and producing artefacts of practice (Table 8.4). Many of these 'artefacts' were *transient forms of professional action*. For example, nursing students were *carrying out* clinical procedures, preservice teachers were *delivering* simulated lessons and pharmacy students were *dispensing* medications. However, some of the artefacts they produced had 'thing-like' qualities. In most cases, the artefacts they created were symbolic products rather than real material things. Some of these artefacts served the function of tools or mediating artefacts for carrying out professional work in the physical world. For example, preservice teachers were *creating handouts*, assessment tasks and other materials for their lessons. Pharmacy students were *creating pamphlets* for health promotion campaigns. These artefacts were not the final goals of their work, but were tools for carrying out specific actions. While most of these artefacts are symbolic in nature, in essence they function in similar ways to physical tools and are used for carrying out actions in the physical world.

In contrast, other artefacts created by students were outcomes of professional work. For example, social work and counselling students were assessing family difficulties, student literacy levels and behaviour problems and *producing assessment reports*. Pharmacy students were conducting medication reviews and *producing medication review reports*. In short, students were creating knowledge products about concrete objects that belong to the physical world, and these artefacts were

Table 8.4 Different kinds of artefacts produced by students and their links to the tasks that draw on the three kinds of perception

Artefact	Description and example(s)
Professional problem tasks that draw upon primary professional perception	
Action artefacts	Transient artefacts that are results of professional actions carried out in the physical world: a role play of oral communication with a patient, a simulated lesson
Artefacts–tools	Concrete artefacts made by a professional that are used as tools in further professional actions: an eResource designed by a teacher to teach English grammar, an assessment task designed to assess students' understanding of the taught topic
Constructive knowledge artefacts	Symbolic knowledge artefacts about phenomena produced as a result of (knowledge) work carried out by a professional in the physical world: a child behavioural assessment by a psychologist, a patient pre- and post-operative assessment by a nurse, family assessment by a social worker
Understanding tasks that draw upon and link primary and secondary professional perception	
Descriptive artefacts	Descriptions of actions and artefacts that embody professional skill: a guide for teachers on how to use case study materials
Reflective artefacts	Reflective products of organisational forms, ways of acting and skills: a reflection on one's own teaching practice
Deconstructive artefacts	Deconstructions of specific existing physical and knowledge artefacts that embody professional skill or knowledge: deconstructions of lesson plans or of medication information leaflets
Projective tasks that draw upon and link primary, secondary and tertiary professional perception	
Projective professional artefacts	Artefacts that project ways of carrying out professional action: a lesson plan, an aboriginal excursion kit, health promotion program, a plan for disease state management service, an artist case study package, nursing guidelines
Projective artefacts–extensions	Symbolic knowledge artefacts that extend knowledge, produced as a result of (knowledge) work carried out in the physical world, and going beyond the traditional professional domain of action: pre- or post-operative teaching plan *for* a patient based on nursing assessment; pharmacist's recommendations *for* a doctor based on the medication review

intellectual products representing knowledge about these objects (medications, families, students with behaviour issues).

In the understanding tasks, students were creating artefacts that represented modes of organisation and forms of action in the physical world, i.e. secondary artefacts. One group of artefacts included descriptions of specific *existing things* and ways of acting, such as reports about the roles and responsibilities of an aboriginal officer, attributes of a school in relation to aboriginal issues, community pharmacy reports comparing their characteristics, etc. Some of these included reflections on *professional practice* and deconstructions of intellectual products created in, and for, professional practice, such as a critique of lesson plans and teachers' reflections on their own practice. While these artefacts drew on the reflective (secondary) perception of the professional world, they were grounded in concrete professional artefacts and skills to act in the physical (primary) world.

In the projective tasks, students created artefacts that represented professional things which do not exist yet in the world, but *project* them (including skills, knowledge and actions). Such artefacts included lesson plans, designs for school excursions, designs of health promotion programs and plans for implementing a disease state management service. While some of these products were specifically linked to particular situations and contexts (e.g. lesson plans), some of them had a broader function beyond the immediate, specific context (e.g. nursing guidelines). Most of these artefacts were based on the knowledge of contexts and patterns of action in the physical world, as well as knowledge of the conceptual world (constraints, affordances, epistemic tools, ontologies of professional praxis, etc.). For example, preservice teachers created lesson plans taking into account constraints of prevailing teaching contexts in schools (e.g. 45 min lesson), knowledge of how to sequence activities (e.g. new material is followed by students' practice) and forms for presenting professional knowledge (e.g. to plan on paper).

Some students who were creating primary knowledge artefacts were also simultaneously creating artefacts that go beyond primary perception and do not fit neatly in the category of traditional primary artefacts – they were what we call *knowledge-based projective artefacts–extensions*. These artefacts included different recommendations that are based on results of their own professional inquiries. They are *projections of action for other people*: such as a pharmacist's recommendations for doctors based on medication review; a psychologist's recommendations for parents and teachers, based on assessment of a student's behaviour; or a nurse's preoperative guidance to a patient about how to care for themselves after an operation.

Most of the projective artefacts were imaginary artefacts, freed from the direct constraints of existing routine behaviours and practices, and, in this respect, were similar to Wartofsky's (1987) tertiary artefacts. However, these artefacts were not detached from projected use; rather they were designed for a specific purpose. Also, they were not products of free creativity and disinterested perception, but were intertwined with structures, rules, available tools and other aspects of professional practices as well as constraints of the practical world.

Furthermore, some assessment submissions produced by students in a single professional activity included sets of artefacts from different categories. For example, a behavioural assessment of a child (a primary artefact) was followed by recommendations to parents and teachers (a tertiary artefact); a case study for arts teaching included handouts and other classroom materials (primary artefacts), a teacher's guide (a secondary artefact) and lesson plans (a tertiary artefact).

In summary, the distinctions between primary, secondary and tertiary artefacts provide some insights into how the artefacts that students create relate to skills and understandings for carrying out action in the physical world. However, as our investigation shows, while the objects, and students' professional actions, are often located in the physical world, they create artefacts that are not solely products of direct perception, and they do not only create physical products. They also create different kinds of knowledge products. Some of these are reflections of the world and modes of action created for others. But many of them are primarily reflective and projective embodiments of their own professional actions – and are created to help with the carrying out of those actions.

Wartofsky primarily wrote about artefacts that embody and carry over skills and ways of acting involved in creating physical (and social) artefacts. Wartofsky's insights become less illuminative in the context of *knowledge work*: when actions are carried out in mental and physical worlds simultaneously and when the final product is understanding not only of action but also of the world. Further, Wartofsky acknowledged the human ability to go beyond experiences and the physical world and construct alternative rules and operations (tertiary artefacts). He also noted that this free imagination is not completely separated from existing modes of praxis. However, he focussed more on free creativity than on deliberative, systematic knowledge work.

Consequently, we now turn to literature that provides some insights into the nature of knowledge artefacts and tools used to create knowledge – knowledge that is a product of deliberative work.

8.8   Knowledge Work and Conceptual Artefacts from the Perspective of Professional Practice

In contrast to Marx Wartofsky (1987), Carl Bereiter (2002) writes about artefacts that are the products of deliberative knowledge work and which embody knowledge about the world rather than about actions or skills. For Bereiter, knowledge is constituted through discourse. While empirical observations can inform discourse, they do not themselves constitute knowledge.

Bereiter talks of 'conceptual artefacts', which are:

> ... human constructions like other artefacts except that they are immaterial and, instead of serving purposes such as cutting, lifting, and inscribing, they serve purposes such as explaining and predicting. (Bereiter, 2002, p. 58)

Conceptual artefacts include such things as factual claims, concepts, theories, models, vision statements, debatable propositions and recipes. Just as physical artefacts are created and used for producing the means of existence, conceptual artefacts are created and used for producing knowledgeability. In Bereiter's view, conceptual and material artefacts share some common characteristics, but conceptual artefacts are different, in important ways, from material things and from knowledge in the mind. They differ from the latter in so far as they have material representations: they are more tangible than are inner mental states or unarticulated working practices.[9] (A model or a plan is more tangible than a hope or a hunch.) Crucially, their autonomous objective life renders them shareable and open to study, discussion, critique, comparison, testing and improvement.

Bereiter also distinguishes between knowledge as the product of knowledge work and knowledge used for knowledge work. He is more interested in the former, and especially in the fact that it can travel beyond the site of its production, and be open to improvement by others.

Conceptual artefacts are commonly inscribed in media – for example, a recipe may be printed in a cookbook or posted on a web page; a new scientific theory may be published in a journal paper or (later) expressed in a school textbook. It is important, however, to distinguish between the conceptual artefact and its material inscription. A recipe for *aubergine cassoulet* is a conceptual artefact that exists independently of any particular inscription. Conceptual artefacts retain their identity even when their representations change (e.g. a recipe printed in a book or on a website). They are immaterial but real.

Bereiter argues that much of the work in a knowledge society is done on conceptual artefacts, rather than on the physical materials in the world to which these conceptual artefacts are related. For instance, if a hospital building needs to be recabled, much of the work will be done using plans of the network. If expensive mistakes are made, it will more likely be while working with the conceptual artefacts than when working with the physical cables.

Bereiter's ideas provide powerful concepts for making sense of knowledge practices that work solely in the symbolic world, which might be said to include a major part of school learning and also some modern professions that predominately use symbolic tools and produce symbolic products, such as software engineers, or opinion research companies. However, if one tries to apply these ideas directly to some other contemporary professions – such as nursing, teaching, counselling or pharmacy – several major challenges emerge.[10] First, professional conceptual artefacts are not created by, or for, working entirely in conceptual domains. Rather, they emerge from many interactions between the conceptual and the physical world in specific contexts and conditions. Second, while parts of

---

[9] From our perspective, as researchers interested in professional work and knowledge, Bereiter's (2002) take on conceptual artefacts has a few limitations. We develop this argument more thoroughly below, but a key point to make just here is that much of the knowledge work that takes place in professional settings involves complex, dynamically changing mixtures of 'knowledge in one's mind' and 'knowledge in the world'.

[10] Bereiter (2002) defined knowledge work as a rather specific and specialised kind of work 'that creates or adds value to conceptual artefacts' (p. 181). He conceived knowledge very specifically as 'real stuff that is possible to work on' (loc. cit.): a product to which one can attach the label of 'intellectual property'. From our perspective (informed also by our empirical evidence), professional workers create a much broader range of intellectual products that have a broad range of uses, including for their own action, as with a lesson plan used by a teacher. Even such occupations as 'brain surgery', in Bereiter's view, did not involve knowledge work – they are 'knowledge-demanding manual occupations' (loc. cit.), making *knowledge work* a completely disembodied, specialised part of *knowledgeable work*.

professional work may draw upon, and include, the production of knowledge, much of this work involves a constant move back and forth between routinised, rule-based choices and complex decisions: intellectual and manual. Not all of this knowledge will be coherently represented in one 'thing-like' artefact; it will be distributed between 'things' that represent various aspects of the knowledge created and the transient forms of epistemic practice. The following examples help illustrate these points.

8.8.1 *Materiality, Embodiment and Context*

Consider a pharmacist who is asked to review the medications of a patient who has multiple diseases. The patient takes a range of medicines prescribed by different doctors, but the overall treatment is proving to be ineffective. The pharmacist is called in to review medications, detect possible pharmaceutical issues and produce recommendations for a doctor that will help the doctor to resolve the issue. Such a medication review might be seen as a piece of straightforward pharmaceutical 'knowledge work' that could be done in front of a computer screen, such as reviewing medications listed in the doctor's referral, figuring out chemical interactions between medications, and producing recommendations for the doctor (i.e. which medication needs to be changed and to what, etc.). Nevertheless, the pharmacist goes to the patient's home to interview the patient. This step of the medication review is not just a 'social activity' – it is a critical aspect that contributes to the knowledge work. The pharmacist needs to see the actual medications, to check expiry dates and to see the conditions in which they are kept, as he needs to make sure that the patient takes the medications as they are prescribed by the doctors. He also needs to know enough about the patient's living conditions and discuss her preferences and other issues that might not (indeed cannot) be made explicit in the doctor's referral, yet which are essential inputs to the pharmacist's decision and recommendation.

The pharmacist constructs a report and recommendations. They are complex 'knowledge products', but they are not objective 'conceptual artefacts' in Bereiter's sense. It would be difficult to locate this knowledge work entirely in the conceptual world without taking into account the contexts and situations – such as medical insurance and local pharmaceutical compensation schemes. While the pharmacist will almost certainly draw on objective concepts of pharmaceutical knowledge, it would be difficult to exclude from his decision factors such as the patient's living conditions and preferences or try to 'objectify' these into universal constructs. As one pharmacy lecturer explained:

> Now the *reference* [in pharmacist's findings] could be '*the patient told me*'. Or the *reference* could be '*The Australian Medicines Handbook* says the first line treatment for this is this drug' – and then the recommendation is what can I do with that finding. I like to think about the findings as being all the evidence – so if you were a lawyer, your finding is all the evidence that you have in order to make the recommendation that this person should

be put in jail or be fined. So it's the same – this is all the information that I have to say that this medicine is not right for this person. So the person told me they didn't like it, they weren't taking it, they were getting side effects. The book tells me, you know, all my reference books tell me that there's interaction with this and, you know, so it's everything.

In short, there is much that is local, material and embodied in this knowledge task.

There are many other kinds of professional knowledge work that one might find hard to locate in a conceptual plane without also considering knowledge that is created in interactions with tools, people and the material world.

Bereiter has in mind a rather different kind of knowledge work. He talks about one 'elite' type of knowledge work that is specifically directed at building and improving conceptual artefacts. He argues that knowledge should not be situated, but knowing should be situated. In our view, Bereiter's definition of knowledge work is different from the nature of knowledge work that we see in professional practices, and the form of knowledge artefacts that are produced in those practices is also different. Professional knowledge work is situated, and the knowledge itself – as a raw material and an outcome of knowledge-building processes – is distributed between non-situated and situated. In short, the knowledge work of professionals cannot be reduced to the work of 'pure' knowledge workers who deal with formal knowledge.

However, professional knowing is also not at the strong end of situative learning (and knowing). It is different from learning the environment by relying on biological perception – as animals do – and from unreflective, direct perception, as lay people habitually do. What is taught and considered essential in pharmacy we could call 'the generative context-sensitive principles of situated knowledge work' – like communicating in the right way with different clients and creating knowledge that is right in the context. These capacities allow one to get the right information for making decisions about the suitability of medications. They draw upon general generative principles for constructing situated knowledge that are sensitive to the context, rather than, as Bereiter claimed, a kind of non-situated knowledge.

An additional complexity of knowledge work in professions is that the knowledge created is within the process, not only in the final product.

8.8.2   Hidden Knowledge Work

Second, consider an example from more routine aspects of the pharmacist's practice. A typical pharmacist does not live only from the fees for medication reviews. They earn much of their income from dispensing medicines. As our study participants explained, 'An individual [pharmacist] may dispense 100, 200, 300, 400 different items per day'. And every prescription involves some knowledge work:

You have to gather the information even it's 'Are you taking any other medicines?' – even if it's one medicine, you've got to gather the information. <...> So you need to work out 'Is this right or wrong', 'Does this seem right' – and then you need to deliver. You need to the tell patient how are they are going to take it. What are they going to do. So even the most

> simplistic pharmacy service, whether it be responding to a cough and cold request or
> whether it be dispensing a prescription, has those three elements. (Pharmacy Lecturer)

This knowledge work does not involve the construction of any substantial 'thing-like' conceptual artefacts. It may require little more than just writing down, and explaining briefly, how to take a medication. In many cases, this might be a rather routine task. Nevertheless, it does involve construction of knowledge for taking a responsible, consequential decision, and it would be difficult to reduce the complexity, contingency and implications of this work to (say) the tasks of a shop assistant. In short, the pharmacist does knowledge work, and this involves various physical and material artefacts (medication, prescription, etc.) and various sources of knowledge (consumer medicines information, information from a client, pharmaceutical databases, etc.). This knowledge work is different from the way pure knowledge workers construct knowledge artefacts.

8.8.3   Materiality of Inscription

It can also be difficult to draw a sharp division between conceptual artefacts and their inscriptions. Consider a doctor who receives from a pharmacist a recommendation letter. This recommendation letter may involve an assessment and a set of specific recommendations, written in a non-prioritised order, or it might be a report and recommendations that are structured and prioritised. While both may contain similar information, the way the report is written (i.e. the representations used) may influence the doctor's decision. (In a similar way, consider a recipe written in a narrative style that runs over two pages and a recipe that is structured in bullet points. While this might be an identical recipe, one form might prove to be much easier than the other to understand, to use in cooking and to improve. Bereiter did not make this distinction.) One pharmacy lecturer explained to us a typical challenge for pharmacists – to learn to inscribe knowledge and produce written medication review reports:

> ... the knowledge is important but that's the easiest thing to get. But it's more the
> communication – the *written communication skills* – because pharmacists have not written
> letters to doctors or reports very often, that's not a skill that they've ever had to use in their
> day to day practice. But that's the thing that we find – so a lot of the times they can pick up
> 'yes, this drug interacts with this drug' and we need to do something about that. But they're
> very used to getting on the phone and saying 'there's a drug interaction' but not necessarily
> solving that or communicating that in a good way.

Further, she explained that this capability to create effective written inscriptions is inseparable from some fundamental pharmacists' capabilities to produce actionable solutions to complex problems encountered in the world, such as capacities to deal with multiple issues simultaneously, see the big picture and prioritise issues and solutions:

> But in particular that *skill of prioritising* what's the most important problem for this patient.
> So when you do the medicines review, you might find 20 problems. But there's no point like
> reporting all 20 of those in no logical order to the doctor because sometimes one of the
> problems if you've suggested a solution for that, it might then upset another problem further

down the track – so you've actually got to put it altogether, prioritise it and say 'ok, this would be how I would deal with it'. And I think pharmacists are very used to *dealing with one prescription at a time* and not having to look at the big picture. So I think they are the skills that the older pharmacists who haven't done this need to practice.

The artefacts produced by professionals are also not so universal that they can be separated from the people and community in and for which they were produced. Of course, they must have an existence out in the world, but to a degree that is practical and functional rather than universal. Professionals must create artefacts that are accessible for those who will use them – a requirement that goes beyond consideration of the mind of the person who produces them.

The quality of a medication review report needs to be judged by quite localised criteria, based on purpose and local 'epistemic culture' in Knorr Cetina's (2007) terms, rather than on the requirements of a universal 'knowledge culture'.

> Interviewer: That [in the table] seems a bit easier to kind of find, for the doctor, [all the information] rather than in that whole letter?
> Lecturer: Yes. It is. But then other people find that writing a *letter is more acceptable. So it's also about when you're a real accredited pharmacist, is finding out how your doctor would prefer the report.* So it's actually what the doctor would prefer. So I quite like it like this because it's broken up into point forms into a table. But some doctors would much prefer to have it, a documented letter like they get from a specialist. So you know, when the specialist is – *so they're used to reading letters.* (Interview with Pharmacy Lecturer)

While we will elaborate on each of these points later (Chap. 15), for now we need to say that work on producing conceptual artefacts is an important part of professional practice and education. However, if we try to apply the notions of 'knowledge building' and 'conceptual artefacts', any sharper separation between knowledge building and practices embodied in tools and embedded in specific contexts and learnt in communities of practice breaks down quite quickly.

If we want to consider other types of professions – ones that involve many diverse tasks that draw on multiple bodies of knowledge and create knowledge products with 'thing-like' properties, of different sizes and shapes, and which are also entangled within interactions with humans, tools and materials – then we need to rethink the concept of 'conceptual artefact' again. Human service-oriented professions, such as nursing, teaching, pharmacy and counselling, draw upon and produce actions in the real world, and considerable amounts of this work involve a mix of complex specialised knowledge and simple knowledge of things around, routinised tasks and complex unpredictable tasks.

When we consider Wartofsky and Bereiter's ideas together, a number of useful insights emerge. Bereiter's notion of conceptual artefacts shares some common properties with Wartofsky's tertiary artefacts: they are both abstract products; they are products of human consciousness and efforts; they have 'thing-like' properties; they are relatively autonomous from context and present actualities. However, these two notions also differ in some important respects. While Bereiter's conceptual artefacts are mainly *stable* external representations of knowledge, Wartofsky's artefacts also include *transient* objects and modes of representation such as bodily gestures and ritual performance.

Wartofsky (1979) is primarily concerned with human actions in their social and historical contexts and with relations between human perception and praxis. He took 'the artefacts (tools and languages) to be objectifications of human needs and intentions; i.e. as *already* invested with cognitive and affective content' (p. 204, original emphasis) and focussed primarily on cultural evolution: 'adaptive changes in the modes of social-historical praxis' (p. 205). Representations, from this cultural–historical point of view, are primary means through which skills and other characteristic modes of action are preserved and transmitted. In contrast, Bereiter (2002) primarily focussed on purposeful knowledge improvement and intentional change. He called this mode of action 'disciplined progress' – 'deliberative and orderly pursuit of solutions to theoretical and technical problems' (p. 71), rather than adaptive historical changes. While Wartofsky focussed on artefacts that preserve *skill, process and modes of action* or human praxis, Bereiter focussed on artefacts that inscribe human *knowledge about the world* in an objectified form – *independent* from the machineries in which it was produced.

The crucial challenge in making 'knowledge work' concepts more suitable for understanding professional work is to acknowledge the contingent and diverse nature of knowledge work and the knowledge products (i.e. conceptual artefacts) produced in professional practice. In this, both *process*, articulated by Wartofsky, and final *product*, articulated by Bereiter, matter. We also need to consider the nature of the artefacts and tools used in this process and the contexts in which they are produced and used. In short, we need to consider practice and the whole epistemic system together with the final product. We turn to this in the next chapter.

References

Adler, P. S. (2005). The evolving object of software development. *Organization, 12*(3), 401–435.

Akkerman, S. F., & Bakker, A. (2011). Boundary crossing and boundary objects. *Review of Educational Research, 81*(2), 132–169.

Argyris, C., & Schön, D. A. (1996). *Organizational learning II: Theory, method and practice.* Reading, MA: Addison-Wesley.

Barad, K. (2003). Posthumanist performativity: Toward an understanding of how matter comes to matter. *Signs, 28*(3), 801–831.

Bereiter, C. (2002). *Education and mind in the knowledge age.* Mahwah, NJ: Lawrence Erlbaum Associates.

Biggs, J., & Tang, C. (2007). *Teaching for quality learning at university: What the student does* (3rd ed.). Buckingham, UK: Open University Press.

Boivin, N. (2008). *Material cultures, material minds: The impact of things on human thought, society and evolution.* Cambridge, UK: Cambridge University Press.

Checkland, P., & Poulter, J. (2006). *Learning for action: A short definitive account of soft systems methodology and its use for practitioners, teachers, and students.* Hoboken, NJ: John Wiley & Sons.

Checkland, P., & Scholes, J. (1999). *Soft systems methodology in action* (New ed.). New York, NY: John Wiley & Sons.

Engeström, Y. (2001). Expansive learning at work: Toward an activity theoretical reconceptualization. *Journal of Education and Work, 14*(1), 133–156. doi:10.1080/13639080020028747.

Engeström, Y. (2004). New forms of learning in co-configuration work. *Journal of Workplace Learning, 16*(1/2), 11–21.

Engeström, Y. (2008). *From teams to knots: Activity-theoretical studies of collaboration and learning at work.* Cambridge, NY: Cambridge University Press.

Engeström, Y., & Blackler, F. (2005). On the life of the object. *Organization, 12*(3), 307–330.

Engeström, Y., Miettenen, R., & Punamäki, R.-L. (Eds.). (1999). *Perspectives on activity theory.* Cambridge, UK: Cambridge University Press.

Eraut, M. (2009). Understanding complex performance through learning trajectories and mediating artefacts. In N. Jackson (Ed.), *Learning to be professional through a higher education e-book* (Ch. A7, pp. 1–17). Guildford, UK: Surrey Centre for Excellence in Professional Training and Education (SCEPTrE). Retrieved from https://www.learningtobeprofessional.pbworks.com

Ewenstein, B., & Whyte, J. (2009). Knowledge practices in design: The role of visual representations as 'epistemic objects'. *Organization Studies, 30*(1), 7–30.

Fenwick, T., & Edwards, R. (2010). *Actor network theory in education.* London, UK: Routledge.

Fenwick, T., Edwards, R., & Sawchuk, P. (2011). *Emerging approaches to educational research: Tracing the sociomaterial.* Abingdon, UK: Routledge.

Ginestié, J. (2008a). From task to activity: Redistribution of roles between teacher and pupils. In J. Ginestié (Ed.), *The cultural transmission of artefacts, skills and knowledge: Eleven studies in technology education in France* (pp. 225–256). Rotterdam, The Netherlands/Taipei, Taiwan: Sense.

Ginestié, J. (Ed.). (2008b). *The cultural transmission of artefacts, skills and knowledge: Eleven studies in technology education in France.* Rotterdam, The Netherlands/Taipei, Taiwan: Sense.

Goodwin, C. (1994). Professional vision. *American Anthropologist, 96*(3), 606–633.

Goodwin, C. (1997). The blackness of black: Color categories as situated practice. In L. B. Resnick, R. Säljö, C. Pontecorvo, & B. Burge (Eds.), *Discourse, tools and reasoning: Essays on situated cognition* (pp. 111–140). Berlin, Germany: Springer.

Goodwin, C. (2005). Seeing in depth. In S. J. Derry, C. D. Schunn, & M. A. Gernsbacher (Eds.), *Interdisciplinary collaboration: An emerging cognitive science* (pp. 85–121). Mahwah, NJ: Lawrence Erlbaum Associates.

Goodyear, P. (2005). Educational design and networked learning: Patterns, pattern languages and design practice. *Australasian Journal of Educational Technology, 21*(1), 82–101.

Hall, S. (Ed.). (1997). *Representation: Cultural representations and signifying practices.* London, UK: Sage, in association with The Open University.

Hall, R., Stevens, R., & Torralba, T. (2002). Disrupting representational infrastructure in conversations across disciplines. *Mind, Culture, and Activity, 9*(3), 179–210.

Hallden, O., Scheja, M., & Haglund, L. (2008). The contextuality of knowledge: An intentional approach to meaning making and conceptual change. In S. Vosniadou (Ed.), *International handbook of research on conceptual change* (pp. 509–532). New York, NY: Routledge.

Hutchins, E. (1995). *Cognition in the wild.* Cambridge, MA: MIT Press.

Ingold, T. (2000). *The perception of the environment: Essays on livelihood, dwelling and skill.* London, UK: Routledge.

Ingold, T. (2010). Working paper #15. Bringing things to life: Creative entanglements in a world of materials. *NCRM Working Paper Series.* Manchester, UK: University of Manchester.

Ingold, T. (2011). *Being alive: Essays on movement, knowledge and description.* Oxon, OX: Routledge.

Ingold, T. (2012). Toward an ecology of materials. *Annual Review of Anthropology, 41*(1), 427–442. doi:10.1146/annurev-anthro-081309-145920.

Jensen, K., Lahn, L. C., & Nerland, M. (Eds.). (2012). *Professional learning in the knowledge society.* Rotterdam, The Netherlands: Sense.

Kaptelinin, V. (2005). The object of activity: Making sense of the sense-maker. *Mind, Culture, and Activity, 12*(1), 4–18.

Kaptelinin, V., & Nardi, B. A. (2006). *Acting with technology: Activity theory and interaction design*. Cambridge, MA: MIT Press.

Keller, C. M., & Keller, J. D. (1996). *Cognition and tool use: The blacksmith at work*. Cambridge, NY: Cambridge University Press.

Knappett, C. (2010). Communities of things and objects: A spatial perspective. In C. Renfrew & L. Malafouris (Eds.), *The cognitive life of things: Recasting the boundaries of the mind* (pp. 81–89). Cambridge, UK: University of Cambridge, McDonald Institute for Archaeological Research.

Knappett, C. (2011). Networks of objects, meshworks of things. In T. Ingold (Ed.), *Redrawing anthropology: Materials, movements, lines* (pp. 45–63). Farnham, UK: Ashgate.

Knorr Cetina, K. (1997). Sociality with objects: Social relations in postsocial knowledge societies. *Theory, Culture & Society, 14*(4), 1–30.

Knorr Cetina, K. (1999). *Epistemic cultures: How the sciences make knowledge*. Cambridge, MA: Harvard University Press.

Knorr Cetina, K. (2001). Objectual practice. In T. R. Schatzki, K. Knorr Cetina, & E. von Savigny (Eds.), *The practice turn in contemporary theory* (pp. 175–188). London, UK: Routledge.

Knorr Cetina, K. (2007). Culture in global knowledge societies: Knowledge cultures and epistemic cultures. *Interdisciplinary Science Reviews, 32*, 361–375.

Latour, B. (1991). Technology is society made durable. In J. Law (Ed.), *A sociology of monsters: Essays on power, technology and domination* (Sociological review monograph 38, pp. 103–132).

Latour, B., & Woolgar, S. (1979). *Laboratory life: The social construction of scientific facts*. Beverly Hills, CA: Sage.

Lave, J. (1988). *Cognition in practice*. Cambridge, UK: Cambridge University Press.

Lave, J., & Wenger, E. (1991). *Situated learning: Legitimate peripheral participation*. Cambridge, UK: Cambridge University Press.

Law, J. (2002). *Aircraft stories: Decentering the object in technoscience*. Durham, NC: Duke University Press.

Leontiev, A. N. (1978). *Activity, consciousness, and personality*. Englewood Cliffs, NJ: Prentice Hall.

Leontiev, A. N. (1981). *Problems of the development of the mind*. Moscow, Russia: Progress.

Ludvigsen, S., Lund, A., Rasmussen, I., & Säljö, R. (Eds.). (2011). *Learning across sites: New tools, infrastructures and practices*. Oxon, OX: Routledge.

Miettinen, R. (2005). Object of activity and individual motivation. *Mind, Culture, and Activity, 12* (1), 52–69.

Miettinen, R. (2006). Epistemology of transformative material activity: John Dewey's pragmatism and cultural-historical activity theory. *Journal for the Theory of Social Behaviour, 36*(4), 389–408.

Miettinen, R., & Virkkunen, J. (2005). Epistemic objects, artefacts and organizational change. *Organization, 12*(3), 437–456.

Mol, A. (2002). *The body multiple: Ontology in medical practice*. Durham, NC: Duke University Press.

Nersessian, N. J. (2006). The cognitive-cultural systems of the research laboratory. *Organization Studies, 27*(1), 125–145.

Nicolini, D., Mengis, J., & Swan, J. (2012). Understanding the role of objects in cross-disciplinary collaboration. *Organization Science, 23*(3), 612–629.

Nonaka, I., & Takeuchi, H. (1995). *The knowledge-creating company: How Japanese companies create the dynamics of innovation*. New York, NY: Oxford University Press.

Nonaka, I., & Toyama, R. (2007). Why do firms differ? The theory of the knowledge creating firm. In K. Ichijo & I. Nonaka (Eds.), *Knowledge creation and management: New challenges for managers* (pp. 13–31). Oxford, UK: Oxford University Press.

Paavola, S., & Hakkarainen, K. (2005). The knowledge creation metaphor – an emergent epistemological approach to learning. *Science & Education, 14*(6), 535–557.

Paavola, S., Lipponen, L., & Hakkarainen, K. (2004). Models of innovative knowledge communities and three metaphors of learning. *Review of Educational Research, 74*(4), 557–576.

Pels, D., Hetherington, K., & Vandenberghe, F. (2002). The status of the object: Performances,
mediations and techniques. *Theory, Culture and Society, 19*(5–6), 1–21. doi:10.1177/
026327602761899110.

Prosser, M., & Trigwell, K. (1999). *Understanding learning and teaching: The experience in
higher education.* Buckingham, UK: SRHE and Open University Press.

Rheinberger, H. (1997). *Toward a history of epistemic things: Synthesizing proteins in the test
tube.* Stanford, CA: Stanford University Press.

Roth, W.-M., & McGinn, M. K. (1998). Inscriptions: Toward a theory of representing as social
practice. *Review of Educational Research, 68*(1), 35–59.

Säljö, R. (1995). Mental and physical artifacts in cognitive practices. In P. Reimann & H. Spada
(Eds.), *Learning in humans and machines: Towards an interdisciplinary learning science*
(pp. 83–95). London, UK: Pergamon Press.

Schatzki, T. R., Knorr Cetina, K., & von Savigny, E. (2001). *The practice turn in contemporary
theory.* London, UK: Routledge.

Scribner, S. (1997). *Mind and social practice: Selected writings of Sylvia Scribner.* Cambridge,
NY: Cambridge University Press.

Sørensen, E. (2009). *The materiality of learning: Technology and knowledge in educational
practice.* Cambridge, NY: Cambridge University Press.

Star, S. L. (2010). This is not a boundary object: Reflections on the origin of a concept. *Science,
Technology & Human Values, 35*(5), 601–617.

Suchman, L. (2005). Affiliative objects. *Organization, 12*(3), 379–399.

Suchman, L. (2007). *Human-machine reconfigurations: Plans and situated actions.* Cambridge,
UK: Cambridge University Press.

Tweney, R. D. (2002). Epistemic artifacts: Michael Faraday's search for the optical effects of gold.
In L. Magnani & N. J. Nersessian (Eds.), *Model-based reasoning: Science, technology, values*
(pp. 287–303). New York, NY: Kluwer Academic/ Plenum.

Vygotsky, L. S. (1978). *Mind in society: The development of higher psychological processes.*
Cambridge, MA: Harvard University Press.

Wartofsky, M. W. (1979). *Models: Representation and the scientific understanding.* Dordrecht,
The Netherlands: D. Reidel.

Wartofsky, M. W. (1987). Epistemology historicized. In A. Shimony & D. Nails (Eds.), *Naturalistic epistemology: A symposium of two decades* (pp. 357–374). Dordrecht, The Netherlands:
D. Reidel.

Wenger, E. (1998). *Communities of practice: Learning, meaning, and identity.* Cambridge, UK:
Cambridge University Press.

Chapter 9
Epistemic Tools and Artefacts in Epistemic Practices and Systems

> ... what we wanted our [nursing] students to do is not – is to be thinking, to be able to think – and not because somebody tells you to do something, that you should do a particular procedure in a particular way. So in the clinical environment, a lot of the time the students come back and say 'we were told to do it this way'. And I say 'well you have to think about why – there are many ways of doing things. If you were to adhere to the principles of what you doing'. (Nursing Practice Coordinator)

Bereiter's (2002) focus on conceptual artefacts puts the emphasis on building non-situated knowledge – scientific mental habits for knowledge production – locating knowledge at some remove from practices and from the contexts in which it is produced. Wartofsky (1987) focusses on artefacts as 'genes' of cultural evolution that transmit modes of action, rather than knowledge, across generations. In this chapter, we extend our analysis of knowledge work as situated practice, sketching epistemic practice (Sect. 9.1), and we introduce some organising ideas about the special roles and qualities of *epistemic tools* (Sect. 9.2) and *epistemic artefacts* in the accomplishment of knowledge work. We frame this in ways that connect epistemic tools and artefacts to the larger systems of epistemic practice in which they function. Section 9.3 establishes some relationships between action, meaning and epistemic practice. In Sect. 9.4, we use interview and observational data from our research with nurse educators to analyse the epistemic qualities of artefacts produced by students as part of their preparation for practice. We show how such artefacts combine multiple epistemic functions and support multiple forms of perception. Section 9.5 introduces ideas about the *epistemic openness* of systems for education, work and scientific research, drawing implications that are relevant for rethinking curriculum in professional education programs.

© Springer Science+Business Media Dordrecht 2017
L. Markauskaite, P. Goodyear, *Epistemic Fluency and Professional Education*,
Professional and Practice-based Learning 14, DOI 10.1007/978-94-007-4369-4_9

9.1 Epistemic Practice

Some studies of scientific practices in research laboratories have tried to reconcile the tension between seeing products of human knowledge as being abstract and independent from their production and seeing them as inextricably intertwined with the practices within which they have been produced (e.g. Knorr Cetina, 1999, 2001; Nersessian, 2005; Rheinberger, 1997). They help make a conceptual shift in how one thinks about knowledge work, moving it from the non-material, idealised realm of symbols to the material settings of epistemic practice – which Rheinberger (1997) calls 'experimental systems':

> First, experimental systems are the genuine working units of contemporary research in which the scientific objects and the technical conditions of their production are inextricably interconnected. They are, inseparably and at *one and the same time*, *local*, *individual*, *social*, *institutional*, *technical*, *instrumental*, and, above all, *epistemic units*. Experimental systems are thus impure, hybrid settings. (Rheinberger, 1997, pp. 2–3, emphasis added)

Experimental systems, thus, provide a 'linking tissue' between the fluid dynamically changing, yet materially and symbolically defined, epistemic things situated within particular practices and the generic knowledge objects which people try to create and which are shared across communities.

Knorr Cetina (2007) – partly reflecting on the link between knowledge as non-situated accomplishment and knowledge work as situated practice – makes a distinction between knowledge production and *construction of machineries for knowledge production*. She points out that the former is a feature of 'knowledge culture' and the latter is a feature of 'epistemic culture':[1]

> If the focus in such early studies [of knowledge culture in the early 1970s] was on knowledge construction, the focus in an epistemic culture approach by contrast is on the construction of the *machineries* of knowledge construction, relocating culture in the micropractices of laboratories and other bounded habitats of knowledge practice. (Knorr Cetina, 2007, p. 361, original emphasis)

In epistemic culture, knowledge work is not abstract symbolic work, but a practice located in specific knowledge settings, where material and symbolic practices come together. She says:

> One other feature of the epistemic culture approach should be mentioned up front. It pertains to the understanding of culture. One of the more consequential moves … [is] to switch from an understanding of knowledge as the representational and technological *product* of research to an understanding of knowledge as *process*, or in other words, to knowledge as practice. (op. cit., p. 364, emphasis added)

Knorr Cetina, however, does not see the two approaches as incompatible. She continues:

> Culture, from the present viewpoint, includes practice, though I want to understand epistemic cultures as a *nexus* of *lifeworlds* (contexts of existence that include material

---

[1] We discussed the notions of epistemic culture and knowledge culture in Chap. 5.

objects) and *lifeworld processes* rather than as practice per se. (loc. cit., emphasis added)

Studies that have adopted this view and investigated knowledge production in specific settings have often focussed on knowledge work as practice. However, Knorr Cetina (2001) notes that 'epistemic practice' is different from 'practice' as conventionally conceived. The traditional view of practice emphasises *rule-governed, habitual processes*. She agrees that routine processes that are specifiable by certain schemata are dominant in social life and in some occupations. However, Knorr Cetina contrasts these habitual practices to practices in situations where people and organisations *confront nonroutine problems* and need nonroutine (differentiated) solutions that build on a significant knowledge base. She points out that some occupations and organisations deal exactly with these kinds of problems and engage in a rather different kind of practice. She argues that such practices then acquire quite different features, require different skills and have different relationships with the objects than do the traditional practices. She calls such practice 'epistemic practice' and its objects 'epistemic objects':

> ... I see epistemic practice as based upon a form of relationship that by the nature of its dynamic transforms itself and the entities formed by the relationship. (Knorr Cetina, 2001, p. 185)

> Epistemic objects frequently exist simultaneously in a variety of forms. They have multiple instantiations, which range from figurative, mathematical, and other representations to material realizations. (op. cit., p. 182)

Rheinberger (1997) helps ground this more deeply:

> To enter such a process of operational redefinition, one needs an arrangement that I refer to as the *experimental conditions*. <...> It is through them that the objects of investigation become entrenched and articulate themselves in a wider field of epistemic practices and material cultures, including instruments, inscription devices, model organisms, and the floating theorems or boundary concepts attached to them. It is through these technical conditions that the institutional context passes down to the bench work in terms of local measuring facilities, supply of materials, laboratory animals, research traditions, and accumulated skills carried on by long-term technical personnel. <...> The technical conditions determine the realm of possible representations of an epistemic thing [such as a complex research question]; and sufficiently stabilized epistemic things turn into the technical repertoire of the experimental arrangement. (Rheinberger, 1997, p. 29, emphasis added)

Constructing appropriate conditions for knowledge work is a part of knowledge production. The notion of 'epistemic practice', thus, relocates knowledge work back into the settings of practical action. Such work is, at the same time, both symbolically and materially defined, open as well as shaped by multiple epistemic systems, general *and* inseparable from the context. It involves not only the *production of knowledge* about the phenomenon but also *production of practices to create* this knowledge.

The notion of epistemic practice also shifts the very foundations of the traditional view of practice. Traditional notions of practice acknowledge customary and habitual forms of human activity, drawing on shared interpretational frameworks and firmly embodied in shared, materially mediated contexts (Cook & Brown, 1999; Henning, 2004; Schatzki, 2001). Epistemic practice, in contrast, involves a more dynamic and reciprocal relationship between shared interpretative and material contexts and differentiated knowledge-producing activity (Knorr Cetina, 2001).

Knowledge work in *professional workplaces*, by being materially grounded and situated in specific practice settings, is by its nature an epistemic practice, rather than 'mere' routine practice or 'pure' knowledge practice.

This shift of seeing professional knowledge work as epistemic practice is not just a rhetorical shift. This view has implications for what and how students should learn, in what kinds of practices they should engage and what kinds of artefacts they should produce. To learn to produce knowledge then means to learn to engage in *epistemic practice* – not only to engage in knowledge building with technological tools and symbolic representations but to learn to adapt ('tweak') existing epistemic tools and *construct machineries for* knowledge production in specific situations and settings.

Another important point to make about epistemic practices in the social or caring professions that have been at the core of our empirical work is that innovation within them characteristically involves the production of new *practices* rather than (just) new material or symbolic products. (Examples would be how to create an effective, ongoing treatment regime for a patient, or how to improve a procedure for giving injections safely, versus how to fix or improve a car headlight or a can-opener.) So, looking at epistemic practice in these professions shows how they create knowledge for, and of, the *production of practices* rather than (just) of material products. In this respect, professional practitioners innovate and create a category of knowledge products which is distinct from those products created in research laboratories and industrial R&D units: *techniques* or artefacts of skills and practices, rather than *technologies* or artefacts pertaining to propositional knowledge about the world. In short, our practitioners produce *process artefacts* of, and for, practice, rather than only *state artefacts* about the world.

That said, we should note that there is often a close relationship between process and state – for example, an effective treatment relates to a precise diagnosis. This kind of knowledge work is based on the understanding of *practice* as it is based on the understanding of *phenomena in the world* that relate to this practice. Thus, there is close constitutive entanglement between knowledge work to produce understanding of the world and knowledge work to produce understanding of, and for, practice in the world. We cannot improve techniques unless we understand technologies which make those techniques possible.

The epistemic system for such epistemic practice is also not constituted from exclusively local arrangements, conditions and culture, but is inextricably interconnected with other systems and cultures that constitute linked sites of practice, including a variety of global knowledge cultures, trans-epistemic cultures and local cultures (Knorr Cetina, 2007; and see Chap. 5). Epistemic artefacts, whether produced in professional workplaces or university settings, need to be sufficiently flexible and open to accommodate the different cultures that constitute the setting and, when necessary, should be able to enter into multiple discourses, representations, ways of acting and other 'technical conditions' of those cultures. For example, an assessment task that a future social worker does in their work placement needs to meet criteria of higher education and the professional workplace and standards of accreditation bodies. A pharmacist who works in a rural community pharmacy should be able to deliver services that mesh with *global* knowledge cultures and systems (e.g. what are the best medications, what are the best community health improvement practices, how to access this global information), *trans-epistemic* cultures (e.g. how databases for dispensing medications work) and *local* cultures (e.g. how to share knowledge and co-deliver services with a local medical centre). In short, epistemic artefacts constructed within university and professional settings have to be open enough to deal with the multiplicities of epistemic cultures and systems that constitute new learning and workplace settings.

9.2   Epistemic Tools

In this section, we develop a set of ideas concerning the nature and functioning of a special category of tools – which we call 'epistemic tools'. To do this, we provide some foundational ideas and make some useful distinctions involving tools and artefacts, tools and symbolic signs and epistemic tools and other kinds of tools.

The role of tools in the history of human social and cognitive development is well acknowledged. As Säljö (1995), drawing on other socioculturalists, puts it:

> In the creation of human culture, tool-making can be seen as one of the most powerful achievements. The difference between digging with one's hands and with a shovel of some kind or between hunting by throwing stones and using a bow and an arrow are profound also from a psychological point of view. Changing tools alters the structure of work activity (Scribner & Cole, 1981, p. 8) and, thus, the cognitive and communicative requirements of our actions. (Säljö, 1995, p. 90)

He extends this argument pointing to the fundamental role of tools in human cognition:

> What is interesting from the point of view of cognition and learning is that tools cannot be conceived as external to cognition, on the contrary they are integral parts of *our cognitizing* as well as of *our physical action*. <. . .> [The tool] gains its power as a device for orienting oneself and for relating to the environment only when integrated into a human practice and when used by a cognitizing subject engaged in a purposeful activity. The tool and the human being operate in a system that cannot be divided if one wants to understand cognition and practical action, rather there is a *seamless co-functionality* in which the mediational means form part of actions in situated practices. (op. cit., p. 91, emphasis added)

However, the role of tools in knowledge-generating activity is far from being well understood. The first question that one could ask is: what counts as a tool in such activity?

A number of scholars use the words 'tool' and 'artefact' interchangeably (Engeström, 1999; Säljö, 1995; Wartofsky, 1979).[2] For example, Wartofsky (1979) explicitly locates artefacts and tools in the same category of 'primary artefacts' and states:

> ... in more generic terms, the 'tool' may be *any* artifact created for the purpose of successful production and reproduction of the means of existence. (Wartofsky, 1979, pp. 200–201, original emphasis)

We accept that defining a tool is partly a matter of purpose, but not all tools are artefacts: a rock casually picked up and used to hammer open a coconut is a tool (while being so used), but it is not an artefact – the rock itself is not a human creation.

The same entity may play different roles – e.g. of a tool or of an artefact that instantiates the object of inquiry – in different situations (Knorr Cetina, 1999, 2001; Miettinen & Virkkunen, 2005; Rheinberger, 1997).[3] For example, 'the diagnosis' of a patient with health issues may initially be seen as an object of inquiry (with a corresponding epistemic artefact to be constructed), but once a diagnosis has been reached, it can be seen as an epistemic tool, used in the doctor's subsequent decisions, constructing the 'treatment'.

In talking about tools, Wartofsky (1979) includes not only material artefacts but also 'language', 'modes of social organisation', 'divisions of labour' and other artefacts that extend the human organs and are instrumental in the satisfaction of human needs and reproduction. We rather question the helpfulness of this all-encompassing position on tools – but will turn now to relations between tools and language: an important topic in clarifying the nature of *epistemic* tools.

9.2.1 Tools and Symbolic Signs

Different views have emerged about the relationship between tool-using and sign-using activity – including activity involving spoken and written language, drawing, symbols and other kinds of self-generated stimuli for guiding behaviour and social intercourse. Vygotsky (1978) noted that tools and signs play similar mediating functions, but argued that tools and signs are not identical and they play different roles in human activities. He made several specific contrasts between tools and signs: (a) tools are a means for labour, while signs are a means for psychological activity; accordingly (b) tools are used for 'mastering nature', whereas signs[4] are

---

[2] A detailed review of different definitions and usages of terms 'tool' and 'artefact' can be found in McDonald et al. (2005).

[3] Bereiter (2002) also agrees there are benefits in regarding conceptual artefacts in a similar way, such that one can see the same object as a tool in one situation and as an object of inquiry in another, depending on their function at the time.

[4] He referred to 'language' in his text.

used for social intercourse; and (c) while tools are directed towards an external object, aiming to change it, signs are directed internally with an aim of mastering oneself (one's behaviour).

Despite these different mediating roles of signs and tools, Vygotsky acknowledged that there is a close tie between them in activity:

> The mastering of nature and the mastering of behaviour are mutually linked, just as man's alteration of nature alters man's own nature. (Vygotsky, 1978, p. 55).
>
> ... the dialectical utility of these [speech and tool use] systems in the human adult is the very essence of complex human behaviour. (op. cit., p. 24, original emphasis)

He specifically argued that symbolic activity has a special 'organising function' and, when this activity accompanies tool use, it produces fundamentally new forms of behaviour.

Some of Dewey's (1929/2008) insights can be seen as extending this link between language and tools to human learning and practice. He specifically argued that language is a tool, but it is 'the tool of tools' and humans master other tools by virtue of language:

> ... at every point appliances and application, utensils and uses, are bound up with directions, suggestions and records made possible by speech; what has been said about the role of tools is subject to a condition supplied by language, the *tool of tools*. (Dewey, 1929/2008, p. 134, emphasis added)

So while many commentators acknowledge the close relations between tools and language, they are commonly regarded as two ontologically independent kinds of mediators.[5]

However, the distinction between tool-using activity and sign-using activity becomes less explicit in the context of knowledge work, when both tools of practice (and skill) and tools for meaning-making have the same symbolic origin and expression, but are also embodied in external material or digital media. For example, such tools for knowledge work as problem-solving strategies, heuristics, patterns of explanation, models, inquiry frameworks, concepts and patients' histories are symbolic, but they can also be 'objectified' and instantiated in concrete tools, such as guidelines, books, computer models, business plans or patient databases. Whether a patient's history, stored in a database, is a material tool or a symbolic tool when it helps a doctor arrive at a certain diagnosis and treatment is far from easy to say. Clearly, the record is used to communicate the information about the object, but the database is also a tool for sorting all records, making links and deciding about the diagnosis.

---

[5] This view may be traced back to ancient insights into human practical activity. For example, Aristotle (1934), describing human practice, made a similar distinction between two fundamental instrumentalities: 'making' or production (i.e. tool use) and 'doing' or communication (i.e. language). While the former instrumentality is a part of productive practice, the latter instrumentality is a part of practical wisdom – a rarer and higher 'intellectual virtue'.

Knowledge work involves psychological phenomena and, thus, involves mastering and acting with 'psychological tools' (Vygotsky, 1930) – such as concepts and representational frameworks:

> By acquiring concepts and discursive tools, we appropriate ways of understanding reality that have developed within particular discursive practices in different sectors in a complex society. When faced with identical problems or situations, people differing in expertise will construe the objects very differently depending on the conceptual frameworks they are familiar with and are able to draw upon. What is a chaotic and completely unintelligible picture to an outsider, as in the case of an X-ray, is highly meaningful and relevant for action for the expert nurse or physician. Even though individuals may be exposed to identical stimuli, these will mean very different things depending on experiential backgrounds and the conceptual resources we bring to the situation. (Säljö, 1995, p. 87)

While discourse is often seen as playing the main role in higher-order learning and understanding (e.g. Ohlsson, 1995), there is also a general recognition that language is not the only tool for generating knowledge. Complex problem-solving often includes a range of physical and digital tools as well as physical surroundings – notebooks, calendars, handbooks, material anchors, experimental instruments and other experimental arrangements (Clark, 2011; Dunbar, Gamble, & Gowlett, 2010; Hutchins, 2005; Kirsh, 2009; Knorr Cetina, 1999; Nersessian, 2006; Rheinberger, 1997; Salomon, 1993; Säljö, 1995). Some of these tools allow one to 'offload' some cognitive tasks from the mind to external devices: such as performing calculations, as calculators do, or keeping information, as handbooks and databases do. Some other tools have an even more central role and participate as 'cognitive partners' *capable of some agency* and helping solve problems, shaping experimental setups or creating knowledge on a par with human beings. Examples might be modelling and simulation software, used in predicting future market trends or projecting a company's annual earnings.

There is a constitutive entanglement between the design of the physical tool, the generated sign and the human capability involved in acting knowledgably with the tool. For example, Pea (1993) vividly illustrates how cognition is distributed across humans, tools and environment – using the example of a forest ranger measuring trees to estimate the amount of lumber on a patch of land. If the ranger measured using a conventional measuring tape, she would need to know the formula for calculating diameters and making other estimations. However, the tape can be scaled up, and the algorithm for calculating the diameter can be built directly into the tape. Then, figuring out the diameter of a tree would rely only on direct perception and getting the measurements right:

> [The] phases of the intelligent activity of measuring trees are distributed in the *object used for measuring*, its social *history* of practices for engaging that embodied intelligence, and the *user's memory* for how to engage that tool in activity. (Pea, 1993, p. 70, emphasis added)

> ... activity is a product not of intelligence in the individual mind, but of one's *memory*, the structure of the *resources* available in the environment at hand, and one's desires, which guide the *interpretation* of these structuring resources. Through processes of design and invention, we load intelligence into both physical, designed artifacts and representational

objects such as diagrams, models, and plans. We exploit intelligence from objects when we use them instrumentally in activities. (loc. cit., emphasis added)

However, Pea notes that intelligent tool use cannot be decoupled from the understanding of intelligence embodied in the design of such tools. He continues:

... we often need to decouple intelligence from such objects to reuse them in novel ways. Once such intelligence is designed into the affordance properties of artifacts, it both guides and constrains the likely contributions of that artifact to distributed intelligence in activity. Obviously the measuring tape, once the formula has been compiled in its design, cannot readily be adapted to linear measurement without recrafting its scale. (op. cit., pp. 70–71)

Most views of practice primarily emphasise the *communicative* role of language for sharing of ideas and social intercourse. However, Andy Clark (1998) warns:

... the emphasis on language as a medium of communication tends to blind us to a subtler but equally potent role: the role of language as a tool that alters the nature of the computational tasks involved in various kinds of problem solving. (Clark, 1998, p. 193)

The more obvious 'communicative' view of language overshadows the *generative* role of language – particularly the role of external symbolic inscriptions – which complements basic human cognitive capacities. While Clark (1998) argues that language does not necessarily alter in any profound ways the brain's own representations and mechanisms, language nevertheless provides 'the rich environment of manipulable external symbolic structures' (p. 200) to support cognition. In short, sign use for communication (traditionally expressed in common views of language) is not the same as sign use for scaffolding of human cognition and knowledge generation in action – the use of signs as epistemic tools capable of bringing forth meanings.

9.2.2   Epistemic Tools as Bridges Between Physical and Mental Worlds

Should we treat tools that are used for creating knowledge as signs (i.e. solely symbolic psychological tools) or as physical tools that involve perception and manual skill? Some of these tools – such as concepts, heuristics or formulae – are predominately symbolic. Some others – such as forceps or a flask – are predominantly physical. But many have qualities of both – such as a measuring tape that needs both the physical act of measuring and symbolic interpretation of scales and numbers or a blood pressure monitor that requires physical manipulation but also generates a symbolic output.

If we apply the criteria that Vygotsky (1986) used for making a distinction between the tool and the sign (primarily as language), we can see that *knowledge-generating tools* are distinguishable from both physical tools and signs. We call these knowledge-generating tools 'epistemic tools' (Table 9.1). That is, while the psychological and physical aspects of these tools could be separated, at least theoretically, in classical practices, it is hard to do this in epistemic practices.

Table 9.1 Locating epistemic tools between other mediating tools

Function	Signs	Epistemic tools	Physical tools
For mastering...	Self	Knowing of nature	Nature
Means for...	Psychological activity	Epistemic work	Physical labour
Directed...	Inwards	Towards dialogic relationship between sign and world	Outwards
For creating and changing...	Social intercourse	Knowledge of the world and for the world, through social intercourse	World

The second and the fourth columns are based on Vygotsky (1986)

By 'epistemic tools', we mean all classes of material and symbolic entities, including those employed in human discourse, that are used to shape inquiry and knowledge-producing action. In professional learning and work settings, this includes structuring resources and other tools that shape professional inquiry – such as concepts, standards, frames of inquiry, heuristics and codes, as well as other knowledge resources in external media – such as professional manuals and databases. We use the modifier *epistemic*, rather than *cognitive*, as notions of knowledge and ways of knowing that are instantiated in such tools are not defined solely by embrained properties of the mind or physical properties of media, but are also social and cultural products – of epistemic cultures.

Epistemic tools are a means for engaging in authentic knowledge work. They are directed towards establishing dialogic relationships between known and unknown, discovering unknown phenomena and producing new relationships between the world and social intercourse. In this respect, *tools for knowledge-generating work constitute a distinct functional category* that, together with discursive activity (language, gestures, etc.) and physical tools, participate in knowledge(able) practice: knowledgeable action and actionable knowledge. They are directed inwards and outwards at the same time.

However, epistemic tools are not the only kind of tools that participate in productive professional inquiry. *Neither practice, nor discourse, nor mental work alone can produce understanding in a professional context*; rather, understanding comes from the interaction between all three kinds of tools and coordination between three kinds of actions: communicative, pragmatic and epistemic.

In fact, one could claim that 'knowledge work' can be regarded as the third instrumentality of human practice. Consider a pharmacist who reviews medications for a patient: she uses her perception and the physical environment to collect information (e.g. drug boxes, a cupboard where medications are kept, in order to check if the medications are kept in appropriate conditions); she uses language to communicate with the patient (for social intercourse), but also uses a range of epistemic tools (e.g. interview schedules, review worksheets, and medication databases) to establish the relationships between disparate and not necessarily consistent knowledge about the world (e.g. patient's feelings, his medical diagnoses and available medications) in order to solve the problem and come up with a better treatment for the patient. Epistemic tools perform a dual coordinating function between the external unknown world (perception) and the internal known world (knowledge) and between the external action (skill) and the internal cognition (coming to understand). This understanding fuses the state of mind and action, complex knowledge and complex process (cf. Ingold, 2011; Ohlsson, 1995).

9.2.3 How Epistemic Qualities of Tools Arise in Practice

There is an advantage in seeing epistemic tools as special tools that play a specific – epistemic – role in knowledge(able) practice. When we understand the structure, function, mechanisms and conditions under which such tools generate productive practice, we are better placed to say what should be learnt and how it could be taught in higher education. However, the distinctions between different kinds of tools are useful as long as we are careful to see and acknowledge their diversity, their dynamic and relational nature and their constitutive entanglement with human action and the environment.

Consider a pharmacist who looks in a medication database trying to figure out possible interactions between several medications. Such a database is simultaneously a technological device that requires skilful physical manipulation (e.g. typing and using a cleverly designed interface to the database), a symbolic tool that requires mastery of pharmaceutical knowledge (e.g. knowledge of medication names and active ingredients) and an epistemic tool that requires a skill for juxtaposing physical and symbolic affordances in order to figure out possible causes of the problem and come up with a possible solution (e.g. searching, sorting, comparing, seeing chemical interactions, putting together evidence and decisions).

Whether the pharmacist will primarily rely on physical interrogation of the database, or will embrace, in significant ways, the mental resources of her pharmaceutical knowledge, will depend on the situation rather than on the database per se. Thus the difference between the symbolic tool, epistemic tool and physical tool is *primarily functional* (based on the role in practice) rather than *solely ontological* (embedded in the nature of the database).

Similar points can be made about the nature and distinctions between 'artefacts' and 'tools', or 'things' and 'objects' more generally. The boundaries between them are rarely clear-cut: they emerge and disappear in activity. Consider the doctor in the example earlier – they have just came up with a diagnosis for a patient. The diagnosis – a constructed epistemic artefact – of course could now be seen as a tool for decisions about the treatment. However, seeing the diagnosis as a stable tool in the doctor's hands misses a key point. One has also to take into account that the patient's health – and so the diagnosis – will change over time and the treatment will require ongoing adjustment. While it can be useful to regard artefacts as the targets of activity, and tools as 'partners' in activity, we should note that this distinction is functional and perspective dependent rather than an inherent feature of the mediating entity (Knorr Cetina, 1999; McDonald, Le, Higgins, & Podmore, 2005; Miettinen & Virkkunen, 2005; Rheinberger, 1997).

Clark (2011) makes a similar point, linking diverse mediating tools with human knowing and action, in the following way:

> ... the proper response is to see mind and intelligence themselves as mechanically realised by complex, shifting mixtures of energetic and dynamic coupling, internal and external forms of representation and computation, epistemically potent forms of bodily action, and the canny exploitation of a variety of extrabodily props, aids, and scaffolding. Minds like ours emerge from this colourful flux as surprisingly seamless wholes: adaptively potent mashups extruded from a dizzying motley of heterogeneous elements and processes. (Clark, 2011, p. 219)

However, as Pea (1993) reminds us, intelligence is accomplished rather than possessed:

> [We] should strive toward a reflectively and intentionally distributed intelligence in education, where learners are *inventors of distributed-intelligence-as-tool*, rather than *receivers of intelligence-as-substance*. In the court of worldly experience, such learners may be far more ready not only to adapt to change but to contribute substantially to it. (Pea, 1993, p. 82, emphasis added)

We should also remember that innovation and learning do not create isolated products or single tools, but integrated instrumental ensembles – constellations of tools – which offer practitioners multiple, variable and flexible ways to answer different questions and accomplish different kinds of tasks (Engeström, 1990, 2006). Such instrumental ensembles range from broad models that help answer the question 'Where to go?' to more specific models, scripts, classifications and prototypes that *help answer* more specific questions of 'Why?', 'How?', 'When?', 'What' and so on. Using, tweaking and creating tools within, and to enhance, such constellations are an essential aspect of professional learning.

Drawing on Merlin Donald's (1991) exploration of the evolution of culture and cognition, Andy Clark (1998) distinguishes between two types of scaffolding that language provides for human cognition – 'the mythic' and 'the theoretic'. Donald notes that, before the Greeks, written formalisms were mainly deployed as tools for the communication of narratives, myths and finished theories such that they could be passed on and learnt. The Greeks, in contrast, started to use the written medium to record *processes* of thought. Records began to include arguments and evidence for and against conjectures and other unfinished ideas, to be amended and completed by others. In short, the written medium was used to record, create and change the very process of thought and discovery.

9.3   Action, Meaning and (Epistemic) Practice

How does our view of epistemic practice relate to other notions of practice, including the classical views of *habitual* practice (Cook & Brown, 1999; Henning, 2004; Nicolini, 2013; Schatzki, 2001) and more recent views of *knowledge-creating* practice (Bereiter, 2002; Engeström, 2008; Nonaka, 2004; Paavola & Hakkarainen, 2005)? Some key differences and relationships can be understood by depicting the main relationships between skill (or ways of doing) and the resourceful mind (ways of knowing), within the exercise of a profession.

On the traditional perspective, practice is 'action informed by meaning drawn from a particular group context' (Cook & Brown, 1999, p. 143) and involves everyday activities organised around shared understandings and material arrangements (Fig. 9.1). The relationship between action and practice is established by skill, mediated by shared tools and material arrangements, whereas the link between meaning-making and practice is established by simultaneous discursive activity, mediated by shared language and other kinds of discourse. Actions in the material world require competence and fine-tuned skill to follow rules, structures, constraints and affordances of the physical world and tools. Whereas meaning-making activity requires mastery of tools for social intercourse, including syntactical and grammatical structures, rules of language and rules of community discourse. Such practice results in public goods – including material, social and cultural products. It also generates artefacts of practice that embody shared interpretative frameworks and routines. Such shared cultural artefacts can be seen as by-products of practice, generated by general (biological and historical) thinking ability to notice patterns and form habits. Nevertheless, these artefacts are the main mediators between mind and skill in the fine-tuned exercise of expertise.

The knowledge-creating perspective (e.g. Paavola & Hakkarainen, 2005) extends the traditional framework of practice by adding to it an additional

Fig. 9.1 The link between action and meaning from a traditional practice perspective

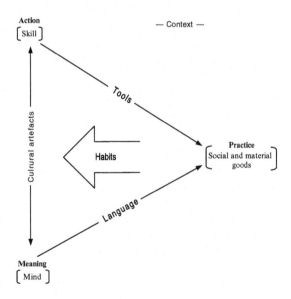

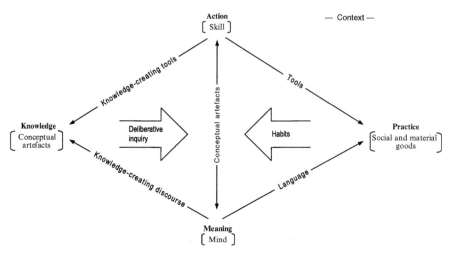

Fig. 9.2 The link between action and meaning from the knowledge-creating practice perspective

element – new knowledge (Fig. 9.2). From this perspective, the link between mind and skill is no longer a by-product of simultaneous acting and meaning-making, but a product of deliberative inquiry aimed at constructing knowledge. Such knowledge-building activity is mediated by a different kind of language – knowledge construction discourse – and by use of a different kind of tool, epistemic tools. Its main product is knowledge embodied in conceptual artefacts: plans, concepts, ways of structuring problems, etc. Such conceptual artefacts extend the link between mind and skill by giving explicit meanings to actions and building instrumental ensembles for activity informed by these shared meanings. Conceptual artefacts are products of deliberative knowledge work and constitute instrumental ensembles for activity informed by shared meaning.

The knowledge(able) practice or *epistemic practice* perspective (Fig. 9.3) shifts the focus of knowledge-creating practice from knowledge production in a largely transparent epistemic system to knowledge creation as situated, embodied epistemic work within action.

On this view, meaning and action are expressed not only in practice or in deliberative knowledge construction but also in the *simultaneous assembling of an epistemic system* for creating meaning (for and within action). This epistemic system is constructed by juxtaposing heterogeneous affordances available for action and meaning-making in a situation. This includes tools, language and other resources for discourse and the production of signs, skills and existing meanings. It also includes epistemic tools, skills and other personal mental resources for

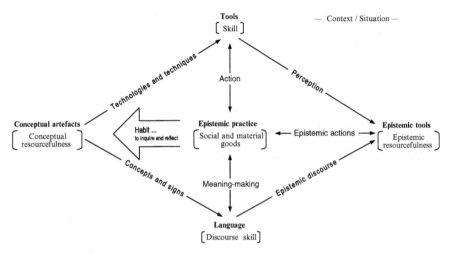

Fig. 9.3 The link between action and meaning from a knowledge(able) practice or epistemic practice perspective

producing new meanings. It is not that tool use and language use are directed by meanings that have been assigned to activity prior to actions; rather, meanings are established during tool use and interaction within concrete situations. Knowledge, practice and ways of knowing are constituted simultaneously by perceiving, assembling the affordances, making sense of the situation and acting. Such knowledge (able) work is *constructed from meanings* assigned to actions and *mediated by tools and skills* (including language), rather than *constituted from tools and skills* and *mediated by actions*. In short, actions give meanings to tool use, and tools give meanings to actions. Knowledge is not so much *embedded* in cultural or conceptual artefacts as *dynamically assembled* through practice, through knowing while acting and acting while knowing.

Ingold (2011) talks about this by contrasting 'thinking through making' and 'making through thinking'. He argues that the latter often overshadows the former, in accounts of (creative or innovative) practice:

> It is because analysts have typically adopted this latter orientation that they have been so inclined to locate sources of creativity in images and objects rather than in things and performances. (Ingold, 2011, p. 6)

However, in knowledgeable action, people face the world simultaneously as 'analysts' and 'makers' of the world and of their own practice.

9.4   Understanding Epistemic Qualities of Artefacts: Results from Artefact Analysis

Wartofsky's (1979) and Bereiter's (2002) classifications of artefacts (Chap. 8) help us see some essential qualities of knowledge products by making distinctions between knowledge in a person's mind and skills and objectified knowledge inscribed in the artefacts and between knowledge that is a reflection of the world and knowledge that is a product of authentic, deliberative knowledge building.

However, these classifications need some further refinement to capture epistemic qualities of artefacts that students, scientists and other knowledge workers produce. Why might we want to consider these qualities? Let's take an example from a non-professional domain, like two contrasting recipe books for the home cook. One includes a set of recipes with all the ingredients and step-by-step instructions on how to cook each dish. Thus, the 'user's' job is to take the recipe and with minimal alteration try to reproduce the dish. It is relatively easy for its producer (the recipe writer, cf. the knowledge worker) to provide the required account of a typical procedure.

In contrast, the second recipe book includes similar information to the first, but also explains the role of each ingredient and of each step in the cooking procedure – how each contributes to the taste, texture and other important qualities of the resulting dish. These additions are anticipatory responses to questions of the following kind: Can I still make a reasonably good dish if I don't have garlic? How does garlic actually contribute to this dish? What are the alternatives? Why should I cook this on a low temperature for a long time, rather than increase the temperature and cook it for a shorter time?

In this case, the cook needs to know 'functional' properties, and perhaps even deeper 'conceptual' qualities, of the ingredients, cooking times and temperatures, so that she can reproduce similar dishes in different ways in various situations while preserving critical qualities of the dish. The job of using such a recipe book shifts from reproducing steps mechanically to knowledgeable adjustment of the unfolding situation, taking into account available ingredients and their freshness, taste, the time available, etc. In short, this kind of recipe book becomes not only a carrier of practice and skills but a carrier of *epistemic* practice. Producing such 'carriers' of epistemic practice requires rather different kinds of knowledge and understanding: not just about cooking itself or simple listing of ingredients and steps.

Before we turn to deeper epistemic qualities, we need to make a further (quite simple) distinction between artefacts embodying *understanding of things* and artefacts embodying *understanding of actions*. There is more to this than the difference between 'learning for understanding' and 'learning for doing' (Ohlsson, 1995) or 'knowledge' and 'knowing' (Cook & Brown, 1999). 'Doing' can also be understood and things are known *by* 'knowing'. Consider an example of a freshly cooked dish. The primary artefact or object in this case will be a prepared meal. This is different from the 'live' artefact embodying the chef's distinct way of preparing this dish. If one may find it hard to call the cooking process an 'artefact',

Table 9.2 Some parallels between artefacts for representing objects and artefacts representing human actions

Type of artefact	Artefacts of phenomena (objects)	Artefacts of process (actions)
Primary	*Real experiential things* For example, prepared meal; a child with behavioural difficulties	*Real skills, ways of doing* For example, skill to prepare a meal; skill to do a behavioural assessment
Secondary	*Mimetic symbolic representations of objects* For example, list of ingredients in the recipe; symptoms of a behavioural disorder, test results, diagnosis	*Mimetic symbolic representations of actions, ways of doing* For example, steps involved in cooking; testing instruments and guidelines
Tertiary	*Symbolic representations of mechanisms, principles and meanings behind functioning of phenomena* For example, essential features of ingredients that make the meal taste as it tastes; causes of behavioural symptoms	*Symbolic representations of rules, principles and other meanings behind operation, actions and other observed processes* For example, cooking heuristics, rules and other principles; behavioural assessment principles

let us imagine it is captured in a video recording, thereby taking on a material form. Of course, the dish and the video-recorded procedure are not the same – one can taste and smell the dish, but one cannot smell and taste the actions. The knowledge embodied in each artefact is very different too – it is easy to talk about the taste by trying the dish, but not much could be said about the taste just by observing the chef's actions. Nevertheless, if one is to reproduce the dish, it may be easier to do it by having an artefact that represents actions, rather than having a sample of the prepared dish (a.k.a. knowledge) or even tasting the prepared dish (a.k.a. knowing).

This example is broadly illustrative of Wartofsky's (1979) primary artefacts (see Chap. 8), but it is clear that the understanding of things and understanding of actions take distinct artefact-like forms. We can also construct secondary and tertiary artefacts for objects and actions (Table 9.2). Simple, abstracted mimetic inscriptions – the secondary artefacts – will be different too. The dish as an object may be represented by listing ingredients, whereas the cooking actions could be captured by outlining the step-by-step procedure for preparation and cooking. Even at a deeper – tertiary artefact – level, the underpinning qualities that make the dish taste as it tastes are different from the cooking principles that the chef should adhere to in order to achieve the desired flavour. The accounts of objects and actions are broadly similar to the representation of mechanisms and other principles behind the *functioning* of the object and representation of processes, rules and other meanings that underpin *human operation* with the functions of this object – between technology and technique.

Much of the knowledge embodied in skilful professional work has similarities with our example about the dish and cooking. In Table 9.2, we use both the cooking example and a professional example: a counsellor's work assessing a child with behavioural difficulties.

9.4.1   Epistemic Qualities of Artefacts Produced by Students

Further examination of the artefacts produced by students in their assessment tasks (Chap. 8) reveals that they exhibit very different *epistemic qualities*. We have identified four broad groups of artefacts, which we label direct, inscriptional, functional and explanatory. These are summarised in Table 9.3 and explained in the text below:

1. *Direct* artefacts are produced by exercising professional knowledge and skill through action.
2. *Inscriptional* artefacts describe phenomena or action.
3. *Functional* artefacts explain relationships between characteristics of phenomena or characteristics of action and its outcome.
4. *Explanatory* artefacts explain underlying principles and causes.

Direct artefacts are material things and skills embodied in producing material, social and cultural goods. The qualities of the artefacts produced, and skills used to produce them, directly embody professional knowledge. *Things* include material artefacts created in action and cultural artefacts created for the purpose of use in professional action. Drugs, lesson handouts, PowerPoint slides and feedback for (school) students on an assessment task are examples of things that pharmacists and teachers commonly produce. *Skills* for the production of direct artefacts have slightly different epistemic qualities. Teaching a specific lesson, explaining a specific concept, dispensing a medication and providing counselling for a family illustrate epistemic work involved in producing these kinds of social goods.

Inscriptional artefacts are literal and abstracted representations of things and phenomena that exist in the physical world (what's there; what steps need to be taken to get something done). Examples include a list of ingredients in a medication or recipe, a list of materials needed during a lesson, a photo of a device or the name of a device. These artefacts also include representations of actions and skills needed to get something done: a (conventional) recipe describing how to prepare a dish, a guide for a teacher on how to use a teaching aid, a prescription for a patient with information about how to take a medication, a step-by-step description of how to produce a medication, a sequence of learning activities, a step-by-step guide for a nurse and an excursion plan ready to be used by teachers.

Functional artefacts are representations that carry over functional information or purpose (how something works; how to combine actions to achieve a goal). They are reflective embodiments of the physical word; abstract inscriptions that represent functional qualities linking characteristics of phenomena (structure) and function, such as models of specific things and prototypes; a list of active ingredients in a drug; and an explanation of what specific test results mean. They also include representations of knowledge for actions that represent functional qualities (purposes) of action: a cooking guide with a description of the roles of ingredients or functions of each action, a medication assessment report with findings explicitly linked to the recommendations for a doctor, and a lesson plan linking a rationale

Table 9.3 Epistemic qualities of professional artefacts

Artefact	Description	Examples
Direct artefacts. Material things, embodied skills, social and cultural goods		
Material and cultural artefacts Direct knowledge embedded in qualities of an artefact	Material artefacts and things created for the purpose of use in direct action, including tools	Drugs, lesson handouts, PowerPoint slides, a corrected student assessment with feedback
Skills used in professional work Direct knowledge embodied in action	Skills for the production of primary artefacts and tools in direct action	Teaching a specific lesson, explaining a specific concept, dispensing a medication, providing counselling for a family
Inscriptional artefacts		
Inscriptional–representational artefacts What's there?	Literal representations of primary artefacts and tools	A list of ingredients in a drug or recipe, a list of materials needed during a lesson, photo of a device, a name of a device
Inscriptional–operational artefacts What steps need to be taken to get something done?	Representations of actions for the purpose of use or production of primary artefacts and tools in direct action	A guide for a teacher on how to use a handout, a prescription for a patient on how to take a medication, a recipe for a meal, a step-by-step description of how to produce a specific medication, a sequence of learning activities, a step-by-step guide for a nurse, an excursion plan
Functional artefacts		
Functional–representational artefacts How does something work?	Representations of structure that carry over functional information	Models of specific things and prototypes, maps, active ingredients in a drug, an explanation of what a test result of a child's reading skills shows or means
Functional–operational artefacts How and why to combine actions to achieve a goal	Representations of knowledge for actions in construction of (specific) primary artefacts or further direct actions	Justification of recommendations for a doctor, cooking guide with description of the roles of each ingredient or functions of each action, a lesson plan linking rationale with learning activities and actions, what students learn by doing a specific activity
Explanatory artefacts		
Explanatory–representational artefacts Why does it work in this way?	Representations of conceptual knowledge behind the structure and mechanisms in the design of an artefact	A psychological assessment report providing evidence and explaining principles behind the conclusions and recommendation, a working sheet for a medication review – with evidence
Explanatory–operational artefacts Why one should act in this way	Representations of conceptual knowledge behind actions	A clinical performance package in nursing, providing conceptual knowledge (or evidence) underpinning specific actions; a practice development portfolio with explanation and justification of taken actions

with learning activities, actions and outcomes. In short, the links among different parts and the logic of how certain initial conditions produce certain outcomes, at least on the observed level, are clear.

Explanatory artefacts carry over meaning (why it works in this way; why to act in this way). They include representations of what we could call conceptual and explanatory knowledge behind the structure and design of an artefact. For example, a psychological assessment report may explain a diagnosis as well as principles behind the recommendation. This category also includes artefacts that explain the rationale behind actions. For example, a nursing guide could provide biomedical knowledge explaining why an infection causes certain symptoms, as well as biomedical knowledge or best evidence explaining why one should take certain actions in order to prevent it. Such explanations go beyond what could be easily noticed by just looking at things, phenomena or actions, into the internal mechanisms that constitute the very essence of how things work and why certain actions will lead to certain outcomes.

While *direct* artefacts are broadly associated with Wartofsky's primary artefacts, *inscriptional, functional and explanatory* have epistemic properties of secondary and tertiary artefacts.

We are not arguing that one specific kind of artefact is better than others at assisting in the learning of professional knowledge. Rather, we note that it is the *epistemic qualities* of the artefacts that provide important bridges between 'learning to do' and 'learning to understand'. These bridges underpin epistemic fluency.

We illustrate this with some observations taken from our research in nurse education – specifically in the context of preparation for clinical practice – by elaborating on the case that we introduced in Chap. 8.

9.4.2   A Case: Constructing the Nursing Guidelines

The nursing course coordinator explained a number of the main challenges in preparing nurses for clinical practice. First, nursing students need to learn skills to carry out clinical procedures. Such skills could be conveniently taught as a step-by-step procedure following guidelines. However, the course coordinator noted that there are many ways to carry out each procedure and each hospital has different protocols for doing this. It is not possible to say if the procedure is correct or not merely by noting that the steps are different. The coordinator explained:

> ... there's many ways of drawing up an injection. You don't always have to do it exactly the same way. <...> We're [nurses] not robots and that's the thing too. There are principles of safety. <...> But the way you – the steps that you get to go there – you and I might do it differently but we would still maintain that level of safety.

She argued that nurses should be critical thinkers – 'not robots'. They should base their decisions and actions on fundamental principles of clinical practice and the available clinical evidence, not on the following prescribed steps:

> ... the whole thing again is to get them to think about – just because somebody says 'you
> have to pick up forceps this way', 'why do you have to pick up the forceps that way?'.

On the other hand, she was concerned about the difficulties entailed if students have
to learn to do clinical procedures just by learning conceptual principles. The course
coordinator reflected on a core tension between teaching underlying general principles of clinical practice and specific clinical skills that nursing students need to
develop by practising physical embodied skill without procedural guidelines. She
observed that students simply struggle to link principles to practice and to learn
practical skills. She noticed that some students even started to construct their own
guidelines:

> ... a group of students last year, of the Master students, when I first got here, they were
> actually taking pictures and making their own [guidelines of clinical procedures].

A similar challenge was to engage students with declarative knowledge:

> ... they come here to do nursing so we want to make it interesting and when I looked at, I
> thought if I hit them with too much heavy theory straight up, you'll lose them.

Her decision was to set an assessment task that requires students to *carry out* a
procedure in the laboratory and to *develop a guide* that illustrates and explains how
to carry out specific clinical procedures while also *providing evidence* about why it
should be done in this way.[6] The coordinator explained:

> This is a step by step guide for them [showing the example of the assignment]. This is how
> we do it. This is a visual. <....> So the thing is I don't know how to take a temperature so I
> wanted them to create with evidence of what is the best – what would I do? I'd wash my
> hands first. I'd take the thing out. I'd put a probe cover on. I'd do all these sorts of things. So
> step by step clearly looking at what you do.

She particularly stressed the importance of evidence:

> We didn't want the whole step by step thing. We wanted them to view the important bits,
> the critical elements of their particular skill. <...> We wanted them to talk about the
> literature. Again, that came into – I wanted them, in that area, to talk about what the
> literature said and what was the best support from literature.

While typical nursing guidelines belong to the category of inscriptional artefacts,
the nursing students, in this particular case, were asked to develop an explanatory
artefact. At the same time, their guidelines were not 'pure' *explanatory* artefacts,
but linked representations of conceptual principles behind the phenomena
(e.g. infection) and behind the skill (e.g. how to prevent it) with direct skills to
carry out these procedures in the material world. In short, they had *direct, inscriptional* and *functional* features, such as the performance of specific actions in the lab,
and visual representations illustrating how to carry out specific procedures.

This example illustrates several other important matters. There is a tension
between three different aspects of actionable knowledge – 'knowing what to do',

---

[6] We return to this case and discuss the design features of the assessment task in detail in
Chapter 11. For a quick preview, see the description of the task in Fig. 11.2.

'knowing how to do' and 'knowing why to do in this particular way'. They are irreducible to each other: 'know-what' takes the form of steps, 'know-how' takes the form of rules or heuristics behind the skills and 'knowing why' takes the form of conceptual principles and evidence. Further, the nurse's actionable knowledge, enabling her to carry out the procedures, cannot be separated from knowledge embodied and enacted in the actual 'doing'.

The nature of inscriptions of practical knowledge embodied in skill and actions is very distinct. These can be captured quite well by visual media (video or photo), but not so well in language or other symbolic forms. Conceptual knowledge, in contrast, is best communicated via language, not through direct representations of skills (Goodyear & Steeples, 1998). Returning to Wartofsky (1979, 1987), the guidelines produced by the students – unlike traditional guidelines that are *imported into* learning settings rather than *produced in* them – are not classical secondary artefacts. They also provide *connections* to primary and tertiary artefacts. Images capture skills in the physical world (primary artefact); step-by-step instructions represent and preserve these skills in an 'objectified', ready-to-transfer form (secondary artefacts); conceptual principles abstract the guidelines from specific representations and open them up for further 'offline' improvement and adaptation to different situations (tertiary artefacts).

So, in this specific example, students create 'unnatural' (extended) secondary artefacts of professional practice ('epistemic artefacts') that 'leak' into primary and tertiary spaces and – as Wartofsky (1987) argued – draw on different kinds of perception. Thus, by creating such guidelines, students have a possibility of discovering the links between all three ways of seeing and representing.

However, we should not lose sight of the distinction between epistemic qualities *of the artefact that embody certain kinds of perception* and epistemic qualities *of perception and skill that are embodied in the very production of the artefact*. In short, these guidelines not only *inscribe* epistemic processes – 'ways of thinking' – that underpin three kinds of professional perception and action, they are *produced by* these very 'ways of thinking' – acting and perceiving. It is this 'juxtaposition' and 'hybridisation' of epistemic features of the action and of the artefact that permit linking the direct experience of the 'thing' with the specific goal of professional action (directed towards a concrete *objekt*) and the broader aims and motives of learning activity (directed towards a broader *predmet*) (see Chap. 8). One of the common faults in higher education is that it tries to educate professionals by getting them to engage with objects directly through tertiary kinds of perception. It would be better to help people build relations between *objekt*, *predmet* and *things* and by coordinating the three kinds of perception: primary, secondary and tertiary. 'Learning for doing' and 'learning for understanding' become captured in coordinated 'thinking through making' and 'making through thinking' (cf. Ingold, 2011; Ohlsson, 1995).

Of course, it would be an oversimplification and overstatement to think that, by creating such guidelines, nurses will become knowledgeable creators and innovators of their practice. Nevertheless, it is likely to be a step in the right direction.

This classification of epistemic features of artefacts also broadly reflects the positioning of students in relation to a discipline that has been characterised by Pickering (1995) as 'a dance' – involving material, disciplinary and conceptual agency.

Material agency is involved when the material system – experimental apparatus and configuration of practice setting – determines the action. *Disciplinary agency* is involved when established ways of doing things, methods and procedures carry humans along and determine the outcomes of their action. Whereas *conceptual agency* is involved when individuals constructively engage with subject matter by interpreting meanings, choosing and adapting methods and making other constructive decisions. Greeno (2006) argued that traditional learning tasks aim to grant students more disciplinary agency and material agency – how to perform procedures and how to set up things in order to get certain empirical outcomes – but give little conceptual agency, how to interpret meanings and design methods and apparatus.

Material, disciplinary and conceptual agency mirror three different roles of epistemic artefacts: inscriptional, functional and explanatory. It is clear that performing tasks and constructing artefacts that have only inscriptional and functional qualities may not take us far when preparing students to innovate. But can construction of *explanatory* artefacts do this? Of course, it depends of how far we stretch the boundaries of conceptual perception. If we consider conceptual as something settled, as a set of 'technical objects' that enter knowing and action, then they may be sufficient to solve problems that are settled in specific – and, thus, by definition closed – systems (or domains) where encountered problems can be perceived as objects rather than things. But when we enter a domain where problems are encountered as *things* – the domain of 'epistemic things' in an open world – then we should not be tempted to reduce the 'epistemic' work to the traditional notion of 'conceptual'. 'Conceptual' is the kind of perception where 'free creation' is made possible by fusing conceptual operations and rules for free creation within the domain. 'Epistemic', in contrast, is the kind of perception that guides coordination among (multiple) primary, secondary and tertiary ways of seeing the world. It enables construction of actionable knowledge.

9.5 Epistemic Openness: Knowledge Practice Systems

University is an odd space in which to learn professional knowledge. It is a hybrid space where three epistemic cultures of learning, research and the profession come together. We should perhaps celebrate this convergence – hybrid sites are places for creativity and innovation. However, as Goodwin (2005) notes, knowledge does not float in some context-free domain, but is situated, and the space and place where work is done have consequences for the knowledge produced.

Such spaces and places constitute and are simultaneously constituted by actions:

> ... relevant spaces are reflexively constituted through the organization of the actions that simultaneously make use of the structure(s) provided by particular places while articulating and shaping them as meaningful entities appropriate to the activity in progress. (Goodwin, 2005, pp. 85–86)

He describes this space as a space for action:

> ... a diverse patchwork of different kinds of spaces and representational technologies by differently positioned actors working together. (op. cit., p. 86)

Heterogeneity is a key characteristic of such workspaces as the university. On the one hand, science, the profession and education each share and value three common phenomena: knowledge, work and learning. On the other hand, there are some significant differences among the knowledge creation and inquiry practices in the scientific world, educational institutions and organisational and professional settings. One of the qualities that makes them distinct is the 'epistemic openness' of their knowledge production *systems*: objects of inquiry, tools and environments.

9.5.1   Science and Research

At one end, in scientific inquiry, cutting edge innovations emerge from discoveries of new ways to look at objects of inquiry and by creating new objects of inquiry – new concepts, new tools, new discovery routines, etc. – rather than doing more of the same with what is already known. That is, knowledge emerges from what Rheinberger (1997) called 'differential reproduction' (p. 75). Changes in experimental systems are important. It is not only that the greatest scientific discoveries were made by formulating new concepts and creating new research methods and tools – such as the microscope, telescope, computer and data-driven research techniques (Hey, Tansley, & Tolle, 2009). What persists are powerful ways to look at things. Instruments, maps, concepts, algorithms, methods, classification systems and other tools and infrastructures for discovery and 'sorting things out' often outlive the original purposes for which they were invented (Bowker & Star, 1999; Clarke & Fujimura, 1992; Lampland & Star, 2009). In short, progress in science is made by creating *new epistemic objects* and *new epistemic tools* – from smaller technical objects to entire infrastructures – simultaneously. They are epistemically open spaces and knowledge creation systems.

9.5.2   Education

In contrast, learning – particularly as it is expressed in the discourses of technical rationality and representational views of professional knowledge – is more about mastering the use of existing technical and symbolic systems and tools that already exist in various domains of inquiry, and applying them to known objects, rather than creating new ones. This view of knowledge is nicely mirrored in some of the 'discovery-based' pedagogical approaches in higher education, such as problem-based learning, case-based learning and discussion (Biggs & Tang, 2007; Goodyear & Ellis, 2007; and see Chap. 2). A number of studies show that when students discuss their experience of such pedagogical approaches, they usually talk about how, through hands-on experience and collaboration, they came to understand certain pieces of knowledge (e.g. concept, formula, theory) or learn to apply certain techniques, but they rarely mention that they created, or learnt to create, new knowledge. And students rarely if ever mention that they invented new methods or tools for creating knowledge (Goodyear & Ellis, 2007; Limbu & Markauskaite, 2015).

Many approaches to learning and instruction, even those strongly influenced by constructivism, show at least some of this inclination to limit students' learning to mastering what is already known – be it content, material tools or methods – rather than creating new knowledge. As an example, take the 'knowledge integration' approach which focusses closely on students' existing knowledge and their ability to generate new authentic (theoretical) ideas (Linn, 2006; and see Chap. 19). According to this approach, four interleaved processes jointly lead to integrated understanding: (a) eliciting current ideas, (b) adding new *normative* ideas, (c) developing criteria and evaluating ideas and (d) sorting out ideas. In this approach, knowledge representation in its 'naïve' original form plays an important starting role, but the target is to learn 'normative' ideas and link them to those other experiences and understandings. In short, the main outcome of such learning is mastering what is already known.

That is, learning via knowledge integration, problem-based learning and other similar approaches is tightly linked to reapplying knowledge creation routines and (re)discovering knowledge created by scientists, but learning them in a constructivist way. In this form, knowledge creation is still about learning about the world, by mastering – in an indirect way – tools that are already shaped to discover true knowledge of the world. That is, knowledge objects and systems in which they are situated are still *epistemically* closed. Note that these objects, in various projects given to students, could be loosely defined (as a broad motive rather than a specific goal) and students could have a lot of freedom for their agency in a given disciplinary space, yet they are not open to novel epistemic reframings. Rather, they are firmly situated in epistemic systems that are full of relatively well-defined 'technical objects'.

We are not saying that all learning should involve new knowledge creation – rather we want to say that educators, particularly in university settings, rarely think about education as an epistemically open space and students would benefit if they did so more frequently.

Of course, it is necessary to acknowledge that the view is not so absolute. For example, some literature on representational literacies emphasises very explicitly the importance of fostering flexibility and creativity in representational practices. This includes not only mastering existing representations but also learning to create one's own representational forms of knowledge (diSessa, 2004; Greeno & Hall, 1997; Roth & McGinn, 1998). This epistemically more open view of learning is nicely illustrated in diSessa's (2002, 2004) approach to learning as fostering and creating 'meta-representations'. As he argues:

> Learning about representation should go beyond learning specific, *sanctioned* representations emphasized in standard curricula (graphs, tables, etc.) to include *principles and design strategies* that apply to any scientific representation, including novel variations and even completely *new representations*. <...> In using the prefix *meta*, we do not mean to invoke the idea of metacognition. Instead, meta is used generically as it is in metascience or metaphysics (and also metacognition), purviews that *transcend the mere practice* of science or of physics, or, in this case, purviews that *transcend the mere production and use of representations*. (diSessa, 2004, pp. 293–294, emphasis added)

However, this view of learning as 'meta' knowing, as an open epistemic practice, is the exception rather than the rule in teaching and learning in higher education.

9.5.3   Organisation and Profession

In contrast, in organisational settings, much of the knowledge building and innovation work is located between the two positions sketched above (science and education). On one hand, knowledge building on its own is never an ultimate goal; rather it is linked to a particular *problem*, to a purpose of achieving efficiency or greater effectiveness. Thus, there is a motivation to reuse existing knowledge creation models, concepts and other knowledge inventions. (This is in addition to a strong motivation to maintain continuity and connection to the rest of the body of knowledge, ways of knowing and practice within a specific organisation or profession through reusing established ways to do things.) Therefore, an epistemic closeness naturally exists in the systems of practice.

On the other hand, the need for innovative solutions to unexpected problems necessitates an approach to problems as epistemic objects, in the way that scientists approach their questions in research. That is, organisations 'objectualise' issues into open-ended shared epistemic objects and work with them in somewhat similar ways to scientists (Checkland & Scholes, 1999; Engeström, Nummijoki, & Sannino, 2012). Similarly, there is an intrinsic motive to 'objectify' successful knowing practices into shared epistemic tools and systems within an organisation or a larger professional community, thereby allowing 'mass production', 'mass customisation', 'mass configuration' (Victor & Boynton, 1998) and other kinds of 'massification' – including situated knowledge work (see Chap. 3).

In short, in organisational/professional settings, both epistemic objects and epistemic systems are partly open and partly closed. While there have been various attempts to identify distinct profiles of knowledge workers and classify them into those who are engaged in routine knowledge work versus those who are reliant on fluid expert judgement, studies demonstrate that such classifications rarely survive empirical testing – knowledge workers engage in individual and collaborative work, both routine and novel (cf. Davenport, 2005; Margaryan, Milligan, & Littlejohn, 2011). Much of what we call 'knowledgeable practice' is broadly entangled in a productive tension between continuity (copying, reproduction) and innovation (variation in practices) (Suchman, 2005). Such knowledge practices as (re)creating a lesson plan, or producing a medication review recommendation, may not be seen as innovations in the classic innovation sense, but they are not routine in the standard (habitual) practice sense either. They (re)create knowledge again and again and do this each time in new ways. Knowledge objects are (re)produced and copied differently to different situations, as epistemic systems are tweaked to specific questions, problems and situations. Epistemic objects and epistemic systems are deeply grounded in the material and social particularities of workplace environments.

9.5.4 Commonalities Across Science, Education and Profession

Of course, science, education and workplace are not each homogenous – in terms of how knowledge and their production systems are perceived and constructed, or how problems and epistemic objects are formulated. For example, sociologists of scientific knowledge have offered a distinction between two modes of knowledge production: so-called Mode 1, investigator-initiated and discipline-based knowledge, and Mode 2, interdisciplinary, problem focussed and context driven (Gibbons et al., 1994; Nowotny, Scott, & Gibbons, 2001) (see also Bresnen & Burrell, 2013). While Mode 1 production primarily focusses on rather systematic and disciplined advancement of epistemic objects and epistemic systems, Mode 2 production is more open to ad hoc formations of epistemic things and interdisciplinary assemblages of epistemic systems for their production – in order to solve specific problems. Further, much practical innovation comes from development and research, rather than research and development, where practices and things are developed and epistemic objects are formulated simultaneously (Bentley & Gillinson, 2007).

Similarly, professional knowledge practices range from what could be regarded as more genuine knowledge work on creating knowledge objects first, rather than direct solutions to specific practical questions. At one end, some knowledge practices include more direct work with knowledge objects – this is what business analysts and other knowledge workers do when they work with information (Knorr Cetina, 2010). At the other end, they involve more routine knowledge work such as applying professional knowledge when looking at new problems and formulating specific solutions (Goodwin, 1994). A range of design practices sit in between: including more traditional design-focussed knowledge work (Schön, 1985), product or service innovation (Nonaka, 2004; Victor & Boynton, 1998) and organisational change (Argyris & Schön, 1996; Checkland & Poulter, 2006; Engeström, 2001).

Similarly, learning as knowledge work ranges from learning to solve common cases and problems (Biggs & Tang, 2007) to learning knowledge structures and inquiry frameworks of the domain (Collins & Ferguson, 1993; Linn, 2006; Morrison & Collins, 1996; Schwab, 1962) to discovering and building genuinely new knowledge (Bereiter, 2002; Paavola & Hakkarainen, 2005).

In short, the differences in views of knowledge around educational sites, working organisations and research institutions are not so much in terms of whether they focus on specific problems (a.k.a. practice) or knowledge problems (a.k.a. theory), but in terms of *how open their epistemic objects and systems* are (Fig. 9.4).

However, openness of the epistemic system should not be confused with the absence or invisibility of this system. Rather, creating an (explicit) epistemic system is the core feature of deliberative innovation and collaborative knowledge work.

Glick (1995) provides an insightful comparison of ordinary practices and broader institutional agendas in school and work locations. He notes that for most teachers and professors, school is also a workplace and the workplace is really a school. However, schools and universities are often seen as:

> ... *transitional institutions from which people eventually are expected to leave.* (Glick, 1995, p. 364, original emphasis)

Glick contrasts schools as educational institutions with workplaces as places for learning and development (Table 9.4, columns 1 and 2):

> The academic form privileges knowledge of a certain type, and elevates that form of knowledge to universal and moral status as the kind of knowledge that people should have if they are said to have knowledge at all. In Wittgensteinian terms, some language games count more heavily than others as the only game in town. (op.cit., p. 361)

The contrast between learning in educational sites and workplaces, however, obscures some essential qualities of constructive knowledge work. Practices that

		Epistemic openness of epistemic systems and objects		
		Low ⟵——————— Epistemic system ———————⟶ High		
		Low ⟵——————— Epistemic object ———————⟶ High		
		Education	Organisations and professions	Research
Focus on knowledge object vs. problem	Problem	Case-based and problem-based learning	Routine knowledge work Design work	Development and research
		Learning knowledge structures and inquiry structures	Product and service innovation Organisational change and expansive learning	Research and development (Mode 2)
	Knowledge	(Re)discovering and building knowledge	Analytical knowledge and information work	Foundational research (Mode 1)

Fig. 9.4 Epistemic openness of epistemic systems and objects

Table 9.4 Comparison of the notion of development in school, work and research settings

Schools (learning institutions)	Work	Research
A place in which people grow up but then graduate and leave	A place where people stay	A place in which people grow up and stay
Guided by the notion of multiformed future: preparation for unknown destination	Guided by the notion of rationalised future: progress is defined by organisational routines	Guided by the notion of epistemically bounded future: progress is defined by creative variation within an epistemic space
Knowledge to be carried with the person: transportable, generative skills	Knowledge as part of the environment: efficient artefacts, effective skills, technology solutions	Knowledge is a part of and to be carried with 'episteme': transportable generative knowledge artefacts embedded in 'epistemic ensembles'
Organisation for flexibility: generalised skills, progressive achievement, transferable knowledge	Organisation for efficiency: specialised skills, maximally adapted, some transfer from person to machine	Organisation for effective flexibility: specialised flexible skills, maximised progress, constitutive reconfiguration of personal knowledge and devices
Architectural notion of progress: younger to older, agenda for progress, progress in person	Historical notion of progress: novice to expert, agenda for success, progress is not necessarily individual	Historical progress based on architecture: agenda for successful progress
Efficacy seen in individuals: measures of success are based on individual behaviour	Efficacy seen in organisations: measures of success are based on profit/loss, organisational worth and other tangible outcomes	Efficacy seen in knowledge products: measures of success are based on contributions to knowledge, esteem, credentials
Focus on knowledge acquisition: competences, integrity	Focus on knowledge integration: adaptedness, coordination	Focus on knowledge production: creativity, contribution

Columns 1 and 2 are adapted from Glick (1995, p. 366)

generate knowledge objects, including those that are in the research world, do not silently privilege one kind of knowledge, so much as they privilege an epistemic system that allows people to (co)construct knowledge. In fact, as Column 3 of Table 9.4 shows, these knowledge practices fuse individual learning, collective work and public knowledge.

References

Argyris, C., & Schön, D. A. (1996). *Organizational learning II: Theory, method and practice.* Reading, MA: Addison-Wesley.

Aristotle (1934) Nicomachean ethics (H. Rackham, Trans.) (2nd ed.). Cambridge, MA: Harvard University Press.

Bentley, T., & Gillinson, S. (2007). *A D&R system for education.* UK: Innovation unit.

Bereiter, C. (2002). *Education and mind in the knowledge age.* Mahwah, NJ: Lawrence Erlbaum Associates.

Biggs, J., & Tang, C. (2007). *Teaching for quality learning at university: What the student does* (3rd ed.). Buckingham, UK: Open University Press.

Bowker, G. C., & Star, S. L. (1999). *Sorting things out: Classification and its consequences.* Cambridge, MA: MIT Press.

Bresnen, M., & Burrell, G. (2013). Journals à la mode? Twenty years of living alongside Mode 2 and the new production of knowledge. *Organization, 20*(1), 25–37. doi:10.1177/1350508412460992.

Checkland, P., & Poulter, J. (2006). *Learning for action: A short definitive account of soft systems methodology and its use for practitioners, teachers, and students.* Hoboken, NJ: John Wiley & Sons.

Checkland, P., & Scholes, J. (1999). *Soft systems methodology in action* (New ed.). New York, NY: Wiley.

Clark, B. (1998). *Creating entrepreneurial universities.* Amsterdam, The Netherlands: Elsevier Science.

Clark, A. (2011). *Supersizing the mind: Embodiment, action and cognitive extension.* Oxford, UK: Oxford University Press.

Clarke, A. E., & Fujimura, J. H. (Eds.). (1992). *The right tools for the job: At work in twentieth-century life sciences.* Princeton, NJ: Princeton University Press.

Collins, A., & Ferguson, W. (1993). Epistemic forms and epistemic games: Structures and strategies to guide inquiry. *Educational Psychologist, 28*(1), 25–42.

Cook, S. D. N., & Brown, J. S. (1999). Bridging epistemologies: The generative dance between organizational knowledge and organizational knowing. *Organization Science, 10*(4), 381–400.

Davenport, T. H. (2005). *Thinking for a living: How to get better performance and results from knowledge workers.* Boston, MA: Harvard Business School Press.

Dewey, J. (1929/2008). *Experience and nature.* Republished in *John Dewey: The later works, 1925–1953.* Carbondale, IL: Southern Illinois University Press.

diSessa, A. A. (2002). Why "conceptual ecology" is a good idea. In M. Limon & L. Mason (Eds.), *Reconsidering conceptual change: Issues in theory and practice* (pp. 28–60). Dordrecht, The Netherlands: Kluwer.

diSessa, A. A. (2004). Metarepresentation: Native competence and targets for instruction. *Cognition and Instruction, 22*(3), 293–331.

Donald, M. (1991). *Origins of the modern mind: Three stages in the evolution of culture and cognition.* Cambridge, MA: Harvard University Press.

Dunbar, R. I. M., Gamble, C., & Gowlett, J. E. (2010). *Social brain, distributed mind.* Oxford, UK: Oxford University Press.

Engeström, Y. (1990). When is a tool? Multiple meanings of artifacts in human activity. In Y. Engeström (Ed.), *Learning, working and imagining: Twelve studies in activity theory* (pp. 171–195). Helsinki, Finland: Orienta-Konsultit.

Engeström, Y. (1999). Activity theory and individual and social transformation. In Y. Engeström, R. Miettenen, & R.-L. Punamäki (Eds.), *Perspectives on activity theory* (pp. 19–38). Cambridge, UK: Cambridge University Press.

Engeström, Y. (2001). Expansive learning at work: Toward an activity theoretical reconceptualization. *Journal of Education and Work, 14*(1), 133–156. doi:10.1080/13639080020028747.

Engeström, Y. (2006). From well-bounded ethnographies to intervening in mycorrhizae activities. *Organization Studies, 27*(12), 1783–1793. doi:10.1177/0170840606071898.

Engeström, Y. (2008). *From teams to knots: Activity-theoretical studies of collaboration and learning at work.* Cambridge, MA: Cambridge University Press.

Engeström, Y., Nummijoki, J., & Sannino, A. (2012). Embodied germ cell at work: Building an expansive concept of physical mobility in home care. *Mind, Culture, and Activity, 19*(3), 287–309. doi:10.1080/10749039.2012.688177.

Gibbons, M., Limoges, C., Nowotny, H., Schwartzman, S., Scott, P., & Trow, M. (1994). *The new production of knowledge: The dynamics of science and research in contemporary societies.* London, UK: Sage.

Glick, J. (1995). Intellectual and manual labor: Implications for developmental theory. In L. Martin, K. Nelson, & E. Tobach (Eds.), *Sociocultural psychology: Theory and practice of doing and knowing* (pp. 357–382). Cambridge, UK: Cambridge University Press.

Goodwin, C. (1994). Professional vision. *American Anthropologist, 96*(3), 606–633.

Goodwin, C. (2005). Seeing in depth. In S. J. Derry, C. D. Schunn, & M. A. Gernsbacher (Eds.), *Interdisciplinary collaboration: An emerging cognitive science* (pp. 85–121). Mahwah, NJ: Lawrence Erlbaum Associates.

Goodyear, P., & Ellis, R. A. (2007). The development of epistemic fluency: Learning to think for a living. In A. Brew & J. Sachs (Eds.), *The transformed university: The scholarship of teaching and learning in practice* (pp. 75–86). Sydney, Australia: Sydney University Press.

Goodyear, P., & Steeples, C. (1998). Creating shareable representations of practice. *Association for Learning Technology Journal, 6*(3), 16–23.

Greeno, J. G. (2006). Learning in activity. In R. K. Sawyer (Ed.), *The Cambridge handbook of the learning sciences* (pp. 79–96). Cambridge, UK: Cambridge University Press.

Greeno, J. G., & Hall, R. P. (1997). Practicing representation: Learning with and about representational forms. *Phi Delta Kappan, 78*, 361–367.

Henning, P. H. (2004). Everyday cognition and situated action. In D. H. Jonassen (Ed.), *Handbook of research for educational communications and technology* (2nd ed., pp. 143–168). Mahwah, NJ: Lawrence Erlbaum Associates.

Hey, T., Tansley, S., & Tolle, K. (Eds.). (2009). *The fourth paradigm: Data-intensive scientific discovery*. Remond, WA: Microsoft Research.

Hutchins, E. (2005). Material anchors for conceptual blends. *Journal of Pragmatics, 37*(10), 1555–1577.

Ingold, T. (2011). *Redrawing anthropology: Materials, movements, lines*. Farnham, UK: Ashgate.

Kirsh, D. (2009). Problem solving and situated cognition. In P. Robbins & M. Aydede (Eds.), *The Cambridge handbook of situated cognition* (pp. 264–306). Cambridge, UK: Cambridge University Press.

Knorr Cetina, K. (1999). *Epistemic cultures: How the sciences make knowledge*. Cambridge, MA: Harvard University Press.

Knorr Cetina, K. (2001). Objectual practice. In T. R. Schatzki, K. Knorr Cetina, & E. V. Savigny (Eds.), *The practice turn in contemporary theory* (pp. 175–188). London, UK: Routledge.

Knorr Cetina, K. (2007). Culture in global knowledge societies: Knowledge cultures and epistemic cultures. *Interdisciplinary Science Reviews, 32*, 361–375.

Knorr Cetina, K. (2010). The epistemics of information: A consumption model. *Journal of Consumer Culture, 10*(2), 171–201. doi:10.1177/1469540510366641.

Lampland, M., & Star, S. L. (Eds.). (2009). *Standards and their stories: How quantifying, classifying, and formalizing practices shape everyday life*. London, UK: Cornell University Press.

Limbu, L., & Markauskaite, L. (2015). How do learners experience joint writing: university students' conceptions of online collaborative writing tasks and environments. *Computers & Education, 82*, 393–408. http://dx.doi.org/10.1016/j.compedu.2014.11.024

Linn, M. C. (2006). The knowledge integration perspective on learning and instruction. In K. Sawyer (Ed.), *The Cambridge handbook of the learning sciences* (pp. 243–264). Cambridge, UK: Cambridge University Press.

Margaryan, A., Milligan, C., & Littlejohn, A. (2011). Validation of Davenport's classification structure of knowledge-intensive processes. *Journal of Knowledge Management, 15*(4), 568–581.

McDonald, G., Le, H., Higgins, J., & Podmore, V. (2005). Artifacts, tools, and classrooms. *Mind, Culture, and Activity, 12*(2), 113–127.

Miettinen, R., & Virkkunen, J. (2005). Epistemic objects, artefacts and organizational change. *Organization, 12*(3), 437–456.

Morrison, D., & Collins, A. (1996). Epistemic fluency and constructivist learning environments. In B. Wilson (Ed.), *Constructivist learning environments: Case studies in instructional design* (pp. 107–119). Englewood Cliffs, NJ: Educational Technology Publications.

Nersessian, N. J. (2005). Interpreting scientific and engineering practices: Integrating the cognitive, social, and cultural dimensions. In M. E. Gorman, R. D. Tweney, D. C. Gooding, & A. P. Kincannon (Eds.), *Scientific and technological thinking* (pp. 17–56). Mahwah, NJ: Lawrence Erlbaum Associates.

Nersessian, N. J. (2006). The cognitive-cultural systems of the research laboratory. *Organization Studies, 27*(1), 125–145.

Nicolini, D. (2013). *Practice theory, work and organization: An introduction*. Oxford, UK: Oxford University Press.

Nonaka, I. (2004). The knowledge creating company. In H. Takeuchi & I. Nonaka (Eds.), *Hitotsubashi on knowledge creation* (pp. 29–46). Singapore, Singapore: John Wiley & Sons.

Nowotny, H., Scott, P., & Gibbons, M. (2001). *Rethinking science: Knowledge in an age of uncertainty*. Cambridge, UK: Polity.

Ohlsson, S. (1995). Learning to do and learning to understand: A lesson and a challenge for cognitive modelling. In P. Reimann & H. Spada (Eds.), *Learning in humans and machines: Towards an interdisciplinary learning science* (pp. 37–62). London, UK: Pergamon Press.

Paavola, S., & Hakkarainen, K. (2005). The knowledge creation metaphor – an emergent epistemological approach to learning. *Science & Education, 14*(6), 535–557.

Pea, R. D. (1993). Practices of distributed intelligence and designs for education. In G. Salomon (Ed.), *Distributed cognitions: Psychological and educational considerations* (pp. 47–87). Cambridge, MA: Cambridge University Press.

Pickering, A. (1995). *The mangle of practice: Time, agency, and science*. Chicago, IL: University of Chicago Press.

Rheinberger, H. (1997). *Toward a history of epistemic things: Synthesizing proteins in the test tube*. Stanford, CA: Stanford University Press.

Roth, W.-M., & McGinn, M. K. (1998). Inscriptions: Toward a theory of representing as social practice. *Review of Educational Research, 68*(1), 35–59.

Säljö, R. (1995). Mental and physical artifacts in cognitive practices. In P. Reimann & H. Spada (Eds.), *Learning in humans and machines: Towards an interdisciplinary learning science* (pp. 83–95). London, UK: Pergamon Press.

Salomon, G. (1993). *Distributed cognitions: Psychological and educational considerations*. Cambridge, NY: Cambridge University Press.

Schatzki, T. R. (2001). Introduction: Practice theory. In T. R. Schatzki, K. Knorr Cetina, & E. V. Savigny (Eds.), *The practice turn in contemporary theory* (pp. 1–14). London, UK: Routledge.

Schön, D. A. (1985). *The design studio: An exploration of its traditions and potentials*. London, UK: RIBA Publications for RIBA Building Industry Trust.

Schwab, J. J. (1962). The concept of the structure of a discipline. *The Educational Record, 43*, 197–205.

Scribner, S., & Cole, M. (1981). *The psychology of literacy*. Cambridge, MA: Harvard University Press.

Suchman, L. (2005). Affiliative objects. *Organization, 12*(3), 379–399.

Victor, B., & Boynton, A. C. (1998). *Invented here: Maximizing your organization's internal growth and profitability*. Boston, MA: Harvard Business School Press.

Vygotsky, L. S. (1930). The instrumental method in psychology. *Text of a talk given in 1930 at the Krupskaya Academy of Communist Education*. Retrieved from http://www.marxists.org/archive/vygotsky/works/1930/instrumental.htm

Vygotsky, L. S. (1978). *Mind in society: The development of higher psychological processes*. Cambridge, MA: Harvard University Press.

Vygotsky, L. S. (1986). *Thought and language*. Cambridge, MA: MIT Press.

Wartofsky, M. W. (1979). *Models: Representation and the scientific understanding*. Dordrecht, The Netherlands: D. Reidel.

Wartofsky, M. W. (1987). Epistemology historicized. In A. Shimony & D. Nails (Eds.), *Naturalistic epistemology: A symposium of two decades* (pp. 357–374). Dordrecht, The Netherlands: D. Reidel.

Chapter 10
Inscribing Professional Knowledge and Knowing

As Merlin Donald (2001) argues, almost any advance in human intellectual enterprise – such as the development of navigational techniques that allowed great ocean voyages to be made, and accounting techniques that made international banking possible – can be traced back to certain, sometimes very small, even trivial, symbolic innovations which, after many refinements, now allow people to think and work in ways that were previously unthinkable. However, the invention of symbolic technology is not enough to achieve change in human practices. In order to explore the full potential of symbolic inventions, both individually and collectively, human minds have to learn 'countless invisible habits' to use symbols effectively (p. 307).

Symbolic competence is a well-recognised part of 'workplace literacy', and practitioners, in every professional field, are expected to master a certain set of inscriptional skills needed to carry out their activities and engage with collective work effectively (Belfiore, Defoe, Folinsbee, Hunter, & Jackson, 2004). Furthermore, as knowledge workers, professional practitioners are expected to be adept at managing their knowledge by creating a range of inscriptions that allow retrieval and application of this knowledge quickly and effectively when needed (Eraut, 2009; Schwartz, Varma, & Martin, 2008). However, as Eraut (2009) notes, how this is done in practice can be uncertain.[1] This is not to say that professionals do not create written records or students do not engage in symbolic learning tasks. (One could even claim the opposite – students spend too much of their learning time

---

[1] As Eraut (2009) says, 'All vocational and professional practitioners are knowledge workers, who are expected to recognise or find out what knowledge is most relevant for their current learning goals, track down that relevant knowledge and make appropriate notes for speedy retrieval at a later date. Information from several sources may be required and, if concept maps of the topic and/or notes on its evidence base are constructed as these investigations proceed, they will greatly enhance the usefulness of their inquiry. Managing one's knowledge adds value to the time spent acquiring and refining it, but this approach is rarely found in practice. Hence it is important to develop a repertoire of these approaches to knowledge representation' (p. 6).

© Springer Science+Business Media Dordrecht 2017
L. Markauskaite, P. Goodyear, *Epistemic Fluency and Professional Education*,
Professional and Practice-based Learning 14, DOI 10.1007/978-94-007-4369-4_10

producing inscriptions, such as essays, reports and other literary artefacts.) What we would argue is that the symbolic nature of professional work in workplace settings and learning in higher education is largely taken for granted and the nature of inscriptional work is therefore quite a mysterious part of professional teaching and learning. How *do* students learn the inscriptional competences needed for their daily professional work and for workplace innovation?

This chapter and the next focus on the role of inscriptional competences in professional practice and look more deeply into the 'representational' qualities of epistemic artefacts used and produced in professional learning in higher education. We ask the following questions:

- What kinds of knowledge, experiences and 'slices' of the real world get inscribed in the artefacts created on the boundaries between higher education and the workplace?
- What kinds of signs are used to encode knowledge?
- What kinds of decoding do these inscriptions afford and restrict?
- What enables epistemic artefacts produced by students to function as professional inscriptions and also as learning artefacts?

We address these questions from two perspectives: functional and semiotic. In this chapter, we take the functional perspective and discuss *what* inscriptions *do* and *how* they obtain their particular roles in practice. In Chap. 11, we take the semiotic perspective and explore *what* inscriptions *mean* and *how* they mean what they mean. That is, by combining two perspectives, we explore how inscriptions, through their pragmatic and semiotic features, become part of a larger epistemic conceptual fabric that provides the foundations for actionable knowledge and knowledgeable action.

We use the word 'inscriptions' to refer to representations of phenomena recorded in some artificial memory medium, as with notches on a tally stick, print on paper or text on a computer screen (Roth & McGinn, 1998).[2] Our perspective on inscriptions in intellectual activity brings together cognitive, social and material views.[3] Inscriptional work (inscribing) is taken as an important *form of*

---

[2] More specifically, by 'inscriptions', we refer to a broad class of human memory representations that draw on human capacities to utilise symbolic technological devices in an external memory storage system. Inscriptions, therefore, are different from other human memory representations (such as mimesis and speech) which draw only upon human biological capacities to use the body and brain as (internal) memory storage systems. In this sense, the former representational system is technological, while the latter representational systems are biological (see Donald, 1991, 2001; and Chap. 5).

[3] *Traditional cognitive (information processing) views* of inscriptions primarily associate inscriptional capabilities with the ability to establish connections between individual mental processes and external symbolic expressions. The *social view* of inscriptions and inscriptional capabilities focusses on the capabilities needed to participate in socially shaped inscriptional practices (Roth & McGinn, 1998). The *enactive material view* moves away from the arbitrary meanings of inscriptions and looks for the source of meanings and, therefore, capabilities in a dense structural coupling between the human mind and its engagement with the physical world (Malafouris, 2013).

thinking which draws on the human capability to establish dynamic connections between the capacities of the internal memory system, affordances of the external inscriptions and engagement with the physical world more generally.

In this chapter, our aim is to make the representational qualities of professional inscriptions, and inscriptional practices in professional work and learning, more visible. We are interested in how professional inscriptions function in professional work and learning and how students learn the capacities for inscribing that are vital for knowledgeable work and innovation. We look into the properties of inscriptions, the nature of inscriptional work and the relationships between inscriptions created and professional action. More specifically, we discuss what gets inscribed and when, what the purposes of these inscriptions are and how the symbolic artefacts that have been created relate to 'real-time' knowledgeable action.

We have two complementary objectives. First, we articulate some traditional functional qualities of inscriptions and inscriptional practices. For this we draw on the literature about inscriptions in scientific knowledge work and in professional practice. Second, we reveal some often obscured, yet critical, features of inscriptions and inscriptional work within professional learning and innovation that have important implications for how inscriptional work is seen and taught in higher education. For this, we draw on some examples from our empirical studies and extend them with our reinterpretations and reframing of inscriptional work from the enactive knowledge perspective.

We show that professional innovation and knowledgeable action are deeply intertwined with inscriptional work. We make four main arguments:

1. Inscriptional practices in professional work are multiple and heterogeneous. Thus, becoming 'inscriptionally literate' requires mastering skills to create, switch between and join together a broad range of inscriptions and ways of inscribing.
2. Inscriptional tasks in learning settings are different (on a deep epistemic level) from the inscriptional tasks in workplace settings (i.e. they are idealised and epistemified).
3. Canonically, the role of inscriptions in knowledge work and innovation has been associated with the view that inscriptions are tools for creating and representing *order in the world*. In contrast, we argue that one additional – and indeed the main – inscriptional skill for professional knowledgeable action and innovation is learning to *inscribe work*.
4. In the past, inscriptions that support work have been seen either from 'the person's perspective' (i.e. practitioners', insiders', first-person singular perspectives) or from 'the system's perspective' (i.e. neutral observers', outsiders', third-person plural perspectives) (Norman, 1991). We extend these views with an additional 'enactive' perspective. We *reframe* how inscriptional capabilities are usually seen and taught in higher education. We argue that for creating inscriptions of actionable knowledge and for knowledgeable work, students should learn to see their inscriptional work in these 'enactive' terms.

In Sect. 10.1, we offer a broader review of why inscriptions and inscriptional skills matter in professional work. In the next Sect. 10.2, we review common (functional) properties of inscriptions that make knowledge work possible. In Sect. 10.3, we turn from inscriptions themselves to the knowledge and skills involved in inscriptional work. In Sect. 10.4, we look more closely at 'inscribing for professional learning'. We step away from the theoretical argument and describe a case that illustrates some common features of inscriptions and inscriptional work in professional learning. In Sect. 10.5, we return to the theoretical argument and discuss how knowledge related to professional work itself gets inscribed (i.e. in contrast to the inscription of knowledge about the phenomena in the world on which the work is operating). In Sect. 10.6, we share some empirical results from our studies that illustrate how students learn to inscribe work and learn through inscribing work in higher education. In Sect. 10.7, we link the insights from the foregoing sections and start to draw some pedagogical implications. In Sect. 10.8, we introduce the enactive perspective for reframing inscriptional pedagogies in higher education.

10.1 Inscriptions in Professional Work and Learning

The theme *inscription*, as the central element of knowledge practices, emerged in science and technology studies (STS). Latour and Woolgar (1979) in their book *Laboratory Life* illustrated the case that much of the knowledge work in scientific laboratory settings is carried out by producing, moving around and sharing various documents such as research papers, preprints, drafts, research protocols, presentations and the outputs of automatic inscriptional devices that transform 'pieces of matter into written documents' (p. 51). Many subsequent studies of scientific work have also shown that one cannot understand scientific knowledge work without understanding how individual scientists, scientific laboratories and larger disciplinary groups shuffle around and manage inscriptions (Knorr Cetina, 1999; Rheinberger, 1997).

Inscriptions and inscriptional work play a significant role in a number of professional domains (Eraut, 2009; Goodwin, 1994; Goodyear & Steeples, 1998; Hall, Stevens, & Torralba, 2002; Sarkkinen & Karsten, 2005). For example, various studies of skilled vision in professions such as Medicine, Biology and Law are arranged around shared representations, and effective participation in such work and discourse depends on the ability to read and create shared inscriptions (Goodwin, 1994; Grasseni, 2010).

However, the extent and nature of inscriptional practices varies across different professional fields and settings. For example, Carberry (2003) shows how the work of clinical chemists, who do biochemical tests in medical laboratories, can be understood as the work of 'symbolic analysts'. Most of their work is done by manipulating and interpreting the symbolic outputs of measurement devices and other professional inscriptions. Work of such a thoroughly symbolic kind is also common in other modern-day, hi-tech, hi-skilled professions, such as in finance and accountancy and in information technology (Knorr Cetina, 2007; Nerland, 2008). In contrast, inscriptional work has a more uneven place in other professions. For example, nurses inscribe only small fragments of their work, though daily handover sheets and other similar symbolic records can play an important role in their practices (Billett, 2014; Eraut, 2009). Some professionals engage with a broad range of representational practices. For example, architects, building engineers and information system designers usually work in multi-professional teams (Adler, 2005; Hall et al., 2002; Sarkkinen & Karsten, 2005). Much of their work is done by juxtaposing multiple kinds of symbolic representations and switching between inscriptions and real-world things. Further, they use inscriptions not only for 'core' knowledge work but also for coordinating their work, planning and managing their cooperation.

Learning to engage with inscriptional work involves several dimensions, including the cognitive, social and material. From the cognitive perspective, external representations mediate perception; and problem-solving requires skill to find effective ways of representing encountered problems in a specific situation.

From the social perspective, the relationship between an inscription and a phenomenon is not fully determined by nature, but established through experience and talk (Roth & McGinn, 1998). Further, complex problems often can be represented simultaneously in a variety of forms – such as textual, figurative and mathematical – and from multiple perspectives, such as engineering, aesthetic and psychological. Creative thinking, inquiry and other higher-order epistemic activities require flexibility in representing problems in multiple ways and seeing connections among diverse ways of inscribing (Verschaffel, de Corte, de Jong, & Elen, 2010). Learning to participate in the inscriptional practices of heterogeneous communities involves mastering a social capability to engage with discourses that join together these multiple perspectives and mobilise diverse ways of interpreting and creating inscriptions.

From the material perspective, we should emphasise that inscriptions are not disconnected from the physical world. Rather they are tightly linked with perception and human action in the world. For example, describing discoveries in molecular biology, Jacob (1988) observes:

> ... everything depended on the representation we formed of an invisible process and on the manner of its translation into visible effects. (Jacob, 1988, cited in Rheinberger, 1997, p. 102)

However, visibility and representations of professional knowledge are often in an uneasy tension with professional action, particularly in skilful embodied work. On the one hand, as Nonaka (2004) argues, knowledge creation – as the central activity of the knowledge-creating company – depends on making one's knowledge visible and available to others. On the other hand, paradoxically, one of the most evident features of well-done professional work is that, as Suchman (1995) notes, *how* it is done remains invisible to others:

> In the case of many forms of service work, we recognize that the better the work is done, the less visible it is to those who benefit from it. (Suchman, 1995, p. 58)

For example, the smoother the clinical handover, the less visible clinicians' work (and the knowledge involved in this complex process) is, to patients and others. What is written in a medical handover record, how it is written and what is discussed during ward rounds rarely become a focus of attention unless things go wrong. In short, production of knowledge inscriptions is an important aspect of safe, efficient and innovative professional work. Yet, inscribing is not always a natural part of work routines, and when it is, it often stays unnoticed in skilful professional work and is taken for granted (or overlooked) in professional learning. This is particularly the case in social professions where inscribing is fused with ongoing work and inscriptions, despite their critical role in this work, are not the main *outcome* of this work.

We now discuss some important properties of inscriptions that underpin how they function in professional work.

10.2   Functional Properties of Knowledge Inscriptions

Science and technology studies (STS) have a long tradition of looking at knowledge practices not only as a distinct kind of mental work but also as material and mundane activity: as 'writing and imaging craftsmanship' (Latour, 1990, p. 3), in which people work using and producing various documents, texts, prints, figures, diagrams, signs and other representations of what has been seen in, and known about, the world. Latour (1990) identified a number of advantages of visual inscriptions in knowledge production, such as their ability to be 'immutable' and preserve things as they are and to be 'mobile' and have a property of being easily multiplied, disseminated and transported. As he observed, cultures, planets and microbes cannot easily be moved, but pictures, maps and other inscriptions of these things can.

However, Latour also argued that it is not only materiality that makes inscriptions in scientific practice important but also other deeper qualities of inscriptions (Table 10.1). He listed a range of materially bounded yet immaterial properties, such as the possibility of reading inscriptions, of combining inscriptions with one another, of translating from one to another and of presenting things in such a way that they can be 'dominated by hand and eye', independent of the actual shape and size of the things represented – whether a building, a city, the entire world, a tiny chromosome or international trade.

Latour (1990) primarily looked at how scientific visualisations and inscriptions allow the creation of shared scientific knowledge. Knorr Cetina (1999, 2001) and others (Ewenstein & Whyte, 2009; Miettinen, 2005; Nersessian, 2008), who are interested in knowledge work in more dynamic environments, such as laboratories, financial markets and architectural teams, 'corrected' Latour, arguing that immutability is not the only feature of material and digital instantiations that makes knowledge work possible. Their incompleteness, openness and lack of stability are also important. For example, Ewenstein and Whyte (2009) point out that visual

Table 10.1 Some properties of inscriptions in scientific work

Functional properties of inscriptions in scientific work
1. Inscriptions are made 'flat' by removing ambiguities from phenomena; thus, 'nothing is hidden', 'no shadows', 'no *double entendre*'
2. Inscriptions are scalable and this scale can be changed without changing internal proportions. They always can be of a size that can be 'dominated hand and eye', no matter whether the original size is small or large
3. Inscriptions can be recombined, as they have optical or metaphorical consistency which enables the human mind to reshuffle connections in many different ways
4. Inscriptions can also be superimposed on one another combining representations of knowledge from different domains, scales and origins (e.g. combining geological and economic information in one map)
5. Inscriptions allow one to represent three-dimensional objects on a two-dimensional surface (keeping proportions consistent with the three-dimensional space) and investigate them using geometry
6. Inscriptions can also be arranged in cascades and show a phenomenon at different levels of detail or represent its different aspects
7. Visual inscriptions can be made a part of a written text, which allows transfer of both the original inscription and any comment made upon it
8. Inscriptions can be reproduced and distributed at little cost – making copies independent from the time and place where they were originally produced
9. Inscriptions are *mobile* and can be moved from one location to another
10. Inscriptions are also *immutable*, as everything is done to preserve things in inscriptions as they are

After Latour (1990)

representations assist knowing and learning in architectural design teams in at least six different ways. Like Latour, they claim that representations are mobile and that they can have many dimensions and layers and embody a range of knowledges. Nevertheless, these representations are also open and incomplete; they can be read by professionals with different areas of expertise, in different ways, and they emerge in joint meaning-making that is often distributed in time and space.

Inscriptions are common in deliberative knowledge work and also in many other aspects of professional practice. As Wenger (1998) notes, the process of giving form to our experience by producing objects is central to everyday practice.[4] He calls this process 'reification' and includes a range of inscriptional practices and processes, such as:

> ... making, designing, representing, naming encoding, and describing, as well as perceiving, interpreting, using, reusing, decoding and recasting ... from entries in a journal to historical records, from poems to encyclopaedias, from names to classification systems, from dolmens to space probes, from the Constitution to a signature on a credit card slip, from gourmet recipes to medical procedures, from flashy advertisements to census data, from single concepts to entire theories, from the evening news to national archives, from the lesson plans to the compilation of textbooks, from private address lists to sophisticated

---

[4] It is probably most straightforward to think of Wenger's (1998) reified objects here in the sense of 'objects' that we introduced in Chap. 8.

credit reporting databases, from tortuous political speeches to the yellow pages. In all these cases, aspects of human experience and practice are congealed into fixed forms and given the status of object. (Wenger, 1998, p. 59)

Irrespective of their diverse 'surface' shapes, such reifications of experience have shared 'deep' qualities that support knowing, such as succinctness and the power to evoke meanings, and a focussing effect that allows the making of important distinctions. These features provide possibilities for ongoing cumulative knowing and learning. Nevertheless, all inscriptions are 'double edged', and, as Wenger reminds us, there is no inherent correspondence between the symbolic representations and the objects to which they refer. Inscriptions acquire meanings, properties and functions within cultures, within human intentions and within embodied, embrained, situated actions that bring what was fixed back to life.

Further, there are different kinds of inscriptions, and the generativity of different features depends on who is using the inscriptions and what they are used for. For example, Greeno and Hall (1997) point out that inscriptions are used for both (a) constructing understanding and (b) communicating and sharing.[5] They are embedded within an individual's activities as well as within collective work. When inscriptions are used for individual knowledge work – for representing problems, for articulating important properties of the objects and for figuring out possible solutions – then they can be constructed and adapted for the purpose at hand using standard *and* nonstandard ways of representing. Indeed, nonstandard representations may turn out to be better for such individual work than the standard ones. However, when representations are used for communicating and sharing knowledge with a sizeable community, then inscriptions have to follow conventions for interpretation that are shared within this community.

However, supporting the construction of knowledge and supporting its sharing are not necessarily incompatible features of inscriptions, just as individual and collective work are not necessarily incompatible ways of carrying out inscriptional knowledge-generating work. As Roth and McGinn (1998) point out, some inscriptions act as 'boundary inscriptions' that are used simultaneously to coordinate and carry out joint distributed work. Such inscriptions serve as interfaces between different communities, allowing knowledge and other resources 'to flow' between different actors and different 'social worlds'. Well-studied examples of such 'boundary inscriptions' include the creation of shared museum collections (Star & Griesemer, 1989), flight and airport management and operations routines (Suchman & Trigg, 1991) and design work in architectural teams (Ewenstein & Whyte, 2009). Inscriptions support shared knowledge work in such teams in a variety of ways:

- They provide mutual focus for meaning-making in face-to-face work and coordinate interactions, gestures and other exchanges when things are talked about and co-created.

---

[5] These two roles of inscriptions draw upon and mirror the two similar roles of signs and language that we discussed in Chap. 9.

- They allow asynchronous work on joint ideas, in groups whose activity is distributed in time and space.
- They help to coordinate diverse activities of people, with various roles and areas of expertise, involved in joint work.

These inscriptions are not only representations of knowledge but also co-configured spaces for carrying out collaborative knowledge work (We elaborate on the nature of inscriptional work in such spaces in Chap. 11.)

Now, we turn from the functions of inscriptions to their deeper qualities, and the knowledge and skills that allow professionals to carry out inscriptional work.

10.3   Skill for Seeing, Inscribing and Knowing the World

What makes inscriptional knowledge work possible? How much of what professionals do with knowledge in their various workplaces is similar to what scientists do in labs? How much resemblance is there between ways of seeing and knowing within practice fields? To better understand the links between knowledge work, professions and inscribing it is worth looking at inscriptional practices in both sciences and professions. As Lynch and Woolgar (1990) claim, if one wants to create knowledge, then it is not enough to represent the object – mere surface resemblance has to be disregarded in favour of deep (theoretical, mathematical) reconstructions of a phenomenon's organisation. The latter opens up the object to active manipulation and exploration of its fundamental organising principles. Latour (1990), drawing on Dagognet (1969, 1973), points out:

> ... no scientific discipline exists without first inventing a visual and written language which allows it to break with its confusing past. (Latour, 1990, p. 36)

He specifically stresses the importance of shared inscriptional systems that allow representation of the structural and functional qualities of phenomena, while abandoning direct visual resemblance and physical relationships with the represented object. As Latour (1990) puts it:

> Chemistry becomes powerful only when a visual vocabulary is invented that replaces the manipulations [of materials] by calculation of formulas. (loc. cit.)

The importance of explicit and implicit shared ways for 'sorting things out' in everyday life and work and the role of common vocabularies and codification systems that 'open up' possibilities for creating shareable knowledge inscriptions are also acknowledged in many domains of professional work and professional learning (Bowker & Star, 1999; Goodwin, 1994, 1997; Lampland & Star, 2009; Star, 1989; Star & Strauss, 1999). As Goodwin (1994) observes, professional practices are organised around particular shared ways of seeing, coding and representing. This 'professional vision' includes the ability to structure problems, cognitive activity and future actions by using ways of seeing that are shaped through ongoing historical practices and creating representations that can be recognised in a professional culture. Representations and their purposes in the fields studied by Goodwin – archaeology and jury work – were different. However, he noted three common practices that were used by professionals to structure things and events and explain what had been seen: coding, production and highlighting.

Classification and *coding* is central to human cognition and to socially organised professional practice. Schemes and classifications, as professional and bureaucratic knowledge structures, allow people to structure and reorganise the world and events into 'objects of knowledge' – things that have names, can be compared, can be related, etc. – around which cognitive activity and the discourse of the profession can be organised. The *production* of material inscriptions makes such practice possible as social and cognitive activity. As Goodwin (1994) argues, the ability to create external representations, such as maps and slide rules, that articulate specific ways of seeing and displaying relevant knowledge 'is as central to human cognition as processes hidden inside the brain' (p. 628). However, the human perceptual field is complex. Learning to distinguish relevant things that should be coded, inscribed or (otherwise) used in professional activity involves mastering a set of methods and practices for making specific features of a phenomenon salient and distinguishable – i.e. *highlighting*.

In these respects, knowledge and skill for engaging with inscriptional work, in scientific and professional fields, have noticeable similarities: (a) they both draw on mastery of shared vocabularies, classifications and other tools for inscribing domain knowledge and (b) they both involve similar practices of coding, production and highlighting. However, Goodwin's insights into 'professional vision' are different from Latour's (1990) insights into scientific knowledge production in at least two ways: (a) how things get inscribed and (b) how inscriptions are handled. First, Latour observes that representations of scientific phenomena commonly preserve proportions and other equivalences; thus, 'knowledge discovery' can be carried out by moving around inscriptions without looking back at the world. As Latour puts this:

> If scientists were looking at nature, at economies, at stars, at organs, they would not *see* anything. <...> Scientists start seeing something when they stop looking at nature and look exclusively and obsessively at prints and flat inscriptions. (Latour, 1990, p. 39, original emphasis)

Latour and Woolgar (1979) acknowledge that discovered phenomena not only *depend on* material things, instruments and practices in scientific laboratories 'but are *thoroughly constituted by* the material setting of the laboratory' (p. 64, original emphasis). They nevertheless make a relatively firm separation between the work (and skill) of 'technicians', who handle equipment in laboratories, and the work (and skill) of 'doctors' whose scientific knowledge craft involves reading, writing and shuffling inscriptions.

In short, from this perspective, scientific knowledge discovery is primarily located in the symbolic realm of already inscribed phenomena rather than in the material realm of looking at the world and inscribing what is yet to be known. In contrast, as Goodwin's (1994) notion of 'professional vision' implies, knowledge work in professional settings rarely permits separation of technical and symbolic work. Professional practitioners look simultaneously at the world and at the inscriptions: they look for and see phenomena in the world, highlight and code it.[6]

Latour also emphasises that scientific discovery relies heavily on active exploration of the fundamental principles in inscriptions: 'shuffling' large numbers of documents, making things flat, putting distant things side by side or looking at thousands of records synoptically, etc. In contrast, as Goodwin's notion of professional vision implies, professional knowing primarily involves deep exploration and reading of the world, rather than just what has already been inscribed.

In short, perception and representation of objects in a symbolic form is an important part of the production of professional knowledge. However, connections with the world can only rarely be abandoned, as the action informed by this knowledge takes place in the world. In fact, once the connection between the inscribed knowledge and the world is lost, then this knowledge becomes of little use for the world and for practice. Thus, the skill needed to manipulate symbolic inscriptions, independently from the skill needed to see the inscribed phenomena in the world, is unlikely to be sufficient for creating actionable knowledge.

Before we discuss other qualities of knowledge inscriptions and inscriptional activity in professional work, we need to look more deeply into how inscriptional work manifests itself in professional learning. To do this, we will introduce a case that will also be featured in later chapters. Here, we focus on the inscriptional work involved in learning to do the work of a school counsellor.

10.4 A Case: Becoming a School Counsellor Through Inscribing Students' Behaviour

To get a sense of a range of inscriptional practices involved in professional learning and work, we want to consider the inscriptional work involved in an assignment project given to psychology students who are planning to become school counsellors. The task asks them to complete a behavioural assessment. Counsellors who work in Australian schools sometimes advise on interventions related to behaviour management of children who exhibit behavioural difficulties. This may involve conducting some psychological assessments. The task given to psychology students thus includes selecting a child who attends a regular school and is exhibiting behavioural difficulties, assessing this child and preparing a full assessment report with proposed interventions and other recommendations.

---

[6] Of course, not all features of inscriptions and inscriptional practices identified by Latour (1990) hold for all research fields, but differences between research fields are not our main focus. Here, we want to emphasise the point that inscriptions and ways of inscribing in professional work are different from the ways in which inscriptional work has been characterised in the canon of science and technology studies of scientific research.

We use the pseudonyms 'Jane' and 'Ron' in this case. Jane is a student training to be a school counsellor. Ron is an 8-year-old child. Jane receives *a referral* for assessment of Ron's behaviour. Jane reads the referral and reviews his previous school reports. Ron's mother and teacher are concerned about his slow academic progress, low self-esteem and behavioural difficulties. *School records* indicate that Ron was assessed about 18 months ago, and results then showed 'a borderline intellectual disability'.

Jane starts her assessment with observation of Ron's behaviour in a lesson. She *notes* down what is going on in the class and what Ron does, including when Ron gets distracted, talks with other students and requires teacher attention. Jane notices Ron's lack of engagement and his uncooperative behaviour. She sets up an interview with Ron's mother and teacher to clarify their concerns. During the meeting, she asks questions and makes *notes* about what they say about Ron's behavioural difficulties, Ron's social environment and his learning. On the same day, she asks Ron's mother to *complete a behavioural checklist* about Ron's behaviour at home and the teacher *to complete a report form* about Ron's behaviour in classroom. After receiving these completed forms, Jane *calculates* some scores and notices that the results of both assessments indicate some similar 'borderline clinical' and 'clinical' issues relating to Ron's attention and other behavioural difficulties.

Jane observes Ron's performance in a lesson again, but now encounters a very different behaviour. She *notes down* that Ron is quiet and absorbed in a task throughout the lesson, but she also notices differences in the tasks when compared with the first observation and notes that the class was on an excursion in the morning. She hypothesises that Ron's behavioural problems may be due to low cognitive functioning and lack of engagement.

Now Jane meets Ron and initially *administers a test* to assess his cognitive abilities. The calculated results are again borderline, so Jane decides to assess Ron's academic achievements and *administers a test* for assessing reading, mathematics, written language and oral language abilities. She encounters difficulties both in administering this instrument – Ron gets every other item incorrect – and later in calculating the scores. However, after recalculating scores several times, she sees that Ron's results are again low. She suspects an intellectual disability and decides to assess Ron's adaptive behaviour and to conduct an additional session with his mother and the teacher, to discuss her findings and develop an individual behaviour plan.

However, time and other constraints do not allow Jane to make these further assessments, and she has to complete her report drawing only on the information that she has collected. Jane observes that some results are indicative of a potential intellectual disability, but at this stage she does not have enough information to establish this and so comes to a decision that Ron's academic, social and behavioural difficulties in class are caused by low motivation, concentration difficulties and poor fine motor skills.

She *writes an academic report* that summarises the evidence she has collected, explains the tests and their results, justifies her decisions and suggests follow-up assessment strategies. Her report follows the structure detailed in the *assessment specification* and includes all the information requested, including a self-evaluation, the test sheets and other records. Most of her decisions and recommendations are backed up with references from the psychology literature. The final section of the report contains eight recommendations on how to assist Ron with the management of his difficulties. Jane also *prepares a handout* with a list of strategies for his parents, to assist in developing Ron's verbal comprehension ability (which she found problematic), and she adds this practical tool to the report. She also creates a shorter and simpler version of the *report for the school and parents*.

At the end of the process, Jane *writes a self-evaluation* where she reports on the problems she encountered administering one of the tests and reflects on other challenges and her skills, such as challenges providing reinforcement during testing, and her note-taking skills. For the coursework assessment, Jane submits *the full 'academic' case study* with all the reports, self-evaluation and the practical tools she developed, packaged together.

10.4.1   Some Insights This Case Provides into Learning and Professional Inscriptions

One of the main lines around which Jane's knowledge work evolves is *inscribing*. It is involved when Jane is observing the child with behavioural difficulties, identifying unusual behaviours, coding and drafting a report and in many other parts of her work. The flow of the main inscriptions used and produced by Jane within this task is represented in Fig. 10.1. Jane's work nicely mirrors Goodwin's (1994) account of practices of profession vision: seeing phenomena in the world, highlighting and coding.

However, Jane's work does not stop at *producing* inscriptions, but includes further work *manipulating* inscriptions: calculating test scores, getting results, making hypotheses and planning further tests. This work is not very different from the work of scientists described by Latour (1990), as Jane is indeed fully immersed in making sense of her inscribed and coded data. She reflects:

> Scoring [of one of the tests, (WIAT-II)] is very difficult – I realised that I had looked at the wrong table to convert raw scores to standard scores and hence, had to recalculate all of the data. Also, on a personal note, I'm not sure if I like the WIAT-II. I found it very difficult that some subtests did not have a ceiling level dependent on the student's responses. (From Jane's self-evaluation)

That is, Jane's activity *blends* ways of working with inscriptions that have their roots in both *professional work* and *scientific practices*. This blending goes down deeply to the level of fine-grained inscriptional actions.

Three features stand out in Jane's inscriptional work: (a) switching between various inscriptional strategies, (b) conceptual translation between different kinds of inscriptions and (c) a variety of times and places across which inscriptional activities unfold. We elaborate on each feature below.

> **Main inscriptions in school counsellor's behavioural assessment**
>
> 1. Referrals from child's mother and school teacher
> 2. Review of previous school records
> 3. Notes from the first classroom observation
> 4. Notes from parent and teacher interviews
> 5. Completed Child Behaviour Checklist (CBCL for ages 6-18) with calculated scores
> 6. Completed Teacher Report Form (TRF for ages 6-18) with calculated scores
> 7. Notes from the second classroom observation
> 8. Completed Intelligence scale for children (WISC-IV) with calculated scores
> 9. Completed Individual Achievement Test (WIAT-II) with calculated scores
> 10. A handout with strategies for development of child's Verbal Comprehension Ability for parents
> 11. Self-evaluation
> 12. Academic case study report for course assessment (university teacher)
> 13. School counsellor's assessment report for school and parents

Fig. 10.1 Main inscriptions used and produced during assessment of a child with behavioural difficulties

Note: Inscriptions 11–13 are produced using the specification of case study project and behavioural report (see Fig. 10.2)

Firstly, during this task, Jane constantly *switches between several inscriptional strategies*: reading inscriptions (e.g. reading referrals, Ron's records), generating inscriptions (e.g. making observation and interview notes, recording test results on forms), manipulating inscriptions (e.g. calculating test scores, summarising observations) and reinscribing (e.g. summarising information from the referral and school records). Further, Jane not only reads and creates inscriptions related to Ron's case but also uses a range of generic inscriptions, provided by others, such as checklists, tests and templates. These inscriptional tools[7] guide, in Goodwin's (1994) terms, coding, highlighting and production, and, once they are fused with the specific insights about Ron, they become a part of other inscriptions created by Jane.

Secondly, she constantly switches between reading and generating inscriptions and makes *conceptual translations between inscriptions with different epistemic qualities*: for communicating and collecting data (e.g. referrals, checklists) and for making decisions (e.g. calculation of test scores). The inscriptions for communication allow Jane to exchange information with other people, including the school counsellor, Ron's parents, the teacher and the child (e.g. referral, reports), as well as

---

[7] By 'inscriptional tools' we refer to inscriptions that function as tools. A detailed discussion about tools is presented in Chap. 12.

to collect information from them in a format that is ready for further processing and decision-making (e.g. structured interviews, profile sheets, forms, tests). The inscriptions for making decisions allow Jane to make sense of collected data and make judgements (e.g. using documents with calculated test scores, evidence summarised from observations and interviews identifying behavioural issues). These two kinds of inscriptions are not disconnected, but rather are 'translated' from a language and form that can be understood by 'lay' people (but which often hide professional concepts) to a language and form that make explicit the underpinning features of the observed phenomena and allow generation of professional insights. For example, a set of questions formulated in everyday language in the behaviour checklist completed by parents is translated into the construct 'somatic complaints' and into a calculated score. Jane's findings and diagnosis are then again 'translated' back from the professional jargon into recommendations on how to help Ron to develop his weaker abilities and into a set of specific strategies for parents and teachers who assist Ron on a daily basis. An important feature of such 'reinscription of inscriptions' is that it involves switching between different discourse and linguistic codes and also generates new actionable knowledge (e.g. diagnosis is translated to strategies).

Thirdly, many of Jane's inscriptions are generated in interaction with other people (e.g. the child tests, observation notes, interview notes), and various 'inscriptional lines' are *distributed across places and time* – moving between the prior 'offline' preparation, 'online' actions and subsequent 'offline' work with the collected data and writing. For example, Jane reads the referral; reviews earlier records; formulates her hypothesis; prepares instruments for assessment *before* action; records information *during* observations, interviews and testing in the classroom and other places; and translates data into the findings and recommendations for further actions *after*. Each such inscriptional line involves a series of inscriptional switches and translations.

One of the most remarkable characteristics of Jane's inscriptional work – and of the final report she presents for assessment – is the *blending* of *professional* and *learning* inscriptions and inscribing. While psychological testing is a real professional task and Jane's report is a real professional artefact, inscriptions and inscriptional strategies involved in completing this task in educational contexts are not *exactly* the same as if they were in a professional setting. They could be characterised as *idealised*, *epistemified* and *educationalised*. These three features, which are characteristic not only of Jane's case but to learning inscriptions and inscriptional practices in professional learning settings more generally, are clearly reflected in the design of this task and in Jane's report.

Idealised inscriptions: First, the specification of the assessment task carries many implicit and explicit assumptions about what is considered to be an appropriate professional *School Counsellor's* report. The specification of the assessment task provides firm recommendations on how the report should be written, including the headings of the sections, what kinds of abbreviations can be used and even templates of sentences for reporting results (Fig. 10.2).[8] The course coordinator explained this as follows:

> I don't want to be too prescriptive [specifying the content of the report] but there are certain things in terms of writing reports on kids which are pretty standard but that's just a format. And those are the sorts of things you *have to have* there.

Teaching and learning to create such professional inscriptions extends beyond an objective of developing professional knowledge and skill (in any narrow sense) to a broader objective of developing professional ethics, etiquette and values:

> For example, if that report is on a file and this little boy goes to another school, this report that you've written goes to another counsellor. So you don't want a bad [poor quality] report to go, so we've all a bit of professional pride that we do what we do well, but there are a few people, like any profession, who are different. But there are fairly accepted ways of doing things, good practice.

Jane's report has the canonical structure of a psychological report, which is only lightly tweaked for her specific case. Indeed, the unit outline explicitly says:

> ... you MUST use every heading [of the report], unless it is definitely not applicable; then you MUST justify why there is no information relevant to or pertinent to this point under the appropriate heading. (Behaviour Assessment and Interventions course outline, original emphasis)

Some parts of the report that are not 'exactly relevant' are nevertheless included in Jane's report, but left blank. For example, the section 'Professional referrals' explains 'This section is not appropriate'. In this sense, Jane constructs an *idealised* report, and the inscriptional task given to Jane has a broader implicit agenda. The course coordinator explained this instructional strategy of constructing 'idealised' inscriptions in the following way:

> When people who are already doing it in the field do it, they're probably a bit more haphazard so the students probably do it more thoroughly and fully, but my argument – and the students accept this – is that when they do it, they have to do it more perfectly.

Epistemified inscriptions: Second, there is nothing invisible or accidental in Jane's report. All decisions are explained and all tests are described. Her decisions and recommendations for parents and teachers are justified by providing references to research literature and professional sources. Indeed, as Latour (1990) might say, everything is made flat and transparent, and everything is moved to paper and 'packed' with knowledge. The course coordinator explained that such explicitness and saturation with external knowledge would not be so usual in an experienced school counsellor's report, yet this *epistemification* is an important part of the instructional approach:

---

[8] Overall, a report is a familiar generic inscriptional form that is used widely to present outcomes of completed work in many professions. However, each professional domain has its own kinds of 'professional report'. Learning to read and create such reports, as well as other generic professional inscriptions customised within each profession, is often among the explicit objectives of professional courses.

A case study report: Behaviour assessment

Headings

(a)   identification of your **subject** and the **settings/not real names**

(b)   description of **presenting problem(s):** (i) as described in the referral, i.e., quote and; (ii) in **objective** terms, including an initial hypothesis may be written during the assessment process;

(c)   details of **screening, assessment and diagnostic tests**

     BACKGROUND INFORMATION

     BEHAVIOUR DURING ASSESSMENT

     ASSESSMENT RESULTS

(d)   **Justify** your choice of assessment measures and try to describe and establish a direction and purpose to your assessment using an hypothesis testing approach; this can be combined with your assessment data;

(e)   **details of professional referrals**, if appropriate, recommended and/or undertaken, with indication of outcomes; state why if none appropriate;

(f)   **summary** of assessment findings, i.e. a brief recapitulation, a short paragraph or a summary list (APA format); can combine with conclusions;

(g)   **conclusions,** i.e. what do you interpret from these findings, what does all the presented and summarised assessment data mean;

(h)   **recommendations** which might include making a referral for extra support, features of a class-based program, etc.

(i)   **sign** your report and put your **qualifications**;

PLUS

(j)   **provide a detailed, clear justification** for the interventions/recommendations which have been chosen for this child, including the justification for any resources used/recommended; i.e., **the theoretical and practical bases for your recommendations**

(k)   **evaluation of the assessment work** and recommendations, i.e. having finished – what would you consider was appropriate/good/went well? What would you do differently or add or subtract? What did you learn at a personal level?

(l)   **references in APA 5th edition style**

(m)   **appendices –** include protocols, and possibly copies of relevant research articles and/or chapters, etc.

Fig. 10.2 Headings given to students as a form for writing behaviour assessment report (a slightly edited and abbreviated version)

> Well that's different – in a report, if you're a professional, you don't have to justify
> it. Whereas they have to say to me – I don't want them just to sort of grab everything
> they've got in the cupboard and do it. I want them to think about why they're doing it.

In this sense, this professional inscriptional task simultaneously carries three instructional agendas of learning (a) professional skills to inscribe, (b) professional values and (c) professional ways of thinking. That is, students not only *learn to inscribe* but also *inscribe to learn*.

Educationalised inscriptions: Third, as the course coordinator explained, some sections of the report are 'obviously for learning' and clarified that she needs to see not only the final product but also students' work process:

> Yeah. And that [a self-evaluation section] obviously is just for the assignment. Because I
> need to see their *processes* as well as the *product*.

The invisibility of work that goes into the construction of professional knowledge products requires this melding into professional inscriptions of additional *educational* features. However, the question of how professionals inscribe knowledge that underpins processes of their work, rather than professional knowledge products that they create, extends far beyond solely educational concerns – it is an important aspect of professional inscriptional work and, particularly, professional innovation. We turn to this aspect next.

10.5   Skill for Seeing, Inscribing and Knowing Work

Much of the literature on inscriptional practices has focussed on inscriptions representing knowledge of the world (microbes, diseases, etc.) and outcomes of professional work related to this world (diagnoses, treatments, etc.). However, professional practice involves not only knowledge related to the world but also knowledge related to the work (processes, actions, strategies, etc.). Work involves knowledge that underpins transient actions in the world – that is, knowledge that underpins *performance*. Inscribing the world and inscribing performance require mastering different kinds of 'vision'. In fact, much of the literature acknowledges that inscribing work requires mastering three rather different ways of seeing and inscribing performance – creating inscriptions *for*, inscriptions *of* and inscriptions *within* the ongoing work.

To illustrate this, let's consider some examples. A *plan for* creating a new health service is not the same as a *report of* how such a service was established. Planning involves creating inscriptions *for* the work that will become an intrinsic part of this work. Reporting involves providing analytical insights into how things were done. The former is a projective view of imagined actions that will change the world; the latter is an analytical view of the performed actions that have changed the world. In short, inscriptions *for actions* and *of actions* have different temporal and material relationships to the experienced world, and their production constitutes two different modes of perceiving work and the world.

Both – the plan and the report – are also different from *the documentation* (*records*) produced as a part of the ongoing work of establishing such a health service. The latter is an inscription *within action and within an emerging world*. That is, this kind of inscription is simultaneously for and of action. Inscribing knowledge for, within and of accomplished work constitutes three ways of seeing and relating action to the material realities of the existing world.

This temporal perspective gives a handy way to look at the functions of work inscriptions in knowledgeable action and how work gets inscribed. We briefly elaborate on each of the three ways for seeing and inscribing work in the next three subsections (Sects. 10.5.1, 10.5.2, and 10.5.3), and after that we discuss how these professional visions are reflected in professional courses (Sect. 10.6).

10.5.1 Inscriptions for Work

Norman (1991) notes that inscriptions created for action, such as plans and checklists, have several potential strengths, some more obvious than others. For example, planning can be done before the actual task is carried out and can itself be distributed across time and space; work can be distributed among people; useful inscriptions for work can be created by people who are not directly involved in carrying out the work. Most importantly, the inscriptions change the nature of the task that an individual has to do in action, and simultaneously change the nature of the skill needed to perform that action – for example, cooking without a recipe or navigating without a map. Such inscriptional tools for work can also serve two other purposes: (a) the evaluation of environmental states and (b) the execution of the acts. The former inscriptions mediate perception and interpretation of the world or changes within it; the latter inscriptions mediate actions that result in changes in the world. For example, a checklist can be a tool for shaping 'professional vision' and detecting issues, but it might not assist much with the execution of actions to address those issues. A guidance note about how to do a certain job can assist with the execution of actions, though it *may* not support the development of an understanding of when these actions are appropriate.

One of the most common professional inscriptions used in work is the *plan* (Agre & Chapman, 1990; Schank & Abelson, 1977; Suchman, 2007). However, what plans are, how they are used in human sense-making and how they are embedded within actions are still rather open questions.[9] Many human actions are

---

[9] The main opinions from research on this matter are distributed along a continuum from the view that plans and other symbolic devices can represent human thought and action (Vera & Simon, 1993) to the view that human thought and action are fundamentally situated and meanings emerge directly in action (Suchman, 2007). We do not want to repeat this debate here (see, e.g. the special issue edited by Koschmann, 2003). We believe that, at this point in time, most of those who have been involved in this debate have more or less agreed that, irrespectively of how plans are weaved into the human cognitive 'fabric', they are always both contingent and important.

carried on without having a plan or planning; and overall, real-world situations and problems are too complex and dynamic to be represented fully in an object-like symbolic form. Nevertheless, plans are important cultural and symbolic resources for guiding human meaning-making, inquiry and action:

What plans are like depends on how they're used. (Agre & Chapman, 1990, p. 17)

Yet, as Sharrock and Button (2003) put it:

... a plan is a technique for the organization of action ... plans are not *theoretically* adequate devices for depicting cases of action but can only be *practically* adequate. (Sharrock & Button, 2003, pp. 260–263, original emphasis)

Collective planning as an activity and plans as shared inscriptions often function as 'activity objects' for joint organisational learning and as 'boundary objects' for orchestrating collective work (e.g. Engeström, 1999, 2001; Miettinen & Virkkunen, 2005; Nicolini, Mengis, & Swan, 2012). Planning and creating other inscriptions for work are also often used as instructional approaches for professional learning (Michael, 1973; Mutton, Hagger, & Burn, 2011). However, their functions in supporting learning, beyond the basic acknowledgement that plans mediate it and their roles depend on the environment, are far less clearly understood.

10.5.2 Inscriptions of Work

Capturing and representing how work is done, and the knowledge that is used in this work, play important roles in improving professional practice and designing new tools for this practice (Falconer & Littlejohn, 2009; Goodyear & Steeples, 1998; Suchman, 1995; Szymanski & Whalen, 2011). The professional capabilities needed to represent one's 'know-how' are increasingly viewed as one of the core professional skills needed for sharing 'best practice' and for developing personal professional knowledge.

Cases, portfolios and videos, as Shulman (2002) notes, are among the inscriptional artefacts used for representing practice. However, capturing work in meaningful ways, such that it can be used beyond one's personal learning, tends to be a complex task. For example, Sharpe, Beetham and Ravenscroft (2004) show how knowledge artefacts used in academia to inscribe knowledge usually take the form of books, papers, case studies, guides, principles, databases and other textual abstractions. While these knowledge inscriptions 'travel' well, they tend not to be very suitable for representing practical knowledge. In contrast, practitioners find it easier to represent and share their practices through images, interactive and video media, narratives, dialogues, presentations, performances and other 'active' inscriptions (Goodyear & Steeples, 1999). Further, effective representations of practice have additional important features that traditional knowledge inscriptions do not possess: (a) they convey the context within which they were created and practitioners' real-life experiences; (b) they are contingent and dynamic, allowing

Table 10.2 Some features of representations of practice

Features of productive representations of practice and practitioners' working knowledge
1. Ownership – representations of knowledge, or at least interpretations of knowledge, should be created by practitioners
2. Reflection and review – representations are needed during reflection of practice, and reflection is important
3. Contingency – less complete representations are better, as they offer more 'room' for the practitioner
4. Dynamism – representations are not locked, but preserve an ability to add, change, improve and adapt them continuously
5. Support for peer learning – networks for creating, sharing and testing representations are a part of representation

After Sharpe et al. (2004)

for practitioners to change them; and (c) they provide opportunities to witness 'the *real thing, in the real context, with the real people*' (Sharpe et al., 2004, p. 18). In other words, such inscriptions of practical knowledge actually allow one to see this knowledge within action, in context and as experienced. As Sharpe et al. (2004) argue:

> ... representations of practice need to become 'living' artefacts, enhanced by their partic-ipation in collaborative activities. (Sharpe et al., 2004, p. 19)

Such representations of professional experiences, including inscriptions that trans-late theoretical knowledge to practice (Table 10.2), are 'active artefacts' enhanced by 'living practice' where open and dynamic knowledge inscriptions are further mediated by interaction, meaning-making and remaking.

However, as Suchman (1995) argues, *representations* of work are *interpreta-tions* of work that are crafted for particular purposes and represent particular interests. She identifies several features of inscriptions (representing work) that are often forgotten in more technical discussions of work inscriptions. First, repre-sentations of work are generated out of ways of knowing through which this work is viewed. Such representations involve certain choices of what gets represented and how and what stays implicit and invisible. Second, there is an intimate relationship between the representation, work and politics of organisations and contexts in which those representations are generated and used. What is represented is not a neutral perception. What is explicit, seen and inscribed represents also what is considered 'as legitimate to be seen, spoken, and thought' (op. cit., p. 61). Repre-sentations of work, in this respect, not only have a rational dimension of creating and sharing knowledge but also carry social order and power and have social and political implications (see also Chap. 2).

So, professional learning is a distinct way of knowing, and inscriptions crafted by students represent their way of seeing and interpreting work and learning. Inscriptions of work and inscriptions of learning to work, as we saw in Jane's case, are often two different interpretations and representations of work and have not only social but also cognitive consequences.

10.5.3 Inscriptions within Work

The two views (above) of inscriptions and inscribing for work, and of work, locate the inscriptional work of a practice outside the time and space of this practice.[10] However, practitioners also create inscriptions to support their knowledge work *within* their situated activity (Roth & McGinn, 1998; Suchman, 1988). They include such things as sketches, drawings, accounting files, daily handover sheets, individual and shared notes and other records. Such inscriptions, generated within daily activities, are often the main carriers of knowledge work and learning (Engeström & Middleton, 1996; Ewenstein & Whyte, 2009). For example, even Jane's case, discussed above, illustrates that her work is a flow of inscriptions, where one inscription (e.g. calculated test scores) informs what should be done and inscribed next (e.g. observation). Such inscriptions closely relate to the inscriptions of (classical) knowledge about the world that we discussed earlier. However, they are not necessarily final products of knowledge work. Rather, they are inscriptions of work generated for work within this work. These inscriptions support situated knowing.

Indeed, while the separation of inscriptions of, for and within work is theoretically possible, they often intersect in practice. For example, Suchman (1995) notes that some technologies and representations created *for* and *in* work are also commonly used as representations *of* work for reporting on those activities. Similarly, Eraut (2009) points out that a range of inscriptions created within professional placements – such as audited accounts, daily handover sheets, building designs, reflective diaries and reflective reports – can be used in higher education as inscriptions of work to represent students' development in work placements and their further learning through reflection. Nevertheless, many inscriptions generated within work often stay inside the work and remain invisible from the outside.

Overall, many accounts of how professional work gets inscribed point to embodied, invisible, local and other situated qualities. These contrast with more idealised accounts of learning for knowledge work – seen as creating knowledge inscriptions that have their own existence outside of the minds, bodies and activities that produced them (Bereiter, 2002). This contrast reflects a tension inherent within professional learning – between inscribing practices situated within educational settings and the need to learn, through them, non-situated skills of inscribing and creating inscriptions of work that can be moved easily across workplace settings. What kinds of inscriptions of professional work and inscriptional skills can travel comfortably across situated practices located and generated in specific contexts? Through what kinds of inscriptions and inscriptional practices do students learn to see and inscribe work?

---

[10] Some of the most rationalistic accounts even locate it outside the minds and hands of those who carry on this practice. That is, inscriptional tools for practitioners, such as plans, are created by 'experts', and professional practices are audited by external accrediting bodies.

Next, we present some common work inscriptions that we found across a range of professional learning situations. This broader sweep complements the more in-depth study of the case of Jane the school counsellor (Sect. 10.4).

10.6 Analysis of Students' Inscriptions of Professional Knowledge and Work

The temporal relationship between inscription and action that we discussed above (Sect. 10.5) provides a useful way of looking at students' learning inscriptions and inscriptional practices. They can be described as *projective* (inscriptions for practice), *productive* (inscriptions within practice) and *illuminative* (inscriptions of practice). While it is impossible to draw precise boundaries, nevertheless different inscriptions serve particular purposes and involve inscriptional practices that have distinctive features (Table 10.3). Furthermore, most of the inscriptions created by students are designed to serve either a generative function or a communicative function in the construction of actionable knowledge (see Sect. 10.2). We call these 'inquiry carriers' and 'discourse carriers', respectively.

While cognitive and social are two interrelated epistemic modalities of inscriptions – and they, of course, have other modalities, including the material (see Malafouris, 2013) – nevertheless putting one modality to the front and another into the background often requires different inscriptional skills. At least, these skills are often learnt by creating different kinds of inscriptions. That is, inscribing to

Table 10.3 Ways of seeing and inscribing work

Inscriptions	Projective	Productive	Illuminative
Purpose	Production, innovation, change	Performative, executive	Scholarly inquiry, reflection
Time of action	Future	Present	From past to future
Nature of knowledge and knowing	Structurally complex phenomena, distributed in space and time	Functionally complex, transient, phenomena	Invisible or complex aspects and relationships between action and phenomena
Learning of	Values, best practice, etc.	Skill, action	Knowledge, understanding
Context for which knowledge is produced	General, imagined	Existing and specific	Existing, but open
What is inscribed	Structures of phenomena	Traces, elements of inquiry	Complete phenomena
Mediate	Future action	Knowing in action	Reflective, analytical perception
Thinking	Projective	Actionable	Interpretative

Table 10.4 Work inscriptions as 'inquiry carriers'

Inscription and description	Examples
Projective inscriptions Products generated prior to work, to plan, imagine, inspire and strategise	*Plans and models of future actions*: new services, lesson plans, guidelines
Productive inscriptions Interim and final knowledge products generated within work	*Traces of productive inquiry and action*: student behaviour tests, measurements, analytical worksheets, assessment interview notes, observations
Illuminative inscriptions Analytical and reflective products based on one's own and others' work experiences	*Reports from analyses of artefacts of professional practice*: analyses of lesson plans and pharmaceutical products *Reports from inquiry into practice*: reports about school practices, comparative analyses of community pharmacies, analyses of aboriginal officer's roles, reports on social and economic implications of a disease *Reflections on one's own learning process, knowledge, skills and practice in a variety of formats*: reflective journals, portfolios, logbooks, action project reports

support (one's own) professional thinking is not the same as inscribing to support professional discourse.

We discuss some common functions of inscriptions and inscribing in professional learning next. We start the discussion with 'inquiry carriers' (Table 10.4) and then move to 'discourse carriers' (Table 10.5).

10.6.1   Inscriptions as Inquiry Carriers

Projective inscriptions are inscriptions of knowledge for future actions. They include specific 'model' artefacts, such as plans for creating new health services and running health promotion programs, course and lessons plans and field trip designs. In learning, projective inscriptional practices are often oriented towards 'best practice' or change, and they serve a visionary function. While projective inscriptions can be specific and quite well elaborated, they are usually less linked to details of the context, and so they often only outline a shape of the problem solution and actions, rather than specifying all the details. One noticeable attribute of projective inscriptional practices in learning is that they tend to convey values of the profession: 'best practice' rather than just realities of the field. The pharmacy students we studied, for example, were involved in producing plans for future community services, not because teachers thought that these tasks are common in current pharmacy practice, but because they wanted to convey a broader vision of the pharmacist in the community, not only as a person who dispenses prescriptions but as somebody who improves the overall quality of health and well-being within a community. Projective inscriptions often carry notions of the 'purposefulness' and 'mindfulness' of professional practice, and of 'improvement' and 'innovation', rather than reflecting the habitual, often reactive, nature of professional work.

Productive inscriptions are representations produced by students as a result of tasks that imitate professional inquiry and other kinds of knowledge-generating work, examples being assessments of child behaviour by school counsellors (as in Jane's case, above), or assessments of family situations by social workers. Productive inscriptions usually form a part of transient professional action, dependent on moment-to-moment interaction and skill. These inscriptions often serve a performative function and accompany habitual, functionally complex tasks (as with conducting professional assessments). They are often linked to specific contexts of action and inscribe elements of knowledge of larger, more integrated, decisions or longer-term actions.

Illuminative inscriptions usually result from purposeful 'outsider' inquiry into, or 'insider' reflection on, certain aspects of professional practice. In such inquiry, things and tools of practice, as well as professional practice itself, become subjects of students' professional scrutiny and interpretation. Illuminative inscriptions of work include three broad groups:

(a) Products of analytical work investigating artefacts and tools of professional practice, such as reports analysing lesson plans and qualities of pharmaceutical products
(b) Products of students' inquiries into professional practice itself (Examples from practicum experiences collected in our empirical studies include student teachers' reports produced as a result of their inquiry into the attributes and needs of a school community and comparative analyses of community pharmacies, produced by trainee pharmacists.)
(c) Reflections by students on their own learning, knowledge, skills and practice – in a variety of formats, such as reflective journals, portfolios, logbooks and action project reports

Illuminative inscriptions are interpretations of work. They often draw upon specific things and relate to specific experiences, whether of students or others. However, these illuminative inscriptions often have a sense of 'openness'. The knowledge created is less tied to the specific contexts and situations in which it was experienced and generated and does not relate to specific, immediate or future professional actions. Rather, the aim is to convey understanding for such actions. In the context of learning, illuminative inscriptions often take the shape of academic-analytical tasks such as deconstructions and comparisons and interpretative reflections. Such tasks help students see some of the less visible features of professional practice and knowledge, and make sense of complex relationships between the phenomena investigated and personal professional action.

One common property of the inscriptions described above is that they are inscriptions through which knowledge work is accomplished. They have what Schnotz, Baadte, Mülle and Rasch (2010) call an 'inferential power' (p. 21), and, in this sense, they are 'inquiry carriers'. As with all inscriptions, they can – and often do – mediate communication and collaborative work with others, but this is not their only – or even their main – function. What is special about 'inquiry carriers' is that they can help their producers to – individually or collaboratively – infer meaning and *create* understanding. For example, a pharmacy student, as a pharmacist, could use a medication assessment report to communicate review findings and recommendations with a doctor, and a student teacher as a teacher might use a course plan to share or discuss their ideas with colleagues and collaboratively improve their planned unit. However, these inscriptions are also 'cognitive partners' through which students – as future professionals – carry out and come to understand their knowledge work.

10.6.2 Inscriptions as Discourse Carriers

The main feature of inscriptions as discourse carriers is that they are purposefully produced to mediate interaction with other people and the environment, rather than for individual mental activity. 'Discourse carriers' are distributed along a similar temporal line as 'inquiry carriers' – they can be created before action, during action or after it – serving projective, productive and illuminative purposes (Table 10.5).

Students produce a range of inscriptions in conjunction with their work designing plans and models for future actions (i.e. in conjunction with *projective* inquiry carriers). For example, our empirical studies showed that designs for health promotion programs and other prospective actions were often complemented with the development of specific discursive tools that could be used to deliver them, such as pamphlets and handouts.

Table 10.5 Work inscriptions as 'discourse carriers'

Inscription and description	Examples
Projective inscriptions Inscriptions for mediating discourse: 'boundary artefacts', instruments via which action will be carried out	*Specific inscriptions for action*: handouts, assessment tasks, disease monitoring tools
Productive inscriptions Traces of actions produced by others and for others	*Natural inscriptions of transient actions and knowledge*: students' works and assessments, counselling information on a medical prescription
Illuminative inscriptions Purposeful mediators of professional discourse that bring produced artefacts and completed actions back into professional communication	*Professional knowledge products and inscriptions of work rendered for presentation and communication*: presentations of case study results and professional guidelines to peers *Purposeful inscriptions of transient actions and knowledge*: peers' and tutors' assessment sheets of role-play performance

Various *productive* inscriptions are created by clients and students themselves through action. Examples include counselling notes on a prescription, students' worksheets and tests. Much of the verbal communication and translation between professional and lay ways of knowing tend to be mediated by such productive discourse. This occurs in many social professions, such as teaching and counselling.

A range of special discursive inscriptions is also created to communicate the results of students' work – including knowledge work – to teachers, peers and other audiences. Such *illuminative* discourse inscriptions may serve explanatory purposes and take the form of presentations, packages of teaching materials, excursion kits, guidelines and other (re)inscribed representations of students' work, but specially rendered to communicate and share their knowledge products with others. While many illuminative inscriptions produced by students are outward oriented – i.e. they aim to support interaction with the external world and other people – some illuminative inscriptions have an inward orientation. For example, assessment sheets used to grade preservice teachers' role-play performance, or video records and other specially produced external traces of professional action, often have this reflective inward-oriented purpose. In these cases, inscriptions are often produced by teachers, peers and other 'observers' and function as raw material for further reflection, interpretation and generation of professional understanding.

'Inquiry carriers' and 'discourse carriers' need to be distinguished and should not be substituted with one another. Both are needed, and while they are closely related, each has particular properties and roles, and each draws on a particular kind of 'inscriptional literacy'. Students, for example, could represent their entire design for a health promotion program by creating 'discourse inscriptions' to deliver it (e.g. booklets, promotion materials), but such discourse inscriptions will not represent how such a program works, what makes it good and other fundamental mechanisms and qualities.

That is, as Lynch and Woolgar (1990) claim, mere surface resemblance does not represent a phenomenon's organisation. The opposite statement is also true. A good plan produced by students does not mean that the students will be able to materialise and enact their inscribed ideas. (Discourse carriers are not the actions, but nevertheless, they bring the mind somewhat closer to the actions.) What's important in such work is an ability to align two ways of seeing: (re)presenting and (re)inscribing practice.

10.7   Insights into the Functional (Pedagogical) Properties of Learning Inscriptions

We will now briefly turn to connect inscriptional practices of students in higher education with some fundamental dimensions of professional learning. We start from Shulman's (2005) ideas about 'signature pedagogies' – powerful types of teaching that organise professional education. Shulman argues that there are three

Table 10.6 Main qualities of the signature pedagogies

Aspects of professional work	Performance	Integrity	Thinking
Pedagogical routines	Habits of the hand	Habits of the heart	Habits of the mind
Knowledge for...	Action	Judgement	Reasoning
Underlying structure of pedagogy	Surface structure	Implicit structure	Deep structure
Inscriptional practices	Productive (within action)	Projective (for action)	Illuminative (of action)

fundamental aspects of professional work to which future professionals are instructed in professional education: *performance*, *acting with integrity* and *thinking*. He notes that pedagogies have all three dimensions, but pedagogical routines through which students are instructed differ fundamentally in their focus and how they form three kinds of habits: 'habits of the hand' (i.e. structure and concrete acts of the profession), 'habits of the heart' (i.e. professional attitudes, values, dispositions and judgement) and 'habits of the mind' (i.e. professional reasoning). He argues that each of the signature pedagogies has a *surface structure*, *implicit structure* and *deep structure*, through which these three habits are respectively formed.

Acknowledging the unique nature of expertise in various professions and without unnecessarily stretching the parallel, we can extend these three dimensions of the professional habits of action, judgement and reasoning to the inscriptional practices: *productive*, *projective* and *illuminative* (Table 10.6). In other words, different types of inscriptional practices learnt and used for learning at university have different relationships to pedagogy and, subsequently, different relationships to the practices within professional cultures.

10.7.1   Learning Habits Through Inscriptional Work

Tasks that mimic 'real' professional tasks usually evolve around productive inscriptional practices and, as a rule, involve the main aspects of 'professional vision': highlighting, coding and production (Goodwin, 1994). For example, such a task as the production of a professional assessment report inevitably requires the student (a) to identify what is relevant and what is not by employing highlighting strategies, such as structured interviews or tests; (b) to classify and code relevant things in professional language, such as 'reshuffling' what was said by a client; and (c) to inscribe what is seen in a certain way, so as to produce a report that could travel from one setting to another. Such tasks and inscriptional work locate professional learning in close proximity to learning 'habits of the hand' and rely on the 'surface structure' of pedagogy (Shulman, 2005).

The literature provides plenty of evidence about the dangers of any habit in professional work – and particularly the dangers of routine unreflected behaviours that could take the shape of the 'habit of the hand' even when people engage in inscriptional kinds of work (e.g. Wenger, 1998). However, some inscriptional habits, as Goodwin (1994) argued, are among 'the distinctive forms of professional literacy' (p. 612). Further, our studies show that productive inscriptional tasks account for a relatively small part of the inscriptional work done by students, even in courses that aim to prepare them for professional fieldwork.

In professional learning, productive and even projective tasks encountered in workplaces (e.g. planning a lesson and teaching it) are often substituted by the illuminative tasks (e.g. analysing plans, teaching resources and video recordings of lessons). What does this kind of substitution mean for learning inscriptional skills for professional work? Can similar professional vision and inscriptional habits be learnt by engaging with the analytical illuminative tasks? We have doubts.

There are some important similarities and deep differences in both cognitive and social aspects of inscriptional practices. We discuss these next.

From the cognitive *inquiry carrier* perspective, the (analytical and explanatory) illuminative work draws on an external observer's 'scientific vision'. While this is different from the productive inscriptional work that draws on canonical 'professional vision', nevertheless the structures of the two visions have some similarities. For example, when the students completed an analytical task asking them to compare several community pharmacies, they (a) identified essential features in pharmacy layouts by *highlighting*, (b) classified them against the official standards regulating pharmacy design by *coding*, and (c) produced a report. The illuminative work and productive work, in this respect, share an overarching commonality – they both require mastering routine skills of professional seeing, coding and inscribing. Similarly, there is no apparent tension at the level of declarative ('know-that') knowledge. The necessary declarative knowledge could be learnt by doing things and/or by analysing how somebody else does or did this. For example, the counsellor could learn declarative knowledge involved in completing the child's behavioural assessments by producing assessments and writing reports or by analysing reports and other inscriptional traces of behavioural assessments completed by other people.

Illuminative and productive inscriptions and their functions in professional work are very different from those that we typically see in scientific work. Professionals most often engage with productive inscriptional work – where they create knowledge inscriptions to solve specific professional problems; they less often engage with illuminative inscriptional work – where they create inscriptions of knowledge that are unrelated to their immediate action.

These two kinds of inscribing draw on different sets of 'know-how' and result in different kinds of habits. For example, (a) picking up relevant things (i.e. highlighting and coding) from the real world and from the reports is not the same thing; (b) inscriptional skills for producing a behavioural assessment report are not the same as for producing an evaluation report analysing behavioural assessments produced by others. These differences become even sharper from the discourse perspective: ways of knowing and inscribing that are carried over via interacting with people (e.g. children, patients) cannot be learnt by analysing inscriptions, but only by interacting, inscribing and knowing in action.

The importance of illuminative inscriptional practices in learning and professional work should not be underestimated. One could even argue that it is necessary, or at least beneficial, to engage with illuminative inscriptional tasks for learning 'professional vision'. For example, perhaps there is no other good way to learn about the properties of medications, than to analyse available information and complete a report. However, different inscriptional practices assist in learning different kinds of knowing and knowledge – one can't learn habits of the hand by training only the mind.

10.7.2   Linking Professional Inscriptional Work and Innovation

Traditional notions of 'knowledge work' have a rather different character than the knowledge work carried out by professional practitioners as a part of their daily practices and actions – it involves major illuminative inscriptional work, rather than productive inscriptional work. Furthermore, one can see a fundamental difference between professional illuminative work and traditional scientific analytical work. For example, when student teachers learn about the role of an aboriginal officer in a school by completing an inquiry about that role, they do not produce an inscription about 'the role' in general, but an inscription that is about the role of the specific officer in the specific school. That is, professional knowledge that is learnt through analytical inscriptional work involves *forming bridges* between the abstract principles (e.g. the role of such officers, in general) and the situation (a specific officer in a specific school). The nature of such professional analytical inquiry and inscriptions is different from scientific analytical inquiry and inscriptions which normally aim to *break links* between the specific and the abstract, to form abstractions of knowledge that can travel easily beyond the local situation.

One noticeable feature of the illuminative inscriptional practices in professional education is that they are rarely found in just this form in day-to-day professional practice. Professional work does, of course, involve learning and sense-making, but this is rarely accompanied by the creating of inscriptions; it is often done in passing, without much conscious attention. Similarly, professionals do, from time to time, create reflective scholarly inscriptions, but these are usually for sharing their 'know-how' with others, rather than for their own learning (e.g. creating lesson plans and other teaching resources, or guidelines underpinned by best practice, for sharing with other colleagues).

In saying this, we do not want to imply that scientific and professional ways of thinking and ways of doing, or their material and inscriptional practices, are completely different and incompatible. We accept that the contrasts made between rationality and the formal nature of scientific practices vs. the sometimes arbitrary situated nature of actions in professional settings are more artificial than real (both of them are mundane and material) (cf. Latour, 1990); yet the inscriptional practices and products of these two ways of knowing are not the same. The difference between generic inscriptions that are designed for reuse across situations and concrete inscriptions that are designed for immediate specific action is rather easily identifiable. In fact, the question of knowledge use and reuse becomes central for understanding the nature of knowledge work and inscriptional practices involved in producing professional innovations.

Are practices that underpin traditional professional vision sufficient for innovative knowledge work? It seems that one aspect which is 'invisible' in professional vision is how what is known from individual cases and experiences, and is inscribed in a variety of media, suddenly becomes new shared professional knowledge. Latour would say that this is the job of the bureaucrats who shuffle hundreds of inscriptions around; but then, can professionals themselves create new knowledge?

Professional expertise (and habits) also have a similar form of 'knowing' that is achieved by shuffling via experiences. The main difference is that 'normative' scientific knowing is mainly based on *explicit shuffling* across instances distributed *in space* (across places and cases), while professional expertise often involves *implicit shuffling* across instances distributed *in time* (i.e. along the lines of one's experience). These two kinds of illuminative work are particularly visible in the analytical and explanatory vs. reflective inscriptional tasks.

However, in the context of higher education pedagogical practices for students, learning is not restricted to activities that have a routine repetitive character or those that separate habits of hand from habits of mind and other professional qualities. For example, in our studies we have seen that pharmacy teachers chose the medication review task as a tool to learn 'professional vision', not because of its routine character or pervasiveness in pharmacy practice, but because of the complexity, contingency and pervasiveness of the underlying form of thinking and the complexity of the associated discourse, as well as the explicit articulated character of the underpinning thinking (and inscriptions). Medication reviews, according to pharmacy teachers, help students to learn the underlying structure of thinking that organises many decisions in pharmacy practice. Teachers' understanding of deep features of such inscriptional practices is important. Overall, finding a task that requires the creation of an inscription is important from a pedagogical point of view. That is why the medication review becomes important in learning pharmacy practice. (We elaborate on this case in Chaps. 14 and 15.)

10.7.3 Inscriptions of Knowledge and Professional Actionable Knowledge

There are two distinct aspects to 'professional knowledgeable action'. The first of these is the knowledge and action that are required to make sense of the world (i.e. perception or vision). The second is the knowledge and action that are required to change the world (i.e. decisions about the action and its execution). The former is a part of 'professional vision', while the latter is a part of 'professional action'. They are closely related, but not the same, and inscriptions for perception and for action are different: the former have an illuminative character and require an outsider's view, the latter have a projective character and require an insider's view. Vision and action often come together in inscriptional work around productive inscriptions.

In analytical–interpretative work, an inquiry ends with findings. In contrast, the main products of professional inquiry are not the findings but *decisions and recommendations*. In this sense, analytical tasks and inscriptions may help to learn professional vision, but are less likely to assist in making a decision, producing a recommendation or taking an action.

As Norman (1991) has noted, inscriptions for work change the nature of the task being done by the person or group and the nature and level of skill needed to perform the task. For example, teaching a new lesson with a plan requires different expertise from teaching a new lesson without a plan. While one may argue that this means that novice professionals should be equipped with good 'cognitive artefacts' (manifest in inscriptions) that help them to perform their tasks skilfully, even though they have not yet fully developed their expertise, we want to make a different claim – professionals should be fluent in creating and adapting such inscriptions for the situation and for their work.

As we pointed out earlier, a significant part of students' work in professional courses involves creating different kinds of inscriptions – in which they inscribe knowledge related to actions rather than knowledge representing perceptions of the world. In such cases, professional action becomes an object of inscription itself and part of the practice through which such 'work representations' are created.

This includes projective inscriptions for future work: future nurses create guidelines, preservice teachers create lesson plans and pharmacy students create strategies for community health programs. This activity also includes traces and reflective interpretations of how the work was done: future teachers write reflective journals, social workers create field logbooks, etc.

What does it mean to create such inscriptions for and of work? What kinds of inscriptional practices and knowledge work does this involve? The nature and role of projective inscriptions and inscriptional practices are not well understood in education for the professions.

This diversity of inscriptional practices that characterise professional work and learning should not be forgotten. It is this coordination of heterogeneous practices and inscriptions that makes productive inquiry possible and fluent. It is not the *nature of* inscriptions per se but the *consistency between* situational demands and the functions of inscriptions that determines their value in professional practice and learning.

10.8   From Inscribing to (Re)presenting: Personal, System and Enactive Views of Inscriptions

The temporal perspective discussed above gives us one way of seeing functional properties of inscriptions that represent work. It specifically shows *when* knowledge-generating inscriptional work enters a person's activity (i.e. before, within or after execution of action with the inscription) and allows us to see *how the* inscription joins up with a person's action (i.e. by projecting, producing or illuminating actionable knowledge). However, functional properties of inscriptions depend not only on *when* they enter *and how* they relate to a person's actions but also how they enter the person's *way of seeing* inscriptions and inscriptional work within these actions. In short, how are inscriptions seen – *(re)presented* – by the inscribers or those who use these inscriptions in their work?

As a starting point, we can draw on Norman's (1991) distinction between 'the personal view' and 'the system view' of inscriptions.[11]

From the view of a person, who uses an inscription to perform a certain task, the inscription embodies knowledge needed for the task (Fig. 10.3a).[12] As we noted in the last section, the presence of the inscription changes the nature of the task and, simultaneously, changes the personal actor's knowledge and skill needed to perform the task. That is, the inscription permits the achievement of a similar objective as before, but in a different way – and using different personal knowledges and skills – than would occur without the inscription. For example, external memory aids like handover sheets, checklists, to do lists and other inscriptions produced for and used within action, when looked at from the personal viewpoint, change the skills and knowledge needed to perform this action. The actor no longer needs to remember all the information, but instead needs to know how to use these memory aids when performing the job. Such inscriptions could be ready for use (e.g. a lesson plan prepared by somebody else) or could involve some further inscriptional work and thus require a skill to 'complete' the inscription (e.g. a nurse needs the skill to fill in handover sheets). However, the structure of knowledge is embodied in the inscription and is generally stable or, at least, unproblematic (i.e. a nurse does not need to rediscover what to write in the handover sheet and how to write it). Such

---

[11] Norman (1991) uses the term 'cognitive artefacts' to mean things that have similar representational features and functions as inscriptions: 'an artificial device designed to maintain, display, or operate upon information in order to serve a representational function' (p. 17).

[12] It would be more precise to call this view 'the actors' view' than 'the personal view' as similar inscriptions for work could be also used for collective work.

Fig. 10.3 The personal (**a**), system (**b**) and enactive (**c**) views of (re)presenting and inscribing work
Notations: *Brackets* indicate that inscription creates an illusion of stability and independence of the inscribed knowledge from an actor and observer; *dashed lines* show temporality and the relational nature of the boundaries created

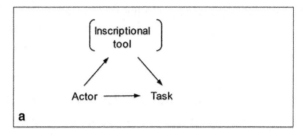

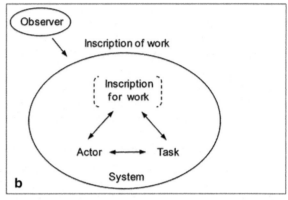

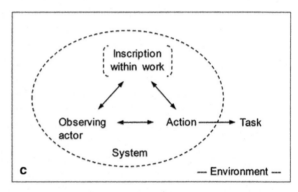

inscriptions created and viewed from the personal perspective may *expand* the person's capacities for action, but they do not present or make explicit knowledge embodied in this capacity. That is, the handover sheet embodies, but does not present, knowledge of how to complete and use the handover sheet for a task.

Once seen from *outside*, the knowledge needed to perform the task by the system is distributed between the actor, the inscriptional tool used by this actor and the task (Fig. 10.3b). Thus, once viewed from the system perspective, the inscription of knowledge for action is inscription *of work* and is different from an inscriptional tool used *for this work*. This inscription of knowledge presents all the activity system – including the actors, tools, tasks and relationships among them. That is, work inscribed from the system view represents knowledge of how the work is done by the whole system. This perspective allows a person to see how inscriptions used within the system relate to the person's skill and the task and how change in one element of the system changes other elements within it. Norman argued that the system view is the representation of the system from outside that system. It is not the insider's view from which the actors see their task and inscriptions used to do it. This view splits inscriptional work into two discrete ways of seeing and representing knowledge needed to perform this work: inscriptions *for* work and inscriptions *of* work.

Inscriptional tasks in professional learning are usually framed from one of these two views. When tasks are framed from the personal perspective, students' learning, as a rule, involves various tasks using inscriptional tools and practices available for tackling such tasks. When tasks are framed from the system perspective, students are thereby asked to step outside the practice and create representations of this practice from the outsider's viewpoint. Jane's inscriptional work nicely represents this gestalt switch: from creating a range of inscriptions using available tools during the behavioural assessment, from the personal view (complete tests, etc.), to the self-evaluation at the end of the project – i.e. from the system view. However, the shared challenge is that knowledgeable action and one's ability to create actionable inscriptions require seeing the system from *within* the system and the inscription not as separable from the task, but as a *part of* the task (e.g. how Jane should tweak the test if Ron missed every item).

Norman's perspectives need to be extended by a third – *enactive* – view. From the enactive viewpoint, cognition is 'an embodied engagement in which the world is brought forth by the coherent activity of a cogniser in its environment' (Di Paolo, 2009, p. 12).

Enactive inscriptions, thus, are dynamic (re)presentations of the work that emerge from the person's actions performed as a part of inscriptional work (Fig. 10.3c). From this perspective, the inscription does not necessarily present how the system works from the outsider's view; it also does not present in advance how the work should be carried on from the actor's view. Rather, it is a dynamic inscription of work which acquires meanings and functional properties within this work. In other words, it is not located outside the system or outside the work, but constituted through action within this work. It is *(re)presentation* of work constituted within this work. This view allows students to see their work – creating and tweaking inscriptional practices and inscriptions for work – as a part of the work that enhances *their* capacity to do the work *and* the performance of the *system* in an environment open for new possibilities and meanings.

References

Adler, P. S. (2005). The evolving object of software development. *Organization, 12*(3), 401–435.
Agre, P. E., & Chapman, D. (1990). What are plans for? *Robotics and Autonomous Systems, 6* (1–2), 17–34.

Belfiore, M. E., Defoe, T. A., Folinsbee, S., Hunter, J., & Jackson, N. S. E. (2004). *Reading work: Literacies in the new workplace*. Mahwah, NJ: Lawrence Erlbaum Associates.

Bereiter, C. (2002). *Education and mind in the knowledge age*. Mahwah, NJ: Lawrence Erlbaum Associates.

Billett, S. (2014). *Mimetic learning at work: Learning in the circumstances of practice*. Heidelberg, Germany: Springer.

Bowker, G. C., & Star, S. L. (1999). *Sorting things out: Classification and its consequences*. Cambridge, MA: MIT Press.

Carberry, H. F. (2003). *Semiotic analysis of clinical chemistry: For knowledge work in the medical sciences*. PhD thesis. Queensland University of Technology, Brisbane, Australia.

Dagognet, F. (1969). *Tableaux et langages de la chimie*. Paris: Le Seuil.

Dagognet, F. (1973). *Ecriture et Iconographie*. Paris: Vrin.

Di Paolo, E. (2009). Extended life. *Topoi, 28*(1), 9–21. doi:10.1007/s11245-008-9042-3.

Donald, M. (1991). *Origins of the modern mind: Three stages in the evolution of culture and cognition*. Cambridge, MA: Harvard University Press.

Donald, M. (2001). *A mind so rare: The evolution of human consciousness*. New York: W.W. Norton.

Engeström, Y. (1999). Expansive visibilization of work: An activity-theoretical perspective. *Computer Supported Cooperative Work (CSCW), 8*(1), 63–93.

Engeström, Y. (2001). Expansive learning at work: Toward an activity theoretical reconceptualization. *Journal of Education and Work, 14*(1), 133–156. doi:10.1080/13639080020028747.

Engeström, Y., & Middleton, D. (Eds.). (1996). *Cognition and communication at work*. Cambridge, NY: Cambridge University Press.

Eraut, M. (2009). Understanding complex performance through learning trajectories and mediating artefacts. In N. Jackson (Ed.), *Learning to be professional through a higher education e-book* (Ch. A7, pp. 1–17). Guildford, UK: Surrey Centre for Excellence in Professional Training and Education (SCEPTrE). Retrieved from https://www.learningtobeprofessional.pbworks.com

Ewenstein, B., & Whyte, J. (2009). Knowledge practices in design: The role of visual representations as 'epistemic objects'. *Organization Studies, 30*(1), 7–30.

Falconer, I., & Littlejohn, A. (2009). Representing models of practice. In L. Lockyer, S. Bennet, S. Agostinho, & B. Harper (Eds.), *Handbook of research on learning design and learning objects* (pp. 20–40). Hershey, PA: Idea Group.

Goodwin, C. (1994). Professional vision. *American Anthropologist, 96*(3), 606–633.

Goodwin, C. (1997). The blackness of black: Color categories as situated practice. In L. B. Resnick, R. Säljö, C. Pontecorvo, & B. Burge (Eds.), *Discourse, tools and reasoning: Essays on situated cognition* (pp. 111–140). Berlin, Germany: Springer.

Goodyear, P., & Steeples, C. (1998). Creating shareable representations of practice. *Association for Learning Technology Journal, 6*(3), 16–23.

Goodyear, P., & Steeples, C. (1999). Asynchronous multimedia conferencing in continuing professional development: Issues in the representation of practice through user-created videoclips. *Distance Education, 20*(1), 31–48.

Grasseni, C. (Ed.). (2010). *Skilled visions: Between apprenticeship and standards*. Oxford, UK: Berghahn Books.

Greeno, J. G., & Hall, R. P. (1997). Practicing representation: Learning with and about representational forms. *Phi Delta Kappan, 78*, 361–367.

Hall, R., Stevens, R., & Torralba, T. (2002). Disrupting representational infrastructure in conversations across disciplines. *Mind, Culture, and Activity, 9*(3), 179–210.

Jacob, F. (1988). *The statue within: An autobiography*. New York: Basic Books.

Knorr Cetina, K. (1999). *Epistemic cultures: How the sciences make knowledge*. Cambridge, MA: Harvard University Press.

Knorr Cetina, K. (2001). Objectual practice. In T. R. Schatzki, K. Knorr Cetina, & E. V. Savigny (Eds.), *The practice turn in contemporary theory* (pp. 175–188). London: Routledge.

Knorr Cetina, K. (2007). Culture in global knowledge societies: Knowledge cultures and epistemic cultures. *Interdisciplinary Science Reviews, 32*, 361–375.

Koschmann, T. (2003). Plans and situated actions: A retro-review. *Journal of the Learning Sciences, 12*(2), 257–258.

Lampland, M., & Star, S. L. (Eds.). (2009). *Standards and their stories: How quantifying, classifying, and formalizing practices shape everyday life*. London: Cornell University Press.

Latour, B. (1990). Drawing things together. In M. Lynch & S. Woolgar (Eds.), *Representation in scientific practice* (pp. 19–68). Cambridge, MA: MIT Press.

Latour, B., & Woolgar, S. (1979). *Laboratory life: The social construction of scientific facts*. Beverly Hills, CA: Sage.

Lynch, M., & Woolgar, S. (Eds.). (1990). *Representation in scientific practice*. Cambridge, MA: MIT Press.

Malafouris, L. (2013). *How things shape the mind: A theory of material engagement*. Cambridge, MA: MIT Press.

Michael, D. N. (1973). *On learning to plan and planning to learn: The social psychology of changing toward future responsive societal learning*. San Francisco: Jossey-Bass.

Miettinen, R. (2005). Object of activity and individual motivation. *Mind, Culture, and Activity, 12* (1), 52–69.

Miettinen, R., & Virkkunen, J. (2005). Epistemic objects, artefacts and organizational change. *Organization, 12*(3), 437–456.

Mutton, T., Hagger, H., & Burn, K. (2011). Learning to plan, planning to learn: The developing expertise of beginning teachers. *Teachers and Teaching, 17*(4), 399–416. doi:10.1080/13540602.2011.580516.

Nerland, M. (2008). Knowledge cultures and the shaping of work-based learning: The case of computer engineering. *Vocations and Learning, 1*(1), 49–69.

Nersessian, N. J. (2008). *Creating scientific concepts*. Cambridge, MA: MIT Press.

Nicolini, D., Mengis, J., & Swan, J. (2012). Understanding the role of objects in cross-disciplinary collaboration. *Organization Science, 23*(3), 612–629.

Nonaka, I. (2004). The knowledge creating company. In H. Takeuchi & I. Nonaka (Eds.), *Hitotsubashi on knowledge creation* (pp. 29–46). Singapore, Singapore: John Wiley & Sons.

Norman, D. A. (1991). Cognitive artifacts. In J. M. Carroll (Ed.), *Designing interaction* (pp. 17–38). Cambridge, MA: Cambridge University Press.

Rheinberger, H. (1997). *Toward a history of epistemic things: Synthesizing proteins in the test tube*. Stanford, CA: Stanford University Press.

Roth, W.-M., & McGinn, M. K. (1998). Inscriptions: Toward a theory of representing as social practice. *Review of Educational Research, 68*(1), 35–59.

Sarkkinen, J., & Karsten, H. (2005). Verbal and visual representations in task redesign: How different viewpoints enter into information systems design discussions. *Information Systems Journal, 15*(3), 181–211.

Schank, R. C., & Abelson, R. P. (1977). *Scripts, plans, goals, and understanding: An inquiry into human knowledge structures*. Hillsdale, NJ: Lawrence Erlbaum Associates.

Schnotz, W., Baadte, C., Mülle, A., & Rasch, R. (2010). Creative thinking and problem solving with depictive and descriptive representations. In L. Verschaffel, E. Corte, T. d. Jong, & J. Elen (Eds.), *Use of representations in reasoning and problem solving analysis and improvement* (pp. 11–35). London: Routledge.

Schwartz, D. L., Varma, S., & Martin, L. (2008). Dynamic transfer and innovation. In S. Vosniadou (Ed.), *International handbook of research on conceptual change* (pp. 479–508). New York: Routledge.

Sharpe, R., Beetham, H., & Ravenscroft, A. (2004). Active artefacts: Representing our knowledge of learning and teaching. *Educational Developments, 5*(2), 16–21.

Sharrock, W., & Button, G. (2003). Plans and situated action ten years on. *Journal of the Learning Sciences, 12*(2), 259–264.

Shulman, L. S. (2002). Forgive and remember: The challenges and opportunities of learning from experience. In B. Chase, M. Cochran-Smith, L. Darling-Hammond, L. I. W. Fillmore, E. Lee, & L. Shulman (Eds.), *Launching the next generation of new teachers. Symposium proceedings* (pp. 59–66). Santa Cruz, CA: University of California.

Shulman, L. S. (2005). Signature pedagogies in the professions. *Daedalus, 134*(3), 52–59.

Star, S. L. (1989). The structure of ill-structured solutions: Boundary objects and heterogeneous distributed problem solving. In L. Gasser & M. N. Huhns (Eds.), *Distributed artificial intelligence* (Vol. 2, pp. 37–54). Pitman, CA: Morgan Kaufmann.

Star, S. L., & Griesemer, J. R. (1989). Institutional ecology, 'translations' and boundary objects: Amateurs and professionals in Berkeley's museum of vertebrate zoology. *Social Studies of Science, 19*(4), 387–420.

Star, S. L., & Strauss, A. (1999). Layers of silence, arenas of voice: The ecology of visible and invisible work. *Computer Supported Cooperative Work (CSCW), 8*(1), 9–30.

Suchman, L. (1995). Making work visible. *Communications of the ACM, 38*(9), 56–64.

Suchman, L. (2007). *Human-machine reconfigurations: Plans and situated actions* (2nd ed.). Cambridge, MA: Cambridge University Press.

Suchman, L. A. (1988). Representing practice in cognitive science. *Human Studies, 11*(2), 305–325.

Suchman, L. A., & Trigg, R. H. (1991). Understanding practice: Video as a medium for reflection and design. In J. Greenbaum & M. Kyng (Eds.), *Design at work: Cooperative design of computer systems* (pp. 65–89). Hillsdale, NJ: Lawrence Erlbaum Associates.

Szymanski, M. H., & Whalen, J. (Eds.). (2011). *Making work visible: Ethnographically grounded case studies of work practice*. Cambridge, MA: Cambridge University Press.

Vera, A. H., & Simon, H. A. (1993). Situated action: A symbolic interpretation. *Cognitive Science, 17*(1), 7–48.

Verschaffel, L., de Corte, E., de Jong, T., & Elen, J. (Eds.). (2010). *Use of representations in reasoning and problem solving analysis and improvement*. London: Routledge.

Wenger, E. (1998). *Communities of practice: Learning, meaning, and identity*. Cambridge, MA: Cambridge University Press.

Chapter 11
Inscriptions Shaping Mind, Meaning and Action

... it gives them the opportunity to basically put one lesson plan on one A4 sheet of paper. Yeah. So that's one A4 sheet of paper. <...> So they intellectualise and then mentally go through the whole lesson. This is what needs to be prepared. This is the knowledge and the content that we need to implement during class and these are the kind of steps that we need to take in order to teach it in a 45 minute period. (An Education Lecturer explaining a lesson plan created by a preservice teacher, see Fig. 11.1)

How does a piece of paper become an intellectual device for constructing professional knowledge and supporting knowledgeable action? How do inscriptions (constructed by students as a part of their learning or by professionals as a part of their everyday innovative work) allow practitioners to bring together various pieces of knowledge and ways of knowing – into a coherent actionable idea that can support knowledgeable action?

As Roth and McGinn (1998) point out:

... inscriptions, like words, are semiotic objects ontologically independent of their referents. For each case where a relationship exists between an inscription and a natural phenomenon, that relationship was established through a considerable amount of situated, lived work. <...> [S]uch work establishes the rules and conditions by means of which an inscription can be said to represent a natural object or phenomenon. (Roth & McGinn, 1998, p. 41)

Professional work and knowledge inscriptions stand in a strange relationship to one another. Work produces actions, but does not necessarily generate inscriptions or other external representations that stand for, or in some other way represent, this work. And when work does generate inscriptions, how it does so is not well understood. Professionals just do it. In contrast, knowledge that comes into this action becomes far more visible when it acquires a symbolic form, inscribed in external media. Most importantly, such knowledge inscriptions acquire their value in professional work not only for what they *represent and stand for* in an objective decontextualised and disembodied sense but also, and particularly, for how they *can be brought forth and enacted* in knowledgeable action in a subjective

L. Markauskaite, P. Goodyear, *Epistemic Fluency and Professional Education*, Professional and Practice-based Learning 14, DOI 10.1007/978-94-007-4369-4_11

Art Practices	

	Date: Lesson 1 (double lesson)
Unit: Introducing Art Practices	**Year:** 7 Stage 4

Focus: The aim of the lesson is to introduce to the students the Art Practices.

Students will be introduced to the concepts of Art Making, Art Criticism and Art History through images (PPT). Students will investigate a range of different art making conventions and procedures of art along with an exploration of the terminology of the critical and historical interpretations of art through a class activity.

Outcomes Lesson:	**Resources Needed:**
Relationship to the syllabus and UoW:	Teaching resources
4.5, 4.7, 4.10	• Blackboard/whiteboard
	• Data projector
Students will be introduced to the knowledge, understanding and skills that are required in order to make artworks informed by an awareness of practice and the critical and historical studies of art.	Student resources:
	• Visual Art Study Journal
	• Coloured texts
	• A3 sheets of paper for mind-map
	• Head bands for Celebrity Head Activity
	• Handout of PPT

Students Learn About:	**Students Learn to:**
Characteristics of Art Practices such as the different conventions, activities, traditions and customs shaped by different values and beliefs.	Investigate Art Practices and approximate some of the conventions, activities, traditions and customs to develop their own art making practice.
The Art Practices response differs to time and place by a range of interests and issues.	Discuss and write about a range of practices in the visual arts in different times and places in consideration of how practices can be interpreted from different points of view.
Art Practices are comprised of different interpretations by artists, writers, critics, historians and other audiences.	

Sequential Learning Activities:	**Self Reflection:**

1. Acknowledgement of country: '*I would like to acknowledge the traditional owners of the land (or country) on which we stand and pay my respects to their Elders and to the Elders past and present.*'
2. Lesson Introduction.
3. Hand out and explain to students their Visual Art Study Journal. Go through some of the booklets early content, e.g. classroom behaviour, OHS, learning areas for the term, important dates, etc...
4. Explain the purpose of the Visual Art Diary (VAD) and why every student must bring their own VAD to class.
5. In small groups of 4-5 students are to discuss and mind-map the concept of art through student's pre-conceived knowledge and understanding. Investigating questions like:
    a) What is art?
    b) What are the types of art made?
    c) Why do people make art?
    d) Who looks at art?
6. Show PowerPoint Presentation (PPT) on Introduction to Art Practices. (Linking key points raised by the class from the previous activity to images of PPT).
7. Deconstruct the concepts of Art Practices – students are to fill out the Art Practices section in their Art Directory in their Visual Art Study Journal.
    a) *Art Making* is a component of Art Practice relating to both your own practical experiences and recognising the approaches and intentions of artists of the world. What are some artistic practices? Traditional? Modern? Contemporary (technology)?
    b) *Art Criticism* another component that deals with the ways in which different meanings are represented in artworks. The role of the Art critic? Art Critics look at things like the quality of an artwork, how an artist develops and produces art and how the audience might view, understand or appreciate the artwork.
    c) *Art History* is the final component which looks at the significance of artworks and artists in relation to events or actions that have taken place that may have influenced or inspired the artwork. The role of the Art Historian? Art Historians analyse and assist in our understanding of the significance of the artwork and to gain an idea of what the artist intended to do.
8. Class involved in a celebrity heads style activity where selected students are given a definition, concept, artist or artwork that was discussed in PPT and are required to give questions as to find out what they have written on their celebrity head.
9. Small recap (hand out notes from PPT).
10. Set homework.	

Homework:
Students are to complete the 4 questions on Art Practice in their Visual Art Study Journal – *1. What are the 3 components of Art Practices? 2. Name at least 2 artists shown in PPT and describe their artmaking practice. E.g. what type of materials do they use? 3. What is the role of the Art Critic? 4. What is the role of the Art Historian?*
Bring to class a Visual Art Diary for next week's lesson.

Follow Up:
Understanding of Art Practices further emphasised through the Introduction of the Conceptual Framework.

Fig. 11.1 An inscription of a lesson plan (Source: example of student's work produced in the Art Curriculum (Secondary) course)

contextualised and embodied sense.[1] If we take seriously the potential of professionals to engage with innovation and the generation of knowledge that can be shared, then we need to understand how professional knowledge products inscribe and bring forth meanings.

In this chapter, we take the semiotic perspective and explore *how inscriptions mean* what they mean and how they become an integral part of the signs through and with which professionals learn and construct actionable understanding. This semiotic exploration extends our discussion in Chap. 10 of *how inscriptions function*. In combination, these two perspectives provide insights into how the diverse inscriptional tasks that are given to students, through drawing on pragmatic and semiotic features of inscriptional work, provide possibilities for learning, knowing and creating new knowledge – in external media and/or in the mind – that is ready to be woven into knowledgeable action in professional settings.

We acknowledge the diversity of situations and ways in which professionals engage with knowledge work and share practice. In this chapter, we primarily focus on those kinds of professional tasks that relate closely to professional innovation and the construction of shareable professional knowledge products. It is not that we see innovation and inscribing as kinds of knowledge work that stand apart from other professional work. Rather, we focus on innovation and knowing through inscribing because they are increasingly seen as a desirable, perhaps an essential, part of everyday professional work and professional education. In contrast, how professional knowledge is inscribed, or should be inscribed, in order to scaffold learning and allow *actionable meanings* to travel is not widely understood within many professions.

One of the best examples to illustrate this is the teaching profession. Innovative behaviour and sharing of practical knowledge are seen as an essential part of teachers' 'know-how': the need to keep up to date with a changing society, new technologies and a richer understanding of how people learn make this professional skill not only desirable but necessary (Thurlings, Evers, & Vermeulen, 2014). However, finding good ways to represent effective practices and share them beyond one's immediate work environment is seen as one of the most wicked professional challenges (e.g. Falconer & Littlejohn, 2009; Goodyear & Steeples, 1999; Sharpe, Beetham, & Ravenscroft, 2004; and see Chap. 10). Inscriptions of *practical* knowledge and innovation tend to stick to the contexts in which they are created and do not travel easily without further human involvement. What is so distinct about inscriptions of knowledge constructed by professionals when compared with knowledge inscriptions constructed by scientists – which travel much more readily? What kinds of inscriptions tend to be effective for learning, creating and sharing professional knowledge?

---

[1] To be clear, we are using 'objective' here to mean 'removed from the mind and experiences' (of a creator or user of the inscription) and 'subjective' to mean 'dependent on the experiential mental resources/mind' (of the user or creator of the inscription).

If we are interested in understanding learning for innovative knowledgeable work, then we need to understand how shareable knowledge products and their production actually support professional meaning-making – how *meanings are constructed* through inscribing and how inscribed *meanings* are *carried over*, reconstructed and re-enacted across time, settings, situations and people. In short, we need to understand the semiotic qualities of inscriptions through which personal professional understanding is constructed and the qualities which make inscribed knowledge, in technical terms, 'transferable'.

In Sect. 11.1, we look at how knowledge gets inscribed in *scientific* work and discuss semiotic qualities of those inscriptions. This is to get an initial insight into the semiotic practices in productive 'knowledge-building sites' and into inscriptions that tend to be efficient carriers of meanings between sites. Section 11.2 builds on some of our empirical data to present and discuss some typical semiotic qualities of knowledge inscriptions that are constructed in *professional learning* sites. In Sect. 11.3, without overstretching the parallels between science, learning and professional work, we provide some insights into the inscriptions of knowledge that are typically constructed in professional learning and work. We show that the apparent symbolic expression of professional inscriptions hides their deeply nonsymbolic character. Professional knowing is not just, or even mainly, about understanding phenomena in the world: establishing links between those phenomena and one's professional action is crucial. We trace some of the implications of this difference, with respect to inscriptions and situated action.

Understanding the nature of inscriptions, and the relationship between an inscription and an inscribed phenomenon, is not sufficient for understanding how these semiotic qualities of inscriptions bring forth meanings and become enacted in professional sense-making. In Sect. 11.4, we turn to the second part of the question: how inscriptions enable productive kinds of professional thinking, from which meanings emerge, particularly when multiple ways of knowing are involved. To do this, we expand the semiotic perspective. We look specifically at what slices of knowledge and ways of knowing get inscribed in the artefacts produced by students as a part of their work on professionally oriented assessments. We show how these inscribed slices, when put together, provide an intellectual platform for knowledge and knowing that *links* – not only linking multiple ways of knowing but also linking knowledge expressed in artificial memory media with the mind, skill and environment. In Sect. 11.5, we specifically turn to how inscriptions bring forth meanings in professional work. We introduce the notions of projection and blending. In Sect. 11.6, we illustrate how different ways of knowing and kinds of knowledge get combined in professional inscriptions. Drawing on this literature, and our examples, we argue that professional inscriptions, instead of being understood and *constructed* in purely representational terms – as entities that emerge from, and will be brought into action following, a 'represent–retrieve–apply' logic – should be understood and *created* in enactive terms, as entities that support emergent meaning-making and which follow an enactive 'pack–unpack–deploy–repack' logic. In short, productive inscriptions that support knowledgeable action cannot just *stand for* but also have to *bring forth* – and afford the possibilities for –

knowing. In professional work, they often provide scaffolds ('anchors') for blending different kinds of knowledge and ways of knowing.

11.1 How Meanings Get Expressed and Inscribed in Knowledge Production

A brief excursion into the territory of semiotics is unavoidable if we are to understand how professional knowledge gets inscribed and how these inscriptions bring forth meanings. To avoid delving deeply in rather complex semiotic terminology, we introduce the basic vocabulary, following and reinterpreting some semiotic ideas applied and elaborated by others (Oakley, 2007; Rheinberger, 1997).

We use the term 'inscription' to mean an entity (external to the human mind) that has a representational function: texts and graphics on paper, images and marks of transient events produced in professional and everyday activities to represent things, actions, thoughts and other phenomena.

Rheinberger (1997) describes three major connotations of representation in scientific work: 'representations of', 'representations as' and 'realisations of'. They offer a good way of understanding how knowledge gets expressed in inscriptions.

A representation, in its conventional sense, means a symbolic entity that is intentionally linked to another entity that already exists, where the two things can be regarded as similar, when understood within some agreed or conventional system. Such representation involves *representation of*. The symbolic entity *stands in for* the entity it represents.[2] The symbolic entity, and its relation to the entity it represents, can be understood by those who know how to 'read' the representation. For example, such *terms* as 'problem-based learning' and 'Jigsaw technique' are representations of pedagogical strategies, but can be understood as pedagogical strategies only by those who comprehend this professional vocabulary.

If someone says that she saw a *demonstration* of the Jigsaw technique, then such a representation is more than a term that stands in (vicariously) for something else. The demonstration embodies (and expresses or depicts) the technique in a visible or even tangible form. This is *representation as* – a demonstration of, or a plan for, something that exists or can come into existence.

If someone says that she has *created* a new pedagogical strategy, then we have a *realisation of* this thing. Such realisations often take over the meaning of 'representation of'. They often entail production of the real thing (or action) and also production of a perceptible trace that represents and signifies its meaning. For example, the Jigsaw technique would produce records of successful student learning, such as their worksheets inscribed with their problem solutions.

---

[2] Rheinberger (1997) calls this 'vicarship' – the pre-existing entity also exists vicariously in the symbolic entity.

Rheinberger draws a broad parallel between the three kinds of representations and three common moves that scientists make when they produce scientific knowledge. *Representation of* relates closely to the creation of analogies, hypothetical constructs and other ideas that are yet to be tested. *Representation as* involves expression and embodiment of these ideas in models, simulations and other tangible but not yet real forms. *Realisation of* often involves concrete models and other experimental realisations that produce traces. These traces serve as proxies of certain (often intangible) ideas or phenomena and signify their presence. The key products of the scientific knowledge work are, thus, 'traces' through which ideas become realised, materialised and expressed.

As Rheinberger notes, these three connotations of representation in knowledge production – representations of, representation as and realisation of – can also be mapped to established semiotic terms for three kinds of signs: symbols, icons and indexes, respectively. We extend this analogy further, to speak of representations of professional knowledge.

1. *Symbols* are representations defined by meanings. They relate to the phenomena by rules, habits or other conventions and have no perceptual similarity or factual connection. Rules and other conventions provide a signification space in which new questions and meanings can be expressed and articulated. Names given to pedagogical strategies, diseases, chemical elements and mathematical expressions are all symbolic representations.
2. *Icons* represent phenomena through their own qualities. They resemble things or processes to which they refer in a direct sense, regardless of factual links and of interpretive conventions. They represent phenomena with the help of structural commonalities and similarities. Pictures, maps and models are all examples of iconic signs. They show properties of a phenomenon directly or by analogy. Models, plans, sketches and other similar depictions of physical entities and courses of action are examples of iconic representations in professional work. They refer to specific things or actions that may be materially instantiated or enacted in various ways, though they are more or less preconfigured by their direct imitative capacity and by how they are sensed.
3. *Indexes* stand for phenomena by certain real connections, rather than interpretive rules or resemblance. They have a capacity to convey experience. In professional practice, such indexical signs appear in concrete material realisations of knowledge and embodied professional actions, such as accounting records, financial statements and other traces of professional work, instantiated in a variety of artefacts produced within this work.

This basic semiotic vocabulary offers some help in thinking about how meanings get expressed and inscribed in professional work. It can be applied to generate some insights into the nature of inscriptions in professional learning. In short: how do work and learning inscriptions relate to phenomena? To start, let's look at the semiotic nature of the epistemic artefacts produced during the carrying out of professional tasks by students involved in professional learning.

11.2 How Meanings Get Expressed and Inscribed in Professional Learning

We can place the majority of the artefacts produced by students in two broad categories: inscriptions that model and bring forth action and inscriptions that trace and represent action. Roughly, these two groups of artefacts correspond to the iconic and indexical inscriptions, respectively (Table 11.1).[3] The first category of artefacts model future professional actions, thus are *iconic representations of* how work should be done. The second category of inscriptions represents accomplished work, thus are *indexical realisations of* professional work. However, once we look beyond their surface meanings into how these inscriptions are produced, on a fine-grained level, it turns out that most professional inscriptions are instantiated in particular symbolic systems and expressed using professional conventions – thus, they are (also) symbolic artefacts. However, symbolic meanings in epistemic artefacts have a secondary character, since symbolic systems are often used at the level of communication rather than at the level of the generation of meanings. We now extend and illustrate this argument.

Inscriptions of knowledge for action include a range of 'model' artefacts, such as plans for new services, promotion programs, lessons and field trips, and more general planning artefacts, such as packages of materials for teaching or guidelines for clinical practice. In a broad sense, these artefacts could be called *iconic* as they aim to model, sometimes in a rather imitative or literal sense, future situations and actions. Some of them do not have a direct sensory resemblance to real things or actions and often are represented using professional conventions and language. In this respect, they are not conventional icons, but are iconic inscriptions generated using symbolic conventions.

Overall, inscriptions of knowledge for action stretch along a continuum from being more symbolic – such as lesson plans, which are expressed using professional conventions and vocabularies – to being literally iconic, such as lesson resources, activity handouts, questions that should be asked, etc., that can be taken 'off the shelf' and brought directly as they are into a lesson. Iconic–symbolic inscriptions usually depict characteristics of work and configurations of things and actions, rather than mimicking them in a direct sensory way. In this respect they need

---

[3] We should note that in this chapter, we are focussing on the nature of the *semiotic reference*. That is, how the *relationship* between the inscription and the professional phenomenon that the inscription signifies is established: by social conventions (i.e. symbolic reference) or by direct resemblance or form (i.e. iconic reference) or by contiguity (i.e. indexical reference). This should not be confused with the nature of the *sign vehicle* itself which we call inscription (in the semiotic literature, often called 'representation' or '*representament*'). Sign vehicles, in most of our analysed cases, were symbolic, i.e. written and graphical conventions. The difference between the semiotic nature of the sign vehicle and its reference could be illustrated using a simple example: the sign vehicle of the text ':-)' is symbolic as it is composed from symbols, but the semiotic reference is iconic as it signifies a smile by a direct resemblance. By this, we do not say that the nature of sign vehicles is not important to the capacities of inscriptions to bring forth meanings and fulfil their epistemic functions. Indeed, it is. But it is not the focus in this chapter.

Table 11.1 Semiotic nature of common professional inscriptions in professional learning

Semiotic nature	Examples
Iconic–symbolic inscriptions[a] Inscriptions that model and bring forth actions	*Plans and models for innovations in professional work*: development of a community-pharmacist led disease state management service, development of a health promotion program *Guidelines and models for professional work*: nursing clinical practice guidelines, unit and lesson plans, educational trip designs for school students *Tools for professional action*: resource packages for teaching about an artist, language assessment tasks *Recommendations*: recommendations for other professionals, treatment and other action plans for clients
Indexical–symbolic inscriptions[b] Inscriptions that trace and represent actions	*Professional knowledge products*: professional field assessments, reviews, case analyses and reports *Assessments of professional work*: assessments of specific professional skills, field performance assessments, peer assessments *Reflective inscriptions*: professional portfolios, professional diaries, practice logbooks *Analytical reports*: analyses of professional practices and artefacts

[a] The examples are sorted from more symbolic–iconic to purely iconic inscriptions
[b] The examples are sorted from purely indexical to indexical-symbolic inscriptions

interpretation and simultaneously are more generic and remote from immediate action than are traditional iconic inscriptions. However, and most importantly, direct resemblance to a 'real' thing or 'real' action tends to be favoured in professional learning. Even in cases where students learn by creating more abstract symbolic inscriptions, later they are often also re-represented in more literal iconic ways. In many examples that we studied, students not only created abstract plans but also produced further artefacts for action – such as handouts and tasks for lessons, disease monitoring tools, patient education resources, tools for implementing promotion campaigns or sample cases instantiating their plans. Fieldwork analyses and other tasks often included production of recommendations and action plans. These are genuine iconic inscriptions that can be 'copied' and used directly in action. They can be seen as bridges between conceptual designs and material arrangements and actions in the real world.

In contrast, the other group of inscriptional artefacts created by students capture *realisations of* work. These realisations include a variety of things – such as authentic professional field assessments and special records of externship[4]

---

[4] These *externships* are short workplace learning opportunities organised as an integral part of a professional course. The better known *internships* typically involve longer periods of placement. Externships in the pharmacy case involved such things as visiting, and carrying out various tasks in, a local pharmacy for 2–4 h every week. One of the main aims is to provide students with opportunities to link their knowledge and skills from coursework with experiences in real workplace settings. Such externships are often integrated with coursework; for example, students could be assigned specific weekly tasks to carry out during the pharmacy visit – these being discussed in preparatory or debriefing tutorials.

experiences. They are inscribed in a range of ways, such as reports, letters, reflective journals, portfolios and logbooks. However, all these inscriptions have a shared *indexical* character. They are 'traces' of professional work and knowledge. Nevertheless, many indexical artefacts are not 'raw' traces of knowledgeable work, but are 'traces' *generated purposefully to represent* professional work and knowledge. We find examples in such things as peer assessments of professional performance and personal reflections recorded in a learning journal.

As with the iconic inscriptions, indexical inscriptions are also often expressed using symbolic professional conventions. They stretch along a line from being purely indexical – such as authentic professional reports and other inscriptions produced during fieldwork – to being purposefully weaved with, and re-expressed in, classification and signification systems of the profession, such as reflections on practical experiences and professional portfolios that purposefully re-articulate work experiences using professional vocabularies.

The semiotic category that we assigned to each epistemic artefact depicts an overarching semiotic relationship between the way knowledge and professional work is inscribed – that is, how an inscription expresses and brings forth actionable knowledge and depicts knowledgeable action. However, we should note that *production* of many of these inscriptions often weaves together multiple ways of signifying. For example, nursing students embed in their constructed guidelines (i.e. icons) conceptual explanations expressed in the professional vocabulary (i.e. symbols) and images of their own performance that show those skills (i.e. indexes). Preservice teachers similarly express their lesson plans (i.e. icons) using pedagogical terms, connotations from the state syllabuses and other professional conventions (i.e. symbols).

11.3   Unpacking the Semiotic Nature of Professional Knowledge Work

Why does professional knowledge work tend to be so difficult and professional knowledge intuitively so different from scientific knowledge? In order to build the basis for this discussion, it is helpful to go back to Rheinberger's (1997) ideas about scientific representations and start from a brief retrospective insight into how scientific knowledge production gets expressed through external media.

Rheinberger argues that the three forms of representation discussed in Sect. 11.1 (representations of, representations as and realisations of) get enacted in the materiality of knowledge work in laboratories in particular ways. Each form has a distinct character, but there is an important continuum between them.

Laboratory work starts from the initial articulation of the objects of investigation and questions by constructing representations within particular signification systems. However, research questions and other ideas become real in the technical sense only as models (a.k.a. icons). These models are both ideal and material. That is, they are embodied in the physical arrangements of the scientific setting. However, even though they are material, they are constructed using 'material generalities' of the scientific culture; thus, they are already 'purified', made transportable and 'particularly well suited for the production of inscriptions' (Rheinberger, 1997, p. 109).

The production of traceable marks is the key quality of the realisations of such models (a.k.a. indexes). If epistemic things do not naturally produce a traceable mark, scientists introduce their production artificially – using pigments, radioactive markers and other such 'tricks of the trade'. Scientific phenomena that are investigated, in this sense, are usually intentionally expressed as idealised semiotic objects – they can be manipulated, investigated, handled and moved around as symbols, traces or other transportable inscriptions, not as physical things. They can be reproduced, if needed, in different contexts and many times.

11.3.1 Comparing Students' Epistemic Artefacts to Those Produced in Science

If we compare the epistemic artefacts produced by students in professional courses and the model of representational practices in scientific knowledge production outlined above, we see some stark differences.

First, the knowledge production cycle follows a different logic. Students' work on professional tasks rarely starts from a problem that still needs to be formulated and expressed in a particular signification system. Rather, assessment tasks usually come with ready-formulated, explicitly expressed problems. (Task descriptions, assessment criteria and other task details usually provide the initial specification and 'coordinates of signification'.) In this sense, students rarely start by proposing truly new theoretical constructs. Rather, they apply pre-existing, familiar constructs to specific situations and contexts. They *do* need to formulate hypotheses or new ideas – indeed they might need to formulate hundreds of them. But these hypotheses are rarely *theoretically* new; they are *practically* new.

So we see that most of the students' intellectual work focusses on the second and third of Rheinberger's kinds of representation or moves: representation as and realisation of. These two moves can occur in separate tasks or they may be linked to one another. 'Representation as' transfers articulations of the problem into abstract embodiments of potential solutions and expresses them in 'model-like' inscriptions, such as plans, specific strategies of inquiry and other models of potential solutions (i.e. iconic–symbolic inscriptions). 'Realisation of' links actions, often brought forth and supported by an articulated model, to the production of 'traces' of action that are finally expressed in the form of reports and other representations of accomplished work (i.e. indexical–symbolic inscriptions).

Second, the production of the iconic–symbolic artefacts tends to be a valuable outcome of professional work – available for sharing and reuse, at least in a specific community. For example, lesson plans, excursion plans, nursing guidelines, packages of teaching materials and other such knowledge products are commonly shared by students as valuable resources for future work.

We also can speak about the epistemic artefacts that have an iconic character as being more open (i.e. iconic–symbolic) and being more closed (i.e. iconic). In students' and professionals' work, they are usually linked together into 'cascades'. For example, preservice teachers often create a lesson plan and then design specific assessment tasks and other teaching materials to implement it; or they create a specific assessment task to assess children's knowledge, but link it backwards to the syllabus, curriculum outcomes and more abstract representations. The link forwards to the iconic artefacts gives concrete material sense to the ideas and structures that guide practical action.

In contrast, the link backwards to the iconic–symbolic artefacts renders already expressed concrete ideas and structures more open to accommodating variations. This creates opportunities for multiple adaptations. Iconic–symbolic inscriptions, in this sense, are like not fully realised models. They are not yet material and not yet actual. But this openness has to be eliminated and things need to be made 'real' before taking action.

Third, the broader applicability of iconic–symbolic artefacts (which adds to their value) contrasts with the local and contextual character of indexical artefacts – realisations of work – produced by students in professional inquiries and other work-related tasks. These outcomes of professional knowledge work are often *situated* – linked to specific settings and situations – and *individual*, oriented to the development of the student's own knowledge and skills. Thus, they do not have the same kind of 'generic' value and autonomous existence as the results of scientific work produced from 'traces'. One might think that the value of professional work producing inscriptions is limited. However, the main worth of professional inscriptional products created in such practical actions and inquiries resides not in the *objectified knowledge*, but in the *indexical links* that are forged between the problem, situation and solution and the personal skill needed to carry out knowledgeable action.

Overall, we might say that there is an irony in this inverted value of models and traces in professional work. An attribute of good (iconic–symbolic) representations is to be and feel like the real and the concrete. When these models are realised in the form of iconic inscriptions, and later in the form of traces of work, the knowledge has only *local* value. But there is a *general* value in the model that generated those results, rather than in the results themselves. This is quite different from scientific work, where the whole 'knowledge game' focusses on the production of 'traces' and the symbolic outcomes generated from these traces and the models of experimental setups are merely interim products (means to achieve ends).

In this sense, while scientists generate traces and move symbols around, professionals generate and move around 'experimental setups'. This irony is reflected in the difficulties of professional communities finding suitable ways to represent and share professional knowledge, which is embodied and situated, while trying to emulate ways in which scientists share theoretical representations (Eraut, 2009;

Falconer & Littlejohn, 2009; Sharpe et al., 2004). Successful attempts at inventing new ways of sharing professional knowledge usually come without an explicit realisation that professionals share semiotically very different knowledges (i.e. iconic) whose imitative capacity to bring forth meaning comes from direct senses and engagement with the phenomena in physical world.

Fourth, the realisation of any 'model' – be this is a design of a new service, a lesson plan or something else – relocates this model into a set of new spaces, such as administrative structures and other local arrangements, material affordances and constraints and characteristics of an individual client. What was planned has to be adjusted to, and blended with, structures from multiple spaces that exist in the context of action. For example, a plan for the development of a pharmacist-led disease management service is only as good as it can be if it is effectively used in a specific situation: for clients with specific diseases and other characteristics, within a specific material setting, and involving specific practitioners. Knowledge is involved in creating a more abstract model *and* then blending it with other structures and grounding it within a concrete situation in an embodied action.

This fragile link (and tension) between the 'general' and the 'specific' is also reflected in the semiotic duality of inscriptions. While models are meant to be iconic, they are not *quite* iconic, as they have to be flexible enough to accommodate new situations. While there is a strong aspiration to make professional knowledge products symbolic, they are not *quite* symbolic, as they have to be indexically linked to specific contexts, situations and embodied actions. A preservice teacher cannot know what a specific lesson plan means, unless he can imagine or experience how it flows and feels in a class. Symbolic inscriptions alone cannot bring forth meaning unless this meaning has been established by creating and recreating – numerous times – indexical associations between the symbols and experiences.

The production of any epistemic artefact inevitably draws upon all three ways of signifying. The semiotic nature of the final artefact says only where the outcome of this intellectual work is located. However, it would be a mistake to take for granted (and not pay careful attention to) the semiotic qualities of these intellectual products. These products can travel from location to location, but how they travel and with whom (i.e. with or without their producers) depends on their semiotic features.

This semiotic duality of professional epistemic artefacts reflects the dual nature of professional knowledge and knowing: neither purely theoretical nor atheoretical and neither purely representational nor purely performative. The epistemic artefacts in professions – particularly those more 'epistemified' artefacts created by students in professional learning (Chap. 10) – often embody meanings that *link* multiple ideas (i.e. symbols), their expressions in tangible forms (i.e. icons) and performed work (i.e. indexes). It is *in the creation of these links* that most professional knowledge and knowing resides. Moreover – when work crosses multiple domains, ways of knowing and expressing knowledge – these links need to be made across the domains too. So the question arises, within professional work and learning: how do inscriptions fulfil this far less familiar epistemic function of *linking*?

11.4 What Ways of Knowing and Slices of Knowledge Get Inscribed?

> ... there is a continuity between the use of *multiple semiotic fields* in institutional settings such as in work based settings and in everyday settings that are not work related. The flexibility that is made possible by the various ways that *these semiotic fields can be combined* and used to construct meaning is thought to produce this continuity across settings. (Henning, 2004, p. 162, emphasis added)

In the sections above, we looked at inscriptions from an instrumental semiotic perspective: how relationships between the inscribed signs and professional actions in the world are established. In short, what is the semiotic nature of the inscriptions through which professional knowledge gets expressed? However, as we noted above, professional knowledge work involves *locating* professional ways of knowing – whether expressed in inscriptions or not – simultaneously in a set of spaces[5] that constitute the situation, including multiple domains of work and their administrative structures, social, cultural and other affordances and constraints. We call these spaces – which people use to structure their perception, thinking, actions and interactions – 'epistemic spaces'. How do these different ways of knowing and kinds of knowledge get combined and expressed with(in) the professional inscriptions? How do they allow the human mind to go beyond what is present?

To make further progress here, we need to expand the semiotic perspective with an epistemic dimension and look specifically at what slices of knowledge and ways of knowing get inscribed in the artefacts produced by students when they are working on professionally oriented assessments. Also, we need to look at how these inscribed slices, in combination, provide an intellectual platform for knowledge and knowing that links multiple ways of knowing and links knowledge expressed in artificial memory media with human minds, skills and environments.

11.4.1 Example of Clinical Performance Package: Blending Epistemic Spaces

To illustrate how assessment tasks in professional learning locate students' knowledge-generating work in a blend of professional, scientific-scholarly and educational spaces, we will offer an interpretation of a single example task. We will consider the content and structure of an assessment task used in the course 'Introduction to Nursing Practice', which we discussed in Chap. 8. This course, as we pointed out, aims to assist nursing students 'to develop a "toolkit" of fundamental

---

[5] In cognitive studies of semiotics, it is also quite common to call similar interconnected knowledge elements 'networks of knowledge' (Hoffmann & Roth, 2005) or 'mental webs' (Turner, 2014).

Clinical performance package-portfolio: Nursing guidelines

The students compile information surrounding the development of a set of clinical skills. This assignment is the combination of team and individual work. Each student is to be responsible for one section of the package, but they will also need to perform as a team for the development of their visual representation and tutorial presentation. Clinical performance packages to be chosen by each group: 1) Infection control; 2) Health assessment; 3) Manual handling; 4) Body care.

There are five components to the portfolio.

Academic learning space

1. **Explore the current literature** that exists in relation to your clinical performance package topic and discuss the implications for patients and others.

Research space

2. **Seek evidence from three of the following sources**: textbook, medical-health related web sites, scholarly article, research paper or systematic review to construct a set of guidelines with rationales from the supporting literature to ensure best practice in your chosen area. Discuss any discrepancies.

Scholarly practice space   **Nursing practice space**

3. **Using a systematic approach develop a set of digital photographs** (or video clips) of your performance in your chosen area and match each visual with your guidelines.

Continuous professional development space

4. **Provide a written reflection** on the development of this portfolio using the following headings: How well did your members function as a team? What contribution did you make as a team member? What have you learned about your topic that you didn't already know? What does the portfolio overall reflect about your learning? What were the weakest (if any) parts of your work for this assignment? What has been the most meaningful part of the portfolio process? What strategies would you use to improve on your knowledge of the topic in the future?

Community of practice space

Scholarly practice space

5.   **Make a presentation** in a tutorial using the following structure: an introduction on the significance of the clinical performance package in relation to best practice; a visual representation of the critical elements of each clinical skill with rationales; conclusion and recommendations.

Fig. 11.2 An example of an assessment task from a year 1 preregistration nursing course (Source: Course outline)

nursing practice strategies and "craft skills", and one of the assessment tasks asks students to create nursing guidelines for an area of clinical skills (Fig. 11.2).

This task is primarily situated in *nursing practice*. The form and content of the task relate to the clinical skills that students learn during weekly 'laboratory' sessions and include such aspects of nursing practice as infection control, health assessment, manual handling and body care. Students are required to perform and demonstrate the embodied clinical skills in the 'lab' using clinical equipment and medium-fidelity mannequins which are programmed to increase the reality of the learning environment (Component 3).

This professional task is also supplemented by a set of knowledge practices that relate to traditional *academic learning*, such as 'explore current literature' and 'discuss the implications' (Component 1). This learning is further extended with knowledge practices that relate to *continuous professional development*, such as written reflection on the development of the guide, including one's learning experience in a group, personal knowledge and skills (Component 4).

Simultaneously, the task is framed as a *research* task, and students are asked to engage in a range of epistemic and representational practices which would be immediately recognisable in scientific communities: 'seek evidence' and 'discuss discrepancies', for example (Component 2). Students also engage with some broader *scholarly* practices of 'knowledge-building communities' such as constructing 'literary' knowledge artefacts for their professional community (e.g. guidelines) and making presentations (Components 2, 3 and 5).

The task fuses these different epistemic practices and signification systems into one inscriptional task. This fusion, as illustrated above, is visible already on a surface structural level of the task, but it extends downwards to specific aspects of knowledgeability and upwards to the whole epistemic practice.

First, it exists at both the instrumental level of creating a literary artefact that belongs to a blended epistemic space and the level of overall *epistemic practice*. For example, while the students' constructed knowledge artefacts are shared online, this is done in a password-protected, course environment, which in itself is a blend of community of practice, and traditional learning environment. For example, this sharing involves only the best of the final products, and the selection work is done by the teacher rather than by the community of students:

> ... so what I'm going to do at the end of semester, so they all have a good set of guidelines is we're going to pick the best ones across the board and put them up on WebCT [online course environment]. So they then have a set of information that they can keep in their portfolio. (Nursing Lecturer)

Second, the inscriptional work also fuses multiple ways of knowing and aspects of knowledgeability that we described in Chap. 4. For example, the guidelines start from broad 'knowledge about' – exploring the literature on the topic and general implications and (re)presenting them in the guidelines (Component 1). This is conceptual 'know-that'. They then progress to the knowledge of 'best practice' in the area (Component 2), which generally relates to 'know-how' and 'know-why' for problem-solving and configuration of the material environment. It goes further down to knowledge embedded in actions, bodily skills and material regularities – captured in the digital photographs (Component 3), which are primarily the 'know-how' and 'know-for' of somatic, social and material knowing. The process ends with a reflective component, which draws upon and builds experiential 'know-what' and extends across all kinds of knowledge from conceptual knowledge (e.g. 'What have you learnt about your topic'?) down to somatic knowledge

('What contribution did you make as a team member'?). Some quotations from the teacher's comments on the guidelines created by a student nurse illustrate a number of these epistemic moves:

> Yeah, they [students] use their labs. And they put their guidelines, and their different positions and their rationales. So you can go 'ok if I'm going to put the patient in the Sims' position,[6] I need to put a pillow under the head, under the flexed arm'. And there's rationales for each one of those. <...> I actually like it like that [how the student combined the images with the explanations]. I think it makes more relevant.

> Temperature. Ok. See she's backed it with her 3 pieces of literature. <...> So they use their three and then she goes 'ensure the patients will not interfere with the accuracy of the temperature' – research agrees that the oral temperature can be affected by drinking hot or cold blah blah blah and she's given – well she's been able to back it with two. 'If the patient has engaged in any ..., there is a recommended wait period' and she's also backed that up. So that's exactly, pretty well what we wanted. 'Explain the procedure to the patient and if possible obtain the consent'. <...> 'Research agrees...'. A good example. And then she's backed it up with references.

The moves between the actions in the material world, such as 'put a pillow', 'flexed arm', and the moves on the level of professional concepts, such as 'Sims' position', and 'scientific rationales' come together as one blended epistemic action, inscribed in the guidelines. As the teacher commented, such guidelines fuse together laboratory skills, images, scientific justifications and other kinds of knowledge, making it all 'more relevant'.

As students' inscriptional activity involves working within and across the epistemic practices of several communities – as practitioners, as learners and as scholars/researchers – the epistemic artefacts they produce are inscriptions that can be apprehended by simultaneously locating their work at the junction of these spaces. However, this blend of spaces is simultaneously both *less* than each individual knowledge practice and *more* than a collection of knowledge and ways of knowing taken from each of them. Moving backwards and trying to locate the created artefact in a space of one specific epistemic practice would produce an image of a recognisable yet partial and often inauthentic artefact. For example, if one interpreted the nursing students' work as a *research* task, then their reflections on their learning experiences wouldn't make sense as an authentic practice in this space. Similarly, to see it as a task for learning and demonstrating clinical skills would also be hugely incomplete, since the representations of the clinical procedures embodied in the images are based on the group's performance in an *artificial* laboratory setting and on actions that have been carried out just a *few* times. However, this task and the inscriptional artefacts make sense when one locates them in a space of *learning for knowledgeable action* which blends different epistemic practices, ways of knowing and knowledge forms and signification systems together.

---

[6] Sims' position: the patient lies on their side with the knee and thigh drawn up towards the chest. The chest and abdomen are allowed to fall forwards.

The notion of *sign*, as it is used in Peirce's semiotic tradition, offers a handy explanation of how construction of such professional inscriptions helps students to become cognisant and make connections between the external representations, experienced professional phenomena and thought. As Peirce (1992) claims, signs play the central role in human thinking and establishing shared meanings. As he puts it:

> If we seek the light of external facts, the only cases of thought which we can find are of thought in signs. <...> The only thought, then, which can be possibly cognized is thought in signs. But thought which cannot be cognized does not exist. All thought, therefore must necessarily be signs. (Peirce, 1992, p. 24)

A sign is not one homogenous entity, but a set of relationships between three elements: *an object* or phenomenon that is being referred to; *a representation*, such as an inscription; and *meaning* that emerges as a result of one's interpretation of the representation (Fig. 11.3). Each sign emerges from the simultaneous presence and relationships among all three elements; and mutual intelligibility of objects and their representations emerge through social and cultural practices for making connections between the objects and their external representations, negotiating and establishing shared meanings. Inscriptional work, therefore, offers a handy means for engaging with shared signification systems, within which specialised professional knowledge is expressed and through which personal meanings are constructed.

However, the question arises of how diverse forms of knowledge become organised when a person encounters a problem which cannot be neatly located within one particular domain with an established signification system (e.g. during inter-professional work). How do both meanings and symbolic systems become reconciled when the epistemological ground is constituted from kinds of knowledge and ways of knowing that are drawn from different domains of human practice, such as work and learning? As Hoffman and Roth (2005) note, how people organise diverse forms of knowledge into what they call a 'knowledge network' is not well understood.

Fig. 11.3 The semiotic structure of the Peircean sign

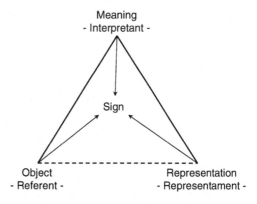

11.4.2   Limitations of the Traditional Semiotic Account with Respect to Innovation in Professional Work

In this respect, the traditional semiotic account is incomplete, in at least two important ways.

First, while it acknowledges the epistemological function of signs, it primarily sees signification systems in their established forms as rather well-defined and stable tools for 'accounting' for the world. It downplays their role as tools for dynamic and flexible generative work that extends beyond what is present in the world. More importantly, it downplays the human symbolic and mental capacity to create new ideas and innovate. As Turner (2014) argues, human capacity for the origination of new ideas is spectacular:

> For us, such extension [of ideas] and innovation is a normal, minute-to-minute feature of thought. (Turner, 2014, pp. 27–28)

Second, the traditional semiotic view – at least as its ultimate goal and 'gold standard' of knowledge (see de Souza, 2005; Hoffmann & Roth, 2005) – maintains quite clear ontological distinctions and mappings between the structure of the object in the world, the representation that stands for it, and its meaning in the mind. From the Peircean perspective, as de Souza (2005) explains, all advanced forms of thought, such as scientific thinking, are fundamentally based on explicit conventions and rule-based representations, within which and through which knowledge is built and expressed.

However, a great deal of professional thinking involves ideas that stretch over time, space, agency, causation and perspectives – ideas which are too complex to be expressed fully in external representations, or thought of, in their entirety, by the human mind on its own. That is, they go beyond human biological capacities for representing and thinking. How does the human mind handle such vast and complex ideas that cannot be thought of without embracing the representational capacities of external symbolic media, objects and other affordances of the environment?

To make further progress on this matter, we need the theoretical constructs of *conceptual integration* and *material blending* (Fauconnier & Turner, 1998, 2003; Hutchins, 2005; Turner, 2014) and *enactive signification* (Malafouris, 2013), which come from the intersection of cognitive linguistics and cognitive anthropology. It turns out that these provide a productive basis for generating insights into how inscriptions and inscriptional work go beyond what is present and bring forth large, far-reaching thoughts, ideas and concepts.[7] We introduce the main theoretical constructs first and then extend them to consider inscriptions.

---

[7] These ideas on conceptual blends have not so far had much impact in education. In addition to our own earlier work (e.g. Kali, Goodyear, & Markauskaite, 2011; Markauskaite & Goodyear, 2009), we note some recent, promising signs of interest (Enyedy, Danish, & DeLiema, 2015).

11.5   Conceptual Integration and Material Blending

Fauconnier and Turner (1998) argue that cognitively modern humans have the ability to entertain simultaneously different, sometimes conflicting, frames of knowledge, and one of the main capacities that enables them (us) to do this is 'conceptual integration' or 'blending' (see also Fauconnier & Turner, 2003; Turner, 2008, 2014). They describe this as follows:

> Conceptual integration – 'blending' – is a general cognitive operation on a par with analogy, recursion, mental modeling, conceptual categorization, and framing. It serves a variety of cognitive purposes. It is dynamic, supple, and active in the moment of thinking. It yields products that frequently become entrenched in conceptual structure and grammar, and it often performs new work on its previously entrenched products as inputs. (Fauconnier & Turner, 1998, p. 133)

Blending is a quite routine mental process and generally does not require much cognitive effort or attention. Blending works on two or more conceptual arrays of already familiar ideas or 'mental spaces'. These provide 'inputs' for new blends. During blending, the structures from several inputs are selectively projected into a separate mental space. This projection carries the chosen elements and relations between them into a new composite space. This blend, through further completion, often develops a new structure that was not provided by the input spaces. This emergent structure can now be further elaborated by performing the necessary mental work within it.

Fauconnier (1997) describes the essence of this process as follows:

> Blending is in principle a simple operation, but in practice gives rise to myriad possibilities. It operates on two Input mental spaces to yield a third space, the *blend*. The blend *inherits partial structure* from the input spaces and *has emergent structure* of its own. <...> This happens in three (interrelated) ways:
>
> *Composition*: Taken together, the projections from the Inputs make new relations available that did not exist in the separate inputs.
> *Completion*: Knowledge of background frames, cognitive and cultural models, allows the composite structure projected into the blend from the Inputs to be viewed as part of a larger self-contained structure in the blend. The pattern in the blend triggered by the inherited structures is 'completed' into the larger, emergent structure.
> *Elaboration*: The structure in the blend can then be elaborated. This is called 'running the blend.' It consists in cognitive work performed within the blend, according to its own emergent logic. (Fauconnier, 1997, pp. 149–151, original emphasis)

To illustrate the point, let's consider a teacher who needs to decide how to teach best clinical practice in a postgraduate nursing course.[8] She says:

> There are various resources about best practice, but they are actually at a very different level to what we need for teaching people to become nurses here in our Master's program. They usually are for people who have background and experience in nursing, and our

---

[8] To make it easier to connect the illustration with the nursing setting that we have been using thus far in this chapter, we have adapted the example here from a quotation we elicited in an earlier study of teaching systems modelling (Markauskaite & Goodyear, 2014).

students come from arts, science and other degrees and, at this stage, they have no clinical experience. They have nothing to hang this on. So we wanted that they actually did it, and connected with it, not just read up on the best way to do it.

Such a decision involves blending (Fig. 11.4). Two input spaces – 'resources for learning best practice for people with a nursing background and experience' and 'a postgraduate student without a nursing background or nursing experience' – are blended together into one composite space. Two frames share some common elements and structures, such as (a) professional field (nursing), (b) taught knowledge (clinical practice), (c) educational level (postgraduate course) and (d) background knowledge and experience (nursing vs. not nursing). They also have some unique elements, such as: (e) anticipated learning outcomes (best practice knowledge).

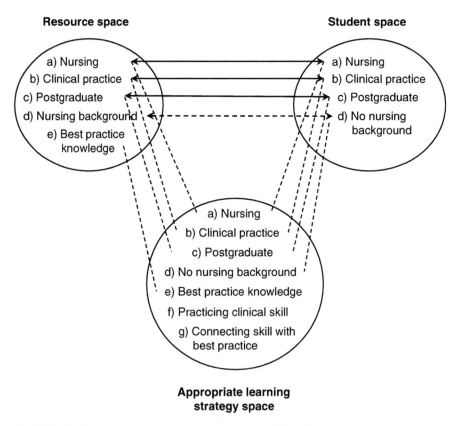

Fig. 11.4 Creating an appropriate learning strategy through blending
Note: Main (shared and not shared structural) elements: (**a**) professional field, (**b**) taught knowledge, (**c**) educational level, (**d**) learner background skill and knowledge and (**e–g**) anticipated learning outcomes. Matching elements are linked with *solid arrows* (**a–c**); non-matching (conflicting) elements are linked with *dashed arrows* (**d**); *dashed lines* show elements projected into the blend (**a–e**)

These selected elements from each space are taken and fused together into a self-contained structure in a blended mental space – 'an appropriate learning approach for teaching best practice for nursing students without nursing experience'. This new self-contained structure in the blend can now be further elaborated. It allows the teacher to anticipate the experience of a student who does not have the background knowledge, skills and experience in nursing, who will use the resources but who will not be able to improve his practice because he has 'nothing to hang this on'. This elaboration results in additional elements in the blended space which allow students to learn the skill informed by best practice: (f) practising clinical skill and (g) connecting skill with best practice. The projection is selective. Many elements from the input spaces are not taken into the blend. For example, specific topics from 'resource space' or students' motives and learning styles or the domain of his earlier experience from 'student space' is not projected into the blended space. Two elements that are in the blend (f and g) were not present in the original input spaces, but emerge from 'running' the blend.

As Fauconnier and Turner (1998) argue, ideas developed in the blend can have an important effect on cognition, which can lead to modifying the initial inputs and in other ways changing the view of the corresponding situations. For example, the teacher's realisation that the traditional learning resources are inappropriate for a non-traditional postgraduate course can lead to restructuring the inputs (e.g. What is an appropriate learning resource for a postgraduate nursing course?) and an overall restructuring of the situation (e.g. How should students who need to learn the background knowledge and skill for nursing, as well as gaining further knowledge of best practice, be taught?).

The critical feature of such blends is that they are tight, manageable and graspable. The complete integration of two inputs with all possible connections would be huge and extremely difficult to imagine, but the blend of two specific spaces selectively projected to the blend is an idea at human scale that could be used to think about vast ideas which are not even present. (And we will argue, when a blend becomes too large and complex to be held and run by the mind alone, inscriptions provide external material–symbolic anchors for scaffolding the blending process).

Blending is one of the key mechanisms enabling innovation and decision-making about future actions. As Turner (2008) argues:

> ... blending is indispensable for many parts of decision and choice. Blending plays a crucial role in running the simulations that result in our sense of possible futures and outcomes that are consequent on different actions. (Turner, 2008, p. 18)

Blending makes it possible to go beyond what is present and immediately available to perception, augmenting the observed or imagined thing with some extra features from another input and seeing what is not there, but what might be (Malafouris, 2013). For example, a teacher who needs to make a decision about whether a learning resource is appropriate 'augments' a situation with an imagined student who uses the resource.

Turner (2014) sums it up as follows, highlighting three characteristic human acts.

Because of blending, we are able to:

- develop new ideas out of old,
- achieve global insight into very diffuse arrays of meaning, in mental webs that arch over time, space, causation and agency,
- and compress diffuse, extended mental webs into compact packages of meaning; we can then manipulate them mentally with greater ease and facility, carry them with us and expand them when we want to think about something we encounter. (Turner, 2014, p. 131).

The central cognitive capacity behind much of the innovative situated work that involves bringing together different kinds of knowledge and ways of knowing is *projection*. It typically involves blending (Fauconnier & Turner, 1998; Malafouris, 2013). As Fauconnier and Turner (1998) put it:

Projection connects frames to specific situations, to related frames, and to conventional scenes. Projection connects related linguistic constructions. It connects one viewpoint to another and sets up new viewpoints partly on the basis of old. (Fauconnier & Turner, 1998, p. 134)

Blending and projection, when compared with the traditional view of knowledge transfer, suggest a rather different mechanism through which knowledge learnt in one situation is brought into play in another. From the traditional perspective, transfer mainly involves 'retrieving' what one already knows and 'applying' it in a new situation. In contrast, from the blending perspective, knowledge transfer involves 'packing' vast ideas into tight conceptual blends that can be carried around and then 'deploying' these compact ideas in new environments by projecting and running new blends (Turner, 2014).

Such blending of thought, however, rarely, if ever, appears an explicit concern in higher education. It is not taught. At best, it might be thought of as a kind of personal skill at which someone is either good or bad.

Much of the literature, particularly from cognitive linguistics, associates blending and projection with mental mechanisms that operate over internal mental structures and cultural models. However, similar mechanisms tend to underpin thinking that runs across internal and external (physical and symbolic) domains (Hutchins, 2005; Malafouris, 2013).

11.5.1 Blending Conceptual and Material Structures

This association of conceptual structure with material structure, as Hutchins (2005) points out, is a general and ancient cognitive phenomenon. For example, consider a clock. Many adults have mental resources to 'read' time from a mechanical clock, but few would have mental resources to tell time without this device. Human use of clocks, dials, slide rules and other similar instruments that rely on stable 'material anchors' (with some dynamic parts) on which cognitive structures are mapped is universal. In such cases, the material device and mental structures are combined into a 'conceptual blend' that performs an operation that would be impossible by the mind alone:

> Thinking processes sometimes involve complex manipulations of conceptual structure. Conceptual structure must be represented in a way that allows some parts of the representation to be manipulated, while other parts remain stable. The complexity of the manipulations of structure can be increased if the stability of the representations can be increased. The stability of the representations is a necessary feature of the reasoning process, but *it is often taken for granted*. The need for representational stability becomes more visible in circumstances where the necessary stability is not present. (Hutchins, 2005, p. 1557, emphasis added)

The material blends are different from the conceptual blends:

> If conceptual elements are mapped onto a material pattern in such a way that the perceived relationships among the material elements are taken as proxies (consciously or unconsciously) for relationships among conceptual elements, then the material pattern is acting as a material anchor. (op. cit., p. 1562)

While conceptual blending *can* be seen as an internal cognitive process, as Hutchins argues, the same kinds of processes operate in situations where one or more of the input spaces to the blend contain material structure that is directly present. Figures 11.5a and 11.5b depict the main difference between the traditional view of conceptual blending and blending through material anchors, respectively. For example, many teachers make decisions about appropriate learning strategies by creating and running such blends in their minds without direct projection to an external material anchor that provides structure for blending. In such situations, none of the material inputs are directly present (i.e. neither the teaching resource nor the student is actually there). Nevertheless, in more complex situations, the teacher could use such external anchors to scaffold thinking and blending. For example, the teacher could have a resource in front of her and project the student directly on this resource. Or the teacher, faced with making complex decisions, could use a checklist to focus on salient features of the resources and students' characteristics and accordingly choose the right 'input elements' for blending.

Malafouris (2013) argues that such material blends are 'material signs' – 'a semiotic conflation and co-habitation through matter that enacts and brings forth the world' (p. 99). Material signs are different from signs that only *symbolise* or represent the meaning. They are *expressive* signs that *bring forth* the meaning:[9]

> ... physical objects become material anchors, thereby enhancing and tightening conceptual blends in a memorable and durable manner. Through this process, the material sign is constituted as a meaningful entity not for what it represents but for what it brings forth: the

---

[9] Malafouris (2013) calls this process 'enactive signification' – 'a process of embodied "conceptual integration" responsible for the co-substantial symbiosis and simultaneous emergence of the signifier and signified that brings forth the material sign' (p. 99).

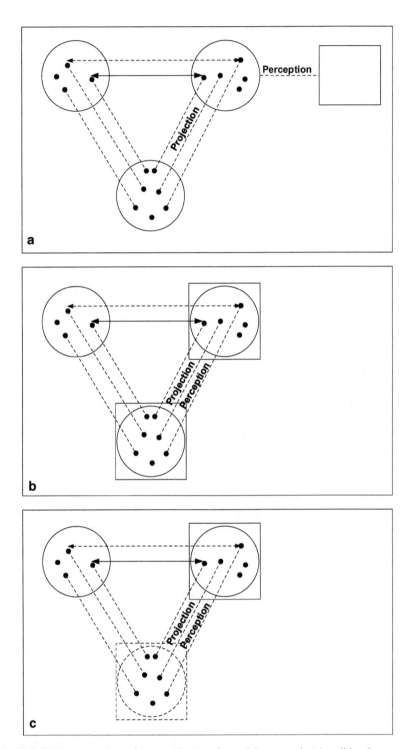

Fig. 11.5 The interpretations of the contribution of material structure in (**a**) traditional conceptual blending (Fauconnier & Turner, 2003), (**b**) blending through material anchors (Hutchins, 2005) and (**c**) blending through inscribing (**a**, **b** images are based on Hutchins, 2005) (By permission of Elsevier B. V.)

Notations: *Circles* represent conceptual spaces and squares material spaces. *Circles* and *squares* drawn with *dashed lines* represent inscriptional–symbolic spaces and structures. Other legends are the same as in Fig. 11.4

possibility of meaningful engagement. What essentially happens in those cases, put in very simple terms, is that the vague structure of a flexible and inherently meaningless conceptual process (e.g., counting), by being integrated via projection with some stable material structure or thing, is transformed into a perceptual or physical process. (Malafouris, 2013, pp. 104–105)

In short, following this logic, inscriptions, as material signs, become meaningful not because one can *read* their meaning, but because one can *engage* meaningfully with otherwise meaningless marks in external media.

The interaction of material structure with mental structure has been illustrated in the anthropological literature using a variety of examples, such as medieval tide computers, Japanese hand calendars, Micronesian navigation systems as well as a sense of weight and learning to count (Hutchins, 2005; Malafouris, 2013). Most of them demonstrate various material blends that draw upon physical things and the human body, such as rulers, sliders, hands and fingers. In such cases, material anchors, which provide an input and material structure for blending, are given and physically present.

But how do people create ideas that far exceed the human biological capacities to be projected in the mind alone, and which extend beyond existing physical reality? For example, how does a trainee teacher plan tomorrow's lesson? While this is under-acknowledged in the literature, in professional work, inscriptions – including inscriptions that are rich in symbols – often serve as 'anchors' for creating such conceptual–material–symbolic blends ('inscriptional blends') that bring forth actionable knowledge and support knowledgeable action. We can call these 'enactive inscriptions'.[10]

To start, consider a checklist for deciding about the appropriateness of a learning resource for a lesson, a learning activity template, criteria for assessing students' performance or other similar prefabricated symbolic tools that teachers use to make instructional decisions. Or consider a simple to-do list that an organised practitioner makes for herself for 'attacking' an important task composed of a vast number of specific steps that need to be done in a particular order to accomplish a task successfully. In such simple blends, conceptual and physical elements are mapped onto a symbolic pattern of the inscription in such a way that the perceived relationships among the symbolic elements are taken as proxies for relationships among the conceptual elements and the entities or actions in the world. In complex and dangerous situations, such as flight control, such to-do lists or checklists become standard inscriptional tools to scaffold blending of the conceptual structure

---

[10] Of course, inscribing also involves 'true' material blending of concepts/meanings with the representational medium. We will not elaborate this point here. However, we should acknowledge that influences of media on cognition in professional knowledge work deserve attention. For example, writing and generating meanings on a computer screen, rather than with pen and paper, changes both the mechanical activity of writing and also the ways in which one generates meanings. (For example, one would struggle to add three comments to explain to oneself a single word in a notebook, but this is easy to do on a computer screen.) That is, by changing media, one changes the blending of meaning and media and, thus, changes enactive engagement with the signs that emerge within this blend. We return to this point in Chap. 16.

(e.g. key aspects of a safe procedure for landing a plane) and material structure (e.g. specific actions checking and preparing the plane). Similar prefabricated symbolic tools are often designed for other practitioners to assist them in making various kinds of complex (yet reasonably standard) decisions. (We return to them later in Chap. 12.) However, creating such inscriptional blends – sometimes partly using prefabricated initial symbolic structures, such as templates, and sometimes from scratch, using symbolic systems of the domain – is one of the central parts of daily innovative and knowledgeable work and learning in many professions. In short, such *inscribing involves enactive projection and blending of meaning, future action and symbolic expression*: it is thinking and projecting actions through mark-making. Figure 11.5c depicts this kind of blending.

Now, consider the rather different situation of a pharmacist who sketches a layout for a new pharmacy. He simultaneously has to consider multiple function-alities of, and multiple aspects of activity in, the future pharmacy, such as security, marketing and selling, formal regulations for dispensary design, dispensing workflows and customer and staff convenience. In more complex blends like this, inscriptions also provide proxies for forming meaningful relationships among different knowledge domains, forms of knowledge and ways of knowing that are brought together in knowledgeable action. Inscribing thus involves *additional blending between epistemic spaces, including blending meanings and symbolic systems for inscribing from these spaces.*

Thinking about important features of enactive inscriptions for knowledgeable action, we can note that they are generated *through* projecting and blending, and – more crucially – the very knowledge that is inscribed is knowledge *for* projection and blending, that is, for enactive engagement. In other words, enactive inscriptions should have the power to be projected to specific situations and bring forth knowledgeable action.

We should note that professionals, including students, create many 'opportunis-tic' conceptual–material–inscriptional blends as a part of routine common-sense intellectual work without conscious attention to blending. But creating generative complex inscriptions is not necessarily such an easy common-sense task, particu-larly when inscriptions need to support cognitively challenging work.

Overall, blending is powerfully expressed in professional inscriptional artefacts. We will illustrate some of their features using the example of a lesson plan.

11.6   An Example: Blending, Projecting and Enacting Through Inscribing a Lesson

Let's return to the lesson plan that we discussed at the start of the chapter (Fig. 11.1) and look at how it blends various spaces and brings forth meanings.

On the broadest level, the plan compactly expresses three main qualities of the conceptual blends. First, it brings together many already known ideas, such as concepts of art practices and pedagogical techniques, and elicits from them a new actionable idea: how to teach a lesson on art practices. Second, it provides a possibility for working with very diffuse arrays of meanings, distributed over time and over a number of epistemic spaces. Third, it compresses these spaces into a relatively small and tight package of meanings that can be manipulated, carried around and expanded to connect the created lesson to the situation encountered when it is taught. The inscription serves as an external anchor both while the idea for the lesson is created (i.e. a lesson plan) and when it is enacted in a classroom (i.e. teaching). The initial inscriptional anchor for choosing inputs for the blend and projecting various spaces into the idea of a lesson, in this case, comes with the template for the lesson plan. That is, some structural elements, like focus, learning outcomes and sequential learning activities, are already in the 'anchor'. However, within this broad structure, many other blends are freely created.

We can illustrate some of the main features of this blend and how it brings forth meanings: (a) compression of the epistemic space; (b) blending of various epistemic spaces; (c) blending within and across symbolic, (d) conceptual and material structures and systems; (e) compression of time; (f) creating inscriptional surrogate situations; and (g) inscribing enactive features for blending the inscription with context and action (Figs. 11.6 and 11.7 show some examples of conceptual projections and blends in the upper and lower parts of the lesson plan, respectively).

(a) The lesson plan tightly *compresses a vast epistemic space* of 'Art Practices' into a small and tight 'lesson space'. Much of this work is done by selectively projecting a small set of concepts from the art practice space and blending them with ideas from other epistemic spaces into the planned activities for the students. Specifically, the broad aim expressed initially as 'Lesson Outcomes' – learning of 'knowledge, understanding and skills that are required in order to make artworks informed by an awareness of practice and the critical and historical studies of arts' – is selectively projected to the lesson's focus and what the students will know and be able to do. This work is done by picking up, from the broad art practice space, specific concepts and specific skills and blending them with the 'pedagogical' space, expressed as 'Focus', and 'students' space expressed as 'Students Learn About' and 'Students Learn To' (see Fig. 11.6). For example, the art practice epistemic space is compressed into three broad art concepts – art making, art criticism and art history – and blending these art concepts with pedagogical techniques, such as demonstration of images and exploration of terminology through other class activities (see 'Focus' in Fig. 11.6). The resulting space, which is still very broad, is further compressed by selecting a small array of concepts and skills that students will learn. For example, art history is projected to four aspects: responses to time, place, interests and issues (see 'Students Learn About' and 'Students Learn To' in Fig. 11.6).

These ideas are carried on into the next step of projecting learning tasks and teaching activities called in the plan 'Sequential Learning Activities' (Fig. 11.7).

(b) Overall, the lesson plan *blends an array of epistemic spaces*. The main epistemic space is art practices, and many concepts and structural elements that

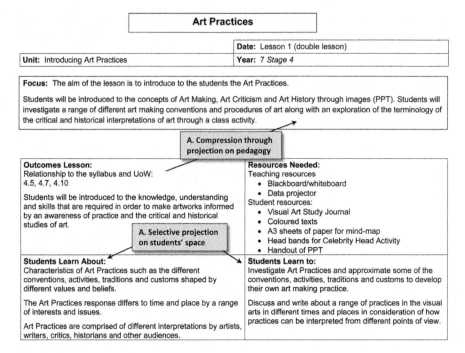

Art Practices

	Date: Lesson 1 (double lesson)
Unit: Introducing Art Practices	**Year:** 7 *Stage 4*

Focus: The aim of the lesson is to introduce to the students the Art Practices.

Students will be introduced to the concepts of Art Making, Art Criticism and Art History through images (PPT). Students will investigate a range of different art making conventions and procedures of art along with an exploration of the terminology of the critical and historical interpretations of art through a class activity.

A. Compression through projection on pedagogy

Outcomes Lesson:	Resources Needed:
Relationship to the syllabus and UoW: 4.5, 4.7, 4.10	Teaching resources • Blackboard/whiteboard • Data projector
Students will be introduced to the knowledge, understanding and skills that are required in order to make artworks informed by an awareness of practice and the critical and historical studies of art.	Student resources: • Visual Art Study Journal • Coloured texts • A3 sheets of paper for mind-map • Head bands for Celebrity Head Activity • Handout of PPT

A. Selective projection on students' space

Students Learn About:	Students Learn to:
Characteristics of Art Practices such as the different conventions, activities, traditions and customs shaped by different values and beliefs.	Investigate Art Practices and approximate some of the conventions, activities, traditions and customs to develop their own art making practice.
The Art Practices response differs to time and place by a range of interests and issues.	Discuss and write about a range of practices in the visual arts in different times and places in consideration of how practices can be interpreted from different points of view.
Art Practices are comprised of different interpretations by artists, writers, critics, historians and other audiences.	

Fig. 11.6 Examples of projections and blends in the lesson plan (upper part of the lesson plan shown in Fig. 11.1)
Note: Examples of projections and blends are marked using capital letters (A, B, etc.) that correspond to features of projections and blends marked by lower case letters (a, b, etc.) in the text

contribute to the blend, such as art making, art history, deconstruction, traditional modern and contemporary art practices, used in the plan come from this
space. The overarching organising structure for sequencing activities in a lesson
comes not from the art practices but from the pedagogical space and follows a
classic pattern: introduction (Activities 1–4), exploration of what students
already know (Activity 5), explanation of new concepts (Activity 6) and
practical activities related to these concepts, for the students to undertake
(Activities 7 and 8). This is followed by a summary of the main points (Activity
9) with follow-up homework (Activity 10). A number of other specific conceptual and structural elements that contribute to the blend also come from the
pedagogical space, such as the use of 'a mind map' (Activity 5) and 'a celebrity
heads style activity' (Activity 8). Some elements that are blended with pedagogical ideas also come from the psychology of learning, such as elicitation of
students' 'preconceived knowledge and understanding' in the mind-mapping
activity (Activity 5). Some other elements that are blended in the lesson plan
come from local cultural practices and institutional arrangements rather than
from disciplinary or professional spaces. An example is the 'Acknowledgement
of country' – referring to a common cultural practice for starting public events

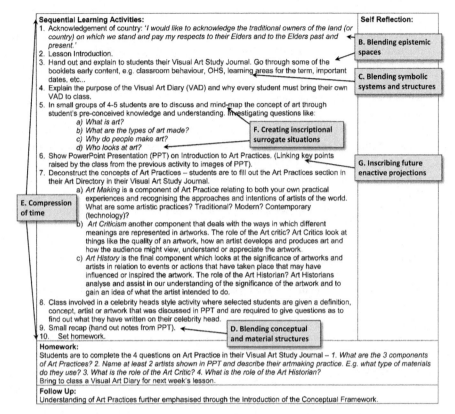

Sequential Learning Activities:

1. Acknowledgement of country: '*I would like to acknowledge the traditional owners of the land (or country) on which we stand and pay my respects to their Elders and to the Elders past and present.*'
2. Lesson Introduction.
3. Hand out and explain to students their Visual Art Study Journal. Go through some of the booklets early content, e.g. classroom behaviour, OHS, learning areas for the term, important dates, etc...
4. Explain the purpose of the Visual Art Diary (VAD) and why every student must bring their own VAD to class.
5. In small groups of 4-5 students are to discuss and mind-map the concept of art through student's pre-conceived knowledge and understanding. Investigating questions like:
   a) What is art?
   b) What are the types of art made?
   c) Why do people make art?
   d) Who looks at art?
6. Show PowerPoint Presentation (PPT) on Introduction to Art Practices. (Linking key points raised by the class from the previous activity to images of PPT).
7. Deconstruct the concepts of Art Practices – students are to fill out the Art Practices section in their Art Directory in their Visual Art Study Journal.
   a) *Art Making* is a component of Art Practice relating to both your own practical experiences and recognising the approaches and intentions of artists of the world. What are some artistic practices? Traditional? Modern? Contemporary (technology)?
   b) *Art Criticism* another component that deals with the ways in which different meanings are represented in artworks. The role of the Art critic? Art Critics look at things like the quality of an artwork, how an artist develops and produces art and how the audience might view, understand or appreciate the artwork.
   c) *Art History* is the final component which looks at the significance of artworks and artists in relation to events or actions that have taken place that may have influenced or inspired the artwork. The role of the Art Historian? Art Historians analyse and assist in our understanding of the significance of the artwork and to gain an idea of what the artist intended to do.
8. Class involved in a celebrity heads style activity where selected students are given a definition, concept, artist or artwork that was discussed in PPT and are required to give questions as to find out what they have written on their celebrity head.
9. Small recap (hand out notes from PPT).
10. Set homework.

Self Reflection:

B. Blending epistemic spaces

C. Blending symbolic systems and structures

F. Creating inscriptional surrogate situations

G. Inscribing future enactive projections

E. Compression of time

D. Blending conceptual and material structures

Homework:
Students are to complete the 4 questions on Art Practice in their Visual Art Study Journal – *1. What are the 3 components of Art Practices? 2. Name at least 2 artists shown in PPT and describe their artmaking practice. E.g. what type of materials do they use? 3. What is the role of the Art Critic? 4. What is the role of the Art Historian?*
Bring to class a Visual Art Diary for next week's lesson.

Follow Up:
Understanding of Art Practices further emphasised through the Introduction of the Conceptual Framework.

Fig. 11.7 Examples of projections and blends in the lesson plan (lower part of the lesson plan shown in Fig. 11.1)
Note: Examples of projections and blends are marked using capital letters (A, B, etc.) that correspond features of projections and blends marked by lower case letters (a, b, etc.) in the text

in Australia (Activity 1). Other examples include occupational health and safety (OHS), term dates (Activity 3) and the state visual art syllabus ('Lesson Outcomes'). All these spaces are fused together by selectively projecting specific elements into the blended lesson space.

(c) In *the inscriptional blend*, many of these elements are compressed by expressing their meanings using concepts and *notational systems* (i.e. *symbols*) that come from the individual spaces that contribute their structural elements to the blend. For example, health and safety procedures are compressed into the tight concept 'OHS', which can be uncompressed and expanded in relevant ways during the lesson. Many specific actions that will be taken during and after the lesson are compressed into the concepts of pedagogical and arts techniques, such as 'mind map', 'deconstruction', 'recap' and 'homework'. Therefore, the lesson plan blends not only conceptual spaces but also notational systems, structures, concepts and other elements from each of the contributing spaces. In this sense, the lesson plan is not only a conceptual or material blend but also a symbolic blend. It comes with its own notational affordances and constraints, for expressing, inscribing and generating meanings within external media – meanings which emerge within the blend. Thus it also comes with expectations for specific kinds of symbolic literacy developed by the teacher who uses the plan.

(d) Almost every activity requires the linking of several kinds of knowledge and ways of knowing. This includes conceptual blending which involves material tools, including symbolic tools inscribed in external media. For example, Activity 7 blends the material structure of the Art Directory in students' Visual Art Study Journals, with pedagogical 'know-how' (how to use the Art Directory for teaching concepts – 'fill out the Art Practices section') and knowledge of content and epistemic practices of the arts ('deconstruct the concepts of Art Practices'). However, other activities involve more unusual conceptual and material blends. For example, Activity 3 fuses OHS requirements and other institutional formalities with the Visual Art Study Journal. That is, institutional arrangements and pedagogical structures are blended not only at the level of conceptual spaces but also at the level of material spaces within which concepts are inscribed.

(e) Symbolic systems and projected material anchors play important roles in the inscriptional blend: not only in compressing ideas but also *in compressing time*. The main principles guiding each activity over the double 90 min lesson period are compacted into a few concepts expressing activities composed of numerous actions: introduction (Activity 2), explanation (Activities 3 and 4), mind map (Activity 5), presentation (Activity 6), deconstruction and filling out the Art Directory (Activity 7), a celebrity heads style activity (Activity 8) and recap (Activity 9). This mix of everyday and specialised words provides a means for expressing lengthy principles and actions in a tight form – one that fits into half page – without the need to lay out steps or even general rules saying what teachers and students should actually do. Each concept simultaneously both *compresses* an activity – into what may be seen as one coherent and well-defined set of actions – and *delineates a much larger space* of possible arrangements. Thus, it can be expanded into a broad set of specific acts when one runs the blend or when one blends it further with specific situations. For example, 'small recap' (Activity 9) can be done in numerous ways, yet the space for actions and arrangements is not infinite – it has to summarise the main points and ideas learnt during the lesson. Further, the material–inscriptional anchor used in this activity ('handout notes from PPT') gives further stabilising structure for projected actions.

(f) However, not everything is (or perhaps can be) compressed into tight concepts, and some aspects of action are delineated by detailing what should be said and done. For example, the mind-mapping activity in Activity 5 provides examples of verbatim probing questions. Also, the deconstruction in Activity 7 is expanded with explanations of the concepts. Such detailed 'linguistic icons', by being blended with compact symbolic expressions, create an inscriptional version of what Andy Clark (2005) called 'surrogate situations' – 'concrete external symbols to support dense looping interactions with a variety of stable external structures that stand in for the absent states of affairs' (p. 233). Such *inscriptional surrogates* make it possible to see how quite dense structures, delineated in the plan, could be projected on, and blended with, specific future situations when the teacher teaches the lesson. That is, they are anchors that help to make future projections of inscriptions onto real-world situations and actions – to enact enactive inscriptions.

(g) The lesson plan is not only the inscription that is constructed by projecting several conceptual spaces into one blended space, it is also the *inscription that literally inscribes further projection*. For example, Activity 6 links knowledge of material tools ('PPT'), knowledge of arts subject matter ('Introduction to Art Practices') and knowledge that will emerge *within action* (i.e. 'key points raised by the class'). In this sense, the lesson plan projects further enactive projection and material blending.

Overall, the plan as inscription of actionable knowledge is, in fact, an unfinished blend. A significant part of actionable knowledge emerges at the intersection of the planned actions with context and embodied skill. As the teacher explained:

> It's not really until they [the student teacher] *actually* have the opportunity to teach it, can I really identify whether the pitch is ok, whether they have delivered it in an *appropriate* manner. And whether, what they set out to do in a 45 minute period is *actually* achievable. Sometimes they grasp too high, put too much in it. And sometimes it's too slow and too low.

This is particularly noticeable in the assessment criteria, where words like 'appropriate', 'variety' and 'range' dominate, and the plan is not only judged as an inscription that stands for what it is; judgements are also made about how it is enacted within a lesson (Fig. 11.8). The context of action and body, thus, provide two additional critical inputs to the final blend of knowledgeable action. In this sense, plans and other inscriptions of actionable knowledge are more complex and open than those which do not have this projective future-oriented intention. As Agre and Chapman (1990) observe:

> Figuring out how a plan relates to your current situation requires a continual interpretive effort. This interpretation is often difficult and can require arbitrary domain knowledge and reasoning abilities. It can also require concrete *actions* such as looking around, asking for help, and manipulating the materials at hand to see how they *relate* to the ones mentioned by the plan. (Agre & Chapman, 1990, p. 29, emphasis added)

Inscriptions, however, are usually weak at supporting fine-tuned perception, projection and blending within embodied action.

From this enactive semiotic perspective, the plan, as with any other cultural inscription, is a part of human constructing and meaning-making activity. How one creates such semiotic inscriptions for action and how one interprets and enacts them rely on certain assumptions about (a) how they relate to the activity and the context in which the inscriptions are used and (b) in what kind of cognitive, reflective and

---

Lesson plan evaluation

Planning and preparation

1. Identified clear and *appropriate* purposes for the lesson

    …

6. Planned *a range of appropriate* assessment strategies to provide feedback
    to students and about their progress
7. Demonstrated an awareness of, and planned *appropriately* for *individual
    differences* and the *varying needs* of students

Teacher–student interaction

1. Planned and implemented *a range* of strategies to motivate and gain
    students' attention and interest

    …

8. *Used voice, gestures, eye contact and movement* to enhance teaching
    effectiveness
9. Developed *a range* of communication strategies, such as questioning,
    exposition and leading discussions, to facilitate student inquiry and
    understanding

Fig. 11.8 An extract from the assessment criteria for evaluating students' lesson plans (emphasis added) (Source: Teaching materials used in Craft Knowledge course)

embodied activity the user will engage while employing these inscriptions in action. As Agre and Chapman (1990) conclude:

> Plan use relies on an unbounded set of assumptions that the plan's maker and user share concerning activity in the world generally and the evolving concrete situation in particular. (loc. cit.)

11.7 Creating Actionable Epistemic Spaces Through Grounding and Blending

The capacity to operate with ideas that overload the biological limits of the human mind – a capacity which is both generative and distributed – can be understood by making a metaphorical move: from seeing the organisation of human thought as a system with a well-defined structure, or a web of fixed, interconnected nodes, to imagining thinking as building and inhabiting a blended space.

We can imagine each classical triad of a sign as three interconnected spaces which are constitutive of each other: a conceptual space for *interpreting*, a physical space for *acting* and a symbolic–notational space for *inscribing*. They broadly

Fig. 11.9 Creating actionable epistemic spaces through blending and inscribing
Notations: *Dashed lines* represent general associations between the spaces; *solid lines* represent projections of selected elements into the blended epistemic space in a specific situation

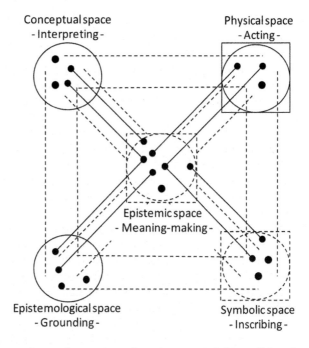

correspond to the object, meaning and representation elements of the traditional sign, respectively (see Fig. 11.3).

These three spaces are usually tightly interconnected with various *epistemological* spaces or grounds – established bundles of ideas through, and with, which people think about knowledge and go about knowing. Examples include disciplines (arts, history, biology, etc.), domains of social activities (culture, politics, economics, etc.) and other perspectives (individual, family, organisation, etc.). People use these bundles of ideas in combinations across various activities for structuring and interpreting situations and events they encounter.[11]

So these four kinds of spaces – conceptual, physical, symbolic and epistemological – are interconnected with each other and operate as a single system (Fig. 11.9). Together they offer a certain field of interpretational possibilities firmly linked to and grounded in physical reality (physical action space) and cultural interpretations (conceptual space), symbolic systems for expression of meanings in discourse and external media (symbolic space) and ways of knowing within various domains (epistemological space).

Each of these four spaces makes certain interpretations, scenarios and outcomes possible and excludes some others. Each of them provides certain affordances and

---

[11] Without regard to their ontology or origin, we call all these different domains 'epistemological spaces'. They are domains of existence that people usually use to structure their perception, thinking and actions. They embody particular ways of knowing that people commonly enact when they make sense of encountered phenomena.

constraints by delineating what kinds of (interpretational, symbolic, physical and epistemological) actions are 'legitimate' or 'feasible' and excluding some others as 'inappropriate' or 'impossible'. In specific situations, these four spaces are combined, making a joint space with specific interpretational possibilities.

The four spaces together delineate *an epistemic space* in which people make sense of encountered phenomena and create knowledge.[12] It is a blended space that combines conceptual, symbolic, physical and other multimodal epistemic affordances for acting and generating meanings.[13]

Each phenomenon – be it a task, a problem or some other entity that demands attention – usually has the potential to be perceived from a range of grounds and, accordingly, located in a range of epistemic spaces. But, in a specific situation and specific moment, these options are reduced to a certain small set – which is humanly manageable – and within which a person makes projections and creates meanings.

Thus, epistemic space is a locally constructed space in which the encountered entity or event is interpreted here and now, in a specific situation. Each entity that demands attention could be located and interpreted in one recognisable epistemic space, in several spaces simultaneously or in a combination of epistemic spaces. In each of these cases, interpretational possibilities, constraints and outcomes will be defined by a specific chosen space, an 'appropriate' intersection of several spaces or a blend of those spaces with new emergent properties.

For example, one may interpret a good behavioural assessment of a child as one that includes the exact diagnosis and suggests the most effective treatment known (i.e. located in a space of *behavioural assessment*), or as one that is well referenced (i.e. located in an *academic space*), or as one that uses locally available services for providing assistance for the child (i.e. located in the *material and social constraints of the world*), or as one that takes into account the parents' willingness to work with the child (i.e. located within *family space*), or as a combination of all or some of these. Some of these spaces are complementary, but some are mutually exclusive.

Epistemic space is primarily a generic *social* construct, not an individual one. It is defined by culture, including the signification systems developed within the culture. (For example, what counts as a professionally written behavioural assessment report is defined by a professional community.) These may be articulated (as in most scientific and professional or other organised communities) or tacit (as in many natural social groupings). So epistemic space generally relates to the notions expressed in artefacts and other inscriptions, rather to the mental resources a person uses to interpret and create those inscriptions. But the two are not independent.

---

[12] Some authors in philosophy and logic also use the term 'epistemic space' (e.g. Chalmers, 2011; Jago, 2009). Our sense of epistemic space has some similarities with what is described there, but the definitions in that literature are diverse and debated and we have not tried to find close alignment with them.

[13] The notion of multimodal affordances was introduced in Chap. 7.

Epistemic space closely relates to the notions of frames and framing used in studies of personal epistemologies (e.g. Elby & Hammer, 2010; Redish, 2004; and see Sect. 7.7). Framing is a *personal* construct:

> ... the set of expectations an individual brings to a social situation, expectations that affect what she notices and how she thinks to act ... a person's generally tacit answer to the question 'What sort of activity is this?' (Elby & Hammer, 2010, p. 413)

It can be seen as an individual response located at the intersection of epistemic spaces in a specific situation. It brings to the situation a person's conceptual, epistemological and other resources that they use to interpret the situation and take actions.[14]

From this viewpoint, framing is a certain personal standpoint through which one construes the situation, blends different structures and constraints and solves the problem. It can be seen as a pattern of activating a certain configuration of mental resources (including knowledge, ways of knowing, beliefs, values, skills, etc.). These are activated in the solving of a problem – engaging with a certain set of tasks in a specific situation. For example, a nurse might see (i.e. frame) a certain problem encountered in nursing practice, such as a patient's complaint about sharp pain, in a variety of ways: as a medical condition that has to be addressed by the nurse himself, as a complex situation beyond the nurse's competence, as an early warning, etc. He might respond accordingly by engaging in a certain set of epistemic practices, such as deciding about and providing a possible clinical treatment, calling a doctor or soothing the patient. Each response will draw on a certain set of mental resources (and skills) including knowledge of medical conditions and clinical care skills, knowledge of the specific medical condition and whom to approach and the skills needed to communicate with a doctor and/or a patient.

If we apply these notions to the assessment tasks in professional courses, we immediately see that most of these tasks are 'multi-space' (and 'multi-frame') tasks that require students to see problems from multiple grounds and to engage in multiple ways of knowing. Consequently, 'epistemic artefacts' constructed by students as inscriptions of their solutions are 'poly-signs'. They are simultaneously construed from a blend of various epistemic spaces that combine elements from diverse epistemological, conceptual, symbolic and physical spaces.

In short, if we see knowledge as certain ways of knowing fundamentally grounded in, and constructed via, our experiences of phenomena in an external world, then the boundaries between symbolic, mental, material, social, embodied, embrained and so on become blurred. Professional epistemic artefacts entangle all of them. However, their meanings, and capacities to support understanding and action, relate to the expectations that a person brings to the situation (i.e. framing) and their personal resourcefulness (to interpret inscriptions and enact).

---

[14] We will return to personal epistemic resourcefulness and framing in Chap. 18.

Why should this matter for professionals? As Marvin Minsky (2006) observed:

> ... self-reflections often fail because one finds it harder to see how one found a solution than it was to solve that problem; this happens when we don't know enough about how our own mental processes work. (Minsky, 2006, p. 274)

The same can be said about inscriptions: professionals create various knowledge inscriptions, but rarely know how they work.

We can end by paraphrasing Malafouris (2013). We are doing this analysis, in part, because we want to show how professionals create meanings through inscribing. Much more important, however, is to show how practitioners could become (more) aware of what they are doing and see how they could learn to do this better. Inscriptions provide scaffolding that enables human perception to become aware of itself and make it visible for others. But *one needs to learn to see inscriptions in this way* (op. cit., p. 239).

References

Agre, P. E., & Chapman, D. (1990). What are plans for? *Robotics and Autonomous Systems, 6*(1–2), 17–34.

Chalmers, D. J. (2011). The nature of epistemic space. In A. Egan & B. Weatherson (Eds.), *Epistemic modality* (pp. 60–107). Oxford, UK: Oxford University Press.

Clark, A. (2005). Beyond the flesh: Some lessons from a mole cricket. *Artificial Life, 11*(1–2), 233–244.

de Souza, C. S. (2005). *The semiotic engineering of human-computer interaction*. Cambridge, MA: MIT Press.

Elby, A., & Hammer, D. (2010). Epistemological resources and framing: A cognitive framework for helping teachers interpret and respond to their students' epistemologies. In L. D. Bendixen & F. C. Feucht (Eds.), *Personal epistemology in the classroom: Theory, research, and implications for practice* (pp. 209–234). Cambridge, UK: Cambridge University Press.

Enyedy, N., Danish, J., & DeLiema, D. (2015). Constructing liminal blends in a collaborative augmented-reality learning environment. *International Journal of Computer-Supported Collaborative Learning, 10*(1), 7–34. doi:10.1007/s11412-015-9207-1.

Eraut, M. (2009). Understanding complex performance through learning trajectories and mediating artefacts. In N. Jackson (Ed.), *Learning to be professional through a higher education e-book* (Ch. A7, pp. 1–17). Guildford, UK: Surrey Centre for Excellence in Professional Training and Education (SCEPTrE). Retrieved from https://www.learningtobeprofessional.pbworks.com

Falconer, I., & Littlejohn, A. (2009). Representing models of practice. In L. Lockyer, S. Bennet, S. Agostinho, & B. Harper (Eds.), *Handbook of research on learning design and learning objects* (pp. 20–40). Hershey, PA: Idea Group.

Fauconnier, G. (1997). *Mappings in thought and language*. Cambridge, UK: Cambridge University Press.

Fauconnier, G., & Turner, M. (1998). Conceptual integration networks. *Cognitive Science: A Multidisciplinary Journal, 22*(2), 133–187.

Fauconnier, G., & Turner, M. (2003). *The way we think: Conceptual blending and the mind's hidden complexities*. New York: Basic Books.

Goodyear, P., & Steeples, C. (1999). Asynchronous multimedia conferencing in continuing professional development: Issues in the representation of practice through user-created videoclips. *Distance Education, 20*(1), 31–48.

Henning, P. H. (2004). Everyday cognition and situated action. In D. H. Jonassen (Ed.), *Handbook of research for educational communications and technology* (2nd ed., pp. 143–168). Mahwah, NJ: Lawrence Erlbaum Associates.

Hoffmann, M. H. G., & Roth, W.M. (2005). What you should know to survive in knowledge societies: On a semiotic understanding of 'knowledge'. *Semiotica, 157*(1/4), 105–142.

Hutchins, E. (2005). Material anchors for conceptual blends. *Journal of Pragmatics, 37*(10), 1555–1577.

Jago, M. (2009). Logical information and epistemic space. *Synthese, 167*, 327–341.

Kali, Y., Goodyear, P., & Markauskaite, L. (2011). Researching design practices and design cognition: Contexts, experiences and pedagogical knowledge-in-pieces. *Learning, Media and Technology, 36*(2), 129–149. doi:10.1080/17439884.2011.553621.

Malafouris, L. (2013). *How things shape the mind: A theory of material engagement*. Cambridge, MA: MIT Press.

Markauskaite, L., & Goodyear, P. (2009). *Designing for complex ICT-based learning: Understanding teacher thinking to help improve educational design*. Paper presented at the ascilite 2009, Auckland, New Zealand.

Markauskaite, L., & Goodyear, P. (2014). Tapping into the mental resources of teachers' working knowledge: Insights into the generative power of intuitive pedagogy. *Learning, Culture and Social Interaction, 3*(4), 237–251. http://dx.doi.org/10.1016/j.lcsi.2014.01.001.

Minsky, M. (2006). *The emotion machine: Commonsense thinking, artificial intelligence, and the future of the human mind*. New York, NY: Simon & Schuster.

Oakley, T. (2007). Attention and semiotics. *Cognitive Semiotics, 1*, 25–45.

Peirce, C. S. (1992). In N. Houser & C. Kloesel (Eds.), *The essential Peirce: Selected philosophical writings (1867–1893)* (Vol. 1). Bloomington, IN: Indina University Press.

Redish, E. F. (2004). *A theoretical framework for physics education research: Modeling student thinking*. Proceedings of the International School of Physics, "Enrico Fermi" Course CLVI, Amsterdam.

Rheinberger, H. (1997). *Toward a history of epistemic things: Synthesizing proteins in the test tube*. Stanford, CA: Stanford University Press.

Roth, W.M., & McGinn, M. K. (1998). Inscriptions: Toward a theory of representing as social practice. *Review of Educational Research, 68*(1), 35–59.

Sharpe, R., Beetham, H., & Ravenscroft, A. (2004). Active artefacts: Representing our knowledge of learning and teaching. *Educational Developments, 5*(2), 16–21.

Tannen, D. (Ed.). (1993). *Framing in discourse*. New York: Oxford University Press.

Thurlings, M., Evers, A. T., & Vermeulen, M. (2014). Toward a model of explaining teachers' innovative behavior: A literature review. *Review of Educational Research, 85*(3), 430–471.

Turner, M. (2008). Frame blending. In R. R. Favretti (Ed.), *Frames, corpora, and knowledge representation* (pp. 13–32). Bologna, Italy: Bononia University Press.

Turner, M. (2014). *The origin of ideas: Blending, creativity and the human spark*. Oxford, UK: Oxford University Press.

Chapter 12
Epistemic Tools, Instruments and Infrastructure in Professional Knowledge Work and Learning

> And when I start talking about LAMS and Moodle and Wikis and they just go 'ohhhh' – and I think that that's another area – that's one of the reasons I pushed the Wiki is for them to overcome some of their technophobia – and actually *think more technological and digital*. I think some of them get that when they go to school where there's lots of Notebooks and they realise that the Notebook is just a resource that they can keep modifying. It's a template for learning. And when then they keep playing with it and save it and keep it. Rather than a lesson plan. If I had a *choice* between writing a lesson plan and doing a Notebook or a LAMS, I'd take the digital one any day. (Education Lecturer)[1]

In Chap. 11, we focussed on inscriptions – and their semiotic features – as epistemic artefacts in professional work and learning. In this chapter, we turn from artefacts to the instrumental ensemble (or epistemic infrastructure) in which the artefacts are produced; from the semiotic features of inscriptions to epistemic features of tools and arrangements within which this inscriptional work is done.

Our aim is to use this *instrumental* perspective to develop a framework for rethinking professional learning as epistemic practice in the hybrid spaces of higher education. Universities are hybrid spaces where diverse histories, and the varied intellectual, social and political agendas of professional communities, disciplinary communities, and society more broadly, coexist. These sites are imbued with distinct sets of physical and conceptual tools, forms of language, social relations and material arrangements conducive to particular kinds of learning and knowing. Such hybrid sites do not and cannot provide students with a full range of authentic

---

[1] *The Learning Activity Management System (LAMS)* is a system for designing and managing collaborative learning activities; *Moodle* is a learning management system used by many educational institutions for developing, managing and delivering online courses; a *Wiki* is a web-based application for collaborative creation of digital online content (e.g. Wikipedia); *Notebook* – SMART Notebook – is an application for creating interactive lessons for teaching with interactive whiteboards and managing lesson content, including storing and sharing lessons in online repositories.

© Springer Science+Business Media Dordrecht 2017
L. Markauskaite, P. Goodyear, *Epistemic Fluency and Professional Education*,
Professional and Practice-based Learning 14, DOI 10.1007/978-94-007-4369-4_12

professional experiences: there are some ways of knowing that only exist in workplace settings. We accept that this is an important challenge, but argue that this is not necessarily an obstacle to preparing fluent, capable graduates who are able to engage productively in diverse work practices. Rather, we suggest that university courses can be sites for some important kinds of epistemic practices involving epistemic fluency, such as mindful problem-solving, everyday creativity and professional innovation. We argue that much of this fluency is grounded in mastering epistemic tools that underpin such work.

In this chapter, we provide a foreground for our focus on physical and mental tools, instrumental ensembles and infrastructures as carriers of professional practices. We start with infrastructure: such an essential part of everyday professional work that it often goes unseen (Sect. 12.1). We move on to look more closely at tools – material and epistemic – and then start to link tools and the ways they are used, drawing on notions about *instrumental genesis* to explicate key tool qualities that are conducive to different kinds of knowledge work (Sect. 12.2). Then, broadly following Goodwin (2005) and Håkanson (2007), we focus on three key elements – tools, infrastructures and work practices – that constitute heterogeneous sites of knowledge work in professions (Sect. 12.3). In Sect. 12.4, we illustrate the key ideas by returning to the example of the school counsellor's behavioural assessment of a child that we used in Chap. 10.

12.1 Epistemic Tools, Infrastructures and Practices

As we have said, the term 'practice' is often used in ways that emphasise its customary, routine character as 'embodied, materially mediated arrays of human activity centrally organized around shared practical understanding' (Schatzki, 2001, p. 2) or as 'the routine, everyday activities of a group of people who share a common interpretative community' (Henning, 2004, p. 143).

Knorr Cetina (2001) reminds us that this focus on recurring habitual performance does not take into account the kinds of creative and constructive behaviour that come into life in nonroutine situations – such behaviour characterises knowledge-centred practices. Actionable knowledge and knowledgeable action are deeply embedded in the relational dynamic between what Knorr Cetina called 'the performance of "packaged" routine procedures and differentiated practice' (p. 187). To enable such work, one needs an *instrumental arrangement* through which knowledge work can articulate itself as more dynamic and fluid epistemic practice. These arrangements include material tools and floating concepts, theories and other conceptual devices that 'within the given standard' maintain connections with 'a wider field of epistemic practices and material cultures' (Rheinberger, 1997, p. 29). In short, tools, ideas and practices, as Goodwin (2005) notes, are among the key interrelated elements that characterise arrangements for such dynamic, joint knowledge work.

12.1.1 Understanding and Encountering Infrastructure

We refer to these arrangements as *epistemic infrastructure*. We use the word 'infrastructure' in the classical sense to refer to:

> The basic physical and organizational structures and facilities (e.g., buildings, roads, and power supplies) needed for the operation of a society or enterprise.[2]

By 'epistemic infrastructure', we point to similar *basic* material, symbolic and organisational structures – including tools, organising ideas and shared arrangements – that underpin and provide the core for the broadly distributed and diverse knowledge practices of a profession. In this chapter, we focus on how material and conceptual tools and practices are brought together in specific tasks and how they link back to a broader infrastructure of the profession. That is, we focus on what might be called *ephemeral microsites* of professional learning that are created when students work on specific tasks and epistemic artefacts.

We need a term like 'infrastructure' to describe instrumental arrangements and epistemic practices in which professionals learn to become professionals – such as in universities. Universities, as places of learning, have several features that make them distinct from other sites of epistemic practice – such as laboratories. First, as we said in Chap. 9, universities are *hybrid places* of professional, educational and scientific work in which these three kinds of practices and arrangements mutually coexist. Second, these learning places are defined by *temporality* – they are places where people come to learn and then leave to work (Glick, 1995). The learning and teaching activities within them have an *ephemeral* and often cyclical nature – which distinguishes them from characteristic activities in some of the sites of knowledge production (such as scientific laboratories) that have been the main focus of empirical research in science and technology studies (STS). There is an *ongoing* quality to 'laboratory life' that contrasts with the staccato and seasonality of educational timetables. Some of what situates educational activity has to be assembled just for that purpose.

Infrastructures are complex and tricky things to analyse, yet are important things to understand and to learn. They evolve gradually and embody much of what could be called 'common sense'; thus, they are rarely completely transparent and can be difficult to articulate (Bowker & Star, 1999; Star & Ruhleder, 1996). Star and Ruhleder (1996) outline a set of qualities that characterise infrastructures – including their reach or scope, links to conventions of practice, invisibility, standards and incremental change – that make them an important entity for, and of, professional knowledge work and innovation.

Infrastructures have a reach or scope beyond a single occasion or a single site. Such infrastructures are often transparent and embedded in professional work arrangements, social structures, material tools and other facilities: in the sense

---

[2] *'infrastructure'*. Oxford English Dictionary. Retrieved June 22, 2015 from http://www.oxforddictionaries.com/us/definition/american_english/infrastructure

that they are not reinvented each time, but can be *brought in* for the task at hand (often invisibly, with little consciousness). This 'taken for grantedness' of professional infrastructures is developed as a part of participation in community practices. However, novices and other outsiders encounter these infrastructures as new and unfamiliar – as objects to be learnt.

Working infrastructures are often unseen in everyday practices, but become visible when they break down, need realignment with other infrastructures or stop functioning for any other reason. New infrastructures do not grow de novo, but often are built upon, and inherit strengths and weaknesses of, the infrastructures that are already in place. They are often 'fixed', 'adjusted', 'plugged into other infrastructures' or 'upgraded' in increments and take on transparency by embodying standards and other agreed conventions. In this sense, professional infrastructures are shaped by, and shape, conventions of the professional community, including conventions that underpin everyday professional knowledge work and innovation.

Infrastructures provide a socio-material basis for shared practices – including knowledge practices – thus, infrastructures are both the *basis for* enabling professional and trans-professional innovation and an *outcome of* such innovation (Edwards, Jackson, Bowker, & Knobel, 2007; Ribes & Finholt, 2009; Star, 1989). Infrastructures that constitute professional practices are constitutively entangled with learning, everyday knowledge work and innovation, yet they are often unarticulated and taken for granted in university learning. A deeper understanding of structures and properties, including intrinsic and extrinsic features of individual tools and their assemblages, and of how students and professionals entangle their epistemic work within those infrastructures, is central for understanding professional learning and epistemic fluency.

12.1.2 Tools

As we said in Chap. 9, an artefact can be considered as a tool by virtue of its mediating role in human activity. Yet making a clear distinction between artefacts and tools proves to be a hard theoretical task (see, e.g. Baber, 2006; Bereiter, 2002b; Clarke & Fujimura, 1992; Rabardel & Beguin, 2005).

As Butler (1912) put it:

> Strictly speaking, nothing is a tool unless during actual use. <. . .> The essence of a tool, therefore, lies in something outside the tool itself. It is not in the head of the hammer, nor in the handle, nor in the combination of the two that the essence of mechanical characteristics exists, but *in the recognition* of its utility and in the forces directed *through it* in virtue of this recognition. (Butler, 2012, p. 24, emphasis added)

Following this definition, tools as a distinct class are distinguished from other artefacts not by their ontological characteristics, but by their function in human activity. Tools extend the capabilities of the person performing the activity. Such capabilities are not restricted to manual skills – tools may also extend cognitive and perceptual skills, for example.

Baber (2006) pointed to another important quality of a tool:

> ... having solved a particular problem by developing a physical device to help us, we then continue to use this device when we next encounter a similar problem. <...> [A] tool *embodies our understanding* of the world; it represents a 'standardised' solution to a given problem and knowledge of how to affect the world in order to achieve that solution. <...> The implication of this statement, as far as ergonomics is concerned, is that far from being merely physical objects, *tools represent both declarative and procedural knowledge* about how we ought to interact with the world and the objects it contains. (Baber, 2006, p. 3, emphasis added)

This statement has at least three implications for learning. First, tools embody professional knowledge. Having a tool to do a task changes the nature of the skills and knowledge needed to perform that task and, thus, changes learning. Second, flexible use of tools that have proved to be effective in the past is not merely a matter of practice but also a matter of learning (some of) the underpinning knowledge. Third, improving professional tools, then, is a very important aspect of professional knowledge building and innovation.

In this part of the discussion, we will return to Vygotsky's (1930) distinction between physical and mental tools – which he called 'technical devices' and 'psychological instruments', respectively (see Sect. 9.2). *Technical devices* are tools used in labour and are directed towards mastery of processes in the natural world. They change the object itself and mediate between the person and the object. A person's *psychological instruments* are 'artificial devices for mastering his own mental process'. They act on the behaviour and thinking process and mediate between oneself and one's mind. Vygotsky argued that when psychological instruments (psychological tools) are included in human activities, they alter the entire structure of mental functioning rather as technical devices (technical tools) alter the manual skills required for skilful performance of physical tasks. He did not claim that all mental activities necessarily require psychological tools, but he noted that psychological tools enhance performance. Further, Vygotsky (1986) claimed that technical and psychological tools are essential for *complex* performance and are necessarily interwoven.

The mediating roles and effects can take a variety of forms: including mediation between *self and object* and *reflective* and *interpersonal* roles (Rabardel & Beguin, 2005; Vygotsky, 1930). Mediation with respect to the *object* includes an *epistemic* dimension, oriented towards getting acquainted with the object and its properties, and *pragmatic* mediation of action, oriented towards transformation and handling. The use of different tools allows one to develop a different understanding of, and relationship to, the object. These epistemic and pragmatic dimensions are usually interrelated, and mediation happens simultaneously. (The classical example is that the use of a hand chisel and the use of a power tool develop very different understandings of the properties of the wood that is being transformed.) *Reflective mediation* allows people to self-manage with the aid of tools. This includes cognitive roles (e.g. use of a colour scheme to help memorise abstract ideas) and metacognitive roles (e.g. use of a plan to monitor one's progress). *Interpersonal mediation* concerns relationships with others and allows coordination of collective activities.

The artefacts that we call 'epistemic tools' are distinguished by their mediating role in mindful symbolic and/or physical work. In our definition, tools – in contrast to other artefacts – are not the main outcome of artefact-oriented work or other human actions; rather they are things with which one performs those actions. To call something an 'epistemic tool' is to refer to the *modality* of the tool in mediating perceptive professional activity. Some of these tools may require significant inter-action and may 'act back' in unpredictable ways. Examples would include an Internet search engine, capable of producing thousands of results (see Orlikowski, 2007), or a complex data analysis instrument, where every step taken depends on earlier outcomes or where a complex tool is being used by several people in a team simultaneously (Derry, Schunn, & Gernsbacher, 2005; Engeström & Middleton, 1996). Nevertheless, the kinds of interactions people have with these tools are generally rather 'settled', and they are directed towards solving a problem, rather than improving the tool.

In educational practices, Vygotsky's distinction between technical and psycho-logical tools is often replaced by a distinction between *physical mediating things* and *symbolic mediating inscriptions* (i.e. written language, representations) or between *physical activity* (skill) and *spoken language* (discourse). That is, when it comes to understanding, the mastery of psychological tools is reduced to mastery of (micro-level) symbols and symbolic systems. This focus overlooks the diverse range of other kinds of tools used in meaning-making and knowledge work. In professional work and disciplines, a range of tools come as 'pre-packaged' generic solutions or semi-generic ways of solving professional problems (e.g. specialised ICT systems, best practices). What we call here epistemic tools are a broad range of tools for constructing understanding.

12.2   Instrumental Genesis: Linking Tool and Game

In order to understand professional infrastructures, we first need to understand their principal elements – mainly tools. Useful insights come from the fields that have been most involved in understanding, designing and improving tools – especially ergonomics and design (de Souza, 2005; Rabardel & Beguin, 2005; and in the learning area; see Ritella & Hakkarainen, 2012).[3] In this section we introduce some ideas from ergonomics about *instrumental genesis*. Our insights about the genera-tive features of different epistemic tools and epistemic games, and how tools and

---

[3] See also other papers in the 2012 special issue of the *International Journal of Computer-Supported Collaborative Learning*. Stahl (2012) provides an overview.

games take on an epistemological unity in specific situations, have been informed by these ideas.

In explaining the idea of instrumental genesis, Rabardel and Beguin (2005) made a distinction between a *tool as an artefact* and a *tool as an instrument*. They think of an artefact as a physical thing, whereas an instrument includes both an artefact and its usage in human activity:

> ... the instrument is a mixed entity born of both the subject and the artefact. (Rabardel & Beguin, 2005, p. 429)

An *instrument* includes two broad intertwined components: an artefact and a scheme. An *artefact component* is constituted of a physical artefact that is used as a tool.[4] A *scheme component* is a behaviour organiser – it both organises past experience and is a resource for future action. So, on this view, an artefact is a physical construct; a scheme is a social *and* psychological construct. An artefact and a scheme are closely related, though this relationship is not 'hardwired' and it allows some independence.

The constructed instrument may be quite ephemeral and constituted in activity by weaving the artefact with relevant action schemes. An example might be a textbook that is used by a teacher to organise classroom activities. The textbook can be used in a variety of ways, such as asking students to read the text and identify contradictions between arguments within it or suggesting to students that they can use the text as a reference in an activity directed towards solving practical problems. An artefact component and a scheme component have different features. The former is mainly intrinsic to the artefact, and the latter is extrinsic.

12.2.1 Tool as Artefact: Intrinsic Features

A set of features intrinsic to the artefact contribute to actions and ways in which the artefact can be used. Rabardel and Beguin (2005) call these features 'modalities of shaping'. Such modalities include several broad categories – such as simple, organised and active shaping – each of which structures the nature of human activity with the artefact in particular ways.

Simple shaping by an artefact steers a user into structuring their activity around a form that is constituted by this artefact. This modality is a common characteristic of manual tools that do not function on their own, such as screwdrivers, whiteboards, forceps or syringes. It is also common in the case of more complex tools that just display certain results, such as thermometers and watches.

Organised shaping by an artefact requires the user to 'fit' his/her actions into a certain procedure that depends on the functioning of the artefact. This modality is

---

[4] We would also want to say that an artefact might be symbolic rather than (or as well as) physical. And what is said here about an artefact might also apply to a *part* of an artefact or a *set* of artefacts.

characteristic of various programmed artefacts. Such tools as video recorders, microwave ovens and blood pressure monitors or database interrogation tools belong to this category.

Active shaping of and by an artefact is a mutual shaping. It requires an artefact to have some 'knowledge' of its user. This knowledge could be fixed and definitive or acquired and updated progressively. In the process of active shaping, the artefact adapts itself to the user and influences the user simultaneously. Intelligent devices for diagnosis, self-adapting learning systems, various expert systems and smart devices (e.g. smartphones) typically have this modality.

12.2.2 Extrinsic Features of Tools: Action Schemes

The second source of activity shaping comes not from the properties intrinsic to the artefact, but from the modes of interaction linked to the artefact, so-called 'utilisation schemes' or 'action schemes'. Rabardel and Beguin (2005) describe them as 'activity's variants that are mobilized by the subject in action' (p. 438). Their key claim is that:

> The introduction of the scheme dimension, along with the artifact dimension, helps one to move from the idea of unilateral activity shaping by the artifact to that of pre-structuring of a broader and far less mechanistic nature since it pertains both to the subject's resources and the characteristics of the artifact. (Rabardel & Beguin, 2005, p. 438).

Drawing on Piaget's ideas, they describe 'schemes' as behaviour organisers that integrate past experience, as frameworks of actions liable to be actively deployed in new situations. *Action schemes* are external to the artefact and are both socially and collectively constructed *and* private to the individual. Accordingly, Rabardel and Beguin identify three levels of schemes:

Usage schemes are specific actions related directly to the artefact, such as handling the control knob. They can be small elementary schemes that cannot be broken into smaller goals and sub-schemes or sets of elementary schemes related to specific characteristics of the artefact.

Instrument-mediated action schemes orient global action and coordinate smaller usage schemes. The coherence among usage schemes is achieved by subordinating them to a global meaning. For example, in order to overtake another car, an experienced driver flexibly coordinates a range of actions: looking ahead and in the mirrors to determine an appropriate moment, indicating an intention to move out, changing gear, etc.

Instrument-mediated collective activity schemes coordinate joint actions and usage schemes in collective work. Such coordination usually takes place (a) when a group shares and works with the same instruments or (b) when individual actions and contributions need to be integrated into a common framework. In such situations, schemes may include specifications of the types of actions, the types of acceptable results and other requirements that guide the conduct of the work.

None of these three kinds of action schemes – whether individual or collective – are developed by people *in complete isolation*.[5] They have a *social dimension*. As Rabardel and Beguin put this:

> Schemes are shared among practitioners of a same skill [*sic*] and among broader social groups. They are 'shared assets' built up through the creations of individuals or groups. They are also the object of more or less formalized transmissions and transfers: information passed on from one user to another; training structured around complex technical systems; various types of users' support (instruction manuals, users' guides and various other supports introduced or not in the artifact itself). (op. cit., p. 441)

12.2.3 Linking Tool and Action Schemes

Action schemes are linked to the *instruments* that provide concrete means for interacting with an entity. They cannot be applied directly, but must be adapted to particular details of a situation. Action schemes are shared, but also have a private dimension. On the individual level, these schemes are grounded in experience and usually enacted in similar situations. In routine expert performance, this generally happens automatically – these constructs are easy to activate and operate with little conscious reflection on the scheme. Nevertheless, they are not hardwired to the tool and can be transformed and adapted to new kinds of situation. Similarly, the properties of artefacts are not necessarily fixed, but can be modified and enriched with new qualities during use.

This view points to important qualities of tools and schemes as means for situated generative work – and less situative resourceful learning – that can be extended towards the future. The social nature, the flexibility and the possibility of 'inscribing' and passing on utilisation schemes, through media and social discourse, give a very special place to the mastering of some kinds of professional tools and related action schemes in higher education. They are things that can be *taught* and *learnt*, and they are tools 'hooked' to professional infrastructure that can be used to create situated knowledge.

Disciplines and professional domains are not just random sets of practices (Fenwick, 2012). They are more than just bundles of concepts and tools (Perkins, 2006). They involve shared practices organised around shared infrastructures, including material and conceptual tools, social arrangements and activity schemes. Describing practices involved in the professional learning of archaeologists, Goodwin (1994) noted:

---

[5] More accurately, let us say that it is only in very unusual circumstances that individuals develop action schemes in isolation. We might call this the 'castaway' case.

> The relevant unit for the analysis of the intersubjectivity at issue here is thus not these individuals as isolated entities but archaeology as a profession, a community of competent practitioners, most of whom have never met each other but nonetheless expect each other to be able to see and categorize the world in ways that are relevant to the work, tools, and artifacts that constitute their profession. (Goodwin, 1994, p. 615)

Perkins (1997), describing epistemic practices involved in a variety of inquiry fields, claimed:

> When investigators know what kinds of characterizations figure in a field, what forms explanation takes, and how to justify conclusions, this helps them to know what to look for and how to go about looking for and verifying it. (Perkins, 1997, p. 50)

Perkins primarily referred to a particular class of conceptual *tools and schemes* – characteristic forms of knowledge and ways of knowledge involved in higher-order thinking – that he called *epistemic forms* and *epistemic games* (see Chaps. 13 and 14). This focus on conceptual tools *may* represent an over-intellectualised picture of professional knowledge, but the general idea is helpful, we believe. These epistemic tools, shared within each profession, help its practitioners build situated professional knowing.

Identifying characteristic tools and characteristic ways of knowing in professions makes it possible to reconcile a major division between:

- The situative view, which primarily sees cognition and expertise as context-sensitive, full of tacit knowledge, nuanced and largely non-transferable
- A view of cognition, higher-order thinking and learning that foregrounds a set of more general productive capabilities that allow a person to adjust their knowledge and capability to new situations

In order to understand the capacities involved in mindful and flexible professional work, we need to understand both aspects of the epistemic infrastructure commonly shared among professionals within the field: shared tools and shared practices – the artefact component and the scheme component, in Rabardel and Beguin's (2005) terms, of epistemic tools.

To summarise, professional fields can be characterised by *shared tools and shared practices*, including epistemic tools and ways of knowing characteristic of professional meaning-making, problem-solving, inquiry and innovation. Both elements – tools with their intrinsic features and shared action schemes – are intertwined. These tools and practices have social and personal components. The social component is partly explicit, inscribed in professional material and symbolic tools, such as tools for crafting legal cases or for conducting medication reviews, and communicated via professional discourse and media – such as handbooks, manuals and learning resources on how to use these tools. The personal component is grounded in personal experiences of using those shared tools in particular situations. This knowledge can be 'meshed' – adapted and used – in other situations, particularly those situations that share similar features and tools.

But this is not to argue that knowledge and capacities for action are inherited in tools and humans as two distinct entities. Rather, we want to reaffirm that the capacity for knowledgeable action is distributed among tools, humans and specific contexts of action. These capacities are both intrinsic to individual elements (humans, tools, etc.) and relational and contingently enacted. The material world of tools and actions has cultural and cognitive consequences, just as sociocultural-cognitive images of the world have material effects (Goodwin, 1994, 2005; Norman, 1991; Säljö, 1995; Scribner, 1997; Suchman, 2007). Nevertheless, tools and infrastructures are more universal than situated practice: professionals move from site to site with their (epistemic) toolbox 'hooked to' their professional (epistemic) infrastructure.

Few, if any, professions have been particularly attentive to the kinds of tools and practices that constitute the core epistemic infrastructure of their fields. In fact they (and we) know very little about what kinds of tools constitute their infrastructures, what their intrinsic features are and what kinds of epistemic actions are involved in fluent performance. So in the rest of this chapter, we aim to establish the ground for some practical 'anthropological work' on professional epistemic infrastructures. We will illustrate some common epistemic tools and their features, drawing on examples that we found in researching professional tasks. We move on, in Chap. 13, to share a taxonomy of characteristic ways of knowing involved in professional work – that is, characteristic epistemic games.

We need to make this part of our argument crystal clear – professional fields are not the same as disciplinary fields, and their epistemic tools and characteristic ways of knowing are different from the disciplinary knowledge that is taught as a part of university courses. Moreover, the professional ways of knowing that are involved in doing specific professional tasks are not the same as the kinds of knowledge specified in professional standards, best practice guidelines or other such 'policy' documents. We are interested in the tools and ways of knowing that are involved in the performative and representational practices that characterise everyday professional innovation and fluent professional work.

12.3 Epistemic Tools and Infrastructures for Professional Work

What are the epistemic tools that people use to produce knowledge and understanding? We can learn something from people who have researched their use in the sciences – in disciplinary fields – but, as we shall point out shortly, careful distinctions need to be made between the production of knowledge in disciplinary and in professional fields.

Schwab (1962) has argued, every *discipline* asks different kinds of questions, collects different kinds of data and formulates knowledge differently. Most importantly, each discipline has particular substantive and syntactic structures. *Substantive structure* refers to a body of concepts that characterises the *nature* of the subject matter and functions as a guide to investigate phenomena. S*yntactic structure* refers to the discipline's *method* or pathway of inquiry which characterises a pattern for the discipline's procedures and describes the ways in which the discipline uses its concepts to attain its knowledge goals. On a similar broad level, Kuhn (1981) defined a 'disciplinary toolbox' using the notions of 'paradigm' or 'disciplinary matrix' – including symbolic generalisations, metaphysical presuppositions and values and exemplars: shared cases of puzzle solution. They argued that within these broad organising structures, people learn and construct cumulative disciplinary knowledge.

More recently, other scholars looked at disciplinary knowledge work at a more fine-grained level and investigated what kind of tools people use when they conduct disciplinary inquiry or solve other disciplinary problems (Collins, 2011; Collins & Ferguson, 1993; Perkins, 1997). Overall, they suggested that disciplinary toolsets are composed from rather diverse tools that are deployed for tackling different challenges. Some of this toolbox tends to be quite universal, such as domain-general strategies, frameworks and epistemic forms and epistemic games (Collins & Ferguson, 1993; Perkins, 1997; Perkins & Salomon, 1989). Some other elements tend to be domain specific, yet broad and overarching, such as discipline-specific conceptions of explanation and causal mechanisms (Russ, Scherr, Hammer, & Mikeska, 2008). Some other tools are content specific, such as disciplinary concepts and theories (Land, Meyer, & Smith, 2008; Meyer & Land, 2006) and theorems and rules of inference that are specific to the domain (Griesemer, 1992).

Accounts of knowledge work often equate it with philosophical and scientific activity: what Griesemer (1992) notes is a 'largely linguistic enterprise' constituted of such elements as a common language, sets of accepted statements and questions within the domain and patterns of reasoning instantiated in answering those questions (pp. 69–70). Some scholars have tried to bring these more idealised conceptions of knowledge work, and its associated toolboxes, back from the cognitive and symbolic domains to material regularities and the social arrangements of knowledge work – invoking the roles of instruments, detectors, devices, models, materials, machines, money, people, etc. (Clarke & Fujimura, 1992; Goodwin, 1994, 1997, 2005; Hutchins, 1995; Knorr Cetina, 1999; Rheinberger, 1997). Goodwin (2005) emphasises two broad kinds of tools – physical tools and ideas – and work practices that constitute heterogeneous sites of knowledge work. Turnbull (2000) similarly identifies two main components in the more mundane practices of building: (a) social methods and strategies and (b) technical devices of the knowledge space. While some studies have investigated the role of tools in practical sense-making and cognition in work settings, and in some learning situations (Bowker & Star, 1999; Engeström & Middleton, 1996; Goodwin, 1994, 1997; Turnbull, 2000), professional knowledge work and particularly learning to be a professional have escaped more detailed analysis of their tools.

Nersessian (2005) underlines the necessity of distinguishing between conceptions of knowledge work that focus on abstract problem-solving and conceptions that acknowledge its emergent, situated quality:

> The structure of an environment provides the constraints and affordances needed in problem solving, including other people, and these cannot be captured in abstract problem representations alone. In traditional cognitive science, problem solving is held to involve formulating in the abstract the plans and goals that will be applied in solving a problem. However … plans and goals develop in the context of actions and are thus *emergent* in the problem situation. Problem solving requires improvisation and appropriation of affordances and constraints in the environment, rather than mentally represented goals and plans specified in advance of action. (Nersessian, 2005, p. 27, original emphasis)

Having established some points of difference between formal discipline-focussed accounts of knowledge work and knowledge work in fields of practice, we can now turn to examine more closely professional epistemic infrastructures.

12.3.1 Elements of Epistemic Infrastructure in Professions

A number of researchers have aimed to describe the sorts of things that are needed to gain *professional* insight or articulate and create new understanding and knowledge. These include such things as tools, templates, maps, codes and standards (Bowker & Star, 1999; Goodwin, 1994; Star & Strauss, 1999; Turnbull, 2000; Weick, 1995).

In reviewing the composition of professional infrastructures in our empirical studies, we found many of the elements could be classified quite simply, using a framework that started with some ideas of Håkanson's. Håkanson (2007) argues that articulation and codification for creating new knowledge involve an interplay among three main elements: *cognitive frames*, *symbolic means* of expression and *technologies* embedded in physical artefacts. He calls these 'theories', 'codes' and 'tools', respectively.

Theory is the main conceptual construct for articulating knowledge. In the broadest sense, theory includes all sorts of conceptual resources – from mental maps to scientific theorems – that are used for making sense and constructing new understanding:

> The concept of practical rules is called theory, when these rules, as principles, are thought at a certain level of generality and when thereby a set of conditions is abstracted that *necessarily* influence their [rules] enactment. (Kant, 1964, p. 127, cited in Roth, 2010, p. 21)

Professional insight and knowledge creation, as many have argued (Bereiter, 1997; Weick, 1995), become possible only in relationship with existing knowledge. Thus, mental models, theories, myths and other similar frames play important roles in articulating or creating new knowledge. Håkanson (2007), Turnbull (2000), Weick (1995), Bowker and Star (1999), Lampland and Star (2009) and others have noted that practical theories do not need to be articulated in order to be used, useful and passed on. However, if they are meant to be stored, or shared beyond local settings, then they need to be codified.

Codes are symbolic, standardised means of expressing knowledge. They can be used for recording, storing and communicating information and for thinking about the practices involved. They involve the use of linguistic systems and conventions of pictorial representation such as common ways of creating graphs, diagrams, pictures and maps and more specialised coding systems, such as mathematics and chemical codes (Håkanson, 2007), standards and classification systems (Bowker & Star, 1999; Lampland & Star, 2009). Suchman (2007) specifically looked at various plans and other artefacts involved in the social ordering of human activity and identified three modes of ordering with associated devices: categorisation (category systems), standardisation (standardised packages, boundary objects) and coordination (templates and plans). Such symbolic means, as Toulmin (1953) and many others have argued, influence the selection of the phenomena that are examined and how they are examined. So they play multiple roles, including epistemic and representational roles (Roth & McGinn, 1998). While many have acknowledged the productivity of natural human capacities to employ 'non-standard' representations for thinking and joint sense-making (diSessa, 2004; Greeno & Hall, 1997), some others have primarily emphasised the importance of standards and other fixed forms while also noting that coding, like theorising, is a local practice and meanings are attached to codes in context-dependent ways:

> ... what is codified for one person or group may be tacit for another and an utterly impenetrable mystery for a third. Thus *context* – temporal, spatial, cultural and social – becomes an important consideration in any discussion of codified knowledge. (Cowan, David, & Foray, 2000, p. 225, original emphasis)

Codes are prerequisites for cumulative knowledge building and learning. Turnbull (2000), drawing on the work of Olson (1994), discusses the role of maps, emphasising several features of codified knowledge that take this form: (a) they serve as theoretical models for considering the unknown, and (b) they provide means for knowledge exploration and coordination:

> The paper world, therefore, did not simply provide a means for accumulating and storing what everyone knew. Rather it was a matter of inventing the conceptual means for coordinating the bits of geographical, biological, mechanical and other forms of knowledge acquired from many sources into an adequate and common frame of reference. This common frame of reference became the theoretical model into which local knowledge was inserted and reorganized. (Olson, 1994, p. 232)

As Turnbull (2000) points out, this is the difference between deliberate and accidental voyages.

Tools, in Håkanson's (2007) account, are various types of man-made *physical* artefacts used to increase the efficiency of the human body, senses and the intellect in human practice. As Håkanson argues, they embody knowledge – including tacit and explicit – and thus can articulate some further dimensions of knowledge that cannot be expressed in symbolic codes. Such tools include a variety of artefacts, from tools for handling materials, measurement instruments and in vitro and *in silica* models used in scientific laboratories (Clarke & Fujimura, 1992) to knives, skimmers and hammers used in manual work (Keller & Keller, 1996). They shape cognition and knowing, like theories and codes do.

In short, knowledge is articulated in a variety of forms – theories (conceptual tools), codes (symbolic tools) and physical tools. All these tools – entangled in different sorts of discursive, material and symbolic expressions – have *epistemic modality*. In short, they are (can be) epistemic tools and have affordances that enable sense-making and the production of new knowledge.

de Souza (2005) can help us pin down the notion of 'epistemic tools' more clearly. de Souza distinguishes two types of tools and calls them 'intellectual artefacts' and 'epistemic tools'. Intellectual artefacts are artefacts that are designed for certain abstract and mental purposes, like logic truth tables, safety measures or a piece of software. Intellectual artefacts encode a particular understanding of a problem situation and a particular set of solutions for the perceived problem. Many intellectual artefacts are used as tools in professional work; however, as de Souza notes, users still often need to make strategic choices about how to use intellectual artefacts. He introduces a second kind of artefact which he calls an 'epistemic tool' – something that can leverage the use of intellectual artefacts:

> An epistemic tool is one that is not used to yield directly the answer to the problem, but to increase the problem-solver's understanding of the problem itself and the implications it brings about. (de Souza, 2005, p. 33)

For de Souza, epistemic tools are metacommunication artefacts. They are linked to specific artefacts. They convey how to operate the artefact and also relevant problem-solving strategies and tactical and strategic choices: not only operational aspects of the artefact but also strategic aspects.

We take a slightly different view on epistemic tools. Rather than seeing them as a *subset* of tools (cf. metacommunication artefacts), *we see the epistemic as a potential modality of all tools* – something that increases the user's understanding of the problem and guides them in taking knowledgeable action. Some of those tools can be what de Souza called intellectual artefacts – we simply acknowledge that *all tools have an epistemic modality* – and some are *deeply epistemic* (e.g. theories, problem-solving heuristics about how to make strategic choices).

12.3.2 Innovation, Tool-Making and Tool Use

Studies of significant human accomplishments – the building of the Gothic cathedrals, discovering new lands, creating new classifications of species, curing diseases and even breaking world records in sport – indicate that much of what has been accomplished has not been the result of changes in innate human mental or physical capacities, but has been made possible through the creation of better tools for this kind of work, such as templates for cutting stones; maps; systems for collecting, cataloguing and note-taking; better skis; or track shoes:

Today's alpine skiers are better able to ski (e.g., faster down steeper hills) than their predecessors not, at least not to any considerable extent, because they are better skiers, but because they profit from the accumulated knowledge embodied in the skis they use. Analogously, today's cars are better than yesterday's not because modern engineers are smarter or more creative than their predecessors, but because they can draw on more knowledge and experience of car making, as articulated and codified in textbooks and engineering manuals and as embodied in components and production equipment. (Håkanson, 2007, p. 71)

As Håkanson (2007) claims, the interaction between theory, codes and physical tools is essential for successful innovation and development, and all three need to be developed simultaneously.[6] The efficient use of tools – be they newly developed theory, codes or physical tools – involves skill that requires experiential and often implicit learning. It involves implicit learning because the skills entail kinds of knowledge that are not (easily) explicable – including complex somatic skills, the knowledge embedded in social interaction and combinations of the two.[7]

These observations are not new. Seymour (1966), comparing activities of experienced and inexperienced workers in repetitive tasks, observed similar qualities of skilled tool use – the smoothness of movement, rhythmic performance, use of sensory data and synergy of responses in relation to the organised whole, rather than individual attributes, of the work:

First, the experienced worker usually employs 'smoother' and more consistent movements, indicating that the patterns of reaction have been more thoroughly organised spatially. Secondly, the experienced worker operates more rhythmically, indicating that a higher degree of temporal organization has been achieved. Thirdly, the experienced worker makes better use of the sensory data. <. . .> Fourthly, the experienced worker reacts in an integrated way to groups of sensory signals, and makes organized grouped responses to them. (Seymour, 1966, pp. 35–36)

Most interestingly, Seymour was struck by the apparent complexity of the manual meat-processing work in a butchery and extremely surprised when one of the foremen told him that there were only six ways of using knives in butchery. As Seymour observed, knowledge of basic knife movements and angles makes learning a simpler and more efficient task:

The careful and detailed teaching of the safe and well-tried methods of the experienced worker contribute considerably to the avoidance of accidents with the knife which might result from haphazard efforts of the untaught learner. (op. cit., p. 188)

However, as Baber (2006) notes:

. . . it is also apparent that some flexibility needs to be incorporated into these movements, e.g., gristle is not distributed evenly across all pieces of meat and so some modification and correction needs to be made when this is present. In other words, a skilled user of a tool is likely to employ a set of actions that are similar across situations, and to be able to modify these actions in the light of changing circumstances. (Baber, 2006, p. 12)

---

[6] Håkanson (2007) argues that American technological industries succeed in theory, but isolate theory from tools, and thus slow down the rate of technological learning.

[7] See also Harry Collins (2010) on kinds of tacit knowledge in Chap. 4.

There is close coupling between tool, skill and tool innovation. As Ingold (2011) argues:

> ... the ways in which tools are to be used do not come pre-packaged with the tools themselves. But neither are the uses of tools simply invented on the spot, without regard to any history of past practice. Rather, they are revealed to practitioners when, faced with a recurrent task in which the same devices were known previously to have been employed, they are perceived to afford the wherewithal for its accomplishment. Thus the functions of tools, like the meanings of stories, are recognised through the alignment of present circumstances with the conjunctions of the past. Once recognised, these functions provide the practitioner with the means to keep on going. (Ingold, 2011, p. 57)

Skill is foundational for revealing those properties of the tool that make tool-making possible:

> ... while hands make gestures, gestures also make hands. And of course they make tools too. It follows that gesture is foundational to both toolmaking and tool use. (op. cit., p. 58)

Ingold's concern here was the manual tools and craft worker's bodily skills, but similar things could be said about the 'gestures of mind' and 'skills of mind' (and discourse) involved in the use of intellectual/epistemic tools. The mind makes epistemic moves, but also the 'movement' of the mind makes the mind. The epistemic functions of tools are not constructed de novo, but are recognised through the alignment of present situations with those of the past. We know much less about epistemic tools than physical tools. Or, more precisely, we know much less about how the conceptual, symbolic and physical are coupled with each other in knowledgeable (epistemic) actions. The skill involved in the use of epistemic tools is foundational to knowledgeable performance. But this is not a skill that involves deploying the same tool (e.g. theory, heuristic or certain kind of symbolic convention) again and again, but rather *recognising* what tools might be right and, most importantly, tweaking them (adjusting or reconfiguring them) to make them right for the current or next job.

Many kinds of tools are taken for granted as 'given'. In large areas of professional practice, the skills involved in conscious and knowledgeable tweaking of tools – let alone creating new tools for new situations – are not given serious consideration; nor do they have much of a place in the corresponding areas of professional education curricula.[8]

Further, 'tweaking' tends to be foundational not only for fluent performance but also for innovation. Bereiter (2002a, 2002b), following Whitehead (1925/1948), argued that, since the nineteenth century, there have been very few radical inventions and the greatest practical achievements have been the result of 'disciplined progress' (see Sect. 3.4).

Whitehead and Bereiter primarily referred to those kinds of innovation that are made possible through formal methods of research and development:

---

[8] This obliviousness to tool shaping and tool invention is not universal across the professions. For example, some areas of engineering and IT see this aspect of professional work as core business.

... by which abstract knowledge can be connected with technology, and of the boundless possibilities of technological advance. (Whitehead, 1925/1948, p. 92, cited in Bereiter, 2002b, p. 71)

However, innovation that requires the creation of new tools, and even new infrastructures, tends to be central to common tasks in professional work – such as interprofessional cooperation and organisational change and learning (Miettinen & Virkkunen, 2005) – which generally are considered as demanding tasks.

There is substantial evidence warning about potential difficulties involved in learning to tweak tools and weave them into skilful performance. First, observations from the neuropsychological field suggest that semantic knowledge about tools is relatively independent from the development of skills (Johnson-Frey, 2004; Menz, Blangero, Kunze, & Binkofski, 2010). The understanding of tool functions can be relatively easy and can sometimes be grasped in a single observation. Understanding the tool is considered to be an essential step in mastering a new tool (Menz et al., 2010). In contrast, competent performance involving the use of complex tools arises from a network of interactive neural systems that cut across a range of processes of the human brain and body – cognitive, motor, social and perceptual processes – and often requires practice and time to develop (Johnson-Frey, 2004). Many people, particularly younger ones, are good 'social learners' – able to grasp and master various tools, including those that involve significant cognitive skill, such as utilising affordances of the environment, just by observing and imitating.

Second, the capacities involved in creating, and learning to create, new tools tend to be distinct from the *use* of the tool. While tool-making is generally perceived as one of the main distinguishing skills of the human species,[9] studies have shown striking evidence that young children encounter substantial difficulties when they are asked to create even a simple new tool, such as a hook to retrieve a bucket from a tube (Beck, Apperly, Chappell, Guthrie, & Cutting, 2011; Cutting, Apperly, & Beck, 2011). Beck et al. (2011) make a useful distinction between two aspects of tool-making: 'tool innovation' – which involves imagining a new tool suitable for solving a problem – and 'tool manufacture', which involves transformation of materials and production of the tool. The main challenge appears not to be the manufacturing – most children tend to do this quite easily once they are shown how – but coming up with an innovative solution.

It is difficult to say whether children's challenges with respect to inventing tools are a consequence of how the brain works or a matter of cultural development. (Our culture generally discourages 'reinventing the wheel' and so may not provide enough opportunities to learn to create and improve tools in conscious and skilful ways.) The research evidence does not tell us if these challenges are specific to children or also apply to adults. In any event, 'tool innovation' is an important

---

[9] A few nonhuman primates make simple tools; creation and use of complex tools, and sequences of tools, is (as yet) only found in humans.

aspect of contemporary knowledgeable work, but is too often overlooked in professional education.

In short, it tends to be easy to do the job when you have the right tool and know how to use it. It is easy to learn to use a tool once somebody teaches you. It is hard to create a new tool, yet new tools are essential.

What kinds of tools constitute epistemic infrastructure for professional work? In this final section, we offer an extended example, drawing on the school counsellor's child behavioural assessment case that we introduced in Chap. 10.

In Chap. 13 we outline two new taxonomies, informed by our empirical studies. The first of these covers epistemic tools and the second epistemic infrastructures.

12.4   An Example: Epistemic Infrastructure for Child Behavioural Assessment

To get a sense of a range of tools involved in professional work and learning, we will return to the example of Jane – conducting an assessment of a child (Ron) with behavioural difficulties.

What kinds of tools does Jane use in accomplishing her task? Jane's assessment work is guided by the objective of 'fully assessing this child' – aiming to produce a 'full descriptive report', through which she needs to present and explain her results and offer conclusions, recommendations and a planned intervention, yet there must be 'no overtesting'. Jane accordingly aligns her actions and decisions using three epistemic tools.[10] First, for 'fully assessing the child', she employs *Sattler's 'four pillars' framework* – which guides her to consider using four modes of assessment: examination of records, observation, interviewing and formal testing (Sattler & Hoge, 2006). Second, for producing 'a full descriptive report', she uses the structure of the case study report for psychological testing that guides what should be achieved. The *form of the behavioural assessment report* guides Jane with respect to how the assessment process and results should be reported, including findings, recommended professional referrals, conclusions, other recommendations and specific interventions (Fig. 10.2). It also guides her to examine and describe the context in which the assessment was conducted, give the reasons for the referral, describe Ron's background and take note of Ron's behaviour during the assessment process. A clear message of 'no overtesting' implies that a test battery approach should not be used. Rather, as the third device, Jane uses a *hypothesis-testing strategy* that guides her to choose the most relevant assessments.

The three epistemic devices provide the general structure for Jane's inquiry process and the final outcome. Jane's assessment starts from Ron's *referral*, which

---

[10] The tools being used here have qualities of what Nersessian (2005, 2006) refers to as devices. A device provides a site for instantiating and generating solutions. We explain and explore this in more detail in Chap. 13.

provides her with initial information about Ron and about the reasons for the behavioural assessment. Then, Jane proceeds with examining Ron's *records*; noting, from two previous assessments, information relevant to her task; and formulating her initial hypothesis. Her choices of assessment modes and tools are guided by the initial hypothesis and by Sattler's three other pillars. Two classroom *observations* conducted over a 2-week period, and observation of Ron's behaviour during assessments, provide her with further information to record about Ron's behaviour. An *interview* with Ron's mother, and the Child Behaviour Checklist (CBCL) she completed, and an *interview* with Ron's teacher, and the corresponding completed Teacher Report Form (TRF), allow Jane to obtain yet more information about Ron's behaviour at home and school. Jane's initial hypothesis that Ron's poor academic performance may be caused by low level cognitive functioning leads her to deploy a set of other *assessment instruments* for formal testing of Ron's cognitive ability. Her initial choice is an Intelligence Scale for Children (WISC-IV). After getting 'borderline' results, she refines her hypothesis and uses an Individual Achievement Test (WIAT-II) to assess Ron's academic achievements. Low results indicate that tools for investigating Ron's adaptive behaviour may clarify the issue, but due to time constraints, she uses data collected from the teacher and Ron's mother to make decisions about Ron's situation and about suitable intervention strategies. Jane's case study report presents key details and assessment results, recommendations, guidelines for intervention and justifications.

The instrumental ensemble in which Jane conducts her knowledge work is depicted in Fig. 12.1. It spans across, and fuses, three broad professional knowledge spaces – instrumental, propositional and social – with situated knowledge about Ron's school, class, teacher, family, child, etc., that Jane finds within this particular place and case.

Jane's inquiry is guided by the combination of three broad-based devices: Sattler's four pillars, a hypothesis-testing strategy and behavioural assessment report. These tools constitute the core of the instrumental ensemble, and each of them plays a specific role in Jane's work. Sattler's four pillars provide guiding *elements* for the inquiry process, but do not actually guide it and do not specify the outcomes. The hypothesis-testing approach gives a shape to the inquiry *process*. It guides decisions about possible steps and choice of instruments, but says little about the outcome. The structure of the behavioural report gives a *form* to the final product. All three devices are relatively free from specific content knowledge, yet the four pillars framework is well aligned with the professional knowledge base that informs Jane about what constitutes a comprehensive behavioural assessment. The form for the behavioural assessment report is saturated with various kinds of socio-material knowledge that renders the report recognisable in Jane's professional community and scaffolds her learning.

Jane also uses the referral letter and previous reports that have been written about Ron. These artefacts each have a recognisable structure and are already full of *situation- and place-specific* knowledge. Jane uses them for their content (situated knowledge) rather than their tool-like properties. For each mode of assessment, Jane further draws on related *instruments* for formal testing, interviewing and

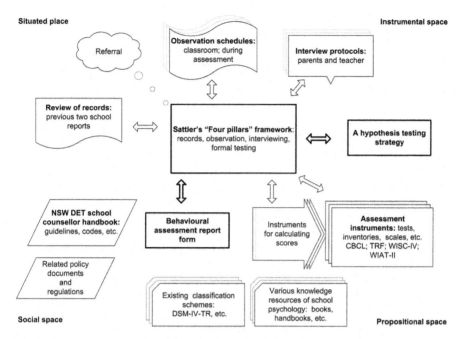

Fig. 12.1 Epistemic assemblage for conducting a child's behavioural assessment

observation. Some of these instruments are relatively open and need to be aligned to specific situations (e.g. observation protocols). Some others are quite rigid and full of psychology knowledge (e.g. behavioural tests). For example, in order to test specific behavioural issues, Jane needs to know how to choose relevant instruments from a large pool of tools designed for assessing cognitive development, achievement, behaviour, mental health and language. She also needs to know how to administer those tests, calculate scores, interpret them and identify specific issues (e.g. anxiety, withdrawal, social problems and attention problems). For making judgements about Ron's disability and offering recommendations, including design guidelines for parents, Jane uses professional journals, clinical assessment and intervention handbooks and other sources. These tools are saturated with general *propositional* knowledge relating to behavioural assessment and psychological intervention.

Many other tools, such as diagnostic and categorisation criteria and practices adopted in the state, regulations, ethical codes, the school counsellor handbook and other manuals, stay in the background for this task. These tools are not necessarily constructed using rational knowledge from psychology, but are saturated with *social* and cultural knowledge of how a school counsellor's professional work should be done.

12.4.1 Concluding Points from This Case

In sum, Jane's knowledge work is constituted of, and instantiated in, a range of epistemic tools. Some of these tools are broad, generic frames and strategies that outline the structure and 'syntax' of inquiry and have only loose connections with a specific professional knowledge base. A good example of this is hypothesis-based reasoning – a strategy that is used in many fields of inquiry. Some other epistemic tools maintain some generic tool-like characteristics (i.e. generic structural and syntax qualities), but are nevertheless also saturated with social knowledge (e.g. the form of assessment report), disciplinary propositional knowledge (e.g. formal testing instruments) or situated case-specific knowledge (e.g. referral or earlier assessment reports). The main point to make is that these tools, being a part of the professional epistemic infrastructure, through material embodiment and social action, allow Jane, who does not know Ron and his situation, to make sense of, and construct, situated case-specific knowledge. Figure 12.2 broadly represents this dynamic movement between the general propositional knowledge and case-specific situated knowledge and knowing through creating and enacting instrumental assemblages of diverse epistemic tools within the epistemic infrastructures of the profession.

These tools are not abstract conceptual entities disconnected from the material world and from social agreements. Rather, they are instantiated in concrete material entities and gain their epistemic power through concrete, socially meaningful, actions. Also, these various tools are not used alone. They are assembled and enacted by Jane in locally relevant ways, in a dynamically unfolding situation. Most importantly, each tool has unique properties and plays a distinct role in the instrumental ensemble. At each stage of the inquiry, different instrumental configurations are assembled and reassembled for the purpose at hand, in a dynamically changing situation. Different intrinsic and extrinsic properties of the tools that constitute the professional epistemic infrastructure – and the heterogeneous organisation of the instrumental ensemble – have strong implications for how the professional work is done and how knowledge and skills for such work can be learnt.

Fig. 12.2 Knowing through creating and enacting epistemic assemblages

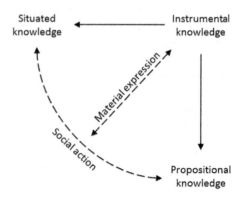

In the next chapter, we present two taxonomies – of epistemic tools and infrastructures – that can be used to carry out further investigations in other professional fields.

References

Baber, C. (2006). Cognitive aspects of tool use. *Applied Ergonomics, 37*(1), 3–15.

Beck, S. R., Apperly, I. A., Chappell, J., Guthrie, C., & Cutting, N. (2011). Making tools isn't child's play. *Cognition, 119*(2), 301–306.

Bereiter, C. (1997). Situated cognition and how to overcome it. In D. Kirshner & J. A. Whitson (Eds.), *Situated cognition: Social, semiotic, and psychological perspectives* (pp. 281–300). Mahwah, NJ: Lawrence Erlbaum Associates.

Bereiter, C. (2002a). Design research for sustained innovation. *Cognitive Studies: Bulletin of the Japanese Cognitive Science Society, 9*(3), 321–327.

Bereiter, C. (2002b). *Education and mind in the knowledge age.* Mahwah, NJ: Lawrence Erlbaum Associates.

Bowker, G. C., & Star, S. L. (1999). *Sorting things out: Classification and its consequences.* Cambridge, MA: MIT Press.

Butler, S. (1912). *The note-books of Samuel Butler.* London: William Brendon and Son.

Clarke, A. E., & Fujimura, J. H. (Eds.). (1992). *The right tools for the job: At work in twentieth-century life sciences.* Princeton, NJ: Princeton University Press.

Collins, A. (2011). A study of expert theory formation: The role of different model types and domain frameworks. In M. S. Khine & I. M. Saleh (Eds.), *Models and modeling* (pp. 23–40). Dordrecht, The Netherlands: Springer.

Collins, A., & Ferguson, W. (1993). Epistemic forms and epistemic games: Structures and strategies to guide inquiry. *Educational Psychologist, 28*(1), 25–42.

Cowan, R., David, P., & Foray, D. (2000). The explicit economics of knowledge codification and tacitness. *Industrial and Corporate Change, 9*(2), 211–253. doi:10.1093/icc/9.2.211.

Cutting, N., Apperly, I. A., & Beck, S. R. (2011). Why do children lack the flexibility to innovate tools? *Journal of Experimental Child Psychology, 109*(4), 497–511.

de Souza, C. S. (2005). *The semiotic engineering of human-computer interaction.* Cambridge: MIT Press.

Derry, S. J., Schunn, C. D., & Gernsbacher, M. A. (Eds.). (2005). *Interdisciplinary collaboration: An emerging cognitive science.* Mahwah, NJ: Lawrence Erlbaum Associates.

diSessa, A. A. (2004). Metarepresentation: Native competence and targets for instruction. *Cognition and Instruction, 22*(3), 293–331.

Edwards, P. N., Jackson, S. J., Bowker, G. C., & Knobel, C. P. (2007). *Understanding infrastructure: Dynamics, tensions, and design.* Ann Arbor, MI: DeepBlue.

Engeström, Y., & Middleton, D. (Eds.). (1996). *Cognition and communication at work.* Cambridge, NY: Cambridge University Press.

Fenwick, T. (2012). Matterings of knowing and doing: Sociomaterial approaches to understanding practice. In P. Hager, A. Lee, & A. Reich (Eds.), *Learning practice.* Dordrecht, The Netherlands: Springer.

Glick, J. (1995). Intellectual and manual labor: Implications for developmental theory. In L. Martin, K. Nelson, & E. Tobach (Eds.), *Sociocultural psychology: Theory and practice of doing and knowing* (pp. 357–382). Cambridge, UK: Cambridge University Press.

Goodwin, C. (1994). Professional vision. *American Anthropologist, 96*(3), 606–633.

Goodwin, C. (1997). The blackness of black: Color categories as situated practice. In L. B. Resnick, R. Säljö, C. Pontecorvo, & B. Burge (Eds.), *Discourse, tools and reasoning: Essays on situated cognition* (pp. 111–140). Berlin, Germany: Springer.

Goodwin, C. (2005). Seeing in depth. In S. J. Derry, C. D. Schunn, & M. A. Gernsbacher (Eds.), *Interdisciplinary collaboration: An emerging cognitive science* (pp. 85–121). Mahwah, NJ: Lawrence Erlbaum Associates.

Greeno, J. G., & Hall, R. P. (1997). Practicing representation: Learning with and about representational forms. *Phi Delta Kappan, 78*, 361–367.

Griesemer, J. R. (1992). The role of instruments in the generative analysis of science. In A. E. Clarke & J. H. Fujimura (Eds.), *The right tools for the job: At work in twentieth-century life sciences* (pp. 47–76). Princeton, NJ: Princeton University Press.

Håkanson, L. (2007). Creating knowledge: The power and logic of articulation. *Industrial and Corporate Change, 16*(1), 51–88.

Henning, P. H. (2004). Everyday cognition and situated action. In D. H. Jonassen (Ed.), *Handbook of research for educational communications and technology* (2nd ed., pp. 143–168). Mahwah, NJ: Lawrence Erlbaum Associates.

Hutchins, E. (1995). *Cognition in the wild*. Cambridge, MA: MIT Press.

Ingold, T. (2011). *Being alive: Essays on movement, knowledge and description*. Oxon, UK: Routledge.

Johnson-Frey, S. H. (2004). The neural bases of complex tool use in humans. *Trends in Cognitive Sciences, 8*(2), 71–78.

Kant, I. (1964). *Werke VI: schriften zur anthropologie, geschichtsphilosophie, politik und padagogik. [works 6: Writings on anthropology, philosophy of history, politics and pedagogy]*. Wiesbaden, Germany: Insel Verlag.

Keller, C. M., & Keller, J. D. (1996). *Cognition and tool use: The blacksmith at work*. Cambridge, UK: Cambridge University Press.

Knorr Cetina, K. (1999). *Epistemic cultures: How the sciences make knowledge*. Cambridge, MA: Harvard University Press.

Knorr Cetina, K. (2001). Objectual practice. In T. R. Schatzki, K. Knorr Cetina, & E. V. Savigny (Eds.), *The practice turn in contemporary theory* (pp. 175–188). London: Routledge.

Kuhn, T. S. (1981). *The structure of scientific revolutions*. Chicago: University of Chicago Press.

Lampland, M., & Star, S. L. (Eds.). (2009). *Standards and their stories: How quantifying, classifying, and formalizing practices shape everyday life*. London: Cornell University Press.

Land, R., Meyer, J., & Smith, J. B. (Eds.). (2008). *Threshold concepts within the disciplines*. Rotterdam, The Netherlands: Sense.

Menz, M. M., Blangero, A., Kunze, D., & Binkofski, F. (2010). Got it! understanding the concept of a tool. *NeuroImage, 51*(4), 1438–1444.

Meyer, J. H. F., & Land, R. (Eds.). (2006). *Overcoming barriers to student understanding: Threshold concepts and troublesome knowledge*. London: Routledge.

Miettinen, R., & Virkkunen, J. (2005). Epistemic objects, artefacts and organizational change. *Organization, 12*(3), 437–456.

Nersessian, N. J. (2005). Interpreting scientific and engineering practices: Integrating the cognitive, social, and cultural dimensions. In M. E. Gorman, R. D. Tweney, D. C. Gooding, & A. P. Kincannon (Eds.), *Scientific and technological thinking* (pp. 17–56). Mahwah, NJ: Lawrence Erlbaum Associates.

Nersessian, N. J. (2006). The cognitive-cultural systems of the research laboratory. *Organization Studies, 27*(1), 125–145.

Norman, D. A. (1991). Cognitive artifacts. In J. M. Carroll (Ed.), *Designing interaction* (pp. 17–38). Cambridge, UK: Cambridge University Press.

Olson, D. R. (1994). *The world on paper: The conceptual and cognitive implications of writing and reading*. Cambridge, UK: Cambridge University Press.

Orlikowski, W. J. (2007). Sociomaterial practices: Exploring technology at work. *Organization Studies, 28*(9), 1435–1448.

Perkins, D. N. (1997). Epistemic games. *International Journal of Educational Research, 27*(1), 49–61.

Perkins, D. (2006). Constructivism and troublesome knowledge. In J. H. F. Meyer & R. Land (Eds.), *Overcoming barriers to student understanding: Threshold concepts and troublesome knowledge* (pp. 33–47). London: Routledge.

Perkins, D. N., & Salomon, G. (1989). Are cognitive skills context-bound? *Educational Researcher, 18*(1), 16–25. doi:10.3102/0013189x018001016.

Rabardel, P., & Beguin, P. (2005). Instrument mediated activity: From subject development to anthropocentric design. *Theoretical Issues in Ergonomics Science, 6*(5), 429–461. doi:10.1080/14639220500078179.

Rheinberger, H. (1997). *Toward a history of epistemic things: Synthesizing proteins in the test tube.* Stanford, CA: Stanford University Press.

Ribes, D., & Finholt, T. A. (2009). The long now of infrastructure: Articulating tensions in development. *Journal for the Association of Information Systems: Special Issue on Infrastructures, 10*(5), 375–398.

Ritella, G., & Hakkarainen, K. (2012). Instrumental genesis in technology-mediated learning: From double stimulation to expansive knowledge practices. *International Journal of Computer-Supported Collaborative Learning, 7*(2), 239–258. doi:10.1007/s11412-012-9144-1.

Roth, W.-M. (2010). Learning in praxis, learning for praxis. In S. Billett (Ed.), *Learning through practice: Models, traditions, orientations and approaches* (pp. 21–36). Dordrecht, The Netherlands: Springer.

Roth, W. M., & McGinn, M. K. (1998). Inscriptions: Toward a theory of representing as social practice. *Review of Educational Research, 68*(1), 35–59.

Russ, R. S., Scherr, R. E., Hammer, D., & Mikeska, J. (2008). Recognizing mechanistic reasoning in scientific inquiry: A framework for discourse analysis developed from philosophy of science. *Science Education, 92*(3), 499–525.

Säljö, R. (1995). Mental and physical artifacts in cognitive practices. In P. Reimann & H. Spada (Eds.), *Learning in humans and machines: Towards an interdisciplinary learning science* (pp. 83–95). London: Pergamon Press.

Sattler, J. M., & Hoge, R. D. (2006). *Assessment of children: Behavioural, social and clinical foundations* (5th ed.). San Diego, CA: Sattler.

Schatzki, T. R. (2001). Introduction: Practice theory. In T. R. Schatzki, K. Knorr Cetina, & E. V. Savigny (Eds.), *The practice turn in contemporary theory* (pp. 1–14). London: Routledge.

Schwab, J. J. (1962). The concept of the structure of a discipline. *Educational Record, 43*, 197–205.

Scribner, S. (1997). *Mind and social practice: Selected writings of Sylvia Scribner.* Cambridge, MA: Cambridge University Press.

Seymour, W. D. (1966). *Industrial skills.* London: Pitman.

Stahl, G. (2012). Cognizing mediating: Unpacking the entanglement of artifacts with collective minds. *International Journal of Computer-Supported Collaborative Learning, 7*(2), 187–191. doi:10.1007/s11412-012-9148-x.

Star, S. L. (1989). The structure of ill-structured solutions: Boundary objects and heterogeneous distributed problem solving. In L. Gasser & M. N. Huhns (Eds.), *Distributed artificial intelligence* (Vol. 2, pp. 37–54). Pitman, CA: Morgan Kaufmann.

Star, S. L., & Ruhleder, K. (1996). Steps toward an ecology of infrastructure: Design and access for large information spaces. *Information Systems Research, 7*(1), 111–134.

Star, S. L., & Strauss, A. (1999). Layers of silence, arenas of voice: The ecology of visible and invisible work. *Computer Supported Cooperative Work (CSCW), 8*(1), 9–30.

Suchman, L. (2007). *Human-machine reconfigurations: Plans and situated actions.* Cambridge, UK: Cambridge University Press.

Toulmin, S. (1953). *The philosophy of science: An introduction.* London: Hutchinson's University Library.

Turnbull, D. (2000). *Masons, tricksters and cartographers: Comparative studies in the sociology of scientific and indigenous knowledge.* Abingdon, OX: Routledge

Vygotsky, L. S. (1930). The Instrumental method in psychology. *Text of a talk given in 1930 at the Krupskaya Academy of Communist Education*. Retrieved from http://www.marxists.org/archive/vygotsky/works/1930/instrumental.htm.

Vygotsky, L. S. (1986). *Thought and language* (2 Revisedth ed.). Cambridge, MA: MIT Press.

Weick, K. E. (1995). *Sensemaking in organizations*. Thousand Oaks, CA: Sage.

Whitehead, A. N. (1925/1948). *Science and the modern world* (Mentor ed.). New York: New American Library.

Chapter 13
Taxonomies of Epistemic Tools and Infrastructures

There are a whole bunch of frameworks. They're like acronyms. I call it the 'acronym game'. <...> In the end, it's a bit, like I've said before, *they walk out with certain messages*. We think they walk out with a *sophisticated scholarly knowledge* after six weeks, and *they don't*. What they try to remember is 'What did Andrew [lecturer] say?' Well he might have said 'Where are we going? How am I going? Where to next?' (Education Lecturer)

The power of tools in making and changing practices and professions is well acknowledged. As Ravetz (1971) argues,

As new tools come into being, and are judged appropriate and valuable by people in the field, they alter the direction of work in the field. (Ravetz, 1971, p. 93)

Surprisingly, the dynamic *properties* of these tools, and the *capacities* they exercise within the work, have rarely been the focus. In fact, as Clarke and Fujimura (1992) observe, two rather different views of tools have emerged in the literature:

- While the creation of new tools – particularly tools for knowledge work, such as theories, models and techniques – is seen as a messy and complex process, once such tools are created, and they become 'black boxes', taken for granted and no longer examined, questioned or modified by those who use them. They are seen as stable, fused with tacit skill and deployed by professionals almost automatically in the right, familiar circumstances.
- However, it is only occasionally that professional work presents professionals with the 'right' circumstances. In order to accomplish their work, in many complex situations, professionals have to construct 'doable problems' (Fujimura, 1987). This often involves actively manipulating and articulating various elements of the situation, and pulling various tools together, in order to construct the 'right' configurations of tools and deploy them at the 'right' times and in the 'right' sequence. This construction of doable problems involves 'tinkering' –

© Springer Science+Business Media Dordrecht 2017   367
L. Markauskaite, P. Goodyear, *Epistemic Fluency and Professional Education*,
Professional and Practice-based Learning 14, DOI 10.1007/978-94-007-4369-4_13

... using what is at hand, making-do, using things for new purposes, patching things together, and so on. (Clarke & Fujimura, 1992, p. 11)

Nevertheless, the knowledge and skills that underpin tinkering have usually been seen as tacit, taken for granted and invisible (Clarke & Fujimura, 1992).

Two approaches to researching tools in work have yielded two contrasting ways of looking at tools: one that focusses on tools themselves, their intrinsic features, and another that looks past these features and focusses on the construction of doable problems and tinkering. In the first case, the focus is on the major classes, elements and standard configurations of tools and their powers; in the second case, the focus is on processes of crafting and tinkering – how tools get entangled in human agency.

Neither extreme feels quite right. If one wants to understand both *what* tools are, and also *how* tools function, *what* human skilfulness looks like, and also *what* underpins this skill to use tools in diverse situations, then understanding both the properties of tools and their emergent capacities becomes important.

Looking at properties and capacities of tools is different from looking at isolated elements (De Landa, 2011). Properties and capacities link what a tool can do with human capacities and intentions, in any specific situation.

Consider a knife. The knife has certain *elements* (e.g. a handle, a blade) and certain *properties* (e.g. sharp vs. blunt, long vs. short, made of steel vs. plastic). It also has certain *capacities* (e.g. to cut bread, to spread butter). Some of these capacities may become *actual* only if the knife is used for this purpose and interacts with other entities (e.g. bread, butter). Nevertheless, these capacities are *real*. The knife may never be used for cutting bread, yet its capacity to do so is still real. In human practices, the *capacities* of tools interact with *human capacities* and *intentions*. A craftsman may be able to carve a spoon from a piece of wood with a sharp knife if he has such an intention, but not everyone will be able to do this even if they have the same sharp knife. Most importantly, *capacities of tools* depend on *properties*, and properties and capacities shape *functions* of tools in skilful human activity. A plastic knife could have the capacity to cut bread, but not wood, and even a craftsman will not be able to carve a spoon with a plastic knife and will not use such a knife for this function.

What kinds of *properties* do epistemic tools have and what kinds of *capacities* and *functions* of these tools emerge in human activity? This understanding of what epistemic tools can do, and what they can't, and how they function, is important if one wants to become skilful at creating 'doable problems' and knowledgeably choosing the right tools for the job.

This chapter falls into three main parts. Section 13.1 describes the main kinds of epistemic tools that we have discerned during our empirical work; then, Sect. 13.2 does the same for epistemic infrastructures. Our focus is the main properties, capacities and functions of various tools and infrastructures in professional work. Section 13.3 brings the different aspects together and discusses how the professional skill needed to master diverse epistemic tools and infrastructures is learnt – bringing us back to the question of constructing doable problems.

13.1   A Taxonomy of Epistemic Tools

We start by outlining three broad types of epistemic tools that provide form and structure to professional ways of knowing: (a) epistemic frames, (b) epistemic devices and (c) epistemic instruments and equipment (Fig. 13.1).

13.1.1   Epistemic Frames

Epistemic frames are the most abstract epistemic tools. They include such things as broad ideas, concepts, metaphors and 'buzzwords'. They act in ways that describe and frame professional knowledge work. They include general epistemic frames and (intra-)professional *epistemes* that provide guidance about how professional problems should be approached.

General epistemic frames provide a shape to intellectual dispositions and professional inquiry across situations and contexts. They include such broad concepts as 'evidence-based practice' and 'teacher–scholar', 'patient-centred care' – which are currently used to describe the nature of professional work and shape professional learning in nursing, pharmacy, teaching and other social professions. They are not tied to a particular epistemic structure or strategy, but define dispositions and the focus of epistemic work.

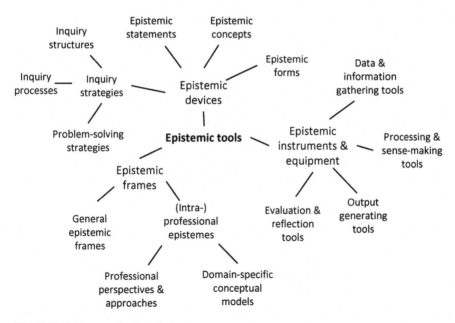

Fig. 13.1 Taxonomy of epistemic tools

(Intra-)professional epistemes are broad conceptual frameworks that are known within a professional discipline or community. Various perspectives familiar in arts education and arts practice, such as structuralist or poststructuralist, and various therapeutic approaches familiar in the health area, such as conventional, natural or homoeopathic treatments or pharmacological and non-pharmacological aspects of managing a disease, are examples of intra-professional epistemes. In contrast with general frames, epistemes define one's epistemic position in relation to a problem and a space of possible solutions. David Perkins (2006) defines episteme as

> ... a system of ideas or way of understanding that allows us to establish knowledge ... manners of justifying, explaining, solving problems, conducting enquiries, and designing and validating various kinds of products and outcomes. (Perkins, 2006, p. 42)

Each episteme comes with its own world view of what constitutes a problem and solution, set of concepts and strategies. Nevertheless different intra-professional epistemes can be practised concurrently. For example, a medical professional could mix conventional and natural therapies for treating lower back pain. Epistemes can be very broad, such as those professional *perspectives and approaches* that we have already mentioned, or they can be *domain-specific conceptual models.* For example, pharmacy students learnt to use a range of theoretical models for designing health promotion activity, such as the Health Belief Model, Socio-ecological Model, Trans-theoretical Model and Tannahill's Model.

Broader professional epistemes define the nature of epistemic space. Some 'threshold concepts' – such as 'ethical reading' in English literature or 'reflexivity' in anthropology – could be further examples of intra-professional and disciplinary epistemic frames that students encounter in higher education (Carmichael, 2012). More specific – model like – epistemes specify the configuration of various ideas in the epistemic space more precisely. They are similar to what Allan Collins (2011) called 'domain frameworks': prior theoretical structures that experts use for guiding their analyses and organising large parts of their inquiry. Such frameworks are usually domain-specific prior theories but also could be various analogies and metaphors of the kind that scientists use to structure the problem space and organise their inquiry. Examples are the law of supply and demand, the frontier metaphor, the light bulb metaphor, the principle of decreasing costs of natural resources and the notion of natural selection.

All epistemic frames 'mount' problem-solving in a specific epistemic space, but they do not necessarily define the nature of this inquiry (nor do they define the inquiry process or the form of a satisfactory outcome). The latter work is done by other kinds of more specific epistemic tools that we call 'epistemic devices'.

13.1.2   Epistemic Devices

Epistemic devices are general-purpose tools that structure and guide professional knowledge work and the production of epistemic artefacts. In the broadest sense, devices provide the means for moving through an inquiry, and they serve as symbolic sites for meaning-making and problem-solving. Similar to the kinds of physical devices that serve as in vitro models for scientific discovery work in research laboratories (Nersessian, 2005, 2006), epistemic devices serve the function of cognitive partners: mental modelling devices for instantiating professional problems and generating solutions. Different epistemic devices have different epistemic affordances: they offer different ways of doing epistemic work. Several broad categories of epistemic affordances are taken up in professional knowledge work, such as inquiry strategies, epistemic statements, epistemic concepts and epistemic forms.

Inquiry strategies include shared ways of undertaking professional inquiry and methods that structure inquiry processes. These devices do not define the target form of knowledge, but suggest one or more of the following: (a) key elements of inquiry, (b) inquiry process and (c) problem-solving strategies.

For example, in our studies, school counselling students used Sattler's four pillars model for behavioural assessment, involving observation, examination of records, interviewing and formal testing as four elements that structured their assessments. Future arts teachers used an arts conceptual framework – which positions artworks in relation to the artist, audience and the world – to structure their analyses of artwork and as a device to be used in teaching art to school students. These general inquiry devices define *key elements*, but do not describe how they are assembled and sequenced in an inquiry process.

In contrast, other inquiry strategies define a *general structure for the inquiry process*. For example, in our studies, pharmacy students were taught to follow a 'working knowledge cycle' that includes three main steps: information gathering, information processing and delivery. Future nurses learnt to structure their every-day inquiry and decision-making using a 'Framework for practice thinking' that includes several questions 'what's going on here', 'what does this mean', 'what could be done' and so on (Fig. 13.2). Similarly, some of the future teachers learnt to structure their professional inquires using Tripp's (1993) critical incident analysis steps: describe, suggest explanation, find more general meaning, clarify and inter-pret, take a personal–professional position and plan a change in practice. Other trainee teachers were encouraged to use an action learning cycle. Such epistemic strategies, as a rule, define key steps or stages of an inquiry process.

Students also learnt to use different *problem-solving strategies* for their profes-sional work. For example, the hypothesis formation and testing approach and the test battery approach, which counselling students learnt to use for psychological assessment, constitute two alternative strategies. Similarly, pharmacy students learnt to use two strategies during the medication review process: going through each disease state or going systematically through each drug to examine possible interactions and other problems. They also learnt to use a range of other strategies to make pharmaceutical decisions, such as prediction of the activity of a drug based on its structure and physicochemical properties or identification of a mechanism of therapeutic action of a selected drug at the molecular, cellular, organ system and whole body levels. The latter group of inquiry strategies is similar to Allan Collins

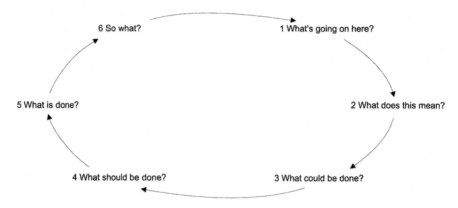

Fig. 13.2 Framework for practice thinking (Source: Curriculum renewal report of a nursing faculty)

(2011) general purpose epistemic strategies – which experts use for making sense of various phenomena. These include: theory and evidence, hypothesis formation and testing, looking for and explaining anomalies, identifying key factors or variables, determining the effect of one variable on another and countering the weak links, segmentation, etc. These epistemic strategies guide how one should approach the problem, but are not tied to particular steps or particular epistemic forms.

Epistemic statements broadly characterise the configuration of a target outcome – the overall configuration of a solution to a particular problem. Examples of such epistemic statements are an artist's case study, health promotion program, critical reflection maze and risk assessment. In contrast to general inquiry strategies, epistemic statements do not offer a structure of inquiry, but broadly define the nature and target form of an acceptable *outcome*. Epistemic statements are loosely structured constructs and professionals usually have a set of more specific criteria for assessing the quality of final outcomes. (These tend to be more domain-specific and/or context-specific than is captured by the epistemic statement alone.) For example, in our studies, the health promotion program reports were characterised by seven core components: title, target, aim, description, tools, theoretical basis and expected outcomes. Three criteria were used for assessing report quality:

- Scope of the project – the project could easily be implemented by a community pharmacy.
- Aims and targeted audience – the project has the potential to be successful in terms of the aims and patient selection.
- Outcome – the project has the potential to positively impact the health of those recruited and possibly a wider audience.

A critical reflection on professional experience was configured or structured broadly as 'a maze', but was also characterised by a set of more specific criteria for assessing reflection on professional experience, including such requirements as that: the case needs to be true; it has to involve a decision-making dilemma; it has to have an interesting plot and descriptive subtitles; the description should be detailed and include concrete assessment artefacts; it should be written clearly and coherently; and it should deepen the writer and the reader's knowledge in the domain concerned.

Epistemic concepts usually play the role of building blocks in figuring out the problem and developing a solution – in the form of an epistemic statement or some other epistemic artefact. For example, in pharmacy practice units, students often used such epistemic concepts as interaction between medications, adverse effects and side effects, family history, lifestyle, diet, symptom control, standard treatment and risk factors. In preservice teacher lesson planning, such concepts included lesson aims, learning outcomes, learning activities and assessment strategies. Epistemic concepts have some similar features to epistemic statements, but they are more specific constructs. Epistemic concepts, like epistemic statements, depict the structure of a solution and broadly characterise an aspect of the targeted outcome. They only acquire a more precise form in concrete, domain-specific situations. For example, a 'risk factor' is a common epistemic concept which is often deployed in 'risk assessment' and then in deciding about an appropriate treatment. However, specific factors, strategies and instruments for assessing risks of different diseases are different. For example, for assessing the risk and severity of community-acquired pneumonia (CAP), our pharmacists learnt to detect risk factors relevant to CAP and to assess overall risk using the Pneumonia Severity Index. They also learnt to consider other assessment techniques, such as history and examination of symptoms, chest X-ray, oxygen saturation (or PaO_2) and investigation for the causal pathogen. In contrast, for assessing cardiovascular risk, the pharmacist learnt to identify a range of factors related to cardiovascular diseases and used various calculators for assessing an absolute cardiovascular disease risk. In short, there is a major difference between general epistemic devices (strategies and concepts) and concrete instantiations in specific tools (instruments and equipment) (see Sect. 13.1.3).

Epistemic forms are characteristic target structures that guide inquiry and give a shape to the final epistemic artefact. A medication review, a lesson plan, a child behavioural assessment report and an excursion plan are examples of such epistemic devices. They are commonly used to produce epistemic artefacts that have a form recognisable in a professional community and which embody solutions to certain kinds of professional problems, plans, designs, cases, etc. Unlike epistemic statements and concepts, which primarily define the shape of the outcome, and unlike general inquiry strategies, which give a shape to the inquiry process, epistemic forms include *both* components: the target structure and a set of rules, strategies and moves (i.e. an epistemic game) coupled with the form of the target outcome. Collins and Ferguson (1993) suggest that such target structures play a critical role in the construction of new scientific knowledge. In the *sciences*, they involve a range of general purpose strategies for analysing phenomena that are associated with particular characteristic forms of outcome, such as comparisons, causal chains, multifactor models, stage models, trend analysis and systems dynamics models. Knowledge work in *professional* fields can also be characterised in terms of epistemic forms and associated strategies, but many of them are more specialised; they are often used in combination with other epistemic devices, and they are tailored to particular kinds of professional tasks. For example, in pharmacy, epistemic forms that guide professional work may include such things as a simple medicines list that a pharmacist could create for a patient in order to assist him to take medications appropriately. (We give examples of such forms in Chaps. 14 and 15.) Such a list is a specialised and elaborated instance of a more general 'list' epistemic form. However, this category may include very specialised forms, such as a medication management review report – of the kind that a pharmacist will produce as the result of a complex examination of drug interactions and other life conditions, calculations of appropriate doses and suggestions for non-pharmaceutical treatments. Such specialised forms, while they may not look very different from other generic epistemic forms, are in fact a complex combination and the product of many separate epistemic games. Despite the situated nature of their production, these forms are widely recognised in professional communities. The coordinator of the behavioural assessment course for school counsellors, for example, said:

> I would say there would be more commonality than difference, I would think so … just because – school counsellors, all our guidelines and training, I would think yes … and also files get shared. <…> Because a psychological report has a certain structure and that's pretty well established.

Epistemic forms are closely associated with epistemic games – which we will discuss in Chap. 14.

13.1.3 Epistemic Instruments and Equipment

Epistemic instruments and epistemic equipment are tools for structuring specific aspects of professional inquiry, such as data and information gathering, analysis, processing, evaluation (and reflection), presentation and sharing. The distinctions between epistemic devices, epistemic instruments and epistemic equipment are broadly similar to the distinction among physical devices, instruments and equipment delineated by Nersessian (2006). In contrast to epistemic devices – that could be merely broad, flexible structures in which, or through which, epistemic artefacts are created and instantiated – epistemic instruments and equipment are already pre-existing instantiations of different aspects of professional inquiry in concrete material or symbolic tools. While many devices are 'intellectual sites' for modelling and creating epistemic artefacts and may not have an independent material or symbolic existence (i.e. an artefact component) without the created artefact, instruments and equipment have both elements – that is, an artefact component and an action scheme (see Chap. 12). For example, a form of a semi-structured interview may act as a generic device for interviewing parents during behavioural assessment review. However, school psychologists rarely start from generic devices; rather, they have a range of more specialised instruments and equipment for conducting such interviews, including the Child Behaviour Checklist (CBCL for ages 6–18) that Jane completed in our example (see Sect. 12.4).

Epistemic instruments and equipment are full of professional heuristics and other kinds of specialised knowledge, including knowledge of how those tools should be used and knowledge about situations and contexts when those tools should be used.

Epistemic instruments and epistemic equipment are specific to the aim or task at hand, but they vary in the degree of epistemic openness and capacity for generative knowledge work. Epistemic instruments are relatively open epistemic tools that themselves require significant mental engagement, human agency and tweaking during the process. Epistemic equipment is usually less mutable: consisting of 'closed' tools for specific aspects of professional inquiry and work. They may require less mental engagement during the knowledge creation process. Epistemic instruments and equipment are usually designed for specific epistemic tasks in the knowledge production cycle: including *data and information gathering, processing and sense-making, generating outputs, evaluation and reflection*. As they are associated with specific epistemic games, we expand on these epistemic instruments in Chap. 14.

In summary, epistemic tools used in professional work vary in their degree of openness and their specificity. Some tools are tied to very specific tasks, providing a well-articulated action scheme (e.g. a checklist); others are more general purpose, offering a broad shape to professional meaning-making (e.g. systems thinking). Different tools play different roles in professional knowledgeable action and require different kinds of professional knowledge and skills if they are to be used productively.

13.2   A Taxonomy of Epistemic Infrastructure

The tools that we described in the previous section constitute the core epistemic toolbox for professional work. Such tools have several features. First, they are largely symbolic. Even if they have a physical manifestation – embodied in a material device – they are still used for their symbolic qualities. (A blood pressure monitor would be a good example. Its symbolic outputs are what matter in knowledge work.) Second, they are directly related to, and/or constructed for, professional knowledge work. However, these pure professional and pure epistemic tools do not exist in a conceptual, social or material vacuum. Rather, they are tightly interconnected with other infrastructures: including the conceptual knowledge bases of other fields and social and material embodiments of professional knowledge. In fact, epistemic infrastructure is interconnected and exists simultaneously with other infrastructures that have a significant epistemic modality (see Chap. 7). The overlaps (blended spaces) of different infrastructures are large. These infrastructures are a part of the same epistemic assemblage when students learn to solve professional problems and create professional artefacts. Broadly speaking, we can

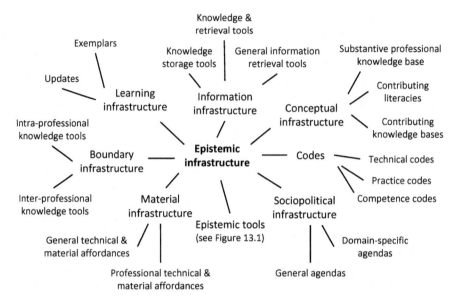

Fig. 13.3 Taxonomy of epistemic infrastructure

discern six types of infrastructures that share thick overlapping borders: codes, conceptual infrastructure, information infrastructure, learning infrastructure, boundary infrastructure, material infrastructure and sociopolitical infrastructure (Fig. 13.3). We describe the main features and functions of each of these in turn in the following subsections.

13.2.1 Codes

Codes are conventions, rules of conduct and other broad macro- or meso-level sociocultural arrangements for coordinating disparate elements of professional work, including outcomes (i.e. products), actions (i.e. processes), practices and individual performances (knowledge, skills, etc.). Drawing on Bowker and Star (1999) and others (Lampland & Star, 2009; Mulcahy, 2011; Timmermans & Epstein, 2010), we define codes as uniformities achieved and maintained across places and time through the generation and enactment of a set of agreed-upon rules.[1] They largely belong to what we called 'sociopolitical knowledge' (Chap. 4)

---

[1] Bowker and Star (1999) put it like this: 'A "standard" is any set of agreed-upon rules for production of (textual and material) objects' (p. 13). We use a broader notion of 'codes' to include both formal standards and informal conventions for production of textual and material objects but also the other discursive activities that underpin professional epistemic practices in the broadest sense.

Recent debate in the sociological literature about this area has been concerned with formal standards and their consequences for professional work (Bowker & Star, 1999; Brunsson & Jacobsson, 2000; Busch, 2011; Lampland & Star, 2009; Timmermans & Epstein, 2010). As Lampland and Star (2009) note, there is a 'leaky border' between formal standards and informal conventions, such as norms and customs, which influence human behaviour (p. 24). Why is a movie often between 90 min and 2 h? Why do many plays last about 3 h? Why are lessons and lectures often 45–60 min? Why is a lesson in one school 50 min and 55 min in another school? Why do many community pharmacies check blood pressure for free, while they charge for other services?

Many such conventions and rules of thumb are widespread, yet not absolute. Some of them are a part of formal systems of models and rules, while some are tacit or unwritten. As Timmermans and Epstein (2010) say

> Although standards are often formally (or legally) negotiated outcomes, they also have a way of sinking below the level of social visibility, eventually becoming a part of the taken for granted technical and moral infrastructure of modern life. (Timmermans & Epstein, 2010, p. 71)

Mulcahy (2011) notes that standards have epistemic consequences as 'standards are not only the objects *of* knowledge practice, but also objects *in* knowledge practice' (p. 96, emphasis added).

They are not only tools that can render professional judgements and decisions precisely in the contexts of shared professional meaning-making and action; they are also active participants in the assemblage of professional epistemic work (Bowker & Star, 1999; Ewenstein & Whyte, 2009; Star, 2005). Extending this view to a broader range of rules, conventions and discursive practices, we can say that codes are a part of professional epistemic infrastructures. What are they and how do they enter the assemblage of professional epistemic work?

We identify three kinds of codes: technical, practice and competence codes.

Technical codes are the various kinds of professional conventions and specifications that regulate and standardise products, services and their elements, as well as other things produced by each profession. Among such conventions can be found various specifications that define requirements for the outcomes and interim results of professional work. They can be relatively broad, such as national curricula, standards, syllabuses and exams. These specify what kind of teaching outcomes are expected. They guide teachers' decisions and work at various levels of granularity, including such things as the content that should be covered during lessons and the achievements students are expected to demonstrate. Some technical codes can be local, such as local hospital guidelines for preoperative and postoperative management. Technical codes can also be related to individual components of professional practice. For example, various standards and other rules for classifying the nature and severity of an intellectual disability, or criteria for deciding about a patient's eligibility for certain medications and services, form part of the epistemic infrastructure on which psychologists and pharmacists depend. Technical codes also include various boundary agreements and rules that allow professionals to work together and achieve compatible outcomes.

Technical codes cover what Timmermans and Epstein (2010) call 'standards'. They distinguish four subtypes: design standards, terminological standards, procedural standards and performance standards. Design standards specify properties of tools and products. They are 'explicit and more or less detailed specifications of individual components of social and/or technical systems, ensuring their uniformity and their mutual compatibility' (p. 72). Terminological standards establish compatibility and stability of meanings between sites and over time and make it possible to aggregate individual elements into a larger whole. They are closely related to what we called boundary agreements. Procedural standards are specifications that delineate how processes should be performed and what steps should be taken under certain conditions. Performance standards specify outcomes, such as the maximum percentage of mistakes deemed to be acceptable for a specific operation. Overall, many technical codes form a part of a codified professional knowledge base: part of an explicit professional epistemic infrastructure that enables mutual compatibility of professional judgements, decisions, procedures and processes.

Technical codes can be thought of as 'tools of the trade' and are to be taught and learnt. For example, school counsellors and pharmacists learn to assess situations using established indexes and classification schemes, and preservice teachers learn to use state curricula, standards and examination requirements to plan their units, lessons and individual assessment tasks. Students should not be mastering technical codes in mechanical or unreflective ways. On the contrary, technical and critical aspects of their use tend to be closely linked in professional learning. Technical codes often come into the epistemic assemblages of professional learning and practical tasks in explicit, clearly distinguishable forms, as things to be learnt. They sometimes shape professional practice and learning in very fundamental ways.

Practice codes define and standardise how professionals *should act*. They range from strict formal requirements to vaguely articulated expectations of professional conduct. Formal practice codes include criminal record checks, occupational screening and vaccination, occupational health and safety and other procedures and checks that have to be followed and met. They also include ethical codes of conduct, privacy codes, child protection policies and other 'moral' guidelines that explicate what is considered to be appropriate professional behaviour and practice. However, these practice codes also comprise of many informal expectations about how professionals should behave and conventions for making professional decisions that are not articulated in any formal documents, such as dress codes. Some practice codes are related to procedural standards (Timmermans & Epstein, 2010) that constitute technical codes. However, practice codes are less concerned about what and when things should be done. They focus on *how* things should be done (and what should not be done). In this sense, explicit practice codes are distinct kinds of procedural specifications, as they represent performative knowledge that goes beyond step-by-step rules and is generally difficult to render explicitly.

Practice codes sometimes feature in professional learning through 'hot' topics, which are often explored in great depth. However, other practice codes seem to avoid or resist direct exploration. For example, in teacher education courses, 'teaching for diverse student needs' tends to be one of the practice codes directly explored in lectures, and it features in assessment criteria in tasks across a range of courses. Some topics, such as principles of social justice, become the focus of whole course units and specific tasks. For example, one of the Professional Practice courses we studied was specifically allocated for work on principles of social justice, such as meeting the needs of students who are living in poverty, fair teaching, student–teacher relationships and classroom management. As a part of their assessment tasks, students analysed their own lesson plans from social justice perspectives, such as equity, access and opportunities for participation. However, in other professions a range of practice codes were given to students as things that they would learn and apply in their practice, without necessarily being taught. This view was summarised by the teacher who coordinated the school counsellors program:

> So this ethical and professional issues. There's a lot of policy and procedure. But you have to know it. So you can't – I mean, it's not just about being a great psychologist at the interpersonal level or intrapersonal level as well, you've got to know all that stuff. Vast amounts of stuff. <. . .> Oh look we do exercises. We give them lots of handouts. I do that one with a colleague – we discuss scenarios. They work in small groups. There's a certain amount of it is just straight inputs, there's so much. They're all given a CD. We burn them a CD on which we have the policies and it's something – I forget the number, it might 200. There's so many. <. . .> If they need to because they're out there with a practising school counsellor. So the practising school counsellor will share a lot with them. But they're expected to know at least enough not to put their foot in it but they're not expected to know it all when they start, no. It wouldn't be realistic. They're there to learn.

Competence codes are professional standards and other agreements that delineate the professional knowledge base, skills, attitudes and other personal professional qualities. As Tummons (2011) says, such standards perform two main functions: 'they inform the public about the claims to competence of the profession' (p. 25) and 'they inform the development of relevant professional qualifications, including the ways in which such qualifications are delivered, mentored and assessed' (loc. cit.).

Competence codes that regulate professional education and claims to professional status include formal requirements, such as competence standards, accreditation and registration standards, graduate attributes and other similar socially agreed outcomes of professional development and education. Competence codes are related to performance standards, but include a much broader set of outcomes than just a set of measurable performances. These include professional attributes, such as roles of professionals in the wider community, and commitments to continuous professional development. Practices associated with how those competence standards and entry requirements should be met and demonstrated include the use of a range of forms. These include such things as individual student logbooks and other records that document students' practical performances. For example, the schools of nursing and social work involved in our studies required their students to keep practicum logbooks. Practices also included use of formal examinations (e.g. in medicine and pharmacy). These competence codes, as a result, find various ways of entering the assemblage of epistemic infrastructures in which students learn professional knowledge.

Competence codes tend to be the most controversial element in the assemblages of professional tasks (Mulcahy, 2011; Tummons, 2011). They tend to be hated, taken into account, sometimes followed, but sometimes abandoned and even ignored. In our studies we saw several distinct patterns of how competence codes have been used to organise professional learning, varying from a dominant role – quite aggressively shaping how and what students do – to being just a broad organiser, added to what students would learn anyway. In some professional tasks, competence standards serve as central organising devices for deciding about learning goals, experiences and achievements. For example, the main assessment task – a placement portfolio – in a field education program for social workers was founded on the basis of *Practice Standards for Social Workers* (Australian Association of Social Workers, 2003; see also Scott, Laragy, Giles, & Bland, 2004). As a part of their field experience, each student prepared an individual learning contract and planned learning objectives around the six areas of the standards (direct practice, system management, organisational change and development, policy, research and education and professional development). The learning plan was then used as the basis for ongoing monitoring and evaluation of students' learning. Students and field educators were required to refer back to the plan during the interim reviews, preparing mid- and end-of-placement evaluation reports. In short, competence standards, through the learning plan, provided the organising framework for professional learning experiences.

In a different yet equally explicit way, practicum assessment criteria entered students' lesson planning in the area of Arts curriculum. For example, the Arts education lecturer used practicum evaluation rubrics that were intended for assessing student teachers' classroom performance during their practicum, as one of the devices for guiding the student teachers' lesson planning and assessment. The Arts education lecturer reflected on the rationale:

> The other thing that I use and that strongly informs my lessons and that's also available to the students is the lesson evaluation from the practicum handbook. *They're being evaluated on specific things and a lot of that is also infused in those lesson plans.* Also because part of lesson planning, apart from them having learning the skills, is to get them ready for their first practicum. If they don't develop a lesson plan according to those criteria, then it's going to be *very difficult.* (Education Lecturer)

In many other units, professional standards were used to frame the broad aims of the course or tasks, but were not very visible in what students actually did. For example, in the Maze task – which required preservice teachers to reflect on their professional experiences – the role of professional standards was described in the following way,

> Develop a narrative maze that demonstrates your deep understanding of Elements Two and Three of the NSW Institute of Teachers professional teaching standards (2005). These Elements are to do with the diverse nature of students, the diverse ways they learn, and the

methods teachers use to know what their students are learning. This means that although a problem behaviour may be the impetus for your narrative, the discussion needs to be phrased in terms of learning. In order to adequately address Element 3, you will need to provide concrete artifacts of teaching (e.g. a variety of assessments, rubrics, and student work). These should be rich in possible interpretations. Your case needs to reflect that learning is a complex, multi-variant business. Your writing should be *rich in detail, nuanced and data driven.* (Professional Experiences course outline, description of a critically reflective writing task 'The Maze')

The competence standards did not just provide a broad framing for students' choice of artefacts and topics for exploration and reflection. Rather, they shaped, in direct ways, what and how students learn and what they actually have to demonstrate.

In summary, technical, practice and competence codes define three different aspects of professional work: (a) objects and procedures, (b) ways of doing and being and (c) knowledge, skills and other attributes. Different kinds of codes consequently have very different intrinsic features and consequentially different roles in the assemblages of professional practice and learning. Mulcahy (2011) uses the distinction between representational and performative ways of thinking to argue that standards are not only a 'technology' for discovering and representing a priori realities, they are relationally enacted in local practices and they produce certain sorts of professional identity.

13.2.2   Conceptual Infrastructure

Conceptual infrastructure (which could also be called 'knowledge infrastructure' or 'cognitive infrastructure') provides the conceptual basis for professional work and connects professional knowledge to other disciplinary knowledge domains. It includes substantive knowledge of the profession and contributing literacies and knowledge bases.

Substantive knowledge of the profession includes concepts, facts and other knowledge resources – including social, cultural, historical and other kinds of knowledge related to the profession. For example, the pharmacist's knowledge base is constituted of numerous knowledge resources, such as pharmacological terms, and knowledge about available medications, prices, substitutes, drug companies, current 'hot issues' in the pharmaceutical field, differences between different kinds of pharmacies and the social organisation of the professional domain, including its history and the role of the pharmacy in the community.

Contributing literacies include knowledge resources related to the adjacent ubiquitous literacies that also provide the basis for professional working knowledge, such as reading, writing, technology use, general communication capabilities, etc. *Contributing knowledge bases* are knowledge resources from adjacent disciplinary domains that contribute to professional understanding and problem-solving. For example, in pharmacy adjacent professional domains include pharmaceutical chemistry, pharmaceutics and therapeutics. While they are separate domains of

---

Information gathering before tutorial

What does an analysis of the structures and mechanism of action of beta agonists and the anticholinergic bronchodilators tell you about their activity?

Before the tutorial: review the chemical structures, thinking about their interactions with target receptors. Be prepared to discuss how these medicines work at the molecular level (including SAR, receptor and cell signalling)

Fig. 13.4 Pre-tutorial task given to pharmacy students (Source: Student resources for Respiratory case)

knowledge they can be used in pharmaceutical decisions. For example, in pharmacy tutorials, students were asked to relate chemical structures and mechanisms of action to the activity of medicines and on this basis decide what kind of medication should be prescribed for a patient with chronic obstructive pulmonary diseases (COPD) (Fig. 13.4).

13.2.3 Information Infrastructure

Information infrastructure is constituted of material and digital knowledge tools for professional knowledge work. For example, during most seminars, pharmacy students constantly consulted the *Therapeutic Guidelines* and *Australian Medicines Handbook* as well as a range of more specialised reference materials related to specific diseases. They also frequently looked on the web for information needed for specific tasks that they had been set. Information devices that constitute information infrastructure are primarily used for their professional knowledge content and information retrieval possibilities. They function as 'cognitive partners' (Salomon, Perkins, & Globerson, 1991) that hold explicit professional knowledge and allow access to this knowledge when it becomes relevant to the task at hand. Broadly, we can distinguish between three kinds of information devices that have different mixtures of knowledge storage and information retrieval functions.

Knowledge storage tools are information tools that are primarily used for their substantive content relevant to professional work: manuals, (text)books, professional journals, newsletters and guidelines. *Knowledge storage and retrieval tools*, in contrast to simple storage tools, are used for both disciplinary content and flexible retrieval opportunities. They include handbooks, disciplinary databases and other resources organised in particular ways (e.g. with good indexes). Such tools have a modular structure, which allows users to retrieve specific knowledge needed for the task at hand, without knowing the rest of the information. *General information retrieval tools* are primarily used for their capacities to locate and retrieve information: by definition, they do not have their own content. Examples include Internet search engines and catalogues of resources.

These three types of information tools have different intrinsic features and structure the nature of knowledge work in ways that broadly are similar to simple, organised and active shaping in Rabardel and Beguin's (2005) terms (see Chap. 12). Knowledge storage tools basically structure the activity around the form distinct to the information (i.e. simple shaping). Storage and retrieval tools broadly structure the activity in ways organised around the structure of this information and tool, and the structure of activity usually depends on the way the tool presents the information and how it is designed to be used (i.e. organised shaping). Retrieval tools, in contrast, are capable of retrieving and presenting information of various kinds and various forms depending on the user interaction (i.e. open shaping). This 'open shaping' is distinct from 'active shaping' (Rabardel & Beguin, 2005). The core feature of open shaping is that not only is the tool capable of shaping and adapting to the user's needs, but also the user is capable of shaping and adapting to the tool. Both the inquirer and the tool weave the fabric of the inquiry.

What are the relationships between information infrastructure, on the one hand, and 'pure' epistemic tools, codes and conceptual infrastructure, on the other hand? The two are closely interrelated. 'Pure' epistemic tools, codes and conceptual infrastructure are brought into the epistemic assemblage for their immaterial (discursive) features. In contrast, information infrastructure comes into this assemblage for its material features. For example, individual technical codes (e.g. national curricula, syllabuses, educational standards) enter teachers' knowledge work as epistemic discourse tools that are capable of generating and shaping meanings, but technical codes are also entangled in material–symbolic tools of the information infrastructure, through which they are shared and brought to life within the profession. They have features (modalities) of both codes (epistemic discourse) and information tools (material knowledge). The two modalities are intertwined – they are a deep blend of socio-material and conceptual parts of professional knowledge.

13.2.4 Learning Infrastructure

Learning infrastructure is an infrastructure that is specially designed for making professional learning possible. This infrastructure is primarily constituted of tools for professional development. These can be grouped into two main classes: updates and exemplars.

Updates are normally used to disseminate and learn knowledge that is new to the field. Most new professional knowledge of this kind involves discrete elements that have a form or structure that is very familiar to experienced practitioners: for example, new facts about a medication. Professionals do not usually encounter any epistemic challenges when integrating these familiar items of knowledge with what they already know. For example, learning about a new medication that has just come onto the market, or about the discontinuation of a medication, would not usually cause epistemic difficulties for a practising pharmacist. Professional bulletins, newspapers, journals, handbook updates and other similar professional learning and development tools play important roles in supporting professional learning of this kind. Such tools are closely intertwined with the information and material infrastructures of the profession. But what we emphasise here is a distinct *modality* – functioning as professional learning infrastructure and as epistemic tools of the profession. For example, in courses we observed, students made extensive use of these professional updates and teachers introduced professional websites and newsletters explicitly as tools to 'watch out for' new knowledge. For example, during the Cardiovascular course, pharmacy students were explicitly introduced to the Pharmaceutical Society of Australia website as a place for hot news that professionals should monitor.

Exemplars, in contrast, are more distinct elements of professional learning and epistemic infrastructure. They are shared learning tools that are intrinsic to a professional episteme. Broadly, exemplars are cases and other examples that are constructed to communicate those aspects of professional episteme that cannot be conveyed by communicating abstract conceptual frameworks and tools of the profession (i.e. substantive and syntactic structures). As Sadler (1987) explains,

> Exemplars are key examples chosen so as to be typical of designated levels of quality or competence. The exemplars are not the standards themselves, but are indicative of them; they specify standards implicitly. (Sadler, 1987, p. 200)

Exemplars are broadly used in many professional domains for conveying practical meaning of abstract professional concepts, such as what counts as 'high-priority problems' in intensive care units (Fig. 13.5) or what counts as 'level 2 students' inquiry skills' in science lessons (Fig. 13.6).

Some such exemplars deconstruct and illustrate professional actions and thinking (e.g. worked out problem solutions), some deconstruct or illustrate specific elements (e.g. how to communicate a specific kind of finding in a letter to a doctor) and the final outcome (e.g. examples of medication reviews, examples of lesson plans and teaching materials). For example, pharmacy students for learning to conduct medication reviews were often referred to a process guide. This guidebook described the medication review process using adaptations of variety of real-life cases (Chen, Moles, Nishtala, & Basger, 2010). These cases modelled different aspects of medication review process, such as what kinds of questions should be asked during the interview if a patient has a particular combination of diseases, what kinds of information should be obtained from pharmacy records, what kind of therapeutic and pharmaceutical knowledge is relevant for making decisions, and how recommendations should be prioritised and delivered to a patient and doctor, up to 'sample' correspondence to the refereeing medical practitioner, illustrating possible communication styles.

Similarly, when arts education students were planning their lessons, it was suggested that they should use an exemplar prepared by the state's Board of Studies (2003) *Visual Arts Years 7–10: Advice on Programming and Assessment*. This document

> ... has been designed to help teachers understand key aspects of the new *Visual Arts Years 7–10 Syllabus* and provide guidance for implementation. <...> The *sample stage* program plans and the sample units of work in this document *demonstrate* ways in which teachers

---

Intensive Care Unit (ICU) problems

High-priority ICU problem characteristics

- Generally fatal without aggressive treatment
- Delays in therapy are associated with worse outcomes
- Frequent data assessment is necessary for clinical decision making
- Significant morbidity often occurs in survivors
- Frequently associated with complications

Examples

Respiratory failure

CV: cardiac arrest, malignant arrhythmia, myocardial infraction

Shock

CNS events: stroke, seizure, meningitis

Massive trauma with haemorrhage

Large body-surface area burns

Fig. 13.5 An extract from the list for prioritising patient problems in the intensive care unit (Based on Hess, 2007, p. 17)

Scientific inquiry skills: Ideas and evidence

Level 2

- Students answer a question using experience

Examples

Teacher: "Which material shall we wrap the hot water bottle in to keep it warm?"

Pupil: "This one because it is like my coat. The fluffy one because it feels warm."

Fig. 13.6 An extract from benchmarks of scientific inquiry skills (Based on a handout used in Science and Technology course for preservice teachers)

can build a teaching and learning program and develop units of work to ensure coverage of the scope of the syllabus. (Board of Studies, 2003, p. 5, emphasis added)

The document includes descriptions of the planning process and annotated examples of the program plans and units of work.

Many similar exemplars are used for teaching in educational institutions, but what we want to point out here is that such learning tools are not just tools for learning at university: they play a much deeper, yet under-acknowledged part, in professional epistemic infrastructure.

Handley and Williams (2011) note that while students in higher education may use exemplars for short-term instrumental reasons – to improve assignments – they also have developmental value 'in that exemplars help students refine their understanding of their discipline and how to communicate within it' (p. 98). The link between the epistemic frames, devices and other symbolic tools that codify knowledge, including rubrics that are used for grading students' essays, and the exemplars is broadly parallel to the distinction between the explicit and the tacit dimensions of knowledge work in professions (Chap. 4). 'Pure' epistemic devices and conceptual infrastructures embody conscious forms of knowledge that can be put into words or other forms of articulated discourse – easing dissemination and the movement of knowledge from one location to another. However, this may obscure many of the surrounding details in which those forms of knowledge make sense. Exemplars, in contrast, tend to obscure underpinning structures and forms, but they are rich in details, tightly linked with the context and other kinds of knowledge that cannot be easily rendered explicit and thus can capture some kinds of knowledge that tend to be tacit.

There is, however, a possible trap. As Handley and Williams note: 'Although exemplars are not models, students may see them in that way' (loc. cit.). That is, exemplars are not objects that have to be precisely reproduced. Rather, they are landmarks which guide improvisatory activity.

13.2.5   Boundary Infrastructure

Boundary infrastructures enable the sharing of information among professionals from different fields who are working on a common problem. They are constituted of different tools for storing, integrating, retrieving and sharing situated, case-specific knowledge. They contain *situated* knowledge needed for *situated* professional work, and they enable its transfer through space and time. Boundary infrastructure is primarily constituted of occupation-specific or workplace-specific knowledge tools for sharing boundary artefacts. These may be quite simple (e.g. handover sheets) or they may be complex, integrated systems (e.g. integrated patient databases). Such infrastructures comprise of tools for inter-professional and intra-professional work.

Inter-professional knowledge tools allow exchanges of situated knowledge across traditional professional boundaries. For example, they include such things as (a) a doctor's referral written for a pharmacist, containing information about a patient (diagnosis, laboratory results, medications taken, reasons for referral, etc.) that is needed for the pharmacist to make appropriate judgements and (b) the pharmacist's medication management review report, sent back to the doctor.

Boundary infrastructures are also used to maintain and share situated knowledge within professional and workplace settings. They allow integration and continuity of professional work across time. Examples of these *intra-professional knowledge tools* include such things as software for dispensing prescriptions used by pharmacists, patient databases used by medical doctors and various files that 'follow' individual students when then move from class to class or from school to school.

Boundary infrastructure is distinct from information infrastructure. The former contains objects of *situated* knowledge and resources for *situated* knowledge work (e.g. information about a student or a patient). The latter contains *generalised* professional knowledge (e.g. information about a curriculum or a medication). Boundary artefacts are created using various epistemic devices, instruments and equipment, such as templates for referrals or templates for keeping records of student progress. The focus here, however, is not so much on the epistemic tools that have been used to produce knowledge embodied in boundary artefacts, but on the artefacts themselves and the infrastructures that enable them to be useful. Boundary infrastructure allows situated knowledge to be passed from one location to another or maintained over the time, integrated, retrieved and understood. This infrastructure is constituted of tools that are broadly similar to what Star (2005; Star & Griesemer, 1989) calls 'boundary objects',

> These are objects that are weakly structured in common usage, and more tightly tailored in the use in one particular line of work. They are ambiguous but they are part of a durable cooperation across social worlds. They facilitate cooperation without consensus. (Star, 2005, p. 171)

13.2.6   *Material Infrastructure*

Material infrastructure is constructed from physical tools and physical things that make epistemic work possible. It includes material (including technical) affordances and related socio-material arrangements that constitute spaces and places for professional epistemic work. Roughly speaking, this infrastructure comprises of two main categories of technical and material affordances: specialised professional and general.

Specialised professional technical and material affordances are specific to a particular domain. Examples would be technical devices, such as inhalers that pharmacists use to demonstrate inhaling techniques; patients' medicines that they would encounter during medication reviews; and blood pressure monitors, mannequins and other such equipment that constitutes the professional environment that nurses encounter in simulated hospital wards during their preparation and later in real hospitals.

General technical and material affordances are not specific to a profession or professional domain. They include such tools as computers that are used for accessing course websites and professional information services and cameras that students use to take pictures when they create their learning portfolios or manuals containing professional guidelines. They also include a variety of very basic material arrangements and tools used in professional work, such as buildings, beds, desks and pens.

In short, material infrastructure is constituted of physical things and arrangements that *embody* 'pure' epistemic tools as well as tools that belong to other infrastructures (e.g. conceptual, information, learning) and that do not have a 'hard-wired' material expression (e.g. a database). But it also includes simple physical spaces and affordances that make human life and work possible. In short, cognition and professional knowledge work do not appear in a material vacuum. Indeed professional knowing and matter are firmly entangled with each other. Many tools – even pure epistemic tools – have a material modality, and many physical things encountered within professional work (medication packages, the patient's body, etc.) have an epistemic modality. We explore this argument more deeply in Chap. 16.

13.2.7   Sociopolitical Infrastructure

In a similar vein, professional work is also entangled with a sociopolitical infrastructure. It consists of a range of cultural and social arrangements that enable society to function as a whole. Such arrangements include broad social agreements that are often simply called 'culture' as well as various more explicit and temporarily bounded political, social and economic agendas, such as general national, regional and local policies and plans, that regulate economic activities, the provision of social services and other aspects of shared human life. While the direct role of this infrastructure in professional knowledge work may be less perceptible, nevertheless these social and political arrangements often have extensive effects on professional knowledgeable actions and work. For example, school teachers' work cannot be separated from the broader social and educational policies that set up expectations, define schools' roles in the overall educational system and in society, regulate school functioning by providing financial resources for particular kinds of activities (and not others) and in other ways shape how teachers see their roles, what they do and what they don't. Similarly, the work of architects and building engineers is shaped by housing and social welfare policies and provisions; energy engineers' work is shaped by energy and sustainability policies, global oil prices and market conditions.

Sociopolitical infrastructures consist of two main components: domain-specific and general social agreements, policies and other agendas.

Domain-specific agendas primarily include policies, strategies, plans and other regulations that directly pertain to the domain of professional activity. For example, knowledgeable actions of professionals working in the telecommunication sector are inseparable from existing universal service policies as well as laws regulating networked industries and monopolies.

In contrast, *general agendas* include various arrangements that run beyond the direct scope of the professional domain, but which nevertheless shape its activities. For example, professional work in the telecommunication sector is also shaped by media, copyright and other policies that are not unique to activities in this sector, but which nevertheless shape consumers' needs for services and choices. Another example would be governmental strategies for lifelong learning or healthcare that could have wide reaching and long-lasting implications for how telecommunications networks are used.

While some aspects of sociopolitical infrastructure could be closely related to codes, particularly technical codes, nevertheless sociopolitical infrastructure and codes have quite different roles in the overall epistemic infrastructure of a profession. Codes provide mechanisms for coordinating and connecting various elements of professional practices and knowledge, including inputs, processes and products. In contrast, sociopolitical infrastructure provides a means for establishing links between, on the one hand, professional purposes and ways of acting and, on the other hand, the broader collective intentions and practices of communities and societies, within which professional work obtains its meaning.

13.3 Learning as Inhabiting an Epistemic Infrastructure

13.3.1 Socio-cognitive and Socio-material Aspects of Epistemic Infrastructure

There are important synergies and tensions between the conceptual, material and social aspects of the epistemic infrastructures of professions. To represent this, we can plot the main constitutive elements of the professional epistemic infrastructures within a socio-cognitive and socio-material space (Fig. 13.7). While some of these contributing infrastructures are strong in cognitive aspects and weak in social and material (i.e. conceptual infrastructure), many other infrastructures that are designed to pass on created knowledge tend to have a very evident material expression (i.e. information, learning, boundary, material infrastructure). Nevertheless, many core epistemic tools for creating knowledge have a strong social dimension (i.e. epistemic frames, devices, instruments, equipment, codes). Yet they are not reducible to the purely social (i.e. sociopolitical infrastructure).

What does this tell us about the nature of tools and infrastructures with(in) which professionals learn and construct knowledge for action?

As Turnbull (2000) argued, about the professional knowledge needed to build Gothic cathedrals,

> It is reasonable to suppose that the Gothic Cathedral builders, as builders of today, did not need a generalised theory in order to achieve successful practice, but case-specific solutions, or exemplars. (Turnbull, 2000, p. 76)

As he noted, such solutions and related knowledge are transmitted in a variety of ways, such as word of mouth, techniques frozen and materialised in portable templates (epistemic tools in our case), education and tradition. Tradition is essential to successful professional work and

> A tradition may or may not include theories and texts but always includes training, development of skills and the knowledge and the observation of other structures and solutions. (op. cit., p. 77)

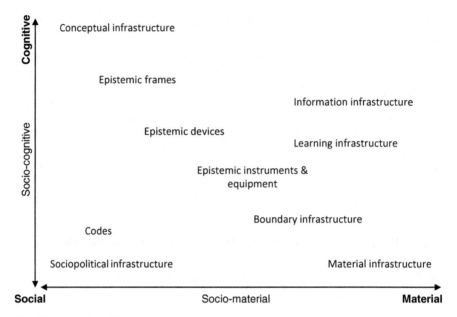

Fig. 13.7 Epistemic infrastructure in socio-cognitive and socio-material spaces

But can conventional material and social traditions be enough for knowledgeable work in rapidly changing knowledge-intensive professions? Indeed, apprenticeship has been one of the main, successful, ways to teach and learn complex occupational skills, across centuries of human history (Billett, 2014). It has not lost its central role in preparing students for complex modern professions, such as medicine and research. However, developing capacities to work with knowledge involves passing on a rather different kind of tradition – an 'epistemic tradition'. Such learning demands new kinds of apprenticeship – 'cognitive apprenticeship' (Collins, Brown, & Holum, 1991) or 'epistemic apprenticeship' – that fuses professional practices, passed through observation, social interaction and material engagement, with observation of largely invisible mental processes, such as thinking, self-regulation and reflection.

What we called pure epistemic tools tend to provide a productive middle zone for developing new kinds of traditions, at the intersection of the conceptual, social and material. These practices build upon and generate knowledge that is connected with material action and the sociopolitical concerns of communities. However, knowledgeable action in a rapidly changing world requires capacities that go beyond the preconfigured core epistemic toolbox, such as ready-made procedures for diagnosing a disease or disability and making decisions about the best treatment. It requires a capacity to navigate among, and flexibly build, assemblages of tools that are 'thick' in the material but also rich in the conceptual – and which therefore can be enacted through a tight alignment between cognitive, social and material practices.

13.3.2 Learning Through Mastering Epistemic Tools

By focussing on the split between disciplinary knowledge, embodied material skill and social practice in higher education, the very essence of professional knowledge is obscured and the epistemic complexity of knowledgeable action is underestimated.

Firstly, different professional tools have different properties. Some tools, in a conceptual sense, are generally straightforward and mastered mainly through extensive social engagement or embodied practice, but some other tools require significant mental engagement. The key danger is that higher education sometimes oversimplifies the *epistemic* qualities of professional tools – treating most of them as purely technical instruments and equipment that do not have an epistemic modality and should be mastered as part of a routine embodied skill. Nevertheless, many professional devices include *various* modalities, such as the conceptual, social and physical. Higher education could do a much better job engaging students in unpacking the epistemology that underpins epistemic tools of practice. Engaging students in *creating* artefacts that can be used as tools for professional work would also bring them closer to a major source of professional creativity and innovation.

Second, little attention has been paid to the diversity of most powerful epistemic tools of professions, such as higher level frames and inquiry strategies used in professional fields: often limiting learning and professional performance to repetitive deployment of one specific (preferred) epistemological frame. What are the different frames and devices that exist in a profession? Why are they different? When and how should they be used and combined?

Third, epistemic forms (and their associated games) are attracting more attention, in science education, as generative structures. They are, as yet, rather overlooked in professional education. Epistemic forms are generic disciplinary tools that help a person develop *generic* capacities for creating *situation-specific* knowledge relevant to the profession and the workplace. A distinguishing quality of these professional epistemic devices is that they allow the creation of situated knowledge but are not themselves situative.

Fourth, epistemic tools are used in an ensemble and are embodied in physical tools and environments in action. Each part is not a whole. As an example, epistemic frames are used in combination with the instruments and codes; they are not separated from conceptual knowledge bases and knowledge embodied in a person's capacities to use information and boundary infrastructures. Epistemic tools are not used in a vacuum; they are used for solving specific professional problems and they are used in material and social environments – they are used to deal with embodied social 'matter' (children, patients, etc.).

Fifth, the professional competence required to weave all the necessary capacities together grows out of practice in such 'weaving' (i.e. in real situated work). But students who are learning to be professionals can, indeed should, also be helped to develop and fine-tune component skills. Their teachers need a good, articulated, understanding of the professional epistemic toolset in order to shape suitable learning opportunities: opportunities to recognise and master the (epistemic) tools of the trade. If higher education relies on the use of traditional situated work-based practice and apprenticeship models, there is little hope of preparing professionals for work and workplace learning better than workplaces themselves can.

Nevertheless, learning to use tools skilfully does not centre on tools as objects, but on developing appropriate action schemes for them, and learning to use these tools in dynamic assemblages within unfolding human activities and interactions, rather than merely in isolation. As Goodwin (2005) observes,

> ... human beings perceive space from within socially organized settings and conceptualise, articulate and traverse space through a rich collection of tools that have been appropriated from the cognitive activities of our predecessors (maps, graphs, ships, etc.). Central to the organisation of space are local activities and processes of human interaction within which different orders of space are tied together into the structures necessary for the accomplishment of relevant action. (Goodwin, 2005, p. 118)

So our focus now shifts from epistemic tools and infrastructures per se to epistemic games – to constructing 'doable problems' by *inhabiting* epistemic spaces.

References

Australian Association of Social Workers. (2003). *Practice standards for social workers: Achieving outcomes*. Canberra: AASW. Retrieved April 14, 2015 from http://www.aasw.asn.au/document/item/16

Billett, S. (2014). *Mimetic learning at work: Learning in the circumstances of practice*. Heidelberg, Germany: Springer.

Board of Studies. (2003). *Visual arts years 7–10: Advice on programming and assessment*. Retrieved June 20, 2015 from http://www.boardofstudies.nsw.edu.au/syllabus_sc/pdf_doc/visual_arts_710_support.pdf

Bowker, G. C., & Star, S. L. (1999). *Sorting things out: Classification and its consequences*. Cambridge, MA: MIT Press.

Brunsson, N., & Jacobsson, B. (Eds.). (2000). *A world of standards*. New York: Oxford University Press.

Busch, L. (2011). *Standards: Recipes for reality*. Cambridge, MA: MIT Press.

Carmichael, P. (2012). Tribes, territories and threshold concepts: Educational materialisms at work in higher education. *Educational Philosophy and Theory, 44*(sup1), 31–42. doi:10.1111/j.1469-5812.2010.00743.x.

Chen, T., Moles, R., Nishtala, P., & Basger, B. (2010). *Case studies in practice. Medication review: A process guide for pharmacists*. Sydney, Australia: Pharmaceutical Society of Australia.

Clarke, A. E., & Fujimura, J. H. (Eds.). (1992). *The right tools for the job: At work in twentieth-century life sciences*. Princeton, NJ: Princeton University Press.

Collins, A. (2011). A study of expert theory formation: The role of different model types and domain frameworks. In M. S. Khine & I. M. Saleh (Eds.), *Models and modeling* (pp. 23–40). Dordrecht, The Netherlands: Springer.

Collins, A., Brown, J. S., & Holum, A. (1991). Cognitive apprenticeship: Making things visible. *American Educator: The Professional Journal of the American Federation of Teachers, 15*(3), 6–11, 38–46.

Collins, A., & Ferguson, W. (1993). Epistemic forms and epistemic games: Structures and strategies to guide inquiry. *Educational Psychologist, 28*(1), 25–42.

De Landa, M. (2011). *Philosophy and simulation: The emergence of synthetic reason*. London: Continuum.

Ewenstein, B., & Whyte, J. (2009). Knowledge practices in design: The role of visual representations as 'epistemic objects'. *Organization Studies, 30*(1), 7–30.

Fujimura, J. H. (1987). Constructing 'do-able' problems in cancer research: Articulating alignment. *Social Studies of Science, 17*(2), 257–293. doi:10.1177/030631287017002003.

Goodwin, C. (2005). Seeing in depth. In S. J. Derry, C. D. Schunn, & M. A. Gernsbacher (Eds.), *Interdisciplinary collaboration: An emerging cognitive science* (pp. 85–121). Mahwah, NJ: Lawrence Erlbaum Associates.

Handley, K., & Williams, L. (2011). From copying to learning: Using exemplars to engage students with assessment criteria and feedback. *Assessment and Evaluation in Higher Education, 36*(1), 95–108.

Hess, M. (2007). *Integrating critical care skills into your practice: A case workbook*. Bethesda, MD: American Society of Health-System Pharmacists.

Lampland, M., & Star, S. L. (Eds.). (2009). *Standards and their stories: How quantifying, classifying, and formalizing practices shape everyday life*. London: Cornell University Press.

Mulcahy, D. (2011). Assembling the 'accomplished' teacher: The performativity and politics of professional teaching standards. *Educational Philosophy and Theory, 43*, 94–113.

Nersessian, N. J. (2005). Interpreting scientific and engineering practices: Integrating the cognitive, social, and cultural dimensions. In M. E. Gorman, R. D. Tweney, D. C. Gooding, & A. P. Kincannon (Eds.), *Scientific and technological thinking* (pp. 17–56). Mahwah, NJ: Lawrence Erlbaum Associates.

Nersessian, N. J. (2006). The cognitive-cultural systems of the research laboratory. *Organization Studies, 27*(1), 125–145.

Perkins, D. (2006). Constructivism and troublesome knowledge. In J. H. F. Meyer & R. Land (Eds.), *Overcoming barriers to student understanding: Threshold concepts and troublesome knowledge* (pp. 33–47). London: Routledge.

Rabardel, P., & Beguin, P. (2005). Instrument mediated activity: From subject development to anthropocentric design. *Theoretical Issues in Ergonomics Science, 6*(5), 429–461.

Ravetz, J. R. (1971). *Scientific knowledge and its social problems*. Oxford: Clarendon Press.

Sadler, D. R. (1987). Specifying and promulgating achievement standards. *Oxford Review of Education, 13*(2), 191–209.

Salomon, G., Perkins, D. N., & Globerson, T. (1991). Partners in cognition: Extending human intelligence with intelligent technologies. *Educational Researcher, 20*(3), 2–9.

Scott, V., Laragy, C., Giles, R., & Bland, R. (2004). Practice standards in Australia: Implications for social work education. *Social Work Education, 23*(5), 613–624.

Star, S. L. (2005). Categories and cognition: Material and conceptual aspects of large scale category systems. In S. J. Derry, C. D. Schunn, & M. A. Gernsbacher (Eds.), *Interdisciplinary collaboration: An emerging cognitive science* (pp. 167–186). Mahwah, NJ: Lawrence Erlbaum Associates.

Star, S. L., & Griesemer, J. R. (1989). Institutional ecology, 'translations' and boundary objects: Amateurs and professionals in Berkeley's museum of vertebrate zoology. *Social Studies of Science, 19*(4), 387–420.

Timmermans, S., & Epstein, S. (2010). A world of standards but not a standard world: Toward a sociology of standards and standardization. *Annual Review of Sociology, 36*(1), 69–89.

Tripp, D. (1993). *Critical incidents in teaching: Developing professional judgement*. London: Routledge.

Tummons, J. (2011). Deconstructing professionalism: An actor-network critique of professional standards for teachers in the uk lifelong learning sector. *International Journal of Actor Network Theory and Technological Innovation, 3*(4), 22–31.

Turnbull, D. (2000). *Masons, tricksters and cartographers: Comparative studies in the sociology of scientific and indigenous knowledge*. Abingdon, OX: Routledge.

Chapter 14
Professional Epistemic Games

> I think that nearly every service that you provide [in pharmacy], even if it was just really quick and you're getting a prescription in and then you're giving it back out – at some stage there needs to be some *information gathering* to find out whether that's appropriate; *the processing* is working out and 'is it appropriate?'; and *then the delivery* is at least giving it back to them and providing some counselling. (Pharmacy Lecturer)

The main aim of this chapter is to explain the function and nature of professional epistemic games. We identify a number of varieties of such epistemic games and we offer a taxonomy to capture their main similarities and differences. We take the view that programs of professional education implicitly involve students in learning to play a variety of epistemic games. Being able to distinguish clearly and explicitly between different kinds of games seems to us to be a prerequisite for a more considered, defensible and effective approach to curriculum planning. The bulk of this chapter is taken up with a presentation of the taxonomy. This is preceded by an introduction to the notion of an epistemic game, with some pointers to the literature in which this construct originates (Sect. 14.1). After that, we offer an extended example, inspired by some of our observational work in pharmacy education (Sect. 14.2). Section 14.3 summarises the rationale for, and approach to constructing, our taxonomy, which is presented in detail in Sect. 14.4. Our taxonomy includes a particularly important kind of epistemic game, which we have named the weaving game. We explain and illustrate this in Chap. 15, which also includes our general conclusions about the importance of epistemic games in professional education and professional work.

14.1 Introducing the Idea of Epistemic Games

The notion of *game* has roots in diverse traditions: game as socially learnt rules and habits (Bourdieu, 1977); language games as a way of meaning-making (Wittgenstein, 1963); game as a kind of formal high-level thinking with abstract schemas

© Springer Science+Business Media Dordrecht 2017

L. Markauskaite, P. Goodyear, *Epistemic Fluency and Professional Education*,
Professional and Practice-based Learning 14, DOI 10.1007/978-94-007-4369-4_14

(Ohlsson, 1993); game as a form of inquiry informed by a set of rules and strategies that guide inquiry around specific forms of discourse (Collins, 2011; Collins & Ferguson, 1993; Ohlsson, 1993; Perkins, 1997); and game as a set of skills, knowledge, values, identity and epistemology that characterise expert behaviour in a particular community (Shaffer, 2006).

Combining those traditions, our emphasis in using the notion of game is on rules and flexibility, a fine-tuned practical sense of a situation and disposition for action. *A game is a form of action that entangles rules of thought and rules of culture with affordances and constraints, symbolic inscriptions and the physical world.*

Wittgenstein (1963) used the notion of a 'language game' to describe the way language combines rules and flexibility. On the one hand, rules that are recognisable in language games make it possible for people to grasp each other's meanings. On the other hand, the flexibility provided by rules enables people to produce an infinite variety of meanings.

Somewhat differently, Bourdieu (1977) used the term 'game sense' to emphasise the routine nature of practical action. He argued that social agents in different fields of modern life (e.g. the economy, politics, science and education) develop certain dispositions for social action. These dispositions combine with each other when the individual engages in a multidimensional (multi-field) social world, eventually forming a 'practical sense' or 'sense of the game' that is based on practical reason for social action and an 'economy of logic', rather than objective, true and complete understanding.

Games can also be seen as abstract structures that operate at the level of generative cognitive mechanisms (Ohlsson, 1993), inquiry patterns structured around specific forms of inscription (Collins, 2011; Collins & Ferguson, 1993) or other forms of discourse (Ohlsson, 1993; Perkins, 1997).

In the context of professional learning, we see a particular value in the *generative* capacities of epistemic games and the discourse structures that guide them. Novices may play these games more consciously, while experts, in routine situations, usually have more finely tuned attention and skill and may play them without (much) deliberative thinking and conscious attention. On this view, understanding that is based solely on abstract generic ways of thinking – technical rationality – is far from sufficient for fluent situated professional work. That said, epistemic games are not purely intuitive or exclusively situated. Each has rules that can be explicated, taught and learnt. Moves can be rehearsed and fluent play can be built up gradually. So actionable knowledge is inseparable from mastery of a certain set of knowledge and skills, but knowledgeable action also involves a competent grasp of the situation and thoughtful local action.

If we accept the existence of epistemic games, as inquiry patterns and characteristic structures that guide human thought and action – and there is enough evidence to do so – the important questions then become: what is the origin of those generative patterns and structures, and how does the human mind work with them and (how) can this capability be learnt?

There are at least several distinct views about how such patterns (i.e. schemas) might arise. Ohlsson (1993) summarises two distinct views. The first is that such schemas have a biological origin. As Hayek (1972) argued,

> Most of the action patterns by which the organism responds will be innate. (Hayek, 1972, p. 317, cited in Ohlsson, 1993, p. 63)

Such patterns may be uncovered in reflection, but, before this, they are created and are used in human discourse. These patterns have biological rather than psychological origins, thus, reflection can only uncover them, and it does not create them.

In contrast, the second view, espoused by Bartlett (1932) and Piaget (1985) and others, says that such schemas are created through conscious reflection by discovering regularities in discourse and in one's own thought. In this case, consciousness allows humans to alter their schemas. Others argue for a middle ground, suggesting that such schemas might have an innate origin, but later are revised, corrected and amended (Ohlsson, 1993; Schank & Abelson, 1977).

Others again have suggested that there is no such direct mapping between the world and the abstract mental schemes that people may use to comprehend the world and to structure discourse and their behaviour. Some deny the very existence of such 'schema-like' mental representations (Greeno & Hall, 1997; Roth & McGinn, 1998; Salomon, Perkins, & Globerson, 1991; Suchman, 2007). In contrast, these researchers focus on the relationship between various visual inscriptions (such as graphs, tables or concept maps) as 'tools for thought' and the unfolding processes of thinking and action – as distinct but constitutively entangled aspects of human thought and the external world.

The debate about whether such generative patterns and structures have similar (isomorphic) representations or are somehow represented differently in the human mind is not so relevant to our argument here. There is enough evidence to suggest that tools of thought that guide human thinking and inquiry exist can be learnt and actively deployed as a part of perception and/or of the thinker's intellectual agenda (Fischer, Kollar, Mandl, & Haake, 2007; Henning, 2004; Moseley et al., 2005; Ohlsson, 1993). A more important and challenging issue is that professional work combines multiple ways of knowing and thus requires the ability to use multiple 'tools for thought' that have diverse epistemic origins and purposes: that is, to engage in different kinds of epistemic games simultaneously.

14.2   Illustrating the Idea of Epistemic Games in Professional Practice: An Example from Pharmacy

In various situations in professional work – as diverse as the dispensing of a single medication by a pharmacist to completing a complex medication review – it is not very difficult to spot some characteristic, recurrent features. Consider the following situation.

Mr Ward comes into the pharmacy with a new prescription for cholesterol. The pharmacist checks his records in a database and recognises Mr Ward as a customer who has come to the pharmacy regularly to obtain his prescriptions for hypertension. The pharmacist asks Mr Ward some questions related to the new prescription and changes in his health conditions (in order to *gather* necessary information), *decides* what and how to dispense, prepares the prescription, writes down information on how and when to take the medication, gives the medication to Mr Ward and *provides* some related counselling.

There are at least three recognisable *moves* made by the pharmacist:[1]

- To *gather* the necessary information from Mr Ward and from relevant databases
- To *process* information and make a decision about the appropriateness of the prescription (what and how to dispense for Mr Ward)
- To *deliver* the medication to Mr Ward and to deliver information to him about how to take this new medication, what kind of changes to make in taking other medications and, overall, how to manage his related health conditions

This mundane form of inquiry and knowledgeable action involves certain characteristic *rules*. The questions to the customer (i.e. gathering) must be relevant to the situation, presented in a logical order and in a language understandable to him. The questioning should provide sufficient information for making a decision and to provide counselling for Mr Ward. For example, Mr Ward would not be surprised to be asked such simple questions as: 'What did the doctor tell you about this medication?'; 'Why has the doctor prescribed it for you?'; 'What have you tried already to lower your cholesterol?'; 'What effect did dietary changes and regular exercise have on your cholesterol?'; 'What was your latest blood pressure reading?'; and 'What other medications do you currently take?' Mr Ward's answers are an essential source of knowledge for the pharmacist.

The pharmacist's decisions (i.e. processing) have to take into account interactions with other medications that Mr Ward is currently using, his other health conditions and risk factors, including his lifestyle and diet. The counselling (i.e. delivery) has to provide clear information about when and how to take this medication, as well as a detailed explanation of possible side effects and actions if they occur.

There are a range of *formal rules* to follow, such as that the medication dispensed should match the prescription and be appropriate for Mr Ward's situation and that the information provided to Mr Ward about the medication and possible side effects should be correct, objective and clear. There are also *semiformal* or *informal rules* that characterise good decisions and good service, such as that counselling should be provided in language that is appropriate for Mr Ward, without pharmaceutical jargon, and avoiding terms that will alarm him.

There are *goals or targets* that guide this pharmacist's inquiry and actions and which characterise the outcome – the medication has been dispensed appropriately

---

[1] Note, this example is based on a case that pharmacy students have been exploring in the Cardiovascular and Renal course and our reinterpretation of key features of epistemic games and forms following Perkins (1997).

if Mr Ward has understood the information and will be able to take this medication in ways that will provide the best health outcomes.

There are characteristic *forms* associated with the outcome. This will include a label with the information on how to take the prescription and more detailed, though standardised, customer information, such as a product description, what the medication is for, when it must not be taken, how it should be taken and what are the known side effects. This characteristic outcome may also include other kinds of verbal and written counselling, such as information about the medication, side effects and relevant actions related to the particular situation of Mr Ward, including aspects of his lifestyle.

Consider now Ms White who comes into the pharmacy with a prescription for a cough medicine. We observe a similar pattern of inquiry again: the pharmacist asks a set of questions, prepares the medication and explains how to take it. Characteristic moves of information gathering, processing and delivery will accompany many other decisions and knowledgeable actions that have a goal of dispensing the right medication and providing appropriate counselling, even if each step is executed in a variety of ways, with a variety of medications, combinations of diseases, clients, lifestyles and other conditions.

This is far from being the only pattern that the pharmacist will follow. For example, the pharmacist may face a situation when he does not have a prescribed medication available and thus will need to *switch* for a moment to another kind of inquiry and to find possible alternative treatments. Occasionally it may turn out that the pharmacist has never dispensed this medication before. This will instigate switching to another kind of inquiry to discover relevant information about the medication before providing appropriate counselling and dispensing the prescription. Or the pharmacist may discover an interaction between the prescribed medication and medications that the customer already takes. This then will initiate switching for a moment to a different form of inquiry, which might involve calling the prescribing doctor to discuss alternatives.

There are very large numbers of such situations and options for inquiry in professional practice. Nevertheless, in each profession we can observe a certain set of core generative patterns of inquiry that underpin knowledgeable actions. Such generative patterns can be characterised with the same notions of *target outcomes*, *forms*, *rules and moves* that apply to different kinds of knowledgeable action and which nicely characterise inquiry in professional work. Some underlying strategies, rules, moves and principles can be quite broad and can be applied with some variations across diverse situations. For example, information gathering, processing and delivery apply to the dispensing of a single prescription, as well as to a complex medication review. Some forms and rules, however, will be more specific to the target outcomes. For example, dispensing a single medication and a medication review will follow specific sets of forms and rules that characterise effective inquiry and outcomes related to each of the two intended outcomes. Some of the moves may be explicit and observable in pharmacists' discourse and actions. For example, we can easily see how the pharmacist asks Mr Ward questions, how he interrogates databases and how he provides counselling. Some other moves will be mental and will not necessarily create a trace in verbal, written or other material form. For example, an external observer would not necessarily see how the pharmacist worked out that two medications will interact.

What characterises the pharmacist's inquiry pattern is that it generates new situated knowledge. The pattern that guides inquiry, however, is neither situated nor hard-wired to a specific context – rather, it is broad and flexible enough to be adapted across medications, customers, pharmacies and pharmacists.

14.3   Creating a Taxonomy of Epistemic Games: Approach and Rationale

In this section, our purpose is to extend the notion of epistemic games to professional work and to propose a taxonomy of characteristic professional epistemic games. We intend it to serve as a framework to identify different kinds of epistemic games that are at the core of professional epistemic infrastructures and which organise professional knowing in a variety of workplace settings. From this perspective, professional knowledge is constituted from a range of strategies that are deployed in and characterise professional knowledgeable actions and knowledge-rich work, including innovation. These strategies involve specific conditions when they are employed, specific rules and characteristic forms of epistemic outcome. They are guiding knowledge structures and generative strategies for inquiry, knowledge building and other ways of knowing that professionals deploy when they face various tasks. Some of these tasks may be rare and complex. However, many of them are quite mundane. In short, epistemic games are used to make sense of phenomena encountered in professional work and to construct knowledge needed for professional action.

In constructing a taxonomy of epistemic games, we applied two main principles. First, each epistemic game should have a typical functional epistemic goal, a typical form or typical target outcome. Second, each game should involve characteristic moves, rules and other generative mechanisms, as well as principles about how to proceed in various situations (which could be more or less informal heuristics and other principles of procedure).

We used the following four dimensions of variation in epistemic games to place them into different classes:

- Epistemic focus: what sort of knowledge the game produces
- Epistemic agenda: what the game aims to achieve
- Object: nature of the epistemic object around which the game unfolds
- Expertise: the sorts of knowledge and skills expert players use

Before we proceed further, we should acknowledge that our sense of epistemic games runs broader than the descriptions found in early writings on the topic (Collins & Ferguson, 1993; Perkins, 1997). Ours draws on the breadth of professional work and includes various kinds of knowledge that professionals produce within their work. This consists of propositional knowledge that contributes to the professional knowledge base (e.g. articulating rules that prove to be effective in particular situations and creating practical heuristics), as well as solutions to professional problems (e.g. diagnosing, creating a plan), and also other characteristic forms of knowledge which professionals create for informing knowledgeable actions in specific situations (e.g. figuring out why a student did not understand an explanation). Therefore, some of the outcomes of these games belong solely to the professional knowledge base and inform professional actions; others belong on the boundaries between several professions or between professional and public worlds (e.g. a teacher's plan for parents to help a child to improve his reading skills).

We differ from Collins and Ferguson's (1993) original account of epistemic forms and games in four other ways.

First, in our view, epistemic games are not necessarily associated with a distinct representational form that can be expressed in symbolic media. Some are, but some are not. Rather, we suggest that an epistemic game is associated with a particular *epistemic target* that has an established recurring presence in professional discourse and actions. An example of this might be an epistemic game played by a pharmacist while dispensing a prescription. *The final target* of this game is a correctly chosen medication and accurate, accessible information about how to take this medication – tailored to the needs of a particular patient. Some of this information might be inscribed on a label (and such inscriptions usually have a recognisable form), but the target is far broader than the few words written on the medication box.

Second, professional epistemic forms are not generic structures. Rather, they are intertwined with the epistemic frameworks and symbolic systems of inscription of a particular epistemic domain. For example, a map constructed and used by social geographers and a map constructed and used by geologists are both maps, but they are maps that have distinct epistemic forms. The professional games for constructing and reading each map involve very different rules and require different professional expertise. In short, an epistemic form becomes epistemic only when it is embedded in a particular epistemic space.

Third, many epistemic games are associated with particular forms of knowledge that are usually expressed in external media (e.g. a map or a written plan). While there is a relationship between the game and its symbolic form, this relationship is not strict or symmetrical. Rather an epistemic form may be associated with a class of symbolic forms that have similar epistemic affordances. For example, two symbolic forms that guide a teacher's development of a new syllabus (e.g. two templates) may be different if we look at their inscriptions (i.e. sign vehicles) from a strictly proportional or symbolic perspective. Nevertheless, they could have very similar epistemic affordances and, from an epistemic perspective, will be linked to a very similar epistemic game.

Fourth, we extend the notion of epistemic games from characteristic moves and forms that are primarily associated with language and inscriptions to other forms of discourse, including body language and other kinds of material, embodied, dynamic expression that are used in human activity. As Ohlsson (1993) says, discourse refers

> ... not only to spoken and written thought but also to silent thinking – the stream of consciousness. Also, the term is not bound to the medium of language. A computer program, a drawing, a mathematical proof, and a musical score all qualify as discourse. (Ohlsson, 1993, p. 52)

Indeed, professional epistemic games involve all these kinds of discourse. For example, physical actions, verbal exchanges, mental actions, gestures and other transactions that occur during medication dispensing are inseparable aspects of the pharmacist's epistemic game.

From this perspective, professional epistemic games involve strategies, rules and moves associated with a characteristic epistemic outcome (target). This target outcome might be explicit – represented in an articulated epistemic form, inscribed in some kind of medium. Or it might be less explicit – represented in characteristic kinds of artefacts with a loosely articulated form from a symbolic/structural perspective. Or it might just be implied in intentions and actions – tacit.

Why do we need to locate professional epistemic games in particular epistemic spaces? As Ohlsson (1993) argues, abstract schemas provide useful tools for entering into unfamiliar discourse and generating new discourse. Thus, formal thinking, focussed on abstract content and context-free generative structures and rules, might be a reasonable target for learning at school – where the aim to foster general intellectual competence. Expertise, however, as Ohlsson affirms, belongs to the other end of 'high-end' cognition. The purpose of expertise is effective action. It is based on large amounts of domain-specific and context-specific facts and heuristics that are not easily applicable in other contexts. (A good taxi driver operates on a large amount of information about local traffic, intersections, one-way restrictions and so on that allows her to get around smoothly in that city. Similarly, an expert has to operate on large amounts of local knowledge that enables decision-making and acting smoothly.)

Professional expertise – and actionable professional knowledge – sits somewhere between these two ends. So our focus is on the epistemic games characteristic of particular epistemic cultures: ways of thinking that are prevalent within a profession and that inform local action. We are interested in identifying key epistemic games shared among members of each profession – classes and kinds of games that are used in situated professional work and which belong to a professional epistemic infrastructure, not just to a particular setting. Knowledge of such games can be very productive when working on the redesign of professional education programs.

14.4   The Taxonomy of Epistemic Games

Figure 14.1 and Table 14.1 provide overviews of our taxonomy of epistemic games. We distinguish six classes of epistemic games:

- Propositional games
- Situated problem-solving games
- Meta-professional discourse games
- Trans-professional discourse games
- Translational public discourse games
- Weaving games

The columns in Table 14.1 capture the principal distinguishing features of the different classes of games, as explained in the previous section.

The rest of this section introduces each of the six classes of epistemic games. We illustrate each class of games with examples taken from our empirical research. To keep things simple, we draw most of these from pharmacy. Professional tasks which require the construction of situated knowledge by embracing a variety of ways of knowing involve learning to *weave* together diverse epistemic games. Thus, the most complex and important class of epistemic games is what we call the 'weaving game'. It draws upon and coordinates all the other games – which usually belong to several classes – into fine-tuned, fluent, knowledgeable action. In Chap. 15, we present an extended exposition of the weaving game and show how

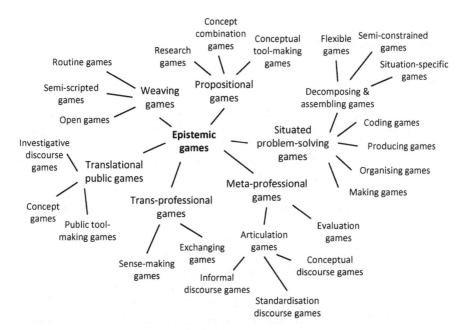

Fig. 14.1   A taxonomy of professional epistemic games

Table 14.1 An overview of the taxonomy of professional epistemic games

Game	Epistemic focus	Epistemic agenda	Object	Expertise
Propositional games	Professional knowledge base	Enhancing conceptual understanding	Generic conceptual tools	Meta-contributory expertise
Situated problem-solving	Solutions of specific professional problems	Enhancing situated understanding	Professional knowledge artefacts	Contributory expertise
Meta-professional discourse games	Understanding of existing professional products and actions	Enhancing professional perception	Meta-professional discourse and artefacts	Interactional expertise
Trans-professional discourse games	Links between different professional knowledges	Enhancing joint knowledgeable action	Boundary discourse and artefacts	Relational expertise
Translational public discourse games	Links between professional and lay knowledges	Extending professional knowledgeable action	Translational discourse and artefacts	Translational expertise
Weaving games	Distributed, embodied knowledgeable action	Enhancing functionality of professional knowledgeable work	Co-constructed epistemic environment	Professional epistemic fluency

various epistemic games, introduced and illustrated in this chapter, are coordinated and 'woven' together into one epistemic game.

14.4.1 Propositional Games

The epistemic agenda for propositional games focusses on enhancing conceptual understanding that informs action.

Propositional games involve strategies, rules and moves for creating general professional knowledge objects and artefacts that can be used across a range of similar situations (theories, models, useful references, heuristics, etc.). They are what might be called 'real' (substantive) knowledge games, as the outputs are conceptual artefacts that codify the professional knowledge base (a.k.a. propositional knowledge). Thus such games rest upon the organisation of professional knowledge as a domain, including (a) how professional knowledge is structured, (b) how new knowledge claims are created and validated as well as (c) knowledge of those concrete knowledge claims. These three elements broadly correspond to the conceptual and syntactical structures as well as the substantive knowledge base of the domain, in Schwab's (1962, 1970) terms.

In professional fields, propositional games also depend upon knowledge of other disciplines related to the profession. For example, in pharmacy, professional knowledge rests on such domains as pharmaceutical chemistry, which provides knowledge about chemical properties of drugs; pharmaceutics, which deals with the formulation of pure drug substances into medications ready for delivery and safe use; therapeutics, which covers how medicines are used in the treatment and management of disease; etc.

Propositional games are not reducible to one particular strategy. Rather, this broad class of epistemic games has a shared epistemic target of creating generic knowledge objects and artefacts. We can identify three more specific kinds of propositional games: research games, concept combination games and conceptual tool-making games.

Research games are mainly empirical games for creating new concepts, theories (including very practical theories) and other evidence-informed kinds of knowledge for the profession, using the accepted inquiry methods of the domain. For example, such professions as education and health often construct their knowledge base by conducting design-based research studies, action research projects and clinical experiments. Health practitioners create evidence-informed knowledge about risks of different treatments by implementing practical risk management and monitoring programs. They are usually composed of a set of heuristic steps and rules for how to conduct the inquiry. For example, an inquiry conducted as a part of risk management and monitoring involves an iterative process composed of five main steps: risk identification, risk assessment, choice and other decisions about risk treatment, implementation of the plan and evaluation (Fig. 14.2). Overall, research games are broad overarching epistemic games, usually composed of a range of more specific games that are called upon at different stages of an inquiry. For example, a step such as *design of risk treatment* is itself an epistemic game, composed from a range of rules and multiple activities.

One may question if such broad research strategies really meet the criteria for epistemic games, as the knowledge created using similar research games may be different and take different forms. For example, a piece of design research may be used to develop and test a new theory, a model or a pedagogical strategy, and the final constructed knowledge may take the form of a taxonomy, a stage model, a situation–action model or some other characteristic form for representing a particular kind of conceptual knowledge. We argue that this is not the case. First, each specific game (i.e. each research strategy) follows a set of rules and moves. Second, the epistemic artefact created will have a distinct characteristic form of the target associated with the particular game (e.g. a research report).

One example of such a game could be a piece of action research implemented by a teacher.[2] Action research follows characteristic steps and other rules for this kind of inquiry, such as (a) identifying the issue that needs to be addressed; (b) locating the issue in the broader context of a school, syllabus or other aspects of an educational system as a context; (c) connecting the issue to the literature and identifying suitable pedagogical approaches; (d) outlining strategies to be

---

[2] In our studies, we saw how this game and form were blended with additional pedagogical elements (such as peer collaboration and feedback from collaborating teachers) employed by preservice teachers in action learning projects implemented during school placements.

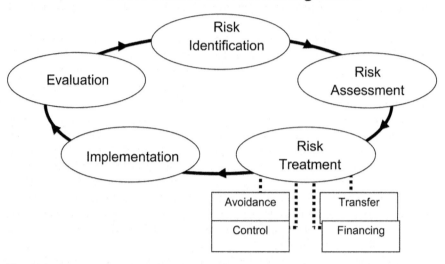

Fig. 14.2 Research game: an example of an inquiry model applied in practical health risk assessment and management (Source: For pharmacists: Code of conduct, March 2014, p. 17) (By permission of Australian Health Practitioner Regulation Agency)

implemented; (e) deciding on what kind of evidence will be gathered; and so on. The report has a typical form for this kind of study, containing such elements as the rationale, context of the project, design, results and implications of findings for practice. That is, it has an agreed *epistemic* form. Various kinds of research games, particularly practice-based inquiries, are an important group of professional epistemic games. Furthermore, these research games are sometimes firmly fused into the practitioner's daily work, as with the example of actions and decisions related to risk management in the health sector (Fig. 14.2).

Concept combination games are more fine-grained propositional games than the research games. They primarily include general analysis techniques for figuring out and describing the structure and function of phenomena, establishing how structure relates to function and in other ways making sense of various dynamic phenomena related to professional work. Many of the games described by Collins and Ferguson (1993) belong to this category. For example, pharmacy students learn theoretical knowledge that informs pharmacy practice by making comparisons between different products and therapies (Fig. 14.3), creating taxonomies of symptoms for a disease, and comparing symptoms of two diseases (Fig. 14.4). These combination games are usually played when one tries to describe, explain or establish new relationships. Thus, they usually involve abstract theoretical constructs. New propositional knowledge emerges from new combinations and representations, even if the contributing knowledges are not new in absolute terms. For example, a comparison between two diseases or between several medications and treatments is new

It is estimated that more than 50% of patients with a malignant illness are using or taking some form of alternative/complementary therapy. There is good evidence to suggest that many patients choose not to discuss taking alternative or complementary therapies with their doctors. Look around your pharmacy, identify at least five treatments which might be used by people with cancer as alternate/complementary therapies. For each product, list how it is used or taken, the dose range which might be being taken, and any advantages or disadvantages which may be associated with your patients using these products.

Product	How used	Dose	Advantages	Disadvantages

Fig. 14.3 Combination game: an example of an inscriptional form that guides an externship task given to pharmacy students (Source: Tutorial and Externship Handbook used in Pharmacy Practice course)

Summarise the main differences between Ulcerative Colitis and Crohn's Disease.

Characteristic	Ulcerative Colitis	Crohn's Disease
Anatomical Location	colon and rectum	mouth to anus
Distribution	continuous, diffuse, mucosal	segmental, focal, transmural
Bowel Wall	shortened, loss of haustral markings, generally not thickened	rigid, thick, oedematous and fibrotic
Gross Rectal Bleeding	common	infrequent
Abdominal Pain	infrequent	common
Toxic Megacolon	occasional	rare
Bowel carcinoma	greatly increased	slightly increased

Fig. 14.4 Combination game: an example of a completed pre-tutorial task given to pharmacy students (Source: Tutorial and Externship Handbook used in Pharmacy Practice course)

knowledge over and above what exists in separate descriptions of the two individual diseases or treatments.

Conceptual tool-making games are design games that result in new practical devices that link propositional and applied actionable knowledge. For example,

Complete the table below to summarise the treatment options for ulcerative colitis and Crohn's disease. Give specific examples of drug therapy and doses.

Ulcerative Colitis		
Acute mild to moderate	short course of oral corticosteroid and/or an aminosalicylate; topical corticosteroid for distal disease	prednisolone 20 to 60mg orally daily, reducing to zero over 8 to 12 weeks sulfasalazine 2 to 4g orally daily in 3 to 4 divided doses; OR mesalazine 1 to 1.5g orally daily in 3 divided doses; OR olsalazine 1 to 1.5g daily in 2 or 3 divided doses prednisolone 20mg/100mL enema rectally at night or bd
Acute severe	hospital admission; short course of IV corticosteroid	hydrocortisone 100mg iv q6h or by continuous infusion
Maintenance	aminosalicylate; immunosuppressant	sulfasalazine 2 to 4g orally in 3 to 4 divided doses or mesalazine or olsalazine
Chronic	immunosuppressant; low dose corticosteroid	azathioprine 1.5 to 2.5mg/kg orally daily or mercaptopurine 1 to 1.5mg/kg orally daily

Fig. 14.5 Conceptual tool-making game: an example of a completed pre-tutorial task given to pharmacy students (Source: Tutorial and Externship Handbook used in Pharmacy Practice course)

creating guidelines for nursing using evidence from best practice, establishing the relationships between treatment options for a disease, and drug therapies and doses are among such tool games (Fig. 14.5). These games usually involve practical cases that portray conceptual knowledge and show how it features in practical decision-making and action. They use conceptual knowledge to explain cases encountered in practice.

Propositional games result in artefacts that articulate the knowledge base of the profession. It is important to note that playing such games involves *meta-professional expertise*, to work with and create conceptual knowledge, but does not necessarily require the professional capability needed to solve concrete professional problems. In other words, the rules and moves involved in *creating guidelines* for nursing, using evidence from best practice, require knowledge and the ability to locate sources of evidence, judge their validity and relevance, describe nursing procedures and justify them using evidence. In contrast, the rules and moves involved in carrying out these procedures depend upon a capability to *see relevant aspects* of a concrete situation and *carry out practical procedures* in ways that are congruent with best practice without necessarily having a capability to create best practice guidelines for others. Of course, in many practical situations, such as in the example of risk management in the health sector, propositional games are played in combination with practical problem-solving.

14.4.2   Situated Problem-Solving Games

The epistemic agenda for situated problem-solving games focusses on enhancing situated understanding of a particular problem.

Problem-solving games are played when practitioners encounter specific professional problems. Examples of such games include creating a lesson plan, creating a floor layout for a new pharmacy, creating a new health promotion program to address certain common health issue in a community, designing a course or sketching a scenario for online resources for teaching this course. These games require knowledge and capability to solve professional problems and produce professional epistemic artefacts that offer, what could be called, 'conceptual solutions for specific problems'. While some artefacts might be quite abstract, the epistemic aim is specific; thus the problem-solving games follow an epistemic path (rules and moves) that draws upon and is rooted in the practitioner's perception of the situation. These rules and moves are different from the propositional games, where they are rooted in abstracts claims.

Perkins (1997) suggested that problem-solving and decision-making are not epistemic games as they do not have an epistemic agenda. We argue that this is not the case in professional work. Such practical strategies of inquiry have an epistemic agenda of producing knowledge for knowledgeable action (see Chap. 7). As with all epistemic games, they involve characteristic rules and moves. They also have a characteristic epistemic target. This is sometimes represented in the particular symbolic form of the artefact. For example, a psychological assessment report, a legal case and an annual financial statement are examples of professional artefacts that express outcomes of problem-solving games in distinct, characteristic forms. In other cases, this epistemic target gets expressed in characteristic discourse and outcomes (e.g. dispensing a medication). The problem-solving games have an epistemic agenda with the target of producing practical solutions, that is, producing actionable knowledge.

Problem-solving games involve the ability to use a range of conceptual devices and representational systems of the profession. They primarily rest upon a professional knowledge base: conceptual and syntactical structures and substantive knowledge of the profession and rather less on the contributory disciplinary domains.

Problem-solving games are a large class of epistemic games. We can classify them in distinct categories along two dimensions: *openness* of the solution space and *aspects* of the problem-solving (Table 14.2).

According to *the openness of the solution space*, games can vary from flexible to situation specific. This dimension shows how tightly the game, and the solution, is linked to the material and social arrangements of a *specific situation*.

Table 14.2 Examples of different kinds of problem-solving games, based on openness of the solution space and aspects of the problem-solving

Openness of the solution space	Aspects of the problem-solving				
	Decomposing and assembling	Coding	Producing	Organising	Making
Flexible games	Creating a health promotion program	Identifying common causes of a particular health issue	Translating identified causes into possible prevention measures	Integrating different prevention measures into one program	Creating mechanisms for implementing a program
Semi-constrained games	Designing a lesson plan	Translating curriculum requirements into lesson aims	Making decisions about content and nature of lesson tasks	Sequencing and integrating lesson content and tasks	Writing lesson plan and making teaching resources
Situation-specific games	Designing an efficient therapy for a patient	Examining a patient and depicting symptoms	Figuring out interactions between medications	Sequencing and prioritising issues and recommendations	Writing assessment report and recommendations

Flexible games are played in a relatively open outcome space with fairly loose constraints from the social and material situation. Creating a program to prevent a common health issue and designing a school library space or a pharmacy layout that meets current regulations, standards and other broad requirements are examples of such games. In these games, rules and moves are generally applicable to a broad class of similar games, and solutions may involve a variety of options. For example, a library space for collaborative work could be designed in many different ways.

Semi-constrained or outcome-focussed *games* are more tightly linked to the outcome requirements and the specific context. Designing a half-day excursion about aboriginal culture for children in a certain school and creating a lesson plan for teaching a particular topic to a specific class of children are examples of such games. The rules and moves of such games usually involve substantial balancing between the aims of the game – specified by the outcome requirements – and the situation. For example, the options for designing and organising the above-mentioned excursion are partly constrained by the school's location and distance to suitable sites, time, available funding and other resources.

Situation-specific games are highly contingent on a specific instance and situation. Figuring out issues and creating a suitable treatment for a specific patient and diagnosing a child's learning difficulties are examples of situation-specific games. Accurate coding of the situation (entry conditions) and then gradual movement towards a specific solution are among the main features of such situated games. These moves commonly involve continuous checking and balancing of the emerging solution with the constraints and affordances of the encountered situation.

The games described above are broad overarching problem-solving games. We call them *assembling and decomposing games* as they are assembled from various components and steps that guide inquiry from the initial specification of the issue or task to the final solution. They do not necessarily have one specific symbolic form for expressing outcomes – some may have several – but they guide the inquiry and solution process from the beginning to the end. For example, designing an efficient therapy for a patient could involve initially investigating and detecting issues and inefficiencies in current therapy, identifying the most important aspects and then creating a better solution. These overarching problem-solving games often involve rules and moves for approaching a broad class of tasks through temporally interleaved decomposition and assembly processes. Problems are tackled by *decomposing* them down into a set of components or steps that can be solved locally and *assembling* the outcomes of those components into a solution: all the time maintaining coherence between individual elements and sensitivity to the needs of the situation.[3] Some key features of decomposing and assembling are nicely captured in lesson planning activities and in the lesson plans thereby produced – some examples of which we presented in earlier chapters (Fig. 11.1).

---

[3] These overarching problem-solving games are broadly parallel to what Ohlsson (1993) called 'compositional schemas'. However, they are situated and mesh together symbolic and socio-material aspects – they are not just mental.

Creating a lesson plan initially involves identifying relevant curriculum objectives and matching with lesson outcomes, decomposing this into decisions about appropriate content and tasks, creating a set of activities and then assembling all the elements into one coherent lesson.

Turning now to *specific aspects of problem-solving* into which problem-solving games are decomposed and from which they are assembled (shown in the horizontal dimension of Table 14.2), problem-solving games can be classified into four kinds: coding, producing, organising and making.

Coding (or translation) games depict relevant information from a discourse, including various symbolic sources and observation of the environment, and (re)present (encode) it using professional coding schemes, such as concepts, categories and symbolic systems, in a different epistemic space. For example, such games include translating curriculum requirements into the aims for a lesson or depicting critical information and symptoms from an interview with a patient and representing them in a form suitable for further processing using professional heuristics, formulas and databases. Rules and moves that professionals apply for shaping perception and depicting relevant information from an interview with a client, observation or working documents belong to this category of epistemic games (Fig. 14.6). (Coding games relate to the public discourse games, described below, but move in the opposite direction – from public discourse to representation using professional coding schemes.)

Producing games involve using epistemic rules and working on a solution primarily in the epistemic space of the task. Making decisions about the pedagogical approach, content and nature of tasks that are appropriate for achieving the aims of the lesson and figuring out interactions between medications, inappropriate doses and other issues during the medication review are examples of such games (Fig. 14.7).

Organising games involve using certain heuristic rules to create the final solution or decision from the heterogeneous pieces that have been produced. Integrating different tasks, curriculum materials, classroom resources and other arrangements into a lesson plan that meets a curriculum goal and ordering issues and recommendations after identifying a range of problems and working out possible solutions during medication review are examples of such organising games. This kind of game includes various strategies, rules and heuristics for highlighting, grouping and prioritising issues and solutions; integrating different aspects of the solution, such as creating priority lists (Fig. 14.8); identifying the main goals; and explicitly working through possible solution options and the reasoning behind each recommendation (Fig. 14.9). Organising games result in decisions about what is most important and relevant and how things fit together into one acceptable solution.

Making games involve creating the final product – a public[4] professional artefact – using discourse forms that are shared within a profession. For example, teachers produce their lesson plans using agreed common formats within a school; psychologists and community workers produce their assessment reports and

---

[4] By 'public' we mean that the artefact moves into a more public arena, though there may nevertheless be strict controls on who can access it.

INTERVIEW GUIDE
(This form is to be used as a guide to the interview, there may be other issues important to the patient)

Placement Type	Residential Facility	Community **Yes**	Hospital	Specialist Clinic	Other
Student Name				GP Code **Dr Excellence**	Patient Code **Jane Edmonds**

Patient understanding of what medications are for
Unclear as to purpose of all of them

Outline of patient's concerns about medication
Has not ever measured peak-flow and doesn't think she could do that. Visits the doctor if she has trouble catching her breath or is coughing more than usual.

Patient problems administering any medication
Denies

Patient perception of medication efficacy
Unconvinced of worth of puffer (Serevent). Ventolin helps when used. She has to use it frequently when she wakes at night.
She thinks cough has been a bit better over the last week since she has been using the prednisone tablets. She has not been waking up as much at night.
She has had various tablets for her blood pressure for years – her GP says her BP is OK lately.

Patient complains of
Constipation ☐ **No**   Diarrhoea ☐ **No**   Drowsiness ☐ **No**   Headaches ☐ **No**
Insomnia ☐ **Just recently** Nasal congestion ☐ **No**   Nausea ☐ **No**   Pain ☐ **No**
Rash ☐ **In past, sometimes gets dermatitis**   Tinnitus ☐ **No**   Urticaria ☐ **No**
Vomiting ☐ **No**
Other ☐ please specify **Cough mainly at night**

Medications (as per patient)
Tritace 5mg 1 d
Serevent 25microgram 2puffs bd
Salbutamol 2puffs prn
Prednisolone 5mg Reducing dose – completed today
Natrilix SR 1 daily
Rani 2 150mg 1 bd
Betagan 0.25% I drop BE bd
Panadol prn

Administration techniques check (if appropriate eg inhaler technique)
Eye drops – husband administers. Patient does not occlude lacrimal duct. **Inhaler technique – cloud of medication obvious – poor coordination and technique.**

Compliance check: (Use dispensing history; dates on patient's medications)
Has no problem taking tablets. Has marked off reducing dose of prednisolone from calendar. Down to last day's dose of pred.

Fig. 14.6 Coding game: an example of the interview template summarising information from the interview with a patient. Extract only (Source: Tutorial and Externship Handbook used in Pharmacy Practice course)

Working sheet for medication review

	Findings	Recommendations
Drug/dosage discrepancies		
Potential therapeutic problems		
Information required from medical practitioner		

Fig. 14.7 Producing game: an example of a worksheet for identifying issues during medication review and potential ways to address (Source: OSCE material used in Pharmacy Practice course)

recommendations following agreed community conventions and standards (Fig. 14.10). Making games require a capability to use professional language, codification systems and rules – and in principle they are specialist discourse games that are played within the profession.

These four different aspects of problem-solving – coding, producing, organising and making – broadly correspond to the *stages* of inquiry in more rigorously codified professions. For example, a medication management review completed by pharmacists usually involves choosing and *recording* relevant information – gathered from interviews and doctor referrals – into a form ready for processing; *figuring out* possible issues by making sense of collected information using knowledge of pharmaceuticals and other relevant knowledge domains; *prioritising* the issues and fitting everything into a possible decision; and *writing* a recommendation in an agreed professional language.

Issues Identified

In point form write down the issues that you have identified. Use the column on the right to prioritise the top five of these issues. Use a number to indicate priority for each issue.

Issues	Priority
Smoker and overweight	
Binge drinker	
Depression	
Weight gain is an issue for him	
Reflux/nausea	
Social issues such as little money and unemployment	
NRT cost vs. cigarettes	
Insomnia	
Missing therapy – aspirin	

Fig. 14.8 Organising game: a worksheet for prioritising issues identified during medication review (Source: Tutorial and Externship Handbook used in Pharmacy Practice course)

Recording, figuring out, prioritising and writing broadly correspond to coding, producing, organising and making games. Coding, organising and making also reflect the three discursive practices for shaping professional perception – coding, highlighting, producing – that Goodwin (1994) used to describe 'professional vision'. However, these aspects of problem-solving do not always appear in the same order, and each task does not always involve all four aspects. For example, the assembling game for creating a pharmacy layout or lesson plan may involve substantial amounts of tinkering where coding, producing, organising and making proceed almost simultaneously or are repeated several times.

Are these different kinds of problem-solving games epistemically distinct from one another? We argue that this is so. For example, pharmacy students, *in the production game* of the medication review, may follow a strategy of either going through each drug or through each disease state in order to identify drug or dosage discrepancies, potential therapeutic issues and recommendations specific to each finding. This game primarily draws on pharmaceutical, therapeutic and other kinds of professional knowledge, as well as strategies for using various devices for extracting relevant information and strategies for meaning-making and inscription. *In the making game*, these same students embrace a set of strategies that primarily involve discursive rules for describing, explaining and justifying professional recommendations. This game diverges from the initial strategies used for meaning-making and follows a distinct set of discursive rules specifically for this kind of professional communication. In our study, pharmacy students learnt such

Goals	Options	Reasoning
1 *Manage the symptoms of PD* *Reduce exacerbations of side effects* *Support for patient with PD and their carer*	*Consider optimal use of medications for PD* *Identify and educate re preventable exacerbations*	*Use lowest dose of levodopa/carbidopa to control symptoms.* *Manage side effect of levodopa (take initially with food).* *Counsel patient and carer on signs of treatment failure and dose adjustment.* *Suggest non-pharmacological measures to maintain mobility and normality.* *Stress importance of adherence to medication regimen.* *Avoid or cease C/I medications in PD – Maxolon, Use domperidone for nausea and vomiting.* *Avoid over the counter medication which may affect PD – overuse of anticholinergics.* *Counsel family and carers re physiotherapy exercises to maintain mobility.* *Advise George and Jemma of support groups and internet sites for more information about PD eg www.pakinsons.org.au; www.parkinsonsnsw.org.au*
2. *Improve patient adherence to medication*	*Suggest DAA* *Improving compliance with medication may restore George's BP control and improve his lipid profile.*	*To minimise impact of caring for her dad Jemma should consider having her father's medication packed in a dose administration aid, particularly since the dosage regimen for levodopa is several times a day and will initially need dose adjustment and future adjustment both in dose and frequency.* *Adherence with medication may mean that George's medications for BP and cholesterol may not need to be increased or changed.*

Fig. 14.9 Organising game: a worksheet for identifying goals and working out possible solutions during medication review (Source: Tutorial and Externship Handbook used in Pharmacy Practice course)

strategies as a part of pharmacy practice. The strategies were outlined and illustrated in their course handbooks and other course resources (see Fig. 14.11). That is, problem-solving games may share the same broad epistemic target, but each of them also has a more specific and distinct purpose, each follows a particular set of strategies (rules and moves) and draws upon a particular set of meaning-making and discursive skills.

How do problem-solving games differ from the propositional games, such as the classic epistemic games identified by Collins and Ferguson (1993) and Perkins (1997)? From a generic perspective – agnostic to the domain of knowledge and practice – many of Collins and Ferguson's games may be played during problem-solving, and description, explanation and justification, which Perkins saw as a 'necessity', will be present in different problem-solving games. Nevertheless, we suggest that professional problem-solving games are distinct in several ways and are unlikely to be learnt merely by learning generic games, such as producing *any*

Medication Review Report Form

Pharmacist Name	

Date of Medication Review	Patient name	Doctor name
	Mrs Greene	Dr S R

Current Medications (including OTC, Vitamins, etc)

Name	Strength	Directions	Indication
Betaloc	100mg	1 bd	Post infarct, angina, hypertension
Pravachol	40mg	1 n	Hypercholesterolaemia
Monodur	120mg	1 m	Angina
Anginine	600mcg	1 s/l prn	Acute chest pain

Previous Medications (including OTC, Vitamins, etc)

Name	Strength	Directions	Start	Stop	Indication
Imdur	60mg	1 m			Chest pain
Isoptin 240mg	240mg	1 m			Hypertension

Renal Function	Normal	30-50ml/min	< 30ml/min	<10ml/min	Unknown
LFT	Normal	Raised (include levels above)			Unknown

REVIEW FINDINGS	RECOMMENDATIONS

References:

Fig. 14.10 Making game: an example of a partly completed sheet for medication review. Extract only (Source: OSCE material used in Pharmacy Practice course)

---

k. *Are there any interactions?*

The references will help you to research each drug.

There may be interactions between two or more of the medications for any given
patient. The GP notes, the nursing care notes and/or the patient interview are a good
source of information. However if there are no particular symptoms noted, it is
important to note that interactions are possible and that monitoring may be advisable.

Example of how your finding may be reported

"When Losec (omeprazole) and Valium (diazepam) are administered concurrently the
half life of Valium may be increased to 90 hours. There will be a significant build-up of
diazepam and an increased risk of adverse effects such as daytime drowsiness, falls,
confusion and respiratory depression."

Fig. 14.11 Making game: an example of recommended professional discourse for pharmacists,
for reporting different kinds of findings. Extract only (Source: Tutorial and Externship Handbook
used in Pharmacy Practice course)

kind of descriptions or *any* kind of explanations, detached from the relevant
professional problem-solving practices. We have two main reasons for taking this
position.

First, problem-solving games are different from propositional games. For example, a school counsellor may analyse changes in students' development by mapping
evidence of their achievements against a certain developmental model or
representing changes in students' results as a graph and exploring change over
time. In their general shape, such games resemble propositional games and may
even use propositional concepts. But problem-solving games are not purely propositional. For example, the school counsellor may add new aspects from empirical
observations or other sources that turn out to be relevant while constructing the
model, while interpreting student progress and making practical decisions, even
though this was not intended initially. Such a game involves concepts and properties, but the rules are not constrained by the rules of the conceptual and inscriptional
spaces; rather they leak into the world.

Second, many epistemic forms used in problem-solving games combine different elements potentially relevant to the decision, as well as relevant to a cultural
practice. For example, teachers include in their lesson plans references to the
national curriculum and standards; school counsellors report their assessment
results in ways that are consistent with 'good practice'; pharmacists include in
their medication review reports not only their findings and recommendations but
also standard information from the doctor's referral, such as the patient's laboratory
results, and prioritised recommendations. Such epistemic forms that guide professional problem-solving are both more heterogeneous, in that they project different
elements relevant for different aims (such as disciplinary logic, politics and culture)
into one inscriptional place, and also they embody unique features of epistemic
practice. That is, these games are not constrained by the conceptual or inscriptional
logic. Which is not to say that they do not have it – rather, they are also governed by

the logic of practicality, usefulness and social agreements, legacy and professional culture. Of course, many problem-solving games involve description, explanation and justification, which Perkins (1997) considered to be an 'epistemic necessity'. But many professional games mix those elements together into one problem-solving game (see, e.g. a completed medication review with the pharmacist's findings and recommendations in Fig. 15.6, Chap. 15). Learning to play these epistemic games goes far beyond having the general competences needed to describe, explain and justify. Professional epistemic forms and games, as occupational and cognitive practices that emerge around different objects of professional work, are products of professional culture as much as of logic (Star, 1989).

Problem-solving games result in artefacts, or other discursive outcomes, that rest on the knowledge base of the profession. The capacity to play such games involves intra-professional expertise to solve professional problems and to complete professional tasks. It requires what Harry Collins and Robert Evans (2007) called 'contributory expertise' (see Chap. 5). Problem-solving games and their associated professional discourse, we argue, are different from specialist and public discourse-focussed epistemic games, which we turn to next.

We identify three classes of professional discourse games: *meta-professional*, *trans-professional* and *translational public discourse* games.

14.4.3 Meta-professional Discourse Games

The epistemic agenda for meta-professional games focusses on enhancing professional perception by redescribing actions and products from a (shared) professional community frame.

Articulation (or intra-professional translation) games are one important kind of meta-professional game. Broadly speaking, they are played when one tries to make tacit professional knowledge explicit and to articulate one's practical knowledge and action in specialist languages and coding schemes. Such articulation results in artefacts and discourse for a specialist audience. The games described by Nonaka and Takeuchi (1995), involved in articulating tacit knowledge, belong to this group. The underlying principle and aim is to articulate, in the language of specialists, what one has done, how it works, what it means, etc. (There is a relationship with conceptual tool games, yet also there is a big difference.) Such articulation may take place in different 'languages' – concepts from the professional knowledge base and codes of various intermediaries, including technical and professional standards – or in more local everyday talk. The shape of the game and epistemic target is broadly the same, but there is a substantial difference between different specialist languages and different specialist discourse games, ranging between what we might call the formal conceptual and the informal situated ends, with a range of standardisation discourse games between.

At the conceptual end, one may use formal conceptual vocabulary in professional discourse. Such games then help understand the meaning of specific professional artefacts and actions in the core propositional system of a profession. *At the situated end*, one may use informal discourses and concepts at hand and try to articulate one's practice and meaning-making without committing to a specific discursive system (often perhaps mixing various languages). Such articulation games are often seen in the discourses of apprenticeship, particularly in early stages (Weddle & Hollan, 2010), but also in various practical professional artefacts, such as guidelines, procedures or recipes for doing professional or semi-professional work.

In professional practice much of this articulation is done using the coding schemes of knowledge *intermediaries* (e.g. technical standards and curriculum standards) and professional intermediaries (e.g. competence standards and accreditation requirements). The existence and important role of such knowledge intermediaries in knowledge domains are well acknowledged (Knorr Cetina, 2007), but their existence has a much longer presence in professional practices (Star & Griesemer, 1989) than in knowledge practices and knowledge society discourses. In short, such coding using *discourses of standards* makes distributed intra-disciplinary work possible, thus, no doubt, is a part of professional discourse. For example, in the professions that we researched, student teachers used technical codes of 'curriculum' and 'standards' to code and share the materials they designed for teaching. Similar strategies and rules, yet very different coding schemes, were used in articulation games that applied professional competence 'codes' for articulating practical knowledge. These discourse games included students' work preparing professional portfolios for formal accreditation but also for less formal reflection and learning. For example, even in action research projects, students used professional standards as language for articulating and reflecting on their learning experiences, knowledge and skills.

There are two important messages here. First, the coding schemes of various intermediaries, and the discourse games that they bring, are a part of professional discourse. In some professions they tend to be a very important part of everyday professional practice. For example, Nerland (2008, 2010) shows that a great deal of knowledge work in computer engineering is associated with sharing and using knowledge products expressed in the discursive language of a global professional community. The professional discourse games that are played to translate back and forth between one's local knowledge and the knowledge expressed in a shared community form are extremely important. Second, games that underpin articulation are games that, at least in part, underpin professional perception, which, following Goodwin (1994), we can call 'coding'

> ... a systematic practice used to transform the world into the categories and events that are relevant to the work of the profession. (Goodwin, 1994, p. 608)

Nevertheless, such articulation in the codes of various technical and professional intermediaries also carries some dangers. The codes of intermediaries do not necessarily come saturated with the deeper principles that underpin a professional knowledge base (see also Nerland, 2008). But the questions here are more general – whose categories and codification systems are relevant to professional work and whether transforming to professional competence codes helps move closer to professional understanding.

Evaluation games are a second kind of meta-professional game. They follow recognised, explicit rules for evaluating certain professional things, resources, actions and other professional objects, from a particular shared perspective. Evaluation games move in the opposite direction to articulation. Some professional evaluation games constitute a specialised area of expertise. (Financial auditing is one such field.) However, many professional and learning tasks follow strategies and rules common to these kinds of games as a part of other tasks. Evaluating a teaching resource, depicting and judging important properties of a pharmaceutical product and various other coding games that use agreed evaluation schemes and criteria belong to this group of epistemic games. Evaluation games draw upon two important principles: (a) a relevant epistemological framework should be applied consistently and (b) work should result in a public artefact[5] (e.g. an evaluation report). That is, professional evaluation discourse can be characterised by such rules as explicitness of criteria and consistency. Evaluation games in professional learning have much broader applicability than evaluation in its traditional sense. In our studies, for example, evaluation games were not usually used by teachers to develop capacities for professional evaluation as such, but to develop capacities for skilled professional perception, such as an ability to notice important features of a lesson plan from a social justice perspective (i.e. 'coding', in Goodwin's (1994) terms). Evaluation games, as they are described here, are a more extreme, explicit form of a large group of games that are evaluative in nature. In practice, some of them are played by experts tacitly, without necessarily making criteria explicit or applying them consistently. Yet the spirit of the game is the same.

14.4.4   Trans-professional Discourse Games

The epistemic agenda for trans-professional games focusses on creating links between different professional knowledges and enhancing joint knowledgeable action.

Trans-professional games are played when professionals engage in interactions with professionals (and their products) from other fields: on boundary topics and issues. Writing referrals and recommendations to specialists in other domains also involve this kind of game.

There are several kinds of trans-professional games. The *exchanging* game follows strategies and rules for articulating and making professional knowledge products accessible for professionals from other domains. This often involves writing for professional others. An example would be when a geotechnical surveyor provides a report to an architect about the suitability of a building site. The

---

[5] 'Public' in the qualified sense, mentioned above.

counterpart to the exchanging game is the *sense-making game*. This commonly involves reading and making sense of products created by experts from other fields, in order to make progress with the task at hand. An example would be the architect making sense of the geotech report, or a civil servant making sense of a legal opinion, or a teacher making sense of scientists' statements about climate change when planning a lesson on this topic. Figures 14.12 and 14.13 illustrate a doctor's referral for a pharmacist to complete a medication review, around which the doctor's exchange game and a pharmacist's sense-making game evolve.

Sense-making games are not necessarily based on exactly the same epistemic frame from which the artefact was created; rather, the artefact can be understood and evaluated from the perspective of the task at hand. For example, a teacher may not be able to make sense of a counsellor's assessment report about a student's learning difficulties in exactly the same way as another counsellor would, but they may not need to do so in order to carry out their professional work as a teacher. Rather, they need to be able to make sense of the report in ways that inform their teaching. Nevertheless, professional sense-making rarely proceeds without some understanding of the epistemological framework of the other. Sense-making games, in this respect, are a trans-professional version of evaluation games. Many of them are at least partly tacit and do not necessarily apply rules consistently or make criteria explicit.

Do professional discourse games, whether meta-professional or trans-professional, constitute separate classes? Using our criteria, yes. They have a specific epistemic target (i.e. exchanging, sense-making, articulation and evaluation) and a set of known strategies and forms. Many professional discourse games are explicitly taught in higher education.

All professional discourse games involve the ability to recognise and adopt an epistemological framework of the domain, as well as the epistemological frameworks of others. However, different kinds of games require different levels of familiarity with the discourse of the field. For example, most complex articulation and evaluation games require a substantial understanding of specialist discourse, including characteristic forms and symbolic systems. It would be difficult to do a financial audit or even to evaluate a financial statement without understanding the professional language and concepts. In contrast, exchanging and sense-making games usually require more schematic understanding of the domain.

Professional discourse games are meta- and trans-professional games involving higher-order thinking. However, it is important to note that these discourse games are not based on the same kind of knowledge and skills that are involved in the propositional games (which are also meta-level games) or problem-solving games. A person may be able to participate in the discourse, evaluate artefacts and knowledge claims, but not have the capacities needed to contribute to it (i.e. solve a problem and use the symbolic systems of the profession). In short, by participating in discourse games, students learn strategies of articulation and evaluation, not knowledge building and problem-solving. (Professional education approaches that give a central place to reflection tend to overlook this important distinction.)

DOMICILIARY MEDICATION MANAGEMENT – HOME MEDICINES REVIEW
Provider/Patient details may be completed by the practice staff

The DMMR referral should include relevant information (e.g. laboratory results) to enable the pharmacist to make a thorough assessment. Please review the patient's medical record and any previous health assessments, care plans, and case conference summaries for relevant information. Completing the referral form* in detail will reduce the possibility of the pharmacist needing to contact you to clarify background information. Relevant information from the patient's medical record may be attached to the referral form e.g. as a printout from your patient record system.

*If you are not using a specific DMMR referral form you still need to provide patient details and relevant clinical information to the pharmacist.
Additional forms are available on the Department of Health and Ageing's website. See www.health.gov.au/mbsprimarycareitems

COMMUNITY PHARMACY /
ACCREDITED PHARMACIST DETAILS
(nominated by the patient)

Name: _____

PATIENT DETAILS
(or affix label with patient details here)

Name: _____

Address: _____

_____

_____

D.O.B.: _____

Medicare No: _____

DVA No: _____

Patient/Carer contact: _____

GENERAL PRACTITIONER DETAILS

Name: _____
Address: _____

_____

_____

Provider No.: _____

Prescriber No.: _____

Phone: _____

Fax: _____

Email: _____

Preferred means of receiving report:

_____

ISSUES THAT MAY INFLUENCE
MEDICATION USE OR EFFECTIVENESS

☐ Vision   ☐ Hearing

☐ Language and/or   ☐ Swallowing
   Literacy problems

☐ Cognition   ☐ Dexterity
   (Memory and   (e.g. manual
   Comprehension)   coordination)

☐ Other

OTHER PATIENT INFORMATION

Height: _____ cm

Weight: _____ kg

Blood Pressure: _____

VACCINATION STATUS
(Tick if up to date)

☐ Tetanus   ☐ Rubella

☐ Hepatitis A   ☐ Hepatitis B

☐ Influenza

DOES PATIENT SMOKE?

☐ Yes   ☐ No   ☐ Ex-smoker

DOES PATIENT DRINK?

☐ Doesn't drink ☐ Approx _____ drinks per week

MEDICATION DOSE ADMINISTRATION:

☐ Self   ☐ Partner/Carer

AIDS OR OTHER EQUIPMENT USED:

☐ Peakflow meter   ☐ Spacer
☐ Nebuliser   ☐ Blood Glucose meter
☐ Multi/unit dose   ☐ Other _____
   DAA e.g. Dosette

INDICATION FOR DMMR

_____

_____

_____

Fig. 14.12 Exchanging and sense-making games: an example of a doctor's referral for medication review to a pharmacist. Part 1 of the extract (Source: Commonwealth of Australia, Department of Health) (By permission of Department of Health Australia)

ALLERGIES OR ADVERSE REACTIONS TO MEDICATION

DRUG	REASON FOR PRESCRIPTION	REACTION

CURRENT CONDITIONS AND MEDICATIONS

CONDITIONS /DIAGNOSIS e.g. DIABETES	MEDICATION OR OTHER TREATMENT e.g. Daonil or Diet	STRENGTH, DOSAGE AND FREQUENCY e.g. 5mg before breakfast	THERAPEUTIC GOALS e.g. Sugar control	ISSUES e.g. Visual problems

RELEVANT LABORATORY RESULTS AND BLOOD DRUG LEVELS

TEST TYPE	DATE	ISSUES

I HAVE EXPLAINED TO THE PATIENT:
- the process involved in having a DMMR and;

THE PATIENT UNDERSTANDS THAT:
- the location of the DMMR is at their choice, but preferably in their own home; and
- the pharmacist who will conduct the DMMR will communicate with me information arising from the DMMR; and

THE PATIENT HAS CONSENTED:
- to me releasing to the pharmacist information about their medical history and medications; and

THE PATIENT HAS/HAS NOT CONSENTED:
- to me releasing their Medicare No. or DVA No. to the pharmacist for the pharmacist's payment purposes. *

Date: _____   General Practitioner's Signature: _____

* If the patient does not agree to release their Medicare No., the DMMR service can still be provided.

Fig. 14.13 Exchanging and sense-making games: an example of a doctor's referral for medication review to a pharmacist. Part 2 of the extract (Source: Commonwealth of Australia, Department of Health) (By permission of Department of Health Australia)

Professional discourse games are closely related to what is known as 'interactional expertise' (Collins & Evans, 2007), 'relational agency' (Edwards, 2010), 'epistemological sophistication' (Bromme, Kienhues, & Stahl, 2008) and other kinds of boundary expertise and meta-level capacities. Ohlsson (1993) persuasively argued that 'powerful thinkers operate with a repertoire of thought forms' (p. 52) that regulate discourse and are able to extract essential properties without a deep understanding of content. This is the critical feature of 'high-end cognition' which Ohlsson contrasts with expertise, that is, 'too domain specific'.

Do professional discourse games draw on similar abstract thought and discourse forms as 'high-end' cognition? One can argue that this is at least partly so, and, in order to engage with the meta- or trans-professional discourse games, professionals should be able to adopt and see the world through the epistemological frames of the domains in which they operate. Yet, it is also important to note that adopting an epistemological frame and mastering rules of the game is not sufficient to operate within this frame. Imagine a math teacher who is asked to evaluate the appropriateness of a lesson plan for teaching arts. She could be perfectly able to identify and make judgements about some qualities of the plan and lesson design and could be perfectly able to appreciate differences between ways of teaching maths and arts and see the plan from the latter perspective. Yet without having deeper knowledge of arts pedagogy and the arts, she will probably not be able to judge the overall quality of the lesson design. That is, one cannot solve a problem with just a game, without a knowledge base. Further, complex professional discourse games involve their own sets of rules and moves for articulating, evaluating, exchanging and sense-making: some of which are outside the epistemological frame within which this knowledge was produced. For example, evaluation in almost any professional field is a specialised domain of expertise that involves mastering specialised meta-discourse games.

As a further point, we can ask what are the differences between specialist discourse games and propositional games? They are similar insofar as both make some use of formal propositional knowledge and language. Yet they are fundamentally different. Discourse games do not aim to *create* general professional knowledge; rather, they *draw upon* this general knowledge to make sense of local situations and align local actions with community knowledge (i.e. code). In Harry Collins and Robert Evans' (2007) terms, the expertise that underpins these games is interactional, not contributory, expertise (see Chap. 5).

14.4.5 Translational Public Discourse Games

The epistemic agenda for translational public discourse games focusses on extending professional knowledgeable action to the actions of others in the everyday world.

Public discourse games are played by professionals when they engage in interactions with clients. They are translational games that underpin professional work in public epistemic spaces. The main epistemic target of such games is knowledge artefacts and objects that emerge from meshing professional and non-professional knowledge and ways of knowing. This class of games involves public tool-making, investigative discourse and concept games.

Public tool-making games result in various professional epistemic artefacts intended for non-specialists' guidance. That is, these artefacts function as epistemic tools to support capacities to act knowledgeably, drawing on the professional knowledge of non-professional people. Examples of such tools include worksheets for students produced by a teacher; a pre- or post-operation plan prepared by a nurse for a patient; an asthma management plan, with personalised instructions for an asthmatic patient on how to improve respiratory inhaler techniques; or a label printed on medication, advising a patient on how often and when to take the medicine. Some of the games involved in creating these tools may be quite open and defined only by the epistemic target. Some may be more tightly or explicitly structured. For example, in an open game for producing a worksheet for teaching students strategies for recognising differences between historical and critical analysis in arts, a teacher might follow a set of strategies, rules, moves and forms defined by the epistemic target – such as that the final form of a worksheet should have a 'compare and contrast' structure. The task should be based on a set of consistent criteria that allow comparisons to be made between the two (e.g. expressed as guiding questions). Students should be engaged in a specific practical task that allows them to practice conducting both types of analysis. In other cases public tool-making games may be more restricted by the targeted form of the tool. For example, a pharmacist or a doctor may create a personalised asthma management and control plan by adapting a generic asthma action plan and giving a patient a personalised sheet outlining (a) characteristic symptoms of different asthma states – when well, when not well, etc.) (Fig. 14.14) and (b) what kinds of medications should be taken and how, depending on the severity of the condition (Fig. 14.15).

The critical feature of these public tool-making games is that they combine professional knowledge forms (e.g. patients should be prescribed symptom preventers, relievers and controllers) and knowledge of public communication strategies, suited to the needs of a specific situation (e.g. the plan should be structured according to different medical conditions recognisable by a patient). The epistemic target, in this case, is also not a specific conceptual artefact, but an artefact that is used as a tool by the public. It allows a non-professional to make similar decisions to those a professional would make, given knowledge of specific circumstances. For example, an asthma action plan for a patient is not only a professional public discourse product but also a tool that a patient uses for producing knowledge about his health conditions and for taking appropriate actions.

In our empirical observations, we noted that pharmacy students are taught a variety of strategies for creating public tools of this kind. For example, in an allergy and asthma tutorial, students were taught that it can be useful to add a colour scheme to a generic asthma plan, where green means 'when well', yellow means 'when not well' and red means 'danger signs'. The tutor also explained to the

ASTHMA ACTION PLAN
what to look out for

WHEN WELL	**THIS MEANS:** • you have no night-time wheezing, coughing or chest tightness • you only occasionally have wheezing, coughing or chest tightness during the day • you need reliever medication only occasionally or before exercise • you can do your usual activities without getting asthma symptoms
WHEN NOT WELL	**THIS MEANS ANY ONE OF THESE:** • you have night-time wheezing, coughing or chest tightness • you have morning asthma symptoms when you wake up • you need to take your reliever more than usual • your asthma is interfering with your usual activities **THIS IS AN ASTHMA FLARE-UP**
IF SYMPTOMS GET WORSE	**THIS MEANS:** • you have increasing wheezing, cough, chest tightness or shortness of breath • you are waking often at night with asthma symptoms • you need to use your reliever again within 3 hours **THIS IS A SEVERE ASTHMA ATTACK (SEVERE FLARE-UP)**
DANGER SIGNS	**THIS MEANS:** • your symptoms get worse very quickly • you have severe shortness of breath, can't speak comfortably or lips look blue • you get little or no relief from your reliever inhaler **CALL AN AMBULANCE IMMEDIATELY: DIAL 000** **SAY THIS IS AN ASTHMA EMERGENCY**	**DIAL 000 FOR AMBULANCE**

ASTHMA MEDICINES	**PREVENTERS** Your preventer medicine reduces inflammation, swelling and mucus in the airways of your lungs. Preventers need to be taken **every day**, even when you are well. Some preventer inhalers contain 2 medicines to help control your asthma (combination inhalers).	**RELIEVERS** Your reliever medicine works quickly to make breathing easier by making the airways wider. **Always carry your reliever with you** – it is essential for first aid. Do not use your preventer inhaler for quick relief of asthma symptoms unless your doctor has told you to do this.

To order more Asthma Action Plans visit the National Asthma Council website.
A range of action plans are available on the website –
please use the one that best suits your patient.
nationalasthma.org.au
Developed by the National Asthma Council Australia
and supported by GSK Australia.
National Asthma Council Australia retained editorial control. © 2015

NationalAsthma
CouncilAustralia
leading the attack against asthma

nationalasthma.org.au

Fig. 14.14 Public tool-making game: asthma action plan with characteristic symptoms of each asthma state. Part 1 of the extract (Source: National Asthma Council Australia) (By permission of National Asthma Council Australia)

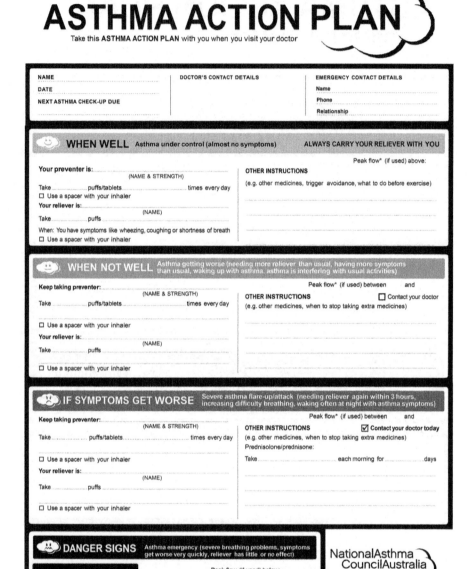

Fig. 14.15 Public tool-making game: asthma action plan with personalised information for asthma state management. Part 2 of the extract (Source: National Asthma Council Australia) (By permission of National Asthma Council Australia)

pharmacy students that, rather than just giving a list with generic symptoms describing each state, it is better to adapt those symptom descriptions to match characteristic symptoms for the specific patient. Another nice example was given by students. They suggested creating a sticker with the steps involved in a correct inhaler technique. Then they would ask a patient to demonstrate her inhaler technique and highlight on a sticker those steps that need attention and improvement. This would be placed on the inhaler. There were a number of very common-sense examples like this that do not seem to have much to do with any 'higher-order' professional knowledge, yet which make a lot of 'higher-order good sense' and draw on a significant body of professional knowledge. The students explained – providing statistics – that, depending on the type of inhaler, 4–94 % of patients have incorrect inhalation techniques and that this can be detrimental to the effectiveness of medications (Lavorini et al., 2008).

Investigative discourse games guide professional interaction and dialogue with a non-specialist audience. In contrast to public tool-making, these games are played when professionals use public discourse to produce final, ready for 'consumption', professional knowledge and understanding. The main feature is that the game is public in nature, but the knowledge that is generated is professional. For example, a pharmacist's communication with a patient (in order to gather relevant information for dispensing a correct medication) or a teacher's questioning strategies (aimed at assessing a student's understanding of a topic) or a counsellor's assessment interview with a client involves instances of these games (Fig. 14.16). The epistemic

Student/s to conduct an interview with Linda to complete *Interview Guide*

Questions to ask the patient
List the questions you would like to ask George and Jemma while conducting the HMR.
These **may include** some general questions and **should include** specific questions tailored to the patient, her conditions and medications.

1. *How are you taking each of your medications?*
2. *Do you take your regular medication every day? (BP still high yet patient on ACEI)*
3. *Can you tell me what each medication is for and how regularly you take them*
4. *Are you currently experiencing symptoms of diverticular disease? Constipation, diarrhoea, abdominal pain?*
5. *Did your doctor check your BP, cholesterol and BGL regularly?*
6. *Has the doctor ever checked your renal function?*
7. *How has your diet been lately? Fluid intake, salt, fat content? Frequency of weight measurement?*
8. *You seem to have some difficulty with your right hand. Is it only in the hand or on the right side? How long have you had the tremor? When does it bother you the most?*
9. *Do you have difficulty walking? Are you unsteady on your feet? Have you ever fallen?*
10. *Have you noticed changes in your voice?*
11. *Have you noticed that you do things more slowly or have difficulty moving (rigidity)*
12. *Do you feel any weakness or lack of coordination?*
13. *Have you had a flu or pneumovax vaccination?*

Fig. 14.16 An investigative discourse game: an example of questions with the patient for a medication review (Source: Tutorial and Externship Handbook used in Pharmacy Practice course)

target, therefore, is professional knowledge and understanding that are created via social interaction. This knowledge is often shaped by specific symbolic epistemic forms and rules (e.g. an interview using a schedule or getting relevant information by asking a patient to complete a questionnaire), but *may* be purely verbal and not mediated by an artefact at all (e.g. questioning during the dispensing process).

Concept games are played when professionals explain professional things in everyday language for a non-professional audience. The epistemic target is, therefore, non-professional knowledge that is created via professionally guided public discourse. These games are characterised by the fact that professionals use specific discourse strategies and rules, such as metaphors, analogies and examples, as discourse tricks. For example, a recommendation to increase intake of potassium for a patient with hypertension could be given by providing examples of products that are rich in this mineral, such as bananas, legumes, meat, poultry and fish. This group of games involves many other strategies that are commonly found in teachers' everyday professional work, such as producing lesson handouts, and in the work of other professionals who are creating similar 'finished' public knowledge products, such as pamphlets to increase awareness about certain diseases.

Are public discourse games epistemic? Yes they are, since they result in actionable knowledge or knowledgeable action, whether by a client or a professional. Are they games? Yes again, since they have an epistemic target and knowledgeable professionals use certain professional strategies and rules when they play these games.

Public discourse games involve what is often called *translational expertise*, as they require an ability to adopt and translate between specialist and lay epistemic frameworks and languages. They involve a professional ability to engage in socio-material interactions and discourse with people who may not be familiar with professional representational systems and discourse. Public discourse games are usually a part of our final major class of epistemic games – weaving games.

14.4.6 Weaving Games

Most professional games are not played alone. Many professional actions involve several epistemic targets, each contingent on the other and constitutively entangled. So they involve discourse games and problem-solving games simultaneously woven together with(in) a range of embodied socio-material professional interactions. Weaving games are those dynamic games experts play by meshing various games together – by fusing perception and conception into knowledgeable action. The epistemic target of such games is characterised by 'rightness', 'relevance', 'doability' and other situated outcomes that enhance professional work. Weaving games often evolve around taking professional actions that harness affordances of the environment and tweaking the epistemic environment in ways that enhance understanding of the situation and the possibilities of taking joint knowledgeable action. They are games that often involve fluent coordination of perception, expert mental resources, bodily skills and discourse.

An example of such a weaving game is administering a reading assessment test that requires noticing and coding different kinds of reading errors, and other features, while the student is still reading. Another example would be teaching a lesson and adjusting pitch, responding to students' performance and behaviour in pedagogically sound ways that are fine-tuned to a particular situation. Weaving games are a diverse and complex class of games – hard to describe in a systematic way. We group them into open, semi-scripted and routine games. Broadly, they can be characterised by three main attributes: (a) *contingency*, (b) *routine character* of the course of action and (c) *explicitness* of the final outcome.

Open games are interactive non-routine games that can be characterised by an open course of actions, high interdependence between related games and low predictability of outcome. For example, an interview with a patient with multiple diseases during medication review has this character and weaves problem-solving with discourse. The target form that characterises outcomes of this game is general and broad, but such an interview needs each time to be redesigned and adapted for a particular patient, and each move during the interview needs to be further tweaked to suit a dynamically unfolding situation. To illustrate this, we can look more closely at a general form used for interviewing patients, shown in Fig. 14.6. The questions asked of a specific patient during an interview are shown in Fig. 14.16, as well as how they are woven together with(in) the pharmacist's work. The former is the target epistemic form of the problem-solving game. It guides coding of the information from an interview and other sources and helps to represent this information in a form suitable for further processing and producing. The latter is the form of the translational public discourse game and guides the pharmacist's investigative dialogue with the particular patient. Thus, the epistemic form is aligned with a specific patient's diagnosis. The two games are woven together with the pharmacist's embodied action and ongoing sense-making, and the overall unfolding game is guided by the pharmacist's mental problem-solving activity, by the dialogue with the patient – collecting verbal information during the interview – and also by a range of moves for 'reading' other relevant verbal and nonverbal cues. Such moves include the pharmacist's investigation of the patient's compliance in taking medications – by reviewing dispensing history, checking the patient's understanding of what medications are for, assessing administration techniques, checking expiry dates of all the medications and observing other relevant condi-tions. What kind of information is relevant, and what can be collected, is contingent on the situation and determined within moment-to-moment interaction. The weav-ing game is generally open to diverse moves and can be adapted flexibly to the situation.

Semi-scripted games have a medium level of interdependence between the related games and actions. A typical example could be a lesson, where the teacher's actions are directed towards particular expected outcomes and what the teacher does is guided by a course of action that is at least partly pre-planned. Nevertheless, individual moves are contingent on moment-to-moment interaction and the specific enacted path that unfolds during teaching can vary a great deal across situations. The need for this flexibility is well recognised by teacher educators:

> ... the less bullet points [in the lesson plan] the better, because you have a little piece of paper on your desk to make sure that you're on track and at the end of the 45 minutes or the double lesson, you've actually have achieved 'I'm going to do this' because if not, sometimes you might depending on what happens in the classroom, you might end up going into a tangent and into a different area which there has to be room for that, to allow that to happen. But you still need, perhaps, to have a reminder of pulling yourself and your students back on track. (Education Lecturer)

Routine games are generally more repetitive, and possible courses of action and outcomes generally involve only a limited set of possibilities and variations. Administering a reading test to a student with learning difficulties can be an example of such a game. The main steps in administering the test need to be adapted to different students, different contexts and different texts, but the variations in the moves that need to be taken in any particular situation are relatively small. In fact, the characteristic procedure and rules should be followed by a counsellor with considerable precision, so that the test maintains its robustness and the measurements do not lose their validity. Routine games do not always imply easy games and they may involve complex weaving of several games and require fine-tuned embodied skill. For example, the reading test procedure involves complex weaving of public discourse and problem-solving (coding) games and usually requires special preparation:

> Lecturer: When I do the – show the DVD of the boy reading and they have to do analysis. They've got the sheets in front of them. The very first time they all nearly pass out because it's quite hard. And then I do it and I slow it all down and get lots of gaps and they relax a bit. They do more practice. And then by the time they get to do their own, I'd say they are pretty much on top of it.
> Interviewer: So they [students] have trouble with like actually conducting tests or interpreting the results?
> Lecturer: No. No. Not the tests so much actually. It's more the child's reading and you've got a copy of what the child's reading. It's just keeping up. So you get a child and they're reading and they're making lots of mistakes. It's very hard to get it all down. And a lot of the tests are like that. So the child's reading aloud and you're trying to record – they're just – a lot of literacy tests, you have to get pretty good at doing them. And that's just *not even choosing* the tests. That's *actually doing* the test. (Interview with School Counselling Lecturer and Program Director)

Learning to play weaving games – including those which look quite routine – tends to be hard for students, as such games inevitably involve contingencies. For example, one school counselling student (Jane) reflected on a challenge administering and making sense of a standard assessment test as follows:

> It was particularly frustrating as Ron scored points on the basal items but then got every other item incorrect, however I still had to continue with the test. (Student reflection on a completed behavioural assessment)

While the test clearly prescribed the moves, it could not help adjust them to a practically encountered situation. Jane continued by noting a number of other similar challenges, most of which also included complex weaving of several seemly simple, yet hard to enact, epistemic games – such as administering interviews with parents and teachers and reinforcing students while administering tests.

Given the challenges that weaving games can cause to novice professionals, we dedicate the whole of the next chapter to them.

References

Bartlett, F. C. (1932). *Remembering: A study in experimental and social psychology*. Cambridge, UK: Cambridge University Press.

Bourdieu, P. (1977). *The outline of a theory of practice*. Cambridge, UK: Cambridge University Press.

Bromme, R., Kienhues, D., & Stahl, E. (2008). Knowledge and epistemological beliefs: An intimate but complicate relationship. In M. S. Khine (Ed.), *Knowing, knowledge and beliefs: Epistemological studies across diverse cultures* (pp. 423–441). Dordrecht, The Netherlands: Springer.

Collins, A. (2011). Representational competence: A commentary on the Greeno analysis of classroom practice. In T. Koschmann (Ed.), *Theories of learning and studies of instructional practice* (Vol. 1, pp. 105–111). New York: Springer.

Collins, A., & Ferguson, W. (1993). Epistemic forms and epistemic games: Structures and strategies to guide inquiry. *Educational Psychologist, 28*(1), 25–42.

Collins, H., & Evans, R. (2007). *Rethinking expertise*. Chicago: The University of Chicago Press.

Edwards, A. (2010). *Being an expert professional practitioner: The relational turn in expertise*. Dordrecht, The Netherlands: Springer.

Fischer, F., Kollar, I., Mandl, H., & Haake, J. M. (Eds.). (2007). *Scripting computer-supported collaborative learning: Cognitive, computational and educational perspectives*. New York: Springer.

Goodwin, C. (1994). Professional vision. *American Anthropologist, 96*(3), 606–633.

Greeno, J. G., & Hall, R. P. (1997). Practicing representation: Learning with and about representational forms. *Phi Delta Kappan, 78*, 361–367.

Hayek, F. A. (1972). The primacy of the abstract. In A. Koestler & J. R. Smythies (Eds.), *Beyond reductionism: New perspectives in the life sciences* (pp. 309–333). London: Hutchimson.

Henning, P. H. (2004). Everyday cognition and situated action. In D. H. Jonassen (Ed.), *Handbook of research for educational communications and technology* (2nd ed., pp. 143–168). Mahwah, NJ: Lawrence Erlbaum Associates.

Knorr Cetina, K. (2007). Culture in global knowledge societies: Knowledge cultures and epistemic cultures. *Interdisciplinary Science Reviews, 32*, 361–375.

Lavorini, F., Magnan, A., Christophe Dubus, J., Voshaar, T., Corbetta, L., Broeders, M., et al. (2008). Effect of incorrect use of dry powder inhalers on management of patients with asthma and COPD. *Respiratory Medicine, 102*(4), 593–604. http://dx.doi.org/10.1016/j.rmed.2007.11.003

Moseley, D., Baumfield, V., Elliott, J., Gregson, M., Higgins, S., Miller, J., et al. (2005). *Frameworks for thinking: A handbook for teaching and learning*. Cambridge, UK: Cambridge University Press.

Nerland, M. (2008). Knowledge cultures and the shaping of work-based learning: The case of computer engineering. *Vocations and Learning, 1*(1), 49–69.

Nerland, M. (2010). Transnational discourses of knowledge and learning in professional work: Examples from computer engineering. *Studies in Philosophy and Education, 29*(2), 183–195.

Nonaka, I., & Takeuchi, H. (1995). *The knowledge-creating company: How Japanese companies create the dynamics of innovation*. New York: Oxford University Press.

Ohlsson, S. (1993). Abstract schemas. *Educational Psychologist, 28*(1), 51–66. doi:10.1207/s15326985ep2801_5.

Perkins, D. N. (1997). Epistemic games. *International Journal of Educational Research, 27*(1), 49–61.

Piaget, J. (1985). *The equilibration of cognitive structures: The central problem of intellectual development*. Chicago: University of Chicago Press.

Roth, W.-M., & McGinn, M. K. (1998). Inscriptions: Toward a theory of representing as social practice. *Review of Educational Research, 68*(1), 35–59.

Salomon, G., Perkins, D. N., & Globerson, T. (1991). Partners in cognition: Extending human intelligence with intelligent technologies. *Educational Researcher, 20*(3), 2–9.

Schank, R. C., & Abelson, R. P. (1977). *Scripts, plans, goals, and understanding: An inquiry into human knowledge structures*. Hillsdale, NJ: Lawrence Erlbaum Associates.

Schwab, J. J. (1962). The concept of the structure of a discipline. *The Educational Record, 43*, 197–205.

Schwab, J. J. (1970). *The practical: A language for curriculum*. Washington, DC: National Education Association, Center for the Study of Instruction.

Shaffer, D. W. (2006). Epistemic frames for epistemic games. *Computers & Education, 46*(3), 223–234. doi: http://dx.doi.org/10.1016/j.compedu.2005.11.003.

Star, S. L. (1989). The structure of ill-structured solutions: Boundary objects and heterogeneous distributed problem solving. In L. Gasser & M. N. Huhns (Eds.), *Distributed artificial intelligence* (Vol. 2, pp. 37–54). Pitman, CA: Morgan Kaufmann.

Star, S. L., & Griesemer, J. R. (1989). Institutional ecology, 'translations' and boundary objects: Amateurs and professionals in Berkeley's museum of vertebrate zoology. *Social Studies of Science, 19*(4), 387–420.

Suchman, L. (2007). *Human-machine reconfigurations: Plans and situated actions*. Cambridge, UK: Cambridge University Press.

Weddle, A. B., & Hollan, J. D. (2010). Professional perception and expert action: Scaffolding embodied practices in professional education. *Mind, Culture, and Activity, 17*(2), 119–148. doi:10.1080/10749030902721754.

Wittgenstein, L. (1963). *Philosophical investigations*. Oxford, UK: Blackwell.

Chapter 15
Weaving Ways of Knowing

A Case: Medication Management Review

Mrs Greene has recently been discharged from hospital following a myocardial infarct (MI). She feels very tired and down since her heart attack. The doctor wonders whether Mrs Greene is depressed, as she is reluctant to go out or attend Cardiac Rehab at the district hospital since her MI. Dr Reid is considering starting Zoloft, but wants to know if Mrs Greene's depression may be drug induced. Mrs Greene lives on a rural property with her son and daughter-in-law, 30 km outside a country town, in a separate dwelling. Dr Reid, asks you – a pharmacist – to conduct a Medication Management Review. He has provided more information for you on the *Referral Form for Medication Management Review*. (Pharmacy Practice: Tutorial and Externship Handbook)

15.1 Medication Management Review as 'Signature Pedagogy'

Medication management reviews – also called home medicines reviews (HMRs) and residential medication management reviews (RMMRs) – are conducted by pharmacists and are intended to give other healthcare providers and patients information that enables them to optimise medication use (Chen, Moles, Nishtala, & Basger, 2010). Medication reviews are usually undertaken in complex medication management cases, such as those involving patients taking five or more medications, or with symptoms of an adverse medicine reaction. Consequently, they require skills and knowledge that are particular to the pharmacist's profession. Pharmacists who provide this service undergo a special preparation and accreditation. However, medication reviews draw upon a range of competences that are also part of skilful and knowledgeable daily practice, such as communicating with and counselling patients, knowledgeably dispensing prescriptions and working in teams with other health professionals. Therefore, the assemblage of epistemic forms,

© Springer Science+Business Media Dordrecht 2017
L. Markauskaite, P. Goodyear, *Epistemic Fluency and Professional Education*,
Professional and Practice-based Learning 14, DOI 10.1007/978-94-007-4369-4_15

epistemic games and other pieces of the epistemic infrastructure that underpin this service is also used as a 'signature pedagogy' for constructing learning tasks that help students to learn professional ways of knowing – 'to *think*, to *perform* and to *act with integrity*' (Shulman, 2005, p. 52, original emphasis). As one of the pharmacy lecturers put it:

> ... my belief is that we use this service as *a tool* for them [students], a learning tool, because *nearly anything that you do, even if it's just dispensing a prescription, has information gathering, processing and delivering components.* So you have to *gather* the information even if it's 'are you taking any other medicines?' – even if it's one medicine, you've got to gather the information. Then you need to *process* it. So you need to work out 'is this right or wrong', 'does this seem right' – and then you need to *deliver*. You need to the tell patient how are they are going to take it. What are they going to do. So even the most simplistic pharmacy service, whether it be responding to a cough and cold request or whether it be dispensing a prescription, has those three elements.

In other words, as we saw in Chap. 14, information gathering, processing and delivery are three core epistemic games within the pharmacist's everyday professional work. However, medication reviews also involve what we earlier identified as the 'hardest elements of professional practice' and thus provide an opportunity for students to learn to play common professional epistemic games, in *complex* professional situations (see Chap. 8). As the lecturer continued:

> We use medication review as the example because the processing is a lot more difficult in medication review because the patient might be on seven medicines at a time. So it's trying to work out if all seven of those fit together. But the process is no different really, just even for dispensing one script.

Our aim in this chapter is to elucidate some qualities of epistemic tools and games that are brought together into assemblages for complex knowledge-rich professional work and to illustrate three main aspects of what is occurring:

- The arrays of *epistemic tools* that are brought together and assembled into specific infrastructures and environments for complex professional tasks
- Some distinct features of *epistemic forms as generative devices* (as modelling sites) that support the alignment of abstract knowledge and actionable knowledge
- How epistemic games are *woven together* with social and material ways of knowing and are thus inseparable from the epistemic practice (and action)

Our reconstruction of the social and epistemic infrastructure (Sects. 15.1 and 15.2) draws on the materials, resources and references collected in one of our case studies, where medication review was used as an approach to prepare students for pharmacy practice and also as a part of a formal exam-based assessment. Our reconstruction draws on an extensive set of materials. However, we illustrate the main epistemic qualities of the epistemic artefacts that were created by using examples of completed works – worksheets, questions for a doctor, reports, etc. – that were included in the package for the exam assessors. (Many of these were presented when we introduced the individual epistemic games in Chap. 14.) These examples, rather than reviews completed by students, are of particular interest here, as they reveal the expectations of the pharmacists' epistemic culture with respect to the key qualities of the epistemic products that characterise 'expert' ways of knowing and making. In Sect. 15.3 – the most substantial part of the chapter – we proceed to show how pharmacy students go about weaving these diverse elements together. Building on this analysis, we explain how epistemic forms need to be understood as both the result of and resources for cooperation, conception and construction (Sect. 15.4). The social infrastructure that we sketch in Sect. 15.1 turns out to play a substantial role in the medication review process, so in Sect. 15.5 we show what is involved when pharmacists – whether experienced or student – weave epistemic games with social and bureaucratic infrastructures. In our concluding section (15.6), we draw some parallels with Andy Clark's (2011) work on the extended mind, pointing out that epistemic games and forms create opportunities to spread problem-solving between mind, body and world: but to take advantage of those opportunities requires one to become a masterly weaver.

15.2   Social Infrastructure

Quality use of medicines is one of the four main elements of the national medicines policy in Australia. A medication management review is one of the services offered by pharmacists that specifically aligns with this goal and thereby aims to improve general health outcomes. Medication reviews may be conducted for patients living at home (the HMR version) or in residential aged care facilities (the RMMR version). If a general practitioner (GP), or the nursing staff in a residential care home, decides that a patient may benefit from a medication review, they refer the patient to an accredited pharmacist.

The medication review is usually undertaken where the patient lives, although it may occur in the pharmacy or in their doctor's surgery. Ideally it includes an interview with the patient. For patients with some diseases, such as Alzheimer's, that make an interview unreliable or impossible, the pharmacist may still visit the patient and/or interview their carer. Once the medication review is completed, the pharmacist provides a report to the doctor. If needed, a case conference involving the doctor, the pharmacist and other health professionals, as well as the patient or carer, may take place.

The formal process of the medication review describes the main steps involved in this service provision (Fig. 15.1).[1] Some of these processes are reified in bureaucratic templates and forms specifying service provision, such as *HMR Claim Forms*. However, as one university pharmacy teacher noted, the formally defined procedure for service provision and the actual medication review that pharmacists carry out (and which students need to learn) are not the same:

---

[1] Outlined, in this case, on the relevant Australian governmental website and in various guidelines for GPs and pharmacists.

The Home Medicines Review (HMR) Process

1. Identification of person requiring HMR service

2. Assessment by GP of clinical need for an HMR from a quality use of medicines perspective with the patient as the focus

3. Formal initiation of HMR

4. Patient is informed and gives their consent

5. Referral by GP to the patient's preferred community pharmacy or accredited pharmacist who must have prior approval from Medicare to conduct HMR services

6. Approved HMR service provider coordinates the HMR service and notifies the GP of the details of the accredited pharmacist who will conduct the service

7. The preferred address and time for HMR are arranged with the patient

8. Pharmacist conducts HMR

9. Review of information by accredited pharmacist and development of suggested management strategies

10. Preparation of report by accredited pharmacist

11. Report provided to and discussed with GP

12. Medication management plan agreed between patient and GP

13. Implementation of agreed actions with appropriate follow-up and monitoring

---

Fig. 15.1 Steps of the home medicines review (Source: Caird, 2012, p. 26)

> Yeah, I mean there are two things. That's referring to the actual *process of the implementation of the review service* in real life – then there's the *process of actually conducting the review*, you know, the building blocks of the review process. So I see those as separate things.

The former constitutes a part of the social infrastructure of the medication review; the latter is a much broader and heterogeneous epistemic assemblage.

15.3   Epistemic Infrastructure

The choice of epistemic tools and strategies for conducting medication reviews is generally left to pharmacists. The infrastructure that provides pharmacists with the core tools for doing this kind of job is partly created and partly assembled from other professional tools by (a) providers of accredited training programs that teach pharmacists to conduct medication reviews and (b) university teachers who teach students to conduct medication reviews as a part of pharmacy practice courses (e.g. Chen et al., 2010). These tools spread across the core epistemic toolbox and related infrastructures – information, learning, boundary, social and material (see Chap. 13). They include tools for various stages of the review, such as templates for writing reports and letters, manuals and cases illustrating the pharmacist's decisions and practices – in other words, exemplars.

What do these different pieces of the epistemic infrastructure look like? It is useful to chart, at least schematically, some key elements of the assemblage that we have reconstructed from the materials we collected and from references used in the pharmacy courses we studied. The configuration of this assemblage is shown in Table 15.1.

The overall process of the medication review is guided by an inquiry framework that focusses on three aspects: (a) information gathering, (b) information processing and (c) information delivery. As explained earlier, these three elements are well known in pharmacy practice, because, as the teacher explained to us, they guide 'nearly anything that you do' in pharmacy. In the HMR case, information gathering includes the patient interview and other strategies to collect relevant data. Information processing involves figuring out issues in current medication use and coming up with possible solutions. Information delivery involves the initial discussion of findings and possible recommendations with the doctor and patient and communication of the final review outcomes in the form of a written report.

Each element of the review process involves a set of form-like templates that give characteristic shapes to the knowledge produced. (We shared a number of examples in Chap. 14 – hence, in the account below, we make frequent references to figures in that chapter.) For example:

1. A general interview form that guides a coding game (Fig. 14.6, coding game)
2. Several forms that guide identification of issues and coming up with recommendations (Fig. 14.7, producing game; Figs. 14.8 and 14.9, organising games)
3. The form for the final report (Fig. 14.10, making game)

The outcomes of the last two interwoven games emerge during information processing and delivery and are illustrated in Figs. 15.4 and 15.5.

Each template reifies different aspects of inquiry and acts as a simple, but powerful, epistemic form that guides a problem-solving or other epistemic processes. Some of these are simple and generic devices that are brought into the assemblage from the generic epistemic toolbox. An example would be the list for prioritising issues (Fig. 14.8). But some of them embody characteristic forms of knowledge and ways of knowing that are specific to the professional epistemic culture. An example of this would be the form instantiated in, and in which is instantiated, the final medication review report (Fig. 14.10). We will return to this particular form later.

Epistemic devices that help organise each step are also accompanied by various other 'pure' epistemic tools and 'exemplars'. For example:

Table 15.1 Medication review: a summary of tools, games and infrastructures

General inquiry framework	Review process cycle: information gathering, processing and delivery		
	Gathering ——>	<—— Processing ——>	<—— Delivery
Tools	• A general interview form • Case-specific interview questions	• Strategies for systematic review: (a) by medication and (b) by disease state • Working sheets for different stages of processing: (a) figuring out issues, (b) prioritising and (c) identifying goals and options	• A medication review report form • A standard letter for a doctor
Epistemic games	• Interviewing a patient and collecting all other associated information	• Identifying issues and generating possible hypotheses and recommendations • Prioritising issues • Identifying goals and matching goals with options	• Communicating and tuning findings and recommendations
Nature of epistemic games	Three interwoven games: • Trans-professional discourse (sense-making) • Problem-solving (coding) • Translational public discourse (investigative discourse and concept)	Two interwoven games: • Problem-solving (producing) • Problem-solving (organising)	Three interwoven games: • Problem-solving (making) • Translational public discourse (concept and investigative discourse) • Trans-professional discourse (exchanging)
Outputs	• Information from the referral: information about patient, lab results, diseases, prescribed medications, medical history, allergies, etc. • Information from the patient and observations: patient's understanding, concerns, problems administering, medication efficacy, complaints of side effects, all medications taken, administration techniques, etc.	• Issues and possible solutions: drug or dosage discrepancies, potential therapeutic issues, lifestyle • Priority of issues • Goals (prioritised and grouped issues), options and reasoning • Additional information required from medical practitioner[a]	• Findings and recommendations for doctor's decision making

	• Information from observations: compliance check, expiry dates, etc. • Other data indicative of possible issues and possible solutions (a possibility space)	• Handbooks and databases (information infrastructure): (a) Medicines complete, (b) eMIMS (monthly index of medical specialties), (c) eTG (Therapeutic guidelines), (d) drug interaction facts, (e) eAMH (Australian medicines handbook online) and (f) the Internet	• Guidelines and exemplars on how to report findings and how to counsel a patient (learning infrastructure) • Further information from the doctor[a] • Interview and interaction with a doctor and patient (social infrastructure, but also human bodies, minds and discourse)
Socio-material infrastructures	• HMR referral (inter-professional boundary infrastructure) • Pharmacy dispensing database (intra-professional boundary infrastructure) • Medications and places where medications are stored, etc. (material infrastructure) • Interview and interaction with a patient (social infrastructure, but also human bodies, minds and discourse)		
General epistemic frame	Improvement of community health outcomes		
Codes	Patient's consent, confidentiality, regulatory framework of HMR process		

[a] 'Additional information required from medical practitioner' and 'Further information from the doctor' – are additional outputs and elements of socio-material infrastructure, respectively, that were added to the standard medication review by university teachers for educational purposes. These elements aim to develop students' capacities to discuss initial findings and possible recommendations (in a case conference with the doctor) before finalising the medication review report and recommendations. In professional practice settings, these elements do not normally exist – case conferences with doctors are rare, or they take place only at the end of the review process (see 'Step 11. Report provided to and discussed with GP' of the medication review process in Fig. 15.1)

1. The general interview form (Fig. 14.6) is supplemented by examples illustrating how one should ask general questions of the patient, as well as case-specific and disease-specific questions (Fig. 14.16).
2. The forms for processing information are extended with several alternative strategies that can help the pharmacist examine the information systematically and uncover reasons for any problems identified. For example, within a producing game, the pharmacist could choose between going through each disease state or going through each of the medications and identifying associated issues.
3. The medication review form for information delivery, used in the making game, is supplemented by examples illustrating how different kinds of findings and recommendations can be reported (Fig. 14.11). The medication review casebook (Chen et al., 2010) provides further examples of letters for a doctor, counselling notes for patients and other exemplars illustrating this element of the review for different combinations of diseases and different situations.

The review process is further supplemented by a list of questions that point to common issues in medication use. This is labelled 'Some questions to ask yourself when conducting medication review' and includes questions such as: 'Is the patient compliant/adherent?', 'Are there signs of drug toxicity?', 'Is any therapy missing?' and so on. Each question is then further described, suggesting specific strategies of where to look for necessary evidence or information, how to figure out answers and how to write these findings into the report (Fig. 15.2).

These epistemic devices and exemplars provide core tools, rules and strategies for the medication review. However, this work does not just draw on a set of general heuristic devices and rules. The tools, rules and strategies are constitutively entangled with the conceptual knowledge base of the profession. Furthermore, the medication review is not just a mental enterprise that draws on conceptual tools, but is constitutively entangled with other infrastructures: information devices, boundary artefacts, other digital and material things and human bodies.

What do we mean by this? First, epistemic forms used in professional work sometimes, but not always, already involve the conceptual knowledge base. However, associated epistemic games inevitably require this knowledge. For example, the interview form is already structured using elements linked to pharmaceutical knowledge, such as concerns about medication, and problems administering medications (Fig. 14.16). In contrast, a list for prioritising issues – as an epistemic form – does not include any reference to disciplinary knowledge and could be used for prioritising any kinds of things (Fig. 14.8). However, both games require this knowledge base – one would not be able to prioritise identified issues unless one understands what these issues mean. Second, epistemic games are fundamentally social and material: they are played in action and interaction with the material and social world. A pharmacist cannot interview a patient, unless there is a patient to be interviewed; she cannot check the expiry dates of medications unless the medications *actually* exist.

Examples of where to find the information and how to write your report

c. Are these the same drugs as prescribed by the GP?

When you examine a medication chart or doctor's referral form you may find that a medication is not listed, but the resident is using it. For example, the resident may have a diagnosis of glaucoma and you notice that there are no eye drops. On investigation you may find that the resident is actually having Timoptol 0.5% administered BD. Your report should note this.

Example of how your finding may be reported

"Timoptol (timolol) 0.5% eye drops are administered twice daily. There is no order for this medication on the medication chart. Recommend medication chart (or notes) be updated."

d. Is the patient compliant/adherent?

Compliance is not often a problem for residents in Residential Aged Care facilities as staff administer medication and each dose is signed for by the person who administers it. However it may be a problem with community-based patients and may be identified by you when you analyse the patient's pharmacy computer history.

In the nursing home or hostel you may find that the chart does not have signatures to show regular administration or that the resident has refused the medication.

Example of how your finding may be reported

"Coloxyl with Senna is ordered 2 BD, the medication chart shows that this medication is not administered. Recommend the GP be notified and the medication reviewed."

Fig. 15.2 Coding and making games: An example of strategies for finding out information and recommended discourse for reporting findings. Extract only (Source: Tutorial and Externship Handbook used in Pharmacy Practice course)

15.4 Assembling and Weaving

How are these different pieces assembled into one coherent epistemic environment and woven into coherent action and, in learning settings, into 'signature pedagogies'? Each step of the medication review draws on different kinds of material and social infrastructures, and each of the three stages weaves together several epistemic games. The process starts from the information provided in the doctor's referral (Figs. 14.12, 14.13, 15.3 and 15.4).

Information gathering is guided by the general interview form and is linked to what we called (in Chap. 14) the *coding game* (Fig. 14.6). This game guides the process of noting and capturing situated information about the use of medicines, such as the patient's understanding of what medications are for, concerns about medications, problems administering any medication, perception of medication

MEDICATION MANAGEMENT - HOME MEDICINES REVIEW

COMMUNITY PHARMACY DETAILS:	GENERAL PRACTITIONER DETAILS:
(nominated by the patient)	Name: Dr Reid
Name: Your Friendly Pharmacy	Address: **50 Main Rd, Beach Junction**
PATIENT DETAILS:	Provider No:
Name: **Nola Greene**	Prescriber No: 610671
Address: **3 Lone Crescent, Special Junction, NSW**	Phone: 02 4908 4888
D.O.B: 03/03/1939	Fax: 02 4953 0276
Medicare No: 81111	
DVA No:	PREFERRED MEANS OF RECEIVING REPORT:
Patient/Carer contact:	**Written report and case conference**

ISSUES THAT MAY INFLUENCE MEDICATION USE EFFECTIVENESS:	Does patient drink alcohol? **Nil** Does the patient smoke? **Nil**
⊓ Vision ⁻ Hearing	
☐ Language and/or ⁼ ⁼ Swallowing literacy problems	
_ _Cognition _ Dexterity (eg manual coordination) (memory and comprehension)	**MEDICATION DOSE ADMINISTRATION** **Self :** Partner/Carer:
⁼ ⁼Other	

OTHER PATIENT INFORMATION:	AIDS OR OTHER EQUIPMENT USED:
Height: **160cm** Weight: **74kg**	_ ⊔Peakflow meter ⊔⊔Spacer ⁻ ⊓Nebuliser Blood Glucose Meter
Blood Pressure: *110/69*	⁼ ⁼Multi/unit dose ☐ Other .... DAA eg Dosette

VACCINATION STATUS (TICK IF UP-TO-DATE)	INDICATION FOR HMR
■ ⁻Tetanus ■ ⁻Rubella ⁼ ⁼Hepatitis A ■ ⁼ Hepatitis B _ Influenza _ _Other .... ⁻ ⁻Pneumovax⊓⊓	• **Recent hospital discharge post MI** • **Depression? (has not attended Cardiac Rehab)** • **Considering starting Zoloft (please r/v if appropriate)**

ALLERGIES OR ADVERSE REACTIONS TO MEDICATION: Penicillin (rash)

Fig. 15.3 Exchanging and sense-making games: an example of a doctor's referral for medication review to a pharmacist. Part 1 of the extract (Source: OSCE material used in Pharmacy Practice course)

efficacy, complaints of side effects, a check on whether the medications are actually being taken, administration techniques, compliance and expiry dates.

The coding game is interwoven with the trans-professional discourse (sense-making) game and the translational public discourse (investigative) game. The pharmacist's work starts with the sense-making game. The referral letter serves as a boundary object for passing over information from the doctor to the pharmacist

CURRENT MEDICATION:

Condition/diagnosis	Medication/treatment	Dose	Goal	Issues
Heart	Betaloc 100mg	1 bd		
Cholesterol	Pravachol 40mg	1 n	Lower cholesterol	
Angina	Monodur 120mg	1 m		
	Anginine 600mcg	1 s/1 prn	Stop acute pain	
Hypertension	Isoptin 240mg	1 d		NB recently ceased in hospital
Angina	Imdur 60mg	1 d		NB recently ceased in hospital

PAST MEDICAL HISTORY:

1985	Cholecystectomy
	IHD
	Hypertension
	Hypercholesterolaemia
2007	AMI
September 2009	AMI

RELEVANT LABORATORY RESULTS AND BLOOD DRUG LEVELS (eg serum electrolytes, liver function test etc. as relevant):

Biochemistry	Date	Result	Reference Interval
Sodium		No results available	
Potassium			
Creatinine			

I HAVE EXPLAINED TO THE PATIENT:	THE PATIENT HAS CONSENTED:
• the process involved in having a HMR; and THE PATIENT UNDERSTANDS THAT: • the location of the HMR is at their choice, but preferably in their own home; and • the pharmacist who will conduct the HMR will communicate with me, information arising from the HMR; and	• to me releasing to the pharmacist information about their medical history and medications; and THE PATIENT CONSENTED: • to me releasing their Medicare No. or DVA No. to the pharmacist for the pharmacist's payment purposes.*
Date: 12th October 2009	General practitioner's Signature: DrS Reid

Fig. 15.4 Exchanging and sense-making games: an example of a doctor's referral for medication review to a pharmacist. Part 2 of the extract (Source: OSCE material used in Pharmacy Practice course)

(Figs. 14.12, 14.13, 15.3 and 15.4). It documents diagnoses, medications, recent biochemistry, allergies and reasons for the medication review. This information is supplemented with records from the pharmacy's dispensing database, which provides additional insights into the patient's compliance with respect to getting prescribed medications, and allows the pharmacist to prepare for the interview (see Fig. 15.2).

A good deal of important information is obtained from the pharmacist's observations and insights during the home visit and the interview. An investigative discourse game played during the interview is interwoven with other forms of active embodied exploration, such as observing and checking medications. Both conversation and exploration are crucial sources of situated knowledge in a coding game: medication boxes with expiry dates, and places where medicines are stored, serve as sources of information about compliance, about difficulties the patient has with taking the medications, potential issues with medication effectiveness and other inefficiencies associated with the therapy. The patient's social and physical environment and their answers to the pharmacist's questions are the main sources of data and clues for detecting discrepancies and issues in medication management, administration techniques, social conditions and other critical aspects that may impact health, but which neither the doctor's referral nor the pharmacy's records can reveal.

Exploration, sense-making and public investigative discourse are all interwoven with the coding game that is gently guided by the interview form (Fig. 14.6). The word 'gently' reflects the critical characteristic of this inscriptional epistemic form, and as the course guidelines say:

> This [form] is by no means prescriptive and serves as a prompt or guide during the interview. There may also be other questions you wish to ask the patient. (Pharmacy Practice: Tutorial and Externship Handbook)

This form is recommended rather than required – acknowledging possible contingencies of the work that may not fit into standard procedures and an inevitable need to mix generic forms and strategies with ways of knowing informed by the situation and by disciplinary knowledge. The guidelines given to students explicitly suggest that specific questions *should* be asked of the patient when completing this interview form:

> These *may include* some general questions and *should include* specific questions tailored to the patient, her conditions and medications. (Pharmacy Practice: Tutorial and Externship Handbook, original emphasis)

Information processing is a problem-solving game. It is what one may call a 'mental game', which may not require material devices; or as a pharmacy lecturer put it: 'They're doing it in their head'. But learning to do such work, which requires orderly – systematic and systemic – problem-solving and well-considered professional judgement, is guided by a set of worksheets, which play the role of epistemic forms and rules. The teacher explained this as follows:

> It's [the worksheet] to help them [students] structure their thoughts. <...> We try to get them into that *habit* so that they can, not because we want them to use that form but just so they have a *structured way* of approaching the review process. We think that's important, otherwise the whole process can be very intimidating for them. They can see a particular clinical intervention but they kind of work out why they haven't seen these other four or five other things.

The course resources suggest several such structuring and ordering devices (Figs. 14.7, 14.8 and 14.9). One of the most frequently used forms guides students through a systematic examination of three areas – drug and dosage discrepancies, potential therapeutic issues and lifestyle – and helps the students who are using it to align their findings for each identified issue with possible recommendations (see Fig. 14.7 and completed version in Fig. 15.5).

Working sheet for medication review

	Findings	Recommendations

Drug/dosage discrepancies	Need to exclude concordance problems:
	  - interview patient
	  - check date of dispensing and amount taken
	  - previous community pharmacy
		Stress compliance to patient.
		
		Once daily medications may help, or dosage administration aid may be of benefit.

	Ascertain usage of Anginine Patient storing Anginine in pill box for up to 3 months	Inform Dr Reid, suggest Nitrolingual as an alternative for acute angina attacks, easy to carry, better expiry and more reliable for Mrs Greene.
	Isoptin still being taken as patient unaware or forgot that it was ceased	Inform doctor, counsel patient and remove Isoptin, with patient's permission
	Missing therapy	Aspirin
	Atenolol may be a better choice than metoprolol in relation to compliance – once daily dosing rather than twice daily.	Consider use of atenolol 100mg daily to improve compliance – discuss with Dr Reid.
Potential therapeutic problems	Beta-blockers offer prognostic benefit following MI, especially in high-risk patients such as those with significant left ventricular dysfunction and/or ongoing ischaemia, and should be commenced during hospital admission unless contraindicated. TG Cardio4 2003 Atenolol may be better choice as less lipophilic and less likely to cause depression The mortality rates for metoprolol and atenolol were equivalent (13.5% vs 13.4% 2-year mortality, respectively).mdx Healthcare Series Vol. 126 2005	Discuss with Dr Reid and suggest use of atenolol 100mg daily to prevent possible metoprolol related depression, whilst retaining mortality risk reduction. Counsel Mrs Greene on the triple role of beta-blockers post MI, angina and for hypertension.
	Loss of drug potency with current storage of Anginine in pillbox, may have contributed to lack of response when taken previously for chest pain.	Discuss with Dr Reid and suggest alternative Nitrolingual, 400mcg.(longer expiry and convenient for patient to carry)
	Combination of beta-blocker metoprolol and verapamil additive negative inotropic and chronotropic effect, combination not advised without monitoring	Cause reduction in HR and BP possible cause of lethargy, See above.
	ADRs; Monodur, check effectiveness (frequency of Anginine use) and monitor for S/E (Orthostatic hypotension, syncope, dizziness, palpitations, light-headedness, headache, and blood pressure).	Regular monitoring of BP, use of paracetamol (not NSAIDs) for mild headache, patient to report if continual headache or dizziness. Mrs Greene to swallow whole Mrs Greene to understand the difference between prevention and treatment and which nitrate to use for attack
	ADRs: metoprolol and lethargy, depression. As this is more lipophilic, possibly more incidence of CNS effects. In US Studies only, depression occurred in 0.6% of patients (n=164) taking atenolol versus 0.5% in placebo patients (n=206) (Prod Info Tenormin(R), 2002).	Consider change to less lipophilic beta-blocker such as atenolol. Equivalent dose is 100mg but may prefer to start at 50mg and titrate upwards pending response. No need to reduce slowly as swapping to another beta-blocker.
	ADRs: Pravastatin, may cause increase in LFT's, myopathy, dose related, possibly contribute to lethargy via weakness	Refer to baseline or previous LFTs and CK, monitor regularly
	Missing therapy: Low dose aspirin is indicated as antiplatelet therapy following an MI.	Suggest commencing aspirin if appropriate.
Lifestyle issues	• Mrs Greene is overweight. Her BMI = $74/1.6^2$ = 28.9. Risk factor for CV disease • Rehab will address low mood post MI	Address modifiable risk factors
Information required from Medical Practitioner	• Mrs Greene's EUC, cholesterol & TG, • Mrs Greene's recent LFTs, ?CK if muscle pain • Iron studies • Assessment of current CV risk (requires results of biochemistry as well as family history, smoking?, level of BP, age > 65 years for females)	

Fig. 15.5 Producing game: an example of a worksheet for identifying issues during medication review and potential ways to address them. Extract only (Source: OSCE material used in Pharmacy Practice course)

This form is included in materials for each tutorial and is also included in the final exam package. Two other forms provided in the tutorial guidelines make thinking about the issues identified in the final report visible. One form simply guides students to prioritise identified issues (Fig. 14.8). The next prompts them to systematically outline the goals and align these with the possible options and the reasoning behind each suggestion, before assembling decisions together into the final recommendation (Fig. 14.9). Some of these epistemic devices are extremely simple, like a table with one column to list all the issues and another column to take a number that indicates priority (Fig. 14.8). Such simple forms, however, are linked to challenging professional games, critical for successful decisions. One teacher explained why prioritising and grouping are so challenging:

> I think, as a student as well, the text books just tell you how to treat all different diseases – like they're all broken up into disease states. So they don't actually say – they never have a text book that says 'if this person has five disease states, this one is the most dangerous' or whatever. <...> To put it all together and say 'ok, let's think about this really logically', 'what's going to happen to this patient if we don't' – because we're dealing often with really chronic conditions that are going to go forever, you know, if someone's cholesterol level is a little bit high but their blood pressure is through the roof, then I would say that the blood pressure is the most important right now. But for some of them, they can't tell – they're just like 'well the cholesterol's high and the blood pressure is high, I don't know which one is more important'. So sometimes they're not very good at working out what's more important.

This stage of the medication review tightly weaves together two kinds of problem-solving games that we called the *producing game* and the *organising game*. The former is mainly concerned with identifying issues and possible solutions to each issue; the latter involves organising all the findings and possible options and combining them together into one solution. These two games, which are quite independent in theory, are closely intertwined in practice. Different issues often have conflicting solutions and thus require constant checking for new potential issues, prioritisation and revision.

The producing game, however, is not entirely a mental game. It is woven together with an extensive and rapidly changing information infrastructure. Three handbooks – the *Australian Medicines Handbook*, *Therapeutic Guidelines* and the *Merck Manual of Diagnosis and Therapy* – serve as key references. As one pharmacy teacher said, these are 'the books that pharmacists will use every day in real life'. This set is extended with a variety of other printed and digital resources, such as drug interaction facts and prescription product guides. This infrastructure provides pharmacists with the information they need about medications, diagnoses, therapies and other relevant medical knowledges and helps them to figure out interactions and other pharmacological and therapeutic issues. The skills pharmacists need in order to use this information infrastructure tend to be mundane, yet they are only a part of a complex epistemic game that requires both figuring out issues and coming up with practical, properly justified, solutions. As one pharmacy lecturer said:

> Anyone can look up whether the dose is appropriate or within the range or not. You have to do that part of the review process. But if you only do that then maybe these are not significant issues. They could be significant but they may not be significant. Likewise,

they can go to a computer program and look for interactions between drugs. But anyone can look for interactions between drugs if they have the program and can type the drug names in. So really, what we're doing is – if you think about those two examples, they're just the finding. Where there's application or where there's integration is making a specific recommendation – once they've found out whether the dose is a problem, what is their recommendation in relation to that? Once they've found out that there is drug to drug interaction, what's their recommendation about what to do about that? So a core concept is that they understand that it's *not about identifying problems*, but it's about *identifying problems which is the finding and then making a recommendation which is the solution*.

Information delivery is the last part of the review. It involves communicating findings with the doctor, and possibly with the patient or carer, fine-tuning recommendations and crafting a formal medication review report and letter to the doctor. Information delivery is a *making game* and is broadly guided by the form for the final report (Fig. 14.10 and completed version in Fig. 15.6). This work requires pharmacists to express their findings and recommendations in the language of medical practitioners *and* lay people; thus, it weaves 'making' with the trans-professional discourse of medical doctors and the translational public discourse of the patient. Crafting the report is not just mechanical work, and the epistemic form that guides this making game is a complex and heterogeneous device: the pharmacist still needs to make final decisions about which findings and recommendations are highlighted, which go first and which follow, which kinds of knowledge and justifications are shown and which are hidden:

> It [the written report] needs to be concise, professional and logical, and there needs to be some sort of order to it, the prioritisation (Pharmacy Lecturer)

The problem-solving (making) and the discourse dimensions are intertwined in this work. The reasoning rules are translated in the discourse; the discourse rules are meshed with the reasoning:

> ... you don't want to just write 'stop this', 'start this', 'change this' – if you write just words like that 'stop', 'start', 'change', then you're actually directing the doctor, which is what you want to do but you want the doctor [to make this decision] – you might not be right. <...> [S]o you need to use words like 'consider' or 'I recommend'. (Pharmacy Lecturer)

Structuring and strategic tools that provide guidance in this kind of knowledge work are both general and local, rational and social, aligned to the broader professional culture and to the local culture, and transferable and constitutively intertwined with the perceived affordances of the situation:

> Yes. It is [easier to have the review report presented in a table format]. But then other people find that writing a letter is more acceptable. So it's also about when you're a real accredited pharmacist, is finding out how your doctor would prefer the report. So it's actually what the doctor would prefer. So I quite like it [the report] like this because it's broken up into point forms into a table. But some doctors would much prefer to have it, a documented letter like they get from a specialist. So you know, when the specialist is – so *they're used to reading letters*. (Pharmacy Lecturer)

Such constructed professional epistemic artefacts are of particular interest here. They have a dual character. First, they embody forms of knowledge characteristic of the pharmacists' epistemic culture and recognisable *within*, and in this case

Medication Review Report Form

Pharmacist Name	

Date of Medication Review	Patient name	Doctor name
	Mrs Greene	Dr S Reid

Current Medications (including OTC, Vitamins, etc)

Name	Strength	Directions	Indication
Betaloc	100mg	1 bd	Post infarct, angina, hypertension
Pravachol	40mg	1 n	Hypercholesterolaemia
Monodur	120mg	1 m	Angina
Anginine	600mcg	1 s/l prn	Acute chest pain

Previous Medications (including OTC, Vitamins, etc)

Name	Strength	Directions	Start	Stop	Indication
Imdur	60mg	1 m			Chest pain
Isoptin 240mg	240mg	1 m			Hypertension

Renal Function	Normal	30-50ml/min	< 30ml/min	<10ml/min	_Unknown_

LFT	Normal	Raised (include levels above)			_Unknown_

REVIEW FINDINGS	RECOMMENDATIONS
1. Depression may be drug induced, some studies show metoprolol associated with a higher incidence of depression as more lipophilic. Depression may be a natural response to MI, SSRIs may eventually be required, but consider other changes first.	Suggest use of atenolol 100mg daily to prevent possible metoprolol related depression, and to improve compliance, whilst retaining mortality risk reduction. Cardiac rehab provides multi-disciplinary support; information and education, behavioural and lifestyle change, exercise, peer support and professional support. Consider Zoloft 25mg m, if other changes ineffective
2. Lethargy and apathy may be due to continuation of Isoptin in combination with beta blocker Betaloc (additive negative inotropic and chronotropic effect) Other possible causes are lifestyle (dietary, lack of exercise, lack of socialization), anaemia, myopathy from statin, side effect of metoprolol	Patient education re action of Betaloc regular monitoring of HR and BP, home monitoring? Removal of ceased Isoptin Recommendation for Webster pack Recommend iron studies, LFTs, CK, ongoing EUC and lipids Consider use of less lipophilic beta blocker such as atenolol Recommend attendance at cardiac rehab
3. Anginine incorrectly stored, may have been inactive when used for recent severe chest pain	As discussed with Dr Reid, a new treatment to be prescribed, Nitrolingual, for acute chest pain. Education re product and why Anginine may have been ineffective
4. Lifestyle modifications/risk factor reductions Aspirin therapy missing	Weight loss, diet exercise, rehab and reduction of risk factors. Suggest attendance at Rehab as will give her confidence to garden and exercise. She will be supervised by doctors, nurses, physio and pharmacist. Attention to diet is important for recovery; instant foods and fried foods have high saturated fats adding to cholesterol and future risk. Healthier eating will facilitate weight loss As discussed with Dr Reid, a new treatment to be restarted, to reduce cardiovascular risk factors.
References used:	

Fig. 15.6 Making game: an example of a completed sheet for medication review. Extract only (Source: OSCE material used in Pharmacy Practice course)

beyond, this culture as genuine professional products. Second, they capture some characteristic features of professional epistemic tools and ways of knowing that were assembled together to produce this artefact. The form instantiated in the report and in which the report is instantiated, as we will explain in a moment, serves as a *modelling site* that aligns abstracted, conceptual, cultural, and social professional knowledge resources with the situation and context of action and provides epistemic bridges between multiple frames of reference and ways of knowing.

Epistemic forms have characteristic features distinct to epistemic devices that immutable instruments and equipment, in Nersessian's (2006) terms, do not possess. They are *modelling sites*. Bertelsen (2000) also noted this feature of some tools that are used in design-oriented work, such as theories, methods, compilers, editors, debuggers and case tools. He called these tools 'design artefacts' and argued that some kinds of objects, such as prototypes, have two roles in design activity: as a design artefact (i.e. a tool) *mediating* the creation and as a continually moving object of this activity, *instantiating* these ideas.

15.5   The Medication Review Form as a Modelling Site

Goodwin (2005) argues that tools instantiate perception. The organisation of perception is not inherent in an individual. Rather:

> In that the separate perceptual frameworks of each participant must be integrated into a common task … the task of translating the view from one perspective into the frame of reference of another is posed. (Goodwin, 2005, p. 105)

In order to unpack this, following Goodwin, we looked at (a) how forms and produced documents are *organised as conjunctions* of diverse spaces with heterogeneous properties and (b) how they are *articulated as frameworks* for the production of meaning and action.

15.5.1   *Structure as a Conjunction of Diverse Epistemic Spaces*

> Interviewer: And in terms of this structure of the report, is it some common structure that you … ??
> Lecturer: It's how we – even professionals that are becoming accredited – it's how we train them to provide the medication reviews. Looking at, first of all, what are the issues? What are your findings? What does – so what's the problem with the patient and what does the book say about, like what do the resources say about that. So what's the fact? And then the recommendation is what can I do about that fact? Either monitor, change, whatever it is that you need to do. *So we get people to try and divide it as to 'ok this is the issue, how do I solve it?'* (Interview with Pharmacy Lecturer)

The epistemic artefact – the final medication review report – brings together different pieces of situated and conceptual knowledge, different structures and different ways of knowing that went into the construction of this artefact.

The report, given as an exemplar of this kind of work that examiners can use in assessing students, first starts from the information about the patient and then lists current and past medications and information from laboratory results (Fig. 15.6). The second core part of the report lists identified issues (called 'Review Findings') and in an orderly fashion aligns each issue with a set of suggested solutions ('Recommendations'). There is an apparent similarity between the first part of the report and the doctor's referral (Fig. 15.4). However, they are not identical. Now, this information about the medications, detailed in the doctor's referral, is amended with the findings from the review – to identify not only the medications that were prescribed by the doctor but those actually taken by the patient. Also, the laboratory results are replaced with a few measurements, some of which are calculated by the pharmacist, that are important for choosing appropriate therapy, such as the renal function and liver function test (LFT).

The second core part of the report (Fig. 15.6) has also an apparently similar systematic structure, linking review findings with the recommendations, to that which was used in the worksheets to guide the examination of issues (Fig. 15.5). But now, the systematic order of going through each medication and identifying drug or dosage discrepancies, and systematic analysis of the therapeutic issues, is replaced with what appears to be a more eclectic list. It starts with the concerns identified in the doctor's referral (i.e. possible causes of depression; see Figs. 15.3 and 15.4) and then goes to the patient's concerns (i.e. possible causes of lethargy) and then to issues related to incorrectly stored medications, lifestyle concerns and missing therapies. This list is organised using the logic of practice, i.e. 'priority of the issues'. There are some repetitions in the recommendations. For example, the recommendations to replace a currently used medication with one that is less lipophilic, and to attend rehabilitation, are repeated, addressing different issues several times. While such a repetitive list is not an ideal list, since it does not follow the core rules of logic for creating lists (see Collins & Ferguson, 1993), it nevertheless follows the rules set by the logic of the situation – i.e. to provide the doctor with information about how each issue could be addressed. Each recommendation for addressing complex issues, such as depression and lethargy, is in itself an assemblage of multiple frames of reference and multiple modes of action, such as modifications in prescribed medications, regular monitoring, patient education, blood iron studies and rehabilitation.

15.5.2 Structure as a Framework for Production of Meanings and Action

Neither the findings nor the recommendations are conclusive. As the report says, Mrs Greene's depression 'may be drug induced', but 'may be a natural response to myocardial infarct'. Nevertheless, the recommendations are sufficiently concrete to propose a sequence of changes: from those which are necessary and easy to try first to those which are possible in the future 'if other changes are ineffective'. Each issue (e.g. depression) has a number of dimensions – such as the biochemical, physical and social – and each solution, including changing one medication to another, has a number of dimensions, biomedical, material and social. Even the exemplary pharmacist's recommendation is not the idealised solution, but a model of how to resolve the issue and how to achieve a reasonably good alignment between the identified issues and practical solutions.

However, these practical recommendations are not atheoretical, unscientific or unjustified. The evidence from various sources has a clear presence in the worksheets and the final report. The report, nevertheless, hides theoretical details by translating them into concrete (material) recommendations for action. For example, the information from studies about the mortality rates associated with two candidate medications are initially documented in the worksheet:

> Atenolol may be better choice as less lipophilic and less likely to cause depression The mortality rates for metoprolol and atenolol were equivalent (13.5 % vs 13.4 % 2-year mortality, respectively).mdx Healthcare Series Vol. 126 2005 (see Fig. 15.5)

However, this background information is omitted from the final practical recommendation and replaced by the statement:

> Suggest use of atenolol 100 mg daily to prevent possible metoprolol related depression, and to improve compliance, whilst retaining mortality risk reduction (see Fig. 15.6)

A section headed *References*, listing handbooks and other information sources used, nevertheless, stands out in this report and in other exemplars as being an unnatural part of a practical recommendation. However, the use of a variety of sources for making decisions, as well as sharing of this information with doctors, tends to be seen as a natural part of the medication review epistemic game and of the epistemic form that gives shape to its outcome:

> Interviewer: And people in practice, would they have to provide references?
> Lecturer: Yes, yes. Because particularly if a doctor gets a recommendation – they're like 'I've never heard of that' and at least it's referenced from somewhere, then they could check it up if they wanted to. (Interview with Pharmacy Lecturer)

In this respect, the medication review report is both (a) *a result of* cooperation, conception and construction and (b) *a tool-like artefact for* cooperation, conception and construction.

First, it is a *site of cooperation* that brings different kinds of evidence and different kinds of knowledge into one place: the doctor's and Mrs Greene's concerns about depression and lethargy are linked with the pharmacist's knowledge of underlying chemical mechanisms of medications. It is also a site of the pharmacist's *conception* and *construction*. The situated evidence is sorted and aligned with the general causes that may underpin depression. The need to control cardiovascular risks, and scientific evidence about which drugs are less likely to cause depression, is used to construct situated recommendations. The information from Mrs Greene and the pharmacist's observations about her difficulties taking some medications are linked to the general common-sense knowledge about which medication might be more convenient to carry (see Figs. 15.5 and 15.6).

Second, the report is also a *tool-like boundary artefact*. The structure of the report, which briefly explains causes and aligns the review findings with suggested solutions, is transparent enough to convey the links that underpin the recommendations – thus providing the doctor with the information that enables further decisions to be made. This contrasts with more traditional forms of professional artefacts that contain 'black boxed' professional knowledge. In this respect, *the report works as a tool* for the doctor's further sense-making and construction.

As Goodwin (2005) argues:

> What is at issue here are *processes of perception*. The organisation of this perception is not, however, located in the psychology of the individual brain and its associated cognitive processes but it is instead lodged within and constituted through situated endogenous social practices. Such perception is a *form of social organisation* in its own right. <...> [T]ools shape perception *through the way* in which they construct representations. (Goodwin, 2005, p. 104, emphasis added)

15.6 Linking Conceptual and Material with Social: Weaving Epistemic Games with Social (Bureaucratic) Infrastructure

We illustrated earlier how the epistemic game is linked with *material* action and is grounded in the context or environment for action. Is this epistemic game played by the pharmacist completely independent from the social orders? Definitely not. Some dimensions of sociality are as follows.

The epistemic game of producing the medication review as a conceptual artefact that embodies solutions is constitutively entangled with the social (or bureaucratic) game of how medication reviews are conducted. At many points, the lines of the two games simply blend and converge. For example, the doctor's referral for the pharmacist to conduct the medication review is a step in the bureaucratic game (see 'Step 5. Referral by GP to the patient's preferred community pharmacy or accredited pharmacist...' in Fig. 15.1). However, the referral meshes (a) the laboratory results, the information about prescribed medications and other medical information that are primarily information for the pharmacist's knowledge work with (b) information about the patient's consent, which is primarily a part of the social order (see 'Step 4. Patient is informed and gives their consent' in Fig. 15.1). The pharmacist's knowledge work intertwines with the instituted bureaucratic process of the medication review at a number of points: 'the preferred address and time for [review] are arranged with the patient', 'development of suggested management strategies', and the pharmacist's report being sent back to the doctor. The knowledge work of the pharmacist, the social order regulating the home medication review process and material action do not only intersect at the 'obligatory points of passage' – certain specific points of an assemblage through which all other relations should flow (Fenwick & Edwards, 2011; Latour, 1987). The conceptual, social and material are constitutive of each other. For example, the address where the medication review is conducted is not just a bureaucratic choice of a place that allows the pharmacist to meet a patient; *the choice of place has epistemic consequences* for what kind of information the pharmacist will be able to gather and how they can gather it.

The epistemic assemblage of tools and practices that are brought together for this kind of work is emerging as a juxtaposition of:

- Governmental policies (e.g. of what counts as a universal health service)
- Bureaucratic decisions (e.g. how the service is provided and remunerated)
- Professional cultures and histories (e.g. what kind of knowledge is valued and what form of discourse is acceptable for communication between the pharmacists and doctors)
- Technical and practical constraints (e.g. what kinds of symptoms can be observed, what kinds of evidence are available, what kinds of recommendations would make sense)
- Professional ways of knowing (e.g. how to figure out the interactions between drugs)

This juxtaposition and convergent diversity of tools and agendas is different from analogous processes in scientific laboratories, which, as Goodwin (2005) argues:

> ... produces a creative synergy, as a tool embedded within the work practices of one discipline provides new resources and opportunities to view phenomena for another. (Goodwin, 2005, p. 99)

This convergent diversity does not require an overlap, but it does require enough synergy among different views and agendas and joint spaces where different lines can intertwine and converge. (In this case, such spaces include both physical spaces, such as the patient's home, and symbolic spaces, such as the referral and the medication review form.) These spaces in professional work are not necessarily natural or easy to create. Overall, in professional work, such juxtapositions (of policy and practice, practice and theory or professional and lay) are often seen as troublesome and disruptive rather than creative and as imposed and necessary rather than natural. Nevertheless, such meshing of various spaces – including the physical, discursive, conceptual and social – is a necessity for productive work. For example, one pharmacy lecturer explained some limitations in medication reviews, as follows:

> That's [case conference] a separate activity. But it's fair to say that is like the exception rather than the rule. Although the process is described as being collaborative, that's probably more cooperative than collaborative in a sense.

Why do case conferences between pharmacists and doctors rarely happen in practice? One lecturer put it this way:

> So the reason case conferences don't happen is because of the payment structure at the moment. However, having said that, in all the research that [my colleague] did, the doctors actually really like the verbal meetings. I mean, it's quicker than reading a report. They can argue – well, not argue but they can discuss different items. If the pharmacist said 'look what do you think about this drug' and the doctor can say 'no I've tried that before' or 'I don't like that' or 'where' – so then the pharmacist can say 'ok well another alternative is this'. But if it's just in a written report, you can't have that discussion.

A possibility for collaboration and constructive discussion between pharmacists and doctors is already a part of the bureaucratic procedure and a part of what is seen as productive knowledgeable action among pharmacists and doctors. That is, there is no deep epistemic tension between policy and practice, or between the ways of knowing of pharmacists and the doctors. However, this collaboration does not (usually) happen in the real world because the joint socio-material space (financial arrangements) for collaborative dialogue does not exist. Policy and practice, pharmacists and doctors have a shared symbolic infrastructure for joint work and agree on epistemic grounds about productive practice. However, they do not have a shared socio-material space – because of payment structures – in which this epistemic practice may happen.

15.7   Concluding Points

A medication review and other similar professional tasks would be unbearably difficult without assembling and using fluently an array of professional epistemic tools – ways of noting relevant clues, ways of asking relevant questions, ways of grouping and prioritising issues and other tools for coming up with practical solutions.

Professional education often looks to scientific fields and established disciplines for a 'knowledge base' and an 'epistemic toolbox' that can underpin knowledgeable professional work. But this perspective easily obscures the fact that knowledgeable action also requires the capability to take personal ownership of an epistemic toolbox and engage in the epistemic practices of professions themselves. In other words, it involves the ability to recognise and use a variety of epistemic tools, as well as to play, switch between and weave together a variety of professional epistemic games.

These epistemic tools serve a *generative* purpose in professional knowledgeable action. Learning to use professional tools is learning *for* situated practice, yet is not the same as learning *as* situative practice. The focus is not on dispensing more medications, but on engaging in the kinds of work that link a professional's action in the material world with their epistemic action (e.g. being alert to situated knowledge, actively using professional ways of knowing or a disposition to seek understanding – in Perkins and Tishman's (2001) terms). We do not deny that such learning is also a practice, but it is a *different kind* of practice – an epistemic practice – that involves *knowledge* of, and the *skill* and *disposition* to use, professional epistemic tools and to engage in professional epistemic games.

Epistemic tools, like other tools, are created for certain purposes. Some are more general, while some are specific to a task. Professions have a range of powerful general epistemic tools, shared across tasks, settings and situations. These include inquiry strategies, frameworks and characteristic forms that guide inquiry and the construction of shared professional epistemic artefacts. These tools are rarely invented from scratch, even for relatively new professional tasks, such as the medication review. Rather, many tools are tweaked and assembled, for specific purposes and tasks at hand, from larger professional epistemic infrastructures. That is, questions that a pharmacist asks a patient during the medication review are not really different from questions that should be asked when the pharmacist dispenses a prescription: 'Do you have any other medical conditions?', 'Do you have any allergies?' and so on. The view of professional practice *as epistemic practice*, in this respect, is quite distinct from the view of professional practice *as purely situative practice*. What is special to epistemic practice is that learning to see when such questions and other generic epistemic tools are relevant, to adjust these questions flexibly for different situations and to ask them and make sense from the answers – that is, learning to use tools for understanding the situation – is the central element of professional learning, rather than merely a tacit skill mastered through a situative act. The key quality of epistemic tools is that they are generic enough to be applicable across situations. However, epistemic games and practices that involve these tools allow the creation of situated knowledge.

Epistemic forms are often heuristic devices, and epistemic games are heuristic strategies and rules in professions. They are neither deeply conceptual, logical or systematic nor completely atheoretical or illogical: they embrace a different kind of logic and a different kind of systematicity. As we explained, the structure that underpins the recommendations of the final medication report is not asystematic, even if it is hard to articulate the exact universal principles used to determine the priority of the issues. The artefact, and the underpinning structure of recommendations, serve as a heuristic device that (implicitly) provides epistemic bridges between the multiple frames of reference, and ways of knowing, embedded in professional action. The structure of the report is logical enough for practical sense-making.

The role of epistemic forms and epistemic games in professional learning and thoughtful, attentive work has some resemblance to the notions of 'ecological control' and 'ecological assembly' that Andy Clark (2011), borrowing from robotics, used to characterise embodied and embedded forms of human cognition:

> ... an ecological control system is one in which goals are not achieved by micromanaging every detail of the desired action or response but by making the most of robust, reliable sources of relevant order in the bodily and worldly environment. (Clark, 2011, pp. 5–6);

It draws on the principle of ecological assembly:

> ... the balanced use of a set of potentially highly heterogeneous resources assembled on the spot to solve a given problem. (op. cit., p. 13)

While this term, as used in robotics, might feel too mechanical to describe the nuanced nature of professional decisions, some principles might nevertheless be relevant. Epistemic forms and games – be they external, inscribed in a symbolic medium or more tacit – give an opportunity to spread problem-solving between mind, world and body.

The medication review process used in this case study may look like an orderly professional exercise – information gathering, processing and delivery and playing one game after another. However, it is also important to acknowledge the 'messiness' permeating much professional knowledge work: incomplete information in the medication dispensing database, unavailable laboratory test results, the patient who cannot remember key information, a natural need for a pharmacist to mix interviewing of the patient with counselling during a home visit, etc. The critical point here is that epistemic tools are only tools. They are things created by a professional culture for guiding problem-solving processes and can be used in variety of ways. As with all other ordering devices – plans, templates, coding systems, etc. – they provide a resource for structuring insights or for giving shape to action, but do not predetermine in any direct sense these insights or actions. In practice, professionals come to each situation equipped with a much larger array of epistemic tools than they will use, accumulated through a variety of miscellaneous experiences. What we have attempted to list here are just those core epistemic tools that were assembled by pharmacy teachers in one specific learning task.

Are epistemic tools necessarily physical or inscribed in symbolic media? Surely not. With experience, people learn to manipulate various epistemic devices within their memory. As Norman (1991) pointed out:

> ... with increasing skill, a person mentally bridges the gulfs, so that the operations upon the artifact are done subconsciously, without awareness, and the operators view themselves as operating directly upon the final object. (Norman, 1991, p. 24)

Our examples illustrate that university teachers introduce into professional tasks some epistemic tools that do not necessarily sit comfortably within the instrumental assemblages for equivalent tasks in authentic professional settings: such as the forms for prioritising issues, or providing justifications for each proposed option, that were used in the pharmacy case. Kirschner, Sweller, and Clark (2006) alert us to the differences between 'learning a discipline' and 'practising a discipline' and between 'learning patterns of inquiry of a domain' and 'learning by using disciplinary frameworks of inquiry as an instructional approach'. Knowledge resources, behaviours and methods of those who are domain experts and those who are novices are rarely the same. Thus, it may not be appropriate to use the inquiry approaches employed by domain experts as instructional strategies for novices, without first modifying them for learning purposes.[2] We do not aim to glorify or romanticise structuring devices or other epistemic tools. We should remember that similar heuristic tools can be used in two very different ways, which de Souza (2005) labelled *technical tools* and *decision support tools*. Technical tools are used in a direct operational sense: as things to follow. (An example would be a checklist, which may be created as a result of extended practice and is used and 'ticked off' without much conscious thinking.) Decision support tools are used to support

---

[2] Andy Clark (2011) speaks to a very similar point, discussing notions of the active self-modelling needed to gain behavioural competence. He contrasts *guided exploration*, which simplifies problem-solving by helping isolate salient aspects of the environment from the mass of experiential inputs to *natural problem-solving* that may require massive prestructuring and prior knowledge (pp. 21–22).

conscious problem-solving. They bring forth meaning. They are not necessarily tools that can operate by themselves, but devices that come with a set of epistemic strategies (or action schemes) for how to engage with a problem. Epistemic devices, in this sense, cannot be mastered as technical tools without also mastering epistemic strategies. As Bachelard (1984) reminds us:

> Simple always means simplified. We cannot use simple concepts correctly until we understand the *process* of simplification from which they are derived. Unless we are willing to make this difficult epistemological reversal, we cannot hope to understand the real point. (Bachelard, 1984, p. 139, emphasis added)

In short, practices, tools and the knowledge that those tools embody 'come packed together'.

We do not argue that a focus on epistemic forms and other epistemic tools alone can provide a solution to professional problems, without substantive knowledge. As Gordin and Pea (1995) note, when scientists use modern, powerful representational devices, they draw on a large amount of background knowledge, just as (other) professionals need to. In a related vein, Falconer and Littlejohn (2009) remind us that representations of practice, used for professional learning, need to represent effective practice and be effective representations of practice.

In short, both form and substance matter. In the next chapter, we argue that matter matters too.

References

Bachelard, G. (1984). *The new scientific spirit* (A. Goldhammer, Trans.). Boston, MA: Beacon Press.

Bertelsen, O. W. (2000). Design artefacts: Towards a design-oriented epistemology. *Scandinavian Journal of Information Systems, 12*(1), Article 2. Retrieved July 17, 2015 from http://aisel.aisnet.org/sjis/vol12/iss11/12

Caird, C. (2012). Home medicine rules: Are you sure your patients are getting the most benefit from their medications? *Health First Network Quarterly Magazine, 19*(1), 26–27. Retrieved April 17, 2016 from http://www.healthfirst.org.au/client_images/339904.pdf

Chen, T., Moles, R., Nishtala, P., & Basger, B. (2010). *Case studies in practice. medication review: A process guide for pharmacists.* Sydney, Australia: Pharmaceutical Society of Australia.

Clark, A. (2011). *Supersizing the mind: Embodiment, action and cognitive extension.* Oxford, UK: Oxford University Press.

Collins, A., & Ferguson, W. (1993). Epistemic forms and epistemic games: Structures and strategies to guide inquiry. *Educational Psychologist, 28*(1), 25–42.

de Souza, C. S. (2005). *The semiotic engineering of human-computer interaction.* Cambridge, MA: MIT Press.

Falconer, I., & Littlejohn, A. (2009). Representing models of practice. In L. Lockyer, S. Bennet, S. Agostinho, & B. Harper (Eds.), *Handbook of research on learning design and learning objects* (pp. 20–40). Hershey, PA: Idea Group.

Fenwick, T., & Edwards, R. (2011). Introduction: Reclaiming and renewing actor network theory for educational research. *Educational Philosophy and Theory, 43*, 1–14. doi:10.1111/j.1469-5812.2010.00667.x.

Goodwin, C. (2005). Seeing in depth. In S. J. Derry, C. D. Schunn, & M. A. Gernsbacher (Eds.), *Interdisciplinary collaboration: An emerging cognitive science* (pp. 85–121). Mahwah, NJ: Lawrence Erlbaum Associates.

Gordin, D. N., & Pea, R. D. (1995). Prospects for scientific visualization as an educational technology. *Journal of the Learning Sciences, 4*(3), 249–279.

Kirschner, P. A., Sweller, J., & Clark, R. E. (2006). Why minimal guidance during instruction does not work: An analysis of the failure of constructivist, discovery, problem-based, experiential, and inquiry-based teaching. *Educational Psychologist, 41*(2), 75–86. doi:10.1207/s15326985ep4102_1.

Latour, B. (1987). *Science in action: How to follow scientists and engineers through society.* Cambridge, MA: Harvard University Press.

Nersessian, N. J. (2006). The cognitive-cultural systems of the research laboratory. *Organization Studies, 27*(1), 125–145.

Norman, D. A. (1991). Cognitive artifacts. In J. M. Carroll (Ed.), *Designing interaction* (pp. 17–38). Cambridge, UK: Cambridge University Press.

Perkins, D. N., & Tishman, S. (2001). Dispositional aspects of intelligence. In S. Messick & J. M. Collis (Eds.), *Intelligence and personality: Bridging the gap in theory and measurement* (pp. 233–257). Mahwah, NJ: Lawrence Erlbaum Associates.

Shulman, L. S. (2005). Signature pedagogies in the professions. *Daedalus, 134*(3), 52–59.

Chapter 16
Rethinking the Material, the Embodied and the Social for Professional Education

I don't think that that's [interviewing] a difficult skill. The thing that I think that most – like pharmacists who haven't done it, that's one of the most daunting things that they do at first, is going into someone's house and interviewing them. But after they've done it for a while, the hardest skill is how to get out of the house because the patient's there and they want you to stay there forever and have two thousand cups of tea and lots of biscuits (laughing). So sometimes it's a very – and it's an important skill to learn how to get out. How to say 'the interview is finished now, I've got to go'. (Pharmacy Lecturer)

Evidence from cognitive sciences, psychology, neurosciences, anthropology, cultural studies and many other domains shows quite plainly – human cognition and behaviour exhibit extensive sensitivity to context (Boivin, 2008; Robbins & Aydede, 2009; Smith, Barrett, & Mesquita, 2010; Streeck, Goodwin, & LeBaron, 2011; Valsiner & Rosa, 2007). This includes the *internal* context created by other processes within the human body and brain (e.g. movement, mood, pain, feeling), the *external* physical things and surroundings and the immediate social environment and culture. In contrast, when it comes to education, it seems that abstract and decontextualised theoretical knowledge and disembodied ways of thinking are often favoured. This fracture between how people really *think* and how they are *taught to think* creates a number of serious challenges. One extreme is that students simply do not transfer what they learn in educational institutions to the tasks encountered in workplaces and everyday settings (see Chap. 6). Another extreme is that people, including scientists, become victims of 'the essentialism error' (Smith et al., 2010). That is, they tend to look for, and focus on, certain universal mechanisms, but fail to see and appreciate how these mechanisms are influenced by context.

Extensive evidence shows that many phenomena encountered in the world and in professional work – from genes and diseases to daily social life and culture – are context-sensitive and dynamic processes. Absolutist thinking simply does not work, and developing sensitivity to social and material contexts and awareness of one's own body and mind are emerging as important educational tasks. But how do the social, the material and the embodied enter professional knowledge work?

L. Markauskaite, P. Goodyear, *Epistemic Fluency and Professional Education*,
Professional and Practice-based Learning 14, DOI 10.1007/978-94-007-4369-4_16

461

In this chapter, we explore more deeply some of the ways in which the material, the embodied and the social are intertwined with professional epistemic practices – knowledge, action and learning – and in particular, ways in which they are enmeshed with professional epistemic games. Specifically, we argue that *professional knowledge work and knowledgeable action are constitutively entangled with embodied practices in the material and social worlds*. Therefore, careful attention to the roles of matter, the human body and social others in situated professional work helps us to understand how to design productive activities and environments for learning professional knowledge and skills. What we care about most is how to create opportunities for students to learn professional knowledge and skills that are simultaneously rich in characteristic ways of knowing and grounded in characteristic embodied, material and social experiences of authentic professional work.

We start this chapter by continuing our discussion of the examples from the Pharmacy Practice course introduced in the previous chapter. In Sect. 16.1, we illustrate how teachers tackled the challenges of creating productive learning experiences for teaching pharmacy practice knowledge and skills, by designing learning tasks that focus on characteristic ways of knowing and acting in the pharmacy profession. They encountered challenges creating suitable, sufficiently authentic social and material environments for such learning, and this opens up some questions related to the social, the material and the embodied nature of professional actionable knowledge. We explore this topic in the rest of the chapter. Specifically, Sect. 16.2 discusses how the material and the social are intertwined with professional actions and cognition. Section 16.3 then explores some dimensions of 'the material' and 'the embodied' knowledge and knowing that are constitutive of professional epistemic practices. Section 16.4 then turns to some dimensions of 'the social' knowledge and knowing. Section 16.5 returns to the question of mediation, which we explored earlier (Chap. 8) and discusses how knowledgeable action is mediated by the social, the material and the embodied. Section 16.6 concludes by discussing some implications for teaching and learning. It specifically draws attention to a central role of professional capacities to create epistemic tools and artefacts for one's own situated knowledgeable action – a topic that has received very little attention in professional education and one we return to at the end of the book.

16.1 Epistemic Games in Course Designs: Some Empirical Illustrations

16.1.1 Epistemic Games and the Material and Social Worlds

The medication management review and many other epistemic games that are played in professional workplaces are weaving games which are played in an ongoing interaction with the material and social worlds. They often proceed simultaneously on many levels, drawing on different kinds of knowing and aspects of knowledgeability (see Chap. 4, Table 4.2). This creates a significant difficulty when it comes to designing authentic tasks in higher education settings. How best can one create learning experiences that help to develop capacities for such epistemically dense work? Does learning really need to proceed in all directions at the same time?

In our pharmacy observations, this challenge was tackled by the teachers through a mixture of lectures that introduced different topics, tutorials that analysed cases and weekly externships accompanied by structured activities guiding students to explore different aspects of pharmacy practice. The tutorial description from the course outline documentation explains this relationship between the therapeutic knowledge, the learning processes of pharmacy practice and the enactment of this knowledge in workplace settings, as follows:

> The tutorials are designed to help students integrate communication skills and therapeutic knowledge in order to solve the *types of problems* they are likely to encounter as a practicing pharmacist. The tutorials will be run in conjunction with the externship and students are encouraged to utilize externship placements to practice the material/processes discussed in tutorials. (Pharmacy Practice course outline, emphasis added)

Most usefully, this blending of different teaching and learning modes nicely illustrates the fact that mastering epistemic devices and epistemic games in professional pharmacy courses is a more universal skill than the ability to apply specific kinds of therapeutic knowledge for specific problems. The description continues:

> The tutorials will be conducted in a way that emphasises *processes* to allow students to practice as a pharmacist. This process will incorporate information gathering, information processing and information delivery. *Not all topics in therapeutics will be covered* in tutorials, but by the end of the semester students *should be able to apply these processes to any situation* that arises in practice (clinical interventions and medication reviews). (op. cit., first emphasis is original, others are added)

In short, learning to play epistemic games – which the pharmacy teachers simply called 'processes' – develops the students' capability to apply learnt propositional knowledge to 'types of problems' and enact learnt ways of thinking and doing within 'any situation that arises in practice'. Further, the tutorial handbook gives an insight into three other features of professional problem-solving and knowing. It explains:

> Many tutorials will be conducted over two sessions. In the first session, the focus of the tutorial should be on gathering and processing information. Prior to the second session for the case, students are expected to further research the case using a *variety of resources* (*including primary references where relevant*) and *document* their findings and recommendations (i.e., written information delivery). Findings and recommendations should be *referenced and prioritised.* <...> In the second session for a case, the focus should be on processing information and delivery of information (*written and verbal communication with medical practitioner and/or patient*). For example, students will be required to role-play a face-to-face case conference with a medical practitioner using their documented findings and recommendations as the basis for the case conference. Students will also be required to role-play a counselling session with a patient *using written information to*

support their counselling (e.g. CMI [Consumer Medicine Information leaflets], Self Care Fact Cards). (Pharmacy practice: tutorial and externship handbook, emphasis added)

First, professional problem-solving is a dynamic, unfolding process, and different ways of knowing are integrated at different stages of inquiry. While 'gathering' focuses on ways of knowing that draw upon various sources, 'delivery' focuses on discursive ways of knowing.

Second, knowledge is created in collaboration and interaction – problem-solving is woven into trans-professional and public discourse games, such as case conferences and counselling, involving the patient, the doctor and other health professionals.

Third, various resources and written information are firm and explicit aspects of this professional knowing and problem-solving: information infrastructure, material–inscriptional devices and inscriptional artefacts, as well as their production, are fused throughout this professional knowledge-making process.

The terms 'prioritise' and 'reference' sit side by side in this description. The first of these terms reflects an expectation that the student will be able to make sensible pragmatic decisions in an 'ill-structured' situation. The second term conveys a firm belief that these pragmatic decisions are not arbitrary – evidence and rigorous defence of recommendations are seen as a natural part of professional pragmatic thinking.

These problem-solving and discourse games are sufficiently independent of each other to be learnt separately, before weaving them into a more complex game. This more complex game is partly an individual mental activity of identifying issues and finding solutions and partly a collaborative discourse game. Thus, the necessary skills can be partly 'unwoven' and learnt skill by skill:

In first semester, we focus less on the communication with the doctor and more on *just identifying the problems*. And in second semester, we hope that they can find the problems. It's more about *how you communicate those problems*. (Pharmacy Lecturer)

16.1.2 Designing Environments for Learning Epistemic Games

Teaching 'process knowledge' can be a difficult task, but assessing it can be even more difficult.

... it takes 2½ full days to get them all through this OSCE exam.[1] It's insane the amount of logistics that you have to do because they all have to start at different times. <...> So we had to have 10 examiners and they all go from station to station. It's like full on. (Pharmacy Lecturer)

---

[1] OSCE – Objective Structured Clinical Examination.

This difficulty is not just because it is a 'logistical nightmare', but because playing professional epistemic games involves space, time and the body. When knowledge and skill involve all three, one needs real time, and (something close to) real bodies and material spaces (environments) for learning, enacting and assessing those skills. In short, the constitutive entanglement between knowledge, matter and the body, involved in knowledgeable action that unfolds through space, time and movement, is a critical problem for the design of learning environments in higher education.

How should such learning environments be designed? Higher education generally tends to overemphasise *language and communication* as the main skill involved in such processes – space and the body are often overlooked. Language and flexible use of other forms of symbolic expression are important, but are not everything. One pharmacy teacher explained, in an unexpected way, why carrying out a medication review in the patient's home can be a complex skill to learn (see also the quote at the start of the chapter):

> Interviewer: And why did you say it [interviewing in the patient's home] may be daunting for them?
> Lecturer: Just because they've never walked into – they've never actually been in their patients' houses before.
> Interviewer: So just the place is different?
> Lecturer: Just the place is different, yeah. It's just something that they're – it's out of their comfort zone. (Interview with Pharmacy Lecturer)

Matter, and material and social space – what is often simply called 'context' – is not some kind of container that can be easily detached from the 'essence' of knowledge and problem-solving. It is an integral and fundamental aspect of this knowledge and knowing. The fine-tuned sensitivity of the pharmacist to the material context is at the core of making sensible professional decisions:

> Now sometimes you could treat something by using an injection but it's not as convenient – so it's not wrong because it would still treat the patient's disease but it's not as practical because the patient's in a home environment. <...> So that's the thing that they [students] – one of the problems that they have is they'll read it in the book and they're like 'that sounds alright' and they'll write that down without thinking about 'can this person really use that [syringe]?' (Pharmacy Lecturer)

Authenticity, as another lecturer pointed out, cannot be reduced to words but also involves bodies and actual situations, and any such reduction could have severe implications for a student's capacity to conceptualise an encountered problem:

> Also they're doing it [exam] as if it's a role play but there's no acting in the role play. So you could have another female member of staff pretending to be an old male doctor. So it's not authentic in that sense. It's authentic in terms of the *words* but not in terms of the *actual situation*. If our students were actually put with a more authentic situation, it could be easier for them to *conceptualise* the issue. It could even be the case that they're role playing with a patient, and the patient they're role playing with is a different gender to the patient. (Pharmacy Lecturer)

Further, would it be possible for students to infer relevant facts about the social and physical environment of a patient's home merely by seeing the boxes with the medications that are usually used as substitutes for the patient's home environment in these role plays? Of course, an interview involving a pharmacy teacher who pretends to be patient is neither a real social practice nor a real material practice, and boxes with medications are not the authentic material and social environment. In this sense, 'role play' pedagogies have an inherent limitation when it comes to creating authentic professional experiences, as they rarely reproduce a sufficient range of epistemic affordances and practical contingencies of the kind one finds in the natural environment.

Why do university courses still try to create such pseudo-authentic environments and even tasks that involve situations that do not exist in the real world? There are several answers to this.

First, while epistemic games may not be the same as well-rounded social and material practice, they nevertheless are epistemic practices that play important roles in 'cognitive apprenticeship'. They make visible some of the habits of mind that would otherwise remain hidden and implicit in fluent expert work. This articulation of thought and various elements in the situation become particularly important when practice is an epistemic practice that couples *actions of mind* – which may not be explicitly expressed in material or discursive forms and moves – with *actions in the social and material worlds* – that are made explicit in discourse and artefacts.

Second, as we noted in Chap. 15, *work* and *learning for work* are not necessarily the same kind of practice (see Sect. 15.6). They are related, but not the same: the latter weaves in an additional game – we might call it a 'pedagogical game' or 'learning game' – and additional tools (learning tools) that are specifically created and used for *learning for transfer* (of knowledge and ways of knowing). Like most tools, they are artificial devices that prove to be effective for a specific purpose, i.e. for learning.

Third, epistemic games are not hard-wired to specific situations and contexts; they are enacted within, and have value across, contexts. Learning to recognise relevant situations, tweak more universal tools and weave professional games across diverse situations are fundamental to professional vision and flexibility.

Fourth, some epistemic games are played not because of their surface resemblance to the professional practice, but because of their ability to convey professional values and habits of mind. For example, the introduction of the case conference into the medication review process is one such game (see Sect. 15.5). The teachers explicitly acknowledged that this game is not common in pharmacy practice, but it is important to the pharmacy profession and it communicates professional values. It embodies the view that pharmacists and doctors should work in teams if they are to achieve better health outcomes.

> ... at university, we still want to train the students to be able to talk to the doctors because we think in the future, perhaps, there may be a better funding model for that. But also it's still a good skill to have regardless of whether it ever gets paid for or not. (Pharmacy Lecturer)

Almost all the teachers we interviewed said something similar – they are trying to equip students with knowledge, skills and dispositions for better future practices.

For example, preservice teachers, in our studies, were often taught to use various innovative pedagogies and technologies in their teaching – even though their university lecturers were well aware that such innovative teaching is not seen as a core capability in current workplace settings.

16.2   Actionable Knowing as Embodied Social Practices in the Material World

How are knowledge work and knowledgeable action intertwined with embodied *material practices* in the physical world and with *social practices*?

> ... thinking, or knowledge-getting, is far from being the armchair thing it is often supposed to be. The reason it is not an armchair thing is that it is *not an event going on exclusively within the cortex or the cortex and vocal organs*. It involves the explorations by which relevant data are procured and the physical analyses by which they are refined and made precise; it comprises the readings by which information is got hold of, the words which are experimented with, and the calculations by which the significance of entertained conceptions or hypotheses is elaborated. *Hands and feet, apparatus and appliances of all kinds are as much a part of it as changes in the brain.* (Dewey, 1916, pp. 13–14, emphasis added)

Cultural contexts, social situatedness, material artefacts and other contextual cues found in workplaces and learning places – in addition to the biology of the human brain and body – are commonly acknowledged as entities that have an impact on human thinking, learning and action. However, they have not always been seen as *constitutive parts* of knowledge, knowing and action or – in the case of the human brain and body – as being at the very core where thought originates. As Damasio (2012) asserts, the construction of a conscious mind – 'the self-as-knower' – depends on a far more basic 'protoself' and 'the self-as-object'.

> The unsung sensory portals play a crucial role in defining *the perspective* of the mind relative to the rest of the world. I am not talking here about the biological singularity provided by the protoself. I am referring to an effect we all experience in our minds: having a *standpoint* for whatever is happening outside the mind. This is not a mere 'point of view,' although for the sighted majority of human beings, the view does dominate the proceedings of our mind, more often than not. But we also have a standpoint relative to the sounds out in the world, a standpoint relative to the objects we touch, and even a standpoint for the objects we feel in our own body. (Damasio, 2012, p. 210, original emphasis)

How are the material and social intertwined with actions and thought (cognition) in professional work? To start, we approach this question by drawing on two related lines of thinking: (a) socio-material organising of action and (b) socio-material organising of cognition.

16.2.1 Socio-material Organising of Action

Revisiting studies of how everyday organising is bound up with materiality in organisational settings, Orlikowski (2007) observes that there are two common perspectives on how technologies and other material affordances shape, and are shaped by, human practices. She calls them the 'techno-centric perspective' and the 'human-centric perspective'. *The techno-centric perspective* takes a functional or operational approach. Its main focus is on how material tools and arrangements have an impact on human organising. From this perspective, technological and other tools are generally determined by their materiality, and their function in human activity is generally predictable, 'black boxed' and exogenous to human intentions and actions; thus, they evolve rather independently of users, contexts and the situations in which they are used.

The human-centric perspective focuses on human interpretations and dynamic interactions with tools and other material arrangements. This approach acknowledges that meanings assigned to technological tools and other material arrangements are shaped by history, culture, social contexts, human interests and other situational configurations. Thus, the ways in which people engage with these tools – and other material arrangements – are generally not determined by what the tools (etc.) are. How they enter into and shape human thinking and action is primarily the result of human sense-making, rather than materiality.

Orlikowski notes that some dynamic social theories have acknowledged that humans and their technological and material environments mutually shape each other. Nevertheless, these theories presuppose an ontological separation of humans and nonhumans: they interact and shape, but are still seen as entities independent from each other. In contrast, Orlikowski argues[2] that material and social, nonhuman and human, are *constitutively entangled* in everyday human organising.

16.2.2 Socio-material Organising of Cognition

A similar argument about the constitutive intertwining of human cognitive activity with culture, tools, contexts and dynamically emerging situations is also familiar in some areas of writing about human knowing and learning (e.g. Goodwin, 2005; Malafouris, 2013; Säljö, 1995).

As Grasseni (2010) puts it, there is a 'unity of cognitive and operative aspects' (p. 10). Technology, knowledge, culture, practice and learning come together in the notions of educating professional vision and skill.

---

[2] She draws on theoretical work on 'actor–networks', 'sociotechnical ensembles', 'the mangle of practice' and other similar approaches that have roots in science and technology studies (STS). Some of these ideas were introduced in Chap. 5.

> ... skilled practices literally shape the way we look at the world. Participating in a richly
> textured environment, full of objects, images and body patterns, structures and guides our
> perception tacitly and implicitly. (Grasseni, 2010, p. 11)

There is a relational dynamic – a deep entanglement – between vision as skill and
skill as vision:

> The notions of *taskspace* (Ingold) and *worldview* thus converge on the issue of practical
> understanding, achieved locally through material and social learning experiences. (loc. cit.,
> original emphasis)

In this 'equation' material things and action schemes – historically and situationally
co-constructed around those things – are usually conceived as constitutive of
human thinking. However, while culture and things matter, less careful attention
is paid to the physical and material properties of the tools and environments through
which things and culture are materialised. As Barad (2003) reminds us:

> Language matters. Discourse matters. Culture matters. But there is an important sense in
> which the only thing that does not seem to matter anymore is matter. (Barad, 2003, p. 801)

Matter indeed matters in professional learning. As one nursing lecturer pointed out,
even the most sophisticated high-fidelity mannequin cannot replace fully the real
body of a patient when nurses learn manual handling skills.

> One of them [mannequin] we can program to speak. It can do anything – it can vomit, it can
> have a heart attack and it can say 'ohhhh'.

Nevertheless, mannequins do not look and feel like human beings, because of the
very matter from which they are built.

> One of the biggest criticisms is [that] with a real patient, if somebody's sick, they change
> colour, they go grey and sweaty, and the mannequin of course can't do that because *they're
> made of rubber*. So that's one of the big criticisms of using simulation. It can't ever really
> 100 % emulate the real situation.

And as Andy Clark (2011) reminds us,

> Cognition leaks out into *body* and *world*. (Clark, 2011, p. xxviii, emphasis added).

How does mind 'leak' into matter in professional work? We discuss this
question next.

16.3   How Matter Matters in Professional Knowledge Work

In professional knowledge work, knowledgeable action and learning, the social,
material and embodied come into play and 'matter' in at least four respects: as
(a) physical tools, (b) inscriptions and inscriptional tools, (c) embodied skill, and
(d) as environment, as knowledge embodied in the world around us. We discuss
each of these aspects in the next four sections.

16.3.1 Knowledge Embodied in Physical Tools

Human knowledge embodied in skills is intertwined with the physical and material properties of tools through which this knowledge and skill are developed. The use of different tools requires different skills and allows the development of different understandings of, and relationships to, the objects entangled in this work. In Chap. 12, we used the classical example of a woodworker's skill and knowledge learnt through the use of different kinds of tools. Rabardel and Beguin (2005) note that the use of a hand chisel and the use of a machine develop very different understandings of the properties of wood. Similarly, in nursing, the use of a finger and watch to take a patient's pulse involves different knowledge and skill, and develops a different understanding about the human body and tools, than is the case with an automatic monitor registering a pulse. However, 'complexification' of technology does not mean simplification of skills and knowledge. Learning to embrace new tools for enhancing human powers, or for inscription, visualisation and manipulation of messages, goes along with the education of new skills, new senses and new ways of meaning-making. As Grasseni (2010) puts it,

> ... there is no fixed algebra of skill and machine by which an increase of technology means a decrease in skill. (Grasseni, 2010, p. 10)

The constitutive role of the material properties of physical modelling devices, and indeed entire experimental setups, in constructing human knowledge and understanding in research laboratories, has been well documented. As Rheinberger (1997) argued, deriving ideas from the material and imposing abstract ideas and concepts on experimental devices and empirical materials are inextricably interconnected in creating new knowledge,

> They [experimental setups] are not simply experimental devices that generate answers; experimental systems are vehicles for materializing questions. They inextricably cogenerate the phenomena or material entities and the concepts they come to embody. Practices and concepts thus 'come packaged together'. (Rheinberger, 1997, p. 28)

This constitutive entanglement between the materiality of symbolic tools (and conceptual artefacts) and knowledge is not universally recognised. For example, as Bereiter (2002) argued, conceptual artefacts, which are often used in creating new knowledge, are commonly inscribed in certain media – paper, video or digital file, for example – but, in Bereiter's view, conceptual artefacts should be distinguished from their representations:

> ... the representation or concrete embodiment is *not the knowledge*. (Bereiter, 2002, p. 64, emphasis added)

In contrast, Latour (1990) made a distinction between 'mentalist' and 'materialist' notions of inscriptions and, acknowledging the vital role of material practices in knowledge work, argued that powerful explanations could be found in imagining and writing craftsmanship,

... in the way in which groups of people argue with one another using paper, signs, prints and diagrams. (Latour, 1990, p. 21)

Latour noted that the qualities of inscriptions as real physical things are consequential. Others have pointed to the ways that perceptual and other material qualities of symbolic tools are entangled with human thought. For example, Gleick (1993) recounts an insightful exchange between the physicist Richard Feynman and the historian Charles Weiner. In response to Weiner's note that Feynman's materials represent 'a record of [Feynman's] day-to-day work', Feynman reacted,

I actually did the work on the paper. (Gleick, 1993, p. 409)

To Weiner's, comment 'Well, the work was done in your head, but the record of it is still here', Feynman reacted,

No, it's not a *record*, not really. It's *working*. You have to work on paper, and this is the paper. Okay? (loc. cit.)

While the Weiner–Feynman exchange concerned the mediational role of inscriptional media in general, others have specifically focussed on the physical and structural qualities of physical representational devices.

Hutchins and Klausen (1996), observing the movement and distribution of information among pilots and devices during a flight simulation, argue that the structure and physical properties of representational tools and media, and the specific organisation of the representations supported by different media, have consequences for the cognitive processes of individual pilots and of the cockpit system,

Every representational medium has *physical properties* that determine the availability of representations through space and time and constrain the sorts of cognitive processes required to propagate the representational state into and out of that medium. (Hutchins & Klausen, 1996, p. 32 emphasis added)

Summarising research on visual representations, such as diagrams, Nersessian (2005) points to their perceptual cognitive qualities, noting particularly that

... external representations differentially facilitate and constrain reasoning processes. Specifically ... diagrams can play more than just a supportive role in what is essentially an internal process; these external representations also can play *a direct role in cognitive processing*, without requiring the mediation of an internal representation of the information provided in them. The external representation can change the nature of the processing task. (Nersessian, 2005, p. 28, emphasis added)

She continues by pointing out that there is no clear boundary between internal and external, and the notion of memory and its workings naturally extends outside the human mind,

... to encompass external representations and cues; that is, specific kinds of affordances and constraints in the environment are construed, literally, as memory in cognitive processing. (loc. cit.)

Nersessian develops this argument further by observing that inscriptional matter does not *always* matter. Depending on circumstances, a diagram can be inscribed

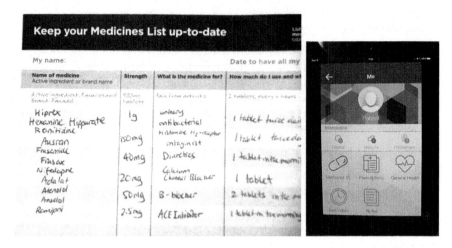

Fig. 16.1 Medicine lists in different material bearers

and discussed with equal success on a piece of paper or a whiteboard. But some-times – for example, if a diagram is inscribed in computational media or if it needs to be seen by large numbers of people at once – then the material qualities of the inscription can make a huge difference, affecting thought and outcome (see also Coopmans, Vertesi, Lynch, & Woolgar, 2014; Nersessian, 2008).

The skill needed to recognise the 'rightness' ('fitness') of media is important not only for professional vision but also for action. This fitness varies in rich, multi-modal and textured ways that are not easily reducible to one denominator.

For example, one of the pharmacy students in our study found himself thinking about the choice of giving a patient a 'Medicines List iPhone App' rather than completing a conventional printed Medicines List to help the patient keep track of medicines taken (Fig. 16.1). The student spent a while figuring out how this digital Medicines List actually works and concluded that 'reminder functions' would be very useful for older people who have difficulties remembering which medicines they should take and when they should take them. But then, the student asked himself a rhetorical question: 'Do older sick people really have iPhones?' – observing that this unlikely to be so. A small misalignment between the material modality of the inscriptional medium ('What can it do?') and its social modality ('Who can afford it and is willing to use it?') changes the epistemic capacities of a tool in radical ways.

16.3.2 Knowledge Embodied in Inscriptional Tools

A lot of attention has been paid to how codification systems (Bowker & Star, 1999), images (Coopmans et al., 2014) and physical tools (Clarke & Fujimura, 1992;

Keller & Keller, 1996; Vaesen, 2012) shape perception and cognition in human development and in professional epistemic work. In contrast, the cognitive consequences of the *structure* and *matter* of various structuring inscriptional devices and structured inscriptions have not received much attention in research on professional work. For many teachers, worksheets and other guiding structures are primarily tools for learning – though choices about them are often made intuitively. ('It just feels right'.) However, professional inscriptions often go unnoticed in their daily epistemic work. Asked about their role, teachers (and other professionals) would often answer: 'It is just a set of boxes' or 'It is just a form'. But what *form* should an effective lesson plan take? Why is it important to have it on an A4 piece of paper? What does a good medication review report look like? What are the epistemic consequences of the structuring devices within which such effective professional inscriptions are constructed? When one stops and reflects on such questions, the answers are far from straightforward.

As we said at the end of the last chapter, in order to be effective, such inscriptions should be inscriptions of competent and effective solutions and also competent and effective inscriptions of professional solutions. In short, what matters is the combination of the 'right' content, 'right' form and 'right' matter (Falconer & Littlejohn, 2009).

But what does this 'right' form and 'right' matter look like and how does it shape knowledgeable action? Consider a lesson plan. Should it be detailed and elaborate? One lecturer explained to us:

> Well, there are – I think there [in a detailed, long plan] are two traps there. If it's too long, students *might feel very constrained* by this and might not allow a natural flow of teaching and questioning from the students on the floor to come back and to devote time to that. So there's the one thing. Or they *might get really anxious* because they might see half way through the lesson they're not going to get there and then they might either leave things out or dismiss things or get really into a state because it means they haven't allowed perhaps down the track enough time to catch up. So that's all a balancing act. (Education Lecturer)

Having just a few points on a piece of paper, as the lecturer explained, is usually a more effective inscription of a plan than having something more complicated:

> And the less bullet points the better, because *you have a little piece of paper on your desk* to make sure that you're on track and at the end of the 45 minutes or the double lesson, you've actually have achieved 'I'm going to do this' because if not, sometimes you might depending on what happens in the classroom. (Education Lecturer)

In this regard, experts, as Clark (2011) puts it, are 'doubly expert'.

> They are expert at the task in hand, but also expert at using well-chosen linguistic prompts and reminders to maintain performance in the face of adversity. <...> the linguistic tools enable us to deliberatively and systematically sculpt and modify our own processes of selective attention. (Clark, 2011, p. 48)

Moreover, the symbolic-visual shape of epistemic tools, and epistemic forms in particular, has both cognitive and social consequences in professional knowledge work. For example, a form that prompts students to align identified problems with possible recommendations (Fig. 14.7) or a list that students use to prioritise problems (Fig. 14.8) has this cognitive purpose – which is achieved via a combination of *linguistic* and *spatial organisation* that 'sculpts attention' (Clark, 2011, p. 48). As Norman (1991) argued, in well-designed artefacts and tools that serve a cognitive function, the form of representation is an important choice:

> The form of representation used by an artifact carries great weight in determining its functionality and utility. *The choice of representation is not arbitrary*: Each particular representation provides a set of constraints and intrinsic and extrinsic properties. Each representation emphasizes some mappings at the expense of others, makes some explicit and visible, whereas others are neglected, and the physical form suggests and reminds the person of the set of possible operations. Appropriate use of intrinsic properties can constrain behavior in desirable or undesirable ways. (Norman, 1991, p. 34)

Furthermore, a lesson plan and a medication review template become effective epistemic forms not only because they sculpt the user's perception but also because – through their shared and recognisable material forms – they sculpt the joint perception and cognition of people working together.

In summary, the cognitive and social are constitutively entangled within material–symbolic professional epistemic devices. For example, an effective form for a medication review should have a socially recognisable *shape*, should guide a pharmacist in prioritising and aligning problems with solutions, should be concise and in any other consequential ways should guide perception. From this perspective, effective epistemic devices are effective material and symbolic embodiments that can be effectively entangled with epistemic work and action.

16.3.3   Knowledge Embodied in Bodily Skills and Senses

Various *embodied experiences* that are seemingly unrelated to the human mind – such as not getting anxious if a lesson does not go according to plan or not getting daunted by an unfamiliar environment – as well as *bodily movements* are also entangled in the very act of knowing. What is this knowledge – embodied within human flesh and feelings?

The human body and embodied knowledge are a focal area in various domains, including feminist, materialist and post-humanist studies, cognitive sciences, philosophy and neurosciences.

Davis (1997), drawing upon contemporary feminist scholarship, describes embodiment by taking seriously into account individual experiences and practices, as 'individuals' actual material bodies or their everyday interactions with their bodies and through their bodies with the world around them' (p. 15) and as 'the relationship between the symbolic and the material, between representations of the body and embodiment as experience or social practice in concrete social, cultural and historical contexts' (loc. cit.).

Similar interests in human embodied experiences appear in materialist and post-humanist theoretical accounts. Here, however, as Mulcahy (2000) concludes, embodiment primarily implies socio-material practice that produces 'knowing locations' (see also Law, 2003). This embodied knowledge may not necessarily imply unique individual experience, but it implies a *performative* knowledge, and locations imply not only physical spaces but various kinds of embodied phenomena experienced in the world, including human and nonhuman bodies, routines, texts, tools, organisations and economies. A 'knowing location' as Law (2003) notes is not about 'cognitive knowledge' that can be written down as a set of rules or principles, but a kind of tacit knowledge that resides in a person and their relations. This knowledge is in the relations between the person and a whole array of external things,

> ... knowing may be understood as an effect of recognition and consequent possible intervention generated at a particular location by a heterogeneous array of materials. (Law, 2003, p. 11)

Mulcahy (2000) draws a distinction between 'universalistic' knowledge (which is usually explicit) and the (often tacit) 'particularistic' knowledge involved in embodied performance and experienced judgement. Defining competence, she notes,

> ... competence is a complex outcome or, better perhaps, event. Competence development in its 'richest' sense involves a number of processes – discursive and material – which are only partially assimilable. Rather than regarding competence as something individuals or organizations *have*, it might be better to regard it as something that they *do* and provide products which can assist training practitioners and participants to analyse the dynamics of the processes through which competence is achieved. Perhaps we should think more in terms of competence *through* work than competence *for* work. Or, better again, regard it as both product and process and provide strategies for managing the tension between this double reality. (Mulcahy, 2000, pp. 521–522, original emphasis)

She argues that particularistic knowledge, being hard to express, is often marginalised or ignored in competency standards and similar formal accounts of learning. Such accounts have an overriding concern for outcomes and evidence, rather than the processes through which these outcomes were achieved, thus they overlook embodied kinds of knowledge that are central to competent performance.

Agreeing with, and extending, this materialistic account, Beckett (2004) suggests that embodied competence and generic skills can be reconciled by putting the emphasis on 'inferential understanding',

> ... a form of doing ['knowing how' to go about], where there are distinctive reasons articulable in that process of doing (the 'knowing why'). (Beckett, 2004, p. 505)

In a nutshell, according to Beckett's view, inferential understanding emerges from judgements-in-context, by articulating 'what is done (materially)' in public professional language, i.e. expressing 'what is done (discursively)' (op. cit., p. 499). This view of embodied performance implies that understanding is developed by doing and then giving 'epistemological significance' to certain kinds of decisions and experiences. Embodied competencies are passively constructed by doing and then reflecting, rather than actively 'engineering the self' and 'engineering the environment' in order to gain this situational understanding and insight.[3]

---

[3] In other words, we would say that people create actionable knowledge and learn for action not by acting and then reflecting (a.k.a. representing) but by *enacting*: by bringing forth meanings and the world.

Some neuroscientific, cognitive and philosophical accounts offer other useful views on how bodily senses and environmental supports are intermingled in human cognitive activity (Clark, 2011; Damasio, 2012; Hutchins, 2010). Neuroscientific studies provide increasing evidence that bodily states are inseparable from human consciousness and intelligent behaviour. As Damasio (2012) argues, we all have our bodies in our minds and, at all times, bodies provide a backdrop for human feelings, conscious experiences and interactions with the world:

> Body mapping of the most refined order undergirds *both* the self-process in conscious minds *and* the representations of the world external to the organism. The inner world has opened the way for our ability to *know* not only that very inner world but also the world around us. (Damasio, 2012, p. 114, original emphasis)

Extending this line, Andy Clark (2011) argues that human reasoners lean heavily on bodily senses and environmental supports. Following Kirsh and Maglio (1994), he distinguishes between 'merely pragmatic actions' that involve physical change desirable for its own sake (e.g. giving a box with medications) and 'epistemic actions' that 'alter the world so as to aid and augment cognitive processes' (Clark, 2011, p. 222) – e.g. using a formula to calculate a renal function, checking expiry dates on the medications). These latter cognitive processes (epistemic actions) are not necessarily wholly in the head, but often involve parts of the world. They are rearrangements that may not be seen as a core part of the 'real' action, but are a part of thought or mental action and mental perception. Andy Clark underlines the importance of bodily experience and situated knowledge in this regard,

> With time and practice, enough bodily fluency is achieved to make the wider world itself directly available as a kind of unmediated arena for embodied action. At this point, the extrabodily world becomes poised to present itself to the user not just as a problem space (though it is clearly that) but also as a problem-solving resource. <...> At such moments, the body has become "transparent equipment" (Heidegger, 1927/1962): equipment (the classic example is the hammer in the hands of the skilled carpenter) that is not the focus of attention in use. Instead, the user "sees through" the equipment to the task in hand. (Clark, 2011, p. 10)

However, referring to active sensing and the extended mind, he introduces a different kind of experiential and bodily knowledge than is usually implied in the notions of tacit knowledge and in the different kinds of environmental knowledge found in more established situative accounts. He describes 'real cognition' as processes in the head that are 'portable' and offers a broader concept of the 'naked mind' – 'a package of resources and operations we can always bring to bear on a cognitive task, regardless of the local environment' (op. cit., p. 224). Brain and body comprise of a package of basic portable cognitive resources that incorporate bodily actions into cognitive processes. The external coupling between mind and environment is a part of this basic package – the fish's capacity to swim involves the capacity to couple its swimming behaviours to the externally occurring processes and obstacles (swirls, rocks, eddies, etc.); similarly, a coupling of the human body with the external world (and symbols) constitutes human thought.

Epistemic fluency inevitably involves bodily 'knowing' that is grounded in a deep sense of context and self. The embodied performative skill is important. For example, preservice teachers need to get the pitch and timing right in order to be able to deliver a lesson competently and fluently; nurses need to get a sense of the human body in order to perform fluently their various procedures; the psychologist needs to be able to learn to 'hear' reading mistakes while a child reads, in order to carry out a reading assessment; and so on. This kind of embodied knowledge is particularly important in professional learning, but often considered as 'lower-order' knowledge, and it rarely gets sufficient attention in higher education. However, having an instrument that guides perception helps the pharmacist to focus his attention on carefully checking medication expiry dates, storage conditions or inhalation techniques; seeing what kind of medication would be most convenient to take because of social conditions, etc.; and not feeling overwhelmed with details of the unfamiliar environment of the patient's home. Such a distribution of embodied knowledge is particularly critical for its learnability and its grounding in the epistemic tools. This kind of embodied knowledge and knowing underpins knowledgeable action. It is active embodiment rather than passive embodiment, or more precisely, skilled, knowledgeable embodiment.

That said, it is insufficient to focus only on educating the 'human body' alone. More relevant is the triplet of 'body–mind–environment'. The environment of action (things in this environment) is the key for learning this kind of knowledge: medication boxes, assessing the patient's ability to take medications, access/distance to a health service centre, etc. – all of this is in the assemblage within which knowledge is constructed and enacted. We are speaking of more than just 'a context', but rather of real things that enter knowing and knowledge production.

16.3.4   Knowledge Embodied in the World

Empirical encounters with the world provide an essential experiential resource for knowledge and learning. But where do the experiential resources of the environment come from in university settings? This is not easy. Affordances and constraints that are natural in professional worksites and pervasive in professional knowing cannot be relied on to occur naturally in university settings. Thus, the affordances and constraints essential for a skill and knowledge (and task) have to be artificially created. Universities do this in a variety of ways. Here we should be explicit that 'authentic environments with affordances and constraints' and 'affordances and constraints of environments relevant for the task' are not the same. While the two are intertwined, they are not identical. (The distinction is like that between possible affordances and perceived affordances or those affordances of the environment relevant for the skill. Not everything that exists in the environment enters perception and professional vision.) To construct an authentic workplace environment in the university environment is an impossible, and perhaps an irrelevant, task. People come to university *to learn* for work, not *to work*.

But to assemble a learning environment with professional affordances and constraints (or perhaps, reconstructed professional affordances) in order to support the learning of specific kinds of skills or specific kinds of tasks is a more feasible and relevant aim.[4] Yet an 'experiential' context, on which knowledge and skills can be 'hooked', is essential.

How do university teachers do this? The counselling psychology course, which we discussed in Chap. 10, nicely illustrates the range of approaches that teachers take in creating environments for learning embodied kinds of knowledge.

In order to learn how to do behavioural assessments, students went out to schools: that is, to the real environment. The learning environment was created in a workplace setting, rather than the other way around. To carry out the reading assessment, students picked out a child whom they knew. So this was not necessarily a child with any reading difficulties, yet a real child providing the necessary key 'affordances' of a workplace environment for doing this kind of assessment and learning the relevant set of skills.

Before this, for practising literacy assessment, students used a tape recording that could be 'slowed down', 'paused', 'replayed' and so on. While such affordances have some natural qualities, in this case, they are blended deeply with additional learning affordances. Such 'artificial remaking' is not a limitation, but a necessity for learning, sculpting perception and rehearsing.

To learn to carry out other kinds of assessments and tests, counselling students tried them out on each other during tutorials. This approach has limitations, but it also has learning affordances: such as making it possible to experience how it feels to be tested and engagement in joint reflection.

In the teacher education programs we observed, students' past experiences as learners were also used as an experiential resource for them to reflect and think about how they might teach.

In short, different kinds of 'substitutes' – or blends of authentic work situations and learning situations – are dynamic multimodal affordances that have modalities relevant to learning certain kinds of skill and certain kinds of knowledge. They are not real and not authentic in a simple sense, but they are made for learning a real professional skill and vision – a more universal competence that, in any case, has to draw on a small selective set of affordances available in natural workplace contexts.

Of course, sometimes these substitutions can be very crude (remote) and lose key affordances that configure professional perception: they break the ecology of perception. As in the pharmacy case, with a tutor role-playing a patient and a doctor, the voice, physical appearance, discourse, way of seeing the world and other personal characteristics are critical perceived affordances for a pharmacist in this task, yet cannot be acted out with sufficient accuracy. Or in other situations, the

---

[4] Indeed, there is a very fundamental human capacity, on which the modern mind has historically developed, that is largely ignored in professional education. This is the 'mimetic skill' used in rehearsing and fine-tuning the body and mind in systematic and voluntary ways (Donald, 2001). Billett (2014) is helping rescue the concept.

entire home environment of the patient is substituted by a couple of boxes with medications, or the interview with the patient is replaced by a narrative description of what was said by a patient and what was observed during the home visit.

In short, affordances of the context and experiential resources are important for learning to use professional tools and to do professional tasks. Lack of experience and lack of real environments to get this experience are a challenge for learning, but things are not so 'black and white' when the purpose is to learn, to sculpt perception and to rehearse skill, rather than learn by mere doing. Effective tasks and environments for learning – for sculpting attention, for seeing relationships, for rehearsing – are not necessarily the tasks and environments of authentic workplace settings or the real world.

Overall, different kinds of epistemic games, by their nature, involve different relationships between the mental and experiential aspects of knowledge work. Some epistemic games, such as those involved in lesson planning, are played prior to the action, even by professional teachers. Thus, they build heavily on previous experiences, imagined contexts and projected situations. Other epistemic games, such as in medication assessment, are played mainly in direct interaction – in the unfolding experience – and therefore, many parts of this game, such as information gathering and delivery, need socially and materially real and rich environments and real interactions. In contrast, the environment for what pharmacy teachers called 'information processing' (the processing part of the game) can be recreated in a university setting, as this environment is tightly linked to an information infrastructure that is now quite universal, including handbooks, databases, manuals and so on.

16.4 Learning and Thinking with Social Others

One cannot really talk about the 'social' professions without taking a serious look at the 'social'. Professional thinking and action encounter the social in a variety of ways. Here we concentrate on two main aspects of this encounter: (a) how the human mind and professional meaning-making are *extended by* the social (Sect. 16.4.1) and (b) how professional learning and meaning-making are *enacted with and through* the social world (Sect. 16.4.2). Then we discuss implications for learning (Sect. 16.4.3).

16.4.1 The Socially Extended Mind

If the mind can be extended with the body and the external physical world, then similarly it can be extended with the minds and bodies of other people, through symbolic human actions and social worlds. As Andy Clark (2011) puts it, one's mind is 'partly constituted by the states of other thinkers' (p. 231). He goes on to say

> ... if [this] view is taken seriously, certain forms of social activity might be reconceived as less akin to communication and action, and as more akin to thought. (Clark, 2011, p. 232)

From Clark's perspective, there is not a strong distinction between social and material (including symbolic) extensions of the human mind, such as notebooks or to-do lists. As Clark argues,

> What is central [for the socially extended mind] is a high degree of trust, reliance and accessibility. (op. cit., p. 231)

From this perspective, the social is not just a context in which a self-contained mind operates using its own intrinsic powers, but rather it is a sufficiently stable, transparent, tangible extension of the mind. Humans can extend their minds with other humans' minds in ways that are similar to material extensions. For example, why should a doctor bother learning how to sort out complex issues with medications if she could ask a pharmacist to do this? From this perspective, humans and nonhumans are a part of the instrumental assemblage that is weaved into one's cognition. The relation between the 'knower' and the rest of the social world tends to feel asymmetrical: others might be thought of as a part of the epistemic environment for a person's own knowledge work. While knowledge work is seen as social activity, knowing is generally a mono-agent (person-solo) activity – something that happens in an individual, albeit socially extended, mind.

However, if we acknowledge that the *generative mechanisms* of meaning-making (*how* we know) 'leak' into the social world, then we need to go beyond this basic functionalist extension and accept that knowing is not only a monological person-solo activity, characterised by an internal monologue and *intra-action*, but also *interaction* with social 'others'. So we need to reconsider the roles of social interactions in professional knowing and learning.

16.4.2 Dialectical, Dialogical and Trialogical Perspectives

The literature offers three main views on how personal and shared knowledge are constructed through social interactions: the dialectic, dialogical and trialogical views.

Ravenscroft, Wegerif, and Hartley (2007) distinguish between *dialectical* and *dialogical* stances towards thinking and learning. Dialectic and dialogic are two different ways of seeing the role of social others in constructing shared knowledge and personal understanding. Both views agree on the point that knowledge and understanding are primarily products of social interaction, but the views differ in some other important ways.

The *dialectical* perspective is based on a coherence view of knowledge and truth. On this view, knowledge involves an entire system of propositions with its own structure and rules. Understanding arises in the dialectic interaction between humans and the world. From this perspective, learning is mediated by tools, including words as sign tools, and higher-level mental processes – such as articulated thought, logical memory and selective perception. It is constructed from 'outside' to 'inside'. Tools are learnt through a social process, as one participates in an activity with a more knowledgeable 'other' and, through external interaction, learns and internalises those tools. Development of one's understanding (and similarly expertise) progresses from participatory, heterogeneous thought towards increasingly more rational, systematic, internally mediated thinking and reasoning. On this view, professional learning involves developing expertise in the use of a range of epistemic tools and in how to play a range of epistemic games, be they propositional, problem-solving, professional or involving public discourse. The guiding principle for success is an ability to choose the right tools and use them correctly.

The *dialogical* view, in contrast, opposes the possibility and primacy of a single perspective as a basis of understanding and argues that learning is mediated by the perspectives of others. The main mechanism for understanding and learning involves taking the perspectives of real or generalised others. Learning is not so much about mastering a coherent set of tools, but developing an ability to see things from a new point of view and change one's way of seeing. Dialogue, here, is a source of new perspectives. Expertise, creativity and learning primarily emerge from participation in dialogue and from being open to the emergence of new ideas.

Ravenscroft et al. (2007) argue that dialectical and dialogical views are not in opposition, but that they have different emphases. While the dialectical approach emphasises intrapersonal cognitive and epistemic aspects of knowledge, the dialogical approach emphasises intersubjective and interpersonal aspects.

> The desire to reason to progress towards a rational synthesis does not have to override the need to understand others, and likewise, the desire to understand others does not have to override the often pragmatic need to reach a rational consensus that links to purposeful action in a context. <...> [D]ialogic relations precede and exceed dialectic ones, as they are the necessary medium of reflection and therefore of understanding. On the other hand, the construction of useful cognitive artefacts and tools that embody shared understandings and carry them forward between dialogues occurs through dialectical processes. <...> [D]ialectic without dialogic is blind (as in machine cognition), dialogic relations without dialectic is empty of content. <...> [I]t is through their union that new shared understanding can arise. (Ravenscroft et al., 2007, p. 47)

Paavola and Hakkarainen (2005) extend these two common views of perceiving thinking, knowing and learning by suggesting a *trialogical* perspective. They argue that knowledge advancement and learning to create knowledge involve collaborative processes through which shared *objects* of activity are developed. Such processes do not focus solely on the interaction and dialogue between people but also on the interaction through, and the creation of, shared objects of joint activity and mediating conceptual and material artefacts.

> *Trialogue* means that by using various mediating artifacts (signs, concepts and tools) and mediating processes (such as practices, or the interaction between tacit and explicit

knowledge) people are developing common objects of activity (such as conceptual artifacts, practices, products, etc.). <...> Artifacts are object-like things that are produced by
humans, and the models of innovative knowledge communities concentrate on processes
where people collaboratively create and develop such conceptual and material artifacts and
related practices for a subsequent use. (Paavola & Hakkarainen, 2005, pp. 545–546)

On this perspective, learning and expertise involve a mastery of shared tools,
engagement in dialogue with social others and a capacity to develop concrete
shared objects that integrate individual situated understandings and produce new
conceptual meanings that are objectified in the mediating artefacts.

16.4.3 Implications for Professional Work and Learning

How does this notion of the social enter into the practices of teaching and learning
to play professional epistemic games? The distinction between dialectical, dialogical and trialogical views is useful. The *dialectical* approach would foreground
individual learning (from more knowledgeable others) of the available professional
tools and of rules for engaging in professional epistemic games. The *dialogical*
approach, in contrast, would foreground playing these games collaboratively with
social others in various epistemic spaces. The *trialogical* approach – focussed on
the joint creation of epistemic artefacts – involves developing the skills needed to
coordinate one's unique individual capacities with the capacities of others, by using
shared tools.

The main difference between dialectical and dialogical forms of knowing is the
distinction between single-agent and multi-agent views. In the dialectical case,
agency is attributed to the solo professional as a problem-solver who brings
established professional ways of knowing to the situation. In the dialogical case,
agency is attributed to multiple agents who may bring to the situation *different*
knowledge resources and perspectives. New shared meanings emerge from successful relationships between the two.

As we showed in Chap. 14, professional work involves epistemic games that,
from the social perspective, involve interactions with different sets of people. We
can focus here on three such sets: intra-professional, trans-professional and public
(see Table 16.1).

Intra-professional knowledge work primarily involves propositional knowledge
and problem-solving epistemic games and meta-professional dialogue for individual (monological) or collaborative (dialogical) work. The way such mono-professional knowledge is constructed and learnt could be monological, dialectical or
dialogical. The product of such games will usually be real epistemic professional
artefacts, e.g. reflective journal entries, nursing guidelines or lesson plans.

Trans-professional work draws on an ability to participate in professional discourse across professions. This involves mastering the rules of trans-professional
discourse games, in shared epistemic spaces, using and creating various

Table 16.1 How the social enters knowledge work: dialectical, dialogical and trialogical perspectives

Nature of knowledge work	Nature of learning and knowing		
	Dialectical	Dialogical	Trialogical
Intra-professional Propositional, problem-solving, meta-professional epistemic games	Learning focussed on individual skills, knowledge, preparing for monological problem-solving (e.g. discussion with more knowledgeable others, apprenticeship)	Learning focussed on one's engagement in intra-professional discourse (e.g. collaborative problem-solving, peer feedback)	Learning focussed on production of professional artefacts (e.g. conceptual games, development of characteristic professional epistemic artefacts)
Trans-professional Trans-professional discourse games	Learning focussed on mastering rules of trans-professional discourse (e.g. simulated case conferences with doctors)	Learning focussed on engaging in trans-professional work, forming relationships, knowing others (e.g. field experiences, interviewing)	Learning focussed on engaging in joint problem-solving and knowledge creation with other professions (e.g. project-based interdisciplinary tasks)
Public Public discourse games	Learning focussed on mastering rules of public discourse epistemic games and skills (e.g. simulated case conferences with patients)	Learning focussed on doing, engaging with contingencies of real situations (e.g. completing a behaviour assessment, teaching a lesson)	Learning focussed on joint creation of shared knowledge (e.g. learning to take the patient's perspective, educating the patient and generating joint solutions)

trans-professional or boundary epistemic artefacts (e.g. referrals from a GP to a specialist, geotechnical reports from a surveyor to an architect).

Public knowledge work primarily involves mastering the rules of social discourse and playing games in the social world. Various social discourse games and constructed artefacts are the main objects that guide this kind of knowledge work (e.g. interviews, medication lists for patients and guidelines for parents).

To some degree, all social professions involve all these kinds of knowledge work. Consequently, they also involve various social embodiments of professional knowledge, such as colleagues, other professionals and clients and also various social extensions of knowledge (i.e. dialectical, dialogical and trialogical). Nevertheless, there is a challenge in creating university learning environments for professional education, such that they provide opportunities to engage and mesh multiple, socially extended ways of knowing. The reason for this is that professional learning environments in higher education are historically constituted for learning mono-professional knowledge.[5] The move from dialectical forms of

---

[5] The distinction between mono-professional and mono-disciplinary knowledge is important here. For example, pharmacy is a mono-professional field even though it draws on knowledge from multiple disciplines.

learning[6] to dialogical, collaborative forms (such as group projects) changes the *way* students learn, but does not necessarily change the *kinds of knowledge-building* in which they engage or the kinds of knowledge work for which they are preparing (i.e. knowledge still remains mono-professional).

To create authentic learning environments for trans-professional and public knowledge work is a very challenging task in higher education, as situational contingencies are an essential part of such knowing and learning. From this perspective, different dialectical forms, such as role plays and simulations, are forms for dialectical learning of discourse tools and rules, but they cannot replace the dialogical and trialogical forms of knowing in an open epistemic space. It is the situational contingencies that make new trans-professional and public perspectives visible, possible to articulate and mesh together.

16.5   Four Kinds of Mediation: Tools, Social Others, Artefacts and Self

Before finishing we should revisit the relationships among material, embodied and social aspects of knowledgeable action. As we saw in Chap. 15, many epistemic games are 'weaved' games, which are played in dynamic social, embodied inter-action between people. The social, the material and the embodied are often too tightly woven into human actions, and with each other, for them to be decoupled. If one thinks of a doctor interviewing a patient or a schoolteacher teaching in a classroom, these games – and the knowledge, knowing and action created through such games – are social, material and embodied at the same time. They are social in a number of respects: action schemes that emerge in such games owe much of their origin to human social interaction; much of the understanding comes from the discourse; the understanding thereby created itself takes the form of discourse.

However, these games are also deeply material and embodied. Firstly, the physical and symbolic *tools* embody understanding in material things. Second, the patient who participates in the interview and the children in the class are embodiments of social knowledge in the deepest sense – discourse embodied in the 'matter' of the human body. Patients, children and other *social others* are objects and subjects at the same time. Knowledge comes from coupling what they say and what they do. Such kinds of epistemic games are genuine multi-agent epistemic games, a kind of socially distributed, embodied, dynamic knowing and knowledge.

Thirdly, epistemic games often evolve around, and produce, *epistemic artefacts*. These are not *usually* the ultimate objects towards which action is directed. Rather,

---

[6] Be they teacher-led methods, such as apprenticeship or Socratic dialogue, or student-led methods, such as students writing reflective journal entries on which they get teacher feedback.

they are dynamic, materially embodied, mediating things through which knowledge for action is constructed.

Fourth, knowing humans are themselves embodied, socially constructed entities within which consciousness ('self') and action originates. As Damasio (2012) argues, we could consider 'self' from two vantage points:

> One is the vantage point of an observer appreciating a dynamic *object* – the dynamic object constituted by certain workings of minds, certain traits of behavior, and a certain history of life. The other vantage point is that of the self as *knower*, the process that gives a focus to our experiences and eventually lets us reflect on those experiences. (Damasio, 2012, pp. 8–9, original emphasis)

These two perspectives produce the dual sense of conscious 'self': 'self-as-object' capable of interacting with the environment and responding to it and 'self-as-knower' capable of reflecting and constructing a conscious self. But 'self' – whichever perspective we take – is anchored in the *protoself* with its primordial feelings and senses, generated within the living body and the brain.

Traditionally, the mediating role in human sense-making is attributed to tools, including psychological tools (Vygotsky, 1930, 1978) and perspectives of social others (Wegerif, 2011). However, if we see knowledge, not as already given out in the world, but rather as constructed and re-enacted by a knower within a richly sensed environment, then a much richer picture of the mediation emerges.

As pictured in Fig. 16.2, there is a relationship between subject and object: a result of human senses, biological perception and learning. This knowledge is grounded in what Damasio (2012) called *protoself*: human body and the brain capable of sensing its environment. Subconscious perception of the situation,

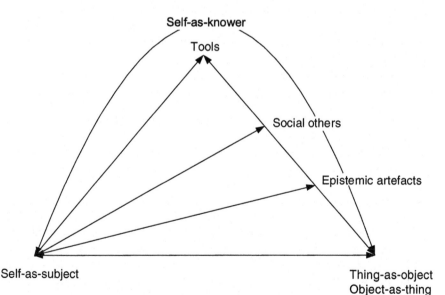

Fig. 16.2 Self and knowledgeable action: four kinds of mediation

spontaneous feelings and other bodily states are often coupled instantly with the encountered object, resulting in a certain immediate reaction. This relationship is often regarded as non-mediated. (But perhaps it would be more accurate to say that there is a relationship between 'self' and 'thing' mediated by the material body and protoself.) Then there are at least four kinds of *mediated* perception and knowing, consequent upon the presence of tools, social others, epistemic artefacts and (not to be overlooked) the self.

There are *tools* (symbolic and material). Tools here could be seen as relatively stable entities with related action schemes. Tools are material or at least are inscribed in some symbolic medium external to the brain, but action schemes are at least partly social: they are learnt in the past, usually through social interactions (see Instrumental genesis in Chap. 12). The relationship here between the subject and the object is mediated by the tool and is dialectical.

There are *social others* in the situation: people who have agency. They have a body (thus, are physical) and use discourse (thus, are social). They are sources of new perspectives, new frames, new ways of looking at and doing things and new feelings. Crudely, they are sources of new ideas and experiences for modifying existing, and creating new, action schemes. As Wegerif (2011) claims, the possibility to see an encountered thing from two perspectives –'the self' and 'the other's' – makes things thinkable and opens up mental space for new creative thoughts. This opens up dialectical space for a dialogue. Social others mediate not only the relationship between the self and the thing but also between the tools and the thing. That is, they have a capacity to change how one uses a tool.

There are *epistemic artefacts* – dynamic physical or symbolic embodiments of the perception and evolving understanding of the object. An epistemic artefact, in this case, is a thing 'meshing' a person's resourcefulness (including her knowledge and embodied skills), tools, perspectives of social others and the object itself. Epistemic artefacts are simultaneously physical things and social constructs that come into being and embody tools and discourse. In the everyday situations of professional work, epistemic artefacts are sometimes coupled with the physical object or action. These artefacts mediate and change not only the relationship between the self and the thing but also between the tools, social others and the thing.

There is also *self-as-knower* with a resourceful mind and bodily skills capable of perceiving the self within the environment and of acting. The self-as-knower builds upon the protoself, with its generated feelings, as well as the self-as-object, with its interpretations of the world, that emerge through the embodied interactions with the thing, tools, social others and epistemic artefacts. The self-as-knower has a capacity to sense and interpret the whole environment, including the encountered thing, epistemic artefacts, perspectives of social others, tools and embodied self by linking all that is experienced as one sufficiently coherent pattern. The emerging pattern gives a standpoint and generates a sense of knowing what it makes sense to do next, within the encountered situation. In short, people understand the world by interacting with the world and interpreting their experiences through their own standpoint: the perspective of the mind relative to the rest of the world, including their body and social others. Such experience is grounded in a variety of sources

(sight, sound, spatial balance, feeling, conscious thought, etc.), but always originates within the head and body of a singular organism (Damasio, 2012).

Our view partly contrasts with, but also extends, traditional sociocultural
(Vygotsky, 1930, 1978) and dialogical (Wegerif, 2011) notions of mediation. It
does this in six ways.

First, our approach is different from the traditional dialogical approaches that see
human discourse as the main mediator of learning. For example, Wegerif (2011)
argues that mediation by cultural tools and dialogic relationships with others are not
equal and/or mutual: 'dialogic relations *precede* and *exceed* tool use and are not
reducible to tool use' (p. 207). From this perspective, dialogue and knowledge
come first, and skilful engagement with tools and actions follows. This view
obscures the fact that many important aspects of human thinking, skilfulness and
learning are as much biological as they are cultural and linguistic (Ingold, 2000;
Tomasello, 2014).

Second, knowledgeable action is mediated by *epistemic artefacts*. These 'epistemic artefacts' can be immaterial, but they are usually inscribed in material or
symbolic (including digital) media. They are model-like dynamic artefacts through
which object and thing come together. Such artefacts embody intelligent perception
of the situation constructed through a conscious mind and link perception with
knowledgeable action. Epistemic artefacts are essential mediators of knowledge
construction and action. They are different from the object/thing, different from the
(stable) tools and different from the ephemeral dialogic relations. They *stand for*
objects, rather than *are* objects; they are dynamic and they persist through space
and time.

Third, tools, social others and objects/things have *not only cognitive but also
material, social and other modalities*. What epistemic capacities they have, and
what role they play in mediating knowledgeable action, is inseparable from what
they are, what kind of feelings they generate, what kinds of action they permit in the
physical world and what kinds of discourse they enable. For example, as Wegerif
(2011) observes, emotions, smiles and other facial expressions are inseparable parts
of a person and of a relationship with that person within a learning dialogue, and the
quality of these relationships determines whether or not the perspective of the
'other' is taken up. This can be extended to other modalities and other elements
of the environment mediating knowing – tools, etc.

Fourth, there is a *distinction between the isolated object and the thing encountered within the environment and specific situation*. The general context in which
the object sits – and where the action takes place – is important. (It is one thing to do
the medication review in the patient's home, quite another to do it in the pharmacy.)
Further, the specific situation, within a textured, perceptually rich environment,
cannot be reduced to an abstract, formally perceived context. For example, it is one
thing to do a medication review in a wealthy, comfortable, quiet, well-maintained
home, quite another to do it in a busy, run-down care home. Formally, the contexts
may be similar but the situations for a practitioner are very different. And the
decisions may end up being very different.

Fifth, the *subject is not an undifferentiated entity*, but has a body and a mind tightly coupled together within a singular organism (with skills, mental resources and other capacities for perceiving, knowing, acting and reflecting). Skills, mental resources and other capacities are the property of the subject: of their 'self'. They are a part of a transferable toolbox for knowledgeable action. The self, of course, cannot be reduced to a stable entity. Rather, as Damasio (2012) points out, the self is not a *thing*, but a *process* which presents when we are conscious. However, a human's embodied brain has a remarkable capacity to learn composite information and reproduce it later with considerable fidelity and in a variety of ways and combinations.

Sixth, the feeling of knowing generated within the self is not reducible to a non-mediated experience and not reducible to an experience mediated by tools, social others and created epistemic artefacts. It is experience mediated by the self as knowing, embodied agent having a standpoint towards the encountered situation *as a whole* and coming to see how individual aspects – tools, social others, self, etc. – fit into a meaningful pattern that informs action. *Seeing the acting self as an actor, mediator and coordinator of its own knowing, within the environment,* changes the way the self sees not only the object but also its relationships with tools, social others, epistemic artefacts and the overall environment. This view of embodied self-as-knower allows flexible movement between seeing things as objects and objects as things.

16.6   Concluding Points: Learning in 'Thin' and 'Thick' Social and Material Environments

The way we have presented epistemic games and epistemic forms, here and in Chaps. 14 and 15, is of course rather idealised and somewhat 'sterile'. Epistemic practice, as with any other practice, is always more messy, fluid and contingent than the action scheme presupposed by any epistemic tool.

For example, would it be practically possible and meaningful, during the medication review, to separate the interviewing of a patient – finding out about her medications and checking her medication administration techniques – from counselling her about how to take medications? Such a separation is usually neither possible nor desirable. However, the weaving of the game that is designed to collect the initial information (i.e. the interview) with the game that is designed to deliver the outcome (i.e. counselling) is not what the medication review procedure prescribes.

However, epistemic tools (frames, forms, strategies, etc.) and their preassembled and inscribed counterparts (plans, procedures, templates, coding schemes, etc.) are not hard-wired structures in the mind or human skills that should be replicated on each occasion, but tools with a spectrum of flexible usage schemes that have a capacity to bring forth multiple meanings and actions. Epistemic and material tools are assembled into instrumental ensembles for a task; usage and action schemes are blended and meshed together into the instrumental act (in knowledgeable action).

We should remind ourselves that various role plays, and other pseudo-authentic learning tasks within simulated environments, are not real professional epistemic games. Rather they are games for learning professional epistemic games – which, through certain idealised qualities, help students to educate their senses and develop professional vision. Yet, real material and social contexts are important. The difference here is between 'thin' and 'thick' versions of experience. The 'thin' version gives focus and form to thought and action. As Håkanson (2007) notes, expertise is not just about what to notice but also what to ignore. The 'thick' experiential version gives embodied experience, within which the 'thin' versions gain full meaning.

Vygotsky (1930) compared the development of a child with the education of a child, saying that the natural development of the child happens anyway, but education has a special function and tries to restructure those natural processes through bringing in the psychological tools:

> ... natural mental processes are not eliminated. They join the instrumental act, but they turn out to be functionally dependent in their structure on the instrument being used. (Vygotsky, 1930, para 22)

This captures one of the main reasons for bringing epistemic tools and games into professional learning. Natural learning would happen in a situated professional context anyway, but the purpose of higher education is 'education' not just 'plain' natural professional development.

While some substitution and simplification of the context can be done for good pedagogical reasons, this is not always the case, particularly when we talk about the social – collaborative learning and collaborative work. The *social* is an important part of knowledge work in professions, and the social is not eliminated from higher education. However, there are different shapes to the social, including intra-professional, trans-professional and public interactions and joint work. Each of these comes with different sets of epistemic games, epistemic tools and socio-material contexts. Students often collaborate and engage in dialogical activities of learning and knowledge production. (At least, getting students to share the artefacts they produce – such as lesson plans and various guidelines and resources – for their future professional work is often perceived as useful and authentic in professional learning.) We do not deny that this may be good, but this kind of collaboration often invokes two associated paradoxes.

Firstly, collaboration among students is usually an intra-professional dialogical form of knowledge construction, such as collaborative problem-solving or peer feedback. In contrast, large parts of real practice in these professions are often (and inevitably) quite lonely, requiring sharp personal professional vision and good mastery of professional tools. Intra-professional collaboration may involve some selected parts of such work (e.g. lesson planning, solving complex problems), but it is not necessarily the core part of everyday professional workplace activities (e.g. dispensing a medication, classroom teaching). Furthermore, such intra-professional collaboration tends not to pose many epistemic challenges among colleagues who share a similar professional instrumental infrastructure. (The main challenge reported in the literature, and anecdotally, is that they do not collaborate and do not share their knowledge products.)

Secondly, *trans*-professional and public forms of collaboration tend to be an important part of professional work in organisations – particularly during organisational change (Miettinen & Virkkunen, 2005) and in the joint solution of complex practical challenges (Edwards, 2010; Hall, Stevens, & Torralba, 2002) – where professionals with different areas of expertise work together or interact with their clients. Intra-professional collaboration and dialectical forms of learning may help to develop some epistemic tools for these kinds of tasks, but they are unlikely to be good substitutes for dialogical or trialogical trans-professional and public forms of work. Developing relational expertise, seeing things from a different perspective and meshing other perspectives with one's own involve more than just mastering the rules of discourse games but also, as we wrote earlier (Chap. 15), juxtaposing tools, agendas, perspectives and practices and assembling an environment for joint epistemic work (Goodwin, 2005). It turns out to be challenging to create learning tasks and environments for learning such expertise (which extends beyond dialogical and trialogical ways of knowing, to the entire environment).

However, if we accept that learning is a 'second-order' phenomenon and learning these 'second-order' capacities is the main aim of higher education, then the opportunities to develop habits of mind associated with playing various epistemic games, particularly those that are central to innovation, are a valuable focus. What is more, if higher education is serious about dialogical and trialogical forms of knowing, that cross the boundaries of intra-professional work, then its focus should be on 'third-order' games (Argyris & Schön, 1996; Turnbull, 2000) – learning about the epistemic games and tools themselves, learning to construct these games and tools – games that are productive in organisational learning and change.

To put it concisely, much of the attention in professional learning is allocated to learning to use epistemic tools. However, it is important to remind ourselves that understanding professional tools, and the ability to choose the right tools and tweak those tools to meet the needs of the situation, is also important. It is this understanding of the deep properties and capacities of the epistemic tools – and how they fit the requirements of a particular situation – that might help professionals to advance from being tool users to tool builders. This could also foster both general ways of thinking and also thinking contextually.

Clark (2011) notes that 'active externalism' or 'active environmental engineering' is actually 'self-engineering'. Or as Wartofsky (1979) has it:

> ... our own perceptual and cognitive understanding of the world is in large part shaped and changed by the representational artifacts we ourselves create. *We are, in effect, the products of our own activity*, in this way; we transform our own perceptual and cognitive modes, our ways of seeing and of understanding, by means of the representations we make. (Wartofsky, 1979, p. xxiii)

In professional education it is not enough to learn to *use* epistemic tools and artefacts. Knowledgeable action also depends on an ability to construct them. We make our artefacts, and then our artefacts make us.

References

Argyris, C., & Schön, D. A. (1996). *Organizational learning II: Theory, method and practice.* Reading, MA: Addison-Wesley.

Barad, K. (2003). Posthumanist performativity: Toward an understanding of how matter comes to matter. *Signs, 28*(3), 801–831.

Beckett, D. (2004). Embodied competence and generic skill: The emergence of inferential understanding. *Educational Philosophy and Theory, 36*(5), 497–508. doi:10.1111/j.1469-5812.2004.086_1.x.

Bereiter, C. (2002). *Education and mind in the knowledge age.* Mahwah, NJ: Lawrence Erlbaum Associates.

Billett, S. (2014). *Mimetic learning at work: Learning in the circumstances of practice.* Heidelberg, Germany: Springer.

Boivin, N. (2008). *Material cultures, material minds: The impact of things on human thought, society and evolution.* Cambridge, UK: Cambridge University Press.

Bowker, G. C., & Star, S. L. (1999). *Sorting things out: Classification and its consequences.* Cambridge, MA: MIT Press.

Clark, A. (2011). *Supersizing the mind: Embodiment, action and cognitive extension.* Oxford, UK: Oxford University Press.

Clarke, A. E., & Fujimura, J. H. (Eds.). (1992). *The right tools for the job: At work in twentieth-century life sciences.* Princeton, NJ: Princeton University Press.

Coopmans, C., Vertesi, J., Lynch, M. E., & Woolgar, S. (Eds.). (2014). *Representation in scientific practice revisited.* Cambridge, MA: MIT Press.

Damasio, A. R. (2012). *Self comes to mind: Constructing the conscious brain.* New York, NY: Vintage Books.

Davis, K. E. (1997). *Embodied practices: Feminist perspectives on the body.* London: Sage.

Dewey, J. (1916). *Essays in experimental logic.* Chicago: University of Chicago.

Donald, M. (2001). *A mind so rare: The evolution of human consciousness.* New York: W.W. Norton.

Edwards, A. (2010). *Being an expert professional practitioner: The relational turn in expertise.* Dordrecht, The Netherlands: Springer.

Falconer, I., & Littlejohn, A. (2009). Representing models of practice. In L. Lockyer, S. Bennet, S. Agostinho, & B. Harper (Eds.), *Handbook of research on learning design and learning objects* (pp. 20–40). Hershey, PA: Idea Group.

Gleick, J. (1993). *Genius: The life and science of Richard Feynman.* New York: Vintage Books.

Goodwin, C. (2005). Seeing in depth. In S. J. Derry, C. D. Schunn, & M. A. Gernsbacher (Eds.), *Interdisciplinary collaboration: An emerging cognitive science* (pp. 85–121). Mahwah, NJ: Lawrence Erlbaum Associates.

Grasseni, C. (Ed.). (2010). *Skilled visions: Between apprenticeship and standards.* Oxford, UK: Berghahn Books.

Håkanson, L. (2007). Creating knowledge: The power and logic of articulation. *Industrial and Corporate Change, 16*(1), 51–88.

Hall, R., Stevens, R., & Torralba, T. (2002). Disrupting representational infrastructure in conversations across disciplines. *Mind, Culture, and Activity, 9*(3), 179–210.

Heidegger, M. (1927/1962). *Being and time* (J. Macquarrie & E. Robinson, Trans.). New York: Harper & Row.

Hutchins, E. (2010). Cognitive ecology. *Topics in Cognitive Science, 2*(4), 705–715. doi:10.1111/j.1756-8765.2010.01089.x.

Hutchins, E., & Klausen, T. (1996). Distributed cognition in an airline cockpit. In Y. Engestrom & D. Middleton (Eds.), *Cognition and communication at work* (pp. 15–34). Cambridge, NY: Cambridge University Press.

Ingold, T. (2000). *The perception of the environment: Essays on livelihood, dwelling and skill.* London, UK: Routledge.

Keller, C. M., & Keller, J. D. (1996). *Cognition and tool use: The blacksmith at work.* Cambridge, UK: Cambridge University Press.

Kirsh, D., & Maglio, P. (1994). On distinguishing epistemic from pragmatic action. *Cognitive Science, 18*(4), 513–549. doi:10.1016/0364-0213(94)90007-8.

Latour, B. (1990). Drawing things together. In M. Lynch & S. Woolgar (Eds.), *Representation in scientific practice* (pp. 19–68). Cambridge, MA: MIT Press.

Law, J. (2003). *Political philosophy and disabled specificities.* Retrieved from http://www.comp.lancs.ac.uk/sociology/papers/Law-Political-Philosophy-and-Disabilities.pdf

Malafouris, L. (2013). *How things shape the mind: A theory of material engagement.* Cambridge, MA: MIT Press.

Miettinen, R., & Virkkunen, J. (2005). Epistemic objects, artefacts and organizational change. *Organization, 12*(3), 437–456.

Mulcahy, D. (2000). Body matters in vocational education: The case of the competently trained. *International Journal of Lifelong Education, 19*(6), 506–524.

Nersessian, N. J. (2005). Interpreting scientific and engineering practices: Integrating the cognitive, social, and cultural dimensions. In M. E. Gorman, R. D. Tweney, D. C. Gooding, & A. P. Kincannon (Eds.), *Scientific and technological thinking* (pp. 17–56). Mahwah, NJ: Lawrence Erlbaum Associates.

Nersessian, N. J. (2008). *Creating scientific concepts.* Cambridge, MA: MIT Press.

Norman, D. A. (1991). Cognitive artifacts. In J. M. Carroll (Ed.), *Designing interaction* (pp. 17–38). Cambridge, UK: Cambridge University Press.

Orlikowski, W. J. (2007). Sociomaterial practices: Exploring technology at work. *Organization Studies, 28*(9), 1435–1448.

Paavola, S., & Hakkarainen, K. (2005). The knowledge creation metaphor – an emergent epistemological approach to learning. *Science & Education, 14*(6), 535–557.

Rabardel, P., & Beguin, P. (2005). Instrument mediated activity: From subject development to anthropocentric design. *Theoretical Issues in Ergonomics Science, 6*(5), 429–461. doi:10.1080/14639220500078179.

Ravenscroft, A., Wegerif, R., & Hartley, R. (2007). Reclaiming thinking: Dialectic, dialogic and learning in the digital age. *Learning Through Digital Technologies, 1*(1), 39–57.

Rheinberger, H. (1997). *Toward a history of epistemic things: Synthesizing proteins in the test tube.* Stanford, CA: Stanford University Press.

Robbins, P., & Aydede, M. (Eds.). (2009). *The Cambridge handbook of situated cognition.* Cambridge, UK: Cambridge University Press.

Säljö, R. (1995). Mental and physical artifacts in cognitive practices. In P. Reimann & H. Spada (Eds.), *Learning in humans and machines: Towards an interdisciplinary learning science* (pp. 83–95). London: Pergamon Press.

Smith, E. R., Barrett, L. F., & Mesquita, B. (Eds.). (2010). *The mind in context.* New York: Guilford Press.

Streeck, J., Goodwin, C., & LeBaron, C. (Eds.). (2011). *Embodied interaction: Language and body in the material world.* New York: Cambridge University Press.

Tomasello, M. (2014). *A natural history of human thinking.* Cambridge, MA: Harvard University Press.

Turnbull, D. (2000). *Masons, tricksters and cartographers: Comparative studies in the sociology of scientific and indigenous knowledge.* Abingdon, OX: Routledge.

Vaesen, K. (2012). The cognitive bases of human tool use. *Behavioral and Brain Sciences, 35*(04), 203–218. doi:10.1017/S0140525X11001452.

Valsiner, J., & Rosa, A. (Eds.). (2007). *The Cambridge handbook of sociocultural psychology.* Cambridge, UK: Cambridge University Press.

Vygotsky, L. S. (1930). The instrumental method in psychology. *Text of a talk given in 1930 at the Krupskaya Academy of Communist Education.* Retrieved from http://www.marxists.org/archive/vygotsky/works/1930/instrumental.htm

Vygotsky, L. S. (1978). *Mind in society: The development of higher psychological processes.* Cambridge, MA: Harvard University Press.

Wartofsky, M. W. (1979). *Models: Representation and the scientific understanding.* Dordrecht, The Netherlands: D. Reidel.

Wegerif, R. (2011). From dialectic to dialogic. In T. Koschmann (Ed.), *Theories of learning and studies of instructional practice* (Vol. 1, pp. 201–221). New York: Springer.

Chapter 17
Conceptual Resourcefulness and Actionable Concepts: Concepts Revisited

Nat: That'd be good. I like Jigsaw activities.
Agi: I know ((*reluctant tone*)).
Jill: It could get messy, I know, I know, *but just as theoretical* – it sounds like it could work, but *I don't know in practice*.

(From preservice teachers' discussion of the 'Jigsaw' technique)

17.1 Concepts Revisited

Why does theoretical thought feel so different from practice for university students? How do theory (knowing a concept) and practice (acting with a concept) become fused together and indistinguishable in expert performance? We call those people who draw on a broad range of conceptual knowledge[1] when they engage in action 'resourceful practitioners'. They know, and enact what they know, sensibly. But what does it take for university students to become resourceful professional practitioners? What does it take for them to put to work what they have learnt in university lectures when they find themselves facing professional challenges?

Knowing how much energy university teachers put into teaching disciplinary concepts and how much time and effort university students spend learning this kind of knowledge, it feels irresponsible not to try to deal squarely with these questions. This is the purpose of the current chapter.

---

[1] As a reminder: we use the term 'conceptual knowledge' quite broadly to refer to kinds of knowledge that are also called in the literature 'declarative knowledge', 'theoretical knowledge', 'propositional knowledge', 'formal knowledge', 'abstract knowledge', 'general knowledge' and other similar names. We are mainly thinking about the kinds of professional knowledge taught in formal university courses, e.g. by providing formal definitions and explanations, rather than by engaging in professional practice (see Chap. 4).

© Springer Science+Business Media Dordrecht 2017
L. Markauskaite, P. Goodyear, *Epistemic Fluency and Professional Education*,
Professional and Practice-based Learning 14, DOI 10.1007/978-94-007-4369-4_17

As we said in Chap. 6, the meaning of the notion of 'concept' varies quite widely, depending on who is defining the term and how they are using it. Some authors have been very meticulous in defining what a concept is and what it is not (e.g. diSessa & Sherin, 1998; Keil & Silberstein, 1998); others have been inclined to keep this term open for diverse meanings (Schön, 1963). Those who adopt the former view usually see 'true' conceptual understanding only as a certain kind of mature, articulated thought which is guided by theoretically precise meanings. Those who adopt the latter (softer) view usually include in the notion of concept quite a broad range of ways in which people grasp and express meanings. For example, Schön (1963), discussing processes that underpin theoretical developments in science and practical inventions in industry, suggests the following possible meanings:

> I want to use the word 'concept' broadly enough to include a child's first notion of his mother, our notion of the cold war, my daughter's concept of a thing-game, Ralph Ellison's idea of the Negro as an invisible man, the Newtonian theory of light, and the idea of a new mechanical fattener. These are all concepts as we ordinarily use the term. <...> Whether they are to be regarded exclusively as language, behaviour, images, logical terms, or the like, is not the issue. These are all ways of looking at concepts which may from time to time be useful. (Schön, 1963, p. 4)

Given the salience of conceptual understanding in professional education – indeed in education generally – it is worth looking more closely at what this term 'concept' means and how people enact their conceptual understanding.

This chapter is dedicated to constructing and sharing a richer view of what concepts are and how they function. In Sect. 17.2, we provide some examples of different possible meanings of 'concept' and their functions. In Sect. 17.3, we examine the nature of concepts – as constructs of discourse and as constructs of mind – and then continue this discussion in Sect. 17.4 by looking into the capacity of conceptual knowledge to span across contexts. In Sect. 17.5, we integrate the main points and reintroduce the notion of *actionable* concept. In Sect. 17.6, we illustrate some of these ideas, showing how some preservice teachers draw upon and construct concepts within their practical knowledge work. In Sect. 17.7 we return to the notion of actionable concepts and argue that conceptual resourcefulness cannot be said to arise solely from the semantic meaning of conceptual constructs: it arises within situated work where concepts are enacted meaningfully. Let's start from some examples.

## 17.2	Some Examples: 'Constructivism' and Other Concepts in Abstract Notions, Contexts and Actions

Consider the concept of 'constructivism' taught to preservice teachers in a way that is meant to inform and guide their practice. What shapes does 'constructivism' take in a teacher's meaning-making and action? There are at least three easily discernible possibilities.

Firstly, a teacher may be quite good at giving a formal definition of constructivism – thus they may be said to know or have a *formal* (*abstract*) concept and be able to participate in discourse practices that refer to this concept.

Alternatively, the teacher might be good at understanding the sorts of pedagogical practices that count as constructivist – that is, they may be able to make sense of recurrent patterns and purposefully use pedagogical strategies in different teaching situations that belong to this category; but they may not necessarily be able to state precisely what 'constructivism' is. Thus, one may say that the teacher has a good *functional* (*contextually appropriate*) grasp of the concept 'constructivism'.

A third way is 'to be' a constructivist teacher without consciously applying a specific set of constructivist strategies – perhaps without even knowing that this word exists. This teacher would organise their classroom practices in such ways that emerging patterns of situated practice could be recognised by others as 'constructivist'. In this third case, 'constructivism' can be seen as a *situated concept* that dynamically emerges in action from diverse context-sensitive interactions.

The differences between these three ways of grasping the concept are crucial. In the first two cases, one may see abstract (formal) and contextual (functional) concepts as 'built in' recurring constructs that structure sense-making and action. In the third case, the stability is not built into (or by) a concept that is used and imposed 'top-down' on actions. Instead, it is a recognisable pattern that (re)emerges 'bottom-up' as relatively coherent from numerous fluid and context-sensitive actions and interactions. For example, a constructivist teacher may sometimes 'tell' students a definition or a formula or use a textbook or other kinds of strategies that are generally associated with a transmissionist pedagogy, while the overall emerging pattern of activities in their classroom would be still recognised as 'constructivist' teaching.

What we have said about 'constructivism' can also be said about almost any abstract actionable construct, such as 'fairness', or any practical concept – such as the 'Jigsaw' instructional technique. One may not be able to give an abstract definition of what 'fairness' is in teaching or in the provision of other social services, yet one may still know and apply a set of recognisable strategies that can be described as fair, such as 'always treat all students equally' and 'always recognise your own mistakes'. But what does it mean to treat students equally if those students come from very different social and cultural contexts, have different motivations and aims or have other reasons to act and think differently? What does it mean to act fairly when the situation encountered today is different from the one that was encountered yesterday? Rather different views of the concept 'fairness' emerge in the ability to make fair decisions case-by-case and moment-by-moment and to act fairly in specific situation-sensitive ways.

Consider now a longer extract from the planning meeting cited in this chapter's opening quote. Three preservice teachers were preparing for a science lesson in a primary classroom.[2] They were trying to come up with an idea for how they could create opportunities for students to share results from their group work and consolidate what was learnt.

Agi: … How 're they [students] gonna present their information to the rest of the class? How're we gonna bring them together?

Jill: Um like in table ((tries to make sense what Agi has said)), is that what you?

Nat: Maybe what we can do, when those kids are in their groups, we give them big butcher's paper, and then they write it in, and we can stick it up on the board as each of them discuss it.

Jill: You could have a *Jigsaw kind* of thing happening.

Jill: Where you take, so if you've got groups, you've got everyone in their individual groups and then you switch it around so that you share it with the other people that were not in your (…) group.

Nat: That'd be good. I like Jigsaw activities.

Agi: I know ((reluctant tone)).

Jill: It could get messy, I know, I know, *but just as theoretical* – it sounds like it could work, but *I don't know in practice.*

Agi: No, I like it though … [5 seconds] the other thing – 'cause they could share their results in Jigsaw type of thing.

Jill: Yeah, but kids, I don't think there's gonna be that much discussion, I just think that's gonna be more "show me your thing" and then ((shows writing gesture)) copy, copy, copy ((all laugh)). *You know how it is.* (From preservice teachers' discussion of the 'Jigsaw' technique)[3]

As with the examples we gave above, about 'constructivism' and 'fairness', this extract shows that the preservice teachers know and are able to provide an explanation of the 'Jigsaw' instructional technique – 'when you've got everyone in their groups and then you switch it around'. They are able to identify some principles that make 'Jigsaw' functional – "'cause they could share their results'. But they still feel challenged to see how this instructional method will work in a primary classroom – 'Yeah, but kids … It could get messy'. Knowing 'Jigsaw' 'in theory' is different from knowing it 'in practice' in a primary classroom.

The students appeal to their personal experiences – phrases like 'You know how it is' and 'I like it' may look unimportant, yet they offer a powerful insight into how abstract concepts get 'hooked' onto, and extended by, concrete situated feelings of what the concept may mean and how things could work in practice.

---

[2] This example is inherently and unavoidably complicated because there are two layers of teaching and learning: the preservice teachers are learning to teach primary school students. We are also aware that terms for these various learners and teachers vary from country to country. Primary school here can be read as elementary school, teacher as preservice teacher and student as primary school student. For those who don't know it, Jigsaw is a technique for structuring small group learning activities. Its details are not important for understanding the case we are analysing in this chapter.

[3] Transcripts provided in this chapter and Chap. 18 use Jefferson's conventions. Some have been abbreviated and edited for clarity.

After a while, the students continue this discussion:

Nat: But maybe ... [4 seconds] I was just gonna say, maybe don't give them a sheet till like filling a table or whatever, so they don't just copy like – 'cause I remember with – when we did Jigsaw – like the kids'd actually test, like we were tested like when we did it in a tutorial, we were tested on it, so it wasn't just procrastination. They must have actually done something.

Agi: Yeah.

Nat: But that 'd be too hard, like, "testing them" afterwards.

Agi: The only thing with Jigsaw is that I don't think we're gonna have time.

Nat: Yeah, it does take. (From preservice teachers' discussion of the 'Jigsaw' technique)

The experience of being taught using Jigsaw – "cause I remember' – gives a powerful anchor for grounding the abstract concept: 'it wasn't just procrastination', 'we were tested'. This also gives a powerful ground for imagining how Jigsaw could be meshed with other concepts and enacted in practice – 'may be don't give them a sheet', 'testing them'. They can also project how Jigsaw would work in a new context and can anticipate practical constraints – 'Yeah, it does take [time]'.

In short, if we look at concepts at work in fluent, knowledgeable, professional action and learning, we soon discover a more fluid, sensitive and dynamic notion of 'concept'. It is in sharp contrast with homogenised views of what conceptual knowledge is, how it is learnt and how it is transferred (see Chap. 6). Without this sharper understanding about what sorts of constructs we are dealing with, deeper analytical insights into how concepts are learnt and enacted in professional practice, and how they should be taught, become elusive. To help with this task, we need to look a little more deeply into some common notions of 'concept'.

Mainstream psychological and sociocultural accounts provide a good point of departure. To organise our discussion of conceptual resourcefulness, we compare these two views along two main lines:

(a) The *nature* of concepts: concepts as constructs of mind vs. concepts as constructs of discourse (Sect. 17.3)

(b) The *generality* or *span* of concepts: concepts as universal constructs vs concepts as situated constructs (Sect. 17.4)

Table 17.1 provides a concise advance organiser for our discussion in the next two sections. We elaborate upon it at the end of the chapter.

Table 17.1 Overview of the nature of conceptual constructs

| | Nature | |
Generality	Discourse	Mind
Abstract concepts	Normative formal concepts	Stable theory-like mental models
Contextual concepts	Context-specific concepts in practice	Mental generalisations of context-specific experiences
Situated concepts	Situated concepts as arenas of practice	Dynamic, situated conceptualisations

17.3   Concepts in Mind and in Discourse

In educational psychology, 'concept' has primarily been defined as an individual *mental* construct. For example, Goldstone, Hills, and Day (2010) define 'concept' as

> ... *a mentally possessed idea* or notion that can be used *to categorize* information or objects. (Goldstone et al., 2010, p. 381, emphasis added)

Barsalou, Kyle Simmons, Barbey, and Wilson (2003) similarly describe the traditional notion of concept as

> ... knowledge about a particular *category* (e.g. birds, eating, happiness). (Barsalou et al., 2003, p. 84, emphasis added)

This conceptual knowledge supports all cognitive activities about the category.

> Thus, knowledge about birds represents bodies, behaviours and origins of the respective entities. (loc. cit.)

Whether one has, or does not have, a concept is primarily determined by one's behaviour with respect to recognising certain patterns, categorising and acting according to certain rules. For example, in the rule-based account of concepts, Bruner, Goodnow, and Austin (1956) used an individual's ability to discover and apply rules for classifying stimulus cards as evidence of their acquisition of a certain concept (see Goldstone et al., 2010).

In contrast, sociocultural accounts primarily relate the notion of concept to *language and discourse*, including the mastery of words and their abstract meanings – going beyond purely perceptual associative connections. For example, Vygotsky (1986) claimed

> Real concepts are impossible without words, and thinking in concepts does not exist beyond verbal thinking. (Vygotsky, 1986, p. 107)

The development of 'real', 'scientific' or 'genuine' concepts is the development of words as conceptual means for abstract reasoning and discourse. In this account, psychological aspects have an important role, as abstract reasoning is the key feature of conceptual thinking. However, mental changes are an integral part of, or even a precondition for, a 'fully fledged' conceptual understanding rather than a sign of actual 'historically developed *human* intelligence' (op. cit., p. 139).

This distinction between the view of conceptual knowledge as *ideas in people's minds* and conceptual knowledge as *modes of discourse* is very salient in the literature on learning and conceptual change.

Much of the mainstream literature in educational psychology focusses on explaining how the human conceptual system is organised and how it functions: proposing various models of the human mind. Examples include semantic memory and rule-based models, prototypes, exemplars, boundary models and situated simulations (see Goldstone et al., 2010; Holyoak & Morrison, 2005; Vosniadou, 2008/2013).[4] Whichever model we take, one key assumption is consistent – humans have a certain system and mechanisms in their minds that *represent* conceptual knowledge and *produce* conceptual understanding. Thus, conceptual learning, change and transfer primarily involve changes in this system: such as adding new elements, replacing one 'theory' with another or reorganising existing representations.

In contrast, the discourse views tend to shift away from representations and systems in the human mind and look for explanations of peoples' conceptual understanding and change in their social interchanges and discourse. For example, Säljö (1999) argues,

> ... we need to move away from interpretations of concepts and conceptual change that put concepts solely into the minds of individuals and that disregard the intimate connections between discursive practices and individual learning. We need to consider the situated nature of human conceptual knowledge and that *the medium that enabled people to come into contact with concepts is language*, or rather communication, and communication is – by definition – first and foremost a collective activity. (Säljö, 1999, p. 84, emphasis added)

Coming back to our example of mastering the concept 'constructivism' by a preservice teacher, the mind and discourse views of conceptual understanding would imply two rather different processes. From the mind perspective, this understanding primarily relates to changes in the representations and operations in the teacher's memory, which then provide the cognitive and behavioural foundations to act as a constructivist teacher. From the discourse perspective, this mastery is inseparable from the linguistic competences needed to participate in the community's interchanges about constructivism. In short, language comes first and understanding will follow.

Other researchers have tried to integrate the two approaches, suggesting that there are close and intimate relationships between mental representations and discourse (Brown & Hammer, 2008; Nersessian, 2008b, 2012). As Brown and Hammer (2008) put it,

> ... there is an interdependence ... between conceptual dynamics and discourse dynamics. (Brown & Hammer, 2008, p. 135)

Beckett's (2004) work provides a nice philosophical expression of this more integrated view of conceptual understanding in professional learning: in relation to what he calls 'inferential understanding'. Beckett argues a generic skill is a linguistic expression of embodied competence and the two are inseparable. That is, competence and generic skill are not only an outcome of situated action but are shaped by a sensitivity to the process. Although his overall approach gives a distinctive place to language, reason, consciousness and explicit inferential

---

[4] Concise reviews of different models of the human conceptual system can also be found in Barsalou (2003) and diSessa and Sherin (1998). Both are very accessible to an education audience.

understanding in human intelligence, he clearly signals that understanding is inseparable from embodied action, perception and feeling for the context.

> ... *'inferential understanding', grounded in embodied practice,* can provide a strong basis for articulating both statements of outcome (competence), and statements of expectation (generic skills). We get *from the materiality of workplace learning,* to *its discursive nature,* not the other way around. (Beckett, 2004, p. 501, emphasis added)

On this view, even the most abstract kinds of conceptual understanding achieved by means of classical logic are inseparable from a 'practical mastery' – a kind of 'know-how' that enables one to discriminate what does and does not follow from the claim. Beckett (2004) here is directly concerned with what we have called *actionable concepts* (Chap. 6). But before we expand on the notion of actionable concepts and implications for learning, we need to introduce the second dimension that deals with the generality or span of concepts.

17.4   Abstract, Contextual and Situated Concepts

This dimension is broadly parallel to the distinctions referred to by others as 'formal' and 'functional' (Greeno, 2012), 'normative' and 'descriptive' or 'ought' and 'is' (Elqayam & Evans, 2011), 'semantic' and 'situated' (Barsalou, 2009) and 'concepts as things' and 'concepts as tools' (Schön, 1963).

17.4.1   Abstract Concepts

Many accounts of human and social cognition presuppose that concepts – be they internal psychological constructs or discourse constructs – are *well-established* constructs, such as those that can be found in the natural sciences, mathematics, logical deductive reasoning and other domains of human intellectual activity in which a normative system with explicit definitions and formal rules of reasoning are integral parts of discourse and presumably of expert thinking. As Greeno (2012) noted, such concepts have formal explicit definitions and are used for categorisation, formal deductive reasoning and argumentation. They are *abstract concepts* that 'are used formally' (p. 311).

Similarly, a number of established cognitive psychological accounts of the human mind suggest that the human conceptual system is based on quite firmly structured and well-integrated mental mechanisms such as 'ontologies', 'theories' and 'frameworks' (Chi, 2005; Chi & Roscoe, 2002; Vosniadou, 2013). On this view, mastering a concept such as 'constructivism' would imply possession of a generic, well-organised system or framework of constructivist pedagogy that is independent from specific contexts of application and which can be deployed across a wide range of situations.

Others have made a close link between concepts as discourse and concepts as cognitive constructs. For example, Vygotsky (1978, 1986) argued that the dialectical unity between sign use and practical intelligence is the very essence of complex human behaviour.

> Words and other signs are those means that direct our mental operations, control their course, and channel them toward the solution of the problem confronting us. (Vygotsky, 1986, pp. 106–107)

17.4.2 Contextual Concepts

In contrast, as Engeström and Sannino (2012) note, many areas of human activity are full of concepts that are

> ... inherently polyvalent, debated, incomplete, ... loaded with affects, hopes, fears, values, and collective intentions. (Engeström & Sannino, 2012, p. 201)

Hall and Seidel Horn (2012) define 'concepts' of this kind as

> ... *recurring patterns* of purposeful activity that are distributed over people and technologies in work practices. (Hall & Seidel Horn, 2012, p. 241)

On this view, concepts are constructs that contribute to the way people make sense of the situation, negotiate with each other and 'organize their understanding of what they are doing' (Greeno, 2012, p. 311). They are concepts that are 'used functionally' (loc. cit.).

Hutchins (2012) refers to them as 'concepts in the wild' or 'concepts in practice' – linked firmly to concrete situated contexts. He explains,

> Concepts in the wild are manifest in practices, and practices include the social and material settings in which they are situated. (Hutchins, 2012, p. 315)

Hutchins (2012) argues that this view of concepts differs in important ways from the concept of 'concept' in cognitive psychology. In contrast to abstract, formally defined concepts, concepts in practice are more context-specific and dynamic constructs. The formation of such *contextual concepts* is a social and collective process, not reducible to individual learning and not governed by formal discourse rules and meanings assigned by definitions.

Concepts 'in practice', however, cannot be detached from the individual mind. Formal and functional concepts, as Greeno (2012) claims, are 'cognitive entities'. The social is not reducible to the individual, yet it emerges from, and constructs, the individual. There is close coupling between the mechanisms that work at the (individual) meaning-making level and at the (collective) social-discursive level of material practice. Individual people construct their own, often partial and situation-specific, versions of such practice concepts. And they operate in activities with a partial grasp, frequently reconsidering, renegotiating and adapting their meanings to the situation in dynamic interaction with conceptual, social and material affordances of the environment and each other. Such concepts, as Greeno suggests, include a broad aggregate of constructs that help people make sense and organise activity. Some of these are cognitive constructs, grounded in concrete experiences but not usually considered as 'genuine concepts'. Examples include 'complexes'[5] (Vygotsky, 1986), 'coordination classes' (diSessa & Sherin, 1998) and conceptual constructs that might be seen as too flimsy to be called concepts, such as 'p-prims' (diSessa, 1988). These preconceptual mental resources may differ in important ways from the mental constructs that are posited to guide experts' behaviour, thought and discourse. They could include both different kinds of intellectual operation (i.e. mind) and different kinds of language used to express that concept in words (i.e. discourse). Nevertheless, such preconceptual constructs, as Vygotsky acknowledged, are common not only in children's but also in adults' thinking, including thinking at very advanced levels. Others even argue that various 'naive' conceptual constructs that are generally incompatible with normative disciplinary concepts could be a productive, perhaps essential, resource for the dynamic flexibility required of experts (Gupta, Hammer, & Redish, 2010). Whether such primitive conceptual resources are required for expert thought or not is one question, but there is sufficient evidence to say that they play important roles in human sense-making and learning. As Vygotsky (1986) argued,

> Analysis of reality with the help of concepts precedes analysis of concepts themselves. (Vygotsky, 1986, p. 141)

In short, from the contextual perspective, mastering a concept, such as 'constructivism', is not reducible to the acquisition of abstract linguistic or mental models, but is a much more situated and fragmented process. The contextual concept of 'constructivism' would not necessarily be underpinned by an a priori coherent generic structure; rather it is constructed from a range of smaller experiential generalisations about what it means to teach in a constructivist way in specific contexts.

Much of the literature on conceptual change and professional learning has focussed on how people master and use formal concepts. However, as Engeström and Sannino (2012) emphasise, the importance of understanding functional concepts is undeniable:

> Functional concepts encompass a huge variety of practices and epistemologies. The challenge is to start digging into and making sense of this variety. It is too valuable to be neglected. (Engeström & Sannino, 2012, p. 201)

They argue for a

> ... new field of inquiry, namely, the study of the formation of functional concepts embedded in various collaborative activities, organizations, and societal institutions. This field of inquiry cannot be built primarily on theories dominant in traditional studies of the formation and change of formal concepts. (loc. cit.)

---

[5] 'Complexes', according to Vygotsky (1986), are less mature constructs than concepts and are rooted in practical experience of relations observed between objects. They are more like collections of complementary things that cooperate in the same operation.

Indeed, when one looks at concepts in practice, there is more of a dynamic between mind and discourse than one might expect.

Philip (2011) makes an important link between collective and individual conceptual change (i.e. discourse and mind), noting that individual change often gets overlooked in collective processes, such as 'ideological change':

> Rearticulation involves changes in collective meaning that challenge social forms of power. Collectively rearticulated meanings shape how individuals make sense of their social world. In turn, it is from changes in individuals' sensemaking that collectively rearticulated meanings emerge. The nuances, challenges, and barriers to how people appropriate and further transform rearticulated meanings are largely ignored. (Philip, 2011, p. 301)

Concepts in practice are seen as being flexible and responsive to contexts, yet there are two rather different ways to see how this conceptual flexibility functions. One way is to see concepts as recurring patterns of practice and sense-making that are specific and sensitive to particular contexts. Such concepts are composed of a certain set of smaller elements (i.e. context-specific patterns) that are deployed consistently when the context feels right. Such elements may not necessarily have distinct formal definitions, but they function differently and are deployed only in particular contexts. For example, a teacher may draw on two rather different notions of what constructivist learning means in science lessons and in arts lessons and may accordingly draw upon two different sets of strategies when teaching science and arts. We have labelled these concepts 'contextual concepts'. A rather different perspective is to see functional concepts as dynamic constructs that are enacted and indeed (re)created 'in action' in specific situations: 'situated concepts'.

17.4.3   Situated Concepts

Nancy Nersessian (2012), describing the formation of scientific concepts, claims

> ... novel scientific concepts arise from the interplay of attempts to solve specific problems, [and the] use of conceptual, material and analytical resources provided by the problem situation. (Nersessian, 2012, p. 222)

When scientists construct new concepts from their empirical observations, they often start by formulating a 'germ cell' or a 'placeholder concept' – a concept that captures their 'rudimentary idea' and preliminary understanding, but which still needs proper articulation. The action then proceeds in parallel along two lines: (a) transfer of the rudimentary concept to the concrete situation and action, so that the rudimentary concept can be seen in the material world, and (b) simultaneous modification and re-articulation of the concept to account for new observations. Such concept formation is an ongoing dynamic process

> ... as scientists grapple with the dual tasks of trying to understand and make sense of complex, novel phenomena and conceiving and building the artefacts by means of which they do their sense-making. (op. cit., p. 238)

In short, cognitive processes and conceptual notions are not stable patterns, but are situated and co-constructed dynamically in an ongoing process within the environments comprising people (with embodied minds), tools and artefacts.

> Concept formation is not something that takes place just "in the head" of researchers; rather, concepts are formed by a coupling of researchers and models in problem-solving processes. (op. cit., p. 237)

In short, they are dynamic *situated concepts*. However, Nersessian (2012) claims that scientific practice in laboratories is different from mundane practices in other problem-solving environments. She argues that, in the latter case, people create their cognitive powers by 'making use of *existing* representational artefacts' where 'the artefact component of the system is relatively *stable*' (p. 229, emphasis added). On this view, concepts and material tools that enable knowing are *given*. In contrast, Nersessian says of laboratory work that the problem-solving environment is itself ill-structured and not stable – people design and build their representational artefacts while they solve problems. That is, the problem is solved, the environment is created, and the concept develops at the same time. She articulates this difference by making a metaphorical comparison between 'flying a plane' and 'building the plane while it is flying',

> The comparison is akin to that between flying the plane and building the plane while it is flying – and with only a vague idea of what a flying vehicle might look like. (op. cit., p. 229)

This contrast – between the uncertainty, instability and ill-structuredness associated with scientific inquiry and the more settled practices of everyday professional work – may hold true for some cases, but not for all. The professional workplace and its ongoing activities may look stable and orderly to an external viewer, and many of the daily experiences of expert professionals may feel to them well-structured, even routine and humdrum. But things can look and feel very different to the novice professional or to the seasoned practitioner who finds herself taking on a challenging, unprecedented case. In such situations, it is rare that a newly encountered problem can be expressed in terms of a single, coherent conceptual system. What could be seen as a concept is not a construct with a single and stable meaning, but rather a dynamic construct coupled with different conceptual neighbourhoods and contexts. The notion of a 'concept' then becomes far less firm in its internal workings and external powers.

Consider a preservice teacher who has just heard about constructivist pedagogy and is about to design and teach a science lesson that should adhere to this pedagogical approach. The student may ask themselves: 'How should I design classroom activities for introducing students to a new topic without becoming too transmissionist? How could I explain to students how they should carry out a scientific experiment, without being too didactic?' From the perspective of this preservice teacher, who has yet to form an understanding that would look (to an external observer) like a 'full concept' of constructivism, the metaphorical picture is far more similar to 'concept formation' in the scientific lab and may be even more challenging. There may be a *placeholder* – a formal definition of a concept with some contours of its meaning – but it is yet to be filled in with the actions and experiences that embody that concept in material and social worlds. The preservice teacher has to solve the problem with the concept and modify this concept at the same time.

Nersessian's (2008a, 2012) main concern was how the discourse concepts (or indeed formal scientific concepts) are formed in action when scientists try to articulate their understanding in shared (formal) representational systems. How is a concept formed in action on an individual scale, when a practitioner is making sense *and* taking action, without there being an explicit attempt to articulate what he is doing, how he is doing it and why he is doing it in this way?

Dynamic accounts of the human conceptual system give an insight into how such concepts may originate and function. Linda Smith (2005) argues that thought is a unique moment-to-moment event that is open to the continually changing world. What can be seen as a concept and knowledge is an inherently variable phenomenon of dynamic cognition that is

> ... emergent from, embedded in, distributed across, and inseparable from the real time processes of perceiving, remembering, attending and acting. (Smith, 2005, p. 279)

The concept that emerges in action is not a stable construct – a shared mental structure constant across repeated instances – but the continuing coupling of the particularly structured mind to the particularly structured world via a particularly structured body. In short, what might be seen as a concept in action is not separate from perception and action in-the-moment, in the unique situation. Smith illustrates this by pointing out that what is usually considered as evidence that a person (a child) has a concept of an 'object' – that is, he or she behaves in ways that evidence the grasp that material 'objects' persist in space and time – is not a result of a single cognitive mechanism underpinning a stable mental structure of the concept 'object'. Rather, it emerges from multiple components – such as body position, the distance to the object and many other contributing processes that 'make knowing in the moment' (op. cit., p. 284). Stabilities (i.e. transfer) and instabilities (i.e. potential for change) emerge from the interactions of many heterogeneous components, within the human mind, body and environment, rather than from the operation of, and change in, a single construct.

> Each individual experience, each moment of wakeful living, changes us, at least a little. (op. cit., p. 290)

Furthermore, as Barsalou, Breazeal, and Smith (2007) argue, people do not perform tasks or construct conceptualisations in a vacuum or in isolation. Rather

> ... they perform *sets of coordinated tasks* that produce coherent behaviour. For example, organisms do not produce categorisation alone. Instead, they perform categorisation together with perception, inference, action, reward, and affect. (Barsalou et al., 2007, p. 83, emphasis added)

From this perspective, nothing can be explicitly labelled as a 'concept'. The question shifts from being about the entity that constitutes the concept within the human mind to the mechanisms that produce conceptual understanding and from learning detached abstract concepts to developing the ability to construct productively situated conceptualisations (see also Chap. 6).

The concept of 'constructivism', on this view, would not imply a mastery of detached definitions and patterns of constructivist pedagogy, but rather a mastery of certain principles for situated actions from which constructivist pedagogy dynamically emerges.

Two mechanisms play important roles in the productivity of the human conceptual system: (a) *coordination* of cognitive processes with those that are usually considered as noncognitive, during real-world cognition, such as perception or kinesthetic skills (Barsalou et al., 2007), and (b) *combination* of existing concepts to form new ones, by embedding the mechanisms that produce different concepts in

Table 17.2 Summary: conceptual resourcefulness as discourse and as cognition

	Nature	
Generality	Construct of discourse (Social, external)	Construct of mind (Individual, internal)
Abstract concepts Models	Normative discourse constructs that have a formally defined semantic meaning: formal concepts (Greeno, 2012); scientific concepts (Vygotsky, 1986)	Stable, theory-like mental constructs that are insensitive to the context: mental models, frameworks, prototypes, exemplars (see for reviews Goldstone et al., 2010; Holyoak & Morrison, 2005; Vosniadou, 2008/ 2013)
	Abstracted traits that are linked with words and used to direct abstract thinking: 'genuine concepts', 'real concepts', 'true concepts' (Vygotsky, 1986)	
Contextual concepts Modules	Context-specific, social-discursive constructs in shared practical activity: concepts in practice (Hutchins, 2012); concepts as recurring activity patterns (Hall & Seidel Horn, 2012)	Context-specific mental generalisations of experience: functional concepts, concepts in use (Greeno, 2012); pseudoconcepts, complexes (Vygotsky, 1986); coordination classes, p-prims (diSessa & Sherin, 1998)[a]
	Discourse constructs that link collective structural and individual cognitive dimensions of change: naturalised axioms, pivotal concepts (Philip, 2011)	
Situated concepts Modalities	Situated dynamic discourse constructs: concepts as arenas of shared human practices (Roth & Duit, 2003; Säljö, 1999)	Situated dynamic cognitive constructs: concepts as a capacity to construct situated conceptualisations (Barsalou, 2003; Barsalou et al., 2003); dynamic concepts as a moment-to-moment coupling of perception and action (Smith, 2005)
	Authentic construction of socially shared meanings: formulating new scientific concepts (Nersessian, 2008b, 2012); conceptual and discourse dynamics during conceptual change (Brown & Hammer, 2008)	

[a]diSessa and Sherin (1998) argue that p-prims are not concepts, as they are too small and situation specific. However, from our perspective, such constructs still belong to this category as they are small context-specific mental generalisations, relatively similar to Vygotsky's (1986) 'pseudoconcepts'

one another (Barsalou et al., 2003). From this perspective, conceptual understanding is not a representation of an abstract category in the human mind, but rather a performative skill to construct situated conceptualisations by combining different elements and coordinating different processes.

> A concept is not a single abstracted representation for a category, but is instead *a skill* for constructing idiosyncratic representations tailored to the current needs of situated action. <...> [A] concept is a *simulator* that constructs an infinite set of specific simulations. (Barsalou et al., 2003, p. 521, emphasis added)

From the learner's or novice professional's perspective, this process is likely to involve quite similar epistemic actions to those which allow scientists to create novel concepts: abstraction, integration of knowledge and constraints from multiple domains, conceptualisation, etc. (see Nersessian, 2012). It is also likely to involve other kinds of complex epistemic mechanisms through which, as Hutchins (2012) argues, 'conceptual structures in the wild achieve and maintain organisation' (p. 314).

Table 17.2 provides a synthesis of the views described above. To summarise, the two main dimensions organise the kinds of conceptual constructs on which professional knowledge could operate and how it operates. They can be seen as:

- *Mental* constructs or *discourse* constructs
- *Abstract* knowledge constructs that function in a broad range of situations, *context-specific* constructs that function in specific groups or communities and are sensitive to the context or *situated* constructs that are assembled dynamically from different multimodal mental resources and environmental affordances in specific situations

Abstract, contextual and situated concepts also closely mirror three different views of transfer: model, module and modality (see Chap. 6).

On what kinds of conceptual constructs is fluent and knowledgeable performance likely to draw?

17.5 Actionable Concepts

In Chap. 6, we introduced a useful distinction made by Jim Greeno between formal and functional knowledge. Greeno (2012) suggests that formal concepts (or more exactly 'concepts that are used formally') should be considered as a subgroup of functional concepts (i.e. 'concepts that are used functionally') (p. 310). As discourse concepts could be considered to be a subgroup of mind concepts, so abstract 'fully fledged' concepts could be considered as a subgroup of contextual concepts and situated concepts. In short, the embodied mind does more work than the formal systems of language and articulated thinking could afford.

In his account of the relationship between generic skills and embodied competences, Beckett (2004) points out that formal and embodied (a.k.a. actionable) mind and discourse play important roles in professional learning and, indeed, emerge from each other.

> What it is to be a lawyer, or a mason, is largely to be immersed in socio-cultural experiences, which shape more immediate skill formation. These experiences are not merely of a single time and (work) place. An individual *inherits* and *modifies* 'knowing how' as her/his practice in the broad sense of a workplace (the 'craft' of lawyering, or masonry) as well as in the narrow sense (in 'reading' what a current employer or client specifically requires). (Beckett, 2004, p. 504, emphasis added)

Similarly, while some concepts can be seen as 'situated', they are simultaneously embedded in workplace contexts and in the sociocultural practices and discourses of professions – they are expressed in, and meshed with, 'contextual' and 'formal' ways of meaning-making.

Overviewing recent developments in research on concepts in cognitive psychology, Murphy and Hoffman (2012) observe that, for a long time, psychologists mainly studied concepts of *objects* rather than *events*, *situations* or more abstract entities, such as the aesthetic. And they did this by studying simplified concepts in constrained experimental settings. Nevertheless, even this kind of research generated many valuable insights into the richness and diversity of the human conceptual system. As Murphy and Hoffman conclude,

> There is no single type of concept or single way of learning and representing concepts. Indeed, it is remarkable that almost every study that has looked at individuals (rather than averaging over groups) has found that people differ in how they learn. <...> More and more often, formal models of category learning are turning to mixtures of different processes, with the hope that they can predict when one form of learning (rule testing, prototype extraction, exemplar learning) is preferred. (Murphy & Hoffman, 2012, p. 166)

Studies of professional learning and cognitive psychology are generally in agreement that if conceptual articulated knowledge matters (and it does), then there is a need to think more deeply about what shapes it takes and *how* it matters. It is a mistake to try to reduce this knowledge a priori to one particular kind or model.

Rather than trying to explain dynamic, complex processes of conceptual learning, change and transfer handicapped by subscription to a single view of concepts, we suggest considering the notion of 'actionable concepts'. These help us talk more clearly about the skill of drawing upon and enacting diverse conceptual resources – resources that span across discourse and mind, the abstract and the situated. The notion of actionable concepts can be applied in the case of concepts of objects and also to concepts of processes, actions, situations and events.

For example, Ingold (2011), drawing on similar dynamic qualities of skilful practice, speaks of the education of 'whole body intelligence' – an intelligence in motion that is capable of responding to a changing environment. He points out that learning cannot be understood as internalisation of a motor schema or imitation (in the sense of 'replication') of a schema 'housed in the minds of experts and expressed in bodily execution' (pp. 9–10). While learning requires repetitive practice,

> To copy, however, is not to replicate a pre-existing schema but to align observation of the
> model with action in a world suspended in movement. Any formal resemblance between
> the copy and the model is not given in advance but a horizon for attainment. <...> [I]n
> practice regardless of the number of times you make a move, each time is the first, every
> copy is original. (Ingold, 2011, p. 10)

This applies to knowledge that is strictly grounded in kinaesthetic experiences but
also to virtually any professional knowledge that informs professional sense-
making and action. For example, Philip (2011), drawing on Stuart Hall (1982),
notes that explanation or interpretation of ideological meanings cannot be understood from individual words, that is, from 'concepts' as isolated linguistic units.
Key pivotal concepts are mutually articulated in particular physical and conceptual
contexts and form distinct chains of meanings.

> ... the meanings of words and phrases exist in articulation (i.e., interconnectedness) with
> other images, stories, conversations, anecdotes, and concepts, into a 'distinctive set or chain
> of meanings' <...> Developing a well-elaborated and internally consistent system of
> thought involves learning to see key pivotal concepts in particular contexts and for these
> concepts to become mutually articulated. (Philip, 2011, pp. 303–305)

In short, not only the *contexts* but *the lines* along which sense-making and action
unfold form a part of conceptual understanding for action.[6]

This view of learning and conceptual understanding contrasts with the view of
conceptual understanding as an ability to grasp the abstract schema behind the
particularities of the situation and extract an individual concept from the messiness
of multiple meanings. Rather, it calls for a careful attention to how abstract
concepts become mutually articulated and meshed within professional meaning-
making.

17.6   A Case: Constructing Actionable Concepts

How do students learn to construct actionable concepts? We return to the conversation between the student teachers who are planning their Jigsaw activity. In the
lesson that these preservice teachers are designing, the primary school students are
to learn about the properties of materials. Following their lecturer's suggestion
(described briefly in a 'mini-unit'), they use a nappy (diaper) as the object with

---

[6] Philip (2011) gives an example: 'within contemporary free market arguments about education in
the United States, 'competition is good' is arguably articulated in a chain of meaning with notions
of privatizing public institutions, greater parental choice in where children go to school, the
reduction of taxes, merit pay for teachers, testing of students, and so on. Words and phrases,
such as 'competition is good' are also articulated with meanings from 'all phases of histories'
(Gramsci, 1971, p. 324). Therefore, when one makes sense about an issue at hand, words and
phrases that are used may vacillate between meanings that are differently nuanced or significantly
different in ideological positioning' (Philip, 2011, p. 303). Philip refers to the varied meanings that
a word or a phrase might take within different chains as 'multiplicity of meanings'.

which to demonstrate that different materials have different properties. The different properties of the materials in each layer in the nappy can be tested by the school students.

At this point, their focus is on how to shape an activity that will allow each of the working groups of children to report and share their results with the whole class.

Agi: Let's say we had um – this is . . . Say we cut it up ((*looks at her drawing of nappy*)) and we're doing the cross-section . . . And we can identify the three layers, maybe if we made like a big ((*hand gestures for* "*big*")) cross-section for the board. ((*all nod*)).

Agi: And then we'd – when we're talking at the beginning about the different sections, we could sort of stick them up on the board, big versions ((*shows with her hands*)).

Nat: Big nappy ((*laughs*)).

Agi: But after they've drawn, otherwise they'd copy it.

Jill: Yeah.

Agi: So we stick those up, and maybe we could literally give each section to the groups, and they write stuff on them. They come back as a class, stick them up, and they talk about all these things ((*hand gestures for all activities*)).

Nat: That's good.

Jill: Yeah, that's probably better 'cause otherwise they'll be copying.

Agi: ((*all smile*)) They'll still copy, but we can get them not to.

Jill: You know you'll have discussion about it, not just copying.

17.6.1   Creating Actionable Pedagogical Concepts for Teaching by Combining Concepts

In the initial part of this episode, presented earlier in Sect. 17.2, the teacher team tries to come up with a way for each of the school student groups to report their results back to the whole class. Each member of the team comes up with a different suggestion for a possible strategy. Nat describes her suggested strategy as 'give them a big butcher's paper' so the groups can write what they have found, stick it on the board and discuss with the whole class. Jill initially proposes: 'like in a table' and later 'Jigsaw kind of thing'.

Agi describes her suggestion as 'a big cross section for the board' showing separate layers of the nappy. So each section could be given to each team to write their results and then discuss with the whole class. Agi assembles her suggestion by selectively taking features from the previous suggestions from Nat and Jill and integrating and combining them together with the idea of using a diagram of a nappy. (In one of the preceding episodes in the planning, just few minutes previously, but not included in the transcript here, Agi described this as 'a good visual thing'.)

The three different pedagogical concepts – visual representation with some layered table-like qualities, Jigsaw and presentation to the whole class using butcher's paper – are combined into one pedagogical approach and blended with a specific material structure (a cross section of a nappy). That is, an actionable pedagogical concept has been created from a mix of everyday experience and formal concepts, not just formal concepts alone.[7]

What this demonstrates is that different pedagogical concepts are flexibly combined by the preservice teachers into one decision. These are not static concepts, but flexible resources from which actionable knowledge, appropriate to the situation, can be created.

These initial pedagogical plans are followed by a long discussion that goes back and forth. There are still arguments for Jigsaw – as a good technique – and against its use, because it takes too much time. And it is not very clear what Agi is suggesting. The student teachers nevertheless decide to write into the lesson plan what they have already agreed. After about 20 min, once the other activities are in the plan, they return to this point about how results will be reported back to the class. Agi again proposes that the student groups need to report back to the whole class, thus they need a big image of a cross section of a nappy, with separate sections. Nat asks why.

Nat   Yeah ((nods)) What? ((suddenly realizes that she doesn't understand what Agi has said)).

Agi   I've got a nappy to give you ((all laugh)). Okay, I really don't know what the nappy is gonna look like ((draws now)), but okay, we've got like – we kind of make it like a hamburger. Like that. So then (...) umm these are separate bits of paper, so put together, we stick them up to the board – but I umm (thinks) – 'cause we need to get somehow – they need to report back to the group ((looks at mini-unit)) what they found.

Jill   So why 're they not Jigsawing it?

Agi   (Ohhhh) ((shakes her head agreeing)) but that's – oh, oh, oh! ((remembers)) (the progressive brainstorming!) It's not progressive brainstorming.

Nat   Oh oh ((remembers)) we did it!

Jill   We never did Jigsaw before and (I'd love about it) ((all laugh)).

Agi   This is not Jigsawing, // but ((Nat interrupts)).

Nat   // We did it in TESOL.

Jill   Was it in Professional Experiences though?

Agi   No.

Jill   Ah.

Agi   This is the – let's say this is the umm // like ((tries to draw something on paper but seems not very sure what to draw and Nat interrupts)).

Nat   I like how we go, I can see what you're doing ((all laugh)).

---

[7] In Stella Vosniadou's experiments on students' conceptions of the shape of the earth, similar kinds of combinations or blends – mixing formal knowledge and everyday experiences – are called 'synthetic models' (Vosniadou & Brewer, 1994). They are regarded as something transitional that students hold or create on the spot as they don't have the right framework, as a kind of immature knowledge. But looking at the professional context, such combination/blending may well be one of the essential capacities that underpin professional sense-making and creativity – an ability to see the opportunity points and combine/blend structures and mechanisms and coordinate related actions.

17.6.2 How Actionable Concepts Are Grounded in Experiences and Actions

The experiences and pedagogical concepts expressed through actions have a prominent role in the team's discussion. In the previous episode, Nat describes the group presentation by explaining in detail, and gesturing, what 'the kids' will do, but she never labels her suggested strategy as a 'presentation' nor does she use any similar abstract concept to convey the gist of the strategy. Similarly, Agi proposes a blended version of earlier suggested strategies by plainly describing steps, resources and classroom arrangements. Initially, she does not have a label for this, but when the team comes back to it after about 20 min, she suddenly dubs her proposed strategy as 'progressive brainstorm' – without really being sure if this *is* a progressive brainstorm. The concept has clear experiential roots, as Nat immediately picks it up: 'Oh Oh!... We did it in [a] TESOL [tutorial]'.

Nat, who until recently looked completely puzzled when trying to make sense of Agi's idea, now reacts: '*I like* how we *go*, *I can see* what you're doing'. Being able to link Agi's initial abstract description of actions with a compact familiar concept and then link to her embodied experience and affective states ('I *like* how we *go*') makes a powerful bridge.

What does this show about transfer? The 'progressive brainstorm' label helps Nat to bridge from her previous experience of the enacted concept to a new projected experience. From the transfer point of view (Chap. 6), Nat constructed her actionable understanding by transferring her grounded experience of the concept from situation to situation, not actually from the abstract concept 'progressive brainstorm' to a new concrete situation. What this suggests is that traditional pedagogies and research that focus on how to help students transfer abstract knowledge and skills to new specific situations may overlook an important point about how transfer (and learning) of actionable concepts actually works from the learners' perspective: not from an abstract principle to a concrete situation, but from one situation/context to a new situation/context, building new connections to (and via) what might be called an abstract principle or 'concept'. Thus, it invites a rethinking of transfer of professional conceptual understanding as transfer from one context to another, as Wagner (2006; 2010) and Lobato (2012) suggest (see Sect. 6.7).

17.6.3 How Are Actionable Concepts Linked to Language?

Do language and concepts – as *discourse* constructs – play any role in constructing actionable knowledge? Our analysis of this and other episodes of preservice teachers' planning gives some valuable insights into three aspects: (a) links between actionable concepts and articulation of actions; (b) some powerful communicative functions of formal linguistic labels and (c) multimodal multi-experiential nature of conceptual understanding.

Actionable Concept as Action: In most of the observed situations, all the preservice teacher team members start their constructive work from descriptions of activities and specific actions and then attach to them a pedagogical label like 'progressive brainstorm' or 'working scientifically'. In many situations, these teachers use pedagogical, and even disciplinary, terms to label actions that have already been described in everyday language or in sketches, gestures and other actions that embrace those concepts. Rather than starting from the normative concepts – i.e. 'scientific inquiry', 'validity' and 'progressive brainstorm' – and moving on to the design of activities, preservice teachers do this other way around. That is, the conceptual vocabulary follows perception and follows action. In contrast, animated everyday vocabulary, drawings and body language are used to express and generate their ideas. For example, Jill, and later Agi, describe 'surface learning' as 'copy, copy, copy' with gestures of grabbing a worksheet from someone else. 'Instructivist or transmissionist pedagogy' appears as 'tell them', and a 'constructivist approach' is encapsulated in 'come up' (with ideas). Agi describes the representation of a cross section using the metaphor of 'a big hamburger'. Many pedagogical ideas are never expressed in professional vocabulary: 'show', 'tell' and 'being at the front' persist as pointers to instructivist teaching; 'come up', 'discuss' and 'small group' are used consistently to refer to constructivist learning. However, the lesson plans they create are well grounded in constructivist approaches; they are well designed and well written up. In essence, they draw on a set of experiential mental resources that have a family resemblance to diSessa's (2000, 2002) social p-prims. In recent work we have referred to these as *pedagogical* p-prims (Kali, Goodyear, & Markauskaite, 2011; Markauskaite & Goodyear, 2014).

Concepts as Communicative Devices: Nevertheless, our data suggest two evident roles for linguistic concepts and labels in *constructing* jointly actionable knowledge. That is, the label helps: (a) to *see* the *structure* of a concept that might be obscured by other details and (b) to *feel* a concept as a *multimodal whole*. These two roles are almost opposites, but they are essential parts of the construct 'concept'. Agi's abstract explanation of how she suggests they organise the (student) groups' presentations to the whole class does not make full sense for Nat until Agi gives a label to the activity that she has already described in detail – a 'progressive brainstorm'. First, the label activates Nat's TESOL experiences and now she also 'can see' where Agi 'is going'. Similarly, the term 'Jigsaw' activates Nat's experiences of learning in a Jigsaw situation: 'not procrastinating' and 'being tested'. That is, on the one hand, Nat feels 'conceptually present' – experiencing Jigsaw and progressive brainstorm. On the other hand, Nat is now able to make specific distinctions in her less articulated experience and 'sees' properties of the situations in which she experienced Jigsaw and progressive brainstorm (i.e. structure) that can be transferred to a new situation – e.g. 'there is a test' that prevents procrastination. These pedagogical concepts have features of what Barsalou (1999, 2009) called 'situated concepts' (see also Barsalou et al., 2003; Barton & Hamilton, 2005). They include amodal symbolic structures and also situated (modal) simulations that include conceptual properties relevant to the situation, information about the background and possible actions associated with the goal and introspective states, including cognitive operations, evaluations and emotions (see Chap. 6). Nat is perceptually and conceptually 'there' – within the concept.

Nat   This is good, this is good. Good job, Agi.
Agi   It's from TESOL, it's a TESOL thing.
Jill   I could swear we did this in (professional string). What was the other – blah blah, you know how we did.
Nat   No.
Agi   No, we didn't do it.
Nat   We've never done progressive.
Jill   But we did something.
Agi   Let's write.
Jill   OK!

Multimodal Multi-experiential Concepts: Concepts linked to linguistic labels are not exact copies of past experiences nor are they abstract, idealised symbolic structures. Rather, they are generalised selective and multimodal experiences of similar phenomena from multiple situations – multimodal, multi-experiential concepts. Nat initially reacts to 'Jigsaw' using one generalised affective state: 'I like Jigsaw activities'. This is followed by activating other modalities of her experience, such as cognitive states 'it wasn't just procrastination' and actions 'being tested'. These experiences are not necessarily exact, but are abstracted from multiple events, and are selective. For example, Jill feels that she had an experience similar to being engaged in a 'progressive brainstorm' in her Professional Experiences course. But Nat and Agi contradict this: it was in the TESOL course. Nevertheless, even after discussion, Jill mutters: 'I could swear we did this. . .'. Not having the exact experience of 'progressive brainstorm' in TESOL does not stop Jill from feeling that she has similar experiential understandings. Jill's latter statement reflects the fact that such experiential concepts are multimodal and at least partly overlapping. It is not about precision, but about having sufficient (selected) related experiences that permit a simulation of a feeling of 'being conceptually' there. Agi, in fact, never explains if her proposed pedagogical strategy is a 'progressive brainstorm' or 'not'. (The pedagogical literature proposes many variants of this pedagogical strategy.) But once some common ground and links to shared experiences are established, the team successfully uses the label 'progressive brainstorm'.

The importance of shared normative professional language is undeniable. Yet, this role is different from the role given to language and professional discourse in the 'threshold concept' literature. Linguistic labels are not attached to purely abstract constructs (a.k.a. symbolic structures of concepts), but are much richer: grounded in, and generated from, a variety of situated experiential constructs. The preservice teachers' minds operate on constructs that are more likely to have the form of grounded (modal) 'situated concepts' that share mechanisms with perception and action (Barsalou, 1999, 2003, 2009) than they are to take the form of autonomous (amodal) 'symbolic concepts' that have their own representations, independent of perception and operating according to different principles from those of action. Linguistic labels are not constructs that 'kick off' certain sequences of symbolic operations in teachers' minds. They are constructs and events that activate much richer selective simulation of past and projected experiences. In these terms, linguistic labels as well as idealised normative patterns ('theoretical patterns') that underpin concepts are 'bridges' between the past, and new projected experiences, abstracted (or perhaps integrated) and concrete, that share similar conceptual and contextual properties – i.e. grounded, situated concepts.

> A fundamental problem in situated action is mapping action effectively into the world, and an intriguing possibility is that the conceptual system develops to facilitate this mapping. In particular, ad hoc and goal-derived categories develop to bind roles in action with instantiations in the environment. As systems of these mappings develop, the conceptual system becomes organised around the action–environment interface. (Barsalou, 2003, p. 522)

If we accept this view – and we do – normative concepts in preservice teachers' thinking are not an abstract 'infrastructure' on which sophisticated pedagogical/ professional thinking runs, but compact constructs for communicating, making bridges across diverse experiences, modalities, situations and frames of reference and integrating these and other otherwise fragmented pieces of articulated and intuitive understanding. What is most important here is that much productive actionable thinking (simulation) is done using preconceptual, in classical terms, grounded constructs that have traditionally been dismissed as 'naïve knowledge'. For example, 'naïve pedagogy' and 'expert tacit knowledge' are often regarded as two distinct ways of organising conceptual knowledge and understanding that have to undergo conceptual discontinuation – abandoning the former. Alternatively, they can be viewed as a constitutive mesh of diverse experiential and linguistic resources, constructed through integration and restructuring rather than replacement (see also Markauskaite & Goodyear, 2014).

Much that we see in successful performance is underpinned by combinations of different conceptual constructs – including actions related to them – rather than by the consistent deployment of abstract concepts.

17.7   Actionable Concepts as Concepts That Mean and Matter

To summarise, fluent professional performance is most likely to draw on different kinds of conceptual constructs and different ways of constructing actionable conceptualisations – spanning across discourse and mind, abstract notions and situated meanings.

We can take this argument a little further by drawing on an observation from DeLanda (2012) that there are two different meanings of the word 'meaning'. This can help tease apart two rather different notions of 'conceptual knowledge' and what it takes to become a resourceful practitioner. There is meaning as 'signification' and meaning as 'significance'. In the first case, the word 'meaning' is used in *linguistic* terms to refer to semantic content; in the second case, the word 'meaning' is used in *pragmatic* (actionable) terms to refer to the relevance or importance of the perceived world – to the perception of capacity to make a difference. In the first case, a grasp of meaning is inseparable from a conscious mastery of language; in the second case, it is inseparable from perception of affordances for action in the world – a capacity to see what makes a difference.

Figure 17.1 captures the relationship between significance and signification of the concepts. Concepts that have low significance and low signification are usually embodied in habitual patterns of professional action – they do not require much additional reworking before deployment and usually work well in routine situations. Concepts that have low significance, but high signification, are rich in semantic meaning – but do not have much practical value in the practitioner's meaning-making and actions. Theoretical concepts and sociopolitical concepts that practitioners know, but do not enact or enact without much attention to situational details, have this quality. Concepts that have high significance, but low signification, are usually expressed in the practitioner's fine-tuned perception and attuned skill – they require attentive engagement with whatever the unfolding situation brings. Such concepts are usually learnt through apprenticeship by observing and imitating rather than by being told and explained. Complex kinaesthetic concepts usually have this quality. Concepts that have high significance and high signification require active engagement with their semantic meanings. Such meanings are not fully given, rather semantic meaning has to be (re)constructed or (re)discovered through enacting meaning within work. Such concepts are usually encountered in knowledge-demanding novel professional challenges and in joint inter-professional work.

In Fig. 17.1, dark arrows indicate the path of how conceptual learning is traditionally understood in professional education: students initially learn formal theoretical concepts (high in signification, but low in significance) as well as skills

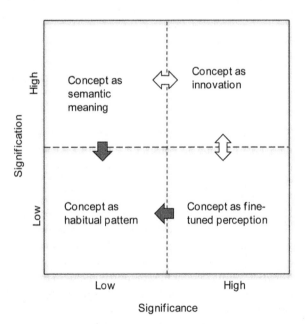

Fig. 17.1 Constructing actionable conceptualisations: relationship between significance and signification

(low in signification, but high in significance). Such learning may initially require apprenticeship and reflection to link theory with practice, but after some time, theory and skill become meshed together into habitual patterns of performance which can be deployed as needed without much thinking. Expertise is habit that neither challenges experts' perception nor requires articulated thinking. The white arrows indicate the view of learning and knowledgeable action as educating intelligent perception. Concepts are never fully given in the mind or in the world; they are (re)enacted by (re)creating situated conceptualisations of their meanings. Such learning is not an event, rather it is a process (a practice) of simultaneously constructing shared meanings and fine-tuning situated perception.

Dominant views of concepts as 'classifiers' of the world into predefined categories, or as 'recurring patterns' of actions that underpin professional habits, tend to introduce an unproductive and misleading notion of conceptual knowledge and its relationship to action. The understanding of how students learn conceptual knowledge, and teaching them to do so, requires a much more action-oriented and meaning-oriented notion – an understanding of the concepts in terms of a capacity to actively engage with conceptual work and construct meaningful, actionable conceptualisations of the situation. The key educational question this raises is what teachers of new professionals should emphasise when talking about concepts: stressing their fluidity and potential or their 'frozen' stable forms and canonical meanings.

Further, it is important to note that the movement from abstract (formal) to situated (functional) concepts is not simply movement in one dimension – from local to general knowledge or from general to local. It is movement along at least two intertwined lines: discourse and meaning (signification and significance).

A skill to construct situated conceptualisations is inseparable from perception and action and couples internal meaning and sense-making with the external world and action. What comes next is that the human conceptual system should also perform a *coordination* of context – concept – actions. Such coordination involves a different kind of knowledge and draws upon different kinds of mental constructs from the traditional concepts that are held to allow people to deal readily with phenomena encountered in the world.

DeVries and Triplett (2000) capture this difference nicely:

> ...*direct knowledge* does not have to be achieved or arrived at by inferring, pondering, sorting of evidence, calling forth memories, comparing data, or using other *constructive cognitive processes*. All it has to do is *simply be there*. It requires only the person's *attention*, if even that, in order to be knowledge for that person. As such, *it is given*. And the rest of one's knowledge, the *indirectly known*, has to be built up from what is given by the sorts of cognitive processes just noted. (DeVries & Triplett, 2000, p. xix, emphasis added)

This indirect knowing draws upon additional kinds of mental constructs – for inferring, pondering, sorting of evidence, etc. – that make knowledge creation possible. We call them *epistemic constructs*. Many of these constructs feature in the resourceful mind, and many of them are firmly intertwined with everyday meaning-making. Nevertheless, they often tend to go unnoticed – neither recognised nor analysed.

In the literature that takes innovation and knowledge construction seriously, we see a growing awareness of the importance of cognitive and discursive processes in knowledge creation (e.g. Clement, 2008; Damsa, Kirschner, Andriessen, Erkens, & Sins, 2010; Engeström, Nummijoki, & Sannino, 2012; Hutchins, 2012; Nersessian, 2008a). However, even in this literature, these epistemic constructs are usually set apart from the rest of cognitive and discursive work and rarely, if ever, are seen as being an integral part of the same conceptual system that produces situated conceptualisations. In short, knowledge for understanding the world and knowledge for creating knowledge tend to be separated.

We explore this claim, and argue against this unproductive division, in Chap. 18.

References

Barsalou, L. W. (2003). Situated simulation in the human conceptual system. *Language and Cognitive Processes, 18*(5–6), 513–562. doi:10.1080/01690960344000026.

Barsalou, L. W. (1999). Perceptual symbol systems. *Behavioral and Brain Sciences, 22*, 577–609.

Barsalou, L. W. (2009). Situating concepts. In P. Robbins & M. Aydede (Eds.), *The Cambridge handbook of situated cognition* (pp. 236–263). Cambridge, MA: Cambridge University Press.

Barsalou, L. W., Breazeal, C., & Smith, L. (2007). Cognition as coordinated non-cognition. *Cognitive Processing, 8*(2), 79–91. doi:10.1007/s10339-007-0163-1.

Barsalou, L. W., Kyle Simmons, W., Barbey, A. K., & Wilson, C. D. (2003). Grounding conceptual knowledge in modality-specific systems. *Trends in Cognitive Sciences, 7*(2), 84–91. doi:10.1016/s1364-6613(02)00029-3.

Barton, D., & Hamilton, M. (2005). Literacy, reification and the dynamics of social interaction. In D. Barton & K. Tusting (Eds.), *Beyond communities of practice: Language, power and social context* (pp. 14–35). Cambridge, UK: Cambridge University Press.

Beckett, D. (2004). Embodied competence and generic skill: The emergence of inferential understanding. *Educational Philosophy and Theory, 36*(5), 497–508. doi:10.1111/j.1469-5812.2004.086_1.x.

Brown, D. E., & Hammer, D. (2008). Conceptual change in physics. In S. Vosniadou (Ed.), *International handbook of research on conceptual change* (pp. 127–154). New York, NY: Routledge.

Bruner, J. S., Goodnow, J. J., & Austin, G. A. (1956). *A study of thinking*. New York, NY: John Wiley & Sons.

Chi, M. (2005). Commonsense conceptions of emergent processes: Why some misconceptions are robust. *Journal of the Learning Sciences, 14*(2), 161–199.

Chi, M. T. H., & Roscoe, R. (2002). The processes and challenges of conceptual change. In M. Limon & L. Mason (Eds.), *Reconsidering conceptual change: Issues in theory and practice* (pp. 3–27). Dordrecht, The Netherlands: Kluwer.

Clement, J. J. (2008). *Creative model construction in scientists and students: The role of imagery, analogy, and mental simulation*. Dordrecht, The Netherlands: Springer.

Damsa, C. I., Kirschner, P. A., Andriessen, J. E. B., Erkens, G., & Sins, P. H. M. (2010). Shared epistemic agency: An empirical study of an emergent construct. *Journal of the Learning Sciences, 19*(2), 143–186.

DeLanda, M. (2012). Chapter 2. Interview with Manuel DeLanda. In R. Dolphijn & I. van der Tuin (Eds.), *New materialism: Interviews and cartographies* (pp. 38–47). Ann Arbor, MI: Open Humanities Press.

DeVries, W., & Triplett, T. (2000). *Knowledge, mind, and the given: Reading Wilfrid Sellars's 'empiricism and the philosophy of mind'*. Indianapolis, IN: Hackett.

diSessa, A. (1988). Knowledge in pieces. In G. Forman & P. Pufall (Eds.), *Constructivism in the computer age* (pp. 49–70). Hillsdale, NJ: Lawrence Erlbaum Associates.

diSessa, A. A. (2002). Why "conceptual ecology" is a good idea. In M. Limon & L. Mason (Eds.), *Reconsidering conceptual change: Issues in theory and practice* (pp. 28–60). Dordrecht, The Netherlands: Kluwer.

diSessa, A. A. (2000). Does the mind know the difference between the physical and social worlds? In L. Nucci, G. B. Saxe, & E. Turiel (Eds.), *Culture, thought, and development* (pp. 141–166). Mahwah, NJ: Lawrence Erlbaum Associates.

diSessa, A., & Sherin, B. L. (1998). What changes in conceptual change? *International Journal of Science Education, 20*(10), 1155–1191.

Elqayam, S., & Evans, J. S. (2011). Subtracting "ought" from "is": Descriptivism versus normativism in the study of human thinking. *Behavioral and Brain Sciences, 34*(5), 233–248. doi:10.1017/S0140525X1100001X.

Engeström, Y., Nummijoki, J., & Sannino, A. (2012). Embodied germ cell at work: Building an expansive concept of physical mobility in home care. *Mind, Culture, and Activity, 19*(3), 287–309. doi:10.1080/10749039.2012.688177.

Engeström, Y., & Sannino, A. (2012). Concept formation in the wild. *Mind, Culture, and Activity, 19*(3), 201–206. doi:10.1080/10749039.2012.690813.

Goldstone, R. L., Hills, T. T., & Day, S. B. (2010). Concept formation. In I. B. Weiner & W. E. Craighead (Eds.), *The Corsini encyclopedia of psychology* (pp. 381–383). New York, NY: John Wiley & Sons.

Gramsci, A. (1971). *Prison notebooks*. New York, NY: International Publishers.

Greeno, J. G. (2012). Concepts in activities and discourses. *Mind, Culture, and Activity, 19*(3), 310–313. doi:10.1080/10749039.2012.691934.

Gupta, A., Hammer, D., & Redish, E. F. (2010). The case for dynamic models of learners' ontologies in physics. *Journal of the Learning Sciences, 19*(3), 285–321.

Hall, S. (1982). The rediscovery of "ideology": Return of the repressed in media studies. In M. Gurevitch, T. Bennet, J. Curran, & J. Wollacott (Eds.), *Culture, society and the media* (pp. 56–90). London, UK: Methuen.

Hall, R., & Seidel Horn, I. (2012). Talk and conceptual change at work: Adequate representation and epistemic stance in a comparative analysis of statistical consulting and teacher workgroups. *Mind, Culture, and Activity, 19*(3), 240–258. doi:10.1080/10749039.2012. 688233.

Holyoak, K. J., & Morrison, R. G. (Eds.). (2005). *The Cambridge handbook of thinking and reasoning*. Cambridge, MA: Cambridge University Press.

Hutchins, E. (2012). Concepts in practice as sources of order. *Mind, Culture, and Activity, 19*(3), 314–323. doi:10.1080/10749039.2012.694006.

Ingold, T. (2011). *Redrawing anthropology: Materials, movements, lines*. Farnham, UK: Ashgate.

Kali, Y., Goodyear, P., & Markauskaite, L. (2011). Researching design practices and design cognition: Contexts, experiences and pedagogical knowledge-in-pieces. *Learning, Media and Technology, 36*(2), 129–149. doi:10.1080/17439884.2011.553621.

Keil, F. C., & Silberstein, C. S. (1998). Schooling and the acquisition of theoretical knowledge. In D. R. Olson & N. Torrance (Eds.), *The handbook of education and human development* (pp. 621–645). Malden, MA: Blackwell.

Lobato, J. (2012). The actor-oriented transfer perspective and its contributions to educational research and practice. *Educational Psychologist, 47*(3), 232–247. doi:10.1080/00461520.2012. 693353.

Markauskaite, L., & Goodyear, P. (2014). Tapping into the mental resources of teachers' working knowledge: Insights into the generative power of intuitive pedagogy. *Learning, Culture and Social Interaction, 3*(4), 237–251. doi:http://dx.doi.org/10.1016/j.lcsi.2014.01.001.

Murphy, G., & Hoffman, A. B. (2012). Concepts. In K. Frankish & W. Ramsey (Eds.), *The Cambridge handbook of cognitive science* (pp. 151–170). Cambridge, UK: Cambridge University Press.

Nersessian, N. J. (2008a). *Creating scientific concepts*. Cambridge, MA: MIT Press.

Nersessian, N. J. (2008b). Mental modeling in conceptual change. In S. Vosniadou (Ed.), *International handbook of research on conceptual change* (pp. 391–416). New York: Routledge.

Nersessian, N. J. (2012). Engineering concepts: The interplay between concept formation and modeling practices in bioengineering sciences. *Mind, Culture, and Activity, 19*(3), 222–239. doi:10.1080/10749039.2012.688232.

Philip, T. M. (2011). An "ideology in pieces" approach to studying change in teachers' sensemaking about race, racism, and racial justice. *Cognition and Instruction, 29*(3), 297–329. doi:10.1080/07370008.2011.583369.

Roth, W.-M., & Duit, R. (2003). Emergence, flexibility, and stabilization of language in a physics classroom. *Journal of Research in Science Teaching, 40*(9), 869–897. doi:10.1002/tea.10114.

Säljö, R. (1999). Concepts, cognition and discourses: From mental structures to discursive tools. In W. Schnotz, S. Vosniadou, & M. Carretero (Eds.), *New perspectives on conceptual change* (pp. 81–90). Amsterdam, The Netherlands: Pergamon Press.

Schön, D. A. (1963). *Displacement of concepts*. London, UK: Tavistock.

Smith, L. B. (2005). Cognition as a dynamic system: Principles from embodiment. *Developmental Review, 25*(3–4), 278–298. doi:10.1016/j.dr.2005.11.001.

Vosniadou, S. (Ed.). (2008/2013). *International handbook of research on conceptual change*, (1st and 2nd eds.) New York, NY: Routledge.

Vosniadou, S. (2013). Conceptual change in learning and instruction: The framework theory approach. In S. Vosniadou (Ed.), *International handbook of research on conceptual change*. New York, NY: Routledge.

Vosniadou, S., & Brewer, W. F. (1994). Mental models of the day/night cycle. *Cognitive Science, 18*(1), 123–183. doi:10.1207/s15516709cog1801_4.

Vygotsky, L. S. (1978). *Mind in society: The development of higher psychological processes*. Cambridge, MA: Harvard University Press.

Vygotsky, L. S. (1986). *Thought and language*. Cambridge, MA: MIT Press.

Wagner, J. F. (2006). Transfer in pieces. *Cognition and Instruction, 24*(1), 1–71.

Wagner, J. F. (2010). A transfer-in-pieces consideration of the perception of structure in the transfer of learning. *Journal of the Learning Sciences, 19*(4), 443–479.

Chapter 18
Epistemic Resourcefulness for Actionable Knowing

Agi: Have you ever pulled apart a nappy?

Jill: No, I haven't.

Agi: Does it come apart? Does a nappy come apart? ((...)) ((Turns to Research Assistant)). You've probably never cut one in half. Like, are there very distinct layers?

RA: No.

Jill: What happens if we (...) can't find the layers?

Agi: Well, we've got to do this prior to ... Ok, I will, next time (...) we come together (...) I'll bring a nappy. (()) So, nappy ((writes it down)), cause it's kind of – if we can't get distinctive layers or if they can't see it ... [4 seconds].

> (From preservice teachers' lesson planning conversation trying to design a lesson about material properties. Slightly abbreviated)

18.1 Understanding Epistemic Resources

To illustrate our main arguments in this chapter, we draw on the same empirical source as we used in Chap. 17 – that is, the team of preservice teachers who are planning an inquiry-based science lesson for some primary school children. In this chapter, the focus shifts from their discussion about Jigsaw groups to the core subject matter of the lesson they are planning. The lesson is about properties of materials, how properties of materials are important in everyday life and how to 'work scientifically'. The preservice teachers have been given a brief 'mini-unit' by their education lecturer. This includes a short description of possible activities and suggests using a baby's nappy (diaper) as the object with which to demonstrate how different material properties are utilised in the design of everyday things. The 'mini-unit' also suggests to the preservice teachers that they could use a worksheet with a diagram in the lesson activities they are planning. The rest of the lesson details are left up to the preservice teachers to design.

What kind of mental resources do these preservice teachers need in order to design and teach this lesson successfully in a classroom which they have not yet seen, using a nappy which they have never cut apart and a worksheet that they still

L. Markauskaite, P. Goodyear, *Epistemic Fluency and Professional Education*, Professional and Practice-based Learning 14, DOI 10.1007/978-94-007-4369-4_18

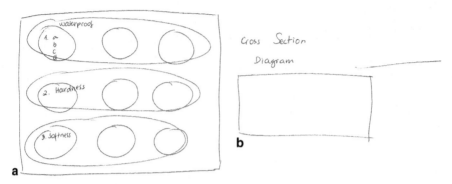

Fig. 18.1 The initial sketch of the worksheet (**a**) and the final worksheet (**b**)

need to create? Or let's make it simpler: what kind of mental resources does one need to translate the idea of using a nappy, and the diagram of a nappy, into knowledgeable teacher actions?

One might argue that the preservice teachers need conceptual resources for identifying the underpinning pedagogical concepts – pedagogical knowledge or pedagogical content knowledge, in Shulman's (1986) terms. The members of the team, it seems, have this kind of knowledge or at least have sufficient functional[1] mental resources to successfully recognise the rationale for the suggested pedagogical techniques. For example, after reading the instruction: 'Students should add comments about the properties to each layer of their diagram', one preservice teacher immediately identifies the underpinning pedagogical rationale and says: 'it's a good visual thing'.

However, the team's design conversation begins with a very chaotic exchange, during which Agi starts sketching the worksheet (Fig. 18.1a).

Agi: Okay, I'll do it, okay. Here is your nappy (. . .) ((Agi draws it now, Nat laughs and asks Jill to look at the nappy as well)). So they [students] look at it, and they draw their nappy. Okay, it's not really what a nappy looks like ((laughs)). They draw their nappy. ((. . .)) So that's gonna be a (worksheet). The second one – don't inquire now how it works – there's the second worksheet, and they've got three tests. ((. . .)) And so they've got four – I don't know how many layers in a nappy. This is layer A, B, C, D. So then they test A, B, C, D, for . . . [4 seconds] I don't know what it is, like hard err waterproof I think. Maybe we can divide them into groups. Maybe so, group 1 // test. . .

Despite this apparently chaotic start, after just two short meetings, the team ends up with a carefully designed inquiry-based lesson and teaching materials and, later, with a lesson which is judged to be taught excellently. Their worksheet goes through numerous revisions, but at the end it turns out to be a blank page on which the primary school students will draw their cross sections (Fig. 18.1b).

---

[1] Note, we are not arguing that the team members have abstract (formal) conceptual knowledge. They do not express their understanding in any normative language. However, they have sufficient contextual (functional) knowledge to be able to see the pedagogical value of visual representations in this activity.

Agi:	We need to go through it one more time. So we need worksheet // wise.
Agi:	We need a cross-section worksheet for them just to draw it on *((writes it in her notes))*. It just needs basically to be =
Jill:	=A box – with a name tag.
Agi:	Yep. The name and a title *((see Agi's drawing.))*.

What kinds of mental resources allow the preservice teachers to move through a series of confusions, uncertainties and decisions to reach the final successful practical solution? In short, how do preservice teachers bridge between the 'abstract concept' – *a visual diagram that is useful for learning* – and the 'actionable concept' – *how students will learn about the material properties by using a diagram*?

In Chap. 17 we explained that actionable concepts are not stable and that conceptual understanding is not something that is constructed from pre-existing constructs by a simple replication process: it is *assembled* by a knower. This means that a human conceptual system that supports action does not just have domain-related mental constructs – abstract, contextual or situated concepts – that allow a person to make sense from, and act in, the socio-material world. The conceptual system also has to have the kinds of mental constructs that allow the person to *build knowledge* – to make sense of, and act in, *the knowledge world* itself. In short, the human conceptual system is unlikely to function without a rich array of *epistemic* and *meta-epistemic constructs* that assemble those (abstract, contextual and situated) concepts into an ecologically rational and sensible decision that supports competent action. Such constructs allow a person to align their existing conceptual understandings with social and material situations and actions.

In fact, there is plenty of evidence to show that, for making conceptual knowledge actionable, professionals need far more than just abstract concepts and far more than just the skills involved in habitual actions. They need *epistemic resourcefulness* in order to make *concepts for and through action*.

In Sect. 18.2 we examine epistemic resources as constructs in discourse and in the mind, mirroring the treatment of conceptual resources in Chap. 17. We bring them together at the end of Sect. 18.2 by synthesising some theoretical accounts in which ways of thinking combine with ways of acting. Section 18.3 looks at epistemic resources as *actionable*. Actionable knowledge in professional work involves both multiple, changing, interacting (sometimes conflicting) framings of the world. It also involves multiple modalities. So in Sect. 18.3 we look more closely at epistemic actions and the integrated involvement of multiple senses – the body – in epistemic action. Section 18.4 is where we start to bring the epistemic and conceptual together, with a dynamic view on conceptual learning. Thereafter, our main concern is to develop some arguments about framing: looking at how the preservice teachers in our study shift and combine frames in developing their designs for the class. Section 18.5 looks at framing as (a) the imposition of rigid structures or (b) a more flexible, emergent process. It uses an analysis of the preservice teachers' framing and reframing of their work as 'following instructions' or 'sense-making' to show their epistemic resourcefulness in action. Finally, Sect. 18.6 returns to the epistemic and conceptual dynamic. It looks at epistemic resourcefulness in terms of a coordination of diverse ways of knowing and a simultaneous combination of diverse kinds of knowledge.

18.2   Epistemic Resources in Discourse and the Mind

The broad field of social, psychological and cognitive epistemology has created a 'world' of epistemic constructs that is, in nature, very similar, almost parallel, to the 'world' of concepts. Table 18.1 captures the essence. It mirrors Table 17.1.

18.2.1   Epistemic Knowledge as Discourse

Sociologists remind us that every discipline can be characterised by a certain formal *episteme*. Each discipline has a distinctive conceptual structure, asks particular kinds of questions, collects only some kinds of data and formulates knowledge in its own way (Donald, 2002; Kuhn, 1981; Maton, 2014; Schwab, 1962, 1978). As Schwab (1962, 1978) puts it, disciplines have their own 'syntactical structures' – orders of method, pathways of inquiry or patterns of procedure that represent ways that they use their concepts to attain their goals and create knowledge. In short, the inquiry process, as a social phenomenon, has a certain formal pattern or structure, and mastery of *abstract* epistemic constructs is an essential skill for those who work in the domain. This view is reflected, in various forms, in contemporary sociological claims about disciplinary knowledge as 'socially powerful knowledge' (Wheelahan, 2010) and the role of legitimation codes in education (Maton, 2014). As Wheelahan (2010) says:

> ... all workers need access to the theoretical knowledge that underpins their occupational field of practice if they are to participate in debates and controversies within field ... they need to be able to access *decontextualised disciplinary systems of meaning* if they are to select and apply contextually specific applications of that knowledge. (Wheelahan, 2010, pp. 2–3, emphasis added)

> ... [the] disciplinary basis of academic, and vocational/professional qualifications needs to be restored and made explicit. (op. cit., p. 16)

Table 18.1 Overview of the nature of epistemic constructs

Generality	Nature	
	Discourse	Mind
Abstract epistemic constructs	Formal 'epistemes' and other epistemic systems of disciplinary fields	Epistemic beliefs and other stable model-like mental constructs
Contextual epistemic constructs	Epistemic practices in specific knowledge settings	Epistemological frames and other coherent context-sensitive generalisations from experience
Situated epistemic resources	Epistemic agency in individual and collective knowledge work	Epistemic resources activated moment-to-moment in epistemic activity

From this perspective, a teacher who chooses to use visual representations in her lesson should understand the underpinning cognitive theories of visual information processing, or a teacher who chooses to design an inquiry-based lesson should have a good grasp of psychological, social and cultural theories that underpin this pedagogical approach. Most importantly, such a teacher should have a foundational understanding of how knowledge for teaching is produced. For example, Janet Donald (2002) claims that professionals in education draw on a method of inquiry that relies on a sense of the relevant context parameters and on well-developed representations of knowledge and action schemas:

> Experts recognize patterns and solve problems efficiently and effectively. They have a sense of the context, select the appropriate information, recognize organizing principles, and verify their inferences. They are equipped with representations and thinking strategies or action schemas for applying these representations to problems. (Donald, 2002, p. 25)

Laurillard (2012) argues that teaching, as a profession which deals with unstructured problems, should draw on the epistemological foundations and methodologies of 'design science' and should use principles of inquiry, knowledge building and sharing similar to those used in other design professions, such as architecture, engineering or computer science.

Other accounts express a more *contextual* epistemic view. They shift the focus of epistemic knowledge to the application of various disciplined ways of knowledge building and to modern methods of technological innovation. The constructs that underpin such *epistemic practices* range from quite generic epistemic schemes that are shared across disciplines and settings – such as systems methodologies (Checkland & Poulter, 2006; Checkland & Scholes, 1999; Collins, 2011b) – to quite local epistemic understandings embedded in the practices of workplace and organisational settings. Examples include such things as methods for setting up an experimental apparatus, handling data and interpreting outcomes of experiments in laboratories (Knorr Cetina, 1981, 1999; Latour & Woolgar, 1979), handling claim forms in insurance companies (Wenger, 1998) or doctors, social workers and community care personnel working across professional boundaries and domains of expertise to agree a care plan for an elderly person (Edwards, 2005; Meads & Ashcroft, 2005).

On this contextual view, the epistemic constructs become fused with material, social and other regularities of the practice. In learning settings, this view of epistemic knowledge often takes the form of learning through engagement in practices and discourse that resembles shared knowledge building in research or workplace settings. This includes the range of views that focus on the kinds of knowledge and knowing that can grant students more 'conceptual agency' – the agency which is involved

> ... when individuals or groups interact with subject matter constructively – interpreting meanings, formulating questions, choosing and adapting a method, designing an apparatus, and so on. (Greeno, 2006, p. 88)

The main focus here is not the *origin* of the epistemic constructs, but their *use* in practice. In this case, the shared epistemic constructs – including those that are generally formal (Collins, 2011a; Collins & Ferguson, 1993; Perkins, 1997; and see Chaps. 13, 14 and 15) – are used functionally.

From this perspective, a knowledgeable teacher making actionable decisions would need to master certain functional strategies and heuristics – such as pedagogical patterns (Goodyear & Retalis, 2010; Laurillard, 2012) – that allow them to build on shared 'know-how' and create the necessary practical knowledge.

A range of epistemic constructs also exists at a *situated* action level. For example, Engeström, Nummijoki, and Sannino (2012) note that ascending from the abstract to the concrete in forming new concepts is achieved through specific 'learning' or 'epistemic actions', such as questioning, criticising or rejecting previous practices; analysing the situation; constructing an explicit model of the new idea; examining and experimenting with the model; concretising the model by applying it in practice; and reflecting, evaluating and consolidating the outcomes. Coming from a very different theoretical position, Ohlsson (1995) similarly argues that epistemic tasks that people carry out when they are involved in producing discourse or understanding involve seven kinds of epistemic activities: describing, explaining, predicting, arguing, critiquing, explicating and defining. There is no one fixed order or pattern in these situated actions – the goals for actions are learnt micro-genetically in interaction with other people and with epistemic objects and the environment.

From this perspective, the teacher who wants to produce actionable knowledge needs to master principles and strategies that allow them to engage in shared, knowledgeable, professional work, in a situated activity. Damsa (2014) and Damsa, Kirschner, Andriessen, Erkens, and Sins (2010) refer to such capacities using the notion of *shared epistemic agency*

> ... the capacity that enables deliberate collaborative efforts of groups to create shared knowledge objects. (Damsa et al., 2010, p. 143)

Epistemic agency is not characterised by particular abstract or generalisable patterns, but by epistemic actions that participants take when they engage in knowledge work. This includes a number of knowledge-related actions – such as searching for information, sharing ideas, structuring ideas and producing ideas – and process-related actions, such as projecting goals, regulating collaborative efforts and negotiating relationships.

18.2.2   *Epistemic Knowledge as Cognition*

What we have discussed so far are primarily discursive epistemic constructs that could be observed at the level of language and *action*, but the cognitive and epistemic literature also suggests a similar set of 'constructs of the mind' for epistemic and meta-epistemic understanding (cf. our treatment of concepts in Sect. 17.3).

An abstract view is broadly adopted in the discipline-specific and general *epistemic beliefs* literature. Learning outcomes within the disciplines in higher education, while usually extending beyond raw cognition, are nevertheless often framed in terms of 'learning to think' in a particular disciplinary or professional way, which learners often find challenging. For example, Jacobson (2001) argues that the way in which people approach problems dealing with complex and dynamic systems is underpinned by one of two generally consistent mental model frameworks, composed of associated epistemological and ontological component beliefs. His examples are the 'clockwork mental model' which involves a reductive understanding of complex phenomena as a system composed of isolated parts and the 'complex systems framework' which acknowledges that the whole is greater than the sum of the parts and involves non-reductive thinking. While the 'clockwork' mental model was found to be typical for novice university students, the 'complex systems' model was typical for experts.

At a meta-epistemic level, much of the literature in psychology has similarly argued that human epistemological understanding is composed from a few well-integrated coherent constructs, such as generic or discipline-specific beliefs, frameworks or epistemological theories that guide how a person approaches key intellectual tasks, such as learning, judgement of knowledge claims, use of authority sources or knowledge construction (Kuhn, 1999; Perry, 1970; Schommer, 1990). For example, if a person believes that knowledge is produced externally, rather than being something they can construct for themselves, they would probably apply similar beliefs in their epistemic work across contexts and situations (Hofer, 2001) (we reviewed some of these theories in Chap. 7).

From this perspective, teachers are often seen as possessing distinct, rather broad, conceptions of teaching, learning and educational design that substantially shape how they approach practical teaching and design tasks (Ellis, Hughes, Weyers, & Riding, 2009; Kember & Kwan, 2000; Prosser & Trigwell, 1999; Trigwell, Prosser, & Taylor, 1994). On this view, the preservice teachers' decisions, in our example, would be shaped by their conceptions of what visual representation means in teaching and learning, how important the design of the activity and the worksheet is and how one should use a diagram in practical teaching activity.

In contrast, at the *contextual* or functional level, a person's intellectual activity seems to be informed by more context-sensitive, yet coherent, constructs. They are often associated with a notion of frame, such as 'epistemological frame' used in studies of personal epistemologies (e.g. Elby & Hammer, 2010; Redish, 2004) and 'framing' in psychology (Kahneman & Tversky, 2000), anthropology and other domains (Bateson, 1972/2000; Tannen, 1993).

Framing is generally an implicit answer to the question 'What sort of activity is this?'

For example, Hammer, Elby and many others have consistently shown that the ways in which students and adults approach intellectual tasks are guided by their ways of making sense of what sort of activity they face – their epistemological framings or mindsets (Bing & Redish, 2009; Elby & Hammer, 2010; Hammer, Elby, Scherr, & Redish, 2005; Louca, Elby, Hammer, & Kagey, 2004). This

... refers to the student's *perception or judgement (unconscious or conscious)* as to what
class of tools and skills is appropriate to bring to bear in a particular context or situation.
(Bing & Redish, 2009, p. 1)

Elby, Hammer and colleagues (Elby & Hammer, 2010; Hammer et al., 2005)
specifically show that when students solve physics problems, they frame their
activity in epistemically distinct ways, such as doing formal calculations or engaging in an intuitive sense-making process.

Seen this way, our preservice teachers may frame the instructions they have been
given – to use a graphical representation in a lesson and other things that they are
supposed to do – in a number of different ways and from many different viewpoints,
such as 'We have to give students a worksheet with the diagram, thus we simply
need to find a good accurate representation' or 'We need to understand the role of
the diagram in students' learning, thus we need to model the design of the activity
and a worksheet simultaneously'. While different framings are not necessarily
incompatible, not all of them are equally productive. Framing is 'sticky' and people
do not always move naturally between different ways of approaching problem-
solving (Elby & Hammer, 2010).

As Kirsh (2009) says:

> When people think about something they see as problematic, they typically frame their
> difficulty in terms of their immediate understanding of their situation, an understanding that
> comes with perceptions of what is relevant and potentially useful. This is often
> constraining. Problems of cooking, for instance, are framed in terms of ingredients, flame
> size, and pots and pans, rather than in terms of concepts in chemistry (e.g., reaction
> potential, catalyst) we may have learned in school and that are, in principle, relevant to
> understanding the cooking process. Expert chemists may bring such domain-external views
> to the cooking process. And expert mathematicians or modelers may bring the capacity to
> neatly formalize the concrete. But for the rest of us it is hard to get beyond the concrete to
> the abstract and general. (Kirsh, 2009, p. 269)

However, as Elby and Hammer (2010) note, if prompted, people usually have
mental resources for making such moves. Further, Schön and Rein (1994) claim
that frame reflection and reframing are among the central principles in solving
complex problems of the kind that are typically encountered in design work, policy-
making practices and other public spheres of practical action.

Resources that underpin epistemic understanding do not necessarily come in
ready-to-use modules. Problem-solving and other knowledge-building activities are
situated activities that people encounter in a variety of everyday situations. Most of
us have a rich set of *context-specific* intuitions about how people come to know. As
with the 'knowledge-in-pieces' perspective, an 'epistemology-in-pieces' perspective argues that people's epistemologies, including epistemic frames, generally are
not stable structures or objects. Rather, they are 'cognitive states' that are formed in
the moment of the interaction from the activation of smaller, fine-grained context-
sensitive epistemological resources. Epistemological resources are diverse. While
some of them may be formed via explicit learning, people generally develop many

of them intuitively from their everyday encounters with epistemic phenomena. For example, Hammer and Elby (2002) argue that most people come equipped with at least four kinds of epistemic, epistemological and meta-cognitive resources, such as resources for understanding:

- The source of knowledge ('How do you know this?' – 'Dad told me' or 'I made it up')
- Forms of knowledge ('How did you make it?' – 'This is the fact' or 'I followed the rules')
- Knowledge-related activities ('What are you doing?' – 'I am checking' or 'I am looking for information')
- Stances towards knowledge ('Do you understand this?' – 'I am puzzled' or 'I agree')

Thus, people have epistemic resources needed to make distinctions between, and understand the nature of, knowledge constructs, including the sources of knowledge, knowledge forms, ways of constructing knowledge and possible meta-cognitive states. At least, they have resources to recognise 'knowledge as transmitted from others' ('Dad told me') and 'knowledge as invented by themselves' ('I made it up'). They have many other similar and contrasting fine-grained constructs that are usually linked to specific situated activities and which – in classical theories of epistemological development – are attributed to very different, often conflicting epistemic beliefs or stages of epistemological development. People simultaneously possess epistemic resources that allow them to relate to 'knowledge as insights provided by an authority figure' and 'knowledge as something I can construct for myself'. For example, in the episode from our data that started this chapter, the preservice teachers call upon a number of such intuitive epistemic resources for figuring out what the nappy's cross section might look like: such as using their previous experience, asking others for an explanation, bringing in an example of the object and conducting observation and using imagination and sketching. That is, they fluently move between using and substituting knowledge which is 'transmitted from others' and knowledge that is 'authentically constructed' by themselves (see Chap. 7).

18.2.3 Epistemic Knowledge: Bridging Discourse and Mind

A number of established models and theories place the epistemic constructs that enable a person to create conceptual understanding and solve problems either as constructs of discourse or as constructs of mind. However, some scholars have offered more integrated accounts. For example, Janet Donald (2002), in her examination of how teachers teach and students learn to think in eight different university disciplines, found five common methods and modes of inquiry –

hermeneutic (English literature), critical thinking (English literature), problem-solving (engineering, physics), scientific method (hard sciences) and expertise (physics, education, English literature). These methods and modes of inquiry represent structures that disciplines use to construct and validate their knowledge claims. They specify processes of thinking and operations used to describe them. For example, the *critical thinking* mode seeks evidence and critically scrutinises assumptions; *problem-solving* supplements critical thinking with implementation and testing, *scientific method* focusses on universal standards and a disinterested attitude to inquiry, and *expertise* draws on a combination of sensitivity to the context, selection of appropriate information, recognition of organising principles and verification of inferences. Donald argues that these different methods and modes of inquiry are underpinned by six common 'ways of thinking' that represent mental processes through which individuals construct meanings: description, selection, representation, inference, synthesis and verification. While the 'methods and modes of inquiry' analysis emphasises the social-discursive aspects of knowledge construction in different disciplines, 'ways of thinking' puts the focus back on individual cognitive representations and processes.

Other more integrative models offer extensions that go beyond the discourse and cognitive epistemic constructs directly involved in knowledge work, to include dispositional, motivational and other meta-epistemic constructs involved in making decisions about what kind of thinking activity is appropriate and worthwhile to pursue. For example, Kuhn and Park (2005) argue that intellectual values – defined as the extent to which different kinds of intellectual engagement are regarded as worthwhile to a cultural group – have similar patterns of variation as epistemological understanding across cultural groups. They argued that

> ... epistemological understanding and intellectual values are not constructs located primarily at the individual level. Rather, they are constructs that have social and cultural meaning. (Kuhn & Park, 2005, p. 123)

These views, while they integrate and extend sociocultural and cognitive dimensions of epistemological understanding, nevertheless still maintain a strong commitment to a generalised view.

Others have put forward more malleable views of the epistemic constructs that underpin intellectual activity. For example, Zhang and Sternberg (2005) linked preferred ways of dealing with tasks to *intellectual style*. They suggested that intellectual styles are not completely stable personal traits, but are more flexible and modifiable states that include cognitive, affective, physiological, psychological and sociological dimensions and relate to personal characteristics, experiences and environment. Zhang and Sternberg (2005) regard intellectual styles as *relatively* fixed. They may undergo periodic changes, yet tend to remain stable unless there is a need for change.

However, status [of intellectual styles] as states does not mean that intellectual styles constantly change. They can normally be rather stable, except when there is a demand for change of styles by specific situations. Therefore, to be more precise, we posit that intellectual styles largely represent *relatively* stable states. (Zhang & Sternberg, 2005, p. 39, emphasis added)

Using an example from teaching, they illustrated this as follows:

... new teachers need to keep trying different teaching strategies and adopting various teaching materials until they become comfortable with their teaching. On the contrary, experienced teachers already know what works best for them and thus may stop being creative in their work. Therefore, with increasing teaching experience, teachers' thinking styles in teaching may change from being more creative to being more conservative. (op. cit., p. 14)

Others again have suggested that epistemic constructs and processes involved in an intellectual activity may be more *sensitive to the context*. For example, Perkins, Tishman, Ritchhart, Donis, and Andrade (2000), rather like Kuhn and Park (2005), point to the role of dispositions in intellectual performance and make a distinction between intelligence 'as ability' and intelligence 'as thinking disposition'.

Perkins et al. (2000) argue that it is difficult to explain intelligent performance in real-life contexts solely based on a person's ability to deploy cognitive processes or strategies. The important question is what people are inclined to do and *how* they deploy their abilities. Passions, motivations, sensitivities, values and other similar dispositional constructs play the central role in this process. Perkins et al. suggest that thinking dispositions – what people are disposed to do – include three aspects: (a) *ability*, a capacity to carry out certain behaviour; (b) *inclination*, the motivation and impulse to engage; and (c) *sensitivity*, noticing occasions to engage. For example, a disposition such as 'open mindedness' includes the ability to see the situation from different perspectives but also the inclination to consider different views and – most importantly – *noticing* the moments when such deliberation from multiple perspectives is needed.

Their empirical findings showed that people generally have the abilities needed to consider different perspectives; however, they are less inclined to deploy their abilities and usually have very low sensitivity to occasions that are characterised by a 'need for cognition'. Extending this view to 'knowledge-to-go' beyond the learning site, Perkins and Salomon (2012) link these aspects to three – *primarily epistemic* – processes: *detecting* potential connections with prior knowledge (i.e. noticing), *electing* to pursue possible connections (i.e. inclination) and *connecting* between one's knowledge and the current situation (i.e. ability to apply). Detect–elect–connect are not abstract mental operations; rather they are 'bridges' that link knowledge learnt in one setting to actionable knowledge in a new context.

Researchers taking a distributed cognition perspective have made similar links between cognitive constructs and processes operating at the individual level and cultural practices operating at the level of the community, notably when people engage in situated epistemic activity, such as concept formation 'in the wild'. For example, Hutchins (2012) review of processes involved in creating situated conceptual knowledge lists such epistemic constructs and operations as analogy, metaphor, blending, dimensionality reduction, filtering, positive feedback and design. He notes that these mechanisms operate, and are observable, in situated activities at the community level, but they share striking similarities to the cognitive processes which cognitive scientists claim operate at an individual level.

> The mechanisms that increase order in the systems ... are enacted in cultural practices and operate at the level of the community rather than the individual. It is quite likely that formally similar processes, operating via very different mechanisms, exist within individual persons. Both systems are, after all, composed of complex networks of elements. (Hutchins, 2012, p. 316)

Nersessian (2008a, 2008b) specifically focusses on micro-scale thinking processes involved in conceptual innovation and in problem-solving activity using models. She discerns such operations as model construction, simulation, evaluation and adaptation. These processes simultaneously involve physical rearrangements of the models, cognitive mechanisms at an individual level and conceptual reordering of individual and community understandings.

In short, epistemic constructs span across discourse and mind. Domain knowledge, dispositions, culture and environment serve as 'bridges' that connect epistemic activity to practical action. Table 18.2 presents a summary running across these different perspectives (cf. Table 17.2).

18.3   Actionable Epistemic Resources

> How words are understood is not told by words alone. (Wittgenstein, 1967/2007, §144, 26e)

While many socioculturalists focus on language as the dominant modality of discourse and socio-cognitivists focus on cognitive resources as key 'executives' of epistemic work, researchers who take a situated perspective point out that the resources involved in human sense-making extend to different modalities. For example, Hammer et al. (2005) argue that a person's framing of the situation includes not only epistemological framing ('What do I expect to use to answer questions and build new knowledge?') but also social framing ('Whom do I expect to interact with here and how?'), affective framing ('How do I expect to feel about it?') and more (p. 98). Hammer et al. see these dimensions as relatively independent of one another. For example, one student may frame the situation in a lecture from a social perspective as a set of expectations about sitting still and speaking only if asked and from an epistemological perspective as recording the information carefully. Another student may socially frame the situation in the same way, but epistemologically may see themselves as deliberating over what is said in the lecture rather than merely recording.

Shifting attention back to professional work, we might say that actionable knowledge often draws simultaneously on multiple, interacting, mutually changing and often conflicting, framings of the world and on different modalities. Consider

Table 18.2 Summary: epistemic resourcefulness as discourse and as cognition

Generality	Nature	
	Construct of discourse (Social, external)	Construct of mind (Individual, internal)
Abstract epistemic constructs Models	Formal 'epistemes' or epistemic systems that function as normative discourse constructs for knowledge construction: disciplinary matrixes (Kuhn, 1981), syntactical structures of disciplines (Schwab, 1962), epistemic forms and epistemic games (Collins & Ferguson, 1993; Perkins, 1997), legitimation codes (Maton, 2014)	Epistemic beliefs, mental models and other stable model-like mental constructs that predict or explain intellectual behaviour: stages of epistemological development (Kuhn, 1999; Perry, 1970)[a], epistemological beliefs (Schommer, 1990), epistemological theories (Hofer & Pintrich, 1997), epistemological and ontological mental models (Jacobson, 2001)
	Thinking styles and other cultural, dispositional and intellectual parameters of the disciplines, groups and individuals: disciplinary thinking modes and processes (Donald, 2002; Pace & Middendorf, 2004), intellectual values (Kuhn & Park, 2005), intellectual styles (Zhang & Sternberg, 2005)	
Contextual epistemic constructs Modules	Epistemic practices and other context-specific social-discursive epistemic constructs in shared knowledge construction activity: epistemic machineries (Knorr Cetina, 1999), social and relational agency (Edwards, 2005)	Epistemological frames and other coherent context-sensitive generalisations from experience about the nature of epistemic activity (Bing & Redish, 2009; Hammer et al., 2005)
	Thinking dispositions and motivations and other tendencies of individuals to use their intellectual abilities in a certain way in particular situations (Perkins et al., 2000; Perkins & Salomon, 2012)	
Situated epistemic resources Modalities	Epistemic agency: regulative and reflective tasks and actions deployed in individual and collective knowledge work (Damsa et al., 2010; Engeström et al., 2012; Muukkonen & Lakkala, 2009; Ohlsson, 1995)	Epistemic resources: manifold cognitive resources, activated in a moment-to-moment interaction in epistemic activity (Elby & Hammer, 2010; Hammer & Elby, 2002; Kahneman & Tversky, 2000)
	Mechanisms for distributed cognition: socially shared mental constructs and operations involved in creating situated conceptual knowledge such as analogy, metaphor, blending, model construction (Hutchins, 2012; Nersessian, 2008a, 2008b)	

[a] Note, the highest levels of these developmental schemes usually correspond to more flexible and context-sensitive epistemological constructs, but, overall, the stage is considered to be relatively stable for an individual

again the discussion between the preservice teachers trying to decide about the structure of the worksheet and the classroom activity:

Agi: ... And so they've got four – I don't know how many layers in a nappy. This is layer A, B, C, D. So then they test A, B, C, D, for ... [4 seconds] I don't know what it is, like hard err waterproof I think. Maybe we can *divide them into groups*. Maybe so, group 1 // test =

Nat: = Do this layer.

Agi & Jill: Yeah.

Agi: Umm and then we've also // got ((Jill interrupts)).

Jill:	// And then we also *need less stuff*, we don't need to like have … [4 seconds] and if there's three, are *there three things* that are being tested then *one of us can be in each* of these groups.
Agi:	Yeah. Waterproof, what was the other one? But then umm ((thinks)).
Nat:	It will be interesting to look at *how they might vary their results* though if they're all in one group (…) not like we're gonna talk about it, but anyway.
Jill:	Yeah.
Agi:	So but what do you think you'd have ((leaves sentence incomplete thinking about what's written in the mini-unit))
Jill:	So you'd test the waterproofness of each layer, then test the hardness of each layer, then test the softness of each layer.
Agi:	((nods her head agreeing)).
Nat:	*That's gonna take so long.*

While Agi initially frames the activity of worksheet design primarily from *the subject domain perspective* and tries to align the structure of the worksheet to the key elements of the nappy and the test ('This is layer A, B, C, D. So then they test A, B, C, D …'), she suddenly reframes her activity and looks at it from the *social classroom organisation* (socio-pedagogical) perspective ('Maybe we can divide them into groups'). Jill extends her thinking, but reconsiders Agi's design of the activity from the *material perspective*, seeing themselves as teachers as an integral part of the classroom environment ('we also need less stuff', 'there are three things that are being tested', we are three, thus 'one of us can be in each group'). In contrast, Nat notices that Jill and Agi's suggested design may be in tension with *the subject domain perspective* since dividing tests across groups may not allow the students to see variability in the results and explore the question of reliability. But then she relinquishes her concern, rethinking the suggestion from the *practical perspective* and seeing her concern as irrelevant or impractical. Agi, however, picks up her idea and continues her modelling of the worksheet, which now becomes a blended sketch of the nappy's layers, tests and student groupings (see Fig. 18.1).

Agi:	But could you've (…) you've got three groups like this ((draws circles)) with then (…) how many do we have, 27 in the class, we don't like those numbers anymore, we want 30 people in the class now ((laughs)). There'll be so we've got 30 and we've got 10.
Jill:	I wanna look if I can see a nappy ((starts looking on the web)).
Agi:	27 people in the class, then we've got three groups ((draws them again)) – we've got nine groups ((draws more)) this is sounding crazy, I know, but ((leaves sentence incomplete but keeps drawing)).
Nat:	Just a little ((smiles)).
Agi:	'Cause then you've three groups testing, doing the waterproof test ((shows on the drawn circles)), three groups doing the hardness ((shows next row)), three groups doing the softness … so then you kind of – if one group is way out.
Jill:	Yeah.
Agi:	You can do the discussion of what did you all find when you did your waterproof test, which layer did you find was the (…) most absorbent.
Jill:	Yeah. Are you bringing issues of like =
Agi:	= Variability.
Jill:	No, validity, no, validity is testing what's err reliability!
Agi:	Reliability.

Agi imagines how many students will be in the class (and freely manipulates it) in order to simplify her task and see if she come up with a design of *classroom arrangements* where several small groups would do the same test ('Cause then you've three groups testing') and simultaneously switches to the *teachers' roles* ('You can do the discussion'). Prompted by Jill, she reframes and tries to explain what this would mean from the *subject domain* perspective ('Reliability').

In summary, the preservice teachers are not only engaging with relevant disciplinary and pedagogical knowledge and following inquiry frameworks of these domains – they are also simultaneously drawing on epistemic resources and are grounding their shared knowledge construction in their direct perception of the unfolding *drawing*, the imagined *material environment* and *themselves*. They simultaneously consider different modalities of the activity (material, temporal, social, conceptual, pedagogical, etc.), and they incrementally add and combine diverse constraints (the structure of the nappy, the nature of scientific tests, numbers of students and teachers, time available, etc.). Different modalities are not isolated, but firmly and extremely carefully combined together: there is no possibility to bring into the classroom discussion (pedagogy) questions about reliability (subject domain) if group work (embodied social arrangements) would not generate variability of results.

In a similar way, embodied and grounded cognition perspectives do not see the epistemic as ontologically separable from other modalities, such as movement, perception and affect. As Andy Clark (1999) claims,

> ... attention to the roles of body and world can often transform our image of both the problems and the solution spaces for biological cognition. (Clark, 1999, p. 510)

Following Kirsh and Maglio (1994), he emphasises the crucial role of epistemic actions:

> ... actions whose purpose is not to alter the world so as to advance physically toward some goal (e.g., laying a brick for a wall), but rather to alter the world so as to help to make available information required as part of a problem-solving routine. Examples of epistemic actions include looking at a chessboard from different angles, organizing the spatial layout of a hand of cards so as to encode a record of known current high cards in each suit, laying out our mechanical parts in the order required for correct assembly, and so on. Epistemic actions, it should be clear, *build designer environments* – local structures that transform, reduce, or simplify the operations that fall to the biological brain in the performance of a task. (Clark, 1999, p. 511, emphasis added)

This dynamic agent–world interaction brings practical activity into the very centre of epistemic and conceptual thinking:

> Practical activity, understood as a mode of epistemic access to the world, is a necessary underpinning of our general referential capacity. At the highest level, what is at issue here is the fact that practical, bodily activity can have cognitive and epistemic meaning; it can be a part of a particular problem solving routine, as with the use of paper in long division, or be involved in ongoing cognitive development, as with the use of environmental interactions and manipulations to learn to recognize objects, or to come to appreciate their significance and meaning. (Anderson, 2003, p. 109)

While visual perception is often given one of the dominant roles, inquiry and conception are not separable from any of the spectrum of modalities. Sellers-Young (1999) says this about the (theatrical) actor's ways of inquiry:

> Focusing an actor's attention to the sensory attributes of any task immerses her in a dialogue with herself and her environment that includes modes of attention, methods of inquiry and application of information. Somatic explorations rely on an actor's ability to take in, at any given moment, *new information* through her sensory modalities (eyes, ears, nose, tongue, and skin) and process this information with that taken in simultaneously through the proprioceptor or sensing devices located in the skin, muscles, joints and inner ear. This combination of sense and proprioceptor *information is examined* or explored by the memory in order to *take action*. For example, an actor can be asked to attend to questions concerning her gait. In response [with] increased attention to the eyes, ears, skin, joints of the body and soles of the feet, she can transform her basic walk in a variety of ways. While this may sound simplistic, the perceptual experience involved in the act of walking takes place beyond the level of awareness of most actors. The exploration of walking with the reflection on the act of exploration serves three purposes. First, it teaches the actors to explore their sensory system. Second, it constructs new neural images of walking. Finally, it teaches them the act of exploration and reinforces the self-reflective state that is a part of the process. (Sellers-Young, 1999, p. 92)

Such embodied skill is not seen as a tacit and inexplicable, but as a domain of inquiry with its own methods for gathering and processing data.[2] It is a method that actors master in order to get conscious access to their body and foster bodily intelligence:

> Focusing on the modes of attention and methods of inquiry causes actors to ask questions regarding their use of their sensory systems to attain information. These self-reflective questions help actors to understand their perceptual use of their sensory system. By noting her physical response in a situation the actress learns how a habit is related to her method of perception. She begins to understand what frame of intelligence, to use Gardner's words, she is relying upon. She notes, for instance, a tendency in specific situations to repeat a particular motion, such as, rubbing her forehead. (loc. cit.)

The ballet dancer, Tamara Rojo, sums it up this way:

> Life on stage is like nothing else . . . every feeling and sense exploding. Every nerve in your body completely awake. <. . .> It's as if the end of your nerves in your body were completely raw. As if you have no skin. So you feel everything. You feel your partner and you feel his emotions, and you feel the air and you feel the audience. You just feel everything, in such high level. (Young & Rojo, 2014)

In contrast, in the main streams of conventional education, including education for the professions, preference is often given to *formal, decontextualised and disembodied* ways of (professional) knowing and inquiry – with a concomitant undervaluing of the role of everyday experiences and common-sense methods of knowing. Methods that do not have an articulated framework and rely more directly on the senses are often labelled primitive and even misleading. However, as Hammer et al. (2005) claim, expert understanding of complex ideas involves a complex process of integration: reconciling and coordinating what may initially be

---

[2] Cf. Harry Collins (2010) view, which we outlined in Chap. 4.

new counter-intuitive ideas with diverse *everyday common-sense experiences* and with *diverse formal ideas* about the phenomena concerned. Expert conceptual understanding of complex phenomena, such as *force* in physics:

> ... can come into being only in conjunction with epistemological resources activated for understanding consistency and for understanding the value of combining formal and informal knowledge. (Hammer et al., 2005, p. 109)

Consider the following discussion between the preservice teachers, which extends their previous modelling of the class activity. Agi reminds everyone that they should organise the students' discussion of how to test material properties and asks other team members a question 'For the test. Do we do it as a whole class?'

Nat: It has to be as a // class, so everyone is doing "working scientifically".
Jill: // Yeah.
Jill: Yeah ((when Nat finishes saying)).
Agi: Are you gonna get them to discuss it in small groups or just a whole class discussion so just couple of them might contribute?
Jill: I think we need to do it as a whole class discussion.
Agi: Okay.
Nat: Maybe what we can do is *divide them up by three* and then *each of us* (...) can //take a group.
Jill: //That's what I said before, but I think we need to wait until we go and *see how the class is actually* ... [4 seconds] *you know* ... [4 seconds] *how it works*.

In thinking about their lesson design, the preservice teachers draw upon a *formal* epistemological perspective ('working scientifically'), while simultaneously deploying *situated* epistemic resources for making comparisons about the advantages of having discussion in groups or a whole class ('so just a couple of them might contribute'), thinking about *themselves* as an embodied pedagogical resource ('divide them up by three and then each of us (...) can // take a group') and also referring to their *embodied senses* ('we need to wait until we go and *see how the class is actually* ... [4 seconds] *you know* ... [4 seconds] *how it works*'.)

As Kirsh (2009) puts it:

> ... in many naturally arising problems the locus of difficulty may lie as much in the registration process, the activity of selecting environmental anchors to tie mental or physical representations to the world, as it does in searching for paths in representation itself. (Kirsh, 2009, p. 277)

Novices and experts rely on a capacity to notice important features of the environment that allow them to anchor and enact certain modes of working. Conception and perception are tightly entangled, even in the seemingly quite simple teachers' decision illustrated above. Can teachers divide students in three groups if they haven't seen the classroom?

This aspect of epistemic fluency, which we can call *dynamic grounded epistemic flexibility*, involves both an ability to move smoothly between the abstract, contextual and situated ways of knowing and a capacity to employ multiple ways of knowing provided by the senses, environment and imagination to construct actionable understanding.

18.4   Linking Epistemic and Conceptual: Dynamic View of Conceptual Learning

How do epistemic resources and conceptual resources become a part of the same actionable knowing?

The insights into contextual sensitivity and noticing provided by Hammer, Wagner, Lobato and others show that the questions of conceptual change, cognitive flexibility and transfer cannot be reduced to the possession of abstract mental (conceptual and epistemic) constructs (Brown & Hammer, 2008; Hammer et al., 2005; Lobato, Rhodehamel, & Hohensee, 2012; Wagner, 2006, 2010). Rather, the key is in the contextual *sensitivity* that underpins noticing, perception and activation of productive sets of mental resources (including the conceptual and epistemic).

As Hammer et al. (2005) note,

> ... the activation of finer-grained cognitive resources should often depend on the social and physical environment such that the resulting knowledge can coherently be attributed to the overall system (people + environment). (Hammer et al., 2005, p. 117)

This way of thinking about personal mental resourcefulness provides a mechanism for explaining how knowledge could be situated and simultaneously distributed between mind and environment.

> ... elements of an individual's mind interact with elements of the social and physical environment to create knowledge that's situated even distributed. (loc. cit.)

But how do these interactions occur?

Brown and Hammer (2008) argue that scientific understanding of knowledge and learning can benefit from a complex systems account. Order and structure emerge from a large number of independent interactions of smaller agents. A complex system perspective

> ... entails a view of knowledge and reasoning in terms of manifold resources that can activate in various ways at various times, rather than unitary, systematic (mis)conceptions. (Brown & Hammer, 2008, p. 143)

They note that *conceptual change* and *inquiry* are often regarded as two distinct objectives of learning. However, from a dynamic perspective,

> ... epistemological resources may be seen in dynamic interaction with conceptual resources. (op. cit., p. 144)

Epistemic resources mediate the coordination and activation of *relevant* conceptual elements in a new context and play an important role in *dynamic sense-making*. The main idea behind this view is that sound conceptual understanding should develop from existing mental resources. This does not require the replacement of intuitions (a.k.a. 'misconceptions') with theoretical knowledge. We return to this argument at the end of the chapter.

18.5 Framing, Stability and Coherence

18.5.1 Stability vs. Coordination

Stability and variability and coherence and fragmentation have been seen as two incompatible views associated with expert vs. novice thinking (see Chap. 6). We nevertheless should make a distinction between two very different ways of defining and seeing *framing* and other stable patterns in expert actions.

The first view can be found in the organisational literature and in theories of practice. For example, Orlikowski and Gash (1994) define frames of reference as

> ... *cognitive structures* that are shared among groups of individuals. (Orlikowski & Gash, 1994, p. 175, emphasis added)

Or as Gioia (1986) says,

> It is a built-up repertoire of tacit knowledge that is used *to impose structure upon*, and impart meaning to, otherwise ambiguous social and situational information to facilitate understanding. (Gioia, 1986, p. 56, emphasis added)

Such frames are sometimes seen as rigid and constraining and, as Orlikowski and Gash (1994), paraphrasing Bolman and Deal (1991), call them – '"psychic prisons" that inhibit learning' (Orlikowski & Gash, 1994, p. 177).

Alternatively, in shared meaning-making, frames are viewed as more flexible and multidimensional 'webs of meanings' that structure shared experiences, reduce complexity and provide a basis for taking action.

> Frames are *flexible in structure* and content, having *variable dimensions* that shift in salience and content by context and over time. (Orlikowski & Gash, 1994, p. 177)

Nevertheless, frames, from this perspective, have an already-defined structure that is deployed in (or imposed on) epistemic work and sense-making.

The second very different view of frames and framing comes from socio-cognitive studies of personal epistemological resourcefulness (Elby & Hammer, 2010; Hammer et al., 2005). Frames are not rigid or flexible *pre-existing* epistemological structures that are *imposed* on meaning-making or to direct individual epistemic actions. Instead, framings *emerge* from the fine-grained epistemological resources activated in the context. From this perspective, the coherent patterns of meaning-making that are often observed in skilful expert behaviour across diverse situations are recognisable *dynamic configurations* of numerous, situated epistemological resources.

The difference between the two perspectives stems from contrasting views of the ontological basis of the constructs that underpin human knowing. Hammer et al. (2005) call these two sets of views a '*unitary* ontology' and a '*manifold* ontology'. The unitary perspectives see framing – and human epistemic cognition more generally – as guided by abstract, coherent, inflexible, durable epistemic constructs and mechanisms that may reside in the human mind or in discourse or span across both. In contrast, the manifold ontological perspective sees framing as a local co-activation of a range of epistemic resources. Framing and the formation of other cognitive constructs that enable coherent expert decisions and actions are not necessarily prefabricated 'cognitive objects', but rather 'cognitive states' into which a person enters by simultaneously activating multiple epistemological resources and which itself refines and forms new epistemological resources.

From this perspective, a person's capacity for knowledgeable action and coherent professional decisions is not due to having and deploying large unitary epistemological constructs in various contexts. It depends on co-activating and coordinating context-sensitive epistemological resources that together form an emergent coherent pattern. This view does not impose an a priori assumption that the human mind has to operate on large unitary epistemological constructs. It helps us understand the capacity to fuse formal ways of knowing with pragmatic situated action. The epistemic flexibility seen in expert thinking – when someone solves professional questions that cannot be understood and resolved from a single epistemological perspective and when appropriateness of the solution depends on numerous contingencies – has to be understood on a local scale.

How do our preservice teachers frame challenging learning situations when they construct actionable knowledge?

18.5.2   'Following Instructions' vs. 'Sense-making'

We illustrate some central grounded dynamic qualities of their epistemic resourcefulness and framing that features strongly in their productive actionable knowing. The episode comes from the team's early discussion during the lesson planning activity discussed before. The team decided to repurpose the lesson plan template that they had used for planning a lesson before. They made a quick pass through the purpose and outcomes of the lesson and tried to come up with a possible scenario in which they could situate students' activities in order to 'engage' them. But they were not successful in coming up with good ideas, thus they postponed their work on these sections and decided: 'Let's start with the activity'. As a part of their planning, the team used the description of the lesson provided by their university teacher in the mini-unit. This is how they started their work creating lesson activities:

Agi: ((reads her mini-unit)) Let's start with activity 1 (. . .) work with that, and then //
        come back.
Jill: // Come back to this section, OK?
Agi: Cause it's very // sort of
Nat: ((in the meantime, looking with Jill at the laptop)) // Just delete everything
        ((referring to the content of the plan constructed before)).
Agi: So ((in a thinking way)) it's quite unclear. Do you want me to *read* it as you delete?
        ((reads from her mini-unit printout)). So *it says*, "Provide each group with half a
        disposable nappy", in that group students 're to – the first thing is to draw a labeled
        diagram, showing – *well, that's called* "a drawing" actually – showing the different
        layers of a disposable nappy. They need to look at the nappy side on *so they're
        actually* drawing a cross section.

Agi: ((still reading from mini-unit, Lesson Four)) Then they need to separate the layers. For further testing, "Identify the special properties of each layer by comparing the layers based on the following properties. Testing what happens when water is added, use a eye dropper to place water in the centre of the sample, measure the number of drops that fall into the cup" – *obviously, there is a cup under it* (all laugh) – "how many drops were added before the water starts to pass through". The second test is the toughness of each // layer.

Nat: // That's gonna take a *really long time*.

Agi: Yeah, ((keeps reading)) "use a brick" – it's kind of like an activity that they do – "use rough brick across the surface or rub each bag" – bag, *what?* – "across a hard surface, e.g. asphalt playground. // Use" ((leaves sentence incomplete as Jill Interrupts)).

Jill: // Alright kids, get your nappies on the playground ((all laugh)).

Agi: "Use small gardening glove to protect hands in the rubbing process".

Jill: ((looking at Agi, laughing with disbelief)) What's this lesson?

First, the team frames the challenging situation as 'follow instructions' and reads the step-by-step guidelines for the activity given in the mini-unit. These describe what should happen in the lesson.

Nevertheless, the signs of active epistemic engagement appear from the very beginning of this episode. When Agi reads the instructions, the team periodically interrupts the flow of the text, by making comments and jokes that clearly show that they are trying to make sense of the instructions and imagine how the activity might look in a class. For example, Agi immediately notices that what is called a 'drawing' is not a traditional picture of a nappy, but a diagram – a schematic representation of layers of the nappy that shows the hidden structure of the nappy rather than its surface appearance. The instruction 'rub a bag' – a mistake in the activity description left by copying the description of the 'toughness' test from the previous lesson – is noticed and is followed by Agi's puzzlement 'what?' The incomplete explanation of how to test waterproofness is followed by her note filling in the gap: 'obviously there is a cup under it'. Nat further tries to make sense of the whole sequence of instructions and insightfully notes the challenge: 'That's gonna take a really long time'. Such engagement can be characterised as a kinaesthetic simulation – imagining material arrangements, actions and unfolding activity in real time. At this stage, this simulation is not very profound in conceptual or kinaesthetic/embodied terms. Nevertheless, Agi and Nat's comments indicate that reading and following the instructions are not the only epistemic activity in which they are engaged. They try to make sense of these instructions by trying to re-express the instructions in different language and simulating real embodied experiences. At this stage, they are already drawing on a large set of epistemic resources: following the instructions, seeing incomplete information, spotting inconsistencies, raising doubts, imagining the situation, imagining the action and foreseeing the activity unfolding over time. The epistemic constructs on which they draw are not articulated strategies. Rather, these epistemic resources are closely coupled with kinaesthetic experiences of how this feels. A nontraditional object for use in a normal lesson – a nappy – provokes jokes, disbelief and other emotionally charged epistemic states.

In short, the team frames their activity not only as 'follow instructions' but also 'make sense'. They use the step-by-step instructions as a resource for sense-making and for the latter use a range of epistemic resources firmly grounded in projected perception and kinaesthetic experiences (i.e. what the actions and material arrangements in the class will look like).

Much of the mainstream literature on personal epistemology associates the use of instructions and textbooks with a primitive epistemological stance (relying on authority) or with a surface learning approach. What emerges here, however, is different. First, instructions are just one (epistemic) source of ideas, and 'following instructions' is just one of epistemic resources on which the team draws in this planning activity. Second, the epistemic resource 'follow an authority source provided by a teacher' is used in close dynamic interaction with many other epistemic resources that could be called 'making sense', 'being puzzled', 'imagining', 'reframing', 'making up' and 'sketching'.

The team weaves the instructions while adopting a productive epistemic stance – that we can call 'sense-making'. The step-by-step descriptions of the activity are a *scaffold* rather than an authority that should be followed with little awareness. Others have already alluded to similar productive uses of textbooks and similar resources in school classrooms (Elby & Hammer, 2010; Hammer & Elby, 2003; Louca et al., 2004; McDonald, Le, Higgins, & Podmore, 2005). The traditional developmental or epistemic belief frameworks, however, are poorly placed to depict the productivity of the epistemic stance that emerges in this episode.

The preservice teachers in our study did not draw on one coherent 'theory-like' way of knowing. Much of their productivity comes from the team's switching between and coordination of diverse epistemic strategies.

18.6 Learning to Coordinate Diverse Ways of Knowing

18.6.1 Three Kinds of Stability in Situated Knowing

What then becomes critical is the question 'How could the activation of mental resources that enable coherent and productive meaning-making be achieved?' As we mentioned before, Hammer et al. (2005) identify three main ways of achieving coherent framing: *contextual* activation, *deliberative* activation and *structural* activation.

Contextual stability is achieved by a passive, repetitive activation of similar mental resources. Such activation is dependent on the contextual cues that induce a certain mental state, but does not involve meta-cognitive resources that coordinate the co-activation. For example, children and adults could form coherent patterns of thinking and intelligent behaviour – such as building Lego houses, completing income tax forms or creating a lesson plan – mainly by relying on the perceptual affordances of the environment or following instructions they have been given, but without activating their own meta-cognitive resources for coordinating their epistemic actions or reflecting on what they are doing.

Deliberative stability is achieved by active monitoring and attention – aiming to maintain a coherent activation of certain epistemological resources. In this case, the coordination involves a deliberative activation and deployment of epistemological and meta-cognitive resources. For example, less experienced teachers may be conscious that each of their lessons should help students to learn a certain set of skills and concepts and so they might deliberatively map their intended activities (in the lesson plan) against each mandated learning objective.

Structural stability involves a coherent activation, across diverse contexts, of a range of resources that, once they have been formed, behave as a coherent 'cognitive unit'. Such units have their own activation conditions – passive or deliberative – but, once cued, the coherence is achieved automatically without deliberative attention. For example, many experienced teachers achieve coherence between lesson objectives and activities without monitoring and reflecting deliberatively on how they do this.

Given time and repeated practice over a range of contexts, both the contextually and deliberatively activated sets of resources may form their own integrity. While their activation remains sensitive to the context, their functioning becomes less dependent on specific contextual cues and they function without active meta-cognitive monitoring. In short, coherence is achieved by *noticing gaps* and educating sensitivity to specific situations that require deliberative activation of productive epistemological resources, rather than imposing specific coherent epistemological frames.

What are the sources of productive framings and reframings? Let's return to the example.

While we observed many sources in preservice teachers' design work, but two common moves led to the productive construction of actionable knowledge: (a) *seeing opportune points for productive reframing* and (b) moving *between conceptual regularities and material arrangements*.

18.6.2 Seeing Opportune Points for Productive Pedagogical Framing and Reframing

Agi: This is where this is where I got ( ). The third test is the softness of each layer. And there's not (…) a … [4 seconds] what do you call it (…) instructions for the test. ((refers to test c in point 3 in 'mini-unit')). So it's kind of like this =

Nat: = Rub it? ((rubs her check with the finger and laughs)).

Agi: No, no, no, the point of that is (…) the point that is I don't know if they use it in our course, but (…) they've modeled it, they've modeled it, they're on their own ((shows by making gestures with her hands)).

Jill: Oh yeah.

Agi: So we need to – in the worksheet, do we want them to document how – it's like a process of planning – how they're gonna – they come up with their own test.

Nat: Ah, "working scientifically" ((shows her understanding)).
Agi: Yeah, "working scientifically" ((nods, laughs and writes "working scientifically" on her printout of mini-unit)).

Reaching the third test – 'softness' – which does not contain instructions, Agi notices the underlying pedagogical strategy saying: 'they modelled it, modelled it and now they are on their own'. At this stage she activates her conceptual resources trying to articulate: 'what kind of pedagogical strategy is this', as well as her epistemic resources, 'we need to design a worksheet' to support this strategy. That is, she activates the epistemic resource: 'pedagogical knowledge is constructed'.

Agi frames the lack of instructions as a clue for a different kind of pedagogy – not to give the instructions to the students, but to design an activity in a way that students are able to come up with the testing procedure on their own. Note that there was a possibility of using the same epistemic resource that she used before – 'incomplete information' – and to frame this situation very differently, much less productively, 'these are unfinished instructions, thus we need to think how to test softness and give those instructions to students'. The preservice teachers, however, had epistemic and conceptual resources to frame this situation more productively and proceeded to design a 'constructivist' rather than an 'instructivist' activity.

We can call the epistemic strategy that is evident in the team's discussions *seeing opportune points* for productive reframing. At the core of such reframing is an insight into a productive, yet not realised, opportunity (seeing the situation from a broader conceptual perspective) and proceeding (from this conceptual insight) towards specific actions. In this case, the lack of a softness test was such an opportune point, which Agi successfully noted and realised. Hall and Seidel Horn (2012) similarly observe that 'a bug' in a certain procedure or practice can become an entry point or a 'feature' for reconceptualising the situation, 'conceptual change' or even innovation. What we see in the preservice teachers' discussion is that such 'bugs' and 'reconceptualisations' are mundane features of constructing actionable knowledge in this team (the earlier example illustrating how the team embedded concepts of 'variability' and 'reliability' in the students' activity involves a similar epistemic strategy).

18.6.3   Situating Instructions Between the Conceptual Regularities and Material Arrangements

Initially, Agi and other team members switch from framing the situation as *following instructions* to *making sense* of instructions trying to imagine what would happen in the class (see Sect. 17.5.2). At this point, in the episode presented above, Agi starts noticing a more general, higher-level pedagogical principle which is broadly based on 'modelling and imitation' or 'cognitive apprenticeship' pedagogical principles. What is noticeable, however, is that Agi has a mental resource for seeing this pedagogical principle in the step-by-step description, though she does not use a term to describe the pedagogy that underpins these instructions, either in compact everyday language or in professional terms. (One can argue here that Agi has a concept or mental conceptual resource for such a pedagogical principle, in a deep sense, but does not appear to have a linguistic resource to name it.) From the discourse perspective, Agi's talk is a long way from 'professional discourse'. In contrast, Nat is more successful in expressing Agi's insight in professional language, labelling this strategy – not particularly precisely – using the much broader label of 'working scientifically'. Together they successfully connect the instructions to the underpinning higher-level pedagogical principle.

Afterwards, Agi goes in the opposite direction – from the instructions to the socio-material arrangements in the classroom that are needed to support such a pedagogy.

The discussion continues:

Agi: So, however we do the worksheet, that's kind of the // interesting ((leaves incomplete as Nat interrupts)).

Nat: // What number is that? Number 3? ((looks at her mini-unit printout)).

Agi: Yeah … [4 seconds]. "Students ((reading on)) should add comments about the properties to each layer err of each layer to their diagram".

Agi: I think – I also said that it was like a … [6 seconds] it's a good visual thing, the diagram, and then writing comments on layers, so then when they look at it, they can kind of see what each layer does (. . .) cause they've it on the diagram, they haven't just written like, "the middle layer was soft", they write the results onto the diagram ((Nat looking at Agi, Jill is typing)).

Agi's focus is now on the design of the worksheet, and what should be in this worksheet, so that students are able to succeed and 'come up with their own test'. In the next move, Agi makes further sense of the instructions that 'students should add comments. . . to their diagram'. She again makes sense of the productivity of the visual representations in teaching by seeing a higher-level pedagogical principle beneath the surface of the step-by-step instructions to 'use a diagram'. 'It's a good visual thing, the diagram'. This conceptual insight is again expressed in everyday language that is a long way from sophisticated professional discourse or well-justified theory. However, Agi and the other team members, who agree with her, have the conceptual resources to understand that visual representations are 'good'. Once more, this conceptual resource is somewhat intuitive and does not need any further explanation. Nevertheless, despite its primitiveness, it can be seen as productive. Later, Agi directly converts this principle into the practical design of activity. She uses the diagram of a nappy to design the worksheet. In this episode, the way the team and particularly Agi start constructing actionable knowledge gives a further insight into the nature of resourcefulness.

An obvious source of resourcefulness is visible in the fluent moves Agi makes between the three 'levels' of seeing classroom activities: (a) the middle-level step-by-step actions that are already partly expressed in the mini-unit description, (b) the higher-level pedagogical principles that underpin those steps and (c) the socio-material arrangements – worksheets, classroom arrangements and other regularities – that can support those pedagogies in the classroom. Agi has the conceptual resources needed to see classroom activities at the three levels simultaneously and has the epistemic resources that allow her to move smoothly between the step-by-step actions, broader pedagogical principles and material arrangements.

Environment and prompts from the instructions play an important role. But the productivity of the preservice teachers' actionable knowing does not rely solely on the environment.

18.6.4 Resourcefulness as Active Coordination of Concepts, Actions and Situated Experiences

A number of interesting features of the epistemic resources can be observed in these two 'resourceful' seeds. First, *seeing an opportunity point changes the frame*. What is distinct here is that this change of the frame is not entirely external – prompted by affordances or people outside one's head – and not entirely internal and deliberative. Rather, reframing emerges as chains of coordinated epistemic actions closely coupling one's internal mental resources with the material and social affordances of the external environment. The instructions and the external environment provide very minimal, passive 'clues' for seeing such 'opportunity points' or making sense of instructions at a higher conceptual level. Thus, such framing is not independent from the mental resources that one brings to the situation – the epistemic resources that do the framing.[3]

Second, this *epistemic resourcefulness is closely coupled with the conceptual resources*. If Agi did not have the conceptual resources to recognise different kinds of 'drawing', 'modelling pedagogy' or the productivity of representations in teaching and learning, she would not be able to make any of those productive moves. However, what is distinct about these conceptual resources is that they are far from being well-articulated professional concepts expressed in professional discourse. Indeed, they form an intermediate level between experiences of 'how it works' in action and thought.

Much actionable knowledge is constructed through diverse coordinated attempts to make abstract knowledge actionable and actions meaningful.

---

[3] This situation is different from classroom studies in which the main prompt for changing the frame comes from the class teacher (Elby & Hammer, 2010; Louca et al., 2004).

References

Anderson, M. L. (2003). Embodied cognition: A field guide. *Artificial Intelligence, 149*(1), 91–130. doi:10.1016/s0004-3702(03)00054-7.

Bateson, G. (1972/2000). *Steps to an ecology of mind: Collected essays in anthropology, psychiatry, evolution, and epistemology* (New ed.). Chicago, IL: University of Chicago Press.

Bing, T. J., & Redish, E. F. (2009). Analyzing problem solving using math in physics: Epistemological framing via warrants. *Physical Review Special Topics – Physics Education Research, 5* (2), doi: http://dx.doi.org/10.1103/PhysRevSTPER.5.020108.

Bolman, L. G., & Deal, T. E. (1991). *Reframing organizations: Artistry, choice, and leadership*. San Francisco, CA: Jossey-Bass.

Brown, D. E., & Hammer, D. (2008). Conceptual change in physics. In S. Vosniadou (Ed.), *International handbook of research on conceptual change* (pp. 127–154). New York, NY: Routledge.

Checkland, P., & Poulter, J. (2006). *Learning for action: A short definitive account of soft systems methodology and its use for practitioners, teachers, and students*. Hoboken, NJ: John Wiley & Sons.

Checkland, P., & Scholes, J. (1999). *Soft systems methodology in action* (New ed.). New York, NY: John Wiley & Sons.

Clark, A. (1999). Embodied, situated and distributed cognition. In W. Bechtel & G. Graham (Eds.), *A companion to cognitive science* (pp. 506–517). Oxford, UK: Basil Blackwell.

Collins, H. M. (2010). *Tacit and explicit knowledge*. Chicago, IL: The University of Chicago Press.

Collins, A. (2011a). Representational competence: A commentary on the Greeno analysis of classroom practice. In T. Koschmann (Ed.), *Theories of learning and studies of instructional practice* (Vol. 1, pp. 105–111). New York, NY: Springer.

Collins, A. (2011b). A study of expert theory formation: The role of different model types and domain frameworks. In M. S. Khine & I. M. Saleh (Eds.), *Models and modeling* (pp. 23–40). Dordrecht, The Netherlands: Springer.

Collins, A., & Ferguson, W. (1993). Epistemic forms and epistemic games: Structures and strategies to guide inquiry. *Educational Psychologist, 28*(1), 25–42.

Damsa, C. I. (2014). Shared epistemic agency and agency of individuals, collaborative groups, and research communities. In E. Kyza, D. K. O'Neill, & J. L. Taba Polman (Eds.), *Learning and becoming in practice, Proceedings of the international conference of the learning sciences*. International Society of the Learning Sciences.

Damsa, C. I., Kirschner, P. A., Andriessen, J. E. B., Erkens, G., & Sins, P. H. M. (2010). Shared epistemic agency: An empirical study of an emergent construct. *Journal of the Learning Sciences, 19*(2), 143–186.

Donald, J. G. (2002). *Learning to think: Disciplinary perspectives* (1st ed.). San Francisco, CA: Jossey-Bass.

Edwards, A. (2005). Relational agency: Learning to be a resourceful practitioner. *International Journal of Educational Research, 43*(3), 168–182.

Elby, A., & Hammer, D. (2010). Epistemological resources and framing: A cognitive framework for helping teachers interpret and respond to their students' epistemologies. In L. D. Bendixen & F. C. Feucht (Eds.), *Personal epistemology in the classroom: Theory, research, and implications for practice* (pp. 209–234). Cambridge, UK: Cambridge University Press.

Ellis, R., Hughes, J., Weyers, M., & Riding, P. (2009). University teacher approaches to design and teaching and concepts of learning technologies. *Teaching and Teacher Education, 25*, 109–117.

Engeström, Y., Nummijoki, J., & Sannino, A. (2012). Embodied germ cell at work: Building an expansive concept of physical mobility in home care. *Mind, Culture, and Activity, 19*(3), 287–309. doi:10.1080/10749039.2012.688177.

Gioia, D. A. (1986). Symbols, scripts, and sensemaking: Creating meaning in the organizational experience. In H. P. Sims Jr. & D. A. Gioia (Eds.), *The thinking organization: Dynamics of organizational social cognition* (pp. 49–74). San Francisco, CA: Jossey-Bass.

Goodyear, P., & Retalis, S. (Eds.). (2010). *Technology-enhanced learning: Design patterns and pattern languages*. Rotterdam, The Netherlands: Sense.

Greeno, J. G. (2006). Learning in activity. In R. K. Sawyer (Ed.), *The Cambridge handbook of the learning sciences* (pp. 79–96). Cambridge, MA: Cambridge University Press.

Hall, R., & Seidel Horn, I. (2012). Talk and conceptual change at work: Adequate representation and epistemic stance in a comparative analysis of statistical consulting and teacher workgroups. *Mind, Culture, and Activity, 19*(3), 240–258. doi:10.1080/10749039.2012. 688233.

Hammer, D., & Elby, A. (2002). On the form of a personal epistemology. In B. K. Hofer & P. R. Pintrich (Eds.), *Personal epistemology: The psychology of beliefs about knowledge and knowing* (pp. 169–190). Mahwah, NJ: Lawrence Erlbaum Associates.

Hammer, D., & Elby, A. (2003). Tapping epistemological resources for learning physics. *Journal of the Learning Sciences, 12*(1), 53–90.

Hammer, D., Elby, A., Scherr, R. E., & Redish, E. F. (2005). Resources, framing, and transfer. In J. P. Mestre (Ed.), *Transfer of learning from a modern multidisciplinary perspective* (pp. 89–120). Greenwich, CT: Information Age.

Hofer, B. (2001). Personal epistemology research: Implications for learning and teaching. *Educational Psychology Review, 13*(4), 353–383.

Hofer, B., & Pintrich, P. (1997). The development of epistemological theories: Beliefs about knowing and their relation to learning. *Review of Educational Research, 67*(1), 88–140.

Hutchins, E. (2012). Concepts in practice as sources of order. *Mind, Culture, and Activity, 19*(3), 314–323. doi:10.1080/10749039.2012.694006.

Jacobson, M. J. (2001). Problem solving, cognition, and complex systems: Differences between experts and novices. *Complexity, 6*(3), 41–49.

Kahneman, D., & Tversky, A. (Eds.). (2000). *Choices, values and frames*. New York, NY: Cambridge University Press.

Kember, D., & Kwan, K.-P. (2000). Lecturers' approaches to teaching and their relationship to good teaching. In N. Hativa & P. Goodyear (Eds.), *Teacher thinking, beliefs and knowledge in higher education*. Dordrecht, The Netherlands: Kluwer.

Kirsh, D. (2009). Problem solving and situated cognition. In P. Robbins & M. Aydede (Eds.), *The Cambridge handbook of situated cognition* (pp. 264–306). Cambridge, UK: Cambridge University Press.

Kirsh, D., & Maglio, P. (1994). On distinguishing epistemic from pragmatic action. *Cognitive Science, 18*(4), 513–549. doi:10.1016/0364-0213(94)90007-8.

Knorr Cetina, K. (1981). *The manufacture of knowledge: An essay on the constructivist and contextual nature of science*. Oxford, UK: Pergamon Press.

Knorr Cetina, K. (1999). *Epistemic cultures: How the sciences make knowledge*. Cambridge, MA: Harvard University Press.

Kuhn, T. S. (1981). *The structure of scientific revolutions*. Chicago, IL: University of Chicago Press.

Kuhn, D. (1999). A developmental model of critical thinking. *Educational Researcher, 28*(2), 16–26.

Kuhn, D., & Park, S.-O. (2005). Epistemological understanding and the development of intellectual values. *International Journal of Educational Research, 43*(3), 111–124.

Latour, B., & Woolgar, S. (1979). *Laboratory life: The social construction of scientific facts*. Beverly Hills, CA: Sage.

Laurillard, D. (2012). *Teaching as a design science: Building pedagogical patterns for learning and technology*. New York, NY: Routledge.

Lobato, J., Rhodehamel, B., & Hohensee, C. (2012). "Noticing" as an alternative transfer of learning process. *Journal of the Learning Sciences, 21*(3), 433–482. doi:10.1080/10508406. 2012.682189.

Louca, L., Elby, A., Hammer, D., & Kagey, T. (2004). Epistemological resources: Applying a new epistemological framework to science instruction. *Educational Psychologist, 39*(1), 57–68. doi:10.1207/s15326985ep3901_6.

Maton, K. (2014). *Knowledge and knowers: Towards a realist sociology of education.* London, UK: Routledge.

McDonald, G., Le, H., Higgins, J., & Podmore, V. (2005). Artifacts, tools, and classrooms. *Mind, Culture, and Activity, 12*(2), 113–127.

Meads, G., & Ashcroft, J. (2005). *The case for interprofessional collaboration in health and social care.* Oxford, UK: Blackwell.

Muukkonen, H., & Lakkala, M. (2009). Exploring metaskills of knowledge-creating inquiry in higher education. *International Journal of Computer-Supported Collaborative Learning, 4*(2), 187–211. doi:10.1007/s11412-009-9063-y.

Nersessian, N. J. (2008a). *Creating scientific concepts.* Cambridge, MA: MIT Press.

Nersessian, N. J. (2008b). Mental modeling in conceptual change. In S. Vosniadou (Ed.), *International handbook of research on conceptual change* (pp. 391–416). New York, NY: Routledge.

Ohlsson, S. (1995). Learning to do and learning to understand: A lesson and a challenge for cognitive modelling. In P. Reimann & H. Spada (Eds.), *Learning in humans and machines: Towards an interdisciplinary learning science* (pp. 37–62). London, UK: Pergamon Press.

Orlikowski, W. J., & Gash, D. C. (1994). Technological frames: Making sense of information technology in organizations. *ACM Transactions on Information Systems, 12*(2), 174–207. doi:10.1145/196734.196745.

Pace, D., & Middendorf, J. (Eds.). (2004). *Decoding the disciplines: Helping students learn disciplinary ways of thinking.* San Francisco, CA: Jossey Bass.

Perkins, D. N. (1997). Epistemic games. *International Journal of Educational Research, 27*(1), 49–61.

Perkins, D. N., & Salomon, G. (2012). Knowledge to go: A motivational and dispositional view of transfer. *Educational Psychologist, 47*(3), 248–258. doi:10.1080/00461520.2012.693354.

Perkins, D., Tishman, S., Ritchhart, R., Donis, K., & Andrade, A. (2000). Intelligence in the wild: A dispositional view of intellectual traits. *Educational Psychology Review, 12*(3), 269–293.

Perry, W. G. (1970). *Forms of intellectual and ethical development in the college years: A scheme.* New York, NY: Holt, Rinehart and Winston.

Prosser, M., & Trigwell, K. (1999). *Understanding learning and teaching: The experience in higher education.* Buckingham, UK: SRHE and Open University Press.

Redish, E. F. (2004). *A theoretical framework for physics education research: Modeling student thinking.* Paper presented at the Proceedings of the international school of physics, "Enrico Fermi" Course CLVI. Amsterdam.

Schommer, M. (1990). Effects of beliefs about the nature of knowledge on comprehension. *Journal of Educational Psychology, 82*(3), 498–504.

Schön, D. A., & Rein, M. (1994). *Frame reflection: Toward the resolution of intractable policy controversies.* New York, NY: Basic Books.

Schwab, J. J. (1962). The concept of the structure of a discipline. *The Educational Record, 43*, 197–205.

Schwab, J. J. (1978). *Science, curriculum, and liberal education: Selected essays.* Chicago, IL: University of Chicago Press.

Sellers-Young, B. (1999). Technique and the embodied actor. *Theatre Research International, 24*(1), 89–97. doi:10.1017/S0307883300020290.

Shulman, L. S. (1986). Those who understand: Knowledge growth in teaching. *Educational Researcher, 15*(2), 4–14.

Tannen, D. (Ed.). (1993). *Framing in discourse.* New York, NY: Oxford University Press.

Trigwell, K., Prosser, M., & Taylor, P. (1994). A phenomenographic study of academics' conceptions of science learning and teaching. *Learning and Instruction, 4*, 217–232.

Wagner, J. F. (2006). Transfer in pieces. *Cognition and Instruction, 24*(1), 1–71.

Wagner, J. F. (2010). A transfer-in-pieces consideration of the perception of structure in the transfer of learning. *Journal of the Learning Sciences, 19*(4), 443–479.

Wenger, E. (1998). *Communities of practice: Learning, meaning, and identity.* Cambridge, UK: Cambridge University Press.

Wheelahan, L. (2010). *Why knowledge matters in curriculum: A social realist argument.* Abingdon, UK: Routledge.

Wittgenstein, L. (1967/2007). *Zettel.* G. E. M. Anscombe & G. H. V. Wright (Eds.), (G. E. M. Anscombe, Trans.). Berkley, CA: University of California Press.

Young, K. (Interviewer), & Rojo, T. (Interviewee). (2014, June 13). *Kirsty Young's castaway this week is the ballerina Tamara Rojo.* Desert Island Discs, BBC Broadcast. Retrieved from http://www.bbc.co.uk/programmes/b045xz2k

Zhang, L., & Sternberg, R. (2005). A threefold model of intellectual styles. *Educational Psychology Review, 17*(1), 1–53. doi:10.1007/s10648-005-1635-4.

Chapter 19
Teaching and Learning for Epistemic Fluency

19.1 Introduction

In this chapter, we turn from an analysis of the nature of epistemic fluency, actionable knowledge and knowledgeable action to address some implications for teaching and learning. We discuss some of the ways in which the development of epistemic fluency is currently supported in education (even if it does not go under that name) and make some suggestions about how this could be improved with respect to professional education. This is a large topic, for which we can only provide a skeleton treatment. Our intention is that the organising ideas introduced here will be enough to stimulate and guide curriculum leaders in professional education faculties. We address two major questions, primed by the issues raised in Chaps. 17 and 18. How can students develop:

1. Flexible conceptual resources that enable professional meaning-making and action?
2. Flexible epistemic resources that enable inquiry that produces actionable understanding?

We claim that well-designed tasks for professional learning are simultaneously professional (actionable, situated), conceptual and epistemic. Such tasks involve the weaving of epistemic games that are played in professions and a dynamic – embodied and embedded – assembling of actionable concepts. These tasks stimulate discourse that integrates generic (formal) and situated (functional) kinds of knowledge and formal and functional ways of knowing. They involve knowledge that is both coherent and contingent, structured and experiential and explicit and tacit.

Our main extension to this is to propose that epistemic games should not be understood solely as games of discourse and mind: they also involve the construction of material epistemic environments and an embodied conscientious self. We explain this in the final chapter of the book – Chap. 20.

© Springer Science+Business Media Dordrecht 2017   553
L. Markauskaite, P. Goodyear, *Epistemic Fluency and Professional Education*,
Professional and Practice-based Learning 14, DOI 10.1007/978-94-007-4369-4_19

19.1.1   Four Educational Approaches to Teaching and Learning for Epistemic Fluency

To frame the analysis for *this* chapter, we begin by recalling two views on the nature of learning and constructing expertise which can be found in forms of professional education that focus on learning by doing a representational view and a performative view (introduced in Chap. 3).

On the *representational* view, learning starts from fragmented experiences and rather messy, incoherent ways of doing things. But with experience, practice and repetition, knowledge and skill become increasingly coherent and systematic – expressed in routine and reasonably consistent patterns of thinking and doing. Thinking and action, through practice, become more methodical and consistent with the norms of the discipline or profession.

On the *performative* view, which foregrounds perception and action, learning starts from rather coarse perceptions and crude actions which, with experience, become more finely tuned – picking up and aligning to the specifics of each situation. Professional perception and action become more holistic, attuned to a larger number of relevant details.

The representational and performative views are echoed in two traditions of systems thinking, learning and practice, about which we will say more in Sect. 19.5, below. These traditions relate to two world views: the systematic and the systemic (Checkland & Scholes, 1999; Ison, 2008; and see Sect. 19.5.4, below).

A *systematic* approach can be characterised as a linear, step-by-step manner of tackling a problem. The relevant issues are examined in an *orderly* fashion, following recognised procedures and examining each part of the whole. A *systemic* approach also focusses on the whole; however, it focusses on *interconnections* between elements within the larger context of the whole. To understand things systematically means to approach them methodically. To understand things systemically means to put them into relationships with other things, within their larger context (Ison, 2008). There is no need to see these as oppositional approaches; rather, in combination, they constitute a powerful repertoire for purposeful, action-oriented, thinking and practice (Blackmore & Ison, 2012).

Table 19.1 captures the four families of educational approaches that we describe in detail in the body of this chapter. One way to think about them is in terms of their relations to conceptual and epistemic resourcefulness and to emphases in the way knowledge is framed – systematic and systemic.

Table 19.1 Teaching and learning for epistemic fluency: four educational approaches

	Conceptual resourcefulness	Epistemic resourcefulness
Knowledge as systematic (constructed around abstract concepts; representational)	Integrating knowledge	Playing epistemic games
Knowledge as systemic (constructed around the perception-action interface; performative)	Designing knowledge	Designing inquiry

Section 19.2 summarises educational approaches associated with *knowledge integration* and cognitive flexibility. The emphasis here is on how students can be helped to integrate the formal knowledge they encounter in classroom settings with everyday, real-world knowledge: including how they can be helped to learn how to relate formal academic knowledge to problems of practice. The examples we use mainly come from the work of Marcia Linn and Rand Spiro. Section 19.3 focusses on ways of enhancing students' ability to engage in inquiry. We use David Shaffer's interpretation of conducting inquiry through *playing epistemic games* and the work of Armin Weinberger and colleagues on scripting various kinds of collaborative inquiry. The shift of attention from conceptual to epistemic resourcefulness can also be thought of as shift from the systematicity of *knowledge* to the systematicity of *knowing*. The approach in Sect. 19.4 can best be called 'learning by *designing knowledge*' – the emphasis is on professional learning as a 'knowledge construction' task. A variety of educational innovators and theorists can be associated with this broad approach: we draw particularly on knowledge building and knowledge creation (Carl Bereiter, Marlene Scardamalia, Kai Hakkarainen and colleagues) and expansive learning (Yrjo Engeström and colleagues). Section 19.5 introduces 'learning by *designing inquiry*'. Its focus on inquiry places it in the 'epistemic' column of Table 19.1. It is distinguished by a shift in emphasis from creating knowledge by following (established) inquiry methods, to designing novel methods of inquiry, appropriate to the needs of emerging problems. We illustrate this with examples from Soft Systems Methodology, associated with the work of Peter Checkland and Ray Ison.

All four of these families of educational approaches are important. Professional actionable knowledge is not homogenous, so it should not be surprising that some educational approaches are more productive than others when addressing specific kinds of knowledge and specific learning challenges. That said, it should be clear that we have come to believe in the importance of approaches that acknowledge the socially and materially extended and embodied mind. This comes together with an acknowledgement of the central role of the ability to *construct and configure one's epistemic environments*.[1] This is an under-represented concern in professional education as currently practised, which we explore in Chap. 20.

19.1.2 Professional Problems: Structure and Stability

To map educational approaches onto classes of professional problem types, we also find it useful to employ the dimensions of (a) the degree of *structure* to the problem and (b) the degree of *stability* of the problem. The first of these involves distinguishing 'well-structured' from 'ill-structured' problems. The second

---

[1] We are thinking here of both a learner as an emerging professional and a professional as a lifelong inquirer.

distinguishes 'wicked' from 'tame' problems. As will soon become clear, these are poles on continua rather than discrete categories.

Problem structure: Problems are often described as falling on a continuum between well-structured and ill-structured. David Jonassen (2011) summarises key features of well-structured problems:

> Well-structured problems present all of the information needed to solve the problems in the problem representation; they require the application of a limited number of regular and circumscribed rules and principles that are organized in a predictive or prescriptive way; they possess correct, convergent answers; and they have a preferred, prescribed solution process. (Jonassen, 2011, p. 6)

Ill-structured problems are very different. They often involve some or all of the following: conflicting goals, multiple solution methods, unanticipated problems, multiple forms of problem representation, one or more unknown problem elements, multiple solutions, uncertainty about knowledge applicable to the problem and a need for personal judgements or reliance on personal beliefs.

The processes and thinking skills needed to succeed with well-structured and ill-structured problems are not the same. Well-structured problems are sometimes described as transformation problems (Greeno, 1980). That is, they consist of a known initial state, a known goal state and a set of operations for producing the solution from the initial information. The skills needed to solve such problems include being able to recognise the structure of the problem and being able to carry out the transforming operations that produce the solution (Chi, Glaser, & Farr, 1988; Newell & Simon, 1972). In real-world settings, recognising the kind of problem one is facing and knowing what knowledge is applicable to it are often quite difficult. Ill-structured problems cannot be described solely in terms of problem structure and representation or valid transformational moves. Their solution requires other kinds of information. Working out what information is likely to be relevant is a key part of solving ill-structured problems. Simplifying somewhat, we can see well-structured problems as essentially *recognition and knowledge integration* problems, whereas ill-structured problems are better thought of as *knowledge design* problems. We return to this in a moment.

Problem stability: Problems can also be described as falling on a continuum between 'tame' and 'wild' (or 'wicked') (Rittel & Webber, 1973).

> A tame problem is one where all the parties involved can agree what the problem is ahead of the analysis and which does not change during the analysis. In contrast, a wicked problem is ill-defined. Nobody agrees about what, exactly, the problem is. (Ison, 2008, p. 146)

Tame problems, even if they are ill-structured, can usually be solved using established strategies and applying established criteria. Wicked problems often involve defining the problem and solution simultaneously. They change during problem-solving work. Establishing agreement on the nature of the problem, appropriate methods for tackling it and criteria that can be used to know when a satisfactory solution has been reached are key aspects of working on wicked problems. Tame problems require an ability to choose and apply relevant problem-solving strategies – we can see them as *epistemic framing* problems. In contrast, part of how one tackles wicked problems is through setting up an appropriate inquiry strategy – so we see these as *inquiry design* problems.

Each of the next four sections describes one of the educational approaches we listed in Table 19.1. They share a common format.[2] Each section starts with a definition of *purpose* – what kind of problem is addressed by this educational approach? This is followed by an account of the *structure and principles* of the approach – how it works. After that come some *model cases*, usually based around the work of one or two people (researchers and educational innovators). These provide more concrete examples of the approach in action. Finally, each section offers an explanation of the *rationale* for the approach, evaluating its strengths and weaknesses in relation to the professional education challenges we have identified and making connections to key theoretical ideas and values – what kind of thinking informs this approach and what it offers for professional learning.

19.2 Approach One: Learning by Integrating Knowledge

19.2.1 Purpose

This approach is centred on enhancing students' abilities to integrate formal knowledge structures, learnt in academic settings, with their everyday, real-world knowledge. For reasons of space, we focus on two significant instances of this approach, drawing on the work of Marcia Linn on knowledge integration and Rand Spiro on cognitive flexibility and randomised instruction (Coulson, Feltovich, & Spiro, 1997; Linn, 1995, 2006; Spiro, Coulson, Feltovich, & Anderson, 1988/2013; Spiro & Jehng, 1990). Other instances of this approach can be found in Uri Wilensky's work on agent-based embodied modelling and complex systems (e.g. Goldstone & Wilensky, 2008; Wilensky & Reisman, 2006).

Knowledge fragmentation is a widely acknowledged challenge in higher education (Knight & Yorke, 2004; Renkl, Mandl, & Gruber, 1996). The problem takes a number of forms, but one of the most serious arises from the disconnect between students' everyday knowledge and formally learnt scientific principles. Some of the most intensively researched examples arise in areas of science education, where students endeavour to make sense of scientific descriptions and explanations of phenomena and processes by making connections with their existing experiential knowledge. In Linn's (2006) research, we then find students making statements like:

---

[2] Teaching and learning approaches are themselves 'knowledge' that is created by people for a particular purpose, and it is handy to have a tool that helps us to understand such practical knowledge. David Perkins (1986) suggests using these four questions about any knowledge: (a) what is its purpose, (b) what is its structure, (c) what are model cases of it, and (d) what are the arguments that explain and can be used to evaluate it? Our structure echoes Perkins' questions.

'metal feels colder than wood at room temperature' (p. 243) and expressing ideas in colloquial language – for example, treating 'heat' and 'temperature' as synonyms. As Linn notes, 'only heat flows in the classroom, but heat, cold and even temperature flow at home' (p. 244). Not all these ideas are wrong or counterproductive. Expert engineers and computer programmers regularly use a repertoire of strategies and ideas when they solve problems, rather than relying on a single formally correct strategy. It is likely that this is commonplace across all professions. Linn's approach is to use students' initial intuitive ideas as building blocks for developing more *integrated knowledge*: in the sense of knowledge that connects ideas learnt in class to knowledge and skills relevant in personal and professional contexts (Linn, 1995, 2006).

A variant of this approach can be found in Rand Spiro's work on advanced knowledge acquisition – a term he uses to identify learning that sits between introductory and expert levels (Spiro et al., 1988/2013). His focus is on the difficulties students have when reasoning with formal knowledge that they have already learnt when they encounter complex, 'messy' problems in diverse contexts. An example from Spiro's work would be the difficulties medical students encounter when reasoning with biological knowledge in clinical settings. They have been thoroughly tested on the underlying knowledge – that is not the issue. Rather,

> ... many concepts (interacting contextually) are pertinent in the typical case of knowledge application ... their patterns of combination are inconsistent across case applications of the same nominal type. (Spiro et al., 1988/2013, p. 545)

The initial understanding of foundational concepts, which is often acquired studying very clear instances, turns out to be too compartmentalised to function when needed in complex, real-world situations.

The approaches to this issue developed by Linn, Spiro, Wilensky and others fit under our heading of *learning as knowledge integration*: a family of educational approaches which see the disconnection of disciplinary knowledge from real-world experiences as one of the main obstacles to the development of a well-grounded understanding of theoretical concepts and more complex practical problem-solving skills. Despite some differences, these approaches all acknowledge the importance of formal disciplinary knowledge in understanding and solving real-world problems. They focus on the challenge of linking disciplinary generalisations with students' experientially grounded, contextualised ways of reasoning about the phenomena they encounter.

19.2.2 Structure and Principles

Linn and Spiro assign quite different roles to students' prior experiential learning.

Linn's (1995, 2006) *knowledge integration* approach focusses on the productivity of students' prior ideas. The approach is driven by four tenets: (a) make science accessible, by setting up investigations of personally relevant problems; (b) make thinking visible – so that it becomes easier to see and diagnose mistakes and compare alternatives; (c) help students learn from each other; (d) promote ongoing learning by helping students develop better self-regulation skills.

The instructional design that flows from these axioms involves four specific processes: (a) elicit students' initial ideas; (b) add normative ideas that stimulate knowledge integration (e.g. using pivotal cases, bridging analogies); (c) develop criteria for assessing ideas; (d) sort out ideas – building stronger connections between them.

These processes can be embedded in various instructional activities, such as experimenting, creating artefacts, exploring simulations and constructing an argument. The ultimate objective is to help students to make links between the experiential, often intuitive, knowledge that they use in everyday life and the new normative knowledge they are encountering in class.

Spiro's *cognitive flexibility theory* and the instructional approach derived from it (called 'random access instruction') (Spiro et al., 1988/2013) could be seen as having the opposite orientation to Linn's work. Where Linn is concerned with making productive use of students' prior experiential knowledge – moving from the world to the classroom – Spiro is concerned with the difficulties students face in applying formal knowledge to real-world problem-solving, moving from the classroom to the world. Spiro concentrates on what he terms students' 'reductive bias' – the tendency to use simplification strategies badly and overlook important aspects of real-world complexity in solving professional problems. There are seven kinds of common reductive bias and seven instructional principles to address them (Table 19.2).

The key to Spiro's educational approach is that instructional materials for advanced learning in complex professional domains should be represented as a flexible mix of *conceptual knowledge* (representations that are used to organise theoretical knowledge of the domain) and *practical cases* (generalised schemas created from specific events that underpin classical case-based reasoning and learning from experience) (see also Kolodner, 2006).

The overall idea is that advanced knowledge for solving problems in complex ill-structured domains can best be attained by developing mental representations of conceptual (theoretical) and practical (case-based) knowledge that support cognitive flexibility. For this, as Spiro and colleagues suggest, several instructional principles are central: (a) multiple representations of knowledge, (b) multidimensional and multi-perspectival 'crisscrossing' of a complex conceptual and practical territory during learning and (c) fostering students' ability to assemble diverse knowledge sources to the specificities of a particular situation.

So the instructional approach emphasises: (a) learning to apply knowledge flexibly, rather than the creation of new knowledge, and (b) the development of the right kind of mental representations to support this flexibility, rather than learning strategies and skills for assembling diverse knowledge sources. The core assumption behind this is that advanced knowledge for professional decision-making is best instantiated as a well-organised mental apparatus: with a systematic, detailed and well-organised mental map of the landscape, combining knowledge

Table 19.2 Seven sources of reductive bias and instructional principles to address them

Reductive bias	Principles for developing cognitive flexibility
Oversimplification of complex irregular structure – superficial similarities among phenomena are mistakenly taken as essential unifying features	Avoidance of oversimplification and overregulation: demonstrate complexities, irregularities, interactions and other complex features
Overreliance on a single basis for mental representation – complex multifaceted content narrowed down to the understanding of a single, incomplete prototypical case	Multiple representations: represent and revisit the same conceptual landscape and cases from different perspectives, multiple times
Context-independent conceptual representation – learnt knowledge is too abstract for effective application	Centrality of cases: allow learner to see how abstract knowledge is intertwined with cases and case-centred reasoning
Overreliance on 'top-down' processing – reasoning relies on generic theoretical abstractions	Conceptual knowledge as knowledge in use: show how meanings of concepts are connected to their patterns of use and facilitate reasoning from cases
Overreliance on precompiled knowledge structures – rigidly packaged schemata are used as recipes across many cases	Schema assembly (from rigidity to flexibility): shift focus from large precompiled knowledge structures to assembly of different conceptual knowledge and case sources (i.e. small knowledge structures)
Rigid compartmentalisation of knowledge components – interdependent aspects are treated as separable, overlooking connections	Non-compartmentalisation of concepts and cases: show interconnectedness of cases and concepts along multiple conceptual and practical dimensions
Passive transmission of knowledge – passive acquisition and limited personalisation of knowledge representations by a learner	Active participation and guidance: facilitate active learner involvement supported by opportunistic expert guidance and support to manage complexity of information

After Spiro et al. (1988/2013)

created from events (practical knowledge) and conceptual abstractions (theoretical knowledge). Well-organised mental representations allow problems to be approached from many different directions.

19.2.3   Model Cases

The knowledge integration approach has been applied in teaching a broad range of complex science topics, such as planetary motions and seasons, global climate change, principles of thermodynamic, genetics and natural selection. It is focussed on complex conceptual ideas in these domains. The instructional approach is usually implemented in a technology-enhanced learning environment that provides scaffolding for the four main processes: eliciting initial ideas, adding normative ideas, developing criteria and sorting out ideas (Linn & Eylon, 2011).

While much of the work has been in school settings, Linn (1995) also illustrates the use of this approach in undergraduate courses, for teaching ways of thinking rather than specific concepts. This includes teaching programming in computer science and spatial reasoning in engineering. In the engineering example, students are provided with an environment that scaffolds spatial reasoning by offering three-dimensional representations of objects that can be manipulated. The environment supports a repertoire of strategies for spatial problem-solving, such as a holistic strategy, where the whole object is rotated; a pattern strategy, where familiar parts of the object are rotated together and connected to the rest of the object; and an analytic strategy, where the object is rotated by manipulating individual lines and angles. During problem-solving tasks, students are asked to predict how a rotated object will appear, and they then rotate the object on the screen to compare and analyse their results. In tutorials, the students explicitly learn to distinguish among the three strategies, reflect on their methods for spatial problem-solving and discuss how they use the different strategies and the benefits and disadvantages of each. The main purpose is to provide opportunities for the students to share their reasoning strategies and to legitimise the repertoire of strategies rather than emphasise just one holistic strategy which is stereotypically considered as the best. While the goal is to provide students with opportunities to learn the most effective techniques, they are not discouraged from using their intuitive ways of approaching spatial problems – helping them to see the connections and differences between various ways of reasoning.

Cognitive flexibility theory has been applied in the development of learning resources for a range of professional learning areas, including medical reasoning (Coulson et al., 1997; Jonassen, 1992, 1996), teachers' classroom decision-making (Jonassen, 2011) as well as in reasoning about social, cultural and political topics (Jacobson & Spiro, 1995; Spiro, Collins, & Ramchandran, 2007).

These instructional resources are usually organised as hypermedia-based theoretical material that is intertwined with multiple case studies. Both theoretical information and cases are organised in such a way that students are able to explore the materials from many different angles. The main rationale for this format is that ideas and concepts cannot be fully understood from abstractions that are isolated from contextual details, and multiple cases provide opportunities to convey the situational richness in which meanings are embedded. The overall organisation of material aims to provide learners with the opportunity to grasp the complex irregular structure of the presented problems and concepts so they can sidestep the temptations of 'reductive bias'.

Therefore, the materials typically involve broad cases that represent the whole picture; these are then broken down into mini-cases, which include more detailed scenarios for specific themes. These themes represent possible conceptual organisations (schema) used by experts for understanding complex problems and which are common across many cases. They thereby provide opportunities for making comparisons and exploring similar thematic aspects across multiple scenarios. In order to convey the complexity of the problems, cases are usually presented from a variety of perspectives, including personal perspectives relevant to the case, thematic perspectives and theoretical perspectives.

For example, Jonassen illustrates how cognitive flexibility theory has been implemented in a learning environment for an introductory sociology course in which students learn how various sociological perspectives pertain to everyday decisions (Jonassen, 2011; Jonassen & Kim, 2010). Students face the task of making decisions such as hiring a sales director for a job, admitting freshmen to a university and evaluating applications from potential tenants wanting to lease a house. They are provided with a set of applications (cases) and asked to assess them by examining the applications from several sociological perspectives and considering such aspects as the applicants' credentials, gender and social class. In addition to the general application, students are provided with information about each applicant, on these perspectives. Drawing on the case information and relevant theories, students are required to make and justify their decisions. They are asked to identify relevant sociological concepts and facts to support their decisions, as well as concepts and facts that could be used to support alternative choices of candidates. They are also requested to examine and consider decisions from different personal perspectives (e.g. CEO of the company). In addition to these theoretical, thematic and personal perspectives, such analyses could include various disciplinary perspectives or broad paradigmatic ideas that would influence problem interpretation and solution.

19.2.4   *Rationale and Evaluation*

Knowledge integration approaches draw on a range of learning theories, including cognitivist, constructivist, developmental and sociocultural, but overall the core assumptions are deeply rooted in cognitive constructivist ideas. On this view, mind is organised using multiple representational structures, and the main learning challenge is to achieve better integration between them. For example, cognitive flexibility theory sees this as primarily a matter of integrating conceptual and case-based representations. The former representations support top-down reasoning using formal knowledge; the latter representations help with case-based reasoning drawing on precedents.

Both accounts – and the educational approaches they inspire – highlight the importance of being able to connect experiential and formal knowledge in order to make sense of complex phenomena encountered in the world.

> In an ill-structured domain, general principles will not capture enough of the structured dynamics of cases; increased flexibility in responding to highly diverse new cases comes increasingly from reliance on reasoning from precedent cases. Thus, examples/cases cannot be assigned the ancillary status of merely illustrating abstract principles (and then being discardable); the cases are key. (Spiro et al., 1988/2013, p. 551)

A major challenge in regard to reasoning about, and learning from, such cases is the so-called 'indexing problem'.[3] This emphasises two critical moments in learning and reasoning: 'insertion time' and 'retrieval time'. *At the insertion point* the learner interprets the situation in which they find themselves, identifies the main lessons to draw and labels this experience according to its 'applicability conditions'. These 'labels' describe when the experience is relevant and under which circumstances it ought to be applied in the future. While people can do such indexing intuitively, instructional approaches that build on case-based reasoning affirm that such labelling will be most effective if the learner takes time and makes a conscious effort to analyse background information and reflect on the potential applicability of relevant aspects of the experience to new situations. *At the retrieval point*, when the person encounters a new situation, they use their goals and understanding of the situation to identify and access relevant elements of existing, personal knowledge. The more the person is willing and able to engage in interpreting the new situation, the more likely it is that they will find a range of relevant experiences that could be applied productively for reasoning about the new situation and coming up with creative solutions. In short, knowledge integration approaches, by helping students to see links between theoretical knowledge and their experience or practical cases, aim to develop more integrated and flexible mental representations that underpin sound understanding and practical reasoning.

19.3   Approach Two: Learning by Playing Epistemic Games

19.3.1   Purpose

This approach concentrates on developing students' inquiry capabilities. In comparison with the first strategy, this approach shifts the focus from the systematicity of knowledge to the systematicity of *knowing*. Consider the following question.

What were the causes of the French Revolution? (Morrison & Collins, 1996, p. 109)

As Morrison and Collins (1996) note, if the answer to a question of this kind must be discovered rather than remembered, then a recognisable, systematic way of figuring out possible answers from available information, for example, by making

---

[3] See the research of Janet Kolodner (2006; Kolodner et al., 2003) on case-based reasoning (CBR). Research on CBR focusses on processes of reasoning from previous experience (cases) and is a source of educational methods that improve the ability to encode and retrieve relevant features of cases.

a list, is an inquiry process and the resulting, recognisable form for presenting the solution – that is, the list – is new knowledge.

Teaching and learning that regularly involve such work can be seen as shifting the emphasis from knowledge to knowing. As with the knowledge integration account that we discussed in Sect. 19.2, the systematic qualities of knowledge remain important. However, this systematicity is not so much a property of the organisation of conceptual resources (i.e. knowledge about the world) as it is a property of epistemic resources (i.e. knowledge for knowing).

The set of instructional approaches that embraces this view broadly builds on the idea of epistemic games, which we discussed in Chap. 14. On this view, shared knowledge and personal understanding have a structure (i.e. epistemic form): they are constructed by engaging in certain patterned ways of creating knowledge – epistemic games. So mastering the skills and schemas that allow one to play epistemic games well can be seen as an important challenge in education. In general terms, these instructional approaches range from those which focus on students' abilities to engage with certain *broad* forms of discourse (Collins, 2011; Collins & Ferguson, 1993), or to develop *general* mental schemas for solving particular classes of problem (Jonassen, 2011), to those which involve a *richer* mastery of an entire package of cognitive, social and cultural skills, values and other attributes that enable one to become an expert 'player' (Shaffer, 2004, 2006).

At the *broader* end – where the focus is on language and epistemic forms – knowledge is seen as constructed through discourse and interaction with the world. Indeed, knowledge *is* seen as discourse coupled with certain schematised ways of interacting with the world that different communities use to construct knowledge.[4] So the main challenge for students is to master the epistemic tools for engaging in different kinds of shared epistemic games, including through mastery of language and other ways of representing and inscribing knowledge. As Morrison and Collins (1996) are careful to note, this should not be seen as mere learning of a specialised vocabulary. Rather, it involves mastering a shared epistemological framework in which the *meanings* of terms are constructed. The focus for teaching is to devise ways to help students master the rules and principles that guide knowledge-producing conversations in specific epistemological frameworks: to help them become skilful in playing the epistemic games of the discipline or profession. And since professionals create shared knowledge and personal understanding across a broad

---

[4] We are discussing here how this learning approach is represented and enacted in the socio-cognitive literature, rather than reflecting the stronger cognitive accounts that see thinking capacity as primarily an internal mental process (e.g. Donald, 2002; Jonassen, 2011). In so doing, we nevertheless acknowledge that instructional design approaches underpinned by this stronger cognitive perspective also offer many valuable ideas. In their implementation, if not in the details of their theoretical underpinnings, the teaching and learning approaches that eventuate in higher education practices are not so very different. After all, they are inescapably social and discursive.

range of problems, domains, communities and epistemological frameworks, students have to be helped to become skilful players of a broad range of epistemic games.

At the *richer* end, the capacity to construct knowledge is not seen as solely the mastery of discourse structures; instead, it includes a whole package of traits that characterise participants of an epistemic community (Shaffer, 2006). David Shaffer (2009) argues that the professional capacity to solve complex problems depends on an entire 'epistemic frame'. As he explains:

> The concept of epistemic frames begins with the idea that any community of practice has a culture, and that culture has a grammar of: *skills* (the things that people within the community do); *knowledge* (the understandings that people in the community share); *values* (beliefs that members of the community hold); *identity* (the way that members of the community see themselves); and *epistemology* (the warrants that justify actions or claims as legitimate within the community). (Shaffer, 2009, p. 582, original emphasis)

For Shaffer, epistemic frames are more than the epistemic understanding of particular disciplinary ways of explaining and justifying claims and more than the mastery of epistemic structures that guide inquiry, such as 'epistemic forms' or 'epistemic games' as they are described by Allan Collins. Epistemic frames include epistemic understandings and epistemic structures that guide inquiries, but they go beyond this to include other explicit and intuitive principles that guide experts' practice. As Shaffer (2006) puts it,

> ... epistemic frames include methods for justification and explanation, and forms of representation, but orchestrated with strategies for identifying questions, gathering information, and evaluating results, as well as self-identification as a person who engages in such forms of thinking and ways of acting. If epistemic understanding and epistemic structures form the core of disciplines or subjects such as mathematics or history, then epistemic frames are the organizing principle for practices. Geometers, economists, statisticians, and engineers (all of whom use mathematics) have distinct epistemic frames that incorporate different epistemic understandings and structures from the domain of mathematics. (Shaffer, 2006, p. 228)

We might summarise the contrast between the instructional perspectives that are based on Collins' and Shaffer's positions in the following terms. The former focus on building students' epistemic fluency, understood as a flexible and transferable capacity to participate in, and weave, different epistemic strategies and structures, across a range of tasks, in different situations (Morrison & Collins, 1996). The latter focus on students' deep engagement with specific pockets of expertise in an epistemic community (Shaffer, 2004, 2006). Drawing on Crowley and Jacobs (2002), Shaffer (2006) calls such pockets 'islands of expertise' – distinct topics of a domain in which students become genuinely interested and where they develop deep knowledge. The corresponding instructional approach therefore provides students with rich but specific learning environments in which they can immerse themselves in role-playing experiences through which they develop expert skills, values and a sense of identity. On this interpretation, the term 'epistemic game' has more of an immersive, ludic sense.

19.3.2   Structure and Principles

A focus on inquiry processes is common to the various approaches that involve learning to play epistemic games: how does one (learn to) get knowledge? In various combinations, the approaches depend upon (a) an opportunity to work in an authentic inquiry environment and (b) scaffolding – such as prompts and scripts. The minimalist, discourse-focussed versions offer scaffolds that support particular kinds of interchanges. The richer, frame-based versions offer full-fledged learning environments in which a quite authentic experience of being apprenticed in a professional workplace can be had.

A key purpose in all or most versions of this approach is to help instil certain patterns of action that resemble professional problem-solving and interaction: fusing cognition and social aspects of knowing,

> Conversational moves of discourse become the building blocks of knowledge and knowing. (Morrison & Collins, 1996, p. 113)

While many patterns of behaviour and discourse are learnt intuitively, without explicitly noticing and being taught, this instructional perspective points to the importance of making thinking games visible (Perkins, 2009; Ritchhart, Church, & Morrison, 2011).

> *Naming* and *noticing* is a central part of becoming capable in particular activities . . . until students can name *a process* they cannot control it. As our attention is drawn to thinking, we become more aware of it, its uses, and effects. <. . .> Thus the visibility of thinking, both their own and others, provides the foundations for dispositional development. (Ritchhart et al., 2011, p. 29, emphasis added)

Thus, one of the key instructional principles is to provide tools that support productive thinking moves and make students' thinking explicit. As Ritchhart et al. (2011) note, questioning, listening and documenting play central roles in this process. However, one of the overarching strategies that should be fused in these activities is the use of what they call 'thinking routines' – patterns of action which focus students' attention on specific 'thinking moves'. Such thinking routines can be seen as 'pedagogical tools' for structuring and scaffolding learning activity; but, once learnt, they subsequently function as 'thinking tools' that can be used to guide individual and shared thinking and inquiry practices.

This kind of guidance can be implemented in a variety of ways, such as by (a) taking specific roles, (b) providing learners with various kinds of scripts, (c) scaffolding individual moves with prompts or (d) with external representations (Dillenbourg & Tchounikine, 2007; Fischer, Kollar, Mandl, & Haake, 2007; Jonassen, 2011; Morris et al., 2010; Runde, Bromme, & Jucks, 2007; Weinberger, Ertl, Fischer, & Mandl, 2005).

Firstly, as Runde et al. (2007) note, *social roles* that partners assume, or are asked to assume, in collaboration and communication, act as implicit guides that structure interaction and direct the kinds of moves that are seen as desirable. These roles may be quite fixed – as with a doctor and patient in a medical consultation process (Rummel & Spanda, 2007). Or they might be temporarily assumed – as with the roles taken by participants in various collaborative knowledge-generating activities, such as chair, note-taker, analyst, critical friend, writer and peer-reviewer (Gray, Brown, & Macanufo, 2010). Either way, adoption of a role brings with it implicit or explicit scripts that guide individual behaviours and the overall group interaction.

Secondly, learners can be provided with explicit task-specific or generic *scripts* that outline typical phases of an inquiry process. For example, Rummel and Spanda (2007) observe that the collaboration between a medical practitioner and psychologist, aimed at finding a better treatment for a patient – taking into account physiological and psychotherapeutic issues – may progress through 13 stages, starting with an initial coordination of objectives, and mutual questioning and answering, and individual work on diagnosis, up to joint formulation of a therapy. Such scripts can be general and flexible, only broadly outlining the macrostructure of the whole inquiry process, or they may be detailed and rigorous, strictly specifying every step on the way.[5]

Third, instead of providing learners with a complete script outlining the whole routine – including the sequencing of each step – students can be provided with a set of *prompts* that suggest possible moves characteristic of a game. For example, Morrison and Collins (1996) argue that prompts which guide students to label their contributions as 'information', 'commentary', 'question', 'conjecture', 'evidence for', 'evidence against', 'plan', 'step in plan', etc. will help structure their interaction in a way that facilitates a 'theory and evidence' epistemic game – common in constructing scientific understanding. Such scripts and prompts can focus on supporting certain cognitive or epistemic processes that are related to the content or social processes that are related to collaboration and the structuring of an argument. Either way, the main purpose is to make the characteristic moves of the game explicit.

Fourth, inquiry activity can be scaffolded and structured by means of *external representations*, or epistemic forms, such as tables, graphs, diagrams and concept maps (Collins, 2011; Collins & Ferguson, 1993; Okada, Buckingham Shum, & Sherborne, 2008; Runde et al., 2007). While such forms do not rigorously prescribe specific moves and their sequence, nevertheless they provide specific points of reference and, in collaborative activity, can act as scaffolds stimulating negotiation of joint meanings (Runde et al., 2007).

The broader epistemic games perspective and the richer epistemic frame perspective nevertheless suggest rather different educational designs. Reflecting on the affordances of environments that can support the development of epistemic fluency

---

[5] There is some uncertainty about which kinds or degrees of scaffolding are actually most productive (Dillenbourg & Tchounikine, 2007; Noroozi, Weinberger, Biemans, Mulder, & Chizari, 2013; Tchounikine, 2008; Weinberger et al., 2005). In our view, the answers depend in part on what kinds of educational outcomes are most valued. Efficient accomplishment of an individual learning task may be helped by tight scripting; supporting the development of autonomously managed inquiry skills may be better served by looser control.

through epistemic games, Morrison and Collins (1996) suggest that such environments should be quite open, with various kinds of general scaffolding, rather than closed – in the sense of specially constructed for playing one particular epistemic game. They describe several kinds of learning environments and instructional designs that can support learning through playing epistemic games:

Communication environments: offering structure for interactions that correspond to certain classes of epistemic games by providing specific sets of affordances and constraints. For example, an online learning environment may be designed to support discourses that are typical in specific scientific or professional communities, by guiding students to post kinds of messages that are characteristic of this discipline or profession.

Professional tools or construction kits: supporting students in specific kinds of epistemic tasks and enhancing their discourse by providing for it an authentic material basis that organises the inquiry process. Such tools include mathematical modelling environments that are used by mathematicians and spreadsheets and accounting programs that are used by accountants.

Modelling and simulation environments: helping students to conduct various 'thought experiments'. In such environments, students may, for example, create and trial scenarios and examine emerging problems from alternative viewpoints.

While some of these environments and affordances may be quite similar to those used for knowledge integration (Sect. 19.2 above), the emphases with respect to the instruction and learning objectives are quite different. In the current case, the goal is to help students learn to play and understand an epistemic game. That is, the students' developing skills, which enable them to participate in the game, are no less important and may well be of greater lasting value, than the specific knowledge that is constructed during the game. As Morrison and Collins (1996) caution, many environments only support the *playing* of epistemic games; they do not necessarily *teach* students to play them. Thus, the organisation of activities and the teachers' shaping of discourse play important roles. That is, becoming a good player involves not only learning to behave according to a certain set of rules but also mastering a range of strategies and how to choose and fuse them effectively in different situations.

Shaffer's (2006, 2009) approach – centred on epistemic frames – partially addresses this latter challenge by suggesting that such environments should be more comprehensive. They should be capable of supporting specific schematised ways of knowing and acting and also simulate specific rich experiences that students would encounter in the real world of professional practice. (For example, such learning environments should reflect real contexts and specific kinds of mentor support available in the workplace.) Nevertheless, while such environments could support the development of students' professional traits by facilitating their learning of specific strategies, they are not necessarily good at raising students' awareness of how they think and behave and why. (For example, strategies that are appropriate for specific situations can easily be confounded with more generic moves, rules and principles.)

19.3.3   Model Cases

The underpinning principle here is to scaffold patterns of behaviour and thinking in a simulated environment. To illustrate this, we use two sets of example cases, based on scripting and the use of frames.

Script-based methods: There are various template and script-based designs for inquiry and problem-solving tasks (Gray et al., 2010; Ritchhart et al., 2011) and learning environments, particularly in the field of computer-supported collaborative learning – CSCL (Fischer et al., 2007; Strijbos & Weinberger, 2010). These can be used to illustrate the main features of the discourse-centred instructional perspective on epistemic games. Such tasks and environments have been used for teaching and learning a range of inter-professional skills, such as supporting lay people in communication with IT experts, scaffolding net-based medical consultations and facilitating the learning of inter-professional problem-solving in medical education. Weinberger and colleagues (2005) illustrate how this approach has been applied and tested in CSCL, with students on an education course learning psychological theories. Specifically, students participated in an online learning session about attribution theory. The groups – each composed of three students – were given the task of analysing three case problems from an attribution theory perspective and then collaboratively preparing one final analysis for each case. The cases represented typical attribution issues, such as that a student's interpretation of failure is cast in terms of lack of talent. The descriptions of the cases were presented as simple texts. Students worked remotely, communicating with each other via a web-based discussion environment. Some groups of students were provided with two kinds of scripts: social and epistemic.

The *social scripts* included two elements. First, in the analysis of each case, each team member took a specific role: either analyst or constructive critic. One student took the role of analyst and was responsible for preparing the initial and final analyses of a case and responding to the feedback of the two critics. The two other students took the role of constructive critic for that case and had to present a critique of the initial analysis prepared by the analyst. Secondly, case analysts and constructive critics were provided with sets of *prompts* that were implemented as message templates. The template for writing a constructive critique included prompts that invited further elaboration and discussion, such as 'These aspects are not yet clear to me' and 'My proposal for the adjustment of analysis is…' (Weinberger et al., 2005, p. 14). The template for the analyst's response to the critiques included prompts to respond to each aspect of the critique, such as 'Regarding the desire for clarity…' and 'Regarding the modification proposals…' (loc. cit.).

These scripts are aimed at helping students pick up their distinct roles and to stimulate critical negotiation between team members, by encouraging elaboration of their arguments and discouraging premature consensus on a solution.

The *epistemic scripts* prompted students to apply theoretical concepts to cases. They were implemented in the form of a message template with questions and other prompts about the cases from the attribution theory perspective, such as 'Is the attribution located internally or externally?', 'Is the cause for the attribution stable or variable?', 'Prognosis and consequences from the perspective of the attribution theory' (op. cit., p. 14). These prompts were aimed at guiding learners to identify case information relevant to identifying the underlying issue and proposing a pedagogical intervention. The epistemic script was designed to assist with the preparation of the initial analysis of the case, while two social scripts guided students through further discussion of the cases and collaborative problem-solving.

Weinberger and colleagues (Noroozi, Weinberger, Biemans, Mulder, & Chizari, 2012; Weinberger et al., 2005, Weinberger, Stegmann, & Fischer, 2010) build their instructional design of the task and environment on the view that the different perspectives of the three collaborating student partners may prompt each student to reconsider their individual points of view and negotiate and refine their understanding. Such joint engagement with theoretical knowledge and the problem help students both to develop deeper individual understanding and arrive at a better joint solution. However, productive collaboration does not always happen spontaneously.

There are at last two distinct dimensions to successful collaboration: epistemic and social. The epistemic activities relate to how team members deal with the content of the task, for example, how they categorise information and identify relevant concepts. The social activities describe how learners communicate with each other, for example, how they relate their contributions to the joint problem-solving in relation to their partners' ideas. Therefore, providing students with specific scaffolds that help them with each dimension of collaboration may facilitate more productive learning and joint problem-solving. While epistemic scripts aim to assist students with construction of a productive problem-solving strategy, social scripts aim to scaffold productive interaction with each other.

Epistemic frame-based methods: David Shaffer and colleagues have published a number of examples of the use of epistemic game and frame-based methods to provide students with simulation activities that help with the development of epistemic resourcefulness (Shaffer, 2004, 2006, 2009). Most of these are set in K-12 school settings. We have chosen the following example from R&D by Shaffer's team because it comes from a higher education setting.

Chesler, Arastoopour, D'Angelo, Bagley, and Shaffer (2013) discuss a simulator for professional practice in engineering. 'NeproTex' is a fictitious company that offers a virtual internship for first year undergraduate students. During this virtual internship, students are given a task to design a next-generation dialyser membrane. They are provided with most of the resources needed to complete the task, such as technical reports, literature reviews, information about the company, stakeholders and employees; the summary of the requirements for the membrane; and a simulator for the membrane. Students are also given an internship progression chart that depicts the main steps in the internship and the design process: introduction, literature review and data analysis, several cycles of design–build–test and the final presentation of their design. During the internship, each project team of four to five students is mentored by a design advisor and an immediate supervisor with whom they communicate by email or online chat. The membrane simulator allows students to change four parameters of the membrane: material, processing method, surfactant and percentage of carbon nanotube. It represents the performance of the designed membranes using five criteria: biocompatibility, marketability, reliability, ultrafiltration rate and cost. Because of the 'cost' of testing, students are permitted to test only five possible design alternatives in each of two design cycles. During this design process, students evaluate their models against benchmarks for each of five performance metrics that are desired by the various stakeholders involved in the innovation: manufacturing and clinical engineers and marketing and product support teams, for example. The required and desired metrics are different, and, overall, it is impossible to design a membrane that would ideally meet all stakeholder preferences. However, in the last stage of the design, each team must choose 'an optimum device' that best meets stakeholders' preferences and requirements. They present their final design and justification to the class, design advisors and instructors.

As Chesler et al. (2013) state, the task incorporates a number of critical aspects of engineering design, such as exposure to the design process, individual research, exploration of a large and complex design space and stakeholder feedback. Furthermore, the task presents a compelling challenge for first year undergraduates, and the complexity of the design space and competing stakeholder requirements preclude an easy optimisation. Overall, the implemented instructional design of the virtual internship raises many issues that engineering designers would encounter during professional practice, such as working in a team, receiving advice from mentors, gathering information, considering multiple alternatives, iterating through the steps of the design cycle, making and justifying decisions, communicating with clients and so on. A guided virtual internship of this kind helps students master appropriate epistemic frames.

These two examples (scripts and frames) nicely illustrate the core feature of epistemic games: the focus is not only on learning to apply specific disciplinary concepts to the problem but learning rules, moves and strategies of the 'games' that constitute the epistemic practices of the professional community.

19.3.4 Rationale and Evaluation

While the knowledge integration perspective that we described in Sect. 19.2 is primarily based on cognitive constructivist approaches to learning, this epistemic game perspective builds on social approaches, such as sociolinguistic theories of language use and conceptual change (Vygotsky, 1978, 1986). Morrison and Collins (1996) suggest that educational communities can be seen as special instances of communities of practice and learning as an inter-mental process that takes place in specific contexts through real-time discourse. Learning and knowledge work can be thought of as 'conceptual learning conversations' and 'transformative conversations' (Morrison & Collins, 1996, p. 107). On this view, epistemic forms and games are language based, and the ability to play an epistemic game is a linguistic capability, developed through social interactions in a community.

This epistemic games perspective does not dismiss the cognitive dimensions of learning, but sees cognition as primarily happening through discourse. Deep learning and integration of new knowledge or information take place when learners play epistemic games with this information, rather than through mere memorisation. Understanding is more than the accumulation of correct answers – it happens when 'learners participate *in* the information that they have access to' (Morrison & Collins, 1996, p. 114, emphasis added).

Shaffer's (2004, 2006) epistemic framework view extends this approach to learning from language to multimodal interactions in and with a 'thick, authentic' environment – offering access to qualities of epistemic practice that can be hard to articulate, including values and identity. As Shaffer (2006) argues, mastering an epistemic frame means becoming a participant in a particular community of practice. It includes mastering declarative knowledge ('knowing that') and procedural knowledge ('knowing how') and also what Broudy (1977) calls 'knowing with' – a deep understanding of the context, within which one perceives, interprets and judges. This also embraces 'knowing where' and 'knowing when' (Shaffer, 2006, pp. 227–228).

In professional education, the epistemic games approach, with its adoption of the idea of communities of practice, involves a blending of professional practice and learning practice perspectives (see Chaps. 14 and 15). Different communities have distinct epistemologies – distinctive ways to know, justify and evaluate claims. Epistemologies of professions intersect with disciplinary epistemologies that have traditionally provided an organising structure for formal education. And it is important to note that professional knowledge and ways of knowing are not amalgams of disciplinary knowledge and ways of knowing. Productive instructional approaches to professional education are more likely to be based on the organisation of knowledge and ways of knowing of professional communities rather than disciplinary domains. Furthermore, learning is not restricted to educational institutions, but also happens in workplaces. Professional learning communities, in workplace settings, construct their particular epistemologies, and so it is more productive to develop instructional approaches – and learning environments in educational institutions – by building on ways in which successful *professional learning* communities construct their knowledge, rather than on ways in which *established expert* communities organise professional knowledge for real work. Learning in design studios, and in similar sites of apprenticeship, provides good examples. Mentorship, mutual guidance and similar forms of scaffolding for the action of other people are integral to the creation of a learning community's knowledge.

As Stahl (2007) notes, this family of instructional approaches embodies a practical tension. It works well when the learner is engaged in situations where their behaviour cannot be known in advance and where a delicate balance is needed between prior instructional design and support and too much prescription and guidance. Further, reflecting on the state of the art of empirical studies in this area, Spada (2010) remarks that the ultimate goal of roles and other scaffolds is to support students' epistemic agency. Thus, it is not enough to regulate effective student behaviours and goal achievement on a particular task. It is important to encourage students' *mindful* use of these scaffolds in a strategic, self-reflective way. Epistemic agency, as Spada points out, is still a challenge for instructional design – an important 'visionary goal' rather than something we already know how to embed in everyday practice.

To sum up, the epistemic games approach sees inquiry and professional problem-solving as relatively systematic processes. The conceptual space implicated in a problem may be large and complex; many epistemic games may be involved. However – in this family of approaches – it is normal for the conceptual space to be closed. Through participating in epistemic games, students become more skilful at playing individual games and at recognising which games need to be played. It is much rarer for them to be placed in situations in which they have to modify or even invent new epistemic games. (We look at this in Sect. 19.5.)

19.4   Approach Three: Learning by Designing Knowledge

19.4.1   Purpose

> Engineers are not the only professional designers. Everyone designs who devises courses of action aimed at changing existing situations into preferred ones. The intellectual activity that produces material artifacts is no different fundamentally from the one that prescribes remedies for a sick patient or the one that devises a new sales plan for a company or a social welfare policy for a state. Design, so construed, is the core of *all professional training*; *it is the principal mark that distinguishes the professions from the sciences*. Schools of engineering, as well as schools of architecture, business, education, law, and medicine, are all centrally concerned with the process of design. (Simon, 1966/1996, p. 111, emphasis added)

The shared characteristic of this family of learning approaches is that they see professional knowing and learning as a 'knowledge construction' task. They share an epistemology that is heavily shaped by design practice and design thinking. On this view, knowledge is created in response to a specific challenge: as an object shaped to a particular purpose. As Perkins (1986) puts it, knowledge can be seen as 'a tool to get something done' (p. 2).

This perspective includes a variety of approaches, ranging from some that associate learning with an individual capacity to approach problematic situations in a 'designerly' way (Razzouk & Shute, 2012; Schön, 1987) to collaborative engagement in innovation and shared knowledge creation in scientific communities and other workplace settings (Bereiter, 2002; Engeström & Sannino, 2010). More specifically, we include approaches that go under the headings of 'knowledge building' (Bereiter, 2002; Scardamalia & Bereiter, 2006), 'trialogical inquiry', 'knowledge creation' (Paavola & Hakkarainen, 2005), 'object-oriented inquiry' (Muukkonen & Lakkala, 2009; Muukkonen, Lakkala, & Paavola, 2011), 'design thinking' (Brown, 2008, 2009; Brown & Wyatt, 2010) and 'expansive learning' (Engeström & Sannino, 2010).

These approaches have diverse epistemological roots, purposes and commitments.[6] However, despite differences, they have important shared features and synergies (Paavola et al., 2004). They agree on a view that learning is a deliberative process of knowledge construction and knowledge improvement that leads to the formation of new conceptual constructs – theoretical knowledge of various kinds. This knowledge construction process normally follows a heuristic model or pattern that is shared within a community and guides individual and shared knowledge production and discourse. Knowledge improvement is primarily guided by the epistemological agenda of synthetic and integrative ways of designerly thinking, and oriented towards specific conceptual objects. Successful learning is manifested as improvements in the objects. Outcomes are gauged by enhancements in ideas or practices, rather than by progress towards an absolute true or justified belief. Learners are viewed as members of groups or communities with shared purposes, and learning is collective, rather than a matter of individual challenge and achievement.

Shared conceptual objects – 'functional concepts' (Engeström & Sannino, 2012), 'conceptual artefacts' (Bereiter, 2002), 'design concepts' (Cross, 2011), etc. – are at the heart of this approach. However, in contrast with the knowledge integration perspective (Sect. 19.2), this view is less concerned with understanding already known, preconfigured conceptual constructs (e.g. Newton's laws, classic symptoms of a disease) and more interested in the construction of new, functional, conceptual constructs (e.g. a new theory that explains political events or an unusual treatment tailored to the specific needs of a patient). The main goal is to design conceptual blends for problematic situations that are encountered in the world, rather than to fit problems into existing concepts. That is, knowing involves constructing concepts, rather than just linking and applying existing conceptual constructs in encounters with the world.

Some instructional models – particularly those that focus on established scientific disciplines – use the terms 'inquiry' or 'knowledge building' rather than 'design' for describing knowledge work in scientific communities. However, the structures of their proposed models – such as 'progressive inquiry' or 'knowledge building' – have many similarities with the designerly processes we sketch here. As Perkins (1986) asserted,

---

[6] We do not underestimate the importance of such differences, but given space and our purpose we cannot do them justice here. For some illuminating discussions, we suggest the following sources: epistemological roots (cf. Engeström & Sannino, 2010; Paavola, Lipponen, & Hakkarainen, 2004), design vs. scientific research and inquiry (Farrell & Hooker, 2013; Galle & Kroes, 2014; Krippendorff, 2007), design as optimisation vs. design as dialogue (Li, 2002) and learning vs. knowledge building (Bereiter, 2002).

> ... knowledge is not just *like* design but *is* design in a quite straightforward and practical sense. (Perkins, 1986, p. 2, original emphasis)

Or as Glanville (2002) put it:

> ... all research and all knowledge/knowing is a matter of design. (Glanville, 2002, p. 120)

Such pragmatic ways of thinking, learning and acting, which build on the epistemological agenda of practical inquiry and design, at individual and collective levels, are seen as the foundation for more creative and flexible forms of professional work – co-configuration, knotworking, etc. (Engeström, 2008; and see Chap. 3).

19.4.2 Structure and Principles

This 'learning as knowledge design' view broadly builds on the assumption that everyday knowledge problems are generally 'wicked', thus conceptual constructs for solving them need to be constructed rather than taken from the shelf and applied.

These conceptual constructs should reflect the complex nature of the world. That is, problems depend on framing and there is not necessarily one optimal solution – and problem-solving processes should lead to a systemic exploration of the world and the generation of a systemic (satisficing) solution. Specific approaches have their own, slightly different, prototypical models of how this knowledge design process should be carried out, but, broadly, all the approaches suggest that such systemic solutions can be reached by following their recommended heuristics. Examples include 'the expansive learning cycle' (Engeström & Sannino, 2010) and 'the progressive inquiry model' (Muukkonen, Lakkala, & Hakkarainen, 2005). In a similar vein, one might also consider the conventional stage models of 'design thinking' (Ambrose & Harris, 2010; Brown, 2008). These heuristics usually emphasise that thinking should be broad and creative, intended to 'build up' ideas and encourage wide-ranging systemic exploration, including broad participation by a wide range of stakeholders and the voicing of diverse views (see also Paavola et al., 2011).

The proposed models generally include several stages – often between three and eight – with steps, modes or guiding questions that serve as a framework for structuring the overall inquiry or design process. Then, each stage may further involve a set of more specific methods or techniques.

For example, one of the prototypical models, widely known in the design field, includes seven *stages*: define, research, ideate, prototype, select, implement and learn (Ambrose & Harris, 2010). Then, as Waloszek (2012) notes, there is a set of typical *methods* that designers employ when they work on each stage. For example, the definition stage may use a set of heuristic methods and tools for refining the design brief; the research stage may use canonical techniques for observing and interviewing users; and the ideation stage may use various brainstorming, sketching and other idea generation techniques.

These heuristic models generally acknowledge that the design process is not linear – some steps may be skipped, repeated or occur simultaneously. For example, Tim Brown (2008, 2009) says that the process is very different from the 'milestone-based' projects that are typical of the work of many organisations. Design activity often loops back on itself and feels quite chaotic to those who are not used to it.

That said, another common assumption across this family of approaches is that the kinds of processes used to tackle new problems share some stable characteristics and that the methods used in each stage are – in broad terms – known in advance. The choice of specific methods is either a part of an overarching design thinking heuristic or is made by designers subconsciously. That is, the design thinking process is either 'orchestrated' by existing heuristics and learnt through articulated formal discourse or is 'orchestrated' by 'nature and culture' and learnt through participation in design work. Such encounters with the creative minds of experienced designers are necessarily complicated by the tacit aspects of their epistemological and methodological expertise. In either case, the 'good' design thinking that emerges has a reasonably systematic quality: or at least the general form of this process is known in advance. Whatever the nature of such design thinking, in many teaching and learning situations, these systematic processes of good design and discourse are often used as explicit (step-by-step) heuristic models.

19.4.3   Model Cases

This example draws on Muukkonen et al. (2005), who take their inspiration from work on 'knowledge building' (Bereiter, 2002; Scardamalia & Bereiter, 2006), 'knowledge creation' (Paavola & Hakkarainen, 2005) and 'object-oriented inquiry' (Muukkonen et al., 2011). Muukkonen et al. (2005) used a pedagogical model of 'progressive inquiry' in psychology courses at university level. According to this model, learning is organised as a shared inquiry that resembles the processes which expert communities follow when they work with knowledge in ill-defined domains, as is common in the social sciences. Students work together, addressing particular knowledge questions, by constructing shared objects of inquiry such as working theories, explanations and models. This collaborative work includes question–explanation sequences, which are triggered by certain epistemological 'clashes', such as contradictions between two theories or other kinds of problems.

Progressive inquiry is seen as a cyclic process, and the model delineates seven essential elements through which exploration and learning progress: (a) creating the context, (b) presenting research problems and setting up research questions, (c) constructing working theories, (d) conducting critical evaluations, (e) deepening knowledge, (f) deepening problems and generating subordinate questions and (g) developing new working theories (Fig. 19.1). These elements are not necessarily followed stepwise and their importance varies from inquiry to inquiry. Nevertheless, they are seen as 'epistemologically essential elements that a learning community needs to go through' (Muukkonen et al., 2005, p. 530). The

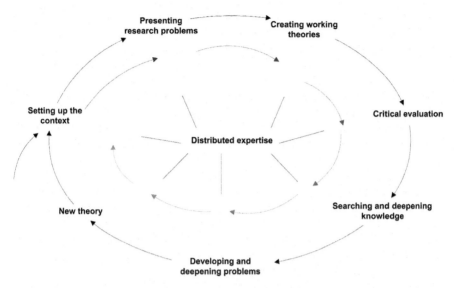

Fig. 19.1   The model of progressive inquiry (Adapted from Muukkonen et al., 2005, p. 531)

core characteristic of the progressive inquiry around which these elements are centred is *distributed expertise*. This notion of distributed expertise points to the learners' cognitive responsibility for discovering knowledge or solutions as well as to a metacognitive responsibility for organising shared inquiry at individual and collective levels. That is, they need to attend carefully to such things as goal setting, planning, monitoring, evaluating and otherwise organising object-oriented, collaborative work over an extended time frame (Muukkonen & Lakkala, 2009). The final product that students create is not a 'true' answer that can be known in advance; rather it is an assembled 'knowledge artefact' – a plausible theory, explanation, etc. – that gives rise to a new shared understanding.

Teachers, and designed learning environments, have several important roles here. Firstly, students are explicitly provided with the progressive inquiry framework for structuring their tasks and activities, so that their investigation follows processes and practices that are similar to experts' work with knowledge in the domain. Second, students are provided with scaffolds that guide the inquiry processes and are offered authentic, situation-specific, expert guidance – which they call 'expert participation during the inquiry process'. The teachers' facilitating role shaping the course of learning is central. As the authors note,

> The most important role of the teacher and the facilitators of collaboration is *to create the context* for this collaboration and *provide anchors* between the theoretical representations, world knowledge, and the real-life experiences that students report. It is also necessary to *structure and scaffold* the process and *keep it active and in focus* during the progression of the course. (Muukkonen et al., 2005, p. 536, emphasis added)

In short, the teacher's responsibility is to set up an epistemic environment and processes that result in a productive expert-like inquiry; the learners' responsibility is to learn their way through, and develop their capacities to engage productively in, these kinds of disciplined and systematic inquiries, including the meta-skills for self-organising knowledge-creating inquiry.

Muukkonen and colleagues illustrate how they applied this model in various university courses (Muukkonen & Lakkala, 2009; Muukkonen et al., 2005; Muukkonen et al., 2011). Initially, students are introduced to the progressive inquiry model and how its heuristics should be used in the inquiry process (i.e. 'setting up the context'). They are also provided with initial resources for generating questions. The students then create their research questions and themes for collaborative inquiry. Throughout the course, students explore their topics by engaging in the progressive question–explanation discussions and producing a joint report or other knowledge artefact, at the end. The work is organised in a collaborative web-based environment, which scaffolds groups' engagement into a certain form of (expert) discourse by asking students to categorise their messages using 'inquiry scaffolds' (e.g. labelling their contributions using tags like: 'Problem', 'My explanation', 'Evaluation of the process', etc.). The tutors' involvement in discussions may vary from general experts' and teachers' guidance to very close involvement and, in some cases, each group of students is supported by a dedicated tutor who organises activities and participates in the discussions.

19.4.4   Rationale and Evaluation

We can identify four quite diverse lines of thinking and educational innovation that actually converge around the notion of learning by designing knowledge. They agree – using their own terminologies and assumptions – that deep learning can result from engagement in the knowledge creation practices of disciplinary and professional communities and that (real-world) processes of professional problem-solving, innovation and invention necessarily entail some learning.

First, there is the line of work associated mainly with Carl Bereiter and Marlene Scardamalia on knowledge building (e.g. Bereiter, 2002; Scardamalia & Bereiter, 2006). Bereiter and Scardamalia talk about two modes for dealing with knowledge – 'belief mode' and 'design mode'. Belief mode foregrounds the truth value of knowledge. In contrast, design mode foregrounds the use value of knowledge. Collective work on the improvement of conceptual artefacts – working with knowledge in design mode – is very much concerned with assessing and improving the usefulness of ideas. Crucially, knowledge work is not seen as detached from the practical world; rather, inquiry is one kind of material practice that is firmly connected to, and grounded in, the challenges of the physical world.

Second, there is Herbert Simon's work on 'the sciences of the artificial' (Simon, 1966/1996). Simon distinguishes the natural sciences, with their focus on what is true, from the sciences involved in making the sociotechnical environment, within which the resolution of complex problems can rarely be done through optimisation.

> Engineering, medicine, business, architecture, and painting are concerned not with the necessary but with the contingent – not with how things are but with how they might be – in short, with design. (Simon, 1966/1996, p. xii)

Simon's view of 'design' and 'curriculum for design' is focussed on the formal knowledge and skills involved in evaluating and synthesising design alternatives, working with arrays of requirements and constraints and arriving at decisions that satisfice conflicting requirements (rather than optimising on single variables).

Third, we can identify a line of thinking with roots directly in the design professions – best articulated in the writing of Donald Schön (1983, 1987; and see Chaps. 2 and 3). Like Simon, Schön argued that all professions are design-like and would benefit from education in design. However, their views separate over the role of formal, technical–rational knowledge in design practice: key for Simon and questionable for Schön. Schön's emphasis is the need (for everyone) to learn how to deal with complex, messy problems in artistic and reflective ways – for example, by conducting 'frame experiments':

> ... [to] impose a kind of coherence on messy situations and thereby discover consequences and implications of their chosen frames. (Schön, 1987, p. 157)

This skill of 'problem framing' – running an experiment on the spot, detecting the consequences and gradually reframing – is at the core of the design professions. It involves special kinds of knowledge and ways of knowing – which Schön (1987) called 'knowing in action' and 'reflection in action'. While these kinds of knowledge and knowing have a verbal component, they are generally tacit. In this sense, designing involves 'professional artistry' which cannot be taught; rather it must be learnt by doing. A productive instructional approach for learning such knowledge is a 'design practicum' where students learn by undertaking simplified projects in a safe, 'design studio' style instructional environment. Such environments approximate to real practice settings (e.g. a design studio in architecture) in which students' project work is accompanied by close supervision and guidance from 'master professionals'. This teaching involves 'coaching', 'joint experimentation' and 'reciprocal reflection' – demonstrating, doing, talking and reflecting while working through problems side-by-side.

The fourth, though by no means the least influential, line of work to be considered here comes from outside formal education, though it is very closely concerned with improvements in professional practice. We refer to work on 'expansive learning' (e.g. Engeström, 2001; Engeström, Nummijoki, & Sannino, 2012; Engeström & Sannino, 2010). Despite many ontological and epistemological differences, the general argument is quite similar. The approach takes what we can call a 'systemic view' of the problematic situation, acknowledging that complex problems can rarely be solved by 'fitting' the problem into a specific, preconfigured set of conceptual constructs or schemas. Rather, problems often need to be solved by designing new 'functional concepts' that fit the encountered situation (Engeström & Sannino, 2012). This kind of problem-solving involves learning to explore the problematic situation from multiple perspectives, framing the problem, and, from multiple pieces of available knowledge, designing a 'solution concept'. That is, the main emphasis of learning and professional skill is on the collective process of assembling in the world, rather than on the representations in someone's head.

Connecting all four of these lines of thinking is a clear sense that there are established procedures for working with knowledge, including creating new knowledge. They do not say much about circumstances in which one needs to be able to deliberatively modify existing inquiry procedures or design *new* kinds of inquiry – new ways to think through encountered challenges.

19.5   Approach Four: Learning by Designing Inquiry

19.5.1   Purpose

This approach aligns with a recognition that many complex problems in the worlds of professional work require *conscious design of the inquiry process* that will be used to tackle them. The design literature talks about 'wicked problems' (Rittel & Webber, 1973; and see Sect. 19.1.2, above). We extend that notion by distinguishing a special class of wicked problems which we call 'wicked systemic problems'. Wicked design problems, in Rittel and Weber's sense, are seen as wicked mainly because they have no clear, uncontestable solution. However, they can often be tackled by using established design methods. We see 'wicked systemic problems' as problematic situations that require the people working upon them to engage in deep learning and in the *design of the methodology* or *method* for tackling the challenge. Blackmore and Ison (2012) talk about it this way, in reference to managing systemic change, which they say is

> ... mainly about developing a critical appreciation of situations with others, recognizing what actions are systemically desirable and culturally feasible and getting organised to affect change in a positive way. (Blackmore & Ison, 2012, pp. 348–349)

So, strategies for investigating and solving shared, systemic wicked problems are much fuzzier than for investigating and solving 'tame' problems (even complex ill-structured ones) and what one might call 'regular' or 'designerly' wicked problems. As with wicked problems generally, they normally entail constructing the *problem* and its *solution* together. But systemic wicked problems are usually distributed across, and solved by, many people over extended periods of time. So they require both joint action and deep learning, which enables all the actors to make sense of the situation and act in alignment with how others think and act. Crucially, systemic wicked problems are dynamic; they change while they are being worked upon and so cannot be tackled by a single strategy that can be chosen in advance. It is not just that the problem and its solution are constructed together, but the problematic situation, the solution and the problem-solving strategy are worked on together.[7]

Wicked systemic problems are increasingly common in many professional domains, particularly in areas of engineering, management and the social/caring professions – information systems, design, environmental planning, health, social work and education, for example (Senge, 2000, 2006; Senge, Smith, Kruschwitz, Laur, & Schley, 2010; Wals & Corcoran, 2012). Here is a representative example from the field of healthcare.

> The home care managers and workers are now struggling to redefine their work and services so as to meet such demanding problems as increasing loneliness and social exclusion, loss of physical mobility, and dementia. <...> *How* can the managers, workers, and clients *learn to work* in such a way that the new needs are met and the society can afford to provide the service? (Engeström & Sannino, 2010, p. 1, emphasis added)

Blackmore and Ison (2012) give an example of a similar challenge encountered in environmental sustainability:

> Should people in Europe welcome the increased availability of biofuels when their production is often considered unsustainable as it is linked to water supply constraints and increased competition for land for food production? (Blackmore & Ison, 2012, p. 349)

Questions like these require that we do more than take into account the interconnections between various systems – such as the social and biological – and acknowledge multiple causes and multiple effects. We also have to work with peculiarities of the problem-solving context, the multiplicity of human perspectives and the requirement for sustainable, joint action. When problem-solving processes are distributed across many domains of professional expertise, and touch on diverse non-professional interests, this demands diverse kinds of knowledge, diverse ways to think and *diverse ways to construct knowledge*. In short, the process of problem-solving is ill-structured, not just the problem itself. And while designerly approaches to solving wicked problems typically result in the production of new objects, systemic wicked problems involve joint learning and design of the inquiry process itself. For example, if one imagines trying to find an answer to the question posed above about biofuels, then one immediately faces the issue of *how* such an inquiry should be conducted. The scale of the problem; the diversity of the cultures, people and interests affected; and the need for shared sense-making and joint action over extended periods of time all combine to make us aware that the processes of learning and knowing involved will be complex, problematic and hard to untangle.

It is increasingly acknowledged that the social and psychological phenomena involved in solving complex issues should be regarded as an integral part of the problematic situation and its solution (Checkland, 1994; Checkland & Scholes, 1999; Ison, 2008; von Foerster, 2003). That is, people who solve the problem, and

---

[7] In the literature on systems inquiry from which we are drawing in this section, people tend not to use the word 'problem', so much as 'problematic situation' or 'challenge' – aiming to emphasise that such complex issues usually require understanding and changing the whole situation rather than fixing one particular 'problem' (e.g. Checkland & Poulter, 2006).

the process that is used to solve it, are a part of the solution. In such situations, the emphasis moves from first-order learning by design (i.e. learning to design complex solutions) to second-order learning by design (i.e. learning to design the learning process).[8] These two learning processes are complementary, but the latter cannot be reduced to the former.

The dominant approaches to professional education certainly acknowledge that professionals have to tackle wicked problems almost every day and that they may have to deal with these promptly and with little time for deliberation. But we have found very few traces in the professional education or instructional design literature of approaches that help students and practitioners learn how to design their own process of inquiry. We explore one promising candidate in the next section.

19.5.2   Structure and Principles

A good candidate to exemplify the approach we have in mind can be found in Soft Systems Methodology (SSM) – see, for example, Checkland and Poulter (2006), Checkland and Scholes (1999) and Checkland and Winter (2006). Checkland describes SSM as a general approach for dealing with situations that are seen to be problematic and which call for action. SSM involves an organised, flexible process for inquiring and learning which helps people to think through the situation and achieve sufficient understanding for taking sensible action to improve it. The process builds on systems thinking and systems practice and includes joint learning. Social situations are seen as complex, with many interactions among different elements which constitute an emergent whole. Furthermore, it regards human sense-making and other actions involved in conducting inquiry as constituting similar, interconnected complex systems with an emergent property of purposefulness. The main conceptual tool for conducting inquiry is model-building. However, the models constructed are not regarded as descriptions of the real world, as it is, or should be. Rather, the models are intellectual devices for organising structured discussion, understanding different world views, learning and finding an accommodation.

The SSM learning cycle usually involves four activities: *exploration* (finding out about the problematical situation), *model-building* (building conceptual models that represent different world views), *structured discussion* (aiming to find an accommodation) and *action* (implementing agreed actions in the real world). See Fig. 19.2.

Checkland stresses that SSM is a methodology not a method – not even a bundle of methods. The emphasis is on general principles of inquiry rather than particular

---

[8] This shift mirrors the difference between first-order and second-order view and first-order and second-order learning that we briefly introduced by drawing on Heinz von Foerster's (2003) work in Chap. 7.

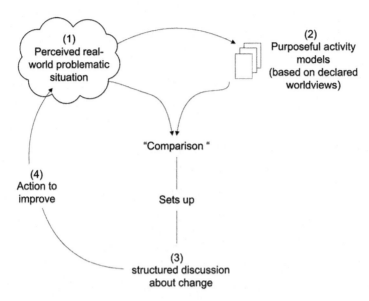

Fig. 19.2 The SSM learning cycle (Based on Checkland & Poulter, 2006, p. 13) (By permission of John Wiley & Sons Ltd)

steps or strategies. While SSM suggests some frameworks, they need to be tailored to the unique features of each situation. To help with this, SSM offers two useful intellectual devices.

Firstly, it emphasises the fact that inquiry is itself a purposeful activity and, as such, learning involves two streams of activity: SSMc (content) and SSMp (process). SSMc deals with the content of the problematic situation; SSMp deals with how the process of inquiry is carried out (see Fig. 19.3).

Secondly, SSM offers the LUMAS model for making sense of relations between the actors, problematic situations and methodologies involved. As Fig. 19.4 shows, learning (L) starts from a user (U) of the methodology, who perceives a problematic situation (S) and appreciates a methodology (M) and weaves these two elements together into an actual situation and user-specific approach (A). This approach simultaneously guides inquiry into the situation and yields improvement and further learning.

In short, this view of systems thinking and systems practice sees the process of acting in complex problematic situations as a form of learning that simultaneously facilitates changes in the situation, understanding and practice: including the way one learns.

This learning how to learn is achieved in two ways: (a) through *retrospective* reflection and an existing intuitive sensitivity to the situation and capacity for reflection in action and (b) through conscious design of the conceptual tools for organising systemic exploration, learning and design – *preceding and accompanying* reflection. Skilful practice is not just an outcome of learning; skilful practice *is* (skilful) learning.

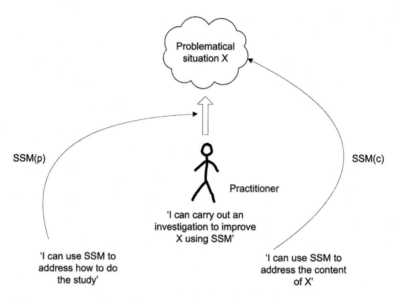

Fig. 19.3 SSM involves two streams of activity, focussed on content and process (Based on Checkland & Poulter, 2006, p. 31) (By permission of John Wiley & Sons Ltd)

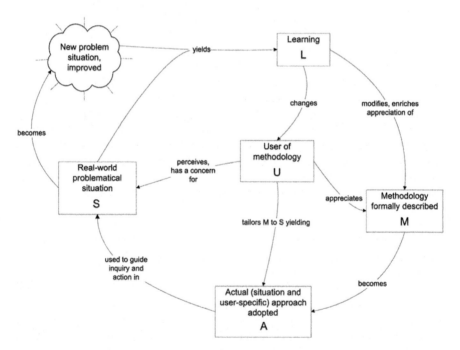

Fig. 19.4 The LUMAS model (Based on Checkland & Poulter, 2006, p. 20) (By permission of John Wiley & Sons Ltd)

19.5.3   Model Cases

We will focus here on a case taken from Ison, Blackmore and colleagues' work in 'systems practice' in the field of environmental decision-making (Blackmore & Ison, 2012; Ison, Blackmore, & Armson, 2007; Ison, Blackmore, Collins, & Furniss, 2007). Among the key elements of their pedagogical design is to create circumstances for the epistemological shift in students' views of practice and learning from first order to second order. This shift

> ... involves the move from seeing *systems as 'real'* (i.e. having some ontological status) to seeing *'systems' as epistemological devices* for learning about situations of complexity (i.e. messes) with a view to changing or improving (transforming) them. (Ison, Blackmore, Collins, et al., 2007, p. 1349, emphasis added)

They extend this view of system to the 'learning system' itself:

> ... we see a 'learning system' as moving from having a clear ontological status (e.g. this course) to becoming an epistemic device, a way of knowing and doing. (op. cit., p. 1344)

One of the main objectives is to create 'an enactive learning system' in which learners experience (environmental) decision-making through engaging in systemic inquiry and systemic practice. As they note,

> A systemic inquiry has to be *designed* not prescribed. (Blackmore & Ison, 2012, p. 349, emphasis added)

That is, one of the aims is to provide students with a learning environment which allows them to see the course as 'an epistemic device' and to begin to become 'learners as designers' – 'to make the material their own and orchestrate their own evolving praxis' (Ison, Blackmore, Collins, et al., 2007, p. 1345).

The overall framework that provides the structure for their course builds on a generic framework for environmental decision-making (Fig. 19.5). It involves four main elements: (a) to explore and re-explore the situation; (b) to formulate problems, opportunities and systems of interest; (c) to identify feasible and desirable changes; and (d) to take action.

At the centre of this model is the use of specific techniques in systems practice. The development of students' systems practice 'know how' is supported by two instructional strategies:

- Students are provided with specific tools to engage in such practice, including the general heuristic model for environmental decision-making and a range of systems diagramming techniques (e.g. systems maps, multiple cause diagrams, rich pictures, metaphors).
- Students are explicitly asked to engage critically with the overall framework and specific techniques. For example, as a part of the project work in which students analyse their selected decision-making situation, they are requested to select, use and evaluate specific techniques that they used for modelling, evaluating and negotiating and to critically appraise the overall decision-making framework.

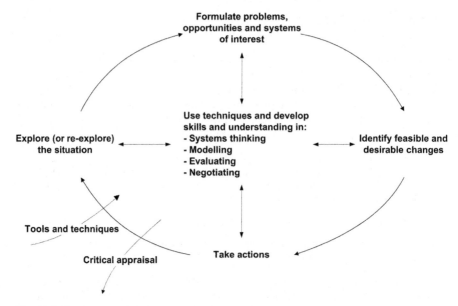

Fig. 19.5 Environmental decision-making framework (Based on Ison, Blackmore, Collins, et al., 2007, p. 1350)

As Ison and colleagues acknowledge, an obvious limitation of the framework is that – as with all frameworks – it has certain systematic features that will not fit every decision-making situation and may lead to a linear step-by-step use. However, the focus on the use of a range of techniques and tools for knowing, the need to choose, and adapt them to the situation, and finally to use them in action, makes explicit the role of the learners as designers of their own epistemic practices.

Ultimately, the students' use of their own (re)designs of the epistemic tools, for their own inquiry and learning, allows them to experience the second-order view of systems practice that entwines inquiry, design and learning: the students are a knowing part of the inquiry that they have designed.

19.5.4   Rationale and Evaluation

This approach of 'learning by designing inquiry' has its roots in constructivist intellectual traditions that build on notions of second-order cybernetics, self-organisation and social learning – including appreciative inquiry (Checkland & Scholes, 1999; Vickers, 1965), trajectories and landscapes of practice (Blackmore & Ison, 2012; Wenger, 1998) and *autopoiesis* (Ison, Blackmore, Collins, et al., 2007; Maturana & Varela, 1980).

These views put social relationships, practical engagement with the world and the evolving nature of human meaning-making at the centre of human knowing. For example, Checkland and Scholes (1999) describe the ontological and epistemological foundation of SSM as follows:

> The view of social reality implied both by the form of SSM and by the way it is used is that it is the ever changing outcome of a social process in which human beings continually negotiate and re-negotiate, and so construct with others their perceptions and interpretations of the world outside themselves and the rules for coping with it. These rules are never fixed once and for all. (Checkland & Scholes, 1999, p. 311)

From this perspective, actions are not driven by certain stable meanings that exist only in the external world. Rather, meanings which are attributed to actions are continuously (re)generated within the system, as people perceive the world, make value judgements and envisage the forms of relationships that they aspire to maintain with the world – within 'the interacting flux of events and ideas unfolding through time' (op. cit., p. A51).

> ... action results from the meanings that members of organizations attribute to their own and each other's acts. Organizational life becomes a collective process of meaning attribution; attention is displaced away from the apparently impersonal processes by means of which, in the conventional model, a reified organization as an open system responds to a changing environment. (op. cit., p. A47).

Overall, this view of learning puts the entanglement of human meaning-making and action at the centre of human knowing. Checkland and Scholes try to convey the nature of this perspective in the following phrases:

> Action not behaviour, Action arises from meanings, Meanings as social facts, Meanings are socially sustained, Meanings are socially changed. (loc. cit.)

Several pairs of foundational concepts characterise this approach and merit closer inspection: *systematic and systemic* views of systems thinking, *hard and soft* systems thinking, *theory and practice, first-order and second-order* views related to the orchestration of learning and *dualism* and *duality*. We introduced the first pair (systematic and systemic) in Sect. 19.1, but we now need to say a bit more.

Systematic and systemic: The word 'system' is often used to refer to things that are *systematic*. 'Systematic' can be taken to mean 'arranged or conducted according to a system, plan, or organized method; involving or observing a system; (of a person) acting according to system, regular and methodical'.[9] When this notion is applied to systems thinking – that is, as systematic thinking – it connotes ways of thinking that are constituted from well-articulated parts or steps, often connected in a linear fashion (Ison, 2008). However, the word 'system' also refers to things that are *systemic*: that is, where they cannot be fully understood through the isolation and examination of individual parts. 'Systemic' here means 'Relating to a system as a whole; inherent in the system; relating to, or affecting more than one system of

---

[9] *'Systematic, adj. and n.'*. Oxford English Dictionary. Retrieved July 09, 2015 from http://www.oed.com/view/Entry/196668?redirectedFrom=Systematic

organs, or the body as a whole'.[10] When this systemic interpretation is applied to systems thinking, it connotes the understanding of things as interconnected wholes.

> ... to understand things systemically literally means to put them into a context, to establish the nature of relationships (Ison, 2008, p. 142).

Ison points out that 'systemic awareness' comes from understanding properties that often characterise complex systems, such as feedback relationships, emerging properties and counter-intuitive effects. It also includes a deep awareness that unintended consequences may arise if multiple interconnected mechanisms and complex feedback mechanisms are not appreciated.

Most importantly, this 'knowledge as inquiry design' view emphasises that 'systemicity'[11] is not only a property of the physical and social world but also a critical property of human inquiry.

Hard and soft systems thinking: As Checkland and Scholes (1999) explain, the distinction between hard and soft systems thinking can be found in the ways systemicity is attributed.

> Hard systems thinking assumes that the world is a set of systems (i.e. is *systemic*) and that these can be *systematically* engineered to achieve objectives. In the soft tradition, the world is assumed to be problematic, but it is also assumed that *the process of inquiry* into the problematic situations that make up the world can be organized as a system. (Checkland & Scholes, 1999, p. A49, original emphasis)

The focus shifts – from assuming the world to be systemic to taking the process of inquiry as systemic.

Systematic and systemic, hard and soft, are often seen as being in opposition. However, practitioners who work in a 'soft' tradition firmly argue that the two views complement each other and that, in professional decision-making, they form a productive duality.

> When understood as a *duality* (a totality), rather than as a *dualism* (a self-negating pair), systemic and systematic thinking and practice create a powerful repertoire for affecting the trajectories of change in a purposeful manner. (Blackmore & Ison, 2012, p. 348, emphasis added)

They also note that systemicity is not best seen as a natural property of the world or of inquiry: rather, it is the observer who gives rise to a particular view of inquiry and a particular form of the world. Thus, as Ison (2008) notes, systems practice requires one to act with 'epistemological awareness' –

> ... to know the traditions of understanding out of which we think and act, including the extent of our epistemological awareness. (Ison, 2008, p. 148)

---

[10] *Systemic, adj. (and n.)'*. Oxford English Dictionary. Retrieved July 09, 2015 from http://www.oed.com/view/Entry/196680?redirectedFrom=systemic

[11] By 'systemicity' we mean 'having the property of system-like characteristics' (Checkland & Scholes, 1999, p. A49).

Indeed, differences in epistemology are a common source of tension and frustration in work practices, particularly in inter-professional work, although the cause is often unnoticed and unacknowledged. As Ison observes:

> Practitioners may not even have the language to speak about it [epistemology]. (op. cit., p. 151)

Theory and practice: This systems thinking and systems practice view does not oppose theory to practice nor does it negate the importance of articulated knowledge. Theory and practice are seen as recursively interrelated and themselves constitute an emergent whole: a 'duality' rather than a 'dualism'. As Ison, Blackmore and Armson (2007) comment: successful innovation in R&D and university education

> ... is not theory without practice or practice without theory but the reflective emergence of both in a situated context ... a capacity to braid theory and practice in novel contexts. (Ison, Blackmore & Armson, 2007, p. 221)

In sum, this view of learning moves from seeing theory, practice and knowledge as being objects to seeing them as things that are continuously (re)assembled in a (recursive) flow of theorising, practising and knowing.

First- and second-order views of learning systems: Ison, Blackmore, Collins, et al. (2007) extend this view of systems to learning systems.

> ... it is a first-order logic that makes it possible to talk about, and act purposefully to design or model a "learning system." A second-order logic appreciates the limitations of the first-order position and leads to the claim that a "learning system" exists when it has been experienced through participation in the activities in which the thinking and techniques of the design or model are *enacted* and *embodied*. (Ison, Blackmore, Collins, et al., 2007, p. 1344)

Following this logic, a 'learning system' can only come into being after its enactment.

> The second-order perspective is not a negation to the first – they can be understood as a duality. This first to second-order shift also enables a more effective engagement with the difficult concept of 'learning'. (loc. cit.)

In other writing, Ison and colleagues describe their view of theory and practice as a 'turn[ing] away from nouns to the verbs associated with what is being done' (Ison, Blackmore, & Armson, 2007, p. 221). In response, we might say that this also risks introducing another unproductive dualism – for practice is both a verb and a noun.

19.6 Concluding Comments

In this chapter, we have outlined four broad families of approaches to teaching and learning for epistemic fluency. In so doing, we have synthesised a range of ideas, educational innovations, theory and practice that originate in a very diverse array of formal and informal educational settings. They also come from other domains of professional practice and the literature on learning and organisation change. In part, we wanted to demonstrate that usable ideas can be harvested from unsuspected places. People involved in thinking about professional education should be able to find inspiration and insight in the literature on primary school science, for example – just as teacher educators should feel confident about drawing on systems thinking, design methodology and theories of learning from biology and organisational science.

We also want to suggest that it is not productive to regard these four approaches as four opposing camps – each demanding exclusive loyalty. Rather, an understanding of what is core to each approach – how it works and why – can inform new and richer versions of education for innovative professional practice.

Learning for knowledgeable action cannot be achieved just by creating better designs, but through embodied enactments of these designs. However, action does not take place in a material or social vacuum. This demands a clear appreciation that human knowing and embodied knowledgeable actions are inseparable from their environments, which brings us to the point where we can present our fifth approach – the main subject of Chap. 20.

References

Ambrose, G., & Harris, P. (2010). *Basics design 08: Design thinking*. Lausanne, Switzerland: AVA Publishing SA.

Bereiter, C. (2002). *Education and mind in the knowledge age*. Mahwah, NJ: Lawrence Erlbaum Associates.

Blackmore, C., & Ison, R. (2012). Designing and developing learning systems for managing systemic change in a climate change world. In A. E. J. Wals & P. B. Corcoran (Eds.), *Learning for sustainability in times of accelerating change* (pp. 347–364). Wageningen, The Netherlands: Wageningen Academic.

Broudy, H. S. (1977). Types of knowledge and purposes of education. In R. C. Anderson, R. J. Spiro, & W. E. Montague (Eds.), *Schooling and the acquisition of knowledge* (pp. 1–17). Hillsdale, NJ: Lawrence Erlbaum Associates.

Brown, T. (2008, June). Design thinking. *Harvard Business Review*, pp. 85–92.

Brown, T. (2009). *Change by design: How design thinking transforms organizations and inspires innovation*. New York, NY: Harper Business.

Brown, T., & Wyatt, J. (2010). Design thinking for social innovation. *Stanford Social Innovation Review, 28*(Winter 2010), 30–35.

Checkland, P. (1994). Systems theory and management thinking. *The American Behavioral Scientist, 38*(1), 75–91.

Checkland, P., & Poulter, J. (2006). *Learning for action: A short definitive account of soft systems methodology and its use for practitioners, teachers, and students*. Hoboken, NJ: John Wiley & Sons.

Checkland, P., & Scholes, J. (1999). *Soft systems methodology in action* (New ed.). New York, NY: John Wiley & Sons.

Checkland, P., & Winter, M. (2006). Process and content: Two ways of using SSM. *The Journal of the Operational Research Society, 57*(12), 1435–1441.

Chesler, N. C., Arastoopour, G., D'Angelo, C. M., Bagley, E. A., & Shaffer, D. W. (2013). Design of a professional practice simulator for educating and motivating first-year engineering students. *Advances in Engineering Education, 3*(3), 1–29.

Chi, M. T. H., Glaser, R., & Farr, M. J. (Eds.). (1988). *The nature of expertise*. Hillsdale, NJ: Lawrence Erlbaum Associates.

Collins, A. (2011). Representational competence: A commentary on the Greeno analysis of classroom practice. In T. Koschmann (Ed.), *Theories of learning and studies of instructional practice* (Vol. 1, pp. 105–111). New York, NY: Springer.

Collins, A., & Ferguson, W. (1993). Epistemic forms and epistemic games: Structures and strategies to guide inquiry. *Educational Psychologist, 28*(1), 25–42.

Coulson, R., Feltovich, P., & Spiro, R. (1997). Cognitive flexibility in medicine: An application to the recognition and understanding of hypertension. *Advances in Health Sciences Education, 2* (2), 141–161. doi:10.1023/A:1009780229455.

Cross, N. (2011). *Design thinking: Understanding how designers think and work.* Oxford, UK: Berg.

Crowley, K., & Jacobs, M. (2002). Islands of expertise and the development of family scientific literacy. In G. Leinhardt, K. Crowley, & K. Knutson (Eds.), *Learning conversations in museums.* Mahwah, NJ: Lawrence Erlbaum Associates.

Dillenbourg, P., & Tchounikine, P. (2007). Flexibility in macro-scripts for computer-supported collaborative learning. *Journal of Computer Assisted Learning, 23*(1), 1–13. doi:10.1111/j. 1365-2729.2007.00191.x.

Donald, J. G. (2002). *Learning to think: Disciplinary perspectives.* San Francisco, CA: Jossey-Bass.

Engeström, Y. (2001). Expansive learning at work: Toward an activity theoretical reconceptualization. *Journal of Education and Work, 14*(1), 133–156. doi:10.1080/13639080020028747.

Engeström, Y. (2008). *From teams to knots: Activity-theoretical studies of collaboration and learning at work.* Cambridge, NY: Cambridge University Press.

Engeström, Y., Nummijoki, J., & Sannino, A. (2012). Embodied germ cell at work: Building an expansive concept of physical mobility in home care. *Mind, Culture, and Activity, 19*(3), 287–309. doi:10.1080/10749039.2012.688177.

Engeström, Y., & Sannino, A. (2010). Studies of expansive learning: Foundations, findings and future challenges. *Educational Research Review, 5*(1), 1–24. doi:10.1016/j.edurev.2009.12. 002.

Engeström, Y., & Sannino, A. (2012). Concept formation in the wild. *Mind, Culture, and Activity, 19*(3), 201–206. doi:10.1080/10749039.2012.690813.

Farrell, R., & Hooker, C. (2013). Design, science and wicked problems. *Design Studies, 34*(6), 681–705. http://dx.doi.org/10.1016/j.destud.2013.05.001.

Fischer, F., Kollar, I., Mandl, H., & Haake, J. M. (Eds.). (2007). *Scripting computer-supported collaborative learning: Cognitive, computational and educational perspectives.* New York, NY: Springer.

Galle, P., & Kroes, P. (2014). Science and design: Identical twins? *Design Studies, 35*(3), 201–231. http://dx.doi.org/10.1016/j.destud.2013.12.002.

Glanville, R. (2002). A (Cybernetic) musing: Some examples of cybernetically informed educational practice. *Cybernetics & Human Knowing, 9*(3–4), 117–126.

Goldstone, R. L., & Wilensky, U. (2008). Promoting transfer by grounding complex systems principles. *Journal of the Learning Sciences, 17*(4), 465–516. doi:10.1080/10508400802394898.

Gray, D., Brown, S., & Macanufo, G. (2010). *Gamestorming: A playbook for innovators, rulebreakers, and changemakers.* Sebastopol, CA: O'Reilly.

Greeno, J. (1980). Trends in the theory of knowledge for problem solving. In D. T. Tuma & F. Reif (Eds.), *Problem solving and education: Issues in teaching and research* (pp. 9–23). Hillsdale, NJ: Lawrence Erlbaum Associates.

Ison, R. (2008). Systems thinking and practice for action research. In P. Reason & H. Bradbury (Eds.), *The Sage handbook of action research: Participative inquiry and practice* (pp. 139–158). Los Angeles, CA: Sage.

Ison, R., Blackmore, C., & Armson, R. (2007). Learning participation as systems practice. *The Journal of Agricultural Education and Extension, 13*(3), 209–225. doi:10.1080/13892240701427599.

Ison, R., Blackmore, C., Collins, K., & Furniss, P. (2007). Systemic environmental decision making: Designing learning systems. *Kybernetes, 36*(9/10), 1340–1361.

Jacobson, M. J., & Spiro, R. J. (1995). Hypertext learning environments, cognitive flexibility, and the transfer of complex knowledge: An empirical investigation. *Journal of Educational Computing Research, 12*(4), 301–333.

Jonassen, D. H. (1992). Cognitive flexibility theory and its implications for designing CBI. In S. Dijkstra, H. M. Krammer, & J. G. Merriënboer (Eds.), *Instructional models in computer-based learning environments* (pp. 385–403). Berlin, Germany: Springer.

Jonassen, D. H. (1996). Scaffolding diagnostic reasoning in case-based-learning environments. *Journal of Computing in Higher Education, 8*(1), 48–68. doi:10.1007/BF02942395.

Jonassen, D. H. (2011). *Learning to solve problems: A handbook for designing problem-solving learning environments*. New York, NY: Routledge.

Jonassen, D. H., & Kim, B. (2010). Arguing to learn and learning to argue: Design justifications and guidelines. *Educational Technology Research and Development, 58*(4), 439–457. doi:10. 1007/s11423-009-9143-8.

Knight, P., & Yorke, M. (2004). *Learning, curriculum and employability in higher education*. London: RoutledgeFalmer.

Kolodner, J. L. (2006). Case-based reasoning. In K. Sawyer (Ed.), *The Cambridge handbook of the learning sciences* (pp. 225–242). Cambridge, MA: Cambridge University Press.

Kolodner, J. L., Camp, P. J., Crismond, D., Fasse, B., Gray, J., Holbrook, J., . . . Ryan, M. (2003). Problem-based learning meets case-based reasoning in the middle-school science classroom: Putting learning by design(tm) into practice. *Journal of the Learning Sciences, 12*(4), 495–547. doi:10.1207/S15327809JLS1204_2.

Krippendorff, K. (2007). Design research, an oxymoron? In R. Michel (Ed.), *Design research now: Essays and selected projects* (pp. 67–80). Zürich, Switzerland: Birkhäuser Verlag.

Li, M. (2002). Fostering design culture through cultivating the user-designers' design thinking and systems thinking. *Systemic Practice and Action Research, 15*(5), 385–410. doi:10.1023/ A:1019933410857.

Linn, M. C. (1995). Designing computer learning environments for engineering and computer science: The scaffolded knowledge integration framework. *Journal of Science Education and Technology, 4*(2), 103–126. doi:10.1007/BF02214052.

Linn, M. C. (2006). The knowledge integration perspective on learning and instruction. In K. Sawyer (Ed.), *The Cambridge handbook of the learning sciences* (pp. 243–264). Cambridge, MA: Cambridge University Press.

Linn, M., & Eylon, B.-S. (2011). *Science learning and instruction: Taking advantage of technology to promote knowledge integration*. New York, NY: Routledge.

Maturana, H. R., & Varela, F. J. (1980). *Autopoiesis and cognition: The realization of the living*. Dordrecht, The Netherlands: D. Reidel.

Morris, R., Hadwin, A. F., Gress, C. L. Z., Miller, M., Fior, M., Church, H., & Winne, P. H. (2010). Designing roles, scripts, and prompts to support CSCL in gStudy. *Computers in Human Behavior, 26*(5), 815–824. doi:10.1016/j.chb.2008.12.001.

Morrison, D., & Collins, A. (1996). Epistemic fluency and constructivist learning environments. In B. Wilson (Ed.), *Constructivist learning environments: Case studies in instructional design* (pp. 107–119). Englewood Cliffs, NJ: Educational Technology Publications.

Muukkonen, H., & Lakkala, M. (2009). Exploring metaskills of knowledge-creating inquiry in higher education. *International Journal of Computer-Supported Collaborative Learning, 4*(2), 187–211. doi:10.1007/s11412-009-9063-y.

Muukkonen, H., Lakkala, M., & Hakkarainen, K. (2005). Technology-mediation and tutoring: How do they shape progressive inquiry discourse? *Journal of the Learning Sciences, 14*(4), 527–565. doi:10.1207/s15327809jls1404_3.

Muukkonen, H., Lakkala, M., & Paavola, S. (2011). Promoting knowledge creation and object oriented inquiry in university courses. In S. Ludvigsen, A. Lund, I. Rasmussen, & R. Säljö (Eds.), *Learning across sites: New tools, infrastructures and practices* (pp. 172–189). Oxon, OX: Routledge.

Newell, A., & Simon, H. A. (1972). *Human problem solving*. Englewood Cliffs, NJ: Prentice-Hall.

Noroozi, O., Weinberger, A., Biemans, H. J. A., Mulder, M., & Chizari, M. (2012). Argumentation-based computer supported collaborative learning (ABCSCL): A synthesis of 15 years of research. *Educational Research Review, 7*(2), 79–106. http://dx.doi.org/10.1016/j.edurev.2011.11.006.

Noroozi, O., Weinberger, A., Biemans, H. J. A., Mulder, M., & Chizari, M. (2013). Facilitating argumentative knowledge construction through a transactive discussion script in CSCL. *Computers & Education, 61*, 59–76. http://dx.doi.org/10.1016/j.compedu.2012.08.013.

Okada, A., Buckingham Shum, S., & Sherborne, T. (2008). *Knowledge cartography: Software tools and mapping techniques*. London, UK: Springer.

Paavola, S., & Hakkarainen, K. (2005). The knowledge creation metaphor – An emergent epistemological approach to learning. *Science & Education, 14*(6), 535–557.

Paavola, S., Lipponen, L., & Hakkarainen, K. (2004). Models of innovative knowledge communities and three metaphors of learning. *Review of Educational Research, 74*(4), 557–576. doi:10.3102/00346543074004557.

Paavola, S., Lakkala, M., Muukkonen, H., Kosonen, K., & Karlgren, K. (2011). The roles and uses of design principles for developing the trialogical approach on learning. *Research in Learning Technology, 19*(3), 233–246. doi:10.1080/21567069.2011.624171.

Perkins, D. N. (1986). *Knowledge as design*. Hillsdale, NJ: Lawrence Erlbaum Associates.

Perkins, D. N. (2009). *Making learning whole*. San Francisco, CA: Jossey-Bass.

Razzouk, R., & Shute, V. (2012). What is design thinking and why is it important? *Review of Educational Research, 82*(3), 330–348. doi:10.3102/0034654312457429.

Renkl, A., Mandl, H., & Gruber, H. (1996). Inert knowledge: Analyses and remedies. *Educational Psychologist, 31*(2), 115–121.

Ritchhart, R., Church, M., & Morrison, K. (2011). *Making thinking visible: How to promote engagement, understanding, and independence for all learners*. San Francisco, CA: Jossey-Bass.

Rittel, H., & Webber, M. (1973). Dilemmas in a general theory of planning. *Policy Sciences, 4*(2), 155–169.

Rummel, N., & Spanda, H. (2007). Can people learn computer mediated collaboration by following script. In F. Fischer, I. Kollar, H. Mandl, & J. M. Haake (Eds.), *Scripting computer-supported collaborative learning: Cognitive, computational and educational perspectives* (pp. 39–56). New York, NY: Springer.

Runde, A., Bromme, R., & Jucks, R. (2007). Scripting net-based medical consultation: The impact of external representations on giving advice and explanations. In F. Fischer, I. Kollar, H. Mandl, & J. M. Haake (Eds.), *Scripting computer-supported collaborative learning: Cognitive, computational and educational perspectives* (pp. 57–72). New York, NY: Springer.

Scardamalia, M., & Bereiter, C. (2006). Knowledge building: Theory, pedagogy and technology. In K. Sawyer (Ed.), *The Cambridge handbook of the learning sciences* (pp. 97–115). Cambridge, MA: Cambridge University Press.

Schön, D. A. (1983). *The reflective practitioner: How professionals think in action*. New York, NY: Basic Books.

Schön, D. A. (1987). *Educating the reflective practitioner*. London, UK: Jossey-Bass.

Senge, P. M. (2000). *Schools that learn: A fifth discipline fieldbook for educators, parents and everyone who cares about education*. London, UK: Doubleday.

Senge, P. M. (2006). *The fifth discipline: The art and practice of the learning organization* (Rev. and updated ed.). Milsons Point, NSW: Random House Business Books.

Senge, P. M., Smith, B., Kruschwitz, N., Laur, J., & Schley, S. (2010). *The necessary revolution: How individuals and organizations are working together to create a sustainable world*. London., UK: Nicholas Brealey.

Shaffer, D. W. (2004). Pedagogical praxis: The professions as models for postindustrial education. *Teachers College Record, 106*(7), 1401–1421.

Shaffer, D. W. (2006). Epistemic frames for epistemic games. *Computers & Education, 46*(3), 223–234. http://dx.doi.org/10.1016/j.compedu.2005.11.003.

Shaffer, D. W. (2009). Wag the kennel: Games, frames, and the problem of assessment. In R. Fertig (Ed.), *Handbook of research on effective electronic gaming in education* (pp. 577–592). Hershey, PA: IGI Global.

Simon, H. A. (1966/1996). *The sciences of the artificial* (1 & 3 ed.). Cambridge, MA: MIT Press.

Spada, H. (2010). Of scripts, roles, positions, and models. *Computers in Human Behavior, 26*(4), 547–550. http://dx.doi.org/10.1016/j.chb.2009.08.011.

Spiro, R. J., & Jehng, J. (1990). Cognitive flexibility and hypertext: Theory and technology for the non-linear and multidimensional traversal of complex subject matter. In D. Nix & R. Spiro (Eds.), *Cognition, education, and multimedia* (pp. 163–205). Hillsdale, NJ: Lawrence Erlbaum Associates.

Spiro, R. J., Coulson, R. L., Feltovich, P. J., & Anderson, D. K. (1988/2013). Cognitive flexibility theory: Advanced knowledge acquisition in ill-structured domains. In D. E. Alvermann, N. J. Unrau, & R. B. Ruddell (Eds.), *Theoretical models and processes of reading* (6th ed., pp. 544–557). Newark, DE: International Reading Association.

Spiro, R. J., Collins, B. P., & Ramchandran, A. R. (2007). Modes of openness and flexibility in cognitive flexibility hypertext learning environments. In B. H. Khan (Ed.), *Flexible learning in an information society* (pp. 18–25). Hershey, PA: Information Science.

Stahl, E. (2007). Scripting group cognition. In F. Fischer, I. Kollar, H. Mandl, & J. M. Haake (Eds.), *Scripting computer-supported collaborative learning: Cognitive, computational and educational perspectives* (pp. 327–336). New York, NY: Springer.

Strijbos, J.-W., & Weinberger, A. (2010). Emerging and scripted roles in computer-supported collaborative learning. *Computers in Human Behavior, 26*(4), 491–494. http://dx.doi.org/10.1016/j.chb.2009.08.006.

Tchounikine, P. (2008). Operationalizing macro-scripts in CSCL technological settings. *International Journal of Computer-Supported Collaborative Learning, 3*(2), 193–233. doi:10.1007/s11412-008-9039-3.

Vickers, G. Sir. (1965). *Art of judgement*. London, UK: Chapman and Hall.

von Foerster, H. (2003). Ethics and second-order cybernetics. In *Understanding understanding: Essays on cybernetics and cognition* (pp. 287–304). New York, NY: Springer.

Vygotsky, L. S. (1978). *Mind in society: The development of higher psychological processes*. Cambridge, MA: Harvard University Press.

Vygotsky, L. S. (1986). *Thought and language* (2nd ed.). Cambridge, MA: MIT Press.

Waloszek, G. (2012, September 1). Introduction to design thinking. *SAP Design Guild*. Retrieved October 1, 2014 from http://www.sapdesignguild.org/community/design/design_thinking.asp

Wals, A. E. J., & Corcoran, P. B. (Eds.). (2012). *Learning for sustainability in times of accelerating change*. Wageningen, The Netherlands: Wageningen Academic.

Weinberger, A., Ertl, B., Fischer, F., & Mandl, H. (2005). Epistemic and social scripts in computer-supported collaborative learning. *Instructional Science, 33*(1), 1–30. doi:10.1007/s11251-004-2322-4.

Weinberger, A., Stegmann, K., & Fischer, F. (2010). Learning to argue online: Scripted groups surpass individuals (unscripted groups do not). *Computers in Human Behavior, 26*, 506–515.

Wenger, E. (1998). *Communities of practice: Learning, meaning, and identity*. Cambridge, UK: Cambridge University Press.

Wilensky, U., & Reisman, K. (2006). Thinking like a wolf, a sheep, or a firefly: Learning biology through constructing and testing computational theories-an embodied modeling approach. *Cognition and Instruction, 24*(2), 171–209.

Chapter 20
Creating Epistemic Environments: Learning, Teaching and Design

We do not just self-engineer better worlds to think in. We self-engineer ourselves to think and perform better in the worlds we find ourselves in. We self-engineer worlds in which to build better worlds to think in. We build better tools to think with and to use these very tools to discover still better tools to think with. We tune the way we use these tools by building educational practices to train ourselves to use our best cognitive tools better. (Clark, 2011, p. 59)

This richly recursive conception of 'self-engineering' provides both resources and challenges for those involved in rethinking professional education. The main goal of this chapter is to introduce a fifth epistemic project and to outline some thoughts on educational approaches which align with this notion of building 'better worlds to think in' – better environments for engaging in epistemic activity.

20.1 From Rational Thought to Embodied Skill to Grounded Actionable Knowledge

In Chap. 3, we described four 'epistemic projects' that can be found in professional education and in writing about the nature of professional work, knowledge and action. These are:

- Reflective-rational
- Reflective-embodied
- Knowledge-building
- Relational expertise

To recap, the reflective-rational project is centrally concerned with connections between theory and practice – between codified academic or professional knowledge and emergent problems of practice; the reflective-embodied project relates to notions of professional identity, being and becoming; the knowledge-building project captures the future-oriented aspects of professional work and includes

© Springer Science+Business Media Dordrecht 2017
L. Markauskaite, P. Goodyear, *Epistemic Fluency and Professional Education*,
Professional and Practice-based Learning 14, DOI 10.1007/978-94-007-4369-4_20

Fig. 20.1 A more comprehensive picture of epistemic fluency

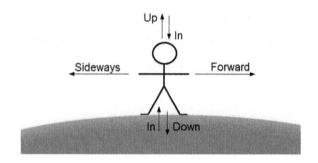

learning to innovate – to work on novel problems, and the relational project fore-grounds working with others, particularly across professional and other boundaries.

We also mentioned in Chap. 3 that we want to add to this set a fifth epistemic project, which we will now label 'grounded actionable knowledge'. This is not a rival to the other four projects: in a sense, it draws them together. It connects them by grounding human knowledge and knowing in the physical environment and the embodied conscious and conscientious self.

We can use the image in Fig. 20.1 to move towards a summarising account of epistemic fluency – one which incorporates the perspectives we described in Chap. 3. On this view, learning to become a capable professional knowledge worker involves development or growth in *five* directions.

We can think of the reflective-rational project as a *growing up* – strengthening the capacity to connect practical application with new theoretical ideas and to integrate personal experiential knowledge with codified knowledge. The reflective-embodied project involves an *inward* turn – sharpening a sense of oneself and one's professional being. The knowledge-building project involves strengthening the capacity to adapt for a changing future: it is a *forward-oriented* growth. And similarly, the relational project is about *growing sideways* – building relational expertise that allows one to work effectively with specialists from adjacent professions.

The fifth epistemic project can be imagined as growth *downwards and inwards simultaneously*. This is not best captured as putting down roots – though aspects of that metaphor do apply. Rather, it is *grounding* oneself: grounding one's professional knowing in forward-oriented actions within the external social and physical world and in a clearer knowledge of one's self, acting in the world. This *grounding* needs to be understood as both (a) becoming more attuned to the affordances, constraints and other significant features of one's epistemic environment, strengthening perception–action loops, and (b) learning how to reshape the ground: to reconfigure one's epistemic environment to better suit the needs of one's current situation.

We have been making parts of the case for this fifth epistemic project in many of the preceding chapters. To start pulling the threads together, we want to use a quotation from Tim Ingold. Ingold (2000) poses a question about what might be seen as hidden choices in the mainstreams of research on the relations between tools, language and mind. How would the focus and history of this field of inquiry look if, instead of foregrounding *technology, language and intelligence*, research had dwelt on *craftsmanship, song and imagination*?

> ... neo-Darwinian biology, cognitive science and psycholinguistics have conspired to produce an extremely powerful approach to understanding the relations, in human evolution, between technology, language and intelligence. <...> Suppose, to pursue my alternative claim, that we set ourselves the task of examining the relation, in human evolution, not between technology, language and intelligence, but between craftsmanship, song and imagination. The resulting account, I suspect, would be very different. (Ingold, 2000, pp. 406–407)

Ingold's writings on craftsmanship are strong on the notion of embodied skill, vividly tracing the perception–action loops that enable the skilled person to work with subtle variations in materials and adjust to subtle changes in the world, more generally. Many of Ingold's examples come from his anthropological research and describe what might seem esoteric skills – traditional within remote communities. But he also speaks of craftsmanship in ways that illuminate discursive work in professional settings. For example:

> We 'feel' each other's presence in verbal discourse as the craftsman feels, with his tools, the material on which he works; and as with the craftsman's handling of tools, so is our handling of words sensitive to the nuances of our relationships with the felt environment. (Ingold, 2000, p. 411)

Of the four accounts of professional knowledge and knowing in our four epistemic projects, two emphasise '*thinking*' or 'reasoning' like a lawyer (or doctor, engineer, nurse, etc.) – the 'reflective rational' and 'knowledge building' – and two emphasise '*acting*' like a lawyer (doctor, engineer, nurse, etc.), the 'reflective embodied' and 'relational'. The literature tends to the view that expertise is either strongly associated with thinking, reasoning and the mind or deeply embedded in tacit skills, dispositions and the material context. It quietly constructs a Cartesian divide between knowledge and skill, mind and context. One can also see a split between views which privilege rational thought and fine-tuned, embrained skills (on the one hand) and views which imply that social and material context and practices matter more than minds and brains (on the other hand).

But what if we take *all* of these seriously: the mind and practice, the body – in which the brain and mind are embodied – and contexts, in which practices are embedded? Mind, body, perception, action and matter all matter. From this perspective, knowledge and knowing involve fine-tuned *coordination*: 'thinking like', 'acting like', 'seeing like' and 'touching like' a professional.

In the following quote, Goodwin (1994) is writing about professional discourse, but his notion of 'professional vision', which we have mentioned before, can help us develop a more general argument:

> Discursive practices are used by members of a profession to shape events in the domains subject to their professional scrutiny. The shaping process creates the objects of knowledge that become the insignia of a profession's craft: the theories, artifacts, and *bodies of expertise* that distinguish it from other professions. Analysis of the methods used by members of a community to build and contest the events that structure their lifeworld contributes to the development of a practice-based theory of *knowledge and action*. (Goodwin, 1994, p. 606, emphasis added)

Goodwin's idea of professional vision as:

> ... socially organized ways of seeing and understanding events that are answerable to the distinctive interests of a particular social group. (loc. cit.)

helps make the point that human knowing and action are not limited to language, but are 'constructed by assembling diverse materials' (Goodwin, 2013, p. 8) including language, prosody, visible embodied displays, tools and material environments through accumulation, differentiation and coordination of these diverse resources over time:

> Individual actions emerge from, and use, *a consequential past* shaped through chains of prior action, providing current participants with a dense, present environment, *a rich now*, containing many different kinds of resources that can be selectively decomposed, reused and transformed to build a next action, a proposal for how the future will be organized. Thus human beings build action by *combining diverse resources* (e.g., language structure, categories, prosody, postural configurations, the embodied displays of a hearer, tools, etc.) to perform both simultaneous and sequential transformative operations on a local, public semiotic substrate brought into existence by processes on many different time scales (from the immediately prior utterance to the progressive sedimentation of structure in tools, languages and settings). To build action participants must know in detail what each other is doing, the kinds of knowledge each can accountably be expected to possess, and relevant features of the materials, whether language structure, artifacts or features of the setting, that contribute to the organization of the action in progress. (Goodwin, 2013, p. 21, emphasis added)

In short, the focus of expert knowing shifts from cognitive operations – what is in the mind – to fluent use of semiotic and material tools, body and environment.

For example, Hindmarsh and Pilnick (2007) have studied the skilful interweaving of professional action among anaesthesia teams during operations. Their descriptions capture our point about professional knowing as entailing the coordination of seeing, feeling and action:

> The tight coordination of action among the anaesthetic team of anaesthetist and ODA [operating department assistant] rests on an intimate understanding of the possible trajectories of delicate shifts in bodily conduct by both anaesthetist and ODA – treated as indicating the need for assistance and the availability of help. Moreover, the resources for the two colleagues to assist are not simply verbal, or even a combination of the verbal and the visual, but rather bring together verbal, visual and tactile resources. The import of tactile knowing in the production, and moreover the interactional organization, of work practice is often overlooked and yet this fragment highlights the critical resource that touch, in the form of finger pressure on a colleague's hand, provides for the anaesthetist in organizing and coordinating the conduct of her colleague. (Hindmarsh & Pilnick, 2007, p. 1408)

This kind of knowing is not a shapeless, moment-to-moment improvisation by the anaesthesia team. Rather, it is an intelligent fine-tuned coordination of manual and perceptual skills with deep understanding of what is happening now and what comes next:

> Knowing the scene rests on understanding the character and sequence of action in the anaesthetic room and recognizing a 'trajectory of action' that he can contribute to. <...> In addition, as he does not explicitly request the instrument, the anaesthetist can be seen to

expect or rely on the ODA knowing what comes next and that he will pass the instrument at just the appropriate moment. However, the timing of the instrument being passed is not all that is relevant here. Indeed the way in which the ODA presents and positions the different instruments to the anaesthetist displays understanding of the other's prospective embodied conduct as well; that is to say, through the manner of the passing of the instrument the ODA displays a sensitivity to what it takes to use a laryngoscope and later to insert a tracheal tube. (op. cit., p. 1404)

This richer, more extensive view of knowledge and knowing (as revealed in perception and action) is nicely captured by both Ingold (2011) and Del Mar (2010):

... it is in the very 'tuning' of movement in response to the ever changing conditions of an unfolding task that the skill of any bodily technique ultimately resides. (Ingold, 2011, p. 46)

Each of our senses – and also the numerous different complexes of them (e.g., hearing-touch) – are skills that can be (perhaps infinitely) improved. Each does already, and can ever more (if it is trained), contribute to our understanding; indeed, understanding consists, *at least to a large extent, in the intelligence of the senses*. (Del Mar, 2010, p. 1, emphasis added)

20.2   What Is Knowledge, Revisited: Dynamic Knowledge, Grounded Concepts and Embodied Epistemic Environments

As we saw in Chaps. 3 and 4, most accounts of professional knowledge give the mind a substantial role. Accounts of what the mind is, how it contributes to intelligent performance, how it learns and can be taught and how it becomes capable of innovation are therefore very salient. Various conceptualisations of professional knowledge have aimed to propose how professionals think in action and in context, but rather few of them have provided explicit accounts of how the mind actually works, changes and relates to skill, movement and social and material context.

Some scholars writing about expertise from a strong psychological perspective can be accused of adopting rather rationalist views of mind (Chi, Glaser, & Farr, 1988; Clark, 2011; Ohlsson, 2011). As a rule they draw a clear division between 'higher-order' conscious thought (cognition, metacognition) involving abstract, systematically organised knowledge constructs (concepts, theories, schemas, etc.) and 'lower-order' cognitive operations (senses, perception, actions, emotions, etc.) which provide an interface with the external world. On this view, the 'higher-order' capabilities do the real intellectual work; the rest are mere inputs for rational expert thinking.

Some scholars who have tried to give a more central role to environment and the human senses in professional work have turned away from mentalist models of cognition, but in so doing have also turned away from serious consideration of a psychological basis for human knowing in general. As a rule, they have dismissed the central role of concepts, theories and other systematically organised knowledge constructs as a basis for expertise, but have said relatively little about what kinds of alternative mental constructs and processes may underpin experts' thinking and performance.

In our view, it is time to find a rapprochement – one that gives due weight to mind and context and which acknowledges the *dynamic* nature of human intellect and its dependence on *grounding* in experiences, environments and embodied action (Barsalou, 2008; Barsalou, Breazeal, & Smith, 2007; Hutchins, 2010; McGann, De Jaegher, & Di Paolo, 2013; Smith, 2005; Smith & Sheya, 2010; Smith & Thelen, 2003). The three core facets of this perspective address (a) how knowledge emerges, (b) the nature of conceptual knowledge and (c) how the environment supports knowing. We have explored each of these topics earlier in the book and recap the key points here.

20.2.1 How Knowledge Emerges

On this dynamic, grounded view, intelligent action is seen as arising in the coordination of the cognitive and noncognitive processes. Traditional theories of cognition commonly focus on stable displays of rational, logical behaviour, but intelligent professional action requires coherence and flexibility in response to a changing world, rather than the exercise of habit. In Chap. 6, we summarised Linda Smith's (2005) critique of conventional explanations of stability in behaviour (across situations and/or over time). This conventional explanation locates the source of stability in the mind – in a central unit that controls and coordinates all actions. The resources with which this control unit works are things like 'concepts', 'habits' and other relatively firm mental representations – theories, mental models, beliefs, frameworks, schemas and so on. These guide behaviour, but exist independently of perception and action. In contrast, Smith argues that much of the apparent stability in human behaviour emerges from the variability and coupling of individual elements distributed across the mind, the body and the world. Smith used the example of a cat's movement over variable terrain as an illustration (see Chap. 6). Smith claims that such apparently stable behaviour can best be understood as a dynamic system – there is no one central control mechanism that has a causal priority (be it a stable concept, theory or plan). An apparently coherent pattern emerges from the interaction and self-organisation of many elements of the system – from the coordinated relationships among diverse components distributed across mind, body and world.

Empirical research is providing more evidence to support this view, demonstrating that creativity, anticipation and intuition are not just a result of independent processes created by a mind; they emerge from the interactions among many other basic systems in the brain, such as perception, goal management, action, motivation, emotions and learning (Barsalou, 1999).

This view shifts the focus of what is central in knowledgeable performance from stable constructs that can (ostensibly) control knowledgeable actions (stable concepts, theories, mental models, etc.) to rich relationships and interactions between elements of a system that spans mind, body and world.

20.2.2 Grounded Concepts: Situated Knowing and Non-situated Knowledge

What then is the role of concepts, theories and other similar well-organised knowledge constructs that have commonly played a role in defining professional knowledge bases and in organising programs of professional education? A grounded cognition view suggests that mental representations (i.e. conceptual knowledge) do have a central role in human cognition (Barsalou, 1999, 2009). However, this conceptual system is unlikely to be composed of abstract self-contained elements operating in a closed system independently from the external world and experiences. Cognition is embedded in actions and the physical world, and this world is the main source of resources from which humans construct and organise their conceptual systems. Along these lines, as we explained in Chap. 6, Barsalou (2009) proposes a view of the human conceptual system in which conceptual knowledge is inherently situated and grounded. He shows how conceptual knowledge remains tightly linked with background situations, experiences and actions.

According to this view, conceptual categories are remembered with at least four types of situated information: (a) selected properties of the conceptual category relevant to the situation, (b) information about the background settings, (c) possible actions that could be taken and (d) perceptions of internal states that one might have experienced during previous encounters with the conceptual phenomena, such as affects, motivations, cognitive states and operations. Such a conceptual system is not abstract and detached from the situated experiences; rather, it is grounded in perception and

> ... constructs situated conceptualizations dynamically, tailoring them to the current needs of situated action. (Barsalou, 2009, p. 251)

These 'conceptual packages' prepare humans for situated action and guide goal-directed activity. Multiple modalities of the phenomena experienced in the world via vision, touch, smell, audition, emotion, etc., are an integral part of knowledge representations and processes through which knowing becomes possible. Such conceptual understanding is not organised around abstract categories, but around the interface between perception and action – understanding the concept is 'being there conceptually'.

20.2.3 How Environments Support Knowing: Embodied Epistemic Environments and Professional Knowledge Work

This grounded view of conceptual knowledge gives us an insight into why professionals find it so hard to bridge between the conceptual knowledge learnt in university settings and the practical problems encountered in workplaces. It is unlikely that gaps between 'knowledge to understand' and 'knowledge to do' create these difficulties (see Chap. 5). Rather, disconnections between the contexts and situations in which the 'theoretical concepts' are learnt and the 'practical concepts' are encountered cause the 'conceptual discontinuities'. Students do not 'see' learnt concepts as professionals do, because educators and employers rarely succeed in creating conditions that allow students to ground concepts in situations that fuse theoretical and practical professional experiences.

What kind of environments may be productive for learning grounded conceptual knowledge and taking knowledgeable action informed by theoretical understanding? Clark (2011) and many others (see, e.g. Hutchins, 1995, 2010; Nersessian, 2012) point to the mutual role of environment, language and embodied interaction, not only for situating but also for *enhancing* intelligent mind–body–world connections:

> ... linguistic tools enable us to deliberatively and systematically sculpt and modify our own processes of selective attention. (Clark, 2011, p. 48)

> ... the intelligent use of space and the intelligent use of language form a mutually reinforcing pair, pursuing a common cognitive agenda. (op. cit., p. 65)

> The environments of human thinking are not 'natural' environments. They are artificial through and through. Humans create their cognitive powers by creating the environments in which they exercise those powers. (Hutchins, 1995, p. 169)

Ingold (2000) prompts us to make one further step beyond the initial contact between 'learning to understand' and 'learning to do' and look into how this relationship may evolve with practice:

> The novice becomes skilled not through the acquisition of rules and representations, but at the point where he or she is able to dispense with them. They are like the map of an unfamiliar territory, which can be discarded once you have learned to attend to the features of the landscape, and can place yourself in relation to them. The map can be a help in beginning to know the country, but the aim is to learn the country not the map. (Ingold, 2000, p. 415)

However, if we step beyond the territory of established professional practices into the territories that are occupied by pioneering 'knowledge workers', then we have quite a different learning challenge. The features of the landscape should be discovered, and the map should be created, simultaneously. Andy Clark's (2011) reminder about the central role of language (and symbolic artefacts) in experts' simultaneous self-engineering of the mind and environment gives us an opportunity to make this further move in the argument:

> Coming to grips with our own special cognitive nature demands that we take seriously the material reality of language: its existence as an additional, actively created, and effortfully maintained structure in our internal and external environment. From sounds in the air to inscriptions on the printed page, the material structures of language both reflect, and then systematically transform, our thinking and reasoning about the world. <...> Linguistic forms and structures are first encountered as simply objects (additional structure) in our world. But they then form a potent overlay that effectively, and iteratively, reconfigures the space for biological reason and self-control. The cumulative complexity here is genuinely quite staggering. (Clark, 2011, p. 59)

One of the key implications of the grounded account of knowledge and knowing is that perception and action are inseparable from, and equally important as, processes in the mind. So professional education cannot be solely concerned with processes in the mind nor solely with actions in the world. It must embrace the coordination of what the mind does with perception and action. If we believe in the usefulness of propositional knowledge in knowledgeable action, then the educational challenge becomes how to link the 'grammar' that underpins these theoretical constructs with the multimodal experiential constructs on which human cognition naturally operates. In short, the focus of attention has to shift from knowledge (concepts, theories) and skill (perception, action) to the constructs, processes and environments for *coordinating* mind–body–world experiences – constructs for knowing, for *conceptually perceiving*, and for *intelligently sensing*.

If we take multiple modalities seriously, then there is no sense in trying to decide which of the five accounts (the five epistemic projects) is 'right' or 'best'. All of them are needed for a comprehensive account of professional knowledge. If one takes a grounded view, and the notion that much conceptual knowledge is organised around the interface between body–world, perception–action and coordination, then it is extraordinary that neither higher education nor employers do much to enable the learning of actionable (conceptual) knowledge, i.e. making concepts grounded and 'educating' 'conceptual perception' in action, in the material environment, in the cultural environment, etc.

Constructing productive learning-epistemic environments is key. And if we are serious about seeing professionals as innovating knowledge workers, then developing graduates' capacities to construct tools and congenial environments for their *own* epistemic work (with *others*) is also vitally important.

20.3 Learning by Creating an Epistemic Environment and Constructing a Conscientious Self

In Chap. 19, we provided an overview of four broad families of educational approaches – illustrating each by the cases drawn from a range of subject areas, sectors and settings – that can each contribute something to the development of epistemic fluency in programs of professional education. We referred to these broadly as learning by:

- Integrating knowledge (Linn, Spiro)
- Playing epistemic games (Shaffer, Weinberger)
- Designing knowledge (Bereiter, Engeström)
- Designing inquiry (Checkland, Ison)

Some of these families of educational approaches map quite well to one of the epistemic projects.[1] Examples would be 'knowledge integration' mapping to the

---

[1] Similarly, as we explained in Chap. 3, each of the epistemic projects also draws on its own historically developed sets of educational approaches. As a rule, these approaches involve a particular configuration of apprenticeship, design, discussion and reflection.

'reflective-rational' project and 'learning as designing knowledge' to the 'knowledge-building' project. But the relationships are not entirely simple or neat. For example, explicit attention to identity, values and other rich professional experiences makes the 'thick' version of epistemic games (Shaffer) closely align with the 'reflective-embodied' project. The focus on generic ways of knowing and discourse characteristics of different disciplines and professions in the 'broad' version of epistemic games (Collins, Weinberger) aligns this approach with 'relational expertise'. The explicit consideration of multidisciplinary and inter-professional collaboration in the 'learning as designing inquiry' approach also makes it relevant to the development of relational expertise. But this learning as designing inquiry approach is also a jumping-off point for educational approaches relevant to our fifth project.

This fifth educational approach could be summarised as 'learning by creating an epistemic environment'. It also involves some important aspects of 'self-assembly' – in the sense of assembling a conscious and conscientious *inhabitant* of epistemic environments. We need to see both environment and inhabitant(s) as one system.

To explain what we mean by creating an epistemic environment, let us return to David Turnbull's (2000) notion of an 'assemblage' of knowledge practices:

> ... the amalgam of places, bodies, voices, skills, practices, technical devices, theories, social strategies and collective work that together constitute technoscientific knowledge/ practices. (Turnbull, 2000, pp. 43–44)

We then need to say that the epistemic is not merely mental, social or technological – it is an interdependent, multimodal, dynamic and complex system. So when we think of an 'epistemic environment', we are thinking of something social and material, in which a rich meshwork of tools and other artefacts, infrastructure, people, inscriptions and speech *afford* epistemic activity.

On the part of the professional worker, this involves both conscious and conscientious habitation. It involves both consciousness, in the sense that this perspective taking is a deliberate, self-aware act.[2] In addition, it involves habits associated with conscientiousness – a desire to do things well and to be orderly, thorough and vigilant – acting with a deep sense of moral responsibility and *moral know-how*. So it depends upon being both systemic and systematic and working with the explicit and the tacit. To express this concisely, we talk about consci(enti)ous inhabiting. Within this term, we aim to wrap the coupled notions of (a) constructing and reconfiguring one's epistemic environments and (b) constructing oneself as skilful inhabitant of such environments – able to act and with senses that are fine-tuned to notice what is important, what should be cared for and what is worth doing.

Constructing, assembling and/or (re)configuring one's epistemic environment are a matter of crafting affordances for both sense-making (i.e. epistemic action) and pragmatic action (Chap. 7).

---

[2] In this, it resembles familiar acts of metacognition or self-regulation – though the focus of attention is on oneself as an agent within a system, rather than on some kind of independent, disembodied mind.

The third of the educational approaches described in Chap. 19 involved creating new knowledge by following established inquiry methods; the fourth approach expanded this conception to include the dynamic (re)design of inquiry methods – as a way of working on what we called 'wicked systemic problems'. But, as with many learning approaches, it mainly focusses on discourse – thereby overlooking the fact that learning does not only take place in the mind and through the discourse, it takes place in the world, through embodied action. Our fifth approach is a way of acknowledging the importance of the environment in which inquiry takes place: hence, the focus is on being able to configure or reconfigure an environment appropriate to the epistemic tasks at hand. Concretely, this includes such things as making sure that all the *necessary* tools, artefacts, infrastructure and so on are in place when needed and that this epistemic environment can be modified in a timely way to match the needs of the evolving inquiry processes at hand.

This concern for the whole of the epistemic environment, not just the focal object in object-oriented inquiry, distinguishes our fifth approach from the 'trialogical' approach to knowledge creation that we discussed in Chap. 19 (Moen, Mørch, & Paavola, 2012; Paavola, Lakkala, Muukkonen, Kosonen, & Karlgren, 2011; Paavola, Lipponen et al., 2004). In addition, this fifth approach is imbued with the sense of cognition as embodied and of interaction with the environment as deeply multimodal. Explicit knowledge is only part of the story; awareness and coordination of cognition and noncognitive states – feelings, motivation, action and so on – are also crucially important.

Del Mar (2010) provides a nice perspective on professional education for the law that aligns with this position and which unconsciously reflects Ingold's (2000) line on 'craftsmanship, song and imagination':

> ... students must be given the opportunity to experience the making of such judgements, i.e., of having such experiences as 'Ah, I see that', or 'Ah, I see that as.' They also need to come to understand the dynamics of legal knowledge, i.e., that the rules themselves to do not delimit or determine anything. What is vital is the activity of seeing, and thus also respecting the potentiality of any rule or any image. It is not students that are 'stupid' if they cannot make the judgement that we want them to make: it is we, the teachers, who are failing to provide them with the right conditions for making judgements for themselves. (Del Mar, 2010, p. 15)

Some of the work involved in configuring and reconfiguring the epistemic environment may well be intuitive. But we want to argue that the capabilities needed can benefit from explicit treatment. That is, it can be very helpful to draw students' attention to ideas that help them recognise, (co)design and (re)design epistemic environments.

Figure 20.2 helps develop the argument a little further. It combines ideas from cybernetics and educational design to map what we propose to call three 'orders' of learning.

The first-order perspective positions the learner as a system that has *no intrinsic capacity* for learning – neither of skills nor for creating its own understanding. The teacher is the main architect and conductor of learning and the main source of knowledge. This may work reasonably well if the environment is stable and the

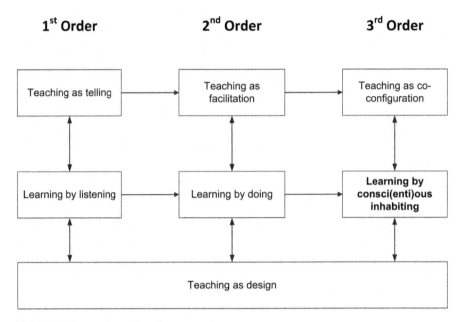

Fig. 20.2 Three orders of learning

teacher can identify gaps or misconceptions in the learner's knowledge. These can be remedied by appropriate variations on 'teaching as telling'.

The second-order perspective positions the learner as a system that has an *adaptive capacity* for learning in response to changes in environment. The teacher is the main creator of environmental conditions conducive to learning; changes in environmental conditions prompt learning. This can work reasonably well in a changing environment, provided that there are appropriate scaffolds for learning. While the learner is engaged in 'learning by doing', the teacher monitors their activity, adds and removes scaffolds and provides hints, as they deem appropriate. This is 'teaching as facilitation' or 'teaching as orchestration' (Dillenbourg, 2013; Dillenbourg, Jarvela, & Fischer, 2009).

The third-order perspective positions the learner as a system that has intrinsic capacities for learning, including for the construction of new understandings and for creating the conditions for its own learning. If a teacher is available, they act as a partner in co-configuring these conditions. However, the learner has the capacities needed to manage their own learning – part of the teacher's *modus operandi* must be to fade their participation over time, strengthening the learners' agency and capacity to (co)construct environments conducive to their own learning–knowing (and their capacity to do this with others). We can call this 'teaching as co-configuration'.

It is probably best to think of the teaching becoming more elaborate and inclusive as we move from left to right in Fig. 20.2. Teaching in the third-order perspective can logically include teaching as facilitation and teaching as telling, for example. But, once approached from the third-order perspective, teaching is driven by more open assumptions: about the learner's agency and about their capacity to engage in weaving epistemic games, for instance (Chaps. 14 and 15).

In addition to the 'real-time' interactive teaching activities sketched in the top line of Fig. 20.2, we see a preparatory activity of 'teaching as design' on the bottom line (Ellis & Goodyear, 2010; Goodyear, 2015). The three instances of 'teaching as design' vary in terms of *what* is designed. In the first-order example, design is focussed on selecting and sequencing elements of an exposition. It is the classic task of instructional design – the design of 'instructional messages' (Briggs, 1977; Reigeluth, 1983). In the middle – second order – instance, design focusses on the learning environment. It works with three main design components – task design and the design of the physical and social situation in which learning activity will unfold. (Goodyear and Carvalho (2014) refer to these as epistemic design, set design and social design, respectively. See also below.) This design activity can also include making preparations for the teacher's later facilitation and/or orchestration work, so that not everything has to be improvised on the fly (Dimitriadis & Goodyear, 2013). In the case of third-order learning, on the right-hand side of Fig. 20.2, the teacher's upstream design work would focus on designing sets of tasks that prompt students both to engage in their learning and inquiry activities *and* monitor and adjust their working methods and working environment. And as with the top-line teaching activities, these teaching-as-design activities also expand from left to right: they are best conceived as becoming more comprehensive rather than as mutually exclusive.

In the next section, we examine more closely this area of designing for epistemic fluency.

20.4 Designing for Epistemic Fluency

In order to explain our perspective on designing for epistemic fluency, we need to take a few steps backwards, into the history of instructional design. The tools, methods and core practices of instructional design began to emerge in the 1940s and 1950s, in circumstances where: (a) large numbers of people are needed to be trained for well-structured military or industrial tasks, (b) acceptable levels of task performance could be defined clearly and tested efficiently, (c) trainees could be assumed to be compliant – that is, they would do what they were asked to do – and (d) trainees could not be assumed to be versatile, self-managing learners. In such circumstances, design could focus on identifying required behaviours and selecting and sequencing expositions and opportunities to practice and be tested. Increasing use of audiovisual resources meant that expositions could be rendered in material form, raising design issues about what should be presented and how (e.g. what mix of text, illustration, film, etc.). Figure 20.3 captures the core design logic.

The upper part of Fig. 20.3 shows a sequence of three learning tasks, each connected to an intended learning outcome. Tasks typically take the form of 'read

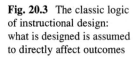
Fig. 20.3 The classic logic of instructional design: what is designed is assumed to directly affect outcomes

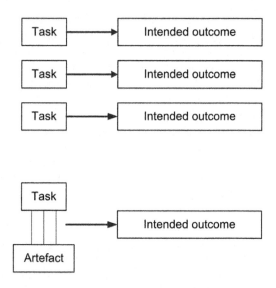

these instructions' or 'examine this diagram' or 'watch this demonstration and then try doing it yourself'. The lower part of Fig. 20.3 shows a tight coupling of task and artefact such as what we find when a demonstration and instructions to practice are embedded in a video clip. The logic animating this conception of design works backwards from an analysis of required behaviours to specifications of intended learning outcomes and to prescriptions for learner activities that align with those outcomes according to some theory of learning (see, e.g. Mager, 1988).

The logic embedded in this classic approach to instructional design breaks down when learners cannot be assumed to be compliant, that is, when – for good or bad reasons – they take more control of their own learning activity. In higher education we generally *want* learners to take increasing control over their own learning, so design approaches have to take a more indirect approach (Goodyear, 2000). Figure 20.4 helps explain this.

Figure 20.4 breaks the direct link between task and outcome by interposing 'learner activity' – meaning *what the learner actually does*. The design logic acknowledges that learner activity mediates between the task as set and the learning outcome. The task specification has to be seen as a *resource* on which the learner can draw in improvising the details of their activity. It is the nature of that activity – including its cognitive, physical, emotional and other qualities – that determines what the actual learning outcomes will be. Design shifts from a deterministic to a probabilistic, or – perhaps better – a communicative mode.[3]

---

[3] This perspective on indirection in design for learning is described in more detail in Goodyear (2000), Goodyear and Retalis (2010) and Goodyear and Dimitriadis (2013). The 'task–activity' distinction comes from Wisner (1995), and the insistence on the centrality of learner activity comes from Shuell (1986). Shuell's exhortation to focus on 'what the student does' is at the heart of John Bigg's work on constructive alignment (e.g. Biggs & Tang, 2007).

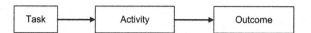

Fig. 20.4 Activity mediates between designed tasks and actual outcomes, an indirect logic for design (After Goodyear, 2000)

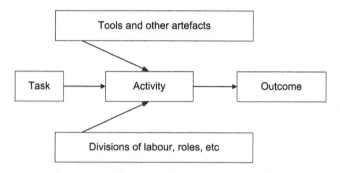

Fig. 20.5 Activity-centred design model (Adapted from Goodyear, 2000)

Figure 20.5 opens up the *scope* of this perspective on design with a reminder that learning activity is both physically and socially situated (Lave & Wenger, 1991; Sawyer & Greeno, 2009). It also acknowledges two extra dimensions to indirection in design. Just as learners adapt task specifications as resources for shaping their activity, so they also make choices about the physical and social resources they will use and how they will use them. The logic of design therefore has to accept that:

- Design should make recommendations about tools and other artefacts that will probably be useful in the learner's activity while recognising that learners will not necessarily use everything that has been recommended and that they may not use what they do select in the ways intended; also, learners will quite probably also bring a selection of their own tools, artefacts, etc., to use in their work.
- In a similar way, design should make recommendations about how learners might best work with one another – suggesting roles to be adopted, divisions of labour, groupings, etc., while also recognising that learners may ignore these recommendations or work in rather different ways.
- The complexity and uncertainty of the design logic is not an excuse for abdicating teachers' professional responsibility to help learners learn.

A key point to be made about the images of design in Figs. 20.3, 20.4 and 20.5 is that they are not intended to represent what actually happens at 'learntime'. Rather, they are a simple representation of the principal design components. They are a prompt to look at the world in a certain way, *when working on design problems.*[4]

---

[4] Designs for learning spend some of their life cycle as *inscriptions*. In Chap. 10, we talked about a number of the ways in which inscriptions function and commented on their relationship to actual activity. For example, we talked about inscriptions that are *idealised* and we talked about *projective* descriptions. These constructs are directly relevant to understanding how *designs* function in professional education settings.

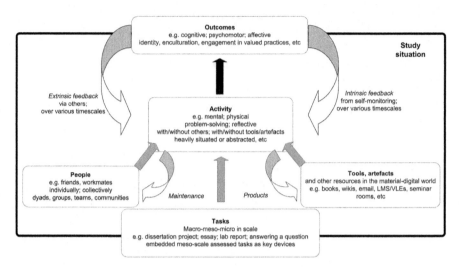

Fig. 20.6 Activity-centred view of a learning situation: tasks, tools and people entangling at 'learntime' (Adapted from Goodyear & Ellis, 2008)

When learning activity gets underway, task specifications (emerging from epistemic design), physical tools, artefacts, etc. (partially resulting from set design), and working relations with others (partially shaped by social design) become intimately entangled.

Figure 20.6 offers a way of picturing the coming together of these components at learntime. It includes some feedback loops, picking up a little of the dynamism of the system at learntime. For example, intrinsic and extrinsic feedback on progress towards intended learning outcomes has the potential to redirect activity. Also, activity is not only shaped by the social and physical environment, it has effects on such things as working relationships (e.g. through group maintenance) and on the tools and other resources available in the setting (e.g. through the production of artefacts).

We can now connect this conception of design to selected aspects of each of the four educational approaches sketched in Chap. 19 and our fifth project. Table 20.1 captures the essence.

For each of the rows in Table 20.1, we can ask: What kinds of task are most appropriate? What kinds of tools (and other physical resources) will be needed? What will be the most helpful divisions of labour and distribution of roles?

Many of the tasks that students are set in professional education courses mix practical and epistemic goals. That is, they blend a pragmatic (sub)task that resembles some aspect of professional practice with a longer-range learning (sub) task intended to build personal knowledgeability that should have broader applicability. As we saw in Chap. 10, the artefacts that students produce may resemble artefacts that would be found in professional workplaces, or more conventional

Table 20.1 Five educational approaches to developing aspects of epistemic fluency

Focus of learning	Approach (Learning as . . .)	Aim
1. Conceptual resourcefulness	Knowledge integration	Strengthening theory–practice connections
2. Epistemic resourcefulness	Playing epistemic games	Participating in established inquiry and problem-solving practices
3. Dynamic conceptual resourcefulness	Designing knowledge	Creating new knowledge
4. Dynamic epistemic resourcefulness	Designing inquiry	Creating new inquiry processes
5. Grounded dynamic resourcefulness	Creating an epistemic environment	(Re)configuring epistemic environments; consci(enti)ous inhabitation of epistemic environments

academic knowledge products, or a mix of both. The types of tasks most frequently found in the *knowledge integration* area (row 1 of Table 20.1), intended to help strengthen theory–practice connections, include (a) tasks that ask students to bring personal experiential knowledge into classroom discussion, where it can be set alongside codified knowledge, and (b) tasks that involve working flexibly with, and reflecting on, conceptual and practical (case-based) knowledge. Unsurprisingly, tasks associated with row 2 in Table 20.1 commonly consist of playing selected kinds and combinations of *epistemic games*. And although the terminology of epistemic games is not widespread in the knowledge-building area (row 3), much of what is actually done when students are learning in the *knowledge designing* paradigm is playing certain kinds of epistemic games in order to construct conceptual artefacts and understanding dynamically. Row 4 (designing inquiry) is where we place the example of using soft systems methodology (SSM) – discussed in Chap. 19 – and tasks here will normally involve *designing and conducting an inquiry* and monitoring, reflecting on and modifying inquiry methods during the inquiry process. As we mentioned in Chap. 19, SSM involves both a *product* (content) focus and a *process* focus – the evolution of both of these is to be monitored, and dynamic adjustments made when needed. In a sense, there is an open dynamic meta-task that shapes the design and redesign of the inquiry tasks. The fifth approach – creating and/or reconfiguring the epistemic environment – (row 5 of the Table) can be thought of as grounding this meta-task (or indeed meta-project) in material and social environment and an embodied self. Whereas in the SSM example the meta-task monitors and adjusts the inquiry *process*, the fifth approach has a meta-task that does this monitoring and adjustment by coordinating and simultaneously adjusting the *environment* in which the inquiry is unfolding.

There is an important switch when we move from row 3 to rows 4 and 5 in Table 20.1. One way to describe this is to say that the locus of design moves from outside to inside the learning system. We made the point earlier in this chapter that design often has to work indirectly and that students will usually customise and reconfigure tasks and the learning environment. But that active shaping work by students is not necessarily carefully considered. It will often be intuitive and immediate, rather than something we would label 'design'.

In contrast, the approaches represented in these last two rows of Table 20.1 *do* ask students to take on a conscious design role. The tasks that are proposed will always include this designerly meta-project: encouraging students to become conscious and conscientious inhabitants of the environments in which they are carrying out epistemic work.[5]

Like all conscientious inhabitants, they take on responsibility for ensuring that the epistemic environment continues to evolve in a way that affords what the work and the people require.

References

Barsalou, L. W. (1999). Perceptual symbol systems. *Behavioral and Brain Sciences, 22*, 577–609.
Barsalou, L. W. (2008). Grounded cognition. *Annual Review of Psychology, 59*, 617–645. doi:10. 1146/annurev.psych.59.103006.093639.
Barsalou, L. W. (2009). Situating concepts. In P. Robbins & M. Aydede (Eds.), *The Cambridge handbook of situated cognition* (pp. 236–263). Cambridge, NY: Cambridge University Press.
Barsalou, L. W., Breazeal, C., & Smith, L. (2007). Cognition as coordinated non-cognition. *Cognitive Processing, 8*(2), 79–91. doi:10.1007/s10339-007-0163-1.
Biggs, J., & Tang, C. (2007). *Teaching for quality learning at university: What the student does* (3rd ed.). Buckingham, UK: Open University Press.
Briggs, L. (1977). *Instructional design*. Englewood Cliffs, NJ: Educational Technology Publications.
Chi, M. T. H., Glaser, R., & Farr, M. J. (Eds.). (1988). *The nature of expertise*. Hillsdale, NJ: Lawrence Erlbaum Associates.
Clark, A. (2011). *Supersizing the mind: Embodiment, action and cognitive extension*. Oxford, UK: Oxford University Press.
Del Mar, M. (2010). *Thinking with the senses in legal playgrounds: A sketch towards multisensory legal education*. Paper presented at the BILETA Conference, Vienna. Retrieved from http:// ssrn.com/abstract=1552349.
Dillenbourg, P. (2013). Design for classroom orchestration. *Computers & Education, 69*, 485–492.
Dillenbourg, P., Jarvela, S., & Fischer, F. (2009). The evolution of research on computer-supported collaborative learning: From design to orchestration. In N. Balacheff, S. Ludvigsen, T. de Jong, A. Lazonder, & S. Barnes (Eds.), *Technology-enhanced learning: Principles and products* (pp. 3–21). Berlin, Germany: Springer.
Dimitriadis, Y., & Goodyear, P. (2013). Forward-oriented design for learning: Illustrating the approach. *Research in Learning Technology, 21*. doi:http://dx.doi.org/10.3402/rlt.v21i0. 20290.

---

[5] It is very risky to assume that the best way for students to learn how to design their future learning and knowledge-building environments is through discovery or by somehow generating their own actionable design principles through reflecting on their experience of designed environments. In short, it makes pedagogical sense to help them become capable designers by using both experience and direct instruction, including through the articulation of some useful design constructs.

Ellis, R. A., & Goodyear, P. (2010). *Students' experiences of e-Learning in higher education: The ecology of sustainable innovation.* New York, NY: Routledge.

Goodwin, C. (1994). Professional vision. *American Anthropologist, 96*(3), 606–633.

Goodwin, C. (2013). The co-operative, transformative organization of human action and knowledge. *Journal of Pragmatics, 46*(1), 8–23. http://dx.doi.org/10.1016/j.pragma.2012.09.003.

Goodyear, P. (2000). Environments for lifelong learning: Ergonomics, architecture and educational design. In J. M. Spector & T. Anderson (Eds.), *Integrated and holistic perspectives on learning, instruction & technology: Understanding complexity* (pp. 1–18). Dordrecht, The Netherlands: Kluwer Academic.

Goodyear, P. (2015). Teaching as design. *HERDSA Review of Higher Education, 2*, 27–50.

Goodyear, P., & Carvalho, L. (2014). Framing the analysis of learning network architectures. In L. Carvalho & P. Goodyear (Eds.), *The architecture of productive learning networks* (pp. 48–70). New York, NY: Routledge.

Goodyear, P., & Dimitriadis, Y. (2013). In medias res: Reframing design for learning. *Research in Learning Technology, 21.* doi:http://dx.doi.org/10.3402/rlt.v21i0.19909.

Goodyear, P., & Ellis, R. (2008). University students' approaches to learning: Rethinking the place of technology. *Distance Education, 29*(2), 141–152.

Goodyear, P., & Retalis, S. (Eds.). (2010). *Technology-enhanced learning: Design patterns and pattern languages.* Rotterdam, The Netherlands: Sense.

Hindmarsh, J., & Pilnick, A. (2007). Knowing bodies at work: Embodiment and ephemeral teamwork in anaesthesia. *Organization Studies, 28*(9), 1395–1416. doi:10.1177/0170840607068258.

Hutchins, E. (1995). *Cognition in the wild.* Cambridge, MA: MIT Press.

Hutchins, E. (2010). Cognitive ecology. *Topics in Cognitive Science, 2*(4), 705–715. doi:10.1111/j.1756-8765.2010.01089.x.

Ingold, T. (2000). *The perception of the environment: Essays on livelihood, dwelling and skill.* London, UK: Routledge.

Ingold, T. (2011). *Being alive: Essays on movement, knowledge and description.* Oxon, OX: Routledge.

Lave, J., & Wenger, E. (1991). *Situated learning: Legitimate peripheral participation.* Cambridge, NY: Cambridge University Press.

Mager, R. (1988). *Making instruction work.* Belmont, CA: Lake Books.

McGann, M., De Jaegher, H., & Di Paolo, E. (2013). Enaction and psychology. *Review of General Psychology, 17*(2), 203–209.

Moen, A., Mørch, A., & Paavola, S. (Eds.). (2012). *Collaborative knowledge creation: Practices, tools, concepts.* Rotterdam, The Netherlands: Sense.

Nersessian, N. J. (2012). Engineering concepts: The interplay between concept formation and modeling practices in bioengineering sciences. *Mind, Culture, and Activity, 19*(3), 222–239. doi:10.1080/10749039.2012.688232.

Paavola, S., Lakkala, M., Muukkonen, H., Kosonen, K., & Karlgren, K. (2011). The roles and uses of design principles for developing the trialogical approach on learning. *Research in Learning Technology, 19*(3), 233–246. doi:10.1080/21567069.2011.624171.

Paavola, S., Lipponen, L., & Hakkarainen, K. (2004). Models of innovative knowledge communities and three metaphors of learning. *Review of Educational Research, 74*(4), 557–576. doi:10.3102/00346543074004557.

Reigeluth, C. (Ed.). (1983). *Instructional design theories and models.* Hillsdale, NJ: Lawrence Erlbaum Associates.

Sawyer, K., & Greeno, J. (2009). Situativity and learning. In P. Robbins & M. Aydede (Eds.), *The Cambridge handbook of situated cognition* (pp. 347–367). Cambridge, NY: Cambridge University Press.

Shuell, T. (1986). Cognitive conceptions of learning. *Review of Educational Research, 56*(4), 411–436.

Smith, L. B. (2005). Cognition as a dynamic system: Principles from embodiment. *Developmental Review, 25*(3–4), 278–298. doi:10.1016/j.dr.2005.11.001.

Smith, L. B., & Sheya, A. (2010). Is cognition enough to explain cognitive development? *Topics in Cognitive Science, 2*(4), 725–735. doi:10.1111/j.1756-8765.2010.01091.x.

Smith, L. B., & Thelen, E. (2003). Development as a dynamic system. *Trends in Cognitive Sciences, 7*(8), 343–348. doi:10.1016/s1364-6613(03)00156-6.

Turnbull, D. (2000). *Masons, tricksters and cartographers: Comparative studies in the sociology of scientific and indigenous knowledge.* Abingdon, OX: Routledge.

Wisner, A. (1995). Understanding problem building: Ergonomic work analysis. *Ergonomics, 38*(3), 595–605.

Related Publications and Presentations

Goodyear, P., & Ellis, R. (2007). The development of epistemic fluency: Learning to think for a living. In A. Brew & J. Sachs (Eds.), *Transforming a university: The scholarship of teaching and learning in practice* (pp. 57–68). Sydney, Australia: Sydney University Press.

Goodyear, P., & Markauskaite, L. (2008). *Epistemic fluency and teaching-as-design.* Paper presented at the Annual Conference of the Australian Association for Research in Education, Brisbane, Australia.

Goodyear, P., & Markauskaite, L. (2009). Teachers' design knowledge, epistemic fluency and reflections on students' experiences. In *Proceedings of the 32nd Higher Education Research and Development Society of Australasia Annual Conference Proceedings, HERDSA 2009. The Student Experience,* (pp. 154–162). Darwin, Australia, 6–9 July 2009. Retrieved from http://www.herdsa.org.au/wp-content/uploads/conference/2009/papers/HERDSA2009_Goodyear_P.pdf

Goodyear, P., & Zenios, M. (2007). Discussion, collaborative knowledge work and epistemic fluency. *British Journal of Educational Studies, 55*(4), 351–368. doi: http://dx.doi.org/10.1111/j.1467-8527.2007.00383.x.

Goodyear, P., Markauskaite, L., & Kali, Y. (2009). Learning design, design contexts and pedagogical knowledge-in-pieces. In *Proceedings of the future of learning design conference,* (Paper 2, pp. 13–19). University of Wollongong, Wollongong, Australia, 10 December 2009. Retrieved from http://ro.uow.edu.au/fld/09/Program/2/

Kali, Y., Goodyear, P., & Markauskaite, L. (2011). Researching design practices and design cognition: Contexts, experiences and pedagogical knowledge-in-pieces. *Learning, Media and Technology, 36*(2), 129–149. doi: http://dx.doi.org/10.1080/17439884.2011.553621.

Markauskaite, L., & Goodyear, P. (2009). Designing for complex ICT-based learning: Understanding teacher thinking to help improve educational design. In Atkinson, R. J. & McBeath, C. (Eds.), *Proceedings of the 26th Annual Conference of the Australasian Society for Computers in Learning in Tertiary Education,* Auckland, New Zealand, (pp. 614–624). Retrieved from http://www.ascilite.org.au/conferences/auckland09/procs/markauskaite.pdf

Markauskaite, L., & Goodyear, P. (2014a). Professional work and knowledge. In S. Billett, C. Harteis, & H. Gruber (Eds.), *International handbook of research in professional and practice-based learning* (pp. 79–106). Dordrecht, The Netherlands: Springer.

Markauskaite, L., & Goodyear, P. (2014b). Tapping into the mental resources of teachers' working knowledge: insights into the generative power of intuitive pedagogy. *Learning, Culture and Social Interaction, 3*(4), 237–251. doi: http://dx.doi.org/10.1016/j.lcsi.2014.01.001.

© Springer Science+Business Media Dordrecht 2017
L. Markauskaite, P. Goodyear, *Epistemic Fluency and Professional Education,*
Professional and Practice-based Learning 14, DOI 10.1007/978-94-007-4369-4

Markauskaite, L., Goodyear, P., & Bachfischer, A. (2014). Epistemic games for knowledgeable action in professional learning. In Polman, J. L., Kyza, E. A., O'Neill, D. K., Tabak, I., Penuel, W. R., Jurow, A. S., O'Connor, K., Lee, T., and D'Amico, L. (Eds.), *Proceedings of the International Conference of the Learning Sciences (ICLS) 2014. Learning and becoming in practice*, (Vol. 3, pp.1289–1292). June 23–27 2014, University of Colorado Boulder. Boulder, CO: International Society of the Learning Sciences. Retrieved from http://isls.org/icls/2014/downloads/ICLS%202014%20Volume%203%20%28PDF%29-wCover.pdf

Index

Printed by Printforce, the Netherlands